AMERICAN HEROES
OF
WORLD WAR II

AMERICAN HEROES OF WORLD WAR II

NORMANDY JUNE 6, 1944

PHIL NORDYKE

PUBLISHED BY
HISTORIC VENTURES

First published in 2014 by Historic Ventures, LLC.
Copyright © 2014 by Phil Nordyke

All rights reserved. With the exception of quoting brief passages for the purposes of review, no part of this publication may be reproduced without prior written permission from the Publisher.

ISBN 978-0-9847151-1-4

CONTENTS

ACKNOWLEDGMENTS 7

INTRODUCTION 9

OPERATION OVERLORD 11

101st AIRBORNE DIVISION 15

82nd AIRBORNE DIVISION 33

UTAH BEACH 43

POINTE DU HOC 63

IN THE AIR OVER NORMANDY 87

OMAHA BEACH 89

APENDIX I – MEDAL OF HONOR CITATIONS 225

APPENDIX II – DISTINGUISHED SERVICE CROSS CITATIONS 233

APPENDIX III – NAVY CROSS CITATIONS 409

NOTES 429

BIBLIOGRAPHY 441

MAP AND CHART INDEX 449

INDEX OF HEROES 451

ACKNOWLEDGMENTS

I am deeply indebted to so many wonderful people who made this book possible. I must first thank my wife Nancy for her tremendous support of my writing projects, for the many hours she has spent with me at the National Archives searching, pulling, scanning, and copying thousands of pages of awards file documents, for providing a critical eye in editing and proof reading of the manuscript, and for a myriad of other contributions to my books.

The format and style of this book is different than my previous works about the World War II 82nd Airborne Division. I have used the outstanding books written by Mark Bando, the renowned historian and author of the 101st Airborne Division, and Michel DeTrez, a leading author in Europe of World War II airborne books, as templates for this book. Mark and Michel are quite simply the best at producing books which contain visually stunning photographs, many of which have never before been published, combined with superb narratives that always contain new information gained through first rate research on their parts.

Doug Sterner has dedicated much of his life to documenting the awards for valor of America's military soldiers, sailors, airmen, and Marines and has been a critical source of information regarding the recipients, the citations of their awards, and identification of the general orders which contain those citations. I want to sincerely thank Doug for his help.

Brandon Wiegand has provided valuable help with general orders containing citations for the awards found in this book and I appreciate his tremendous support of this project.

I am very grateful to Joe Balkoski, the 29th Infantry Division historian and author of groundbreaking books about D-Day and the 29th Infantry Division, who graciously shared his collection of photographs of the 29th Infantry Division's recipients of the Distinguished Service Cross. His outstanding book, *Omaha Beach*, has been a tremendous resource in understanding the details of many of the events that took place on Omaha Beach.

I owe a debt of gratitude to Andrew Woods, Research Historian at the Colonel Robert R. McCormick Research Center of the First Division Museum at Cantigny, in Wheaton, Illinois, who provided many photographs of 1st Infantry Division DSC recipients as well as several written accounts related to the experiences on D-Day of several of the recipients.

The dedicated staff at the National Archives at College Park, Maryland was a vital resource in making this book possible. I want to thank Dave Miller and his team at the Modern Military Textual Records unit for the outstanding help in locating and pulling records relating to the awards file of the recipients. Holly Reed and her team of Jonathan Knorr, Theresa Roy, Carla Sims, Peter Gaynor, and Chanel Sutton at the Still Pictures Reference unit provided a great deal of support in finding and pulling photographs of the recipients and I am very appreciative of their hard work.

I also want to recognize and thank Amy K. Russell, the director of the Barksdale Global Power Museum, as well as Lynn Gamma and Samuel C. Shearin with the Air Force Historical Research Agency for providing general orders for Army Air Corps DSC recipients.

Jonathan Gawne and his book *Spearheading D-Day* have been a valuable resource regarding the many special units which participated in the invasion. Jon has freely shared information and access to his photographs and I appreciate his help.

Sue Ann Dunford, author of *More Than Scuttlebutt*, a fine book about the World War II Naval Combat Demolition Units, Underwater Demolition Teams, and Naval Scouts, has generously shared her extensive knowledge and photographs of those units. I appreciate her assistance.

Doug McCabe, Curator of Manuscripts at the Robert E. and Jean R. Mahn Center for Archives and Special Collections at the Ohio University's Alden Library, made the holdings of the Cornelius Ryan Archive available for not only this book, but for every book I have written. Doug's outstanding support has been pivotal in making those books possible.

Tom Lane very graciously shared his collection of Lieutenant (jg) Stuart L. Brandel's photographs of German defenses of Omaha Beach that were taken shortly after the invasion and I am thankful to him for his generosity.

Coleman Strickland provided a copy of excerpts from Phil H. Bucklew's interview transcript from the United States Naval Academy Library and I appreciate his diligence in doing so.

The family members of the recipients have shared photographs, citation extracts, documents, and background information of the recipients with me and I owe them much. They include Donna Coffman Alexander, Cheryl Assad-Tomczyk, Jacklyn Kay Bahm, Barry Barcellona, Robert W. Bass, Jr., Harold E. Beavers, Erica Beedle, Dr. Claude and Marjorie Beitler, Katie Blum, George and Diane Bolderson, Father John D. Bolderson, Jr., Doris Bonstein, Harriette Brown, Ronald Cavaliere, Michael Cotter, Vinton G. Dove, Patrick Dunagan, Julie Fulmer, Joel Gilfert, Mary S. Gregory, Faith Groce, Barbara Henderson, Willa Bowen

Hensley, Debra Jacobson, Isabelle Ritter Kastak, Ronald Kidwell, Laura Kruss, Kathy Manuel, Gus McKee, Antion Meredith, Kathy Nadel, Robert Orndorff, Victoria Parker-Christensen, Barbara Potter, Trevor Potter, Sterling Proffitt, Mary Caffey Reistrup, Susie Reynolds, David Ritter, Walter Ritter, Jim Roberts, Duane Roberts, Bill Rodgers, Jr., Ed Schaadt, Barbara L. Scholar, Phyllis Shier, Arch Sproul, James Stephens, Reneé Stockwell, Stanley Streczyk, Geoff Taylor, Lynn Towne, Vickie Townsend, Stuart Tribble, Loren Tubbs, Colonel Melvin L. and Jane Turner, Carl Welborn, Kristina Danforth West, Jean A. Whiting, and Amy Wooldridge.

Others such as Paul Adamic, David Allender, Colonel Robert Black, Paul Clifford, Michel DeTrez, Jordan Edelstein, Kevin Frankenfield, Pierre Godeau, Pierre Gosselin, Emily Keating, Joseph Keating, Kevin McKernon, Mark S. Orr, Chris Profota, and General John C. Raaen, Jr. generously provided photographs for which I am grateful.

INTRODUCTION

America has always admired and honored its heroes. Seventy years ago, courageous young men parachuted from the sky in the predawn darkness and stormed the beaches of Normandy to liberate western Europe and end Nazi tyranny. This book honors those greatest of American heroes who spearheaded the invasion of Normandy, France on June 6, 1944 and recounts their acts of extraordinary heroism in combat. These relatively few men were the difference makers—the reason the invasion succeeded. Many of their acts of valor and sacrifice were crucial to the success of the invasion.

The stories of these actions, all of which resulted in the award of the Medal of Honor, Distinguished Service Cross, and the Navy Cross are told primarily through the words of the eyewitnesses whose statements are contained in the award files. Most of these recommendations and witness statements were made just days after the invasion, while still fresh in the minds of the witnesses and are very powerful and compelling. Also included are personal accounts of that day by some of the recipients themselves, all of which reflect modesty on their parts about their own actions on June 6, 1944. There were countless other acts of extraordinary heroism that day which went unrecognized by the award of a medal because the witnesses to those acts were killed in action before they could testify to them. Through the eyewitness and recipient accounts, this book provides a lasting memorial to all of the acts of heroism that day, whether or not formally recognized through the award of medals.

This book does not attempt to provide a complete or detailed history of the invasion of Normandy, but rather includes just enough information to provide the context for these extraordinary acts of valor. For an in depth history of the United States Army's role in the invasion, you may wish to read its official history entitled *Cross Channel Attack*, by Gordon A. Harrison, and two fine books written about the Normandy invasion by Joe Balkoski, entitled *Utah Beach* and *Omaha Beach*. There are many great books regarding various aspects of, and units which participated in, the invasion such as Jonathan Gawne's *Spearheading D-Day*, which does an outstanding job of covering the roles of American special units which took part in the invasion. Mark Bando's *Vanguard of the Crusade* and the *101st Airborne: The Screaming Eagles at Normandy* and George Koskimaki's *D-Day with the Screaming Eagles* are both outstanding books about the 101st Airborne Division's role in the Normandy invasion. I have written a number of books about the 82nd Airborne Division which include its actions in Normandy. Flint Whitlock's *The Fighting First* and more recently John C. McManus' *The Dead and Those About to Die* are both fine books which cover the 1st Infantry Division's experience on Omaha Beach. Joe Balkoski has written extensively about the 29th Infantry Division and its history in Normandy. Colonel Robert Black's *The Battalion* does a superb job of covering the 2nd and 5th Ranger Battalions at both Pointe du Hoc and Omaha Beach.

A number of the recipients received awards for the same action, and as such, I have combined those joint actions into a single narrative where possible. There are a significant number of recipients who received awards for similar actions, such as recipients who saved the lives of countless wounded soldiers or tank commanders who dismounted from their tanks in order to guide them through mined areas or better direct their tanks' fire. Even though it creates a certain amount of repetition, I believe it necessary to detail each of these actions separately.

While eyewitness and recipient accounts were found for over eighty-six percent of the total of 235 recipients and most are included in this book, there are thirty-two recipients for which no first person or eyewitness account could be found. While it is regrettable that these recipients' actions cannot be told through the words of those who were there, the award citations of those recipients describe their respective actions.

In addition, there are a number of recipients who received the Distinguished Service Cross for actions that took place over several days beyond June 6, 1944. Lieutenant Colonel Louis G. Mendez, Jr., Lieutenant Colonel John C. Welborn, Captain Francis L. Sampson, and First Sergeant Herbert A. Tubbs, among others, have amazing stories of heroism that need to be told in the context of the Normandy campaign and will be recounted in a future book. This book focuses solely on and is limited to the actions of June 6, 1944.

Included as a very important part of this book are three appendices containing the award citations for the Medal of Honor, Distinguished Service Cross, and Navy Cross as well as accompanying photographs of 190 of the 235 recipients. Many of the recipient photographs were taken during the award ceremonies and show the recipients wearing their respective medals.

This book is dedicated to all of the American heroes of the invasion of Normandy, both recognized and unrecognized, and their families.

OPERATION OVERLORD

You are about to embark upon the great crusade toward which we have striven these many months. The eyes of the world are upon you...I have full confidence in your courage, devotion to duty and skill in battle. —General Dwight D. Eisenhower

Operation Overlord was the airborne and amphibious invasion of Normandy and the single most critical operation the western Allies executed during the liberation of western Europe from Nazi occupation. It was the largest amphibious operation in history. The scope of the invasion was enormous. The Allied naval armada consisted of 1,089 warships, 4,021 amphibious craft, and 1,373 merchant vessels, totaling 6,483 ships and landing craft. The ships and landing craft were manned by some 170,701 naval and merchant marine personnel (52,889 American, 112,824 British, plus 4,988 from other Allied countries). The Allies had 6,588 bombers, fighters, sea rescue, and reconnaissance aircraft available for the operation. In addition, there were 1,157 troop carrier aircraft to transport the airborne forces. The initial assault landing force consisted of 61,715 British (including 7,900 airborne, both parachute and glider), 21,400 Canadian, and 72,610 American (including 15,110 airborne, both parachute and glider) troops, plus follow-up forces scheduled to land on D-Day, for a total of 174,320 officers and men, plus 20,018 vehicles.

Paving the way for the invasion, the British and American air forces had gained air superiority through a vicious battle of attrition with the German Luftwaffe in which the newly arrived P-51 Mustang proved to be a superior fighter to any propeller driven fighter in the German arsenal. Deep penetration bombing raids had been very costly in 1942 and 1943. However, with Mustangs being able to escort bombers all the way to targets inside of Germany, the Allied bombers had crippled the German war making capability through key industry targets and infrastructure such as railroads and oil storage. During early 1944, the Allies intensified the bombing of transportation system targets in France such as bridges and railroad terminals. Bombing was also increased on German coastal fortifications which were part of what Hitler referred to as an Atlantic wall, which extended from the coast of the Netherlands to the frontier with Spain.

In addition, Allied reconnaissance flights were conducted along the length of the German coastal defenses so as to prevent German intelligence from deducing the planned invasion area by observing where aerial reconnaissance missions were being flown. These aerial reconnaissance photographs provided the Allies with detailed information regarding German defenses in addition to the intelligence provided by underground personnel on the ground in the occupied countries. Allied air dominance over the English Channel prevented German reconnaissance flights, effectively blinding the German military to the enormous preparations being made for the invasion of Normandy.

Allied antisubmarine operations conducted from the air and by Allied warships effectively hunted German U-boats and drove them away from shipping lanes, allowing the flow of men, weapons, munitions, vehicles, fuel, food, and supplies on ships from America across the Atlantic Ocean to England for the massive buildup which would be required for such a large undertaking to succeed on the continent of Europe.

Allied intelligence, counter intelligence, and deception programs were vital factors which paved the way for the invasion. The Allies had broken the German Enigma code used by its military for much of its communications and had done so without the Germans knowing or even suspecting that its code had been compromised. In addition, British counter intelligence had been intercepting virtually every German agent who entered the United Kingdom, turning them into double agents by forcing them to send false information to German intelligence. The Allies also developed and maintained a huge deception program whereby a fictional army group, designated as the First United States Army Group (FUSAG), was created to promote the German military's perception that the landing would be made in the Pas de Calais area of France. The Pas de Calais was the closest point between England and France and was regarded by the Germans as the most likely point for an Allied invasion. The German military therefore heavily fortified this area and the Allied deception program fed this enemy belief in order to tie down German forces and prevent them from being used to strengthen or reinforce the defenses in Normandy.

These factors and more set the conditions by which the Allies could plan and execute an amphibious operation capable of establishing a lodgment large enough to allow the buildup of enough combat power to break out and strike a decisive blow to defeat if not destroy German military forces in France.

The Allied planners designated five invasion beaches covering over fifty miles of Normandy coastline. The United States

First Army was assigned to land on the two most westerly beaches, code named Omaha on the Calvados coast and Utah on the eastern side of the Cotentin Peninsula.

The V Corps would be responsible for assaulting Omaha Beach with two heavily reinforced infantry divisions because the beach was almost five miles wide and the terrain immediately behind the beach consisted of steep bluffs overlooking it, which greatly favored the defenders. The veteran 1st Infantry Division, led by the 16th Infantry Regiment together with the attached 741st Tank Battalion, the 62nd Armored Field Artillery Battalion, the 197th Antiaircraft Artillery (Automatic Weapons) Battalion, elements of the Provisional 397th Antiaircraft Artillery (Automatic Weapons) Battalion, and two companies of 4.2 inch mortars of the 81st Chemical Battalion (Motorized), would assault the eastern portion of the beach. Additionally, the Provisional Special Engineer Task Force's combined teams of army combat engineer and naval combat demolition units designated as gap assault teams, and the Engineer Special Brigade Group's 5th Engineer Special Brigade, the 6th Naval Beach Battalion, the 294th Joint Assault Signal Company, and numerous other units would support the assault.

The untested 29th Infantry Division, led by the 116th Infantry Regiment and the attached 743rd Tank Battalion, the 58th Armored Field Artillery Battalion, elements of the Provisional 397th Antiaircraft Artillery (Automatic Weapons) Battalion, the 467th Antiaircraft Artillery (Automatic Weapons) Battalion, and two companies of 4.2 inch mortars of the 81st Chemical Battalion (Motorized) would assault the western portion of the beach. Additionally, the Provisional Engineer Special Engineer Task Force's joint gap assault teams of army combat engineer and naval combat demolition units, the Engineer Special Brigade Group, the 6th Engineer Special Brigade, the 7th Naval Beach Battalion, the 293rd Joint Assault Signal Company, and numerous other units would support the assault. Additionally, the elite all volunteer 2nd and 5th Ranger Battalions were assigned to capture Pointe du Hoc, which lay about half way between the two American beaches on high ground fronted by a steep cliff at the edge of the water, where a battery of long range artillery capable of shelling both beaches and the troop transport and landing craft loading areas was thought to be emplaced in heavy concrete casemates.

The VII Corps assigned the 4th Infantry Division to assault Utah Beach, led by the 8th Infantry Regiment and the attached 70th Tank Battalion, the 65th Armored Field Artillery Battalion, 474th Antiaircraft Artillery (Automatic Weapons) Battalion, and the 87th Chemical Battalion (Motorized) would conduct the initial assault. The 1st Engineer Special Brigade, the 2nd Naval Beach Battalion, beach obstacle demolition parties of combined teams of army combat engineers and naval combat demolition units, plus numerous other units would support the assault. The 359th Regimental Combat Team of the 90th Infantry Division was also attached to the 4th Infantry Division and was scheduled to land late on D-Day as a follow up force. The 82nd and 101st Airborne Divisions, under the control of the First Army, would become under the control of the VII Corps upon landing by parachute and glider west of Utah Beach. The two airborne divisions would secure the right flank of the invasion, assist the 4th Infantry Division in getting off of the beach, and facilitate cutting the Cotentin Peninsula to prevent German forces from reinforcing the port of Cherbourg on the northern shore of the peninsula.

The 1st Infantry Division, the 505th Parachute Infantry Regiment of the 82nd Airborne Division, the 70th Tank Battalion, and elements of the 1st Special Engineer Brigade had combat experience during campaigns in North Africa, Sicily, and Italy. However, the vast majority of American troops who would parachute into Normandy and assault its beaches had no combat experience. For most, their first day of combat would be on the single most critical day of the war for the western Allies, and for some it would be their last day alive.

The flanks of the invasion were the most at risk of a quick enemy counterattack since German forces defending adjacent beaches and reserve units behind them could quickly drive into the beachheads. Therefore, the invasion planners decided to land British and American airborne forces to block likely enemy counterattacks on the flanks by controlling key bridges and road junctions. The airborne forces would also assist the beach landed forces by destroying enemy coastal artillery batteries and field artillery units within range of the beaches which threatened the amphibious landings.

Major General Matthew B. Ridgway, commanding the 82nd Airborne Division, assigned the most important objective of the American airborne forces—the seizure and retention of Ste.-Mère-Église—to the veteran 505th Parachute Infantry Regiment. Ste.-Mère-Église lay northwest of Utah Beach astride the national highway that ran from Cherbourg south through Carentan to Paris and another road running east from one of two causeways across the Merderet River. Both were chokepoints along primary routes for German counterattacks from the north and west against the Utah Beach landings. In addition, the 505th together with two attached and as yet untested parachute regiments, the 507th and 508th, were ordered to seize the two causeways over the Merderet River to block German counterattacks against Utah Beach from the west. The 508th was also assigned to destroy the Douve River bridges west of the confluence with the Merderet River to block German forces to the south.

The 101st Airborne Division, commanded by Major General Maxwell D. Taylor, would get its baptism of fire during this operation. It was assigned to seize the western ends of four causeways leading from Utah Beach. The Germans had flooded the area behind Utah Beach and were defending the causeway exits to prevent beach landed forces from moving inland. The 101st was also ordered to seize locks at La Barquette on the Douve River to the south, which the Germans had used to flood the Douve and Merderet Rivers. The division's assignments also included controlling or destroying the Douve River bridges east of the confluence with the Merderet River to block a German counterattack against Utah Beach from the south.

OPERATION OVERLORD

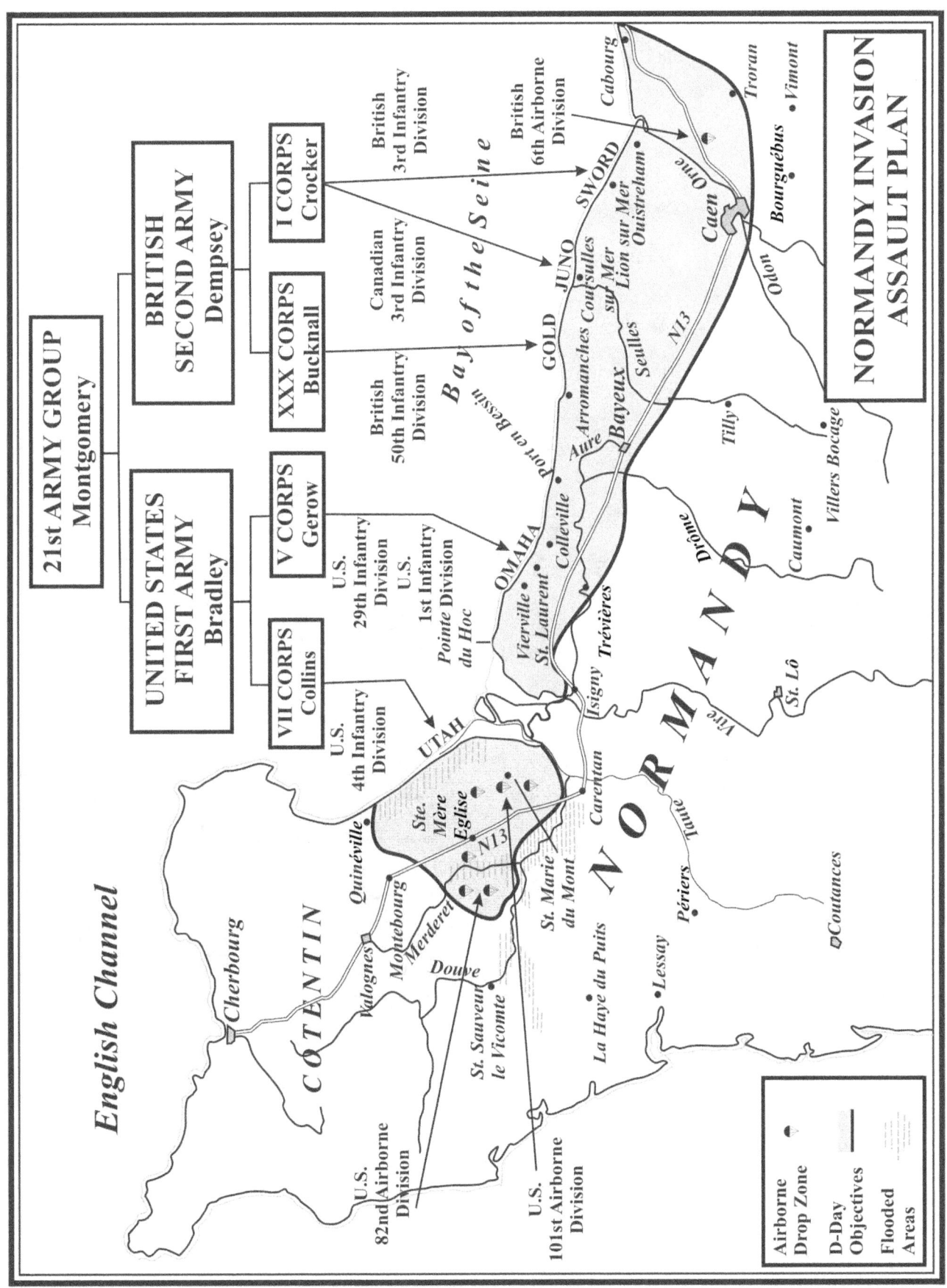

101ST AIRBORNE DIVISION

The 101st Airborne Division…has no history, but it has a rendezvous with destiny.
—*Brigadier General William C. Lee*

The commander of the Allied expeditionary forces that would invade fortress Europe, General Dwight D. Eisenhower, was worried about casualties among the airborne divisions, which were predicted by one of his staff members, British Air Marshal Sir Trafford Leigh-Mallory, to likely be over fifty percent. On the evening of June 5, 1944, Eisenhower visited the 101st Airborne Division's 502nd Parachute Infantry—the Five-O-Duece—at the airfield near Greenham Common to wish those young paratroopers good luck. Hours later, the two American airborne divisions, the pride of the nation, would parachute into the night skies over Normandy, becoming the first American troops to land in Nazi occupied France.

General Dwight D. Eisenhower (center), commander of the Allied Expeditionary Force, visits the 502nd Parachute Infantry at Greenham Common airfield on the evening of June 5, 1944. *United States Army Signal Corps photograph, National Archives.*

General Eisenhower (left center) speaks with Lieutenant Wallace C. Strobel (right center with the Chalk 23 sign) and other paratroopers with Company E, 502nd Parachute Infantry on the evening of June 5, 1944. *United States Army Signal Corps photograph, National Archives.*

Among the first Allied troops to land in France would be the pathfinder teams of the 101st Airborne Division. The American airborne divisions had formed all volunteer provisional pathfinder teams to use electronic transponder beacons and automatic direction finder equipment to guide the aircraft transporting the main forces to the proper drop zones (for troops landing by parachute) or landing zones (for glider landed forces). These pathfinder teams would also mark each drop zone and landing zone with powerful holophane lights in the shape of a "T" to provide visual targets for aircraft crews, jumpmasters, and glider pilots.

The 101st Airborne Division Provisional Pathfinder Company would mark three drop zones and one glider landing zone using eleven battalion teams. Three pathfinder teams would set up navigational aids and lights to guide the 502nd Parachute Infantry Regiment and elements of the 377th Parachute Field Artillery to Drop Zone A, which was southwest of St.-Martin-de-Varreville near causeway Exits 3 and 4 from Utah Beach. Another three teams would guide the 506th Parachute Infantry Regiment, less its 3rd Battalion; and the 3rd Battalion of the 501st Parachute Infantry Regiment to Drop Zone C, which was west of Pouppeville and near causeway Exits 1 and 2. Three teams would guide the 501st Parachute Infantry Regiment, less the 3rd Battalion; the 3rd Battalion, 506th Parachute Infantry Regiment; and the 326th Airborne Engineer Company to Drop Zone D, which was just north of Basse Addeville and near the Douve River bridges and the locks at La Barquette. The two remaining teams would drop on DZ C and mark Landing Zone E, just north of Hiesville and west of Ste.-Marie-du-Mont, for glider landings scheduled for 4:00 a.m.

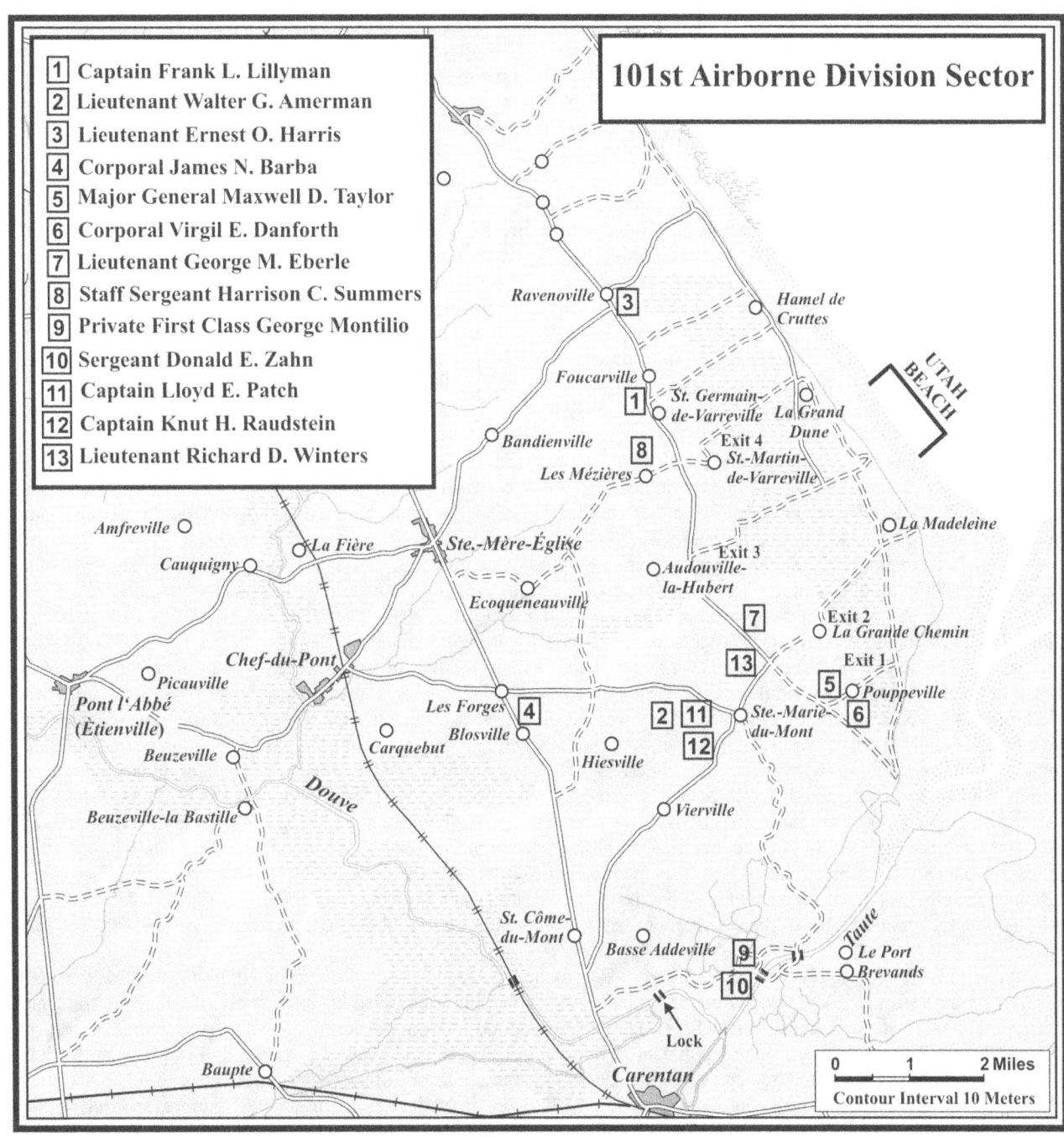

Captain Frank L. Lillyman
Company I, 502nd Parachute Infantry Regiment, 101st Airborne Division and 101st Provisional Pathfinder Company

As darkness approached on the evening of June 5, 1944, the 101st Airborne Division's pathfinder teams boarded eleven C-47 troop transport aircraft. Captain Frank Lillyman, the commanding officer of the 101st Provisional Pathfinder Company, was the jumpmaster in the lead plane. "The lead pathfinder ship took off from North Witham airbase at approximately 21:00. This ship was piloted by Lieutenant Colonel Joel Crouch, pathfinder group commander; Major Vito Pedone, copilot; Captain William C. Culp, navigator. The ship carried eighteen jumpers of which, twelve were pathfinder personnel and the remaining six were a security team of officers and men from the S-2 section of the 502nd Parachute Infantry Regiment.

"From the Midlands of England, the course was generally southwest to near Bristol, thence almost due south to the point west of Southampton, southwest again to a point west of Cherbourg. Here at a submarine marker, the route veered southeast past the coast of Guernsey and Jersey, another change of direction, this time to the northeast and over the west coast of the Normandy peninsula. Crossing the channel, the pathfinder ships kept low, practically on 'the deck' to avoid enemy radar detection, but as they passed between the Guernsey and Jersey Islands, top cover [British Royal Air Force] Sterlings came down and continued on in the direction of Brest, dropping 'window' for diversion.

"The flight climbed to a little over a thousand feet as it crossed the coast and it was here that the first flak was received. The reaction was one of curiosity rather than alarm, but this mainly due to the fact that the heavy stuff was still some distance away. The 40mm was all over and looking down at it, the tracers seemed quite pretty as they came floating lazily upward and then spun over to our rear. The fact that only one out of probably five could be seen did not occur until sometime later. The men in the ship had been flying without their equipment, some sleeping, some watching out the door and others just riding the buckets. As the islands were passed and the shore of France was seen, they were ordered to put on their equipment.

"The strained remarks and corny jokes seemed to accent the tension and when the announcement was made that the ship had just passed over the coast of France, one trooper remarked, 'Well, it's too late to cancel out now.' The sound of Tommy gun slides being tested caused a mild protest of 'Do you want someone to get hurt!' A box of Gammon grenades had been stacked by the door and from the time the ship crossed the coast until Montebourg was sighted, these were promiscuously dropped out door to the ground below without even bothering to observe the results.

"Just below Montebourg, the railroad forms a junction and with this as the turning point, the 'slide' down the coast began. The route now lay parallel to the invasion coast, heading toward Carentan. There is an odd shaped chateau with three ponds in its yard, just outside of Montebourg and from there to the drop zone, the course crossed at right angles eight roads leading to the coast. The ship had slackened its forward speed now and descended to nearly six hundred feet.

"Seven roads to go and the command was given to 'Stand up and hook up!' The speed lessened and the ship was in a mild glide, approaching jumping altitude. The men were crowding the door, eager now, quiet. Six roads to go.

"'Check your equipment' and the long count started way back in the ship. Eighteen OK, seventeen OK, sixteen OK—down it came, each voice increasing in intensity and loudness until [Lieutenant Samuel] McCarter yelled in my ear, 'Two OK!' Four roads to go. The speed was almost down to a hundred and ten and the flak was getting heavier and it seemed—a lot closer. 'Stand in the door' was called and if possible, each man crowded a little closer. I looked back into the ship. The moon was full and bright and I could see some of the faces. They were tense, eager, determined. The caution light flickered and I knew there were but two roads to cross. I yelled at the faces, 'Are you ready?' and the answering shout, both of courage and unintelligible nothings, took any doubt from my mind. The 'butterflies' were really jumping inside of me and I thought of the job to do and the training we had undergone and then the red light was out and there was one more road to go—and there it was. White, inviting but with moving red dots from the intersections rising to meet the plane. Too late now. The green light came on. With a 'Follow me,' that I doubt if any heard I stepped into the cool prop blast and moonlit night. We were about four hundred and fifty feet, no reserve parachutes and over the enemy. It seemed like an eternity until the main [chute] jerked open and without checking the canopy at all I dropped the leg bag. Hand over hand, up the suspension lines and finally the chute spilled air. I slipped past a tree and then the ground came in. I looked at my watch. Fifteen minutes past midnight on the morning of June 6th. The invasion was on."[1]

Captain Lillyman was likely the first American soldier to land in France, north of the intended drop zone, near the village of St. Germain-de-Varreville. After getting out of his parachute harness, he assembled his three sticks of 502nd pathfinders. "We met at the church in St. Germain-de-Varreville and traveled through the fields to the northwest, where we set up lights as markers, along with installation of other special equipment in trees. [Staff Sergeant Thomas C.] Walton and [Technician Fifth Grade Owen R.] Council shinnied up a tree and set up the Eureka for our sticks of jumpers. Our orders were to do no shooting and we had instructed our men to take evasive action if Germans were sighted. A German machine gunner, spotting us through bushes, kept probing with short bursts. This was annoying, and I finally sent two men to convince the Krauts of the 'errors of their way.' Soon, I heard a grenade go off with a 'whumf,' and then everything was lovely and quiet.

"Several of my scouts reported a farmhouse where there were Germans at the edge of the field. Two others and myself went to the house where we met a Frenchman smoking a pipe. He was standing in the doorway. He jerked his thumb toward the stairs and said, 'Boche.'

"We caught the German, in a nice pair of white pajamas, in bed. We disposed of him and expropriated the bottle of champagne beside the bed. We met no more Germans before the main invasion body landed, however one enemy bicycle patrol approached and then turned back. They seemed to not want any part of us and we wanted no part of them.[2]

"Forty-seven minutes later the planes arrived with the main body of troops. This was the longest forty-seven minutes of my life. One Eureka was turned on at 00:30. The first reception was received at approximately 00:45. The lights were turned on at 00:40. Those lights never looked so bright in training, but that night they looked like searchlights. One light went out, and we had to rig an emergency connection. We were silhouetted against it for a few minutes. However, nothing happened.

"The first aircraft flew over the 'T' at approximately 00:57. The groups were scattered and flying fast, with the majority of ships dropping parachutists west and north of the position. Some parachutists were dropped east and some south of the T. The first person contacted from 502nd Parachute Infantry was Captain [Ivan R.] Hershner of Company I and then some enlisted men of Company I. Elements of the 1st Battalion, 502nd were also contacted and several men of the 1st Battalion moved to the lights. All lights and Eurekas remained on until approximately 03:10, at which time the unit assembled at the church at St. Germain. Some jump injuries had been collected and these were hidden in the rear of a house at St. Germain and the balance of the unit moved with Captain [Henry G.] Plitt, Captain [Ivan R. Jr.] Hershner, Lieutenant [Robert G.] Burns (Company I) and approximately 150 enlisted men towards St. Martin-de-Varreville. Upon approaching the position [a German coastal artillery battery emplaced in casemates], Captain Plitt was placed in charge of the main force."[3]

Captain Lillyman then took one of his pathfinders and conducted a reconnaissance of the German casemates and trench system surrounding them. "Upon discovering the position was almost completely demolished and apparently no enemy on the position, [we] returned to where Captain Plitt was waiting and informed him of this fact."[4]

Captain Lillyman then led his pathfinders back to St. Germain-de-Varreville. "On moving north down the road, contact was established with Lieutenant Colonel [Patrick F.] Cassidy [commanding officer of the 1st Battalion] and a small force and it was agreed to establish the road block at CR393-994 for the 1st Battalion until they returned. A CP [command post] was established at St. Germain, and a roadblock of one mortar 60mm, three LMG's [light machine guns] and one .03 rifle grenade was established at the crossroad facing north and northeast. An observation post was established in the church steeple at St. Germain. At 06:40 a squad of the 1st Battalion came down to this position and the weapons were turned over to this squad.

"The pathfinders were then assembled and movement started toward the 502nd CP at Loutres. Four Eurekas were left at St. Germain with one officer and five enlisted men who had sustained jump injuries. These men were hidden in the church along with four of the Eurekas. The unit arrived at 502nd Regimental CP at approximately 08:00 and remained there until approximately 10:00 when movement was started for division CP."[5]

Second Lieutenant Walter G. Amerman
Company B, 506th Parachute Infantry Regiment, 101st Airborne Division and 101st Airborne Division Provisional Pathfinder Company

Second Lieutenant Walter G. Amerman led the security element for the 1st Battalion, 506th Parachute Infantry Regiment pathfinder team, which together with the 2nd Battalion, 506th and 3rd Battalion, 501st pathfinder teams had the mission of setting up Eurekas and lights on Drop Zone C. "A cheer went up in our plane as we left the ground, then there was a grim silence. We skimmed over the channel only ten feet above the whitecaps to avoid radar detection. It was a foggy evening, but soon we could see the coast of France looming ahead. Then the Jerry flak opened up. The black mushrooms of the flak and the red and green machine gun tracer bullets looked perfectly harmless—I even thought how beautiful the tracers looked…

"The five minute red warning light flashed. The jumpmaster barked, 'Stand up!' But we were so weighed down—about 150 pounds with two parachutes, ammunition, weapons, and lights—he had to help us to our feet. He gave the 'hook up' order."[6]

As the plane slowed for the jump, Amerman stepped out into the full moonlit night sky. "It was deep dusk. We could see the field below. I could see two Kraut motorcyclists riding wildly down a road and others running towards the field. We met a hail of bullets. One glanced off my helmet with a terrible clang as I floated down. Bullets ripped through parachutes."[7]

Streams of German tracers rose up as the enemy machine gunners below zeroed in on Amerman and the other pathfinders. "They got four of our men on the way down."[8]

Amerman and his stick descended about a quarter of a mile southeast of the planned drop zone. "With all of that weight, I hit the ground with a terrific jolt. I got to a hedgerow, cutting off the parachute as I ran."[9]

Tracers from German automatic weapons crisscrossed the area as Amerman and the other pathfinders "engaged them and started shooting as we landed, but the Germans sprayed every bush and hedgerow."[10]

Despite the enemy fire, Amerman and the six troopers collected the pathfinder equipment in preparation for setting it up. "We were able to find only six of the marker lights we carried, and only one of the two hand-grinder radio signal sets. We lay hidden under hedgerows and bushes while the Krauts raked the field with fire."[11]

An enemy machine gun pinned down the pathfinder teams and prevented them from setting up and operating the Eureka transponder and holophane lights used to mark the drop zone. Lieutenant Amerman single-handedly attacked the German machine gun team as they sprayed the field. He crept close and tossed a hand grenade into the midst of the crew, killing them. Amerman's destruction of that machine gun nest allowed the surviving pathfinders to set up their equipment.

The 1st Battalion, 506th Parachute Infantry Regiment pathfinder team, designated as Chalk 5, poses on June 5, 1944 shortly before taking off for Normandy. Lieutenant Walter G. Amerman is standing at the far right of the photo. *United States Army Air Corps photograph.*

Lieutenant Amerman remained alert for an attack by enemy troops who he knew were located at various points around the dark hedgerow lined field. "It was pitch black after a few minutes and the Jerries evidently were afraid to come into the field to look for us. We weren't there to fight, but to guide. One of my men got excited and fired his rifle, so I told him to lock it. We worked the hand powered radio which sent a code signal for about one hundred miles."[12]

As planes of the 101st Airborne Division serials approached, intense enemy automatic weapons fire suddenly raked the field, preventing Amerman's team from turning on the holophane lights except for a single green one. A short time afterward, Amerman could see "the dark blur of hundreds and hundreds of planes coming in low. They were met by a regular hell of antiaircraft fire. The first twenty-five or thirty [aircraft] came straight on and their paratroopers jumped pretty accurately."[13]

After completing their pathfinder duties, Amerman and the other troopers stayed on Drop Zone C and guided troopers to their respective units which were assembling in the area of the drop. "The toy crickets we carried for signaling were chirping all over. There was firing everywhere—rifles and automatic weapons barking and r-r-ripping.

"At dawn, I took my six men and tried to find our company headquarters. We found one of our buddies hanging from a tree in his parachute. He had been bayoneted to death. Then we really got mad. We worked our way cautiously through the woods where the Jerries had been and came to a large farmhouse where they had been shooting from all night. I eased along a hedgerow until I came to a gate. Then a Kraut sentry who had been hiding in a foxhole jumped up, shouted, 'Halt!' and shoved his Mauser in my face. The light was still too dim for him to recognize my uniform from more than a few feet away. I was so startled I stepped back and fell over a log—just as his gun went off. My face was almost blown off. Lying on my back, I fired half a clip from my grease-gun right into his face. He was plenty dead. Another German came running around the corner of the house. One of my riflemen and I chopped him down. Then we ran back to the woods. Two other American paratroopers heard the firing, came running up and joined us. One had a Tommy gun. I sent the seven riflemen in a frontal attack on the farmhouse through the woods. The Tommy gunner and I attacked from the left flank, making as much noise as we could to make Jerry think we had a lot more men. Some Germans ran out the back of the house, half dressed. The Tommy gunner and I killed two of them. Then we lobbed five grenades through the windows, while the riflemen poured fire into the front of the house. We killed three more Jerries who were firing from the windows. Then we broke into the house. We found five Krauts hiding in a wine cellar and they came out with their hands up."[14]

THE SERIALS OF C-47 AIRCRAFT transporting the 101st Airborne Division encountered a cloudbank on the western coast of the Cotentin Peninsula and the tight nine plane V-of-V formations dispersed in order to avoid midair collisions. As the planes emerged from the thick cloudbank, extremely heavy enemy antiaircraft fire, ranging from 20mm to 88mm, from Gemischte Flak-Abteilung 153(v), rose up from the area around St.-Sauveur-le-Vicomte. As the planes continued east and approached Pont l'Abbe on the north side of the Douve River, Kompanie 3, Panzerjäger Abteilung 352 of Infanterie Division 352, unleashed devastating fire from nine 37mm rapid fire antiaircraft guns. A short distance later, most of the thirty-seven machine guns of Pionier-Bataillon 191 of Luftlande Division 91, opened fire from positions in the vicinity of Picauville. In addition, there was light antiaircraft fire from the south side of the Douve River from the woods of the Bois de Limors. Later, as the troop carrier aircraft approached the division's drop zones, elements of Bataillons 1 and 3, Grenadier Regiment 919 of Infanterie Division 709 plus elements of Bataillon 3, Grenadier Regiment 1058 of Luftlande Division 91 filled the sky with crisscrossing streams of tracers as the paratroopers exited the planes.

Second Lieutenant Marvin F. Muir
93rd Troop Carrier Squadron, 439th Troop Carrier Group, 50th Troop Carrier Wing, IX Troop Carrier Command

The 93rd Troop Carrier Squadron was transporting troopers of the 2nd Battalion, 506th Parachute Infantry Regiment. The C-47 aircraft designated as Chalk 58 and piloted by Lieutenant Marvin F. Muir, was leading the right V of three planes of a nine plane V-of-V formation. Lieutenant Edward Beauregard, piloting Chalk 59 on the right side of the same three plane V formation, observed that "intense antiaircraft fire was taking place at this time. A few seconds later the bottom of Lieutenant Muir's plane was hit, near the companionway, and the baggage compartment was immediately filled with flames which could be seen through the aerial dome and the radio operator's window. The flames got worse and spread to the cabin very quickly. Almost immediately, paratroopers began coming out the door. I was unable to estimate the number, but it looked like the usual stick. I was unable to tell whether any of the crew jumped. The plane then rose fifty feet on the left wing and seemed to stall. Then it dropped over on the right wing into my path. I dropped under and slid to the left. From then on I saw nothing until the flash of the explosion when the plane hit the ground."[15]

The courageous actions of Muir and his crew had allowed seventeen of the eighteen man stick to successfully jump before the plane crashed, killing Lieutenant Muir and his four crewmen.

First Lieutenant Ernest O. Harris
Headquarters Company, 3rd Battalion, 502nd Parachute Infantry Regiment, 101st Airborne Division

After landing and getting out of his parachute harness, Major John P. Stopka, the executive officer of the 3rd Battalion, 502nd Parachute Infantry, set out to find his plane's stick. "Lieutenant [Ernest O.] Harris with thirteen men out of my stick assembled with me near where we had been dropped. After some scouting of the area we came to the conclusion that we had been dropped in the wrong place, and therefore decided to move in the direction of Ravenoville and down the coast to our battalion assembly area. In our movement, Lieutenant Harris with Lieutenant [Howard D.] Collins were given the mission of leading the group out. Near a place called Marmion, south of Ravenoville, the lead scout, Staff Sergeant [Robert P.] O'Reilly was fired upon and he immediately hit the dirt and fired back killing two sentries. Lieutenant Harris and Lieutenant Collins, who were behind Staff Sergeant O'Reilly, saw the situation at hand and relayed the information back to me, saying that it appeared to be a strongpoint of some sort. I immediately moved to where I could see and also gave some orders. In my movement forward, I shouted to Lieutenant Collins to move across the road, take two men and try to flank the position from the left; and for Lieutenant Harris to take two men and do the same thing from the right. At this time I did not know how large a strongpoint it was, nor how many buildings there were. I told Staff Sergeant O'Reilly to stay where he was and send two more men to bolster his stand and keep up the fire if any more of the enemy came up the road to investigate our firing. Lieutenant Collins and Lieutenant Harris had not been gone more than ten minutes when I heard the chatter of several machine pistols and some machine gun fire coming from the direction where Harris had taken his two men. Not knowing what sort of a situation Lieutenant Harris had gotten into, I immediately took what men I had with Lieutenant [Ralph A.] Watson, and moved on down beyond the crossroad into the barricaded garrison itself and took up some positions behind a stone building. About the time I got into position, I heard some carbine firing and yelling by Harris, and about one minute later I saw Harris come out of the garrison with a group of enemy with their hands up and somewhat worse for wear. There were twenty-four enemy prisoners, several being wounded. Harris said he had gotten behind their position in the garrison, and as they came out, he picked them off and made so much noise that the enemy apparently thought he had a small army with him. After losing six of their own forces, the rest gave up. After turning the prisoners over, Lieutenant Harris said he was going back and mop up the trenches. He then took off with the two men in the direction of the

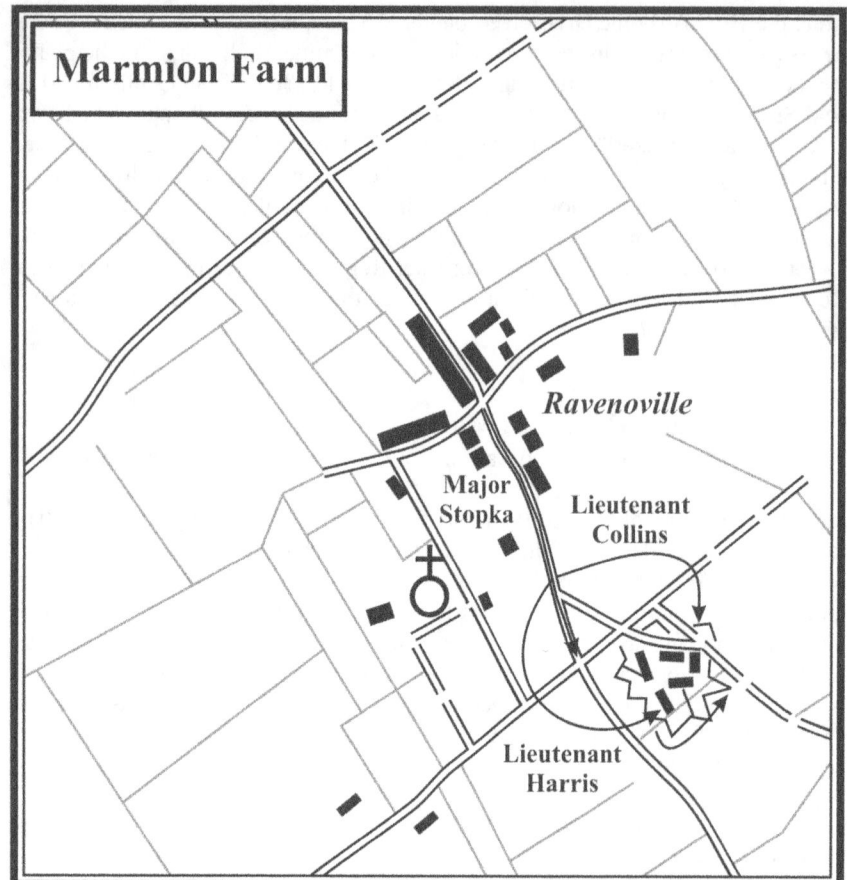

rear of the garrison and shortly thereafter I heard the chatter of machine guns, carbine fire, and shouting by Lieutenant Harris. Thinking that he was now in more serious trouble because the enemy fire seemed to increase, I took two men with me and went forward to try to give him some assistance. When I got to the rear of the garrison, I could see Lieutenant Harris jumping a trench, shouting, firing his rifle, and generally making quite a scene. Following him at about fifty yards were his two men, creeping and crawling on their stomachs, looking rather timid and afraid to get out and move, but in seeing Harris jump up and fire, yell, and carry on like he did, they then got up and did the same thing. All this went on for about ten minutes, in which time I could hear the guns of the enemy stop firing one by one until Lieutenant Harris made a semicircle of the garrison, coming in from the extreme left flank.

"In my questioning Lieutenant Harris and his men, it was found out that one pillbox, two machine guns, and several machine pistols had been knocked out; a total of eight to ten enemy had been killed. Upon checking the area later, I found this to be true. In my questioning the two men who had been with Lieutenant Harris and some of the prisoners he had taken, I found out that Lieutenant Harris' actions, in the face of such apparent great odds, his tenacity, aggressiveness, and sheer guts inspired the two men to do things they would not normally do; and so surprised the enemy that they did not have time to organize properly, and also made them think that there were thirty men instead of only three. After this initial action and the garrison [was] in our hands, it became apparent that the enemy who had escaped and those manning the defenses would try a counterattack. The reason for this belief was the fact that the garrison was the headquarters for about two hundred men, with the ammunition dump, first aid station and some vehicles there. Later, this garrison proved to be the strongpoint for the area from St.-Germain-de-Varreville north to Ravenoville.

"In the preparation of the now captured garrison [area] for defense against counterattacks, Lieutenant Harris was given the mission of organizing some of the outposts, using what few men we had to the best advantage on some commanding ground, making effective use of the enemy's gun emplacements and also some of the enemy's guns. During the thirty hours that were spent in defending our position at the garrison, Lieutenant Harris kept up the moral and fighting spirit of the men by continual visits to the men who he had detailed to man the outposts, and by his utter disregard for the enemy's mortar and machine gun fire which was coming down on the positions he had occupied.

"During the night of 6 June 1944, Lieutenant Harris did not sleep nor take time to get any rest for himself, by his continual checking [of] the men on the outposts, bringing them food, water and even manning their guns while they came back to the garrison to get a break, relieve themselves, or to get something to eat in the kitchen, which had been put into operation by some of the group."[16]

Tragically, Lieutenant Harris was killed in action on June 11, 1944 during the assault to capture the key town of Carentan.

Paratroopers from the 502nd and 506th Infantry Regiments, the 377th Parachute Field Artillery Battalion, and a few from the 82nd Airborne Division gather outside the stone buildings of the Marmion Farm after it had been captured by Major John Stopka's small group earlier on June 6, 1944. *United States Army Signal Corps photograph, National Archives.*

Corporal James N. Barba
Company G, 502nd Parachute Infantry Regiment, 101st Airborne Division

Lieutenant George H. Craft, with Company G, 502nd Parachute Infantry Regiment, landed well to the southwest of Drop Zone A, which was located east of Ste.-Mère-Église. "When I hit the ground the only man in my plane I could locate was Corporal Barba. We both got ourselves oriented and hit the main road to Ste.-Mère-Église. When we reached the road, we ran into several men from G Company. As we proceeded to Ste.-Mère-Église we picked up more men, and finally had around a hundred men. We were trying to get to our company objective at St.-Martin-de-Varreville. Just outside Ste.-Mère-Église and on the main road my lead scouts were fired on. It was determined that in order to proceed with a minimum loss of time we would have to reduce the position (fortified roadblock) in order for troops behind to continue up the road.

"The enemy position was such that no one could advance under such heavy enemy fire. It was determined that a flanking effort should be made and although the flank was heavily covered with fire of enemy automatic weapons, it would draw sufficient fire to make a frontal assault.

This iconic photograph of 101st Airborne Division paratroopers posing with a captured German flag was taken at the Marmion Farm. *United States Army Signal Corps photograph, National Archives.*

"From the time the scouts had been fired on initially, the company was in the ditches along the road. The road was bordered by banks of earth and had hedgerows running along the top of the banks up to the enemy position. During the action the flank patrol was completely out of observation of the remainder of the company, which was pinned down in the ditches along side the road. It was practically impossible to move more than two or three men up across the hedgerow to the flank, for they would be sky-lined and the enemy machine guns would and did commence firing at anything they heard move in the road. The flanking patrol was fired on as they moved over the road and across the hedgerow to the flank of the position.

"Corporal Barba and myself were the only ones able to get across the hedgerow. Consequently, I was the only eyewitness to the action that took place on the flank of the position. Corporal Barba and I proceeded to work up the flank and got to a point fifty yards from an enemy machine gun that immediately drew fire on us. Only one man could proceed. Corporal Barba volunteered to go into the position with a Tommy gun and hand grenades and raise enough hell to reduce the position and create confusion.

"Corporal Barba continued to advance in the face of heavy enemy fire and reached a slit trench in the inner defenses of the enemy. In doing so, he had to go through antipersonnel mines, double apron barbed wire, and final protective line before reaching the inner defenses. He was rushed by enemy personnel in the position and threw hand grenades and fired his Tommy gun into them before he himself was fatally wounded. He succeeded in killing two of the enemy and drawing the bulk of the position fire on himself to enable the company to advance and demolish the position. His action, initiative, and courage have set an example in the eyes of his men long to be remembered."[17]

Major General Maxwell D. Taylor
Headquarters, 101st Airborne Division

The commanding officer of the 101st Airborne Division, General Maxwell Taylor, jumped with the 3rd Battalion, 501st Parachute Infantry Regiment, which was scheduled to jump on Drop Zone C. "I dropped halfway between Ste.-Marie-du-Mont and Vierville, just west of the highway connecting the two villages. I landed alone in a field surrounded by the usual high hedges and trees with a few cows as witnesses. The rest of my stick went into an adjacent field and it took me about twenty minutes to find anyone. The area into which I wandered was covered with field fortifications, newly constructed but fortunately I encountered no Germans. Gradually, I picked up a few men of the 501st and later contacted General [Anthony C.] McAuliffe, who had a group of artillery personnel with him. Still under cover of darkness, we worked our way eastward for about a quarter of a mile and finally halted in an enclosed field where we began to gather stragglers. It was here that I first ran into Colonel [Julian J.] Ewell. We outposted the field and sent out patrols in all directions. They, however, learned very little in the darkness and were driven back by enemy fire that seemed to be on all sides."[18]

General Taylor waited impatiently as the slow process of assembling troopers and equipment took place in the predawn hours. "It was nearly daylight when we had assembled about eighty or ninety men out of the eight hundred troops that were supposed to be there. We had the division commander, McAuliffe, the chief of staff, division engineer—all the brains—radio operators, horseshoers, cooks, K.P.—and only about twenty real soldiers. Never had so few been commanded by so many…

"The question was, 'Where were we?' I am ashamed to say it was daylight before we could discover where we were. Just as dawn was breaking we looked up and saw the large church steeple and knew where we were—Ste.-Marie[-du-Mont]. Originally, the plan was to try to control the operation from Mouesville. The 506th wasn't where it was supposed to be. We thought we would form a combat group and march on Pouppeville and secure one important causeway. It was quite a job making a reasonable combat group out of that heterogeneous collection of soldiers. We went cross country—we didn't want to fight—we wanted to get to Pouppeville. Soon we heard a little firing and encountered our first Germans. About this time the great show started. The naval bombardment started. The Germans were watching seaward to see the show. Five of them were standing in the road when Private [Virgil E.] Danforth of the 501st got all five with a bullet through the head. I thought that was the best marksmanship I saw during the war.

"I was always concerned about new troops, about green troops going into first combat with the enemy. I felt sure of the 101st, but still there is always a question mark. It was about ten o'clock and we still hadn't got to Pouppeville. I saw one of my young parachute soldiers about eighteen years old, who had gotten hungry, sit down on one of the dead Germans with his head spattered across the road. There sat my soldier calmly munching his K-ration. That settled my mind about my new troops. Pouppeville was taken about noon and at about one o'clock the seaborne people came in—the amphibious troops…

"We could tell the machine guns were American guns by their slow rate of fire. Finally, contact was made and we picked up the last Germans—it was a great pleasure to see the shoulder patch of the 4th Division."[19]

Major General Maxwell D. Taylor, the commanding officer of the 101st Airborne Division. *United States Army Signal Corps photograph.*

Corporal Virgil E. Danforth
Company G, 501st Parachute Infantry Regiment, 101st Airborne Division

During the advance to Pouppeville, Corporal Virgil E. Danforth, acting as one of the scouts for General Taylor's group, was fired at by Germans from ditches and the hedgerows lining the road. "We took off for Pouppeville. It was only two miles away. Captain [Vernon] Kraeger [commander of Company G, 501st] insisted on walking down the center of the road toward the town carrying his carbine, which was almost as big as he was. Sergeant Lionel Cole was on his right trying to kill all the Germans in the ditch and hedges on that side while I was on the left side doing the same thing. We kept telling the captain to get back where he belonged, but he kept telling us to mind our own business. He had almost lost his whole company (two planeloads crashed) and he was just plain mad. I had an M1 rifle with [Springfield] .03 clips and I was having a rough time feeding the bullets into the gun one at a time; and at the same time [I] outran the captain and killed a number of Germans on my side of the road. I shot eleven in one group in the ditch—all in the head. That was the only part I could see sticking out above the ground, so it wasn't much of a trick."[20]

After eliminating the opposition along the road, Corporal Danforth continued to scout ahead of General Taylor's group as it approached Pouppeville, which lay at the western end of the southern causeway that ran from Utah Beach, designated as Exit 1. "As we came into the town, the Germans began to withdraw into their headquarters, which was on the edge of the town nearest the beach. Until that time, my squad hadn't lost a man. Their defense in the town wasn't very well organized, so we cleaned them out pretty quickly, but when we hit the headquarters building it was a different story. They had two snipers in a tree that we couldn't see and they killed Lieutenant Nathan Marks, Private First Class Bob Richards, and one other from my squad.

"A sergeant from our headquarters platoon was hit in the open and every time the medic, Technician Fifth Grade Harold Nolicy, tried to get to him, the Germans would drive him back. I got over at the side and tried to draw fire so he could get to the downed men, but they put a bullet in me, too. It hit the ring of my helmet and split in two and half of it went into my skull and I still have the headaches to prove it. Captain Kraeger then got hit in the arm with a wooden bullet. About all this did to him was make him madder. We brought up a bazooka and fired a few rounds into the headquarters building and they decided to surrender."[21]

First Lieutenant George M. Eberle
Company D, 502nd Parachute Infantry Regiment, 101st Airborne Division

Upon landing about five miles south of the Drop Zone A, Captain Carlton P. Chandler, the executive officer of the 2nd Battalion, 502nd Parachute Infantry Regiment, assembled a group of about twenty troopers, including Lieutenant George M. Eberle, a graduate of the United States Military Academy's class of 1943. Lieutenant Eberle was the platoon leader of the 3rd Platoon of Company D, 502nd Parachute Infantry. Captain Chandler led this group north to link up with the rest of the 2nd Battalion. "We had gone about three miles and were approaching Audonville-La-Hubert on our way to the original battalion objective when we were brought under severe enemy machine gun fire along the road about a mile south of the town. This machine gun fire and the fire from accompanying enemy snipers had us pinned down in ditches along either side of the road. We had first tried to knock out the position by hand grenades, as it was still rather dark, but were unsuccessful. About 04:15, while it was growing lighter all the time, I told Lieutenant Eberle to take Sergeant [Bartow R.] Theall and five riflemen from our small group and with this patrol, work up inside the hedgerow that was bounding the road on the right and gave the order for everyone to load their weapons, as we could now distinguish people in the early morning light.

"Lieutenant Eberle, without regard for his own personal safety, personally manhandled the [group's .30 caliber] machine gun, and with his small crew crossed the road and moved up on the enemy position. The rest of the men were with me trying to make a flanking movement on our left flank, but were unable to because of inundation. We were forced to come back to the hedgerow on the left of the road and from there I saw Lieutenant Eberle lead his patrol and knock out the enemy machine gun position.

"The superb initiative and courage of Lieutenant Eberle and his men killed and wounded five of the enemy, disorganized them, caused their withdrawal, and allowed the remaining group then under the command of First Sergeant [John] Wollen, D Company, 502nd Parachute Infantry, to advance up the road and when they tied in with elements of our 3rd Battalion moving south, completed the capture of this main road for use by elements of the 101st Airborne Division.

"Although wounded, Lieutenant Eberle had asked me for the permission to lead this patrol when we were discussing how we were going to knock out this machine gun position after our first attempts had been unsuccessful. Lieutenant Eberle, with his machine gun had only five hundred rounds of ammunition with which to knock out this enemy machine gun position. The enemy must have had many times that number, as they were firing almost continuously on us for an hour from their previously prepared position. Lieutenant Eberle and his crew must have exhibited distinguished marksmanship with so few rounds to knock out a prepared position when that same enemy gun had failed to harm us during the preceding hour."[22]

What happened next is not fully known, but Lieutenant Eberle and the group of five troopers evidently returned to the road after knocking out the German machine gun crew. Private First Class Lemuel L. Nicholas, with Company D, 502nd Parachute Infantry Regiment, stated that "Lieutenant George Eberle, a West Pointer, a good officer and soldier, and well liked by his men, was killed along with his platoon sergeant, Bill Monroe, by a German who rode up on a bicycle and pretended to surrender. The Kraut had a burp gun under his coat and took them by surprise. The German was killed too."[23]

Sergeant Eli Cole, with Headquarters Company, 2nd Battalion, 502nd Parachute Infantry, was south of the point where Eberle was killed. "First Sergeant Wollen asked me to go with the aid man forward as he had seen some of our troops lying in the road ahead. When the aid man and myself crossed the road to the place indicated, there was no enemy fire on us. We found Lieutenant Eberle and Sergeant Theall lying there. The aid man reported that the men were dead."[24]

SEVERAL KEY OBJECTIVES assigned to companies or battalions of the 101st Airborne Division were attacked by small groups of troopers who landed near those objectives. There were also enemy strongpoints and other positions which had not been detected by invasion planners, but nevertheless attacked by these ad hoc small groups of paratroopers.

The 502nd Parachute Infantry Regiment's primary objective was the destruction of a coastal artillery battery of 122mm guns located at St. Martin-de-Varreville. This battery was protected in concrete and steel bunkers and had the range to shell the naval ships and transports, possibly inflicting heavy casualties and disrupting the Utah Beach landing. The 2nd Battalion was assigned to destroy the battery, with the 3rd Battalion as backup if required. The 3rd Battalion was assigned to capture Exits 3 and 4 on the northern side of Utah Beach and block German forces moving south to attack the right flank of the beach landing. The 1st Battalion objective was the capture of a complex of stone buildings at Les Mézières, codenamed Objective WXYZ. The personnel of the German coastal artillery battery at St. Martin-de-Varreville were garrisoned in these buildings which lay a few hundred yards west of the battery and its concrete casemates. The plan called for the 1st Battalion to attack and destroy the garrison prior to H-Hour, before the battery's personnel could deploy to the casemates to man the guns and oppose the beach landing.

Staff Sergeant Harrison C. Summers
Company B, 502nd Parachute Infantry Regiment, 101st Airborne Division

The 1st Battalion's drop was scattered. Lieutenant Colonel Patrick F. Cassidy, the commanding officer, landed about two hundred yards east of the church at St.-Germain-de-Varreville, near the 502nd drop zone. Cassidy proceeded to gather about thirty troopers from his battalion and other units and then moved southeast toward the battalion's objective at Les Mézières.

Private First Class John F. Camien, Jr. was one of a number of Company B, 502nd paratroopers among Cassidy's group as well as troopers who were from other units of the 101st Airborne and at least one officer from the 82nd Airborne Division. "We proceeded along the road to [Les] Mézières, and after arriving there, set up a roadblock at the crossroads, just outside of town. We weren't at this point very long when we received sniper fire. Here, one of the boys from the 506th and I went over to investigate while the rest of the men covered us from the rear. The two of us killed three Germans in the first house. From there we went on to the second house, from which we received no fire, but took two prisoners and killed four sleeping Germans with two hand grenades. The following house was empty, so we went on to the next, where I went upstairs and the boy from the 506th took downstairs. I killed one German and at the same time, I heard someone running up the attic stairs. I went up after him and took prisoner this German officer. While I was upstairs during this action, the 506th boy killed a German soldier and was killed himself by a round from a P-38 [pistol]. Their shots must have been almost simultaneous.

"I turned the officer over to Lieutenant [Elmer F.] Brandenburger, and Sergeant [Harrison C.] Summers proceeded on to the next house with me. There, a French girl told us that there were five Germans hiding in the closet. I put a burst of Tommy gun fire into the door, heard a scream, the door flew open and one German soldier fell dead onto the floor. Another attempted to run up the stairs. Sergeant Summers shot him and killed him. There were three more men in the closet who I kept covered with my Tommy gun. I also turned them over to Lieutenant Brandenburger.

"From there on, Sergeant Summers and myself cleaned out the next four or five houses, taking seven or eight prisoners and killed about ten Germans. That just about completed the group of houses. The last remaining building appeared to be a German barracks, because we encountered heavy small arms fire. At this time, Lieutenant Brandenburger deployed all of his men around the building. A heavy firefight ensued between the Germans and us. This continued for about an hour.

"Then Lieutenant Brandenburger sent me back to the crossroads for bazookas and mortars. There, I ran into Lieutenant [Homer] Combs and some of his men and took them back with me. After we returned, we laid on mortar fire and bazooka fire, setting the house in flames. None of the Germans were left alive."[25]

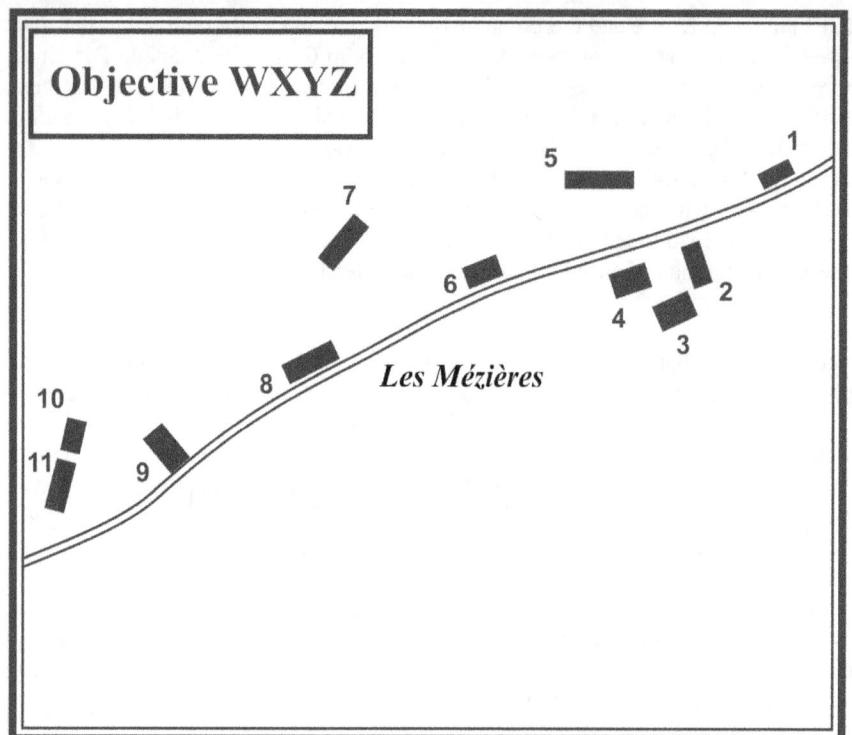

This map depicts the sequence in which Private First Class John F. Camien, Jr. and a trooper from the 506th Parachute Infantry, then later with Staff Sergeant Harrison C. Summers, cleared buildings at Les Mézières which served as living quarters for German troops who manned a coastal artillery battery at St. Martin-de-Varreville. The eleventh building was defended by a large number of enemy troops, and was later attacked by a group of paratroopers who killed all of the German troops defending it.

ON THE SOUTHERN SIDE of the 101st Airborne Division's area of operations, the primary objective of the 3rd Battalion, 506th Parachute Infantry Regiment was the capture of two wooden bridges across the Douve River northeast of Carentan and the high ground overlooking the bridges on the south side of the river at Brévands.

Private First Class George Montilio
Company H, 506th Parachute Infantry Regiment, 101st Airborne Division

Private First Class Donald E. Zahn
Company H, 506th Parachute Infantry Regiment, 101st Airborne Division

Shortly after sunrise, a group of five officers and twenty-nine enlisted paratroopers arrived on the north side of the Douve River, near one of the two footbridges that were objectives of the 3rd Battalion, 506th Parachute Infantry. Like others in the group, Private First Class Donald E. Zahn, with Company H, 506th, didn't know whether the enemy held the other side of the river. "Captain [Charles G.] Shettle was looking for somebody to scout the opposite side of the Douve River. Nobody seemed to be wanting to volunteer, and I remembered that I was a scout, and I decided that being a scout it was my job to do what the captain was asking me to do. I was then armed with a carbine that I had been given by a man that I had met on the way over to the bridge. So, I said I would like a Thompson and somebody came up with a Thompson. I basically ran across the top of the bridge and I sprayed both sides of the bridge embankments thinking there were foxholes there. Then I just dropped down onto the bank of the Douve River and worked my way along the bank—going over, looking up. Eventually I got to the point where I could see some Germans in a wooded area who seemed to be unaware of our presence. They were just very visible to me and it appeared to be a machine gun nest. So, I went a little further past that area to a point where I could see buildings. I don't remember seeing any activity in that area.

"I was working my way back to the bridge with the idea of reporting to Captain Shettle what I had seen. I started back and ran into [Private First Class George] Montilio—then behind Montilio came a group of other men. I remember that [Private Mario J.] Hank DeCarlo was one of the men coming over. Lieutenant [Richard P.] Meason was in the group. They wanted to go back and engage them. Lieutenant Meason wanted to see what was there. The group of us moved back to where I had said the machine gun nest or the group of Germans were [located]. A firefight developed as a result of the group's desire to engage that group of Germans. When we started firing at the group at the strongpoint they came out of there. They came running across the open field and came up the bank. We threw hand grenades and with the hand grenades and all of the firing, they retreated, with the exception of a German who came over the bank with a pistol and shot Hank DeCarlo, who was in front of me. I think he hit Hank in the shoulder. I dispatched the German with the Thompson. Hank was able to move. We all went back across the bridge, and I believe we all crawled underneath the framework of the bridge to get back to the other side. We came under some artillery fire—some fire from the German positions. We got back to the other side and then Captain Shettle promoted me to buck sergeant."[26]

TWO GERMAN ARTILLERY BATTERIES were located short distances west and north of Ste.-Marie-du-Mont that had not been picked up by Allied aerial photo reconnaissance and therefore no parachute units were assigned to attack and destroy them. Each battery consisted of four 105mm howitzers dug in behind hedgerows and connected by trenches and tunnels. The positions were protected by artillerymen armed with machine guns and small arms. Both batteries were firing on the troops landing at Utah Beach that morning. The first battery was located near Holdy, just west of Ste.-Marie-du-Mont and the other was near Brécourt Manor to the north of Ste.-Marie-du-Mont. Captains Lloyd E. Patch and Knut H. Raudstein and a small force of paratroopers with the 1st Battalion, 506th Parachute Infantry Regiment attacked the battery at Holdy. A small force of paratroopers from Company E, 506th, led by Lieutenant Richard D. Winters, attacked the artillery battery positioned near Brécourt Manor, just north of Ste.-Marie-du-Mont.

Captain Lloyd E. Patch
Headquarters Company, 1st Battalion, 506th Parachute Infantry Regiment, 101st Airborne Division

Captain Knut H. Raudstein
Company C, 506th Parachute Infantry Regiment, 101st Airborne Division

West of Ste.-Marie-du-Mont, two officers with the 506th Parachute Infantry Regiment, Captain Knut H. Raudstein, the commanding officer of Company C, and Captain Lloyd E. Patch, the commanding officer of Headquarters Company, 1st Battalion, moved through the hedgerow lined countryside near the tiny hamlet of Holdy looking for their men. As they did this, they heard large caliber German artillery firing. Patch and Raudstein decided to move toward the sound of the gunfire in hope of finding their units.

"When the two officers entered Holdy, Captain Raudstein found "a force of about ten or more men from Headquarters, A, and B Companies, who were attempting to place the battery under fire. This group was immediately increased by two men from the 82nd Division, who were far from their [drop] zones. One of these men had a 1903 rifle with a grenade launcher and some rifle grenades. The other principal armament of the force was a light machine gun with three belts of ammunition.

"This group left the buildings at Holdy and moved to a stone farmhouse about twenty yards from the battery position. The machine gun was set up in the road and one belt fired at the position. The hedgerows on both sides of the road restricted the traverse of the gun to less than ten degrees, and it is doubtful that this firing caused any casualties to the enemy. However, the proximity of the fire did cause the gun crews to leave their pieces and take cover in the ditch surrounding the position and the pieces were thereafter not fired by the enemy. The attacking force realized that it had not yet accomplished anything of real value and would not until the guns themselves were seized. It was decided that a base of fire would be established with the machine gun and the grenade launcher, and the remainder of the force would cross the road and attempt to enter the ditch in which the gun crews were taking cover. The grenade launcher was set up at the edge of the building atop the hedgerow, but while targets were being pointed out to the gunner, he was shot in the neck; whereupon he withdrew to Holdy where aid men had established an aid station. The machine gun and grenade launcher, under the command of one officer, was moved to positions on higher ground across from the farmhouse. The other officer and two men prepared to move along a hedgerow toward the position and then, under cover of the hedgerow surrounding the position, planned to enter the ditch from the northwest. Just as they were moving out, the battalion antitank officer, with one rocket launcher and two men from the antitank platoon arrived in Holdy. They were oriented quickly and sent around a lateral hedgerow to get into position where they could fire into, or preferably enter, the ditch from the southwest. These two flanking elements moved forward while the machine gun fired short bursts at the top of the hedgerow concealing the ditch. Both flanking units crossed the road at about the same time and advanced toward the entrances to the ditch, throwing grenades. The enemy threw grenades back. Although the potato masher grenade could be thrown farther, its effect was not comparable to the fragmentation grenade.

"The ditch was entered from both directions as planned, and the two forces converged toward the center of the position. The ditch had been improved and made into a deep trench in which ammunition for the guns and grenades and small arms had been liberally stocked. The defenders gave little resistance once the trench was entered, because the blast of the rockets from one flank and the continual concussion of grenades from the other took most of the fight out of the artillerymen. Some fled down a drainage ditch to the east. About thirty prisoners were taken and approximately fifty dead or wounded were found in the trenches.

"The reduction of the position permitted many soldiers, who had landed near the position, to leave their cover and proceed toward their assembly areas. Some of these men had lain within fifteen yards of the ditch all night, and would have most certainly been killed or captured had the defenders policed the field instead of attempting to cover the field by fire. Included in those released from their enforced retirement were the battalion S-3, several division staff officers who had landed in the field by glider during the night, about forty 1st Battalion men, and numerous others from other organizations. Total casualties for the attacking force were one man wounded in the neck."[27]

First Lieutenant Richard D. Winters
Company E, 506th Parachute Infantry Regiment, 101st Airborne Division

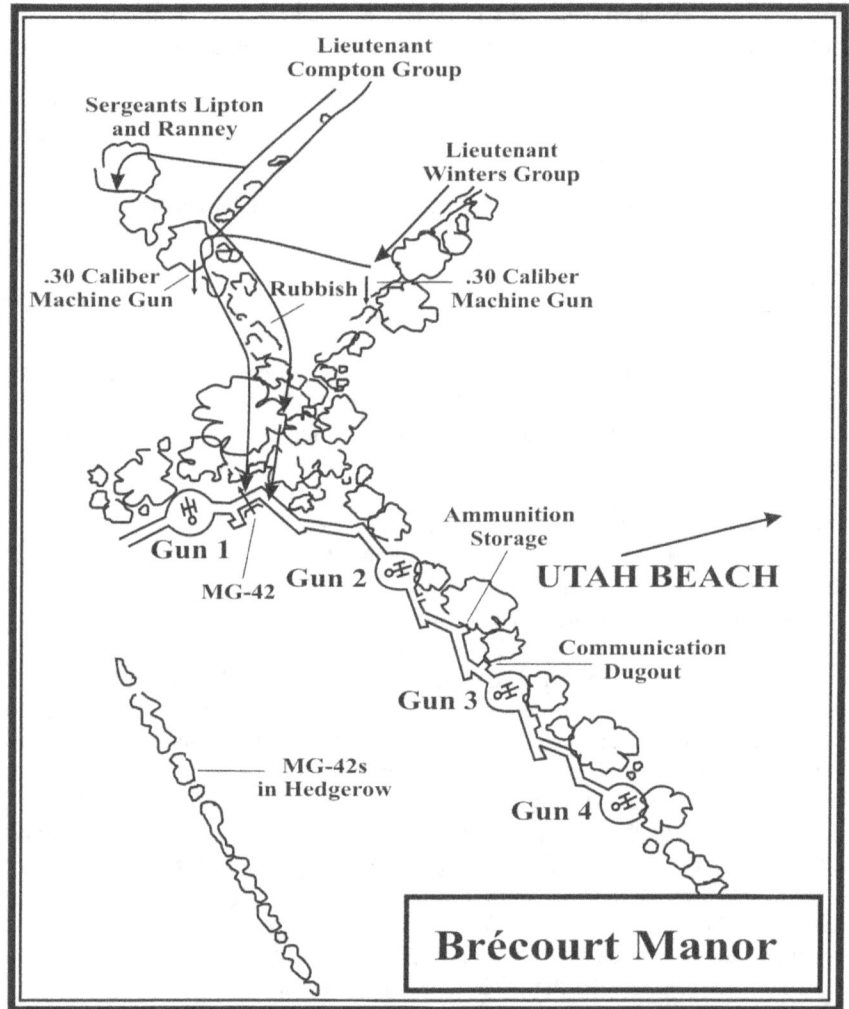

After landing near Ste.-Mère-Église, far to the north of his unit's drop zone, Lieutenant Richard D. Winters, executive officer of Company E, 506th Parachute Infantry, rounded up twelve troopers and after ascertaining his location, led them southeast toward his battalion's objective, the west end of the causeway which ran from Utah Beach to La Grande Chemin, designated as Exit 2. At around 6:00 a.m., Lieutenant Winters and his group came upon about forty troopers from Company D, 506th. Together they moved south and east until finding the main body of the 2nd Battalion, 506th, which totaled about two hundred men and officers. Winters rounded up the Company E troopers from among the assembled group. "E Company now consisted of two light machine guns, one bazooka (without ammunition), one 60mm mortar, nine riflemen and two officers. We were running across a lot of dead Boche as we moved down the road for our objective, but very little fire. Suddenly some heavy stuff opened up on the head of the column as they moved into a small town called La Grande Chemin. The column stopped, we sat down content to rest. In about ten minutes, Lieutenant George Lavenson, (Battalion S-4) came walking down the line and said, 'Winters, they want you and your company up front.'

"So off we went. Up front, I found Captain [Clarence] Hester [the 2nd Battalion S-3], Lieutenant [Lewis] Nixon [the 2nd Battalion S-2], and [Lieutenant John W.] Kelly [with Company D] in a group talking it over. Seemed like Kelly had taken his company up to a position where he could see the [105mm howitzers], but couldn't do anything about stopping their fire. Captain Hester showed me where an enemy machine gun was located and about where [a 105mm howitzer] was situated. That was all I knew.

"First thing I did was to have everybody drop all equipment except ammunition and grenades, for that's all we'd need if things went good or bad. Then I placed one of my two machine guns in a position where he could give us a little covering fire as we went more or less into position. Next, I divided the group into two units. One went with Lieutenant [Lynn C. 'Buck'] Compton, the other with me. He took one hedge, I another. When we reached the hedge that led up to our position, we stopped. Here I placed another machine gunner facing on the [105mm gun] that was pointing straight at us, with instructions not to fire unless he saw a definite target, so he wouldn't give his position away for he was without cover from the gun. Then we worked up to Lieutenant Compton's hedgerow. Here I spotted a Jerry helmet and squeezed off two shots—later found a pool of blood at this position—while the rest of us gave him [Compton] covering fire. I fired occasionally to fill in spots when there was a lull in the covering fire due to putting in new clips. They took too long getting up and we spent more ammunition than we should have, but in return we received no enemy fire. Just as Compton was ready to throw his grenades I started up with the rest of the assault team so that we were all jumping into the position together as the grenades went off. At the same time we were throwing more grenades to the next position, and in return receiving small arms fire and grenades.

"One man, [Corporal Robert] Wynn, of West Virginia, was hit in the butt and fell down in the trench hollering, 'I'm sorry lieutenant, I goofed off, I goofed off, I'm sorry,' over and over again. At the same time, a Jerry potato masher sailed into the middle of us. We all spread out as much as we could, but Corporal Joe Toye of Reading, Pennsylvania, just flopped down and was unlucky enough to have the grenade fall between his legs as he lay face down. It went off as I was yelling at him, 'Move, for Christ's sake! Move!' He just bounced up and down from the concussion, and then bounced up unhurt and ready to go. A couple of us had tossed some grenades at Jerry at the same time, so we followed up our volley with a rush, not even stopping to look at Wynn. Private Gerald J. Lorraine and Sergeant Bill Guarnere were with me as we pounded in on them. They both had Tommy guns and I had an M1 as we came into position. Three Jerries left the [105mm] that we had found working our way up and started running. It took only a yell to the other two and we opened up on our corresponding man for we were strung out, one, two, three, and so was Jerry. Lorraine hit his man with the first burst. I squeezed a shot off that took my man through the head. Guarnere missed his man, who turned and started back for the gun, but he'd only taken about two steps when I put one in his back that knocked him down, then Guarnere settled down and pumped him full of lead with his Tommy gun. This fellow kept yelling, 'Help, help' for about five minutes.

"We had just finished off these three men when out stepped a fourth about one hundred yards away. I spotted him first and had the presence of mind to lie down and make it a good shot. All this must have taken about fifteen or twenty seconds since we had rushed the position. My next thought was, 'Jesus Christ, somebody will cut loose in a minute from further up the trench.' I flopped down and by lying prone I could look through the connecting trench to the next gun position, and sure enough there were two of them setting up a machine gun, getting ready to fire. I got in the first shot however, and hit the gunner in the hip. The second caught the other boy in the shoulder. By that time, the rest of the group was in position, so I put Toye and Compton covering up toward the next position and three [others] to go over and look over the [105mm] and three [more men] to cover to our front. Then I retraced my steps, looked Wynn over, who was still sorry he goofed off, saw he wasn't too bad and told him to work his way out and back himself, for we couldn't spare anybody to help him. He took off.

"Just as I came back, Compton, who had been fooling around with a grenade, let out a yell, 'Look out!' We all hit for cover but there was no cover, for you couldn't get out of the trench, and right in the middle of it was a grenade set to go off, which it did, but for some damn reason nobody was hurt.

"Then, a Jerry, scared to death, came running down the trench with his hands over his head, so he was our first prisoner. We had a lot of trouble getting him out though. Finally, one of the boys hit him with some brass knuckles, and he lay there moaning for about half an hour until I went over, kicked him in the pants, and let him know it was high time he got out and he did as we wanted. No sooner had this happened than I spotted three Jerries for some damn reason walking toward our position along the hedge in a very informal manner. These soldiers were obviously machine gunners protecting the rear of the [105mm] cannon crews. I got two others up there and we set our range for about two hundred yards; somebody must have yelled at them, for they stopped and seemed to listen. That's when I gave, 'Ready, aim,' and just then this guy Lorraine cut loose with a Tommy gun, which wasn't worth a damn over fifty to seventy-five yards. It wounded one of them, but after that it was pure hell, for they had machine guns on us all the time just cutting the top of the trench.

"It was time we took the second gun, I thought, so I left three behind and we charged the next position with grenades and lots of yelling and firing. I don't think anyone got hurt that time, but we did pick up those two I'd wounded when they tried to put the machine gun up. At this time ammunition was low as hell. I needed more men, for we were stretched out too much for our own good and those damn machine gunners never came on up after us as I'd instructed. So I went back for some.

"After about half an hour the machine guns finally got there, so I put them in place and decided to take the next gun. Two men from another company had come up also. On the attack, one of those boys, Technician Fifth Grade John D. Hall, was killed. We took the position and four prisoners and then again had to hold up. I sent four prisoners I had to the back and at the same time asked for more ammunition and men. Finally, I spotted Captain Hester coming up, went to meet him and he gave me three blocks of TNT and an incendiary thermite grenade. I had these placed in the three guns we had already taken. Also he told me Lieutenant [Ronald C.] Speirs [with Company D] was bringing five men up. So while waiting I went about gathering documents and stuffing them in a bag. I found one good map showing all [artillery] positions and machine gun positions on the peninsula. I sent these back and directed the destruction of the radio equipment, range finders, etc.

"Finally, Speirs arrived and led an attack on the final gun, which we took, destroyed, and then withdrew for the machine gun fire we were receiving from the house and other positions was pretty rough. First the machine guns pulled out then the riflemen. I was last, and as I was leaving I took a final look down the trench and here was this one wounded Jerry we were leaving behind trying to put this machine gun on us again. So I drilled him clean through the head—as I found out later—and then pulled out.

On the way, I found Mr. Andrew F. Hill, a Fox Company warrant officer, dead, as he had been killed trying to work his way up to us. In all we had four dead, six wounded, and accounted for fifteen dead and twelve captured. The enemy force numbered about fifty. When I came out I put the machine guns firing on the position as well as a 60mm mortar as sort of harassing fire. The battalion sent for some tanks to help clean this job up and then left for our objective. About that time, Lieutenant Welsh and Lieutenant Roush came down the road with about thirty more men. I organized them into two groups and had them stand by. Lieutenant Lewis Nixon led the 4th Division tanks up from the beach, and I led the tanks into the [105mm] positions to clean them out."[28]

82ND AIRBORNE DIVISION

Wherever you land, make your way to Ste.-Mère-Église and together we will raise this flag, the same one that flew over the post office in Naples, over the highest building in the town. —Lieutenant Colonel Edward C. Krause

The mission of the 82nd Airborne Division was to land astride the Merderet River, west of the 101st Airborne Division to block counterattacks on the forces landing on Utah Beach from German units driving towards them from the north and west. Major General Matthew B. Ridgway, the commanding officer of the 82nd Airborne, assigned the division's key objective, the seizure and retention of the crossroads town of Ste.-Mère-Église, to the only regiment in either American airborne division with previous combat experience, the 505th Parachute Infantry. The 505th had spearheaded the invasion of Sicily and had fought in the mountains around Salerno, Italy and would be making its third combat jump in less than a year. Ste.-Mère-Église lay astride the major highway that ran south from Cherbourg to Paris and one of the two roads that ran east from the Merderet River to Utah Beach. The 504th Parachute Infantry Regiment had been held back when the 82nd Airborne Division left Italy to prepare for the invasion of Normandy. The 504th, badly depleted from fighting in Italy, had arrived in England in April. General Ridgway withheld the 504th from the invasion so that it could be rested and brought back to full strength, too late to participate in the invasion. The untested 507th and 508th Parachute Infantry Regiments had been attached to the division for the invasion and were assigned to jump west of the Merderet River to secure two causeways at la Fière and Chef-du-Pont and establish a defensive line to block German attacks from the west and north.

The division's pathfinder teams would mark three drop zones for the main force. The 505th pathfinders would mark Drop Zone O, west of Ste.-Mère-Église. Upon landing, the 3rd Battalion, 505th would seize the town, the 2nd Battalion would establish a roadblock on the highway about a mile north of Ste.-Mère-Église at Neuville-au-Plain, and the 1st Battalion would secure the east ends of the two Merderet River causeways. The 507th pathfinders would mark DZ T near Amfreville, west of the Merderet River. The regiment's 3rd Battalion would push west and block German attacks from that direction. The 1st Battalion would move northwest and block German attacks from the north and west, while the 2nd Battalion would seize the west end of the la Fière causeway, clear the regimental sector, and then be placed in reserve. The 508th pathfinders would mark Drop Zone N, north of Picauville. Upon landing, the regiment's 3rd Battalion would move west to block German attacks from the west, tying in with the 507th Parachute Infantry Regiment on its right. The 2nd Battalion, 508th would move south and destroy two bridges across the Douve River to block enemy forces from the south. The 1st Battalion would seize Hill 30, which overlooked the Merderet River from the west between the la Fière and Chef-du-Pont causeways.

Private First Class Thomas L. Rodgers
Company C, 504th Parachute Infantry Regiment, 82nd Airborne Division and 82nd Provisional Pathfinder Company

Thirty minutes ahead of the aircraft transporting the main body of the 82nd Airborne Division, nine planes carrying the division pathfinder teams passed over the west coast of the Cotentin Peninsula. Volunteers from among the combat veterans of the 504th Parachute Infantry Regiment served as security for the 507th and 508th Parachute Infantry pathfinder teams. Private Thomas J. McCarthy, with Company A, 504th, and Private First Class Thomas L. Rodgers, with Company C, 504th, were among four 504th veterans assigned to provide security for the 3rd Battalion, 507th pathfinder team.

As the three planes transporting the 507th pathfinder teams approached the drop zone near Amfreville and just west of the Merderet River, antiaircraft fire rose up to meet them. When the green light flashed on, Lieutenant John T. Joseph, the 507th regimental pathfinder leader and jumpmaster of the 3rd Battalion, 507th team stick, went out the door followed by the rest of the stick. After exiting the plane, Private McCarthy felt the sudden jerk of his chute opening. "I looked down and saw that we were not heading for the big field, but were going to land right on top of a German garrison in the farmhouse. The pilot had given us the light too early, and we were coming up short. It was a full moon and with the clouds having moved off, we were coming in low—perfect targets.

The 3rd Battalion, 507th pathfinder team, photographed on the evening of June 5, 1944, shortly before takeoff. Private First Class Thomas L. "Lloyd" Rodgers, from Andalusia, Alabama, who had fought as a member of Company C, 504th Parachute Infantry Regiment in Sicily, at Salerno, in the mountains of Italy, and at Anzio, is standing third from the left on the back row with the blackened face and wearing his helmet. *United States Army Air Corps photograph, courtesy of Bill Rodgers, Jr.*

"I could see the Krauts running around shooting at us with small arms. One of the bullets from the small arms creased my head and I came down a little dazed, but I kept an eye on those birds doing the shooting, and did a little swearing at the pilot, who was now heading for home. The Krauts weren't organized, thank God; they were scared too! I remember seeing Rodgers go down—he was a big guy from C Company—a BAR man. He landed right inside the courtyard of that farmhouse. I remember hearing the BAR going and then the sound of a Kraut burp gun, and it was over."[1]

The recommendation for Rodgers' Distinguished Service Cross stated that "three of his comrades from the pathfinder team were trapped in a dead end street by frontal fire from an enemy machine gun. Private First Class Rodgers, who was present in the immediate area, recognized that his comrades had no means of escape, whereupon he unhesitatingly climbed on a stone wall and from a fully exposed position knocked out the machine gun crew with his BAR. He then crawled under continuing small arms fire from other enemy riflemen to the three man group. With his BAR he afforded covering fire, thereby enabling the two able bodied men of the three to move to a covered position. The third man who had been wounded, he bodily carried out of the danger zone."[2]

The 507th pathfinder teams all landed under intense enemy small arms and machine gun fire, with the 1st Battalion team landing five hundred yards southeast of the drop zone. The 2nd and 3rd Battalion teams' Eurekas were put into operation, but no lights were set up due to the dispersion of the sticks and enemy fire in the vicinity of the pathfinder landings. This resulted in significant dispersion of the regiment's drop, with only two of 117 sticks landing on the drop zone.

The 508th Parachute Infantry Regiment pathfinder teams also were under heavy fire during the approach of its three plane serial and were all dropped south and east of the drop zones and some of the pathfinders remained under fire upon landing. The 3rd Battalion team's Eureka was the only one put into operation and no lights were set up, resulting in a badly scattered drop for the regiment.

The veteran 505th pathfinders landed on the drop zone and put all three Eurekas into operation and set up three sets of lights in the standard "T" configuration. The experienced aircrews transporting the 505th and its experienced jumpmasters contributed to the only thing approaching an accurate drop for any parachute regiment of either division. This contributed to the assembly of the regiment and movement to capture the objectives prior to dawn.

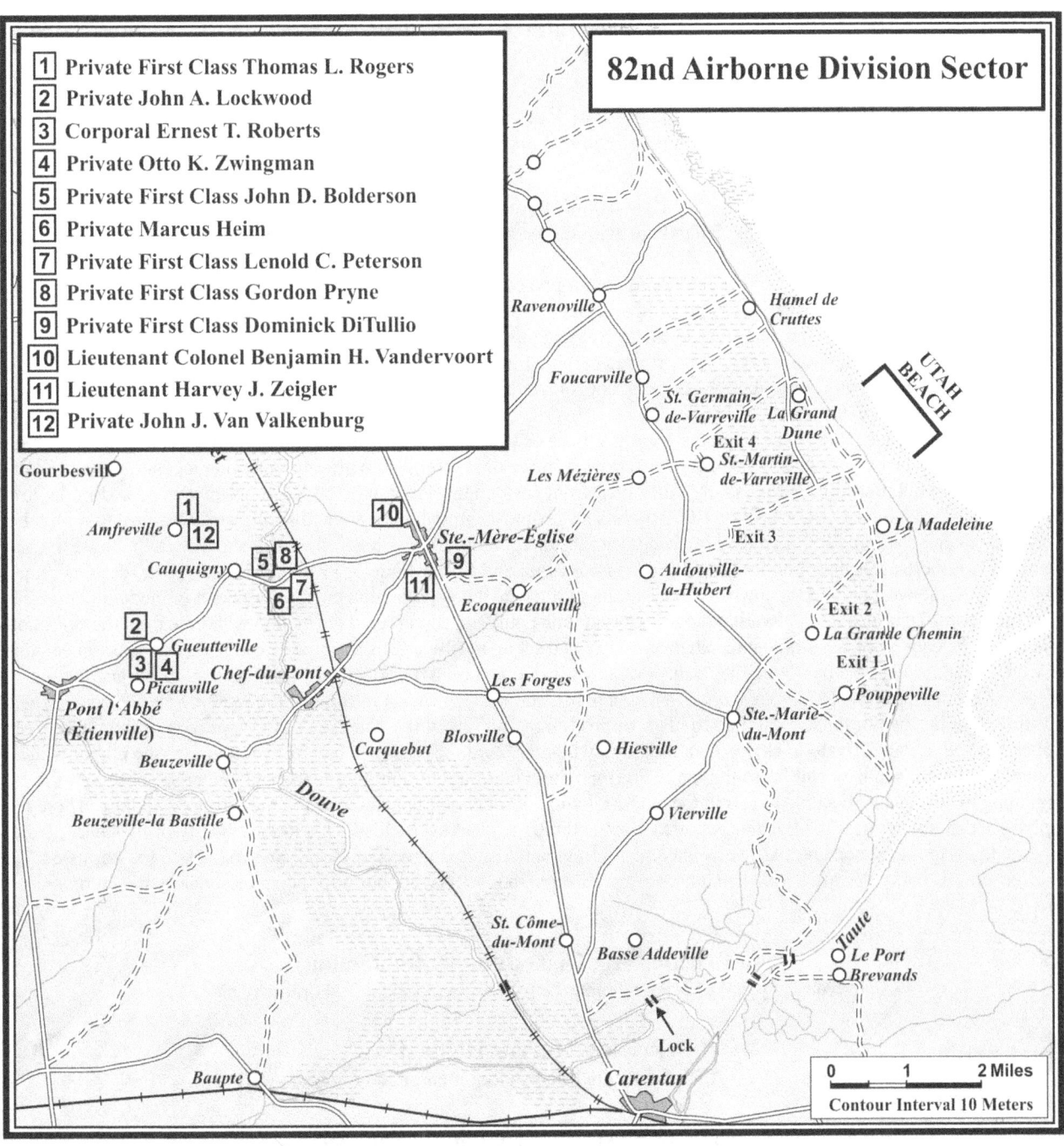

Private John A. Lockwood
Company D, 508th Parachute Infantry Regiment, 82nd Airborne Division

Corporal Ernest T. Roberts
Company D, 508th Parachute Infantry Regiment, 82nd Airborne Division

Private Otto K. Zwingman
Company D, 508th Parachute Infantry Regiment, 82nd Airborne Division

Shortly after 10:00 a.m. on June 6, a German kampfgruppe consisting of Bataillon 3, Grenadier Regiment 1057 of Luftlande Division 91, supported by light tanks of Panzer Ersatz und Ausbildungs Abteilung 100, approached the village of Gueutteville, west of the Merderet River. This force was intent on crossing the river at the la Fière causeway, then pushing east through Ste.-Mère-Église and attacking Utah Beach. A short time earlier, Lieutenant Lynn C. Tomlinson, a platoon leader with Company D, 508th Parachute Infantry, and some thirty paratroopers had arrived in Gueutteville and had established positions blocking the road leading through it.

Lieutenant Norman MacVicar, the commanding officer of Company D, wrote the following recommendation based on a report from Lieutenant Tomlinson regarding the actions of three of his troopers who were manning a position overlooking the main road. "An outguard of approximately thirty men from Lieutenant [Hoyt T.] Goodale's group was posted in the town of Gueutteville under First Lieutenant Lynn C. Tomlinson…Almost immediately after this outguard was posted a battalion of German infantry, reinforced by five tanks, arriving from the direction of Ètienville attacked Gueutteville from the west. Corporal [Ernest T.] Roberts, together with Private [John A.] Lockwood and Private[Otto K.] Zwingman, had been set as an outpost in a building on the west side of the town. They were the first to see the approaching enemy force and immediately opened fire. First Lieutenant Tomlinson, upon hearing the firing, went to the building and ordered the men to withdraw from their position and proceed to the causeway. He saw that the attacking force had set up machine guns and mortars and had two tanks in position, all of which were firing at the building. They called back that they could hold the attack while the other outposts and the remainder of the outguard withdrew. Lieutenant Tomlinson counted fifteen dead Germans in front of the building and decided to hold the position. Lieutenant Tomlinson returned to his own position and directed the defense in other portions of the town. Corporal Roberts, together with Private Lockwood and Private Zwingman, held the enemy at bay for two hours, at the end of which time Lieutenant Tomlinson saw and heard the tanks fire four shots into the building they occupied. When he observed the enemy beginning to advance he decided to pull in the outpost, returned to the building and ordered the men to withdraw. There was no reply. Another soldier near the building reported that the three men had been killed. Due to the severity of the attack, there was no time to verify the statement, and the group under Lieutenant Tomlinson was gradually driven back to the northeast."[3]

Corporal Roberts, Private Lockwood, and Private Zwingman all survived, but were taken prisoner by the German troops.

Private First Class John D. Bolderson
Company A, 505th Parachute Infantry Regiment, 82nd Airborne Division

Private Marcus Heim, Jr.
Company A, 505th Parachute Infantry Regiment, 82nd Airborne Division

Private First Class Lenold C. Peterson
Company A, 505th Parachute Infantry Regiment, 82nd Airborne Division

Private First Class Gordon C. Pryne
Company A, 505th Parachute Infantry Regiment, 82nd Airborne Division

The delay of the German counterattack force at Gueutteville had bought vital time for Company A, 505th Parachute Infantry Regiment, under the command of Lieutenant John J. Dolan, to secure the eastern end of the la Fière causeway. "We dug in, [with] the disposition of my company as follows: 1st Platoon on the north side of the road, the 3rd on the south and the 2nd in reserve, about four hundred yards back, so that it could also protect the rear. On the bridge I had three bazooka teams. Two of them were from Company A and the third was either from B or C Company. The two Company A bazookas were dug in to the left and right of the bridge. Because the road itself was the causeway type, they dug in below the level of the road. The third bazooka was over more to the south where better cover was available."[4]

The bazooka was the primary antitank weapon employed by United States Army and Marine Corps infantrymen during World War II. It was a portable rocket launcher consisting of a fifty-four inch long sheetmetal tube which fired a 2.36 inch diameter rocket with a shaped charge warhead. The high explosive antitank (HEAT) rocket was capable of penetrating up to four inches of armor plate. A two man team made up of a gunner and an assistant gunner was assigned to operate a bazooka. The assistant gunner carried the rockets and was responsible for loading the weapon. The assistant would insert a rocket into the rear of the tube and connect wires from the rocket to battery connections on the tube that provided the ignition source for the rocket when the trigger was pulled.

The Company A bazooka team positioned on the northern shoulder of the causeway consisted of Private First Class John D. Bolderson, the gunner, and Private Gordon C. Pryne, who a short time earlier had been designated as the team's assistant gunner. Private Pryne had been a rifleman with Company A when he jumped into Normandy. "But, on the jump, one of the guys on the bazooka team broke his ankle. They gave that job to me. I didn't want it, really, but they said, 'You got it.' I said, 'O.K.'"[5]

The other Company A bazooka team consisted of Private First Class Lenold C. Peterson, the gunner, and Private Marcus Heim, Jr., the assistant gunner. This team was on the southern shoulder of the causeway. Private Heim, a new replacement, had also recently been assigned as the bazooka team's loader. "There was a concrete telephone pole just in front of us and we dug in behind it. I do not remember how many paratroopers were around; all I saw was a machine gun set up in the Manoir house yard. On the right side down the pathway a few riflemen were placed. We carried antitank mines and bazooka rockets from the landing area. These mines were placed across the causeway about fifty feet on the other side of the bridge. There was a broken down German truck by the Manoir house, which we pushed and dragged across the bridge and placed it across the causeway."[6]

Meanwhile, additional troopers had arrived to strengthen Captain Dolan's defenses. "Down at the bridge now was most of Company A, about one platoon of Company B, a platoon of the division engineers (mission to blow the bridge if necessary), about half of battalion headquarters company with mortars and machine gun sections and several stray men from other regiments. The company dug in well and quickly. West of the Merderet River, was a marsh at least one thousand yards wide at its narrowest point. The road running west from the bridge could better be described as a causeway."[7]

Shortly after his company had dug in, Lieutenant Dolan heard heavy German firing directed at a group of 508th troopers who had crossed the causeway earlier. "They were gone at least an hour when we saw several of them retreating back across the marsh. I remember that we helped several of them out of the river, which was quite shallow.

"Just about a half hour before this attack, a 57mm antitank gun was assigned to Company A. I located this gun about one hundred fifty yards from the bridge on the road where it curves to the right as you approach the bridge. Incidentally, this was my CP and later the battalion CP. This gave the gun excellent cover and a good field of fire."[8]

A short time later, intense German automatic weapons fire was directed from the hedgerow lining the western edge of the Merderet River floodplain against his troopers defending the causeway. "The machine gun fire from the Germans was very heavy by now. We didn't return their fire as there were no visible targets and our ammunition supply was limited."[9]

At approximately 4:00 p.m., a company of German infantry, led by three light tanks, advanced eastward on the causeway. Lieutenant Dolan was about forty yards from the bridge as the German tanks and infantry came into view. "The tanks were firing on us with machine guns and cannons. When the lead tank was about forty or fifty yards away from the bridge, the two Company A bazooka teams got up just like clockwork to the edge of the road. They were under the heaviest small arms fire from the other side of the causeway, and from the cannon and machine gun fire from the tanks."[10]

Getting out of their two man foxhole on the southern shoulder of the causeway, Private Heim quickly loaded the bazooka. "We stood behind the telephone pole so we could get a better shot at the tank. We had to hold our fire until the last minute because some of the tree branches along the causeway were blocking our view. As the lead tank started around the curve in the road the tank commander stood up in the turret to take a look and from our left the machine gun let loose a burst and killed the commander. At the same time the bazookas, 57mm gun, and anything else we had, fired at the Germans and they in turn were shooting at us with cannons, mortars, machine gun and rifle fire."[11]

Private Heim loaded another rocket into the bazooka, connected the wires, and tapped Peterson on the helmet, signifying the bazooka was loaded, as both teams concentrated on knocking out the first tank. "The first tank was hit and started to turn sideways, at the same time was swinging its turret around and firing at us. We had just moved forward around the cement telephone pole when a German round hit it and we had to jump out of the way to avoid being hit as it was falling. I was hoping that Bolderson and Pryne were also firing at the tanks, for with all that was happening in front of us, there was no time to look around to see what others were doing. We kept firing at the first tank until it was put out of action and on fire."[12]

Lieutenant Dolan watched his two bazooka teams courageously continue standing despite the intense enemy fire in order to fire several rockets at the lead tank. "They fired and reloaded with the precision of well oiled machinery. Watching them made it hard to believe that this was nothing but a routine drill. I don't think that either crew wasted a shot. The first tank received several direct hits. The treads were knocked off, and within a matter of minutes it was on fire."[13]

Tanks of Panzer Ersatz und Ausbildungs Abteilung 100 litter the la Fière causeway; knocked out by the two Company A, 505th bazooka teams. This effectively halted the drive by Bataillon 3, Grenader Regiment 1057 of Luftlande Division 91 to cross the Merderet River and drive through Ste.-Mère-Église to attack the beach landings on Utah Beach. *United States Army Signal Corps photograph, National Archives.*

Heim continued to push rocket after rocket into the bazooka. "The second tank came up and pushed the first tank out of the way. We moved forward toward the second tank and fired at it as fast as I could load the rockets into the bazooka. We kept firing at the second tank and we hit it in the turret where the body joins it, also in the tracks, and with another hit it also went up in flames. We were almost out of rockets, and the third tank was still moving. Peterson asked me to go across the road to see if Bolderson had any extra rockets. I ran across the road and with all the crossfire I still find it hard to believe I made it across in one piece. When I got to the other side I found one dead soldier, but Bolderson and Pryne were gone. Their bazooka was lying on the ground and it was damaged by what I thought were bullet holes. Not finding Bolderson or Pryne I presumed that either one or both of them were injured. I found the rockets they left and then had to return across the road to where I left Peterson. The Germans were still firing at us and I was lucky again. I returned without being hit. Peterson and myself, with the new rockets, put these to use against the third tank. This was one of the toughest days of my life. Why we were not injured or killed only the good Lord knows."[14]

Dolan couldn't believe the luck of his two bazooka teams. "To this day, I'll never be able to explain why all four of them were not killed. The 57mm [antitank gun] during this time was firing and eventually knocked out the last tank."[15]

The extraordinary heroism of the paratroopers at Gueutteville had delayed the German force long enough for the troopers at the la Fière causeway to organize defensive positions and repulse the German attack from the west on Ste.-Mère-Église and Utah Beach on June 6.

Private First Class Dominick DiTullio
Headquarters Company, 3rd Battalion, 505th Parachute Infantry Regiment, 82nd Airborne Division

The 3rd Battalion, 505th Parachute Infantry was assigned to capture the key crossroads town of Ste.-Mère-Église. After Lieutenant Colonel Edward C. Krause, the battalion commander, assembled several hundred men and officers, they moved through the town in the predawn darkness and set up roadblocks on all roads leading into the town. He then sent Company I through the village to clean it out, where they killed about thirty of the enemy and captured another thirty. He then supervised the establishment of a perimeter defense on the outskirts of the town, organized around roadblocks on all of the roads which converged on the town. As a part of the defensive preparations, Krause ordered field telephone lines to be laid between his command post in the town and each of the three rifle companies manning the perimeter, one of which was to Company G, which was defending the southern approach to the town along the main highway. "Private First Class [Dominick] DiTullio was a member of the wire section, Headquarters Company, 3rd Battalion, 505th Parachute Infantry, which was ordered to lay a wire to a front line company. The party advanced three hundred yards beyond the front lines in search of the company and was unable to establish contact. It was fired upon and forced to take cover.

"Private First Class DiTullio volunteered to lead the communications officer forward for further information and took the lead when they started out. They immediately drew fire from both their own troops and the enemy because they were well out in front of the battalion's front lines. They discovered that the company they were seeking had withdrawn and while returning to friendly lines were approached by two trucks loaded with Germans. One truck was destroyed by a minefield and roadblock, the other stopping nearby. Private First Class DiTullio opened fire on the Germans without a moment's hesitation and forced them to take cover. They were therefore unable to discover the weakness of the party. He killed one German and forced two to surrender, then advanced with fixed bayonet across the open road to see if there were any Germans remaining. Private First Class DiTullio remained behind to cover the withdrawal of the wire party. The Germans then drove cattle down the road in an attempt to detonate the mines and destroy the roadblock. Private First Class DiTullio came out of his cover, turned the cattle back, and hand grenaded the Germans behind them. When the party had successfully withdrawn, he returned to Ste.-Mère-Église. The road [along which he withdrew] was continually swept by artillery and small arms fire. When he reached the town he discovered that hostile fire around the battalion aid station was so severe as to prevent aid men from securing necessary water. He crossed the fire swept area to a pump and was killed in the act of pumping water."[16]

Lieutenant Colonel Benjamin H. Vandervoort
Headquarters, 2nd Battalion, 505th Parachute Infantry Regiment, 82nd Airborne Division

Lieutenant Colonel Benjamin H. Vandervoort, the commander of the 2nd Battalion, 505th Parachute Infantry, was injured when he landed by parachute on the drop zone. "I landed on about a forty-five degree slope, hit hard, and felt my ankle snap and knew at once it was broken. I got out of my chute in the shadows. I was alone and crawled over to one corner of the hedgerows surrounding the field. The ankle hurt and I shot myself in the leg with a morphine syrette carried in our paratrooper's first aid kit."[17]

Lieutenant James J. Coyle, the platoon leader of the 1st Platoon, Company E, landed nearby. "The first man I encountered was our battalion commander, Lieutenant Colonel Benjamin Vandervoort. He asked me if I had found my medical aid man, but I told him I was alone. At the time, he did not mention that he was injured, but he had broken his ankle on the jump. He ordered me to continue to locate my men."[18]

As the 2nd Battalion was assembling in the moonlit darkness, the battalion surgeon, Captain Lyle B. Putnam, was ordered to report to Vandervoort and found him about an hour after landing. "I located him near a small farmhouse. He was seated with a rain cape over him reading a map by flashlight. He recognized me and calling me close, quietly asked that I take a look at his ankle with as little demonstration as possible. His ankle was obviously broken; luckily a simple rather than a compound fracture. He insisted on replacing his jump boot [and] laced it tightly."[19]

As the 3rd Battalion moved out to capture Ste.-Mère-Église, Vandervoort and his battalion prepared to move northeast to establish a blocking position about a mile north of the town at Neuville-au-Plain. "I think it was about 04:10 in the morning when I felt I completed the assembly sufficiently so that I could move out on our mission and take the town of Neuville-au-Plain. In the meantime, the regiment had told me to stand by. The news from Ste.-Mère-Église was so vague to the regimental commander that he had me stand by. General Ridgway happened to be in my CP during that period and he also directed me not to move without consulting him. It was not until daylight that I received orders to move. We actually started moving at 06:00."[20]

Captain Putnam, the battalion surgeon, watched Vandervoort "pick up his rifle and using it as a crutch, he took a step forward, looked at the men around him. 'Well,' he said, 'let's go!'"[21]

On the way to Neuville-au-Plain, the 2nd Battalion came upon Lieutenant Colonel William E. Ekman, the commander of the 505th, who had been dropped north of the drop zone. Ekman used one of the battalion's radios to attempt to contact the 3rd

Battalion, but was unsuccessful. Fearing that the 3rd Battalion had been misdropped or had been unable to capture Ste.-Mère-Église, Ekman ordered Vandervoort to move the 2nd Battalion south to assist the 3rd Battalion in capturing the town, or reinforce it if the 3rd Battalion was in control of the town.

Vandervoort made a decision that would prove critical to the success of the invasion. "I sent the 3rd Platoon of Company D to Neuville-au-Plain to outpost the area that originally was to have been held by our entire battalion."[22]

As the battalion moved south on the N-13 highway toward Ste.-Mère-Église, Vandervoort "noticed two 101st Airborne Division sergeants moving along with the 2nd Battalion column. They had dropped on the wrong DZ and lost their outfit. They were pulling a wheeled ammunition cart. Since I had a broken leg, I asked them if they would give me a lift into Ste.-Mère-Église. I was told, 'We didn't come to Normandy to pull a damn colonel around.'[23] I persuaded them otherwise."[24]

As the column moved into the town, Sergeant Otis Sampson, with Company E, saw a sight that shocked and infuriated him. "There were [the bodies of] paratroopers still hanging from their chutes where they had been caught in the high trees before they could release themselves.

"Colonel Vandervoort's first command, 'Cut them down!'"[25]

After arriving at Ste.-Mère-Église, Vandervoort released the two 101st Airborne troopers and their ammunition cart from their job of transporting him. "When I got into Ste.-Mère-Église, an elderly French woman, noticing I was using a rifle to hobble about, went into her house and came out with an old fashioned pair of wooden crutches and gave them to me. With these I was able to get about much better."[26]

When the 2nd Battalion entered Ste.-Mère-Église, they found it occupied by Krause's 3rd Battalion. He and Vandervoort met and decided to divide the defense of the town—the 2nd Battalion taking responsibility for the northern and eastern portions, with the 3rd Battalion defending the western and southern approaches.

Later that morning, Vandervoort brought much needed antitank support to the lone platoon which was manning an outpost at Neuville-au-Plain. "About noon I went north to Neuville-au-Plain in a jeep with a 57mm antitank gun and gun crew. I told our 57mm antitank gun crew to go into position on the right of the road where a house offered some concealment. As we drove into Neuville-au-Plain, a French civilian passed us moving south on a bicycle. Lieutenant Turner Turnbull, the platoon leader, told me the Frenchman had just come from the north and had told them that a group of paratroopers had taken a large number of German prisoners and vehicles and were moving south on the highway and would arrive at Neuville-au-Plain shortly. As Turnbull and I walked over his position and talked we kept watching the highway leading from the north. Shortly, a long column of foot troops appeared in the distance with vehicles scattered at intervals through their ranks. If these were prisoners, there was more than a battalion of them. We could make out the field gray of the German uniforms. On their flanks were individuals in paratrooper uniforms waving orange panels that were the recognition signal we were to have used to identify ourselves to friendly aircraft. Somehow, it looked just too good to be true. When the advancing column had closed to within about one thousand yards, I told Turnbull to have his light machine gun fire a burst into the field on the left flank of the column. That did it. The alleged German prisoners deployed instantly on both sides of the road and the leading vehicle, a self-propelled gun, instead of acting like the spoils of war the Frenchman said they were opened fire on our position. Our 57mm antitank gun crew returned the fire and set fire to the leading SP [self-propelled] gun and one more that moved up behind it. A third German SP gun fired smoke shells into the road to its front to screen their position. The German infantry began to move forward on both sides of the road as their 80mm mortars started to range in on the 3rd Platoon position. I told Turnbull to delay the Germans as long as he could, then withdraw to Ste.-Mère-Église. With that, I returned to Ste.-Mère-Église to alert my troops as to what was on the way and to check our positions to meet it."[27]

Later that afternoon, the platoon at Neuville-au-Plain was forced to withdraw in the face of pressure from a kampgruppe under the command of Oberst Kurt Beigang, consisting of Bataillon 1 and Bataillon 2, Grenadier Regiment 1058, Luftlande Division 91; reinforced by Sturm Bataillon AOK 7 (specially trained assault infantry); and with armor support of nine StuG self-propelled assault guns of Kompanie 1, Panzerjäger-Abteilung 709. After capturing Neuville-au-Plain, this kampfgruppe pushed south to the northern outskirts of Ste.-Mère-Église, where it engaged Vandervoort's paratroopers late that day and into the night, before conducting a concerted attack the following morning, with the added support of the Artillerie Abteilung 456 and Artillerie Abteilung 457, plus Artillerie Abteilung 3, Artillery Regiment 243 (less one battery) of Infanterie Division 243. The German attack drove to within fifty yards of Vandervoort's command post before being repulsed with heavy losses.

Lieutenant Colonel Bill Ekman, the commanding officer of the 505th Parachute Infantry Regiment was a witness to the heroism and courageous leadership of Lieutenant Colonel Vandervoort during those first two critical days of the Normandy invasion. "Throughout the continuing engagements with the enemy and under hostile enemy machine gun, rifle, and artillery fire, he moved among his troops directing and encouraging them. He personally inspected the positions of all elements of his command to insure that they were the best available on the terrain. In spite of the pain from his injured foot he was tireless in his effort to maintain his battalion in an offensive defense against enemy repeated counterattacks. Inspired by his ever present encouragement, his men inflicted heavy casualties on the enemy infantry and panzer forces. He maintained a successful defense of the town of Ste.-Mère-Église until the seaborne forces were able to contact his outpost on the 7th of June."[28]

Lieutenant Colonel Benjamin H. Vandervoort, the commanding officer of the 2nd Battalion, 505th Parachute Infantry, 82nd Airborne Division, sits in his command post just outside Ste.-Mère-Église on June 6, 1944. His broken left ankle, wrapped in a gasmask bag, would later be placed in a hard plaster walking cast. *Photograph courtesy of Michel DeTrez.*

First Lieutenant Harvey J. Zeigler
Company H, 505th Parachute Infantry Regiment, 82nd Airborne Division

Late on the afternoon of June 6, several glider serials landed in various fields around Ste.-Mère-Église. Enemy artillery pounded the thinly held perimeter of 505th paratroopers holding the town. From his foxhole near his squad's roadblock on the Chef-du-Pont road southwest of Ste.-Mère-Église, Private First Class Leslie P. Cruise, with Company H, 505th Parachute Infantry, saw a glider descending into a field in front of their position. "One of those gliders had landed about three hundred yards from our roadblock. We could hear the noise as they were getting out and removing equipment. Over their shouting we heard the noise of a jeep motor starting and several troopers left the confines of our position to help.

"Before they reached the landing spot, a jeep rushed down the road passing them even as they shouted a warning about our mines ahead. The occupants of the jeep were in a big hurry as we at the roadblock heard their running motor coming in our direction. Above all the noise, the distinct yells at the block of, 'Hit the ground!' were heard clearly, and we all buried ourselves in the dirt of our foxholes. The driver must have thought our men were Germans and was not about to stop. Down the road they came, full throttle. [There was] a deafening crescendo of explosive sounds as a number of our mines blew the jeep and its troopers into the air. All hell broke loose…flashing lights…with pieces of jeep and mine fragments raining down around us. Directly across the middle of our minefield they drove, and immediately their direction became vertical, and in an arching skyward path they landed in the hedgerow beyond. We could hear the thump and bangs of falling parts all around us. The men had left the jeep on first impact, and they had become the first casualties in our area, but they would not be the last. We had lost about three quarters of our mines, which we had so carefully delivered, and they would be sorely needed in case the Krauts should attack."[29]

Captain Walter C. DeLong, the commanding officer of Company H, 505th, reached the roadblock shortly after the explosion. "A light American truck, loaded with ammunition, accidentally hit an American roadblock and minefield on a road entering Ste.-Mère-Église. The accident dislocated the minefield and damaged the roadblock. The enemy was maintaining accurate fire from artillery and small arms on the damaged truck, which caught fire. At the risk of his own life and with utter disregard for his own safety, Lieutenant Zeigler left cover and personally re-laid the minefield and reconstructed the roadblock. A short while after this action the ammunition in the truck exploded. By his extraordinary heroism, Lieutenant Zeigler reestablished the defensive minefield and roadblock and prevented the enemy from capitalizing its destruction and entering the town."[30]

Private John J. Van Valkenburg
Company I, 507th Parachute Infantry Regiment, 82nd Airborne Division

Lieutenant Robert J. Wilson, a platoon leader with Company I, 507th Parachute Infantry, landed west of the Merderet River and slightly southeast of Amfreville and assembled in an apple orchard east of the town with a group of mostly 507th troopers led by Lieutenant Charles J. Timmes, the commander of the 2nd Battalion, 507th. Lieutenant Wilson observed his platoon medic, Private John J. Van Valkenburg, repeatedly risk his life to treat and evacuate wounded paratroopers on June 6 and later throughout the Normandy campaign. "Before dawn on D-Day, 6 June 1944, elements of the 507th Parachute Infantry landed southeast of Amfreville, France, within enemy lines, and fought for three days west of the Merderet River surrounded by hostile forces until relief reached them on 9 June. During this period, Private Van Valkenburg was the only aid man with the group. He administered first aid and cared for approximately thirty wounded men who had become casualties during this period.

"He worked without sleep, with insufficient rations, with scarcely any medical supplies, and without the help of a doctor. Throughout this period he worked under continuous mortar, artillery, machine gun, and small arms fire, and repeatedly left the defensive area to bring wounded men back within its perimeter. On 6 June 1944, about five hundred yards from Cauquigny, France, Private Van Valkenburg left defensive lines to administer first aid and evacuate two wounded men within sixty yards range of an enemy sniper who had shot them. Without hesitation, and with the sniper firing upon him, he went to the assistance of the wounded men, gave them necessary first aid and effected their evacuation. Later that day, near Le Motey, France, Private Van Valkenburg left the defensive area and went forward to an outpost, where an officer and one enlisted man had been wounded by direct aimed fire of an enemy low trajectory cannon and administered first aid, with shells bursting within five yards of the position. He then assisted them back to the partial protection of buildings on the outskirts of the town. Still later on the same day, he left the defensive area and crossed an open field swept with enemy machine gun fire and brought a wounded man within the defensive perimeter, a distance of more than two hundred yards from where he had fallen."[31]

UTAH BEACH

Almighty God: Our sons, pride of our nation, this day have set upon a mighty endeavor, a struggle to preserve our republic, our religion, and our civilization, and to set free a suffering humanity. —President Franklin D. Roosevelt

The initial objective of the United States Army's VII Corps was to establish a lodgment on the southeastern coast of the Cotentin Peninsula at Utah Beach, followed by a drive to cut the peninsula and capture the port at Cherbourg. The 4th Infantry Division, reinforced by a regimental combat team of the 90th Infantry Division, a combat engineer brigade, a tank battalion, an armored field artillery battalion, a chemical mortar battalion, and numerous other supporting units, would make the assault landing. The 4th Division's 8th Infantry Regiment would make the initial assault following a naval and aerial bombardment of the beach.

Utah Beach was divided into two sectors. The right sector was codenamed "Tare Green" and the left sector was designated as "Uncle Red." Sixteen DD (duplex drive) swimming tanks of Company A, 70th Tank Battalion would launch from four LCTs (Landing Craft Tank) and swim to Utah Beach, with landing scheduled at Tare Green at H-Hour, which was set at 6:30 a.m., while four LCTs would launch sixteen DD tanks of Company B, 70th Tank Battalion to land at Uncle Red at the same time. The DD tanks were M4 Sherman tanks modified with waterproof lower hulls and the addition of a propeller drive system, a collapsible floatation skirt, and an inflation system. The canvas floatation skirt was attached via a horizontal tubular steel frame welded to the tank hull and vertical tubular steel frames to provide rigidity. The inflation system consisted of inflatable rubber tubes attached to the inside of the floatation skirt.

Twenty LCVPs (Landing Craft Vehicle, Personnel) transporting four rifle companies of the 8th Infantry Regiment would also touch down at H-Hour. Companies B and C would land on the Tare Green sector while Companies E and F would land on the Uncle Red sector simultaneously at H-Hour. At H+5 minutes, Companies A and D of the 8th Infantry would land at Tare Green and Companies G and H of the 8th Infantry would land at Uncle Red. Also landing at H+5 minutes with the second wave were eight LCVPs with naval combat demolition units that would begin demolition of the first band of obstacles on the seaward side of the beach. Also at H+5, four LCVPs would land engineers to support the infantry assault on German fortifications and blow gaps in the seawall.

At H+15 minutes, Company C, 70th Tank Battalion would land at both sectors. This tank company consisted of sixteen M4 Sherman tanks that were waterproofed and had special air intakes and exhausts installed which allowed them to wade through water. Eight tank-dozers, which were standard Sherman tanks with front dozer blades and arm assemblies attached, would land with Company C to provide fire support and obstacle clearance assistance for each of the eight combined army-navy demolition teams. Eight LCTs would each transport two wading tanks and one tank-dozer to the beach.

At H+17 minutes, eight LCMs (Landing Craft Mechanized) would land eight combat engineer teams consisting of the 237th Engineer Combat Battalion and Company B, 299th Engineer Combat Battalion. These teams, together with the naval combat demolition units would clear eight gaps in the beach obstacles, each fifty yards wide and 250 yards apart, to provide eight lanes clear of obstacles to the beach for landing craft arriving in later waves. Each lane would be widened by obstacle demolition to the left of the initial gap until all obstacles on the two beach sectors were removed.

The plan called for the 4th Infantry Division to cross an area behind the beach flooded by the Germans to funnel attacking forces onto four defended causeways in order to exit the beach. Elements of the 101st Airborne Division were assigned to seize the western ends of the causeways to assist the beach landed forces. The 4th Division would then drive west to link up with the 82nd Airborne Division.

The German defenses consisted of belts of obstacles located between the low and high water marks, primarily of Element C or Belgian gates, some topped with powerful waterproofed Teller antitank mines to block incoming landing craft and as the tide rose and the landing craft could pass over them, to detonate the mines. Thick wooden stakes were driven into the beach closer to the high water mark to damage the bottoms of incoming landing craft. About one third of these also had Teller mines attached to the tops to detonate and destroy landing craft passing over them.

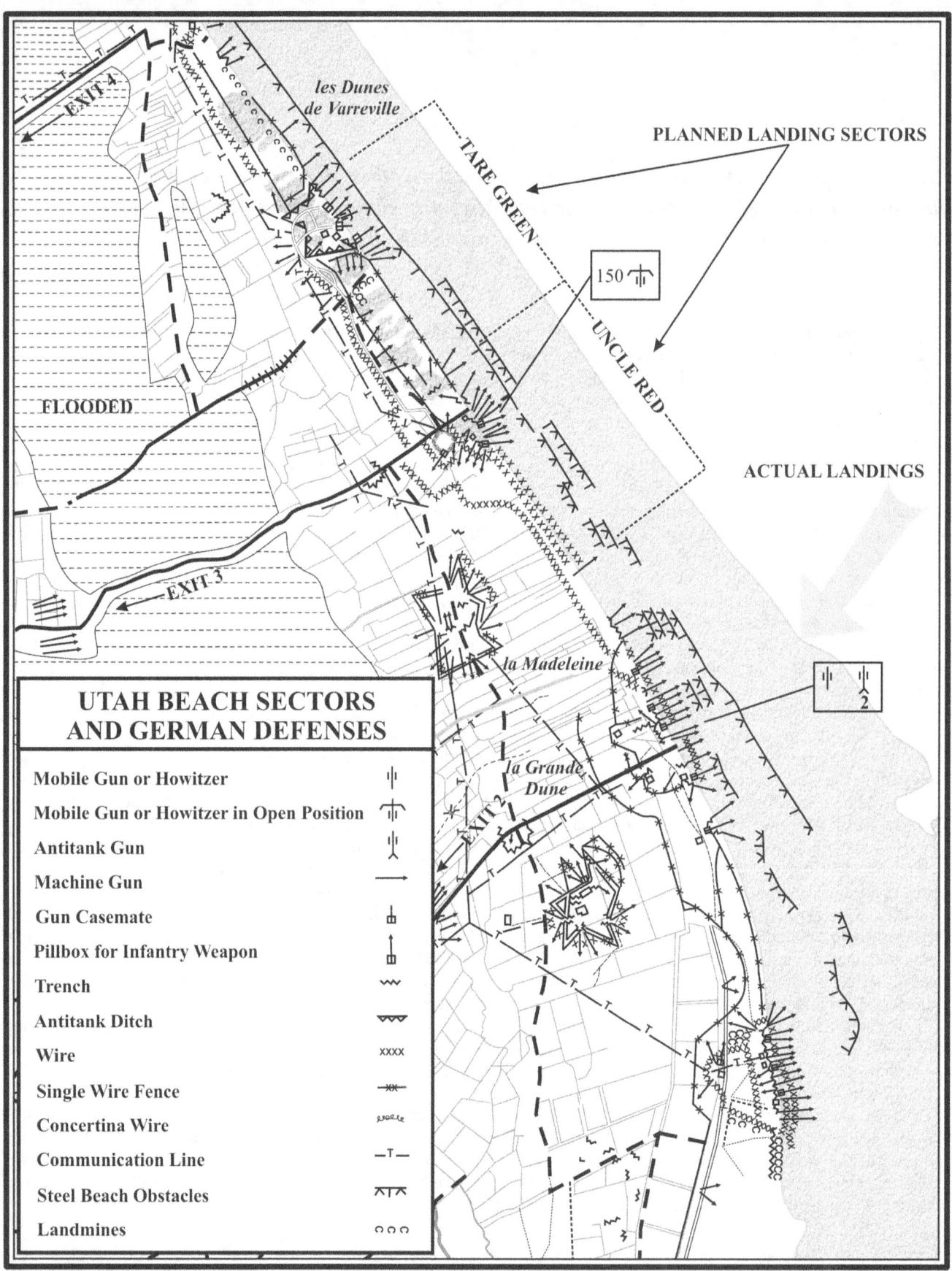

This composite photograph of many aerial reconnaissance photographs shows Utah Beach and the area behind it. These types of photographs were used in the planning of and briefings prior to the invasion. *United States Air Force photograph.*

This type 667 casemate on Utah Beach housed a 50mm PAK 38 antitank gun sited to fire laterally across the beach to place devastating enfilade fire on the less armored sides of landing craft, tanks, and other armored vehicles. *United States Army Signal Corps photograph, www.fold3.com.*

Fortifications constructed behind the beach's seawall consisted of pillboxes, tank turrets mounted on open topped concrete structures called Panzerstellungs, concrete lined open positions for machine guns and mortars called "Tobruks", and a trench system protected by barbed wire, mines, and antitank ditches.

The beach defenses were organized into Widerstandsnesten, or resistance nests. The resistance nest that figured prominently in the fighting on Utah Beach was WN 5, which was defended by a platoon of infantry and in addition had a 50mm PAK 38 antitank gun in a type 667 casemate, two 50mm antitank guns in open concrete emplacements, one French 47mm antitank gun in an open concrete emplacement, a Panzerstellung with a captured French tank turret mounting a 37mm gun, four Tobruks for mortars and machine guns, plus trenches and bunkers for machine guns and small arms.

The fortifications were manned by elements of Bataillon 3, Grenadier Regiment 919 of Infanterie Division 709. The division was known as a static unit which was capable of only defensive operations. The average age of its troops was thirty-six. It also had three Ost (East) battalions of troops from the occupied countries of eastern Europe forced into service with the Wehrmacht. The primary counterattack reserve consisted of Georgian Ost Bataillon 795 located around Criqueville and Bataillon 3, Grenadier Regiment 1058 of Luftlande Division 91, located south of Ste.-Mère-Église.

In addition, the Germans had a number of artillery batteries within range of the beach, including a coastal battery at St. Martin-de-Varreville and several 105mm field artillery batteries located inland from the beach.

This is another type 667 casemate on Utah Beach housing a 50mm antitank gun and sited to fire laterally across the beach in the opposite direction as the one in the previous photograph so as to place incoming landing craft and tanks in a crossfire. A square shaped aperture for a machine gun to protect the gun from an infantry assault is located at the right of the photograph. *United States Army Signal Corps photograph.*

ON THE MORNING OF JUNE 6, the landing plan was almost immediately altered when two naval control vessels experienced mishaps after leaving the transport area. The secondary control vessel for the Uncle Red sector struck a buoy shortly after leaving the transport area, fouling its screw, and was unable to proceed to the control point. The primary control vessel for the Uncle Red sector sunk some seven thousand yards offshore, most likely striking a naval mine. The Tare Green sector's primary control craft, which was one of four LCTs carrying the sixteen DD tanks of Company A, 70th Tank Battalion, struck a German naval mine and broke in two as tanks and men on deck were blown into the air. The area through which these craft were moving had been previously swept for mines, but this explosion and the sinking of the primary control vessel for the Uncle Red sector caused the LCTs to slow down. The secondary control vessel for the Tare Green sector turned about and led the four LCTs scheduled to land at Uncle Red toward the beach. Instead of launching five thousand yards from shore as planned, the LCTs were brought closer to shore in order to make up the time and launched from their respective LCTs. However, this delay caused the DD tanks to arrive almost fifteen minutes after H-Hour.

The naval bombardment of the beach began at H-40 minutes (5:50 a.m.). From 6:09 to 6:27 a.m., 341 United States Army Air Corps B-26 Marauder medium bombers flew over the beach parallel to the coast from northwest to southeast at altitudes ranging from four to six thousand feet, dropping 4,414 250-pound and 2,000-pound bombs on the Utah Beach defenses.

The first wave of twenty LCVPs carrying four rifle companies of the 8th Infantry were dispatched from the line of departure abreast and came in more or less together astride Exit 2, some two thousand yards south of the intended location, a few minutes after H-Hour. The smoke caused by the preliminary bombardment and the lack of natural landmarks along the flat coastline contributed to the navigational error. However, landing at the wrong location was fortunate because German defenses and obstacles were lighter than those at the intended beach sectors. The landing craft ramps were dropped and some six hundred infantrymen stepped into waist deep water about one hundred yards from the shore and made their way toward the beach.

Brigadier General Theodore "Teddy" Roosevelt, Jr., son of the former president, was among the troops in the first wave. Roosevelt, a World War I veteran and former assistant division commander of the 1st Infantry Division, was a supernumerary general officer assigned temporarily to the 4th Infantry Division in an unofficial capacity. Roosevelt had previously requested permission from the 4th Division's commanding officer, General Raymond O. Barton, to land with the first wave troops. Barton had initially turned him down, fearing that the son of a former president would die on the beach. However, Roosevelt appealed to Barton in a letter on May 26, stating the reasons for his request. Roosevelt eventually prevailed and received permission to land with the first wave troops.

Brigadier General Theodore Roosevelt, Jr.
Headquarters, First Army

Prior to dawn, Brigadier General Theodore Roosevelt, Jr. had boarded one of the LCVP landing craft carrying the first wave of troops to Utah Beach. "We passed a capsized craft, some men clinging to it, others bobbing in the waves…As we peered over the gunwale the shore seemed nearer but veiled, as if it was in the smoke and dust of the bombardment, it was hard to make it out. Suddenly the beach appeared before us—a long stretch of sand studded with wire and obstacles. The little boats were now going full speed, slapping the waves with their blunt prows…Then with a crunch we grounded, the ramp was lowered, and we jumped into water waist deep and started for the shore. We splashed and floundered through some hundred yards of water while German salvos fell. Men dropped, some silent, some screaming. Up the four hundred yards of beach we ran—then we reached the seawall. The company CO with whom I was, [Captain Howard] Lees, [commander of Company E, 8th Infantry Regiment] a great tower of a man, led his troops splendidly. He with his men started into the dunes to attack the German strongpoints. There was a house by the seawall where none should have been were we in the right place. It was imperative that I should find out where we were in order to set the maneuver. I scrambled up on the dunes and was lucky in finding a windmill, which I recognized. We'd been put ashore a mile too far to the south. I had to hot-foot it from left to right and back again, setting the various COs straight and changing the task…Stevie [Lieutenant Marcus Stevenson] of course was with me, devoted and competent as always, his Tommy gun ready to defend us if it became necessary. We set up a tiny CP with a radio behind the wall of a house. Most of our work was done on foot. As the succeeding waves landed, I pushed them inland if they halted and redirected them when they started wrong. Shells continually burst around us, but all I got was a slight scratch on one hand."[1]

Lieutenant Colonel Carlton O. MacNeely, the commanding officer of the 2nd Battalion, 8th Infantry, was a witness to the actions of General Roosevelt on Utah Beach that morning. "At 06:30 on 6 June 1944, Brigadier General Theodore Roosevelt, Jr., landed on beach 'Uncle Red' with the foremost assault elements of Company E, 8th Infantry, the right assault company of the 2nd Battalion, 8th Infantry.

"General Roosevelt voluntarily accepted the task of coordinating the initial attack on beach strongpoints by assault troops of the 1st and 2nd Battalions, 8th Infantry at H-Hour, until the arrival of the regimental commander. With complete disregard for his own life and with utter contempt for heavy hostile artillery, machine gun and small arms fires, he immediately went on a personal reconnaissance of the beach to determine the position of the troops in relation to previous designated points of exodus from the beach inland. At the time of General Roosevelt's reconnaissance, strong enemy positions were firing at pointblank range on the assault troops and on him from a distance of little over one hundred yards. Returning to the point of the landing, he contacted the commanders of the 1st and 2nd Battalions and coordinated and personally led the organizations in the assault of the heavy fortified enemy positions.

"General Roosevelt's heroism, leadership and presence in the very front of the attack and his complete unconcern at being under heavy direct fire inspired the troops to the heights of enthusiasm and self sacrifice. Although the enemy had beach 'Uncle Red' under constant direct fire, General Roosevelt moved from one locality to another, and rallying men around him, directed and personally led them against the enemy. Under his seasoned, precise, calm, unfaltering leadership, assault troops reduced beach strongpoints and rapidly moved inland with minimum casualties."[2]

Lieutenant Colonel Carlton O. MacNeely
Headquarters, 2nd Battalion, 8th Infantry Regiment, 4th Infantry Division

Colonel James A. Van Fleet, the commanding officer of the 8th Infantry Regiment, observed the actions of Lieutenant Colonel Carlton MacNeely during the fighting on Utah Beach and beyond it. "Lieutenant Colonel MacNeely was landed with the first elements of his battalion about [two] thousand yards south of the point originally planned where he was met with galling fire of automatic weapons and [50mm] cannon from fixed emplacements in the sand dunes and along the seawall.

He quickly reconnoitered the beach, ascertained his position and although heavy casualties were being suffered, caused his battalion to rapidly advance by the coordinated fire of all arms, passed through the minefields, assaulted and reduced the beach defenses in his sector, crossed the inundated area back of the beach under continual artillery and small arms fire and quickly secured the town of Pouppeville and the commanding terrain nearby. He then moved rapidly inland, overrunning the enemy centers of resistance to his front. His quick determination of the position of his battalion on the beach, his immediate vigorous and determined action in moving inland materially assisted the penetration of enemy defenses, and the rapid advance of the regiment and division and the early establishment of the beachhead."[3]

Captain James W. Haley
Company G, 8th Infantry Regiment, 4th Infantry Division

Captain George L. Mabry, Jr., the 2nd Battalion, 8th Infantry's S-3 (plans and operations staff officer), was transported to Utah Beach in the same landing craft as Captain James W. Haley. "Captain Haley, commanding officer of Company G, 8th Infantry, one of the [four] companies which spearheaded the entire landing operations of the VII Corps on the coast of Normandy, France, landed at 06:37 on Utah Beach; just seven minutes after the first assault waves of his company had waded ashore from the assault craft. As Captain Haley approached the beach in his LCVP just prior to landing, he observed a large group of men congregated on the beach in front of the seawall in the Company G zone of action. Heavy hostile artillery and grazing machine gun fires effectively covered the beach, threatened this group with extremely heavy casualties as they started toward a gap in the seawall, which would afford them access to the inland route of advance.

"As the LCVP on which he and fifteen company headquarters men were passengers hit the beach, Captain Haley led his group through shallow water and up the beach toward the position occupied by his first wave of assault troops. Before he had reached the seawall, heavy direct hostile machine gun and artillery fires had killed or wounded all his headquarters personnel except three men. Upon encountering the group of men behind the seawall, Captain Haley discovered that it comprised elements of E, F, and G Companies. He promptly proceeded to scatter the men to minimize casualties and then, moving from position to position, recklessly exposing himself to increasingly heavy, accurate enemy fire, organized the entire group subsequently separating Company G men from other elements. The enemy at this time was securely emplaced in a series of strongpoints along the sand dunes behind the seawall; and from elevated points of observation and fire was raking the beach with maximum firepower.

"Captain Haley, directly exposed to this murderous fire, organized his men into groups of three and sent them through the gap in the seawall at double time. When the last men had gone through the gap, he gathered the remainder of his headquarters group and attempted to locate the rest of his company so that Company G could be consolidated and without delay, proceed toward the first objective. Turning left at the gap in the seawall, he had advanced only fifty yards when leading elements of his unit became casualties in an enemy minefield. The rest of his men froze in position and hesitated to go forward. Captain Haley, again recklessly exposing himself to increasingly heavy hostile fire and the possibility of instant death from an exploding mine, went into the minefield and after having personally cleared a path through it, returned to his men and led them safely past this obstacle. As part of Company G, led by Captain Haley, who was now with the foremost elements, advanced along the seawall to the south it came within sight of the rest of the company several hundred yards distant. Then, Captain Haley and his men were abruptly pinned down by heavy enemy machine gun fire, coming from a house on the left flank. Captain Haley, in order to organize a patrol to destroy this opposition, again exposed himself to sniper and machine gun fire. The patrol was effectively organized under extreme difficulties and then proceeded to wipe out the resistance. Continuing toward the south, contact was made with the rest of his company. Again, fearlessly exposing himself to hostile small arms, sniper, machine gun and artillery fires, Captain Haley moved from position to position, organizing his company for the assault of Strongpoints 56 and 58. Enemy artillery fire was now heavier and more accurate. Machine gun fire raked the dunes and inland routes of advance, inflicting severe casualties upon 8th Infantry troops. German snipers were delivering deadly accurate fire upon the leading elements of Company G from well concealed positions.

"Captain Haley, again with the leading elements of his company, personally led Company G in the assault of Strongpoints 56 and 58, during which he was subjected to severe hostile machine gun fire directed at him from pointblank range. Captain Haley, displaying the most extraordinary heroism, fought the enemy at these points in hand to hand combat with rifle and bayonet. Entering these desperate conflicts against determined, well disciplined German troops, Captain Haley urged his men to close with the enemy and then fought beside them with tremendous skill and effect. Captain Haley's inspiring example and superb courage fired his men with sufficient determination to enable them to quickly destroy these strongpoints and clear their sector of the beach for subsequent landing, which would have been seriously menaced had not these objectives been immediately destroyed. Captain Haley, having reorganized his company for the advance inland, moved down the beach to the south most causeway and pushed inland against tenacious enemy resistance. After many hotly contested engagements during which Captain Haley and his men had overcome great opposition, Company G reached Ste.-Marie-du-Mont at 14:00 and took up its position for continuation of the advance. The spectacular bravery with which Captain Haley led his company and the brilliant tactical skill which he constantly displayed were a dominant influence upon the success of the 8th Infantry landing operations on Utah Beach."[4]

First Lieutenant John L. Ahearn
Company C, 70th Tank Battalion

The DD tanks landed about fifteen minutes late as a result of the problems associated with the control crafts. As a result, the wading tanks and tank-dozers of Company C, 70th Tank Battalion, under the command of Lieutenant John L. Ahearn, were the first tanks to land. "About 5:30 a.m. or so, we heard the tremendous roar of the bombers going overhead to hit at the beaches. Then particularly to our south, as I recall, we saw the big flashes of light and the thunder of the guns of the battleships as they opened up, and then subsequently there were fighters in the sky, and it was a tremendous sight, of course. As the dawn broke, we got a clearer picture of where everybody was, and it became evident that there'd been some problem with the DD tanks, and that we were not going to come in at H+15, in back of these tanks. But we were indeed going to be the first tanks on the beach, or alongside some of the Company B tanks. As it turned out, we all of course had mounted into the tanks. My tanks did not have this flotation gear, but we had been weatherized, and we were able to get into five or six feet of water, because we had these frontal like objects, which I don't recall the name right now, over our engines, and everything else was sealed.

"All of the eight boats brought us in on the beach just as far as they could and we got off in five or six feet of water, as I recall. Well, as it turned out, [Private First Class] Owen Gavigan, because his tank[-dozer] was in front, was the first tank to land on Utah Beach, and mine was the second. We then proceeded into the beach, and it became evident that the beach area was not the same as it had been planned we would land on. And it was also evident to me that not all of my tanks had got in [to the beach]. As it developed subsequently, about six of the tanks had to return to England because of boat difficulties. I was faced with a decision as to what to do at this time, and I saw General Teddy Roosevelt on the beach, and got out of my tank and reported to him, and told him who I was and what my mission was. He told me to go ahead, the lateral parts of the beach, both north and south, and to take care and to get inland as fast as we could, and to be generally supportive. I then directed my lieutenant, [Preston] Yeoman who was my second in command, and told him to take half of the tanks and proceed up to the north, and I would proceed to the south. At this time I was leading seven tanks. Of the original twenty-four, as I said, six had returned to England. Four of the dozer-tanks under of the scheme of things, had reverted to the control of the engineers, so the remaining fourteen had been divided by me between Lieutenant Yeoman and myself. Anyway, we proceeded southward, trying to find an opening off the beach, and subsequently, I don't know how many yards down the beach, did find an opening.

"However, at this opening, there was a small tank like object that I had never been informed about, and had never seen in the operations in Africa or Sicily. Although I was concerned, my mission was to get in as rapidly as possible so we proceeded through. As it happened, nothing happened. Later on, I read about the fact that there were a number of these so called, 'little Goliaths' that had been controlled from one of the strongpoints of the Germans, and that during the bombing, apparently the controls to these had been severed—luckily for us, as it turned out. We then proceeded when we got inside the seawall; we then again proceeded laterally between the seawall and the road, where we saw a number of infantrymen from the 2nd Battalion of the 8th Infantry, 4th Division who were at this time proceeding northward. As we looked down southward, it became evident to us that there was another strongpoint of the Germans, and although we saw no activity there, I had our tanks fire some shells into it.

"With this, a number of Germans, as it turned out to be, impressed soldiers who were not really of German nationality, came out with their hands in the air and began running towards us. So then I dismounted from the tank to take them as prisoners, and as I did, the most unusual thing happened. I shouldn't say most unusual, because a similar thing happened to me in Sicily, but as I got out of the tank and began to approach them, they began yelling to me and gesturing me to stay still, because they were yelling, 'Achtung Meinen.' With this, I gestured toward them to move toward the road, and the tanks moved toward the road, and we delivered these thirty or so odd prisoners to the infantry."[5]

Technician Fourth Grade Anthony Zampiello was driver of the Lieutenant Ahearn's tank. "Due to limited visibility from within a tank and due to the exuberant natural features of the terrain, Lieutenant Ahearn, in order to reconnoiter properly the route of advance for his tanks often dismounted from his tank in the face of withering enemy fire from automatic weapons."[6]

Lieutenant Ahearn and the seven tanks under his command continued south toward Exit 1. "We came across a country road leading to the town of Pouppeville. At this juncture, I told Lieutenant [Thomas] Tighe, who was one of my junior officers and who was commanding the platoon with which I had associated myself, for him to proceed inward. I would, along with a couple of other tanks, continue to proceed down this rather narrow road, across the dunes and across the hedgerows to see if there was any further strongpoints that we might assault. Shortly after this, as my tank proceeded down this small lane, the tank hit a landmine, and the front left bogie of the tank was blown, and we of course were immobilized."[7]

Upon detonating the mine, Technician Zampiello watched as "Lieutenant Ahearn, again with utter disregard for his own personal safety dismounted under fire to make a foot reconnaissance to observe the enemy, who were close to our front."[8]

As Lieutenant Ahearn was conducting his reconnaissance, he "heard cries for help, and looking toward the beach, I saw three figures who I surmised were paratroopers and had been injured. I immediately returned to the tank and got the rather large first aid kit that we carried in the tanks, and came back, proceeded in back of the hedgerow that separated them from the hedgerow to the north. When I saw a break in the hedgerow, I proceeded to cross it. I was going to try to get as close to them as I possibly could, and at this time, while I was standing there contemplating my next move, a personnel mine went off under me.

An M4 Sherman tank waterproofed and fitted with special air intake and exhaust stacks that allowed it to wade through deep water. These wading tanks were employed by Company C, 70th Tank Battalion on Utah Beach and Company A, 741st Tank Battalion and Company A, 743rd Tank Battalion on Omaha Beach. *United States Army Signal Corps photograph.*

"The mine explosion threw me into the bank of the hedgerows, and I was unconscious for a while. Subsequently I awakened and began yelling, and two of my crew, Sergeant [Technician Fourth Grade] Zampiello and Corporal [Felix] Beard, came out to take a look. It was hard to find me, because I had rolled up against the embankment, but when they did, I cautioned them not to come over, because of the presence of mines. Incidentally, I subsequently learned from our battalion maintenance officer who wrote me a letter back in the hospital, that they had discovered some 15,000 mines in that vicinity. So the odds were not very good that I was not going to be unharmed. Anyway, they went back to the tank and got a long rope, and threw the rope to me."[9]

Technician Fourth Grade Zampiello and the other tanker used the rope to pull him out of the minefield. "When he finally was rescued, he encouraged us by saying, 'We must get in there and take chances, otherwise we'll never get anywhere.'"[10]

Lieutenant Ahearn was subsequently evacuated that morning for medical treatment. "My memory is a little bit fuzzy as to how I got back to the field hospital, which thankfully, apparently had arrived in four or five hours after the invasion and been set up. But I do know that I was on stretchers, and was on jeeps, and had been transferred from one group to another, and subsequently, arrived at the hospital. During that night, it was decided that I would need surgery. As it turned out, I had heavy paratroop boots on, and the one foot was—both feet, I guess were still on at this point, but terribly mangled, and they decided that they would have to operate on me. As I was brought into the tent—before this, I was given about six bottles of plasma, and of course was visited by the chaplain. Then in the early evening, this makeshift tent with white sheets being used as covering the walls of the tent, I was operated on. Subsequently I found from notes that the decision was made that they would just amputate the one foot, because they felt that I would not be able to withstand both operations. So during the night, the one foot was amputated, and I was then prepared for a transport the next day to England."[11]

Duplex drive Sherman tanks with their canvas floatation skirts lowered cover infantrymen advancing to the dune line on Utah Beach. *United States Army Signal Corps photograph.*

There were a number of 70th Tank Battalion commanders who courageously dismounted from their tanks in order to gain a level of observation which was simply not possible using the slits and periscopes from within the tanks. By walking ahead of their tanks, the commanders could more easily spot the signs of buried antitank mines, which were sewn throughout the area of the beach and beyond. However, walking ahead of or beside a tank along the flat beach or an exposed causeway at the point of attack was extraordinarily dangerous. The commanders who did so faced fire from enemy snipers as well as machine guns and antitank fire from well camouflaged pillboxes.

Sergeant Henry V. Nothel
Company A, 70th Tank Battalion

One of the four LCTs carrying four DD tanks of the Company A, 70th Tank Battalion struck a mine offshore, killing sixteen tankers as well as several sailors. The twelve remaining DD tanks were launched from the remaining three LCTs as planned and all of them made it safely to shore. Captain J. Stewart Williams, the commanding officer of Company A, 70th Tank Battalion, was able to observe the actions of Nothel from the turret of his tank. "Under a withering hail of enemy fire, which consisted of flanking coastal guns, mortars and automatic weapons, Sergeant Nothel's tank proceeded across a mined beach and was the first tank to breach the enemy seawall. Then Sergeant Nothel took up position behind the seawall and neutralized two enemy mortars that were delaying the advance of friendly infantry. At this time friendly infantry had not had the opportunity to reconnoiter the route of advance toward the enemy and since visibility was poor within a tank, Sergeant Nothel disregarded personal danger by dismounting from his tank under enemy fire to reconnoiter as his tank advanced through enemy strongpoints. At other times, he advanced with his head exposed from his tank. He led the infantry across heavily fortified terrain bristling with pillboxes, minefields, swamps, and tank traps."[12]

A duplex drive M4 Sherman tank utilized a water proofed hull with the canvas floatation skirt deployed using a steel frame and compressed air pumped into six vertical tubes sewn into the canvas skirt.

A duplex drive Sherman tank with its floatation skirt collapsed after landing on Utah Beach.

This pedestal mounted 50mm antitank gun (right) was protected by a concrete lined open emplacement and was capable of engaging landing craft and tanks. *United States Navy photograph, National Archives.*

Staff Sergeant Darvin D. Purvis
Company A, 70th Tank Battalion

Captain Williams observed that when one of his platoon leaders was seriously wounded, "Staff Sergeant Purvis, on his own initiative, assumed command of the platoon and proceeded over the seawall and down a mine strewn road, leading friendly infantry safely through strong enemy emplacements. At this early time friendly infantry had not had an opportunity to reconnoiter the route of advance toward the enemy and since visibility was poor within a tank, Staff Sergeant Purvis disregarded personal danger by dismounting from his tank under enemy fire to reconnoiter as his platoon advanced through enemy strongpoints. At other times he advanced with his head exposed from the tank as his platoon advanced across heavily fortified terrain bristling with pillboxes, minefields, swamps, and tank traps."[13]

First Lieutenant Francis E. Songer
Company B, 70th Tank Battalion

Lieutenant Francis E. Songer, the commander of Company B, 70th Tank Battalion, ordered the launch of the company's sixteen DD tanks at about 1,500 yards from shore. All sixteen tanks made it safely to shore where Lieutenant Colonel John C. Welborn, the commander of the 70th Tank Battalion, witnessed the subsequent actions of Lieutenant Songer. "In the face of concentrated enemy fire, which consisted of flanking coastal guns, mortars and automatic weapons, First Lieutenant Songer proceeded through the blown gap in the seawall and led his company down a mine strewn road, leading friendly infantry safely through strong enemy emplacements. At this early time friendly infantry had not had an opportunity to reconnoiter the route of advance toward the enemy and since visibility was poor within a tank, First Lieutenant Songer disregarded personal danger several times by dismounting from his tank under enemy fire to reconnoiter as his company advanced in column through enemy strongpoints up the mined causeway that led through dense enemy held swampland in which were concealed many skillfully camouflaged gun positions. While advancing along this causeway his tank was disabled when it was struck a mine. At this point, while he was standing beside his disabled tank, an enemy antitank gun fired upon the tank three projectiles, striking it, instantly killing his driver and wounding other soldiers. After rendering first aid to the wounded he commandeered the next tank in his column and was instrumental in capturing the high ground beyond the swampland, neutralizing several enemy gun positions."[14]

This French 47mm antitank gun was captured by the Germans after the fall of France in 1940 and was pressed into service on Utah Beach where it opposed the tanks of the 70th Tank Battalion during the initial stages of the assault landing. *United States Army Signal Corps photograph, National Archives.*

Tank-dozers were used for obstacle clearance during the beach landing in Normandy. They were standard Sherman tanks modified with the addition of a dozer blade, arms, and controls. *United States Army Signal Corps photograph, National Archives.*

Two German 105mm artillery batteries positioned to the west around Ste.-Marie-du-Mont shelled Utah Beach until they were attacked and captured by the 101st Airborne Division. *United States Army Signal Corps photograph, National Archives.*

Staff Sergeant Richard C. Murrin
Company B, 70th Tank Battalion

Staff Sergeant Richard C. Murrin commanded one of the Company B M4 Sherman duplex drive tanks. Lieutenant John N. Townsend was Murrin's platoon leader. "In the face of concentrated enemy fire, which consisted of flanking coastal guns, mortars and automatic weapons, Staff Sergeant Murrin proceeded on his own initiative across a heavily mined beach and helped to neutralize enemy gun emplacements, thereby facilitating the advance of friendly infantry. At this early time friendly infantry had not had an opportunity to reconnoiter the route of advance toward the enemy. Since visibility was poor from within a tank, Staff Sergeant Murrin disregarded personal danger by dismounting from his tank under enemy fire to reconnoiter as his tank advanced through enemy strongpoints consisting of pillboxes, minefields, swamps and tank traps."[15]

Troops from the 8th Infantry Regiment and one of the Company C, 70th Tank Battalion wading tanks move south across the beach toward causeway Exit 1 which led west across the inundated area to Pouppeville. An American soldier who has been killed in action lies in the foreground. *United States Army Signal Corps photograph.*

Second Lieutenant John N. Townsend
Company B, 70th Tank Battalion

Lieutenant John L. Casteel, the executive officer of Company B, 70th Tank Battalion, observed the heroism of Lieutenant John N. Townsend, during the landing and the drive inland. "Concentrated hostile resistance was encountered on his right flank. He immediately organized his platoon and continued the advance inland while under heavy enemy fire, which consisted of heavy artillery, flanking coastal guns, mortars, and automatic weapons. Since his advance was impeded by extremely poor visibility, Second Lieutenant Townsend, with utter disregard for his own safety, dismounted from his tank while under enemy fire and reconnoitered on foot as his tank platoon advanced rapidly across strongly fortified marshland neutralizing enemy positions, thereby permitting the advance of friendly infantry."[16]

Lieutenant Commander Herbert A. Peterson
Naval Combat Demolition Group, 2nd Naval Beach Battalion, Combined Task Group 125.2.3, Assault Force U, Task Force 125, Eleventh Amphibious Force, 12th Fleet

Eight Naval Combat Demolition Units, each transported in LCVPs loaded with the high explosives required to clear eight fifty yard wide lanes through the seaward obstacle belts, were scheduled to land at H+5. Army combat engineers would land at H+17 in eight LCMs to clear the landward obstacle belts in order to allow succeeding waves to reach the beach as the tide rose. Corporal James H. Burke was a member of Company B, 299th Engineer Combat Battalion. "Commander Peterson was in my boat. I was in a reserve unit, and Commander Peterson, who was in command of all NCDU units, upon finding that all other units had gone ashore took the reserve units and two others and came in. Definite information as to the situation preceding waves was not available at the control point and Commander Peterson assumed responsibility for taking in the reserve units. Coming in to the beach an infantry landing boat about 150 yards from us was hit by an enemy shell and was destroyed. Another boat near us capsized. I saw five men left clinging to this boat. We received fire from rockets coming in from the sea and heavy artillery, small arms, and mortar fire from the enemy inland. The infantry at this time was at the dune line in our immediate front. Tanks in our area were fighting a pointblank battle with pillboxes. After getting on the beach, we blew all the obstacles in our immediate area, of which there were two bands. Our job was to clear a 150 yard lane through the beach obstacles, which was done. We used our remaining explosives to clear an additional area of about 150 yards."[17]

Sergeant Paul Feheley was another engineer with Company B, 299th Engineer Combat Battalion. "The boats of the beach parties had become very scattered. Machine gun fire at the time our boat came in was very heavy and numerous stray shells from what we thought to be navy vessels offshore were hitting in our area. Our unit was working in the center of the group of units under Commander Peterson's command. At the water's edge we picked up a wounded man carrying a flamethrower and carried him in. Machine gun, mortar, and artillery fire was very heavy at this time and interrupted our work after we had destroyed one Element C obstacle. We worked our way up to the seawall and came back and blew the rest of the obstacles. After returning to the seawall, we dug in. At this point, Commander Peterson came along checking on the progress of the work, and stayed with us a short time. He was looking for Lieutenant Smith and another NCDU. He asked us how we were getting along, if we had had casualties and he checked to see if all of the obstacles were demolished and if there was anything we needed. He was exposed to considerable fire in order to come to our location. At the time Commander Peterson came to us we were engaged in carrying wounded men who had fallen on the beach to the aid station. Commander Peterson was ranging up and down the beach all day under fire, checking the work of his NCDU units. The last I saw him was when he checked our unit at about 17:00 on D-Day."[18]

Another Army combat engineer, Sergeant Guido Troiano, with Company B, 299th Engineer Combat Battalion, observed "Commander Peterson working up and down the beach, continually exposing himself to fire in order to check and assist the progress of the work. He was also looking for a medical aid station for wounded men. Commander Peterson and Mr. Padgett, immediate commander of NCDU Number 127, were very steady under fire. Their leadership and calmness under fire was a steadying influence and much appreciated by us. They, by their fine example and exhortation, assisted us to do our utmost."[19]

Captain George L. Mabry, Jr.
Headquarters, 2nd Battalion, 8th Infantry Regiment, 4th Infantry Division

Captain George L. Mabry, Jr., the S-3 (plans and operations) officer of the 2nd Battalion, 8th Infantry Regiment, landed at H+7 in the same landing craft as Lieutenant Colonel Carlton O. MacNeely, the 2nd Battalion commander. After a conference with General Roosevelt, the decision was made to push inland from where the landing had been made.

At that point, Mabry separated from the battalion commander and began moving south "just west of the seawall, hoping to gain contact with Company G. After advancing approximately fifty yards, I saw seven enlisted men of Company G and was about to call to them when a terrific explosion occurred, killing three of the men and wounding the others. It was apparent that one of these unfortunate individuals had stepped on a mine, which caused a number of additional mines to explode simultaneously. Realizing that more mines were probably scattered about the area, I began a circular movement and advanced about fifty yards when small arms fire from an enemy group (estimated to be a squad) pinned me to the ground.

"From the crack of bullets passing inches above my head, I was able to locate the enemy dug in on a sand dune about one hundred yards to my front. Making a hasty survey of my position, I could see mines had been uncovered by strong winds and shifting sand. I now knew that I was in a minefield. A definite decision must be made and quickly! Would it be advantageous to try a withdrawal to the beach, with the possibility of hitting a mine or should I continue the advance towards the enemy position and accomplish my mission? Based on previous training and remembering the necessity of contacting Company G, I elected to push through the mines and engage the enemy. The first rush forward, directed at a shellhole, was begun with good progress in spite of small arms fire; but upon the last leap for the inviting shellhole, my foot set off a mine. The explosion slammed me against the ground with a tremendous thud—no injuries from it—just shaken up a bit. I looked around quickly and hopefully toward the beach in search of a comrade who might help me reduce the enemy to my front. It so happened that a first lieutenant of Company F had seen me and was working his way forward. I called a warning to watch for mines, but it could not be heard above the noise of battle. The lieutenant crumpled under the explosion of a mine. I sprang up and rushed toward the dug in Germans, stopping once to deliver a few rounds of fire before closing in. The last rush of twenty-five yards carried me to the enemy foxholes.

"The first German encountered was quickly exterminated and immediately the remaining six surrendered. At this point a sergeant of Company G, who had been wounded in one hand, was seen making his way back towards the beach. I signaled for the sergeant to join me, which he did. The prisoners were turned over to him and he marched them off towards Beach Uncle Red. A short time later, three men of Company G, having learned from the wounded sergeant that I was by myself, joined me and informed me that Company G had been held up by a minefield and machine gun fire some two hundred yards back. Therefore, I was leading Company G rather than following its advance.

"Since I had met with success thus far, I decided to push on and try to reach Causeway Number 1 as quickly as possible. Our group of one officer and three enlisted men crawled down ditches and along hedgerows, bypassing pillboxes until discovered and taken under fire by a very large pillbox, which guarded the entrance to Causeway Number 1. One enlisted man was dispatched to contact Company G and the DD tanks for assistance. After a thirty minute wait, a platoon of Company G, plus two tanks arrived and brought fire to bear upon the pillbox. The battle raged for about twenty minutes before the Germans surrendered. Thirty-two walking prisoners and four wounded were extracted from their concrete strongpoints.

"Immediately thereafter I, with one enlisted man, made our way toward Causeway Number 1. By crawling along a ditch half filled with water we were able to advance to within ten yards of the important bridge of Causeway Number 1. Upon reaching this point, two Germans were seen running towards the bridge. Fire was withheld until they stopped just short of the bridge and then [they were] cut down by rifle fire. It was discovered later that explosives had been placed to destroy the bridge, but this was not accomplished, since the two Germans were killed before demolition charges were touched off.

"Under the direction of Lieutenant Colonel MacNeely, Companies E and F, with tanks supporting, had completed their turning movement and were driving south, reducing strongpoints and annihilating small groups of enemy. By 10:30 hours, Company E began crossing Causeway Number 1, followed by Company F.

"At this point (at the west end of Causeway Number 1) American rifle and machine gun fire was heard in Pouppeville. This fire indicated that elements of the 501st Parachute Infantry were engaged in a firefight. Company E moved towards Pouppeville and assisted in killing and capturing seventy Germans, who were caught in the nutcracker action of the 3rd Battalion, 501st Parachute Infantry and Company E, 2nd Battalion, 8th Infantry. It was 11:05, 6 June 1944 at Pouppeville that Lieutenant Colonel Carlton O. MacNeely (2nd Battalion, 8th Infantry) and Lieutenant Colonel Julian Ewell (3rd Battalion, 501st Parachute Infantry) established first official contact between seaborne and airborne forces."[20]

Colonel James A. Van Fleet
Headquarters, 8th Infantry Regiment, 4th Infantry Division

Colonel James A. Van Fleet, commanding officer of the 8th Infantry Regiment, was a graduate of the United States Military Academy in 1915 and a World War I combat veteran, having served as a battalion commander. General Raymond O. Barton, the commander of the 4th Infantry Division, witnessed the courage and leadership of Van Fleet on D-Day. "Colonel James A. Van Fleet, with great organizational ability, personal bravery and confidence, gathered together his scattered troops, then engaged in separate firefights and in reducing beach fortifications and quickly organized them into formation and pushed them rapidly off the beach in an orderly and determined manner [then] across the inundated area to inland positions, making very rapid movement, brushing aside the resistance, and thereby greatly expediting the early establishment of the division beachhead. Colonel Van Fleet was always well forward and on a couple of occasions personally went up to check his battalions. He kept in touch with the situation using officer messengers from his staff and kept his rear elements pushed tightly behind the assaulting battalions. At one point, his regimental command post was two hundred yards west of Hébert and the 3rd Battalion was at that moment engaged in reducing a couple of fortified houses to the right front. His superior leadership and personal example of courage aided all to clear the beach with a minimum of casualties and expedited the rapid advance of the division to its D-Day objective, and also enabled the follow-up troops to use the beach which he caused to be cleared of his usable vehicles within a few hours."[21]

Troops pour ashore on Utah Beach and advance over the seawall and the sand dunes immediately behind it to the causeways on the other side that led inland, where elements of the 8th Infantry Regiment of the 4th Infantry Division met elements of the 501st Parachute Infantry Regiment, 101st Airborne Division at Pouppeville. Note the absence of beach obstacles, which were cleared quickly by the Beach Obstacle Demolition Parties, which were joint teams of army combat engineers and naval combat demolition units, aided by bulldozers like the one seen at the right. *United States Army Signal Corps photograph.*

Lieutenant Colonel Fred A. Steiner
Headquarters, 8th Infantry Regiment, 4th Infantry Division

Lieutenant Colonel Fred A. Steiner, executive officer of the 8th Infantry Regiment, had been a successful trial attorney in San Diego, California prior to entering active duty. Colonel Van Fleet was a witness to his heroism on June 6. "As regimental executive officer, Lieutenant Colonel Fred A. Steiner landed in an early wave behind the assaulting troops from a small craft with a detachment of the 8th Infantry regimental CP, as part of the forces assaulting Utah Beach. Although under continual observed well directed enemy artillery high angle and flat trajectory fire, he immediately took command of the situation on the beach. He immediately established a regimental CP in an area across the inundated area close behind the assaulting troops and caused the area to be cleared of snipers and made secure for CP operations." [22]

After the regimental command post was established, Colonel Van Fleet and a skeleton staff moved forward to establish a forward CP. Colonel Van Fleet left Steiner in charge of the regimental CP. "Lieutenant Colonel Steiner discovered a strongly fortified position at Germain near the CP. It had not been fully reduced and was still in position to, and was threatening to cut the axis of communication and advance of the rear elements of the regiment. He quickly organized a force consisting of available personnel of the CP group and two platoons of Company C, 237th Engineer Battalion, then available. He directed their action against the strongpoint, garrisoned by about 120 Germans, effectively reducing it after a firefight, destroying four 88mm field pieces still in position and capable of effective use against the beach installations, and capturing prisoners and important maps and documents, from which accurate information of the German beach and inland defense was obtained and the identity and location of defending troops in the area was established. During the action, he personally engaged in the operation and remained in an advanced position until the action was completed, the weapons destroyed and the position made untenable by the enemy. The information was immediately made available to higher command and assisted greatly in the further movement of the regiment and the reduction of enemy defenses."[23]

A dead German soldier lies outside of one of the pillboxes which defended Utah Beach at la Madeleine. *United States Army Signal Corps photograph, National Archives.*

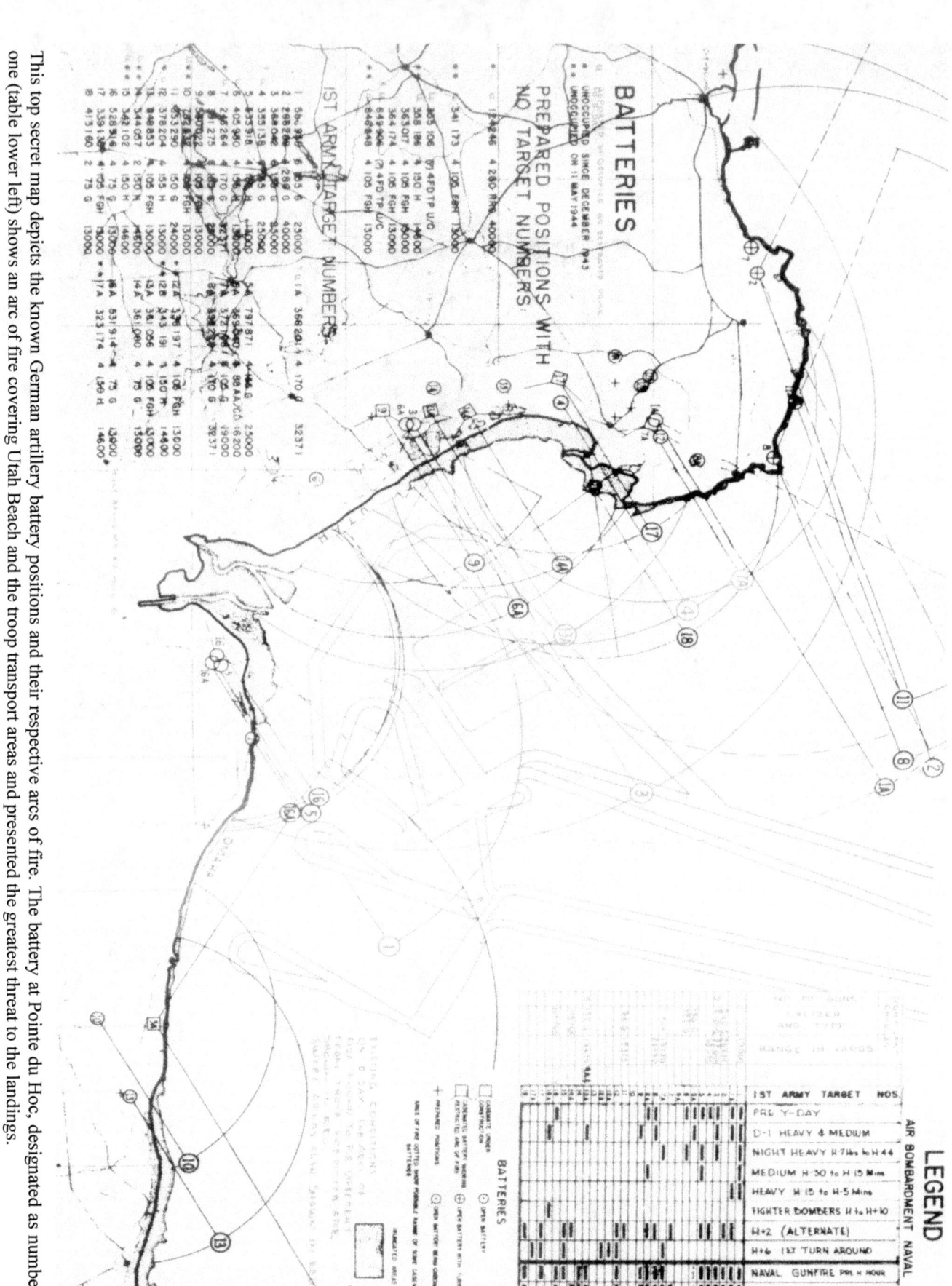

This top secret map depicts the known German artillery battery positions and their respective arcs of fire. The battery at Pointe du Hoc, designated as number one (table lower left) shows an arc of fire covering Utah Beach and the troop transport areas and presented the greatest threat to the landings.

POINTE DU HOC

Rudder's Rangers—in one of the great heroic feats of D-Day—scaled the Pointe du Hoc cliffs —General Omar N. Bradley

A German coastal battery of 155mm French artillery located at Pointe du Hoc, with a range of approximately fourteen miles was the number one priority of the Allied planners. This six gun battery could shell Utah Beach as well as the troop transport staging areas offshore for both Omaha and Utah assault forces. Firing ninety pound shells, these long range guns could wreak havoc on the beach landing operations. As a result, the Allied planners and General Omar Bradley, the commander of the United States First Army, assigned the destruction of the guns at Pointe du Hoc as the highest priority of the invasion.

The battery at Pointe du Hoc was positioned on flat ground along a triangular promontory with 85-117 feet high sheer cliffs overlooking a rocky beach, about four miles west of Omaha Beach. The German army decided that an amphibious assault was not likely because of these cliffs and surf conditions. It therefore constructed the position to defend against a ground attack coming from the landward side of the position. The coastal artillery was manned by Batterie II, Heeres Artillerie Abteilung Küsten 1260, consisting of approximately eighty-five artillerymen. Kompanie 12, Bataillon III, Grenadier Regiment 726, Infanterie Division 716, consisting of about 125 mostly relatively elderly second rate soldiers, provided local defense for the battery. Further protection of barbed wire obstacles surrounded the position and minefields were sewn on the landward sides.

The commander of the 2nd Ranger Battalion, Lieutenant Colonel James E. Rudder, was a tough Texas rancher who had also been a college football coach prior to the war. He had been selected to command and train the new 2nd Ranger Battalion, which was activated on April 1, 1943 at Camp Forrest, Tennessee. The battalion was an all volunteer unit and the training was extremely tough. Lieutenant Sidney Saloman was a platoon leader assigned to Company C. "Rudder really shaped us up. He had expertise in coaching and administration and managerial experience to weld us together as a battalion. We got rid of officers who did not measure up to Rudder's standards."[1]

During the first two months of training, sixteen officers and 227 enlisted men transferred from the battalion. In addition to physical training at Camp Forrest, the Rangers received twelve days of amphibious training at Fort Pierce, Florida at the joint army-navy Amphibious Scout and Raider School, followed by advanced tactical training at Fort Dix, New Jersey, including an emphasis on night attacks and night patrolling. After the 2nd Ranger Battalion arrived in England in early December 1943, it began training with British commandos on the country's southern coast. Over the following months, the commandos taught the Rangers cliff climbing techniques, hand-to-hand combat, and oversaw live fire night exercises and amphibious assaults.

On January 4, 1944, Lieutenant Colonel Rudder and his then executive officer, Major Max Schneider, were ordered to report to General Bradley's headquarters in Bristol, England. Upon arrival at the five story building at Bryanston Square, they were escorted under armed guard to the war room. The room's windows were covered with black cloth so as to preclude spying from outside of the building. On the walls and tables were maps and large aerial reconnaissance photographs marked Top Secret. Bradley's G-3 operations officer, Colonel Truman Thorson, briefed Rudder and Schneider on a two part mission for the battalion. During the briefing, they were shown aerial reconnaissance photos of Pointe du Hoc.

Lieutenant Colonel Rudder was somewhat shocked by what would be the most difficult and dangerous of assignments of the invasion. "When we got a look at it, Max just whistled through his teeth. He had a way of doing that. He'd made three [beach assault] landings [Algiers, Sicily, and Salerno] already, but I was just a country boy coaching football [two and a half years] before. It would almost knock you out of your boots."[2]

The primary mission was to destroy the German coastal artillery battery at Pointe du Hoc with a secondary objective of cutting the coastal road south of Pointe du Hoc to prevent German reinforcements from reaching Omaha Beach from the west. A third assignment was added later, which was the destruction of German positions at Pointe ét Raz de la Percée. This position was also located on a cliff top and could deliver enfilade fire against landings on Omaha Beach, a thousand yards to the east.

Rudder was tasked with developing an assault plan, but left its preparation to the British combined operations headquarters, the organization to which the British commando units belonged. The combined operations headquarters had a great deal of experience in planning amphibious raids by its commando units.

The 5th Ranger Battalion arrived in England on January 18, 1944, and on March 24, Rudder relieved its commanding officer and named his executive officer, Major Schneider, to command it. Schneider was subsequently promoted to lieutenant colonel on May 30, 1944.

At the end of February, the British staff officer responsible for the assault plan presented it to Rudder and Major General Leonard T. Gerow, commander of the V Corps, to which the two Ranger battalions were attached for the invasion. The plan called for Rangers to land in two groups, one about four miles to the east at Omaha Beach and the other to the west of Pointe du Hoc and conduct overland attacks, combined with a thirty-six man parachute assault south of the position. It was rejected because it would take hours to execute and would subject the troop transport staging areas and the Utah Beach landings to heavy shelling during that time.

Lieutenant Colonel Rudder then took over the planning of the assault and after evaluating the very limited options in light of the mission requirements, Rudder decided that a direct assault from the sea would have to be conducted to capture and destroy the guns at Pointe du Hoc. In order to accomplish the three assigned missions, Rudder split the two Ranger battalions into three components. Force A, consisting of Companies D, E, F, and most of headquarters and Headquarters Company, 2nd Ranger Battalion, under the command of the newly named executive officer, Captain Cleveland A. Lytle, would make the assault on Pointe du Hoc. Force B, consisting of Company C, 2nd Ranger Battalion, under the command of Captain Ralph E. Goranson, would land on the right flank of the 116th Infantry Regiment in the Charley sector and move west to destroy the guns at Pointe ét Raz de la Percée. Force C, consisting of Companies A and B of the 2nd Ranger Battalion and the entire 5th Ranger Battalion, under the command of then Major Schneider, would initially be a floating reserve. If a coded message was received from Force A by no later than H+30, signifying that it had successfully ascended the cliffs, Force C would land at Pointe du Hoc and reinforce it to accomplish the missions of destroying the guns and blocking the coastal road. If the code word from Force A was not received by H+30, it would mean that the cliff assault had failed, and Force C would land at the west end of Omaha Beach in the Dog Green sector behind the 116th Infantry Regiment and drive west to attack and destroy the guns at Pointe du Hoc and establish a blocking position on the road.

The plan for a direct assault up the cliffs of Pointe du Hoc precipitated numerous innovations to allow the assault force to quickly scale the cliffs. One was rocket propelled grapnels with hooks to catch at the top of the cliff and with ropes attached that would allow the Rangers to climb if the hooks caught sufficiently. This was followed by the idea of firing the grapnels directly from the landing craft as they approached the cliffs. As a result, their British LCAs (Landing Craft Assault) were fitted with six rocket propelled grapnels per craft. In addition, lighter weight grapnels that would be carried ashore and fired from the beach.

Another innovation was electrically powered extension ladders like those used by the London Fire Department, mounted on to DUKWs, which were amphibious vehicles. These ladders could be raised one hundred feet when these vehicles landed, allowing Rangers to quickly climb the ladders to the top of the cliff. In addition, two British Vickers K machine guns, as well as a protective steel plate, and safety harness were mounted on the top of each ladder for a use by Rangers acting as gunners to spray the cliff top to cover the ascent of the Rangers. Someone also found some modular tubular steel ladders which were made in four feet long sections that could be carried ashore by Rangers and quickly assembled.

To keep the German force defending Pointe du Hoc from firing on the landing crafts as they approached from the sea, the plan called for bombing by two groups of aircraft along with shelling from all of the U.S.S. *Texas* battleship's 14-inch main guns shortly before the Rangers would land.

As the new plan took shape, Companies D, E, F, and Headquarters Company of the 2nd Ranger Battalion practiced cliff climbing, while Company A, B, and C, 2nd Ranger Battalion along with the 5th Ranger Battalion primarily practiced beach assaults, but also some cliff climbing.

Opposite: This top secret map of the German positions at Pointe du Hoc was drawn from aerial reconnaissance photographs taken on April 10, 1944. The heavy steel reinforced concrete casemates were thought to house a battery of six 155mm guns each with a range of fourteen miles, capable of shelling Utah Beach and the troop transport areas offshore for both the Omaha and Utah assault forces. It was assigned top priority by the Overlord planners. It was the initial objective of the Provisional Ranger Group.

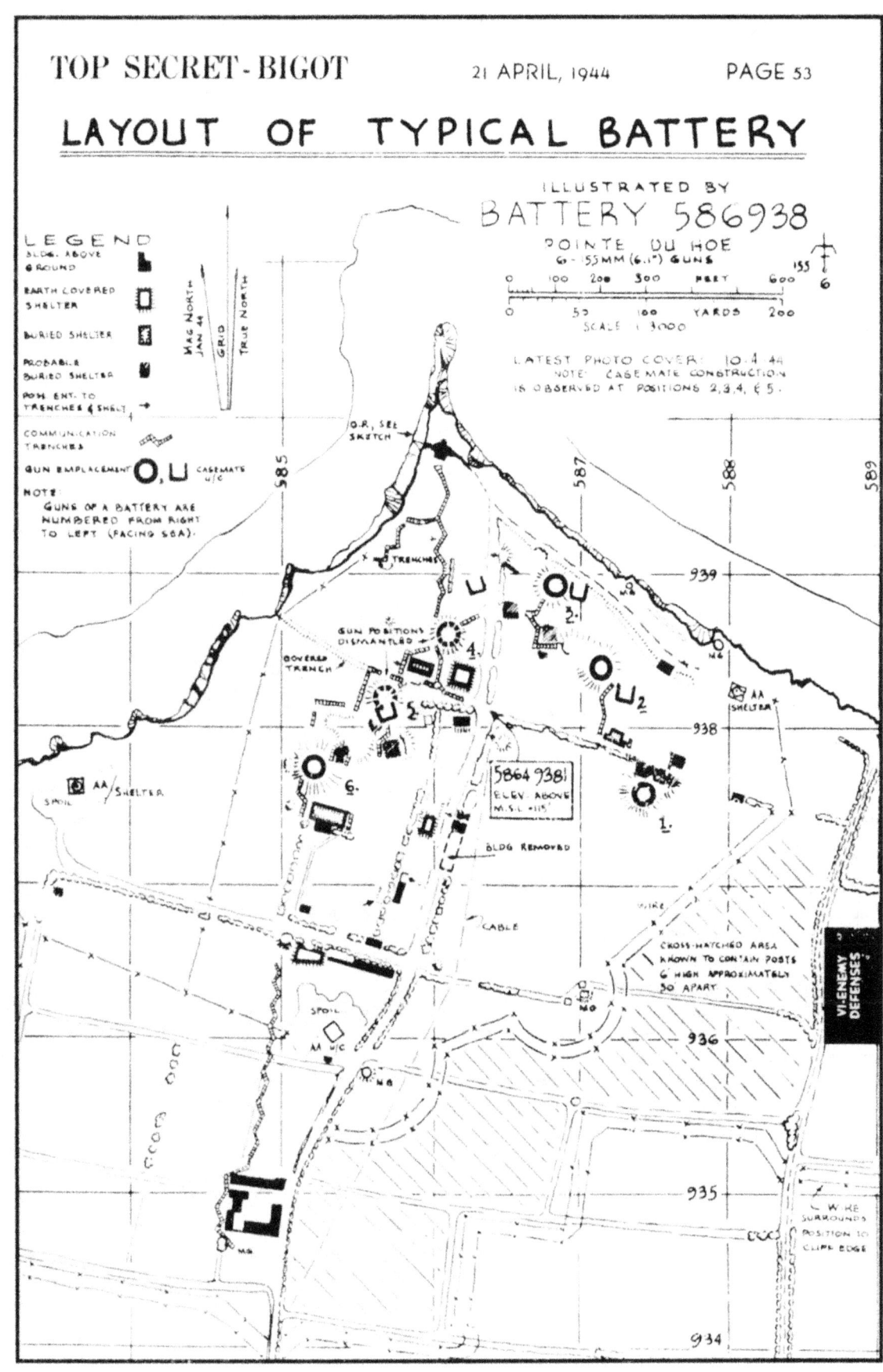

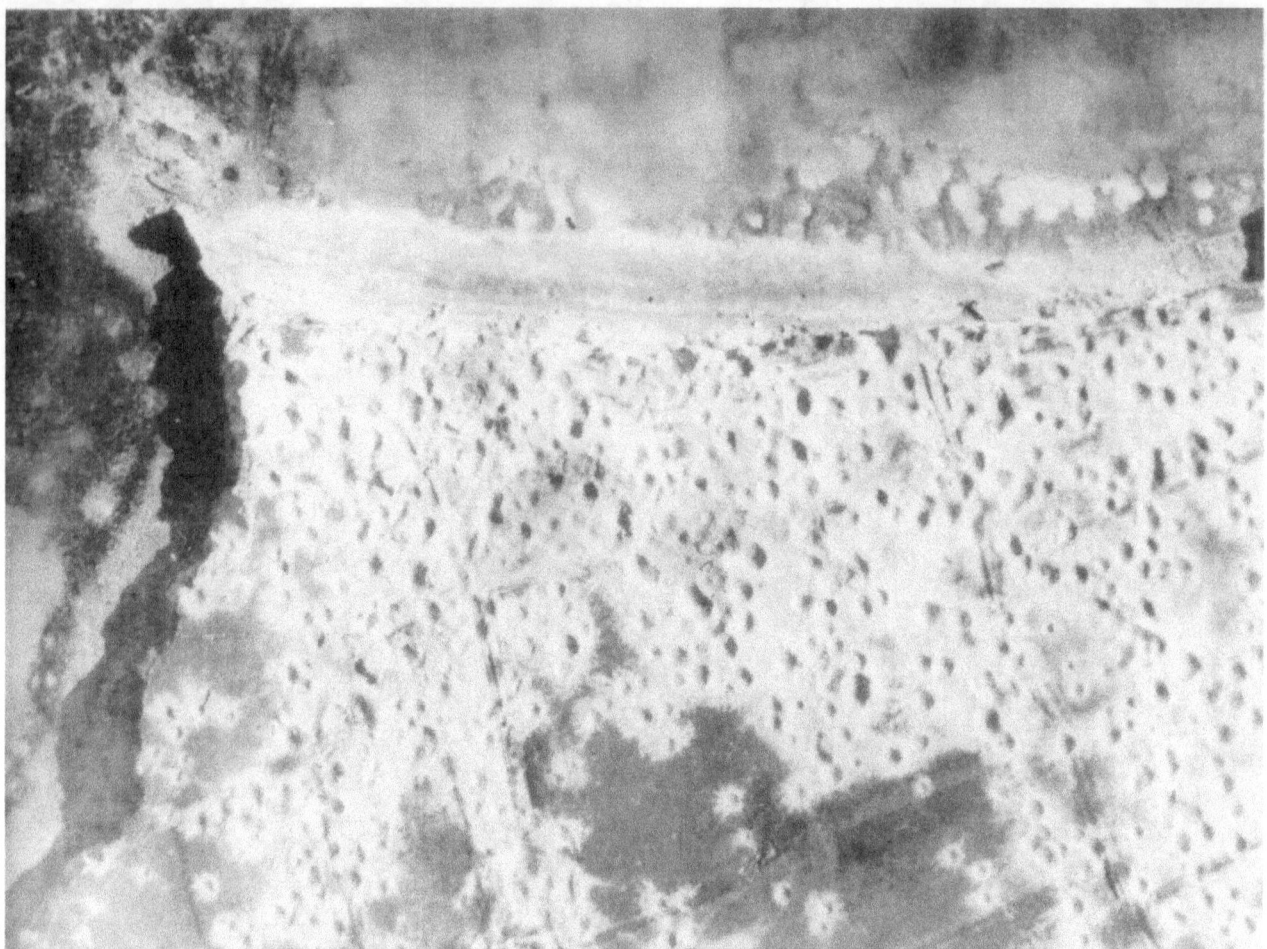

An aerial reconnaissance photograph taken around the time of the invasion shows Pointe du Hoc's landscape. It had been bombed so heavily that the craters gave it the appearance of the surface of the moon and made orientation by the Rangers difficult. *United States Army Air Corps photograph.*

On May 9, 1944, the two Ranger battalions were organized into the Provisional Ranger Group, under the command of Lieutenant Colonel Rudder. A few days prior to embarkation, Lieutenant Colonel Rudder received an unconfirmed report from French civilians that the guns on Pointe du Hoc had been moved from their casemates. However, aerial reconnaissance photos couldn't confirm this because the Germans had replaced the guns with large logs covered by netting so as to appear from the air that the guns were still in place.

Despite the report, Lieutenant Colonel Rudder knew the assault had to made, because the guns could be hidden nearby and because the Rangers had to block the coastal road that ran between Vierville and Grandcamp to block German reinforcements from reaching Omaha Beach and to facilitate the linkup of the Omaha and Utah Beach landed forces. He shared the report with those officers who had a need to know, including the executive officer of the 2nd Ranger Battalion, who attempted unsuccessfully to dissuade Rudder from conducting the assault, calling it unnecessary and suicidal.

On May 29, Rudder visited the 1st Infantry Division headquarters to meet with Major General Clarence R. Huebner, the division's commanding officer, who was in temporary command of all forces landing in the initial assault at Omaha Beach and at Pointe du Hoc, which was, at that time, planned for June 5, 1944. At that meeting, Huebner decided that Rudder should accompany Force C instead of Force A as Rudder had planned, Huebner wanted Rudder to be able to react to circumstances as the assault unfolded and didn't want Rudder to get killed or wounded during the initial assault.

Rocket propelled grapnels with attached ropes fire from an LCA (Landing Craft Assault) as it approaches a cliff lined shore in England during Ranger training in England in the spring of 1944.

A Naval Shore Fire Control Party, part of the combined army-navy 293rd Joint Assault Signal Company, was attached to Force A to provide fire control direction to ships assigned to provide gunfire support for the assault. This team consisted of three officers and twenty-three enlisted soldiers and sailors who had trained with the Rangers and would accompany them, as would a forward observer from the 58th Armored Field Artillery Battalion, which would land on Omaha Beach and was expected to provide long range artillery support for the Rangers. Five soldiers from the Army Signal Corps' 165th Signal Photographic Company would also land with the Rangers to visually document the assault on Pointe du Hoc. A British commando officer, Lieutenant Colonel Thomas H. Trevor, who had previously commanded Number 1 Commando, and who had trained the Rangers in cliff assault techniques, together with his aide would accompany the Rangers he had trained. Each of the three Ranger infantry companies were each composed of sixty-five enlisted men and three officers. An additional fifty Rangers with Headquarters and Headquarters Company, 2nd Ranger Battalion would complete the assault element. Force A totaled slightly more than 250 Rangers, plus about forty attached soldiers and sailors.

All in all, it was a very small number of handpicked and highly trained men to accomplish the most critical mission of the American beach landing forces. The lives of many soldiers and sailors landing at Omaha and Utah Beach hung in the balance if the German guns were able to shell the beaches with those ninety pound high explosive artillery rounds.

On June 1, 1944, the Provisional Ranger Group moved to the port at Weymouth for embarkation to Normandy on several ships in order to provide some contingency in case any of the ships were sunk prior to the invasion. While out to sea on June 3, Lieutenant Colonel Rudder came over from the *Prince Charles* to the *Ben-myChree* to promote the 2nd Battalion executive officer, Captain Lytle, to the rank of major. That evening, after Rudder left, a drinking binge began and Lytle began talking to his subordinates about the French report and told them that the assault was unnecessary and suicidal.

The U.S.S. *Texas*, a World War I battleship, provided naval gunfire bombardment support with its 14-inch main guns to cover the approach of the landing craft transporting the 2nd Ranger Battalion to assault the cliffs of Pointe du Hoc. *United States Navy photograph, National Archives.*

At about 4:30 a.m. on June 4, General Eisenhower postponed the invasion for twenty-four hours to June 6, because of bad weather in the English Channel and in Normandy. The ships transporting the Provisional Ranger Group, along with most of the seaborne invasion forces, returned to the embarkation ports in England.

After docking, Lieutenant Colonel Rudder learned of Major Lytle's conduct the prior evening. He appointed three Ranger captains to investigate and report back to him. They found Lytle locked up on board the *Ben-myChree* by order of the ship's captain because he had been drunk and not in control of his conduct. The three officers determined that Major Lytle could no longer command the officers for whom he was responsible during the invasion.

Lieutenant Colonel Rudder ordered that Major Lytle be relieved of command, taken ashore, and turned over to the military police with orders to take Lytle to a hospital and kept under supervision as a security measure until the invasion commenced. Rudder then informed General Huebner of the situation and that he would personally command Force A during the assault. Of course, General Huebner indicated that he didn't want Rudder to lead the initial assault. However, Rudder was purported to have told General Huebner, "If I don't take it, it may not go."[3]

General Huebner subsequently relented; Rudder would land with Force A and command the initial assault on Pointe du Hoc.

Lieutenant Colonel James E. Rudder (right foreground) marches at the head of his 2nd Ranger Battalion through Weymouth, England along the esplanade to the docks at the Weymouth Pavilion for embarkation to Normandy, on June 1, 1944. *United States Army Signal Corps photograph, courtesy of Jonathan Gawne.*

That night, June 4, Rudder took a small boat from ship to ship in the Weymouth harbor to inform his subordinate officers that he would be replacing Lytle and would personally lead Force A during the assault on Pointe du Hoc. He informed Major Richard P. Sullivan, the executive officer of the 5th Ranger Battalion and also the executive officer of the Provisional Ranger Group, of the change and that Sullivan would effectively be in command of the Provisional Ranger Group during the assault.

On the afternoon of June 5, the ships of the huge invasion fleet sailed from their ports on the southern coast of England, all headed toward Normandy in what would be the largest amphibious operation in history. The massive armada traveled in complete blackout conditions and total radio silence. That night the skies cleared somewhat, the winds abated, and the waves moderated to about five feet. Following behind the minesweepers, the naval task force bound for Omaha Beach and Pointe du Hoc moved into its assigned areas about twelve and a half miles off the French coast.

At about 3:30 a.m. on June 6, the ships weighed anchor in the transport area and the process of offloading the assault troops into landing craft began. The Rangers had already been awakened at 2:30 a.m. and fed a breakfast of two pancakes and coffee, in order to prevent seasickness. By 4:00 a.m., the Rangers were grouped by their assigned boat teams as their LCAs, which were hung from davits on the sides of the ships, were lowered to the deck level. The Rangers boarded them, carrying their normal combat loads, but also some of the specialized equipment they would use for climbing the cliffs, mortar tubes, mortar base plates, mortar shells, and a myriad of other vital gear. Four DUKWs, with their one hundred feet long extension ladders mounted and carrying demolition explosives, extra ammunition, and other equipment waited aboard LCT 46.

Troops with the 2nd Ranger Battalion are loaded in British LCAs (Landing Craft Assault) at Weymouth, England, June 3, 1944. *United States Army Signal Corps photograph, National Archives.*

POINTE DU HOC

A section of Company C, 2nd Ranger Battalion on a British LCA (Landing Craft Assault) at Weymouth, England, on June 3, 1944. These landing craft were armored and had benches upon which troops could sit, with overhead protection. *United States Army Signal Corps photograph, National Archives.*

An aerial photograph with an overlay showing the locations of the individual landing craft that touched down on the beach on the eastern side of Pointe du Hoc. *United States Army Air Corps photograph, United States Army overlay.*

Second Lieutenant George F. Kerchner
Company D, 2nd Ranger Battalion, Provisional Ranger Group

Lieutenant George Kerchner was the platoon leader of the 1st Platoon, Company D, 2nd Ranger Battalion. "On D-Day we were lowered into the water, and our twelve landing craft were moving in two columns of six each, with my craft [LCA 858] in the lead of one of the columns. The craft had a ramp on the front, and these heavy seas would wash up and hit the ramp and wash right up over the top, and very shortly we had six to twelve inches of water in the bottom. As we were going in, the LCA immediately behind mine, which contained my company commander, Captain [Harold K.] Duke Slater, sank from all the water. We immediately began bailing with our helmets and managed to keep the water down."[4] Although Captain Slater and his men were picked up by rescue craft, Company D had lost roughly one-third of its strength before it touched down at Pointe du Hoc.

Due to a navigational error, a strong southeasterly current, and poor visibility, the guide boat was leading the small flotilla of landing craft to Pointe ét Raz de la Percée to the east when Lieutenant Colonel Rudder realized the error about a thousand yards from shore and ordered the coxswain of his landing craft, LCA 888, to change course. Force A now headed for Pointe du Hoc, albeit late due to the navigational error.

Company D was assigned to land on the west side of Pointe du Hoc and attack and destroy the three guns on the west side of the position. However, the navigational error now caused the plan to be modified on the fly. Lieutenant Kerchner's landing craft, which was in the lead with LCA 888 turned with it and the rest of the double column followed. "While running parallel to the coast, the landing craft and DUKWs were taken under fire by machine guns and a 20mm antiaircraft gun, which sunk one of the DUKWs carrying vital supplies and one of the extension ladders, with only one survivor. The double column of landing craft was now approaching Pointe du Hoc from the east instead of from the north as had been planned. So the two landing craft transporting the remainder of Company D came in on the east side of the *pointe* between Company E on its right nearest the *pointe*, and Company F on its left."[5]

Because of the excess water it had taken on, Lieutenant Kerchner's LCA landed a short time after the other craft. "As we approached the beach, I gave the order to fire our rockets and they fired in sequence, two at a time. Out of our six ropes, five of them cleared the cliff, which was a good percentage, because some of the landing craft had a great deal of trouble. Some fired too soon and the ropes were wet and they didn't get up the cliffs. The ramp was lowered and we approached the beach, and the idea and the hope and desire of all of us was that we were going to run right up on the beach and make a dry landing.

"I hollered, 'Okay, let's go' and ran off the ramp, first one out, and immediately sank in eight feet of water. It was a large bomb crater. Everyone else filed around the crater and instead of being the first one ashore, I was one of the last after I paddled in there with all the weight. I was angry because I was soaking wet, and I turned around and wanted to find somebody to help me cuss out the British navy for dumping me, but everybody was busily engrossed in their own duties, so I didn't get much sympathy. Two of my boat crew were immediately hit by machine gun fire and in anger my first impulse was to go after the machine gun up there. But I realized that that was stupid, since our mission was to get to the top of the cliff and get on with destroying the guns.

"Knowing that my company commander had been sunk, I found Colonel Rudder to inform him of this event. He was starting his climb up one of the rope ladders and had his hands full and his mind full. He didn't seem particularly interested that I was assuming command of Company D. He told me to get the hell out of there and get up and climb my rope!

"Climbing the cliff was very easy. The shelling from the warships and the bombing had caused dirt and a large amount of clay and shale to fall down, so that you could almost walk up the first twenty-five feet. I went up a smooth rope and had no trouble. I couldn't understand why the Germans weren't doing more than they were doing, because I thought we were almost defenseless, landing on the shore and climbing the cliff. But I found out that the destroyer *Satterlee* had seen what was going on, and they were very close to shore and they realized that we were without fire support. They saw the Germans on top of the cliff, and they steamed in close and opened fire with their guns.

"Another thing that helped us was that the Germans had never seen anything like our rocket launchers that fired these ropes, and when the nine LCAs fired six rockets, each trailing smoke and fire. I'm sure they thought that this was some sort of weapon and I know some of them hit the ground and took cover. Some of the men had tied pieces of fuse to the end of the grapnel and figured the Germans would see the fuse burning and think something was going to explode any minute and keep away from it."[6]

Lieutenant Kerchner made it to the top of the cliff and started looking for his men. "The ground didn't look anything at all like what I thought it was going to look like. It was one large shell crater after another. I headed toward the portion of the *pointe* where the guns were and every now and then came across other Rangers from one shell crater to the next. I picked up men as I went across the terrain toward the casemated guns and at one time was in a hole with three or four others and we saw a [37mm] antiaircraft gun firing direct fire at the Rangers. This was our first live German and we all wanted to shoot at him, but he turned the gun in our direction and we all took off from our little hole.

"Then one of the sergeants came over and reported that the guns were not in the casemates. There went our initial mission so we set off on our secondary mission, which was to move inland and establish a roadblock on the coastal road that ran along the coast from Omaha Beach. I moved up the road and made contact with the first sergeant, [Leonard G.] Lomell, who was the team commander of the other boat team from Company D. We had a conference and thought we ought to go down this coastal highway several hundred yards to the right and establish a roadblock. Sergeant Lomell and Sergeant [Jack] Kuhn went down the road with the men we had there, and I went back to find more men. I met a man coming forward who told me that a sniper had zeroed the road and had killed a half a dozen Rangers, all shot through the head. I saw some of them and realized it was not a smart thing to walk the road, so I turned back to join the men on the roadblock.

"I felt disappointed that the guns were not there and awfully lonesome realizing how few men we had there and that all three company commanders had become casualties, and lieutenants like myself had taken command in each case. Lieutenant Armen had Company F, Lieutenant Lapres had E, and I was the surviving officer of D. We decided to establish a perimeter around the road and try to defend ourselves and wait for the invading force from Omaha to come up.

This photograph depicts the bomb cratered rocky beach that Rangers had to cross under intense enemy machine gun and small arms fire to reach the cliffs of Pointe du Hoc. This photograph was taken June 7, 1944, during a resupply operation. *United States Navy photograph, National Archives.*

"It was by then 8:30, so we figured that we only had a few hours to hold, and with sixty Rangers, D, E, and F Companies took up positions on the right, center, and left flanks. We saw several straggling Germans coming down the road, which we brought under fire, and then a patrol of Sergeant Lomell and Sergeant Kuhn and one other man decided to look around. They went one hundred yards from where we were along this road leading off of the hardtop coastal road and there, lo and behold, they came on five 155mm guns sitting alongside the road with ammunition stacked alongside of each of them, pointed toward Utah Beach, which was on the other flank, and all ready to fire, but with not a single German around them.

"This was the most fantastic thing that happened in the war, as far as I was concerned. Here were these guns all ready to fire, and Lord knows, the Germans needed them bad enough at this stage, and nobody was there to fire them. The guns were put out of action within a few minutes after they were discovered. We had accomplished our D-Day mission!"[7]

Technician Fifth Grade Rex D. Clark
Company E, 2nd Ranger Battalion, Provisional Ranger Group

As the Ranger LCAs touched down at Pointe du Hoc, the three surviving DUKWs carrying one hundred foot long power extension ladders, additional ammunition, demolition supplies, and the Rangers' backpacks approached the cratered beach. Private First Class Mark A. Keefer, with Company E, 2nd Ranger Battalion, and Technician Fifth Grade Billie Tibbets, from the 234th Engineer Combat Battalion and the vehicle's driver, were in the same DUKW as Technician Fifth Grade Rex D. Clark.

Keefer and Tibbets reported the actions of Technician Fifth Grade Clark to Lieutenant Fred W. Trenkle, who wrote the award recommendation. "Technician Fifth Grade Clark was in command of a DUKW mounting a 90-foot power extension ladder equipped with [twin Vickers K] machine guns [which were] swivel mounted, which was to be used by the Rangers to scale the one hundred foot cliffs at Pointe du Hoc.

The rocky beach and cliffs of Pointe du Hoc on June 7, 1944 as a resupply operation is underway using a part of the cliff that collapsed as a result of the bombardment that preceded the assault. *United States Navy photograph, the National Archives.*

"Due to the pre-assault aerial bombardment, the beach was covered with rubble and bomb craters, and the DUKW could not be employed close enough to the cliff to enable the assault elements to use the extension ladder. However, Technician Fifth Grade Clark, noting the terrific superiority of enemy firepower, ordered himself raised on the ladder so that he could bring his [Vickers K machine] guns to play on the enemy positions. Waving around one hundred feet in the air, firing his guns with deadly effect, Clark voluntarily offered himself as a choice target for enemy machine guns and rifle fire, thereby diverting much of the devastating enemy fire from the troops scaling the cliffs and neutralizing at least two of the enemy's automatic weapons emplacements."[8]

First Sergeant Leonard G. Lomell
Company D, 2nd Ranger Battalion, Provisional Ranger Group

First Sergeant Leonard G. Lomell, the acting platoon leader of the 2nd Platoon of Company D, was on board LCA 668 and carrying a box of rope and a rocket projector for a grapnel in addition to his weapon, ammunition, grenades, and other equipment for the assault. "We got in and our ramp went down and all hell broke loose. The boat leader goes off the front straight away. I stepped off the ramp, and I was the first one shot. The bullet went through what little fat I had on my right side. It didn't hit any organs, but it spun me around and burned like the dickens. There was a shell crater there underwater. I went down in water over my head with the spare rope, the hand launcher and my submachine gun. Keeping in mind that the idea was to get to the top as fast as we could, I got myself together and went up the cliff. Foremost in our minds was the challenge of getting up that cliff, which was wet from rain and clay and very slippery. The Germans were shooting down. They were cutting ropes. They were trying to kill us. I'd already been shot. Were we going to make it to the top? Were we going to get shot? These are the things we were thinking about. I think we were too cocky to be too fearful or frightened. I never thought I was going to get killed. These guys were positive thinkers. I don't think they thought much about getting killed. They thought if they got an even chance in a fight they would win as they always had. Concentrating on what I had to do and climbing the slippery, muddy rope was exhausting.

"Next to me was Sergeant Robert Fruhling, our radio man, struggling with his '500' radio set with a big antenna on it. We were approaching the top, and I was running out of strength. Bob yelled, 'Len, help me. Help me! I'm losing my strength.'

"I said, 'Hold on! I can't help you. I've got all I can do to get myself up.' Then I saw Sergeant Leonard Rubin. He was all muscle, a born athlete, a very powerful man. I said, 'Len, help Bob! Help Bob! I don't think he's going to be able to make it.' He just reached over, grabbed Bob by the back of the neck and swung him over. Bob went tumbling, and the antenna was whipping around, and I was worried that it was going to draw fire. That's all I was thinking about. I was also worried about falling off the cliff with him. I yelled, 'Get down! You're gonna draw fire on us!' You know, you get excited."[9]

When First Sergeant Lomell reached the top of the cliff he dropped down into a bomb crater. "There was Captain Gilbert Baugh. He was E Company's commander. He had a .45 in his hand, and a bullet had gone through the back of his hand into the magazine in the grip of the .45. He was in shock and bleeding badly; and there was nothing we could do other than to give him some morphine and say, 'Listen. We gotta move it. We're on our way, captain. We'll send back a medic. You just stay here. You're gonna be all right.' It was then that we left the crater where we had gathered together as we came over the cliff. We jumped into a bigger crater, and it held maybe a dozen of our guys. We couldn't get all twenty-two together in one crater for the move toward [Numbers] 4, 5 and 6 gun emplacements. We hadn't counted on craters being a protection to us. We would have lost more men, but the craters protected us. We made a move to jump to the next crater. Sergeant Morris Webb was behind me and Corporal Robert Carty was in back of Webb with a fixed bayonet. The Germans opened fire on us as we started out and we jumped back to avoid the fire. Well, Webb jumped onto Carty's bayonet. Carty didn't mean to do it. He was just down behind, ready to come up. I saw the bayonet sticking through Webb's thigh. When I ran by him, I got my morphine and socked him in the thigh. I yelled, 'I can't stay here, Webb, I gotta keep moving! We'll send a medic to you!' At that time somebody else came and took over as we made our way over to the west side of the *pointe* to gun positions 4, 5 and 6. There were no guns there and we thought, 'What the hell? What's happened here? There never were any guns here!' There was no evidence that there were ever any guns there."[10]

First Sergeant Lomell was stunned that the guns were not found in the concrete and steel casemates. "There were no big guns anywhere on the *pointe's* forty acre fortress area that we could see, only telephone poles or something similar sticking out of the bombed out encasements. By this time we were taking mortar and heavy artillery fire, crawling fire to our rear. We moved out of that position fast, hoping to locate the missing guns, thinking they were in an alternate position inland and we would soon hear them firing. It did not happen that way."[11]

"There was an antiaircraft position off to our right several hundred yards and machine guns off to the left of us—maybe a hundred to two hundred yards away. There was another machine gun that we destroyed on our way in. But we did not waste time, we did have some firefights, or little skirmishes, if the Germans had a patrol, or half of dozen of them would pop out of an underground tunnel, you know, they had a lot of tunnels there underground and through hedgerows. Well, when we were confronted, we'd drive them out and fight them and they'd run like rabbits you know, right into their holes and out they went. But we never stopped. We kept firing and charging all the way through their building's area, where they came out of their billets in all states of undress. We were confronted with them there on our way up the road from the *pointe* to the coast road.

"The coast road ran between Utah Beach and Omaha Beach. Our orders were to set up a roadblock and keep the Germans from going to Omaha Beach. We were to also destroy all communications visible along the coast road. *Find the guns,* was our big objective. We were the first ones at the coastal road; in fact there weren't any other Rangers other than D Company men the rest of that morning with us."[12]

"By the time we fought our way about a mile or so to the blacktopped coastal road (about one hour), I had only a dozen men left, some of whom were lightly wounded, but able to fight on. Ten of the original twenty-two Rangers in my boat team had been killed or were very badly wounded. We still had not found the guns nor had any idea of where they were [located]. It seemed we were surrounded and greatly outnumbered by German troops, in broad daylight. We were then behind their second line of defense. Fortunately, the Germans had no idea we were in their midst."[13]

First Sergeant Lomell and his acting platoon sergeant, Jack Kuhn, set up a roadblock on the coastal road and established an observation post. Then Lomell and the platoon sergeant set out by themselves in search of the German guns. "We saw these markings in this sunken road. It looked like something heavy had been over it. We didn't know if it was a farm wagon or what the hell it was. We had to go somewhere looking for the guns because we couldn't hear any big guns firing nearby. There was no firing, just the mortars and 88s coming in.

Machine gun and small arms fire from this concrete and steel observation bunker located at the tip of Pointe du Hoc took the Rangers under enfilade fire as they moved from the edge of the cliff. Two groups from Company E, 2nd Ranger Battalion used hand grenades and a bazooka to silence the Germans firing from it. *United States Navy photograph, the National Archives.*

"And God, we were surrounded by [enemy] troops, a combat patrol of about 40-50 Germans walked in front of us not more than twenty feet away from us. That's how fast they got together. We were badly outnumbered where we were. But our mission was to cut off the road [and] destroy the communications along the coastal road, which Sergeant Harvey Koenig of my platoon did. He was one of our section sergeants. He blew up the telephone poles with all their communications on it.[14]

"Staff Sergeant Kuhn and I started leapfrogging down this sunken farm road heading inland, following wagon tracks between the high hedgerows with trees not knowing where it was going. It led to a little swale, or draw in an apple orchard.

"There was netting with camouflage over the missing guns; their barrels were [raised] over our heads. There was not a shell or bomb crater anywhere that we could see. Looking over the hedgerow, I saw the five big 155mm coastal artillery guns and their ammunition and powder bags neatly in place aimed at Utah Beach. The German gun crew could easily turn the big guns around to fire on Omaha Beach when they so desired. The five big guns were located a little over a mile from where we had landed. About one hundred yards away, a German officer was talking to about seventy-five of his men we believed to be his gun crews, at a farm road intersection.[15]

This is one of the steel reinforced concrete casemates on Pointe du Hoc, which shows the effects of aerial saturation bombing and shelling by the main guns of the U.S.S. *Texas*. These casemates were thought to house 155mm French coastal guns which could shell Utah and Omaha Beaches and the troop transport areas offshore. *United States Army Signal Corps photograph, National Archives*.

First Sergeant Lomell used one of his thermite grenades to disable the first gun. "When the pin was pulled and the incendiary compound was exposed to air it poured out like solder, flowing over the gears and crevices, setting and hardening up like a weld. I used them to weld and fuse fast the traversing mechanisms of two of the guns. I also silently smashed the sights of all five of the guns with my padded gun butt. I had wrapped my field jacket around my submachine gun stock to silence any sound that possibly could be heard. Then Jack and I ran back down the sunken road about two hundred yards, out of sight of the Germans, to the blocking position, got more thermite grenades from our guys and hurried back to finish the job of rendering the remaining three big guns inoperable, several minutes, at most. Since thermite grenades make no noise, we luckily managed to do our job quickly and escaped without being discovered."[16]

Upon returning to his Company D Rangers who were blocking the coastal road, First Sergeant Lomell sent two runners by different routes to the battalion command post to inform Lieutenant Colonel Rudder that the German coastal guns had been found and destroyed.

This is one of the six 155mm long range guns that First Sergeant Leonard G. Lomell, Staff Sergeant Jack E. Kuhn, and later Technician Fifth Grade John S. Burnett destroyed using thermite grenades to disable the gears of the traversing and elevation mechanisms. *Photograph by Lieutenant (jg) Stuart L. Brandel, United States Navy, courtesy of Tom Lane.*

Two views of one of the French 155mm guns that First Sergeant Leonard G. Lomell, Staff Sergeant Jack E. Kuhn, and later Technician Fifth Grade John S. Burnett destroyed using thermite grenades to disable the gears of the traversing and elevation mechanisms. *Photograph by Lieutenant (jg) Stuart L. Brandel, United States Navy, courtesy of Tom Lane.*

Lieutenant Colonel James E. Rudder
Headquarters, 2nd Ranger Battalion, Provisional Ranger Group

Lieutenant Elmer H. Vemeer, the battalion's demolition officer, spent much of D-Day in close proximity of Lieutenant Colonel Rudder. "When I got to the top of the cliff I found that we were in Captain [Otto] Masny's F Company sector. He had already moved his troops in a short distance, so we got to the top of the cliff safely. There was still an awful lot of machine gun fire, and the Germans were also shelling the area from the Maisy batteries near Grandcamp, I think. Colonel Rudder was already top side and he set up a CP in a bomb crater that was right next to an antiaircraft site.

"There were a number of men attached to the Rangers for this mission. One of the groups was a [Naval] Shore Fire Control Party, headed by Captain Jonathan H. Harwood from the artillery and a navy lieutenant, Kenneth S. Norton. They were talking to Colonel Rudder when I came into the CP. They had found out that not one of the radios that were brought in to direct fire from the navy ships was working. They had all become water soaked in the trip across the channel and we didn't have any communication with the ships out at sea. Since we had lost our communication, one of the major problems was the machine gun over to our left, just a little over a quarter of a mile from the CP. This gun could cover the beach area and it was almost impossible for men to cross that beach and get ammunition and supplies up the cliff. The first thing Colonel Rudder asked me to do was to go after the machine gun. [Technician Fifth Grade] Gerald Eberle, whom I had worked with from the T&E section of the battalion, went along and one other man from I think, E Company, who was separated temporarily from his squad. We moved through the shell craters and had just reached the open ground where the machine gun could cover us when we ran into a patrol from F Company, which was on the same mission. Captain Masny had also seen that the machine gun was a real obstacle. The six of us had no sooner got together when a Ranger came running up from the CP saying to back off and wait until they could try and shoot the machine gun off the edge of that cliff with guns from a destroyer.

"Although we were really facing some major problems, such as coming in late, being hit by the machine gun along the coast, losing a number of our supply boats and men at sea (some of them were actually picked up and again came to join us at a later date), one thing seemed to work in our favor. Lieutenant James Eikner, the signal officer, had bought a small lamp with shutters in England for his own personal collection. He did bring it ashore on D-Day and it proved to be the only communication we had with the navy for quite a period of time. He was able with his signal lamp to relay our problem to the navy and one of the destroyers was visually able to see the machine gun and did blow it off of the cliff with its guns.

"I think it would have been virtually impossible for us to knock out that machine gun since the gunner had about three hundred yards of completely open field to fire on us and he was in a fortified position, almost impossible to hit with mortars or any other kind of artillery except the guns on the destroyer. We were so short of mortar ammunition anyway that fortunately we didn't have to use it. Lieutenant Eikner and radio man, [Corporal] Lou Lisko, kept further communications going the best they could.

"We came back with the F Company patrol and stopped at Captain Masny's F Company CP, which was under siege by the Germans from over on the left front and from straight south of where we had landed. The Germans were mounting a very heavy attack with riflemen, machine guns, and mortars. Masny and his men stayed cool and killed a great number of German soldiers, truly displaying the Ranger spirit and training. Captain Masny was an excellent leader. One of his men was operating a mortar by placing it against his knee. He could see where the Germans were and without using a bi-pod or any instruments, he was firing the mortar just by sight. He almost dropped every shell right where he wanted it. Later reconnaissance let us know how effective he had been. An orchard, just beyond where the Germans had attacked was literally covered with dead Germans who had been killed during that raid.

"After the fight, Eberle and I returned to Colonel Rudder's CP. When we got to within about twenty-five yards of the CP, we found a Ranger who had captured a German soldier from an underground pillbox or sleeping quarters. We had just started to question him, since I do speak some German, when the German was shot right between the eyes by someone farther inland. I don't know if it was a German or an American who shot him. He was facing inland, we were facing the channel, and they nailed him right between the eyes while he was standing between us.

"Upon getting back to the CP, we found out that since the only communication we had was Eikner's signal lamp it proved to be impossible to get a message through to higher headquarters telling them that we had landed and were established on the *pointe*. For this reason, headquarters had ordered the remainder of the 2nd Ranger Battalion and the 5th Ranger Battalion to come in on Omaha Beach, which was the alternate plan. Had we been able to report within forty-five minutes of our landing that we had been successful they would have come in to Pointe du Hoc. So we lost all of the reinforcements and supplies when they went to Omaha Beach.

"I remember shortly after returning that Colonel Rudder came back into the CP having been shot through the leg. It was a flesh wound and Doc Block, I think, ran a swab through it and put a little iodine on it. Colonel Rudder refused to stay in the CP and soon went out again with Captain Harwood and Lieutenant Norton. We'd understood that one of the men who were working on the radio in one of the gun emplacements had gotten it operational and the three of them went out to do some fire directing.

Lieutenant Colonel James E. Rudder, commanding officer of the Provisional Ranger Group, at Pointe du Hoc. His gasmask bag is hanging from his neck and he is carrying his map case under his right arm. *Photograph by Major Jack Stree*t.

"One of the shells from the *Texas* battleship hit the gun emplacement the three were in while trying to use the repaired radio. Of course, it was a serious mishap. Evidently the Germans had reoccupied another gun emplacement, which was just farther in from the one where the colonel and the shore fire control party were working. The target number that was given may well have been in error since the area was so thoroughly shelled and bombed. There wasn't a blade of grass to be seen. It was nothing but craters and shellholes and it was difficult to recognize one point from another. The direct hit turned the men completely yellow. It was as though they had been stricken with jaundice. It wasn't only their faces and hands, but the skin beneath their clothes and the clothes which were yellow from the smoke of that 14-inch shell fired from the battleship. It was probably a colored marker shell.

"It wasn't long before Captain Harwood died, and his body was left on a stretcher placed just outside the CP. We could see his body until the third day, when we were relieved. It was again another incident. These things kept happening and at the time we looked at it as part of what was going on. Lieutenant Norton was taken into Doc Block's hospital. The quarters were just behind the CP, down concrete steps and into a concrete bunker which had been the sleeping quarters for the personnel who operated the German ack-ack guns at that point.

"I never saw or heard of Lieutenant Norton again; however, I know he survived and left the *pointe*. At this point I must digress to say something about one of the biggest things that saved our day on Pointe du Hoc. That was seeing Colonel Rudder controlling the operation. It still makes me cringe to recall the pain he must have endured trying to operate with a wound through the leg and the concussive force he must have felt from the close hit by the yellow colored shell. As far as I know, it was the concussion which probably killed Captain Harwood; and Colonel Rudder, I understand, was right next to him when the shell exploded. He was a strength of the whole operation through the next day and a half in spite of his wounds and he was in command all of the time."[17]

Captain Otto Masny
Company F, 2nd Ranger Battalion, Provisional Ranger Group

Lieutenant Colonel Rudder felt that the heroism of Captain Otto Masny was vital to the successful capture of Pointe du Hoc. "[Captain Masny] assisted in holding a firm beachhead approximately four hundred yards long and about fifty yards deep for sixty-six hours under constant sniper, machine gun, and observed artillery fires. Although wounded in action; shot through the shoulder, he remained when he may have been evacuated, and even so handicapped destroyed an enemy ammunition dump within twenty yards of enemy positions. Captain Masny, wounded early during the assault on the cliffs at Pointe du Hoc, on numerous occasions displayed outstanding courage and leadership above and beyond the call of duty. He played an important role in the putting down of three enemy counterattacks during one night.

"On the eve of D+2, Captain Masny, wounded, perceiving that the enemy was procuring ammunition supplies from a nearby ammunition dump, volunteered and led a patrol to destroy the installation. Covered continually by enemy automatic weapons fire and displaying an utter disregard for his own safety, blew up the enemy ammunition dump at Pointe du Hoc. On several other instances Captain Masny displayed courage far above the call of duty; he was finally evacuated under protest by [me] the Ranger group commander."[18]

Lieutenant (jg) Kenneth S. Norton
Naval Shore Fire Control Party 1, 293rd Joint Assault Signal Company, Assault Force O, Task Force 124,
Eleventh Amphibious Force, 12th Fleet

Naval gunfire provided the only artillery support for the Rangers on Pointe du Hoc. The Naval Shore Fire Control Party's communications and fire direction was critical to the survival of the Rangers as the first enemy counterattacks began in the morning and continued throughout the day. Lieutenant Colonel James Rudder was grateful for the heroism of Lieutenant Norton to maintain that gunfire support. "Lieutenant (jg) Norton landed at Pointe du Hoc as forward observer for the Naval Shore Fire Control Party attached to Force A. Without regard to his own safety, on numerous occasions, he exposed himself to enemy fire in order to adjust supporting naval fire. He was wounded in the back by shell fragments and rendered in a state of semi-consciousness (unable to move). Upon recovering somewhat he requested he not be evacuated. Though suffering greatly from shell shock, Lieutenant Norton returned to his post and continued to direct fire effectively against the enemy. Lieutenant Norton's courageous and gallant action, above and beyond the call of duty, greatly assisted Ranger Force A in holding out during the two and one half days it was isolated from friendly troops."[19]

Sergeant Worden F. Lovell
165th Signal Photographic Company

During the assault on the morning of June 6, 1944, Lieutenant Colonel Rudder witnessed a rather amazing act of courage by a soldier who was normally armed with only a camera. "Sergeant Worden F. Lovell, member of Detachment M, 165th Signal Photo Company, landed on Pointe du Hoc with the Assault Force A, 2nd Ranger Battalion. He pressed forward with the point of the attack in order to obtain pictures. His camera was damaged in his hands when it was hit by a shell fragment. The small group that Sergeant Lovell accompanied was subjected to machine gun fire and Sergeant Lovell obtained one of the rifles of a casualty and volunteered to approach the machine gun position and subject it to hand grenade bursts. This gallant action silenced the machine gun fire and allowed the group to move forward."[20]

A Naval Shore Fire Control Party like the one of which Lieutenant (jg) Kenneth Norton was a member, and part of the 293rd Joint Assault Signal Company. This photograph, taken on June 6, 1944 in Normandy, shows the party set up in a shellhole using an SCR-284 radio and an SCR-536 handie-talkie radio to communicate with ships offshore which are providing close gunfire support. The sailor in the center of the photo turns a GN-45 hand cranked electrical generator to provide power to the SCR-284 transmitter. *United States Army Signal Corps photograph, courtesy of Jonathan Gawne.*

Sergeant Worden F. Lovell was a still cameraman assigned to Detachment M, 165th Signal Photographic Company who scaled the cliffs under fire with the 2nd Ranger Battalion.

A 2nd Ranger Battalion non-commissioned officer (right center), identified by the white horizontal stripe painted on the back of his helmet, mans a .30 caliber machine gun from the edge of a crater on Pointe du Hoc. A Ranger officer (lower right) is identified by a white vertical stripe painted on the back of his helmet. *United States Army Signal Corps photograph, National Archives.*

Rangers march German prisoners past the 2nd Ranger Battalion command post, located in a bomb crater on the edge of the cliff, for eventual evacuation to the U.S.S. *Texas* battleship. *United States Army Signal Corps photograph.*

AIR POWER OVER NORMANDY

"The Normandy invasion was based on a deep-seated faith in the power of the air force in overwhelming numbers to intervene in the land battle." —General Dwight D. Eisenhower

The United States Eighth Air Force's 1,864 strategic heavy bombers and its fighter escort aircraft, the United States Ninth Air Force's 3,500 tactical troop carrier, fighter, fighter bomber, and medium bomber aircraft, and the British Royal Air Force dominated the skies over Normandy on June 6, 1944. Just prior to H-Hour, 1,083 B-17 and B-24 bombers flew missions to attack German beach defenses. The Ninth Air Force's light and medium bombers attacked German gun batteries in the Utah Beach area just before the landings commenced and then later in the day attacked communications, command and control, and supply depots. However, poor visibility and fear of bombing friendly forces led the Eighth Air Force's heavy bombers to delay the bomb release over Omaha Beach, resulting in almost all of the bombs being dropped inland, leaving the beach almost untouched.

Some 171 squadrons of British and American fighters and fighter bombers provided massive protection from enemy air attacks. Fifteen squadrons protected shipping, another fifty-four squadrons flew cover over the beaches, thirty-three provided bomber escort and flew offensive fighter sweeps, an additional thirty-three squadrons struck inland targets to interdict enemy traffic and reinforcements, and thirty-six more provided direct air support to the invading ground forces.

Major Paul J. Stach
455th Bombardment Squadron, 323rd Bombardment Group, 98th Bombardment Wing, Ninth Air Force

At 2:00 p.m., a B-26 Marauder piloted by Major Paul J. Stach and the rest of his squadron took off from the airfield at Earls Cole, England on a mission to interdict German reinforcements. Staff Sergeant George W. Fobes was the plane's tail gunner. "We were to bomb a road junction at Caen, France at about 12,000 feet. Due to overcast we had to come down to about 3,000 or 3,500 [feet]. As we came in over the French coast we were shot at by [37mm antiaircraft] guns. This gunfire lasted about one minute and as we came out of it I called each crew member and asked if they were alright. In each case they were, although the plane had been hit in the left wing. A matter of a second [later] we ran into more flak. We were hit in the nose, wings, and bomb bay. Fire immediately broke out in the bomb bay section and the pilot, Major Paul Stach, gave the order to abandon ship."[1]

Staff Sergeant Otis O'Neal was the top turret gunner of the plane flying on the left wing of the stricken B-26 bomber. "We had just opened our bomb bay doors when the flak started coming up into our flight. We were flying on the left wing of Major Stach and the rest of the crew as well as myself saw him get at least three direct hits in the bomb bay or in the left wing. He then put the ship into a climb and they salvoed the bombs. The three gunners bailed out through the waist windows and then three more bailed out of the bomb bays. I remember Captain Seagraves coming out of the bomb bay because of the red scarf he always wears. The ship was hit at 16:16 hours at France. The pilot's escape hatch was opened but it didn't fly off as it is supposed to and I could see someone trying to get out through it, but no one ever got out through the hatch. After six men bailed out, the ship slid down and behind us and went into a spin. It exploded upon hitting the ground."[2]

As he hung in his parachute, Staff Sergeant Fobes saw the plane from which he had just bailed out crash and burst into flames. "As I hit the ground, approximately 200-300 feet away I saw the plane, it was completely enveloped in flames. Twenty minutes later, I was arrested by SS troops and turned over to the German intelligence for interrogation."[3]

Major Stach's gallant actions had saved most of his plane's crew at the cost of his own life.

This B-26 Marauder bomber is like the one flown by Major Paul J. Stach during a mission to bomb a key road junction near Caen on June 6, 1944. Major Stach's plane was struck by antiaircraft fire and he maintained control of the plane while jettisoning the bombs and giving several crewmen time to exit the burning aircraft. *United States Air Force photograph.*

OMAHA BEACH

It was H-Hour. They came ashore on Omaha Beach, the slogging, unglamorous men that no one envied. No battle ensigns flew for them, no horns or bugles sounded. But they had history on their side. They came from regiments that had bivoucked at places like Valley Forge, Stoney Creek, Antietam, Gettysburg, and that had fought in the Argonne. They had crossed the beaches of North Africa, Sicily, and Salerno. Now they had one more beach to cross. They would call this one "Bloody Omaha." —Cornelius Ryan

Of the five Allied assault beaches, Omaha was the most challenging and the most critical. The terrain was a defender's dream. The beach was crescent shaped, which provided outstanding opportunities for enfilading crossfire from both flanks. The beach was gently sloping with a distance of three hundred yards between the low and high tide marks. Just above the high water mark, a sloped shingle or shelf ranging from 4-12 feet in height, rested against a wooden seawall on the western third and against a sand embankment on the eastern two thirds of the beach. This shingle was made up of small shale stones. Beyond the shingle lay flat sand some two hundred yards deep in the center and less at both ends, running to the foot of bluffs. Bluffs ranging from 100-170 feet high dominated the beach, providing great observation for plunging fire and a physical barrier to bottle up attacking forces on the beach. Furthermore, the bluffs were almost vertical cliffs at both ends of the beach. There were only five ravines or "draws" providing natural exits through the face of the bluffs and up to the plateau beyond.

The Germans had taken full advantage of the terrain to turn Omaha Beach into an almost perfect killing ground. The first lines of defense were four rows of obstacles. The first row of obstacles, about 270 yards from the high water mark, consisted of welded steel fences about ten feet wide and seven feet high with steel braces behind called "Element C" or Belgian gates, which had waterproof Teller antitank mines fastened to the outside uprights. About thirty yards closer to the high water mark was a row of wooden posts set at an angle to the sea with waterproof Teller mines lashed to the top of about every third post. About thirty yards closer to the high water mark was a row of ramps, with each consisting of a long telephone pole sized log anchored in the sand on the seaward end and rising to the other end where two supporting logs held it, with a waterproof Teller mine attached to the high end. It was designed to cause a landing craft to roll over on its side or to detonate the mine if struck by a landing craft. The last line of obstacles, about 160 yards from the high water mark was a row of steel hedgehogs constructed of three steel channeled rails welded together, which were designed to rip open the bottoms of any landing craft passing over them.

The first cover beyond the obstacles for an attacking force would be the shale rock shelf or shingle and on the western third of the beach, a 6-12 feet high seawall abutting the landward side of the shingle. On the eastern two-thirds of the beach the shingle was bordered on the landward side by low sand dunes. To deal with this, the Germans sighted indirect fire from mortars and Nebelwerfer rockets and enfilade fire from the flanks to decimate anyone reaching the shingle and seawall.

The area behind the shingle was flat for as much as two hundred yards in the center before giving way to the bluffs. The Germans placed double rows of barbed wire along the landward side of the shingle running the length of the beach and sewed Schu antipersonnel mines and Teller antitank mines on the flat ground beyond and part way up the bluffs. Additionally, they dug ten feet deep and thirty feet wide antitank ditches to block the five draws or exits leading inland from the beach.

There were approximately one thousand German troops defending Omaha Beach. Around 450 were deployed in fourteen *Widerstandsnesten* (or resistance nests) located primarily around the five draws. The remainder of the troops would be deployed in trenches and stone buildings overlooking the beach and in the villages immediately behind the beach. The resistance nests were designated WN 60 on the eastern end to WN 73 on the bluffs west of the beach.

MAP LEGEND

[	Gun Emplacement		xxxx	Wire
⌇	Communications Trench		⊢⊣	Single Wire Fence
⊥⌐	Fire Trench		⌇⌇	Concertina Wire
⊢■	Dugout		—┼—	Communication Line
□	Concrete Shelter		⊼⊼	Steel Beach Obstacles
▭ (dashed)	Concrete Shelter Under Construction		c c c	Landmines
⊢⊣	Mobile Gun or Howitzer		│	Natural Tank Obstacle
⊢⊣	Mobile Gun or Howitzer in Open Position		┃│	Natural Vehicle Obstacle
⊣⊗	Antitank Gun		┼○	Church
⊢○	Antiaircraft Gun in Open Position		■	Building or House
⊢⊣	Antiaircraft Machine Gun		│	Paved Road
⊢○	Antiaircraft Machine Gun in Open Position		┊	Unpaved Road
│	Machine Gun		┆	Tracks
⊟	Gun Casemate		– 30 –	Contour Elevation
⊟	Pillbox for Infantry Weapon			Hedgerow
⊠	Concrete Observation Post		∼	Stream
⋏	Artillery Observation Post		⊁⊁	Bridge
⋛	Antitank Ditch			
K	Fixed Roadblock			

OMAHA BEACH

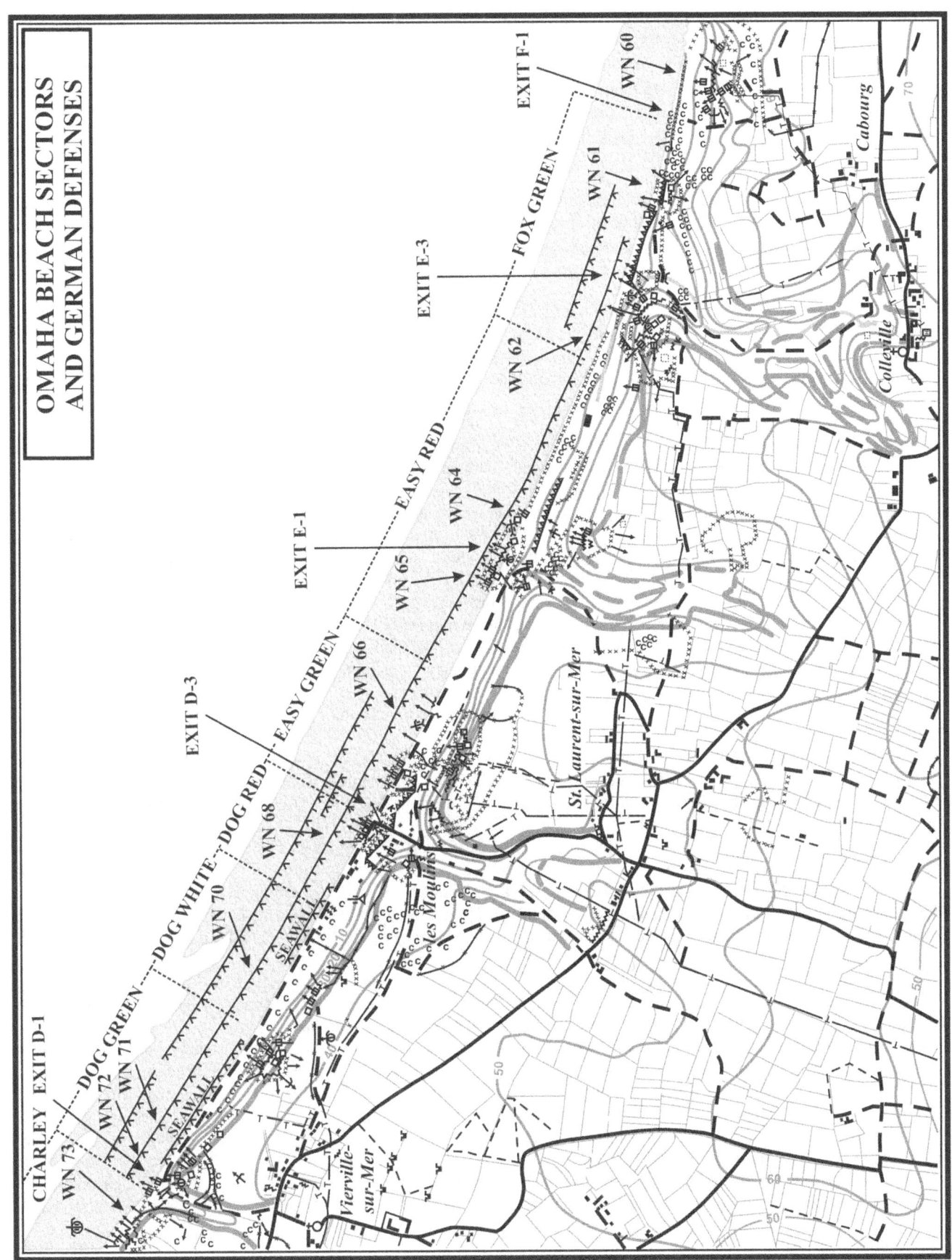

The eastern most resistance nest, WN 60, had armaments of one captured French 75mm howitzer, one 20mm antiaircraft gun, one French tank turret with a short barreled 37mm gun mounted on an open top concrete fortification built flush with the ground (known as a Panzerstellung), four 50mm mortars, and approximately ten machine gun positions. About forty soldiers, mostly from Kompanie 2, Grenadier Regiment 726 of Infanterie Division 716 manned the position, which had a great view of the center of the beach from which to observe and adjust the fire of its 50mm mortars.

Widerstandsnest 61 or WN 61 guarded the eastern side of the Colleville draw, designated by Allied planners as Exit E-3. This position had a type H677 heavy steel reinforced concrete casemate for an 88mm PAK 43/41 antitank gun, which could cover the beach with devastating enfilade fire on approaching landing craft and tanks. In addition, there were two 50mm PAK 38 antitank guns in open concrete emplacements, a French tank turret with a 37mm gun mounted on a Panzerstellung, and approximately nine machine gun positions, some of them located in concrete Tobruks. This resistance nest was manned by around forty soldiers, primarily from Kompanie 3, Grenadier Regiment 726 of Infanterie Division 716.

The largest resistance nest was WN 62, which was located on the western entrance to the Colleville draw. It was made up of two steel reinforced concrete casemates containing two Belgian 75mm FK235(b) howitzers sighted to enfilade the beach to the west and northwest, two 50mm antitank guns in open gun pits, approximately eleven machine guns, and three 50mm mortars. About forty soldiers were assigned to this resistance nest, the majority with Kompanie 3, Grenadier Regiment 726, Infanterie Division 716.

An underground command post located further up the E-3 draw was designated by the Germans as WN 63, but contained no other concrete emplacements and no dug in weapons.

The next resistance nest to the west was WN 64, located on the eastern side of the E-1 exit. This position was composed of a captured Russian IKH 290(r) 76.2mm infantry gun in an unfinished casemate, a 20mm antiaircraft gun, two mortars, and some nine machine guns. Around forty soldiers, primarily from Kompanie 10, Grenadier Regiment 726 of Infanterie Division 716 manned the position.

The resistance nest on the western side of the E-1 exit, WN 65, consisted of a 50mm PAK 38 antitank gun positioned in a casemate, a 50mm antitank gun in an open position, a 75mm PAK 40 antitank gun positioned in an earthen and log covered bunker, two 50mm mortars, and approximately thirteen machine guns. Another forty or so soldiers, mostly from Kompanie 10, Grenadier Regiment 726 of Infanterie Division 716 were assigned to the position.

The WN 66 strongpoint on the east side of the les Moulins draw (designated as Exit D-3 by Allied planners) consisted of one 50mm PAK 38 antitank gun in an unfinished casemate, a second 50mm pedestal mounted antitank gun in an open concrete lined position, two 80mm mortar positions, and approximately fourteen machine guns. About forty troops, primarily with Kompanie 10, Grenadier Regiment 726 of Infanterie Division 716 were assigned to the position.

Located on the plateau behind the bluffs between the D-3 and E-1 exits was WN 67, consisting of a control bunker and thirty-eight Wurfgerät 40 and 41 rocket launchers, each capable of firing four 280mm high explosive or four 320mm incendiary rockets, located in dug in positions in a field.

The west side of the les Moulins draw was defended by WN 68, which was composed of a 50mm antitank gun, a Panzer IV tank turret with a 75mm gun and two French Renault tank turrets with 37mm guns mounted on concrete Panzerstellungs, and approximately ten machine guns. About forty soldiers, primarily from Kompanie 10, Grenadier Regiment 726, Infanterie Division 716 were assigned to the position.

Farther up the les Moulins draw and slightly north of St. Laurent was WN 69, which was composed of two German made artillery pieces and a 20mm antiaircraft gun.

The area between the les Moulins and Vierville exits was defended by WN 70, consisting of one 80mm Czechoslovakian 80mm FK 17(t) field gun in a concrete casemate, a 75mm field gun in an open position, a 20mm antiaircraft gun, two 50mm mortars, and approximately thirteen machine guns and was manned by mostly troops with Kompanie 10, Grenadier Regiment 726 of Infanterie Division 716.

The eastern side of the Vierville draw (designated as Exit D-1 by Allied planners) was protected by WN 71, which had a 75mm PAK 40 antitank gun, one 20mm antiaircraft gun, and about eight machine guns. Around forty soldiers, primarily from Kompanie 11, Grenadier Regiment 726 of Infanterie Division 716 defended this resistance nest.

At the mouth of the Vierville exit, the Germans constructed two steel reinforced concrete casemates; one held an 88mm PAK 43/41 antitank gun and the other held a 50mm PAK 38 antitank gun. The 88mm antitank was sited to destroy incoming landing craft and tanks with enfilade fire from the west. The casemate which held the 50mm antitank gun had embrasures that allowed it to fire toward the sea to the north and also provide enfilade fire on the beach to the east. Two sections of soldiers from Kompanie 3, Grenadier Regiment 914 of Infanterie Division 352 deployed as local defense around the two casemates. This resistance nest was designated as WN 72.

The west side of the Vierville exit was covered by WN 73, which consisted of a 75mm PAK 97/38 antitank gun positioned in a concrete bunker located in a fold of the bluff and sited to enfilade the beach, an 80mm mortar, and approximately eleven machine gun positions. About forty soldiers, primarily from Kompanie 11, Grenadier Regiment 726, Infanterie Division 716 manned this resistance nest.

Aerial reconnaissance photos taken prior to the invasion and a later analysis of German weapons directly defending the beach estimated that there were sixty light artillery pieces, eighteen antitank guns, and no less than eighty-five machine guns.

The resistance nests employed everything the German army had learned in World War I about how to use fortifications and terrain to stop mass infantry assaults. The resistance nests had interlocking fields of fire with pre-sighted targets for most of the weapons to insure that every part of the beach was covered. This included plunging fire from the bluffs, grazing fire from weapons positioned on the beach above the high water mark, enfilade crossfire from fortifications firing laterally across the beach, and indirect fire from mortars, artillery, and Nebelwerfer rockets.

In addition to the three companies of infantry from Grenadier Regiment 726 manning the resistance nests, Kompanie 5, Grenadier Regiment 916 of Infanterie Division 352 was located at St. Laurent-sur-Mer and Kompanie 8, Grenadier Regiment 916 of Infanterie Division 352 was positioned at Colleville. Kompanies 6 and 7, Grenadier Regiment 916, Infanterie Division 352 were positioned 2-3 miles south of the beach. Elements of Kompanie 13, Grenadier Regiment 916 of Infanterie Division 352 manned the howitzers and field guns while Kompanie 14, Grenadier Regiment 916 of Infanterie Division 352 supplied the crews for the antitank guns deployed in the Omaha Beach defense sector. Three batteries of Artillerie Regiment 352 of Infanterie Division 352, each with four 105mm howitzers, were positioned near Formigny, Colleville, and Houteville, within range of Omaha Beach. Two units were in the area constructing additional beach defenses. Kompanie 2, Landesbau Pioneer Bataillon 17 was billeted at St. Laurent-sur-Mer and Kompanie 1, Landesbau Pioneer Bataillon 17 was at Colleville.

In addition to these local defenses, Kampfgruppe Meyer, consisting of Grenadier Regiment 915, Panzerjager Abteilung 352, and Fusilier Bataillon 352, all from Infanterie Division 352 and positioned in the Bayeux area about fifteen miles to the southeast, constituted a reserve counterattack force.

One thousand or so troops defending the beach and sheltered in steel reinforced concrete fortifications, thick walled stone buildings, and trenches, armed with a large number of antitank guns, howitzers, mortars, and machine guns, with substantial artillery support, with the advantages of the terrain, plus the mined obstacles and minefields that would impose casualties and delay, all combined to make Omaha Beach a formidable and almost perfect killing ground.

ASSAULT FORCE O WOULD LAND about 34,000 troops and 3,300 vehicles of the 1st and 29th Infantry Divisions and attached units on Omaha Beach on June 6, 1944. The naval elements to transport the troops and vehicles of Assault Force O across the English Channel consisted of seven attack transport ships, eight LSIs (Landing Ship Infantry), twenty-four LSTs (Landing Ship Tank), thirty-three LCI(L)s (Landing Craft Infantry), thirty-six LCM(3)s (Landing Craft Mechanized), 147 LCTs (Landing Craft Tank), and thirty-three other craft. In addition, the escort, gunfire support, and bombardment missions employed two battleships, three cruisers, twelve destroyers, and 105 other ships. Assault Force "O" also included thirty-three minesweepers and 585 service vessels.

The 16th Regimental Combat Team numbered 9,828 personnel, 919 vehicles, and forty-eight tanks, including 3,502 men and 295 vehicles attached only for movement to the beach. To transport this combat team and the attached units required two transports, six LSTs, fifty-three LCTs (of various types), and five LCI(L)s. Smaller landing craft launched from larger ships in the transport area consisted of eighty-one LCVPs (Landing Craft Vehicle Personnel, eighteen British LCAs (Landing Craft Assault), thirteen other types of landing craft, and about sixty-four amphibious DUKWs.

The naval transport for the 116th Regimental Combat Team was of similar composition and required similar numbers of ships and landing craft.

Lieutenant (jg) Phil H. Bucklew
Naval Scouts, Assault Force O, Task Force 124, Eleventh Amphibious Force, 12th Fleet

Two United States Navy LCS (Landing Craft Support) scout boats commanded by Lieutenants (jg) Grant G. Andreasen and Phil H. Bucklew would be the first to approach Omaha Beach. During one night the previous January, Andreasen and Bucklew had used a couple of thirty-six foot boats equipped with special gear and supplied by the British, to take sound readings measuring the firmness of the sand and collect core samples of the sand on Omaha Beach every twenty yards at a distance of about 150 yards from the high water mark. During a second mission, the two clandestinely swam from a kayak paddled by a British commando to the waterline of Omaha Beach. There, they laid in the water observing and timing the movements of German sentries before going further up the beach to collect additional sand samples to confirm that the beach could support tanks and other heavy vehicles.

A former NFL football player from Columbus, Ohio, Lieutenant Bucklew had received the Navy Cross for heroism during the amphibious assault landing at Sicily and a Silver Star for his actions during the amphibious landings at Salerno, Italy. He would become a legend in the United States Navy, commanding SEAL Team One during the Vietnam War and would be known as the father of naval special operations. The Naval Special Warfare Center at Coronado, California bears his name.

Two United States Navy LCS (Land Craft Support) boats were used by Naval Scouts under the leadership of Lieutenants (jg) Grant G. Andreasen and Phil H. Bucklew to mark Omaha Beach with lights to mark the beach for incoming landing craft.

On the morning of June 6, the two young lieutenants and their scout boats would guide the initial waves of duplex drive tanks and landing craft to the beach. Chief Boatswain's Mate Ray B. Bristol was assigned to Bucklew's scout boat. "Our mission was to provide covering fire for the naval combat demolition units and floating tanks. Then we would set up seaward facing lights at Red Beach Center and guide in the assault waves."[1]

Prior to dawn, Lieutenant Bucklew looked across the dark open water as his scout boat slowly emerged from its LST. "It was souped up for speed. Fifteen knots, which was good for a landing craft then. It was gasoline powered—I had stripped most of the metal armor off it. In moving in we had a longer run for Normandy than we had had for any previous operation, I would say it was twelve to fifteen miles, probably fifteen since I was launched early and while the ship was still under way. I must have been ten miles offshore when all hell broke loose. On my right hand, it must have been ten miles down the beach, there were explosions [of] various types, [and] flares going [up]."[2]

The firing which Lieutenant Bucklew witnessed was the aerial bombardment prior to the 2nd Ranger Battalion's assault on Pointe du Hoc. He was concerned that his scout boat was off course. "I was never more relieved than to see that Vierville church steeple that I had seen during the recon, and it was pinpointed as part of the intelligence chart. When I saw that steeple I was probably the most relieved person in the world, even though it was just the beginning of the fight.

"Then, the next most impressive thing was Admiral [Morton L.] Deyo's fire support; they started hammering the salvos in. As I later saw when I went ashore—I have never seen anything before or since to equal the devastation that a naval salvo from a battleship can do…"[3]

As the LCS scout boat neared the beach, Chief Boatswain's Mate Bristol was able to see that "Omaha Red Beach Center was dead ahead. German shore batteries tried to stop us as we made several passes along the shoreline. One [machine] gun in particular located on the second floor of a building on the beach was coming too close to us. Our crew fired rockets but didn't stop the gun."[4]

Bristol felt the boat abruptly turn toward the beach and gain speed. "We quickly ran into shore and set up our beach lights to guide in the waves of landing craft. Then we headed back out to guide in the floating tanks."[5]

Looking out toward the fleet, Bucklew could see the DD tanks struggling toward the beach in very rough water. "The first troops to land were embarked in DD tanks. Many swamped in the surf line with their crews evacuating through the top hatch and attempting to swim ashore. Only a few DDs made it to the beach under their own power.

"First light revealed the rows of beach obstacles covering the entire shoreline three rows deep and placed at ten to twenty feet intervals, most with Teller mines facing seaward—tetrahedrons—cement and railroad ties improvised to fend off most landing craft in that shallow beach gradient area where tides rose and fell twenty feet."[6]

As the few surviving DD tanks landed, Bristol watched the first wave of infantry come ashore, followed just minutes later by a wave of gap assault teams of army combat engineers and naval combat demolition units. "[Lieutenant] Bucklew directed cover fire for the NCDUs, fixing charges on Teller-mined 'hedgehogs,' large underwater obstacles designed to wreck landing craft."[7]

Lieutenant Bucklew observed the progress of the gap assault teams as his scout boat crew fired at German positions. "The UDTs came wallowing in their old LCMs—nothing glamorous about the way they came in—and they got in trouble right away. They went right into the beach obstacles and detonated some of the Teller mines, took casualties but went to work…

"They were trying to get set up with their demolitions for clearing obstacles and there was heavy strafing going on; there were still pillboxes covering the beaches with [machine gun] fire, and that's where they took their hits—quick—very early in the operation. I know we knocked out one with a rocket—my gunner got it on Red Beach—but that one from a second floor window was just spewing fire as we were just going down the line of the beach, [so we] took a crack at it.[8]

"With Ray King manning our twin .50 caliber machine guns, we made further passes and Ray kept laying in fire until the position was neutralized or abandoned. The noise and concussion of our .50 caliber under a steel canopy almost deafened us, but Cowboy got his man.[9]

"But how many UDT people that machine gunner had hit who were trying to work before we got him we don't know…It was a scurrying proposition. We found where obstacles and mines were exploded and a gap cleared with troops landed. The next craft would follow, like LCVPs, troop loaded. We spent much time with one ship because their troops panicked. They hit the water when mines exploded—of course they had packs and the like—it wasn't a matter of drowning, but the troops didn't know; the troops would be hanging on, they would grab these obstacles with a Teller mine over their heads and they would just cling. We would try to ease the boat in to get them off. I had a scare up there. I was on my belly on the bow of the boat, pulling people up and getting them off the obstacles. I took some flak—it was the closest I ever came to really being hurt. I took a fragment cut on my bald head! I had taken my helmet off because I was hanging over the side. Learned a good lesson there…In pulling people out we were quite busy and I guess we kept that up most of the day."[10]

THE FIRST UNITS SCHEDULED TO LAND were four companies of M4 Sherman DD tanks, which were to be transported to their launch points in sixteen LCTs (Landing Craft Tank). Each of these LCTs had been modified with the addition of a launching gear that was essentially a frame that extended from the bow to keep the DD tanks from nosing down and sinking as they drove off of the end of the ramp. The DD tanks would constitute the only initial close fire support to suppress enemy fire and draw fire away from the infantry and gap assault teams. Thirty-two modified Sherman tanks from Companies B and C of the 741st Tank Battalion were transported in eight LCTs (537, 549, 598, 599, 600, 601, 602, and 603), commanded by Lieutenant (jg) J. E. Barry. These tanks were designated to land in the 16th Infantry Regiment's zone.

Thirty-two DD tanks from Companies B and C of the 743rd Tank Battalion assigned to land in the 116th Infantry's zone were transported by LCTs 535, 586, 587, 588, 589, 590, 591, and 713, with four tanks in each LCT, under the command of Lieutenant (jg) Dean L. Rockwell.

The orders were to launch the tanks from the LCTs at six thousand yards from shore if the sea was calm. If it was too rough in the opinions of Lieutenants Barry and Rockwell, the LCTs were to take the tanks in and launch them from a thousand yards.

Each LCT (Landing Craft Tank) transporting the initial wave of Companies B and C, 741st Tank Battalion and Companies B and C, 743rd Tank Battalion had four DD (duplex drive) M4 Sherman tanks aboard. *United States Navy photograph.*

Lieutenant (jg) Dean L. Rockwell
Group 35, LCT Flotilla 12, Assault Force O, Task Force 124, Eleventh Amphibious Force, 12th Fleet

Lieutenant (jg) Dean Rockwell, aboard LCT 535, was in command of the sixteen LCTs transporting the DD tanks until they reached the transport area at 3:45 a.m. "The force of LCTs split into two previously arranged columns of eight ships each; one under the command of Lieutenant (jg) J. E. Barry aboard LCT 549, was scheduled to launch tanks of the 741st Tank Battalion off Fox Green and Easy Red beaches as part of Force O-1, while I led the remainder to launch tanks of the 743rd Tank Battalion off Dog Green and Dog Red beaches as part of Force O-2. We were met at Point King by LCSs [scout boats of Lieutenants (jg) Andreasen and Bucklew] that were to lead us to the line of launching. Those in Force O-2 proceeded down the fire support lane on the right hand of the assault area, arriving at 05:15 at a point approximately 6,000 yards from the beach so designated by PC 1225, which we had picked up on our way down the [mine] swept lane. The eight LCTs then did a column left movement and proceeded slowly parallel to the beach as we had ample time.

"Long before this time it was apparent that the sea would not be ideal for launching of the tanks. Before leaving Portland, the question had been raised by this command as to the course to pursue in the event of a sea too rough for a launching. Despite the insistence of this command that a decision be made by one senior army officer for both battalions, the question of launching was finally left to the senior army officer of each battalion, in this case Captain [James L.] Thornton of the 741st and Captain [Ned S.] Elder of the 743rd. The decision was agreed upon by Lieutenant Colonels [Robert W.] Skaggs and [John S.] Upham, commanding the 741st and 743rd, respectively.[11]

"The original plans were for our landing craft to proceed parallel to the beach at about six thousand yards off, turn [left] ninety degrees, and proceed toward the beach to the launching point where these tanks would go off of the end of our ramps and over the delicate launching gear one by one, into the sea with their shrouds inflated and their twin screws propelling them to the beach. But the sea was running very heavily, and after launching one [tank] and having [it] become swamped with the water and go down, I was in communication by low power tank radio with Captain Elder of the 743rd Tank Battalion.

"Even though all radio communication was forbidden prior to H-Hour, the decision to launch or not to launch into the sea was absolutely critical to the success of the invasion. We broke radio silence. What the hell—by now the Germans knew what was about to happen. We made the joint decision that it would be insane to launch any more tanks and the signal was given by tank radio to all craft to cease the launch. The next signal to all of our landing craft and to the tank commanders was that we would proceed to the beach, which we did. When our landing craft drove up on the shore, the ramps were dropped and the tanks went off, with their shrouds down, ready to provide coverage for the infantry units that were to come in behind them.

"The LCT(6) 535, from which I commanded these landing craft, touched the beach at H-Hour minus 30 seconds, H-Hour being 06:30 in the morning. As soon as we landed our tanks, we pulled that famous naval maneuver, known through naval history as 'getting the hell out of there.' But not before some of the tanks we landed were already in trouble from a German 88, which was in a pillbox on the extreme right flank of our landing area, protected by heavy overhead concrete shields. It was firing through a slit in the pillbox down the beach, called enfilading fire. Initially it concentrated on our landing craft, two of which were hit by the 88, one of which had three sailors killed and three wounded, but both were able to retract from the beach by virtue of their anchors. The retracting anchor was dropped by every landing craft going in. It drew power from a separate engine, so that even though the three propulsion motors were disabled the craft could get off the beach. Poor LCT 713! All three of its propulsion engines were knocked out by the 88, but it had the auxiliary engine to retract from the beach. It lost three men and three wounded.

"But as soon as the tanks were landed on the beach, the German 88 turned its attention to the tanks. Today in my mind's eye, I can see some of the tanks burning from the direct hits of the German 88. So, our tanks were discharged on the beaches and we returned to a predetermined anchorage area, awaiting our next assignment which was scheduled to be a predetermined wave to go in the afternoon to land jeeps and trailers of the medical detachments that were aboard each of the sixteen landing craft.

"The condition of the sea which necessitated taking the tanks to the beach presented great problems for the succeeding waves of the infantry who were coming in from the infantry ships offshore. I believe naval records will show no succeeding waves of infantry or demolition groups or support groups of any kind were on time.

"Right behind our tanks were to have been 'beach demolition' units, whose task was to destroy and open lanes for the tanks and infantry through the literally hundreds of beach obstacles, which the Germans had erected on the beaches at low tide. These obstacles took the form of tetrahedrons, pieces of heavy angle iron crossed over in a tetrahedron shape and designed to impale a small boat of any kind that came ashore. Many heavy wooden stakes were driven in to the beach at various points. Most of the obstacles carried on their tops small mines or explosive charges, which were to be activated by contact and thereby making the landings at high tide, when just the tops of these might be exposed or just slightly under the water, a very risky endeavor.

"Our landings of course, on the morning of D-Day were at low tide. Since the beach at Normandy sloped very gradually out to sea, it provided a fairly firm surface for the tanks to proceed inland. But as the day went on, the tide rolled in, and the beach obstacles of course, were now dangerous because the beach demolition groups that I had noted earlier were late in arriving. Some of them did not arrive at all. Some arrived at other beaches. Some that got there late, their boats swamped by the sea and as a result there were very few channels through these beach obstacles to allow either the foot soldiers of the military or succeeding landing craft of any kind to get in.

"So, when we were scheduled to go back in the afternoon around 2:00, at a pre-assigned area, with each of our landing craft to put these jeeps and trailers ashore, in many cases there was no way of getting by these beach obstacles. The LCT 535, on which I rode, cruised along the beach parallel for hundreds of yards, looking for an opening through. One time we did try to nose our way in, only to make contact with one of the beach obstacles holding a mine, which exploded and blew a hole in our landing gear. This meant that we could not let our ramp down, and as a result, we kept the jeep and trailers aboard. We were able, however, to put the poor soldiers ashore and let me say that I have never seen anybody more reluctant to execute orders, because at this time the beach was literally covered with military personnel, backed up, held down by enemy fire from the overlooking bluffs that had soldiers, wave after wave of soldiers, pinned down on the beach. And now there were some small craft getting in with jeeps and things, waves of landing craft, etc., coming because they were scheduled to land at specific times. The beach was literally covered with people and material. The enemy was bombarding the beaches with mortars from back over the bluff. They seemed to be located in batteries of four, and when the four shells would come in and land and explode in the pre-targeted areas of the beach, bodies and sand and material would fly. We were trying to guess where these mortars would land. They'd move along, they'd go down the beach, or back and forth. You couldn't tell much where they might come in, but anyway, we put the poor soldiers ashore and we felt very, very sorry for them, but thanking God that we had decided to join the navy instead of the army."[12]

Lieutenant Rockwell's decision to transport the DD tanks of the 743rd Tank Battalion and land them directly on to the beach despite heavy German fire, put him, his sailors, and his LCTs in great danger, but was critical in landing all but one of the thirty-two tanks that would provide close gunfire support for the landing of the 116th Infantry Regiment. It was one of the very critical decisions and actions that made the difference as to whether the invasion was a success or a failure.

The 743rd Tank Battalion was the first unit to land in the 116th Infantry Regiment's zone on the western portion of Omaha Beach. The DD tanks of Company B, scheduled to land at H-5 minutes, were put ashore by Lieutenant Rockwell's LCTs at the Dog Green sector on the right flank of Omaha Beach, slightly east of the D-1 exit. Seven of the sixteen DD tanks of Company B were destroyed or put out of action during and after landing, primarily by enfilade fire from an 88mm antitank gun located in a heavy concrete casemate on the right flank in front of the D-1 exit. Company C's sixteen DD tanks, also scheduled to land at H-5, landed at the Dog White sector to the east, losing no tanks to enemy fire.

First Lieutenant Harold R. Beavers
Company B, 743rd Tank Battalion

Major William D. Duncan, the 743rd Tank Battalion's plans and operations staff officer, was a witness to the actions of First Lieutenant Harold R. Beavers. "The LCTs of his company came under direct and deadly 88mm and mortar fire prior to beaching. During this landing, his company commander [Captain Charles W. Ehmke] was killed in action. First Lieutenant Beavers calmly and courageously assumed command of the disorganized company and moved it forward up the beach. Within an hour after landing, Lieutenant [Donald F.] Turner was killed by the deadly enemy fire and Lieutenant [Robert M.] Hodgson's tank was disabled. Lieutenant Hodgson, while moving on foot up the beach was seriously wounded. Lieutenant Beavers, under intense rifle, machine gun, mortar, and artillery fire, without regard for his personal safety, courageously and with extraordinary heroism dismounted from his tank, lifted Lieutenant Hodgson onto it and moved his tank through the enemy obstacles and mines to a position of safety from the enemy fire where the aid men could collect the wounded officer. Lieutenant Beavers then again mounted his tank and with great courage continuously exposed himself to fire as he displayed exceptional leadership in directing the accurate and intense fire of his remaining tanks. Lieutenant Beavers was the only one of the five company officers who was not killed by the intense enemy fire during the first sixteen hours on the beach. He moved his company through Exit D-1 at 22:30 and bivouacked two hundred yards west of Vierville-sur-Mer on the night of D-Day."[13]

Staff Sergeant John L. Benton
Company B, 743rd Tank Battalion

Major Duncan was also an eyewitness to the heroism of Staff Sergeant Benton, from Lueders, Texas. "When the officers in his organization became casualties, Staff Sergeant Benton took command of the platoon and dismounted from his tank in order to better direct operations and bring fire on the hostile positions. He coordinated his actions with those of the infantry, thus assuring success on that section of the battle line. His outstanding leadership and an utter disregard for personal safety was an inspiration to the assaulting forces on the beach."[14]

On July 9, 1944, during fighting southeast of St. Lo, Company B, 743rd Tank Battalion was pursuing two German Mark IV tanks near Le Désert, France when it was ambushed from the flank by Kompanie 7, SS Panzer Regiment 2, SS Panzer Division 2. In just fifteen minutes, nine Sherman tanks were destroyed, with three more damaged and abandoned. Benton's tank received a direct hit, killing him and the entire crew. The remains of the crew are buried together in a common grave at Zackary Taylor National Cemetery in Louisville, Kentucky.

Captain Ned S. Elder
Company C, 743rd Tank Battalion

Major Duncan, the battalion S-3, wrote the following recommendation regarding the actions of Captain Ned Elder during the landing on the Dog White sector. "Captain Elder commanded a tank company which landed on the Vierville beach at H-Hour. Shortly after landing his company, Captain Elder was wounded in the neck by a fragment of an artillery shell. Though in great pain, he refused to be evacuated and continued to command his company.

"The beach was covered by all types of hostile fire—machine gun, rifle, mortar, and observed artillery fire—but in spite of this Captain Elder dismounted from his tank in order to select enemy targets and direct the fire of his company. When the troops were unable to breach Exit D-3, Captain Elder had a reconnaissance made of Exit D-1 and directed his fire to assist in making an opening in that beach exit. Due to the effectiveness of the fire rendered, the enemy resistance on the beach was overcome and Captain Elder was able to take sixteen tanks through beach Exit D-1."[15]

This is the WN 72 casemate in front of the Vierville draw in the Dog Green sector, from which an 88mm PAK 43/41 antitank gun, the barrel of which can be seen extending from the aperture, inflicted the loss of several of the Company B, 741st Tank Battalion's tanks and numerous landing craft and other vehicles before being knocked out. *United States Army Signal Corps photograph, National Archives.*

This is another view of the casemate shown above. The wing wall at the right hid the gun and its muzzle blast from the observation and gunfire of Allied warships. The remains of an eight and a half feet high and six feet thick concrete wall (left) that blocked the road which ran from the mouth of the draw to Vierville, extended from the casemate to the base of the bluff. The wall was demolished by combat engineers with Company C, 121st Engineer Combat Battalion on the afternoon of June 6 to open the exit to vehicular traffic. *United States Army Signal Corps photograph, National Archives.*

The view from inside the casemate, from which the 88mm PAK 43/41 antitank gun seen in this photograph took landing craft and tanks under enfilade fire across a great portion of Omaha Beach. *United States Army Signal Corps photograph, National Archives.*

Staff Sergeant Gerard B. Peterson
Company C, 743rd Tank Battalion

Staff Sergeant Gerard Peterson, with Company C, 743rd Tank Battalion, was in command of a section of two DD tanks. Captain Ned Elder, commanding officer of Company C, witnessed Staff Sergeant Peterson's extraordinary heroism. "Staff Sergeant Petersen landed with the DD tanks in the assault wave on Vierville beach. He landed his section under heavy hostile fire, both small arms and artillery, and established liaison with the infantry in order to support them in their advance. In spite of the strong hostile fire, he directed and coordinated the fire of his section against enemy installations, which were delaying the advance of the infantry. When the forward advance of his tanks was stopped by an antitank ditch, he dismounted under heavy fire and without regard for his personal safety, assisted in the preparation of a crossing of the obstacle. His outstanding heroism, leadership and coolness under fire were an inspiration to those under his command."[16]

Tragically, Staff Sergeant Peterson was mortally wounded when Allied aircraft mistakenly bombed two Company C tanks on August 8, 1944. At the time, he had been approved for a battlefield commission and promotion to the rank of lieutenant.

This casemate held a 50mm PAK 38 antitank gun which placed deadly enfilade fire on landing craft and tanks landing on the Dog Green sector of Omaha Beach. This concrete emplacement was located west and slightly north of the casemate that held the 88mm antitank gun as part of the WN 72 resistance nest. *United States Air Force photograph, www.fold3.com.*

This is another view of the casemate which held a 50mm antitank gun as part of the WN 72 resistance nest. It was a double aperture casemate, with the second aperture facing north to defend against tanks landing in front of it. *United States Army Signal Corps photograph, National Archives.*

This is a view of the two casemates that protected the Vierville draw as seen from the bluffs east of the draw where the WN 71 resistance nest was located. The casemate holding the 50mm antitank gun is at the right center of the photograph. A section of the Mullberry artificial port that was wrecked during a storm in the English Channel lies on the beach nearby. The casemate containing the 88mm antitank gun is partially seen in the lower right corner of the photograph. *United States Army photograph.*

Company A, 743rd Tank Battalion, consisting of sixteen water proofed M4 Sherman tanks with special air intakes and exhausts installed to allow them to wade through water, was scheduled to land at H-Hour with half of the company touching down on the Dog Red sector and the other half at the Easy Green sector on the left flank. In addition, landing with Company A were the battalion's platoon of six tank-dozers plus two tank-dozers from the 610th Engineer Light Equipment Company. Four of the six tank-dozers from the 743rd would be attached to the 121st Engineer Combat Battalion when it landed for the purpose of assisting with the opening of the two beach exits. Upon landing, the 610th Engineer Light Equipment Company's two tank-dozers would be attached to the 146th Engineer Combat Battalion in order to assist the gap assault teams with beach obstacles. The Company A tanks plus the tank-dozers were transported to Omaha Beach in eight LCTs, each carrying two of the wading tanks and one tank-dozer.

Captain Vodra C. Philips
Company A, 743rd Tank Battalion

Major Duncan, the battalion S-3, wrote the recommendation for the Distinguished Service Cross based on the actions of Captain Vodra C. Philips, which he witnessed on June 6. "Captain Philips commanded a tank company which landed on the Vierville beach at H-Hour. He directed a tank-dozer to move through the beach obstacles in order to clear a lane for his tanks; but the tank-dozer, in attempting to do so, was destroyed by a mine. Though the entire beach area was covered by small arms and artillery fire, Captain Philips, with utter disregard for his own life, dismounted from his tank and led the remaining tanks from his landing craft through the obstacles so that they could move on above the high water mark. Captain Philips then proceeded on foot to mark the routes and lead his remaining tanks from other landing craft up through the obstacles. Upon being informed that the battalion commander was a casualty, Captain Philips took command of the battalion, organized a firefight on the beach, and moved the battalion to a rallying point west of Vierville. His utter disregard for his own safety, his cool and quick thinking, and outstanding example of courage and leadership contributed materially to the successful landings."[17]

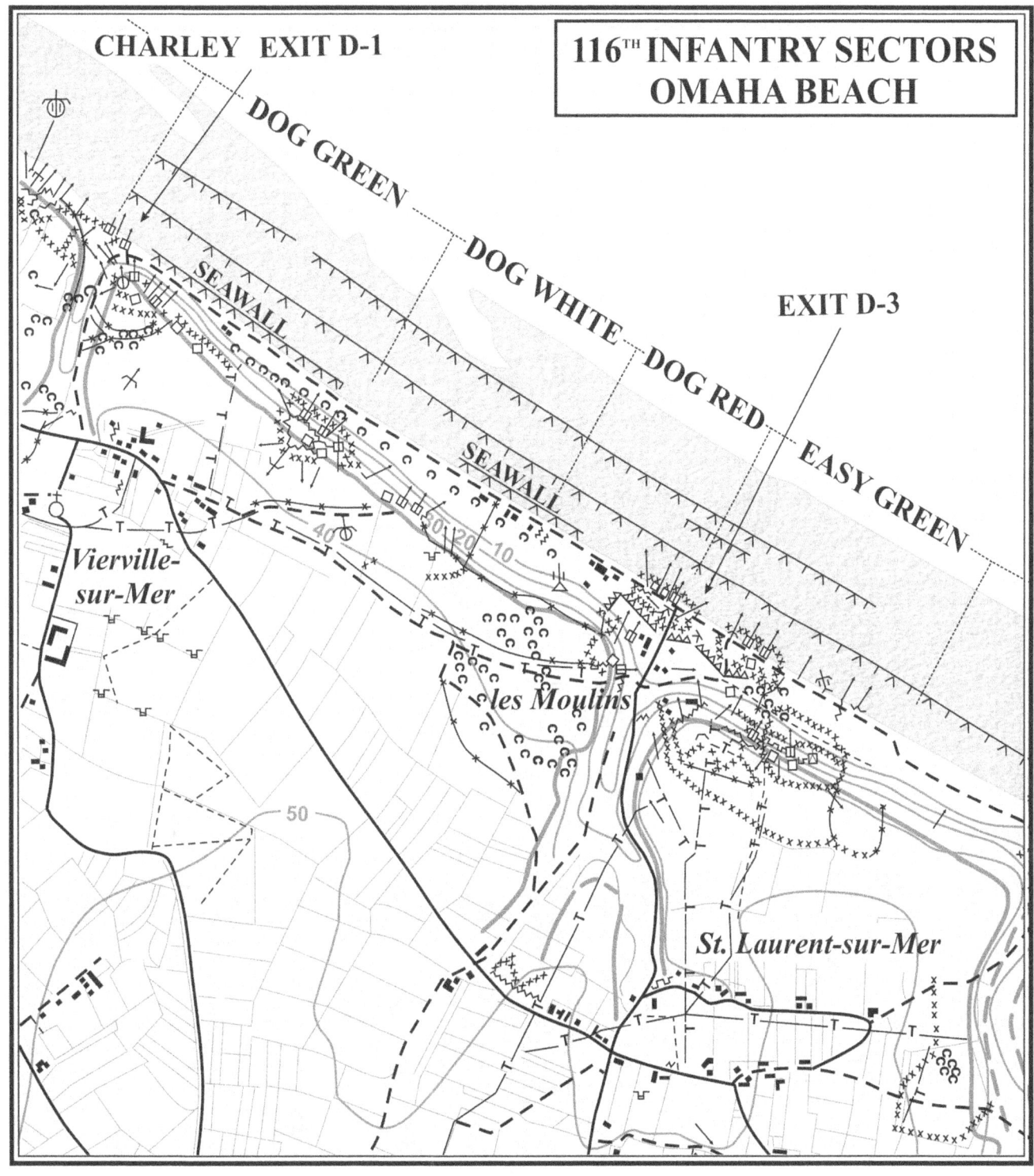

LANDING DIAGRAM 116TH RCT

Time	EASY GREEN	DOG RED	DOG WHITE	DOG GREEN
H-5			Co C (DD) 743 Tank Bn	Co B (DD) 743 Tank Bn
H HOUR	Co A 743 Tank Bn	Co A 743 Tank Bn		
H+01	Co E 116 Inf	Co F 116 Inf	Co G 116 Inf	Co A 116 Inf
H+03	146 ECB / V Corps Control Boat	146 ECB / Demolitions Control Boat	146 ECB	146 ECB / Co C 2 Ranger Bn
H+30	Co H 116 Inf / HQ Co E 116 Inf / 397 AAA (AW) Bn	Co H 116 Inf / HQ Co F 116 Inf / HQ Co 2 Bn 116 Inf / 397 AAA (AW) Bn	Co H 116 Inf / HQ Co F 116 Inf / 397 AAA (AW) Bn	Co B 116 Inf / HQ Co A 116 Inf / 397 AAA (AW) Bn
H+40	149 ECB	Co D 81 Chem Bn / 112 ECB 149 ECB	149 ECB / 121 ECB	HQ Co 1 Bn 116 Inf / 149 ECB
H+50	Co L 116 Inf	Co I 116 Inf	Co K 116 Inf	Co D 116 Inf / 121 ECB
H+57		HQ Co 3 Bn 116 Inf / Co L 116 Inf		Co D 81 Chem Bn
H+60	112 ECB	112 ECB	HQ and HQ Co 116 Inf	121 ECB / Co A / Co B / 2 Ranger Bn / HQ

OMAHA BEACH

	EASY GREEN	DOG RED	DOG WHITE	DOG GREEN
H+65				[A] [A] [A] [A] Co E Co A HQ Co B Co A 5 Ranger Bn [A] [A] [A] [A] [M] [T] HQ Co F HQ 121 ECB Co D Co C Rngr Grp HQ and HQ Co 116 Inf 5 Ranger Bn
H+70	[I] 149 ECB	[I] 112 ECB	[I] HQ and HA Co 116 RCT	
H+90			[T] [T] [T] 58 FA Bn Armd	
H+100			[I] 6 ESB	
H+110	[D][D][D][D][D] 111 FA Bn	[D][D][D] [D][D] [D]← 29 AT Plat 2 Bn AT Plat 2 Bn 116 Inf Signal Bn 116 Inf [T] [T] [T] [T] AT Co 467 AAA 149 ECB 116 Inf (AW) Bn		[D] [D][D][D][D][D] AT Plat 1 Bn Cannon Co 116 Inf
H+120	[T] [T] 467 AAA AT Co 467 AAA (AW) Bn 116 Inf (AW) Bn	[T] [T] DD Tanks DD Tanks	[T] 467 AAA (AW) Bn	[T] 467 AAA (AW) Bn
H+150			[T] HQ Co 116 Inf 104 Med Bn 6 ESB	
H+180 to H+210	[T] [T] DD Tanks DD Tanks [D][D][D] [D][D][D] [D][D] 461 Amphib Trk Co	[T] [T] DD Tanks DD Tanks	[T] [M] [T] [M] [M] DD Tanks DD Tanks DD Tanks Navy Salvage	[T] [T] [T] DD Tanks

◇ DD Tanks   [T] LCT   [A] LCA   [V] LCVP   [M] LCM   [I] LCI   [D] DUKW

Staff Sergeant Floyd M. Jenkins
Company A, 743rd Tank Battalion

Major Duncan saw Staff Sergeant Jenkins in action during the bitter fight for Omaha Beach. "Staff Sergeant Floyd M. Jenkins landed on Omaha Beach at 06:28, 6 June 1944, under intense enemy rifle, machine gun, mortar and 88mm gunfire. Having made a successful landing, he fought an intensive firefight on the beach for sixteen hours and moved off the beach without loss of crew or equipment. Staff Sergeant Jenkins, without thought of his own danger, courageously and heroically dismounted from his tank under sweeping and withering machine gun, sniper, and mortar fire and led the tanks of his platoon through the minefield and obstacles of the beach. During the early action his platoon leader was killed and Staff Sergeant Jenkins assumed command, showing exceptional leadership and willingness to carry the responsibility of command without direction from higher headquarters. Staff Sergeant Jenkins exposed himself to enemy fire several times in order to better adjust fire and locate targets."[18]

First Lieutenant Henry W. Jones
Company A, 743rd Tank Battalion

Major Duncan observed the actions of Lieutenant Henry W. Jones, who was the liaison officer between the battalion and the 116th Infantry. "First Lieutenant Henry Jones landed on Omaha Beach on D-Day and performed outstanding service as a tank liaison officer with the infantry. Carrying an eighty pound 509 radio on his back, along with other combat equipment, he courageously waded through deep water on to a beach which was being raked with mortar, machine gun, rifle and 88mm fire from strong enemy positions which were delivering withering fire upon the infantry. In spite of heavy and accurate fire of enemy guns, Lieutenant Jones remained in an exposed position rather than seeking shelter so that he might better direct the fire of tanks upon enemy positions which were delivering withering fire upon the infantry. Lieutenant Jones was wounded [and despite] his wounds he continued the direction of tank fire, which destroyed and reduced enemy machine gun and 88mm gun emplacements and made possible the advance of the infantry."[19]

Lieutenant Colonel John S. Upham, Jr.
Headquarters, 743rd Tank Battalion

Captain Vodra C. Philips, the commanding officer of Company A, landed with his company's tanks shortly after H-Hour. "The companies began disembarking their tanks onto the beach at approximately H-Hour under intense and accurate enemy fire. Tanks were being hit while still on the LCTs and immediately upon touching the beach. The unloading of tanks and men became increasingly difficult as wreckage and disabled tanks impeded movement on the beach. It soon became apparent that the landing troops would be engulfed by the rising tide if the beach was not cleared. Lieutenant Colonel Upham at this point was directing by radio the landing from his tank on [board] an LCT several hundred yards offshore. Realizing the gravity of the situation he, without regard for his personal safety, dismounted from his tank, leaped over the side of the LCT, and waded to shore in the face of the heavy artillery, mortar, and machine gun fire. He proceeded to the tanks and personally guided them through obstacles and by his outstanding bravery and leadership inspired his tanks to advance up the beach and fight to open the exits. Lieutenant Colonel Upham remained exposed to enemy fire, and disdaining to take cover, continued directing the clearing of the beach until seriously wounded in the shoulder and chest by a sniper. His inspiring bravery and leadership on the beach and the devotion, admiration, and confidence the men had for Lieutenant Colonel Upham was like a beacon of light through those dark hours on the beach that morning."[20]

The 116th Infantry Regiment's plan was for two battalions to land abreast, with the 1st Battalion's Company A assigned to the Dog Green sector. Company G, 2nd Battalion would land at the Dog White sector on Company A's left flank. To the left of Company G, the 2nd Battalion's Company F was assigned to land at Dog Red and Company E was assigned to land at Easy Green on the left flank of the regiment's assigned sectors.

Company A, under the command of Captain Taylor Fellers, was transported in six LCAs (Landing Craft Assault) in the initial infantry wave scheduled to land at H+1 minute. A seventh LCA containing the company executive officer, Lieutenant Elisha R. Nance and company headquarters personnel would land with Company B in the second wave of infantry at H+30.

Second Lieutenant Edward M. Gearing
Company A, 116th Infantry Regiment, 29th Infantry Division

Private First Class John Barnes was an assistant flamethrower operator and a member of Lieutenant Edward M. Gearing's Company A boat section. "Large craft unleashed the massive rockets towards the beach. Smoke clouded the lower coastline and we could just see the bluffs and above that, the single spire of the church. It was Vierville. We knew it. We were right on target. The LCA roared ahead, buffing the waves. Suddenly, a swirl of water wrapped around my ankles and the front of the craft dipped down. The water quickly reached our waist, and we shouted to the other boats on our side. They waved in return. The boat fell away below me, and I squeezed the CO tubes in my life belt. Just as I did, it popped away. The buckle had broken. I turned to grab the back of the man behind me. I was going down under. I climbed upon his back and pulled myself up in a panic. Our heads bobbed up above the water. We still could see some other boats moving off to the shore. I grabbed a rifle wrapped in a flotation belt, and then a flamethrower that was floating around with two belts wrapped around it. I hugged it tight but still seemed to be going down. I was unable to keep my head above the surface. I tried to pull the release straps on my jacket, but I couldn't move. Others shouted at me. Lieutenant Gearing grabbed my jacket and using his bayonet, he cut the straps and others helped release me from the weight. I was alright now. I could swim. We counted heads. One was missing, {Private First Class James M.] Padley, our radio operator. No one saw him come up. He had put the large SCR 300 radio on his back.

"Across the water, we heard the small rapid fire shots. Our company in the other five boats had landed. I felt a sense of strange relief. Sergeant [John] Laird wanted to swim towards the shore. We were roughly a thousand yards out.

"'Too far,' said Lieutenant Gearing. 'We'll wait and get picked up by some passing boat.'

"But no one stopped. They were all loaded down in the water with goods passing in towards the shore. They were on their own mission and their own schedule. Suddenly, we heard a friendly shout of some Limey voice in one of the LCAs, the same type that we had just been on. The boat stopped. It was empty. We were helped to climb overboard. Seven or eight of us got in one boat, three or four in another and the rest in another. We recognized the coxswain. He was from the *Empire Javelin*. He wouldn't return to the beach. How did the others make out? He dropped them off OK. The other boat had two dead A Company men lying in the floor. One [who] we recognized, [Technical] Sergeant [Frank P.] Draper, would live only a few more minutes.

"'How about the others?'

"He couldn't say. We went back to the troop ship, the very same one we had left at 4:00 that morning. How long it had been? It seemed like just minutes. When I thought to ask, it was one in the afternoon. We had been gone nine hours, over three in the water. Gradually, the shock wore off. What could we do? The ship seemed vacant. The British captain wanted us to get off. We had no weapons. Lieutenant Gearing told him we were going to stay on board, go back to England. He had picked up a rifle and said he would hitch a ride in a passing U.S. craft."[21]

Later that day, Lieutenant Elisha R. "Ray" Nance, the Company A executive officer, was lying wounded at an aid station set up on the beach near Exit D-1. "Late that afternoon, 2nd Lieutenant Gearing landed by himself. He came over to me and I got him up on what I knew. I said, 'Hey, I think you're it—company commander.' I never felt so sorry for a person when he left. He didn't know what he was getting into."[22]

As the other five LCAs transporting Company A came to within 700-800 yards of the beach, artillery and mortar fire began to explode in the water as the German observers adjusted the range attempting to zero in on the line of landing craft. As the landing craft closed to within fifty yards of the beach one round struck and killed two of the men in one of the boats. At about 6:36 a.m., the five landing craft touched down and dropped the ramps. As if that was the signal to open fire, German machine gunners raked the landing crafts, killing and wounding many of the Company A soldiers as they ran down the ramps or while they were still in the boats. A vicious crossfire of automatic weapons from the WN 71 and WN 73 resistance nests located on the bluffs above on both sides of the exit to the company's front and right front, as well as from WN 74 at Pointe ét Raz de la Percée about a thousand yards to the company's right rear, and from the left front from the WN 70 strongpoint on the bluff midway between Exits D-1 and D-3 and the defenses on the beach in front of Exit D-3 to the left.

All of Company A's officers and non-commissioned officers who landed in the five landing crafts of the first wave of infantry were killed or wounded. Men were cut down like wheat before a scythe. Ten minutes after the ramps dropped, over one hundred of Company A's officers and men had been killed or wounded and the company ceased to exist as a fighting force. The survivors were in shock and fighting for survival. Some of the wounded would drown as the tide began to rise rapidly.

To the east, the current carried the landing craft transporting Companies G, F, and E eastward of the planned beach sectors at Dog White, Dog Red, and Easy Green respectively. Company G, which was assigned to land on the Dog White sector, landed far to the east on the western portion of Easy Green. Company F landed astride the boundary of its assigned Dog Red sector and Easy Green, and Company E on the eastern portion of its assigned sector of Easy Green.

These LCVPs (Landing Craft Vehicle Personnel) loaded with troops circle while waiting for all of the landing craft associated with its wave and beach sector to assemble before forming a line across and moving toward the beach. *United States Navy photograph, National Archives.*

Sergeant Howard W. Rogers
Company F, 116th Infantry Regiment, 29th Infantry Division

Major General Leonard T. Gerow, the commanding officer of the V Corps, wrote the following regarding the actions of Sergeant Howard W. Rogers. "Sergeant Rogers was a member of one of the rifle companies of the 116th Infantry which made the invasion assault on the beaches of France near Vierville, 6 June 1944. The enemy held [the] beaches by [means of] prepared emplacements, studded with pillboxes, and [by] concentrating a withering small arms, machine gun, mortar, and observed artillery fire over mined and obstacled approaches. Heavy casualties were being inflicted upon the American forces. There was much disorganization of units resulting from enemy action and the rough sea dispersing landing boats. Sergeant Rogers was separated from his unit in the landing and found himself in a group of several other soldiers separated from their organizations. Upon discovering an enemy pillbox from which a devastating fire was being directed on American troops, by heroic leadership and bravery he quickly organized a group of soldiers separated from their units into a raiding party. With disregard for his own safety and with inspiring gallantry led his party in an assault upon the pillbox, which resulted in its destruction with great saving of American lives. It contributed greatly to the successful attack on other enemy positions in that sector of the beach."[23]

Sergeant Lyman K. Patterson, Jr.
Company E, 116th Infantry Regiment, 29th Infantry Division

Lieutenant Donald Casapulla, the adjutant of the 116th Infantry, wrote the following recommendation regarding the actions of Sergeant Lyman K. Patterson, who was a 60mm mortar squad leader. "At the place where Sergeant Patterson's squad landed, the enemy was well protected by underwater obstacles and minefields behind which he was strongly emplaced. At the time of the landing, the enemy was covering the beach with devastating fire from artillery, automatic weapons, and small arms. With utter disregard for his own safety and in spite of the heavy casualties being suffered by his unit, Sergeant Patterson openly exposed himself to the enemy fire in order to encourage and lead the troops about him. As a result of his inspiring leadership and outstanding heroism, troops about him attacked vigorously and gained the beach carrying all enemy positions before them."[24]

This rare image shows the wooden seawall and rocky shingle or shelf that provided defilade for troops who survived the deadly trip across the beach. This photograph was taken on June 7, 1944 in the Dog White sector and shows combat engineers with the 6th Engineer Special Brigade. Tetrahedron obstacles are piled at the right. *United States Army photograph, National Archives.*

COMPANY C, 2ND RANGER BATTALION was scheduled to land on the Dog Green sector at H+3 with the same wave as the gap assault teams. The initial objective of the company, commanded by Captain Ralph E. Goranson, was to eliminate the German defenses at Pointe ét Raz de la Percée to the west of Dog Green. Aerial reconnaissance photos prior to the invasion indicated that the German resistance nest, WN 74, at Pointe ét Raz de la Percée had ten machine guns, four of which were in concrete pillboxes, located along the top of the cliff which could pour enfilade fire into the right flank of the landings at the Dog Green sector. In addition, the photos showed two howitzers of up to 105mm and a cliff top observation post to direct the artillery fire on to Omaha Beach.

The plan called for Company C to pass through the 116th Infantry if it had secured the Vierville exit, which was totally unrealistic since the Rangers were scheduled to land a mere three minutes after the first wave, which was Company A, 116th Infantry. The alternate plan if the Vierville exit was not secured was for the Rangers to move to the west and climb the cliffs in the Charley sector to the west, then turn west and follow the bluffs to Pointe ét Raz de la Percée, where they would assault and eliminate the German defenses and then continue west to Pointe du Hoc to rejoin the 2nd Battalion.

Ranger infantry companies had just sixty-five enlisted men and non-commissioned officers and three officers, organized into two platoons. Company headquarters was comprised of the company commander, the first sergeant, a clerk and a runner. Each of the two thirty-two man platoons had a platoon leader (lieutenant), a platoon sergeant, a platoon runner, a sniper, and two assault sections of eleven men each, plus a 60mm mortar and .30 caliber light machine gun weapons section of six men. A medic and a radioman from Headquarters Company, 2nd Ranger Battalion were attached to Company C for the assault.

It was a very small force for such a difficult assignment. However, these men were volunteers who had survived a grueling selection process to rid the unit of the weaker individuals and had been honed to a razor's edge by extremely demanding training.

This 1945 aerial photograph shows Pointe ét Raz de la Percée (right) and the Vierville draw (Exit D-1) one thousand yards to the east (top left). The Charley sector of Omaha Beach is to the right of the Vierville draw in the photograph. Machine guns and howitzers from resistance nest WN 72 at Pointe ét Raz de la Percée could place deadly enfilade fire on troops landing on the Dog Green sector. Company C, 2nd Ranger Battalion's initial objective on D-Day was the elimination of those defenses. *United States Air Force photograph, www.fold3.com.*

Captain Ralph E. Goranson
Company C, 2nd Ranger Battalion, Provisional Ranger Group

First Lieutenant William D. Moody
Company C, 2nd Ranger Battalion, Provisional Ranger Group

Sergeant Julius W. Belcher
Company C, 2nd Ranger Battalion, Provisional Ranger Group

Private First Class Otto K. Stephens
Company C, 2nd Ranger Battalion, Provisional Ranger Group

Captain Ralph E. Goranson, the commander of Company C, 2nd Ranger Battalion, was a native of Chicago, Illinois and about one month shy of his twenty-fifth birthday on D-Day. "At 04:00 hours on June 6, on the *Prince Charles*, C Company was called to board our assault boats. It was Number 418, which carried the 1st Platoon and I and the radioman, and Boat Number 1038 which carried the 2nd Platoon. At 04:38, the boats were lowered and we went away moving through the rough seas and joined the boats of A Company, the 116th Infantry, for a ten mile trip into shore. It was very rough and we had a lot of seasickness, but as we got closer to the shore we were able to see and hear the bombs coming down on the land behind the beaches. The beaches were not subject to air bombing because of the overcast that morning, and therefore one of the advantages which we would have had on the beach with the resulting craters was eliminated. Therefore, the beaches were as flat as a pool table.

This old Czechoslovakian Škoda 76mm howitzer, part of the WN 74 defenses at Pointe ét Raz de la Percée, was protected by a log and earth covered bunker. *United States Army Signal Corps photograph, National Archives.*

"However, as we started to approach the shore, the big guns opened up with a tremendous bombardment. Rockets were fired from naval ships launching 240 rockets to a wave, per launch. However some of them were hitting in the water and not doing us much good. About two hundred yards to go and there was still no enemy opposition.

"Then all of a sudden in Boat Number 1038, Sergeant [Henry S.] Golas, the first sergeant, said, 'Hey, gee, guys, they're shooting back at us.' In the meantime, in our boat the guys were singing to Sergeant [Walter B.] Geldon because June 6 was Walt's third wedding anniversary.

"We landed exactly at H-Hour and plunged into water chest high—in some cases over our heads. Immediately upon landing, after the first men on the boat that I was on had left the ramp of the boat, it was blown off by a direct hit from an enemy mortar. In a space of sixty seconds, the boat again was hit by mortar fire, this time the midship and the stern. The boat started to flounder and break up as she continued to receive fire.

"The plan for Charlie Company—to go up the Vierville exit was out. There was no way we were going to get over there to our left because of the big pillbox right in the middle of the exit to Vierville. It was sweeping the beach with fire and was controlled from the fortified house up on the top of the cliff.

"Now the men left in Charlie Company made for the protective cover of the cliff. We had trained over and over that in any landing, once you left the boat, get across the beach and to the nearest objective, which of course in this case was at the base of the cliff and get in the safety of the overhang on the cliff. Going across the beach was like a dream. I can only speak for myself. As I went across, I saw men down. However, we had trained that if a man went down, leave him alone. He stayed down. Your job was to get across the beach intact with your weapons and with your knowledge of the job to be accomplished, and then set out to do it. Every man in the company was trained to achieve the company objective, so no matter who fell, the job would get done!

This is a photograph taken well after the landings of Omaha Beach from the bluffs west of the Vierville draw and the location of WN 73. A portion of the Mulberry artificial harbor wrecked by a storm in the English Channel is at the left center. The mouth of the Vierville draw is to the right of the large hut and tents. The rear of the WN 72 casemates is in the center beyond and to the left of the hut. The German troops at WN 73 poured lethal fire on troops landing on Dog Green until Company C, 2nd Ranger Battalion destroyed them in a fight lasting the entire day. *United States Army Signal Corps photograph, National Archives.*

"As I came across [the beach] I went down on the beach once, and machine gun fire started raising sand up all around me, so I immediately got up and made it the rest of the way. It was about 1,000 or 1,500 feet from the boat, where our boat was sinking, to the overhang."[25]

Charlie Company lost nineteen killed, thirteen seriously wounded, and five lightly wounded crossing the three hundred yards of the beach to get to the base of the cliff, just west of the Vierville draw. Upon reaching the cliff the Rangers were soon joined by twenty-five survivors of one of the Company B, 116th Infantry boat teams, led by Lieutenant Leo A. Pingenot, who had landed about H+30. The 29ers attached themselves to the Rangers.

Goranson assessed the situation to determine how to get his surviving Rangers and the 29ers up the cliff to attack the Germans on the high ground. "Once we got under the overhang, we set up protective fire to keep the Germans up on top of the cliff from looking down or dropping hand grenades on us. At one time, when I was flat out trying to scan the situation to my left and right, one of the men in the 2nd Platoon kept—he was a Greek boy, his name was Mike Gargas—kept screaming, 'Mashed potatoes! Mashed potatoes!' and pointing at my rear. I looked back and there was a German potato masher [hand grenade] smoking away. I immediately moved up and spread my legs and when it went off, I was very lucky. All I did was fly up in the air and come down with no injuries. Since it was apparent that moving to our east or to our left was out of the question because of the pillbox, I signaled Lieutenant [William D.] Moody, the platoon leader of the 1st Platoon, to effect Plan 2—straight up the cliff."[26]

Lieutenant William Moody, Sergeant Julius Belcher, and Private First Class Otto Stephens moved west about 350 yards along the base of the cliff before finding a good place to climb. The rest of the surviving Rangers who could move and the Company B, 116th soldiers followed behind them, staying close to the base of the cliff. Goranson watched as "Lieutenant Moody, along with Sergeant Julius Belcher of Schwartz Creek, Virginia, and Otto Stephens of Newcastle, Indiana, scaled the cliffs. These three men free climbed about a ninety foot cliff that was partially an incline and then straight up the last fifteen or twenty feet. We gave them covering fire from down below to keep the Germans off their back. The last ten or fifteen feet they chinned themselves up with their trench knives and secured a series of toggle ropes from the barbed wire emplacement up there, so that the rest of us could immediately move over into this position and climb up the cliff and get into the area around the fortified house."[27]

This is a second view from the bluff west of the Vierville draw showing the trenches of WN 73 (foreground) running along the crest overlooking the beach. The curved trench extending from the right is a communication trench, which provided a covered route to and from the fighting positions and observation posts. The short half circle shaped trench at the lower left connects to a concrete lined and covered artillery observation post located in the center of the half circle and the zigzag trench at the center right is a fire trench, from which machine gun and small arms fire was directed. Both the half circle shaped and zigzag trenches connect to the communication trench via short covered trenches. *United States Army Signal Corps photograph, National Archives.*

Lieutenant Moody, Sergeant Belcher, and Private First Class Stephens were very likely the first Americans to reach the top of the bluffs in the western part of Omaha Beach.

A fortified house anchored the German defenses west of the Vierville exit, designated as WN 73. A series of communications trenches connected it with several pillboxes, concrete lined Tobruks, an antiaircraft gun pit, several dug in machine gun positions, and zigzag trenches used as fighting positions for small arms and machine guns. The resistance nest's weaponry consisted of at least eight machine guns, an antiaircraft gun, two 80mm mortars, and a 75mm PAK 97/38 antitank gun in a casemate positioned on the west side of a gully and sited to fire east down the beach.

Goranson saw Lieutenant Moody, Sergeant Belcher, and Private First Class Stephens toss the toggle ropes down to him and his Rangers waiting below. "Without waiting for more men, Lieutenant Moody [as well as Private First Class Stephens] proceeded to clear the enemy out of the trenches at the top of the cliff.[28]

"Stephens was wounded in the head by a sniper in the performance of this duty. Despite this wound, he killed the sniper and continued to attack so that more men could reach the top of the cliff safely.[29]

"[Sergeant Belcher] stayed there, helping men up the cliff. He then moved into the enemy positions on top of the cliff and cleaned out six snipers. He then cleared a pillbox and a mortar position by using white phosphorous grenades and killing three [of the] enemy.[30]

"Lieutenant Moody immediately when he got topside, killed the officer in charge of the Germans in the fortified house. We found the rest of the area honeycombed with dugouts and trench systems. Immediately, Lieutenant Moody and his men dispatched teams to go and clear up this area. They were followed of course, immediately by the 2nd Platoon with Lieutenant Salomon."[31]

Lieutenant Sidney Salomon jumped into a shell crater with Moody and the two raised their heads over the edge to take a look at the trench system to their front when Moody was killed. Salomon was lucky that he wasn't the one killed. "We were shoulder to shoulder. I was pointing towards a series of trenches when suddenly he rolled to one side. A bullet struck him between his eyes."[32]

The bluffs west of the Vierville draw, where Company C, 2nd Ranger Battalion, led by Lieutenant William D. Moody, Sergeant Julius W. Belcher, and Private First Class Otto K. Stephens scaled the bluffs to assault the German defenses of WN 73, which had been pouring machine gun, mortar, and observed artillery fire onto the west end of Omaha Beach. A casemate positioned on an east facing ridge overlooking the Dog Green sector that housed a French 75mm antitank gun is in the center of the photo about half way up the bluff. *United States Army Signal Corps photograph.*

This knocked out 75mm PAK 97/38 antitank gun positioned in the casemate shown in the photograph above, utilized a French 75mm barrel and a Swiss muzzle brake mounted on a standard German 50mm PAK 38 gun carriage. It was located on an east facing ridge to place enfilade fire on landing craft and tanks on the Dog Green sector. *Photograph by Lieutenant (jg) Stuart L. Brandel, United States Navy, courtesy of Tom Lane.*

After the death of Lieutenant Moody, Goranson's Rangers continued to find and kill the surviving Germans who were holding out. "Lieutenant Salomon immediately went forward and took charge of the perimeter and the groups of two and three Rangers went through the entire network of dugouts and trenches and cleaned it all out, including the fire direction center in the fortified house. This was put out of action by Sergeant Belcher who threw in a white phosphorous grenade, and when the Germans came out they were sent to heaven by Sergeant Belcher's gun. Later on when the total dead were counted in the fortified house and the surrounding area which we neutralized, the count was sixty-eight enlisted men and one officer. One wounded prisoner was taken that morning. C Company unfortunately had high casualties, too. We lost twenty-three men [killed]. We lost about 20-25 more [wounded, of which there were eighteen] who had to be evacuated because they were seriously wounded, and the balance of them were walking wounded. We took care of the objective and solidified the action as we waited to decide what our next move would be."[33]

Later that day, Goranson sat down and realized that as he had crossed that deadly killing ground on the beach that morning he "had picked up nine rounds of shrapnel and bullets in my gear, some of which took care of all of my food in my backpack. My canteen had a couple bullets in it, my recognition safety flare projector on my patch pocket on my right leg had two bullets in it, but they didn't hit the flares or detonate them. The morphine bag (extra morphine for the aid man) strapped to my stomach was shot away by machine gun bullets and all in tatters. So in all, I think I collected eight or nine pieces of metal from all this gear and I thank goodness and thank God I didn't have any—not even a scratch. The only places where I was bleeding were from the barbed wire that we had to work through, but that was all."[34]

This is the type of covered trench that was found in a number of areas of Omaha Beach and was utilized by German troops to infiltrate back into areas of WN 73 previously cleared by Captain Ralph Goranson and Company C, 2nd Ranger Battalion. In this photograph, a medic with the Provisional Engineer Special Brigade Group inspects the trench. *United States Army Signal Corps photograph, National Archives.*

This is the interior of a concrete Tobruk located at WN 73 and overlooking the Dog Green sector, housing an 80mm mortar set up on a platform in the center. Ammunition for the mortar was still sitting on storage shelves (right) that line the position when this photo was taken. The Germans firing from WN 73 inflicted many casualties on troops landing on the Dog Green sector before they were killed by members of Company C of the 2nd Ranger Battalion. *Photograph by Lieutenant (jg) Stuart L. Brandel, United States Navy, courtesy of Tom Lane.*

This is the view from the same WN 73 mortar position as the photo above that overlooked Omaha Beach to the east. *Photograph by Lieutenant (jg) Stuart L. Brandel, United States Navy, courtesy of Tom Lane.*

This is another view of the 80mm mortar position at WN 73. Note the range and direction information as well as photographs of the target areas that have been pre-registered to allow quick adjustment to fire on key target locations. Mortars such as this one fired with deadly effect along the seawall and shingle, which were otherwise in defilade to most German direct fire from machine guns and small arms. The mortar positions at WN 73 were not visible to naval gunfire and were knocked out when Company C, 2nd Ranger Battalion attacked the WN 73 strongpoint west of the Vierville draw. *Photograph by Lieutenant (jg) Stuart L. Brandel, United States Navy, courtesy of Tom Lane.*

Lieutenant (jg) Frank M. Hall
Company B, 7th Naval Beach Battalion, Assault Force O, Task Force 124, Eleventh Amphibious Force, 12th Fleet

Hospital Apprentice Augustus B. McKee, Jr.
Company B, 7th Naval Beach Battalion, Assault Force O, Task Force 124, Eleventh Amphibious Force, 12th Fleet

Lieutenant (jg) Frank M. Hall was a navy doctor and the platoon leader of the medical platoon of Company B, 7th Naval Beach Battalion. Lieutenant Hall and his medical platoon were scheduled to land on the Dog Green sector at H+40. "On the way in, the LCA in which the party was loaded swamped and sank with all equipment and supplies about three miles from shore. Several members of the medical team, including [Hospital Apprentice Augustus B.] McKee [and me] were picked up about ten minutes later by another LCA loaded with [Captain Goranson's] Rangers who were to assault the cliffs of Charley sector to the right of Dog Green. As the LCA approached the beach it came under intense machine gun fire and several men were killed or wounded before the craft could be beached. One of the men became temporarily incapacitated by fear and McKee was assigned to look after him. The intensity of the fire increased and McKee together with the man in his charge were forced to take refuge behind sunken landing craft and beach obstacles for approximately two hours until the tide came in sufficiently to permit him to drag the man ashore.

"When he reached the beach he found himself isolated from the remainder of his unit and unable to rejoin them due to the continued machine gun fire from pillboxes in the face of the cliff. The beach was littered with wounded and dead. McKee aided only by the man he had brought ashore, set about giving medical aid to the wounded. Having lost all his supplies at sea, he had nothing with which to work except such first aid packets containing bandages and morphine as he was able to remove from the wounded and dead on the beach. This required him to leave the shelter of the cliff and run out onto the beach under fire with utter disregard for his own safety.

"He continued to care for the wounded throughout the following night and day without relief, working ceaselessly piling rocks about them to protect them against sniper fire, giving them water and morphine and changing dressings, in the course of which he risked his own life many times in order to reach some men requiring attention. Beyond any doubt, the lives of many men were saved because of his heroic performance and devotion to duty."[35]

Lieutenant (jg) James G. Reid, the commanding officer of Company B, 7th Naval Beach Battalion, landed with the rest of his company later that morning under intense enemy fire. "The only shelter of any kind was the base of the cliff at the back of the beach. Lieutenant (jg) Hall set up his medical aid station there, providing such shelter for the wounded as conditions permitted. There were no litters, bandages, morphine, or plasma, as all had been lost at sea. The only supplies were the first aid packets containing bandages, morphine, and wound tablets carried by the assault troops and prudent judgment precluded using those carried by men able to advance, which left only the dead and wounded as a source of supply.

"The beach was littered with the bodies of dead and wounded men. Lieutenant (jg) Hall left the shelter of the cliff and moved out onto the beach where he was subjected to directed machine gun and sniper fire. Not withstanding the fact that he obviously was being targeted, regardless of his Red Cross armband, he remained on the beach to collect first aid packets and attend some of the more seriously wounded, direct corpsmen and soldiers to others, and drag others behind wreckage for shelter. One wounded man was killed by fire directed at Lieutenant (jg) Hall while he was working over him.

"The original plans for the operation called for two medical teams, including doctors, for Dog Green Beach and adjacent Charley sector beach. The doubling up of medical personnel at this point was due to the difficulties and high casualty rate expected there, in view of the fact that there was located one of the main exits from the beach, and which was to be the scene of a heavy assault upon the defended positions. About 09:00 D-Day, it was decided that the other doctor must be presumed to be missing since he was last seen jumping overboard after his craft had been left burning by shellfire. Lieutenant (jg) Hall assumed command of all medical activities on both beaches and thereafter proceeded back and forth across the two beaches treating the wounded, regardless of the heavy fire from snipers and artillery which persisted through D plus one day. He worked under great physical strain and in the face of almost certain death without relief for more than thirty-six hours."[36]

The next wave, scheduled to land at H+3, consisted of combined teams of army combat engineers and navy underwater demolition personnel, called gap assault teams, under the command of the Special Engineer Task Force. The task force was composed of the 146th Engineer Combat Battalion, the 299th Engineer Combat Battalion (less one company), and twenty-one naval combat demolition units (NCDU). The mission of the gap assault teams was to clear fifty yard wide paths through the bands of obstacles so that landing craft arriving later as the tide rose would not be sunk, damaged, overturned, or have to negotiate through obstacles to land troops and vehicles. Many of the obstacles had Teller mines mounted to the tops, making the demolition of the obstacles more dangerous than would be otherwise. The naval combat demolition unit (NCDU) of each gap assault team would prepare the outer band of obstacles closest to the water for demolition and work toward the shore as the tide rose. The army combat engineers of each team would prepare the landward bands of obstacles and clear the tidal flats of mines. All of the individual charges would be connected using primacord that would allow multiple obstacles to be detonated simultaneously. After all of the obstacles assigned to the army were wired for demolition, a canister of purple smoke would be discharged, providing a two minute warning to troops in the area of the impending detonation. The naval combat demolition units would likewise follow the same procedure prior to detonating their assigned obstacles.

Sixteen gap assault teams, numbered 1 through 16 from west to east would land initially at H+3, followed five minutes later by eight gap support teams, with letter designations A through H, from west to east.

These very courageous gap assault team members would face intense enemy fire, the dangers associated with using large quantities of high explosives, mines mounted on some of the obstacles, and possibility of being struck by incoming landing craft during the course of this vital mission to make the beaches accessible and safer for incoming landing craft and troops.

Despite the rehearsed and timed precision of the naval landing craft waves scheduled to touchdown at precise times at precise points on the beach, twelve of the sixteen gap assault teams landed ahead of the first wave of infantry. Two additional teams landed simultaneously with the infantry. This caused heavy casualties among the teams, as the enemy fire was focused on them prior to the infantry assault wave coming ashore.

Some of the beach obstacles remained intact on Omaha Beach after D-Day. Sloped ramps constructed of large wooden poles were designed to turn landing craft on their sides as the bottoms of the shallow draft boats rode up the ramps which would be partially or entirely submerged as the tide rose. Some of the ramps had very powerful Teller mines strapped to the tops of the ramp logs, designed to detonate as the bottom of landing craft struck them and the resulting explosion would severely damage or destroy them. Shorter wood stakes angled toward the deeper water were planted farther up the beach. Teller antitank mines were strapped to the tops of about one-third of these stakes. *Photograph by Lieutenant (jg) Stuart L. Brandel, United States Navy, courtesy of Tom Lane.*

First Lieutenant William J. Kehaly
Company A, 146th Engineer Combat Battalion, Special Engineer Task Force, Provisional Engineer Special Brigade Group
Gap Assault Team Number 1

Lieutenant William J. Kehaly and his gap assault team were scheduled to land on the Dog Green sector slightly to the east of the heavily defended Vierville exit where Company A, 116th Infantry was quickly destroyed as a fighting force. However, the strong current caused his LCM to bring Lieutenant Kehaly and his team in far to the east in the Dog White sector. Kehaly charged off of the front ramp as soon as it was dropped into the surf. "I knew something happened just after I dashed off the ramp of the LCM, but it was not my duty to check behind me. I heard the cries as machine gun fire wounded two of the men. Sergeant Lewis, who would bring up the rear, would have to handle it.

"I took off like a startled deer and headed for the obstacles which were some two hundred yards up the beach and away from the water at this very low tide. Murphy, the number one primacord man, stumbled as he hit the beach and loosing his stride, did not catch up to me until the obstacles were nearly encircled. Having reached our first obstacle, I quickly threw a clove hitch around one horn of a hedgehog and then rapidly spun the primacord off of the telephone wire reels we had adapted to handle the several hundred feet of primacord necessary to encircle the obstacles. As I sped around the obstacles, I would lay the primacord on a protruding part of the obstacle if possible, otherwise I just kept running.

"You see everything and you really don't see anything but the job for which you have been keyed. I saw the group at the LCM ganged around the two wounded men and it registered on my mind that they should be up here among the obstacles and just then the burst of machine gun fire got them.

"[Corporal John G.] Murphy was with me now and so was Captain [Samuel H.] Ball. Murphy started to lace the middle obstacles to the encircling primacord. He dashed back and forth through the obstacles. At each place, where he came to the existing line of primacord, he would slash his primacord and deftly tie it to the main line. [Captain] Sam Ball, along with the assigned demolition carriers, dropped the charges by the obstacles where all of us set to placing the charges on the obstacles and tying them to the network of primacord.

"When all the charges were about in place I dropped over to the first corner where Sergeant Lewis had tied the igniters. I hit the sand right off. I then noted that the can of violet smoke was not in place. 'Where's the violet smoke, sergeant?' I asked.

"'Hell, I forgot it. It's down at the boat. Shall I get it?'

"'No. Stay here.'

"I then tried to yell at the men to move away from me, as I wanted to set off the charge, but I made no impression in all of the din. I then tried to wave the men to move to the west of where I was, but all my violent antics had drawn fire from up the beach, with no good accomplished in moving the men. The machine gun fire that was directed at Sergeant Lewis and me first just cleared over us, grazing my finger as I tried to signal. The second burst made a uniform pattern in the sand as they fired just under us enough to throw the sand into our eyes. I could not get the men to move without the established signal.

"'Sergeant,' I yelled into the din, 'get the smoke.' Sergeant Lewis, in all the time he played baseball, never moved as fast as he did in his dash to the LCM and back with the violet smoke. Time did not stand still yet it did not rush too rapidly past to prevent my looking around while Sergeant Lewis was going after the smoke signal.

"As demolition charges had all been placed on the obstacles in the engineer section assigned to Boat Team Number One, I unslung my carbine and looked for targets of fire. I actually could see nothing at which to fire.

"I signaled some of the men lying among the obstacles to be blown to move to my right, or to the west, that they might be in a safer place. I looked back at the naval demolition team as they worked rapidly among their obstacles, all of which were still out of the rising water. I could see the dead men lying in the water that gently, but relentlessly, tossed them a little further up the beach with every rising wave. I saw the wounded men dragging themselves across the sands and I signaled them to veer away from the prepared demolition charges. I constantly noticed the crisscrossing on the smooth sands the spray of sand as the machine guns from the dug in positions on the cliff side sprayed the beach. I looked again toward the source of all the machine gun fire and could still not locate it. Murphy, Sam Ball, and [Private Nathan} Levinsky were now by me and none of us could pinpoint a good target, so we guessed where they might be and sporadically fired at these choices.

"While the two minute smoke signal [canister] was throwing its violet smoke into the morning air, we laid behind our various obstacles and continued to seek targets of fire. How so much fire could come at us and our still not see a bit of it was indeed nerve racking. I glanced back at the naval demolition area and could see the CPO [chief petty officer] in charge there still dashing about the obstacles tying the charges to the obstacles. I let out a yell to warn him of the violet smoke, but my voice carried no distance in the hectic morning noise. On his own volition, the CPO took cover and his timing was about perfect. He did not lie in place more than ten seconds and then the whole sky was filled with noise, sand, and debris as our gap was blown. For the next few seconds, the earth and the sky were filled with flying missiles, as what goes up definitely must come down. These huge hunks of steel were still raining down when the CPO in the naval team was again up and against the obstacles, making the last few ties that would clear the naval gap.

"I signaled the men to break for the seawall that paralleled the road along the beach and was still some one hundred feet from where we were scattered. Some of the men had just started their zigzag runs when the violet smoke started belching into the air from the naval gap and this warning was relayed on to the men. Ample time was available to make the seawall and most of the men worked their way to it. I looked back to the tank-dozer where the wounded men were crouching. We laid in the sand immediately behind this protection until the earth and sky were again filled with the obstacles the Nazi war machine had deemed sufficient to stop an invasion.

"The tide had been rising for the twenty-one minutes we had been on this hostile shore and this blast that cleared the gap sprayed water as well as debris upon our LCM as she lay against the beach, just a little south of where it had been dropped…

"I now directed the tank-dozer into the cleared gap and [Private] Levinsky, who seemed to come out of nowhere and to be everywhere there was activity, and I corralled the wounded and aided them on their rough trip up the beach to the breakwater. The tank-dozer had received a direct hit on the mechanism that controlled the dozer blade and the blade could not be raised. I had the tank commander turn his tank around and back up the sloping beach until he reached the breakwater where the blade was jettisoned. As our detonation of the explosive charges had left one hedgehog perforated with one large explosive hole but still menacingly dangerous I had the tank-dozer move back to where Levinsky and I had lashed a heavy rope about it and we drug it up to the beach, which was now rather thoroughly peopled with an ever increasing number of invasion troops.

"About this time a different head popped out of the commander's hatch and the tanker asked me what we should do with the commander. 'Why? What's wrong with him?' I asked.

"'He's dead. He's shot,' was the complete answer. We eased the tank commander out of the tank and on down upon the beach where he was soon forgotten in all the commotion of this unreal history.

"The first aid man who had been assigned our boat team had been seriously wounded in the burst of fire that had hit the group of our men as they had collected about the first wounded men—the two men who had been wounded with the baptism of machine gun fire that hit us as we dropped ramp upon the beach. Now we were faced with the problem of tending to our wounded. The dead we could not help.

"Our wounded had been assembled in a small cove at the edge of the retard that offered ample protection from the enemy fire, and at this point we tended the several men who had so far been wounded. The medic was the most serious case of all and to him went our first efforts. This extremely brave youth gave us instructions and where possible, physical assistance as we rapidly dressed the several gunshot wounds he had received. Other men had been dressing the wounds of the other injured men and as soon as the first aid man had been made comfortable with all of his wounds he insisted that the injured be brought to him that he might expertly tend his injured comrades. This was one of the most spectacular showings of bravery and guts I have ever seen."[37]

Later, Lieutenant Kehaly witnessed an LST approaching the beach through the gap his army-navy team had cleared. As it touched down, it was hit by antitank shells and set on fire. As the men on the LST exited, many of them on fire, Kehaly saw them mercilessly shot down by enemy machine gun fire. Lieutenant Kehaly immediately sprang into action. "The tank-dozer had been standing by and occasionally firing at whatever seemed to move, but no targets were a sure target, so I had the new tank commander move down onto the beach where the wounded were that we might help them to the protective retard. Levinsky and a few other men shared this trip with me and while it was rough on the many wounded, it did get the men up to where they could have their wounds dressed to await evacuation.

"We made three trips down the spit of sand and in all brought back about sixty wounded, burned, and injured men. The wounded men had to help each other. To make this possible, the wounded would lead the blind so that we able people could carry or drag those incapable of any effort. If a man cried and asked for help I would say, 'Get on your feet, you bastard, or stay there and die.' And usually he helped himself. My God, I hated to say that to these men, but Lord, my hands were full.

"One in the first group we brought in was a burned and blinded medical captain who also takes up a page in the book of heroes. In the few minutes we had taken to bring in these men, the captain had had a chance to recover from the shock of the bursting, flaming shells and ocean dunking. We set to work tending the burns about his eyes and as we progressed with the special gauze for burns, he opened his reddened eyes and practically immediately took over his own medication and that of his men.

"First, he must have a bottle of sure-cure from his musette bag. At first, I thought I was mistaken, then I pulled a bottle of whiskey out of the bag, but that officer's eyes were getting better by the second and he said, 'That's it. That's it. Break her open. I brought her for just such an occasion.' The captain took a nice size gurgle and passed the bottle. I took the merest sip to make the captain feel better and passed the bottle on to one of the wounded men, as indicated by the captain. There was only a drop left in the bottle by the time it returned to this wonderful captain and this he drained when all others passed up his offered chance. Between the injured medical corps captain and the badly wounded medical corps first aid man, the wounds and burns of the invading infantrymen were soon nicely dressed and they were eased about our cove until they could be evacuated.

"About this time, I noticed consternation in a group of 29th Infantry men as they deployed at the base of the cliff, some dust as machine gun fire cut through these men and it was apparent the fire was from behind these troops and I quickly looked seventy-five yards across the flat from us and due south of our cove. That one man was wounded I could easily see and while still watching this group, another man was wounded. But it is a strange thing my mind flashed as they were protected from the enemy on the bluff and out of line from enemy emplacements at the end of the beach. As I then watched I could see the puffs of dust as machine gun fire cut through these men and it was apparent the fire was from behind these troops and I quickly looked out to the sea, but there were no craft nearby that could be doing this firing. I then hopped up on the road that ran along the beach and from this better elevation, I again saw the shells striking among these men.

"I don't know where I lost my carbine, but I didn't have it with me and as I turned to drop down behind the retard for a weapon, I bumped into Levinsky. 'What the hell you doing up here?' I yelled at him.

"'I don't know,' was his answer and then he added, 'What the hell you doing up here?'

"I explained to Private Levinsky that there must be a machine gun hidden in some part of the demolished cottage that was strewn about some halfway between us and the group of infantrymen at the foot of the bluff. 'Where's your rifle?' I asked Private Levinsky.

"'I don't know,' he said, 'I guess it's with yours.' We both dropped down behind the retard and picked out one of the rifles that lay strewn about. I checked for ammunition and that the weapon was in mechanical order and then hopped back up on the road. Private Levinsky had mirrored my actions and was on the road with me.

"'Where the hell are you going?' I asked him.

"'I don't know,' he said and added, 'Where the hell are you going?'

"This was Private Nathan Levinsky and without a question of any doubt the bravest man I ever met."[38]

Lieutenant Colonel Carl J. Isley, the commanding officer of the 146th Engineer Combat Battalion, was an eyewitness to Kehaly's heroism. "Lieutenant Kehaly, in command of a demolition team, landed on the Vierville beach at H+03 minutes. Due to confusion which existed at the time of landing, the infantry and Rangers, which were scheduled to land in advance of the demolition team failed to arrive on schedule. The demolition team then landed without the benefit of supporting infantry fire. As the boat beached, it was subjected to extremely heavy small arms and artillery fire. Seven of the original team were killed and at the same time the naval demolition party landing on the same LCM suffered heavy losses. Lieutenant Kehaly promptly reorganized the remnants of his demolition team. He led his team in the successful accomplishment of its mission of breaching a gap through the beach obstacles. During the entire period, he and his crew were subjected to intense hostile fire. The work was conducted without the benefit of supporting fires. Throughout the entire period Lieutenant Kehaly displayed great courage and leadership of the highest quality."[39]

Gunner's Mate Second Class Robert W. Bass
Naval Combat Demolition Unit 11, Naval Combat Demolition Group, 7th Naval Beach Battalion, Assault Force O, Task Force 124, Eleventh Amphibious Force, 12th Fleet
Gap Assault Team Number 1

Gunner's Mate Second Class Robert W. Bass served with Naval Combat Demolition Unit 11, which was attached to Lieutenant Kehaly's Gap Assault Team Number 1. Lieutenant Commander Joseph H. Gibbons was the commander of the Assault Force O naval combat demolition units that were attached to the sixteen gap assault teams. Gibbons went ashore with the command group of the Provisional Special Engineer Brigade Group and was an eyewitness to the heroism of his sailors. "Assigned to clear enemy obstacles from the Omaha Beach at H+03 minutes on D-Day, Bass and his crew were subjected to heavy artillery, machine gun, and rifle fire, and in spite of the intensity of this fire, succeeded in their mission of blowing a fifty yard gap through the obstacles.

"As a result of seven of the twelve men of the crew being killed or wounded, a large share of the extra work fell on Bass, who performed the additional duties capably, coolly, and without regard to personal safety. The courage displayed by Bass was an outstanding example for the rest of the crew and contributed largely to the success of the mission. Upon completion of the work, Bass further exposed himself to enemy fire and was wounded while carrying wounded crew mates to safety."[40]

Second Lieutenant William A. Anderson
Company A, 146th Engineer Combat Battalion, Special Engineer Task Force, Provisional Engineer Brigade Group, V Corps
Gap Assault Team Number 2

The boat carrying Sergeant James E. Lemonds and the rest of Gap Assault Team Number 2 was scheduled to land at Dog Green. "Boat Team Number 2, commanded by 2nd Lieutenant William A. Anderson, was delayed by a faulty LCM, making it impossible to arrive at the scheduled time. After arriving about one hour behind schedule under tremendous enemy fire, we were ordered to take cover. At this moment, Lieutenant Anderson was wounded in the back.

"When the firing slackened, Lieutenant Anderson ordered his men to gather pack charges and commence work on the beach, clearing obstacles and removing mines. Lieutenant Anderson worked right with his men placing charges and at the same time gave instructions. Directly, an order was issued to join the unit. Upon leaving to rejoin the unit, Lieutenant Anderson was wounded in the leg and evacuated."[41]

Lieutenant Colonel Carl Isley, the commander of the 146th Engineer Combat Battalion, wrote the following regarding the Lieutenant Anderson's heroic actions. "Under intense small arms and observed artillery fire, Lieutenant Anderson and his team began the removal of obstacles on the shoreward band, during which time he was wounded in the back. Despite his wound, Lieutenant Anderson continued directing the removal of obstacles until ordered to move his team to rejoin his unit. While moving his team along the beach, Lieutenant Anderson was again wounded and later evacuated."[42]

Gap Assault Team Numbers 3 and 4 were badly shot up during the landing and achieved very little in terms of demolition of obstacles. Incoming infantry taking refuge among the obstacles prevented Gap Assault Team Number 5 from performing its demolition work.

Second Lieutenant Eskell F. Roberts
Company B, 146th Engineer Combat Battalion, Special Engineer Task Force, Provisional Engineer Special Brigade Group
Gap Assault Team Number 6

Lieutenant Ben Bartholomew, with Company B, 146th Engineer Combat Battalion, landed with his Gap Assault Team Number 7 just east of and close to where Lieutenant Eskell Roberts and his Gap Assault Team 6 came ashore. "Lieutenant Roberts was wounded in the legs by mortar fire as he was making his way from the boat to the band of obstacles. Unmindful of his painful wounds, Lieutenant Roberts, with extraordinary heroism and persistence directed his crew in removing a clear gap through the obstacles. As the tide receded, he fearlessly led his crew back onto the beach under heavy enemy fire and directed their efforts until wounded a second time, at which time he was evacuated to a more safe place."[43]

Gap Assault Team 6 was able to blow a fifty yard gap in the obstacle belt in the Dog Red sector, while Gap Assault Team 7 was prevented from blowing obstacles in its area by the presence of infantry among the obstacles.

Second Lieutenant Wesley R. Ross
Company B, 146th Engineer Combat Battalion, Special Engineer Task Force, Provisional Engineer Special Brigade Group
Gap Assault Team Number 8

Lieutenant Wesley Ross, the commanding officer of Gap Assault Team Number 8, was assigned to clear a fifty yard gap in the obstacles on the eastern side of Dog Red. "As we approached the beach, I began seeing splashes in the water from the mortar, artillery, and small arms fire, so I quickly lost interest in being an observer, and ducked down behind the steel ramp and sidewalls. This was really fingernail biting time, as detonation of our explosives by mortar or artillery fire would have been devastating. This unfortunate scenario was visited upon two gap assault teams on the 299th ECB's [Engineer Combat Battalion] eastern sector, when their explosives were detonated prematurely. Both NCDU officers and the majority of their NCDU members were killed. The two army teams to which they were attached must also have suffered similarly as 299th ECB's prorated fatalities were almost double that of the 146th ECB.

"As we came close in, our navy gunner began 'hosing down' the beach ahead with his twin .50 caliber machine guns that were mounted near the stern of our LCM. This certainly was a morale booster, because as we approached the beach we saw several dead GIs [floating] face down, bobbing and rolling in the surf. This was unsettling—this was just a few minutes after our infantry covering force had been programmed to be the first foot soldiers ashore. These men may have been tankers in the DD tanks that sank in the heavy surf. Had they been in our initial infantry cover force, their under the chin assault gas masks should have kept them face up in the water, even though drowned.

"There were no visible tank-dozers or infantrymen near our landing area when we scurried from our LCM, five minutes late from our planned landing time of 06:33—(per Ensign [Harold P.] Blean). This five minute delay had an adverse affect on our mission, as will be seen. Our tank-dozer was late, and I had thought that our infantry covering force was also late. (We had landed on Easy Green, approximately two hundred yards west of our assigned spot, and the infantry may have landed properly.) The fortified house near the mouth of les Moulins draw was a short distance east.

"As for Gap Assault Team 8, its members hurried inland 150 yards near our 'foxhole', and began placing the C-2 charges. Bill Garland, Earl Holbert, Bill Townsley, several NCDU members, and I slid the rubber raft out of the LCM, containing the backup explosives and Bangalore torpedoes. It took some real tugging to skid out the raft, all the while sweating it out while presenting a stationary target with our backs to the enemy. Earl then pulled the raft eastward beyond the edge of our gap and tied the long small-diameter rope to one of the wooden obstacles…

"Running a zigzag path up to our super foxhole located midway between the wooden obstacles and the steel hedgehogs, I found Sergeant W. Grosvenor firing his M1 at the fortified house near the mouth of D-3 draw to our left front, attempting to suppress the machine gun fire coming from there. After a short discussion, I grabbed his big Signal Corp wire reel containing the primacord ring main (two strands of primacord friction-taped at two foot intervals to a small rope), and took off in high gear. Running in multiple short dashes and hitting the ground often denied the enemy gunners an easy target. Bullets knocked splinters from the wooden obstacles overhead after I hit the ground—or so I heard later! I ran the ring main clockwise around the wooden obstacles and Sergeant Bill Garland ran his main around counterclockwise. We square knotted the ring mains together where we met. We then joined the team, who had almost finished tying on the C-2 charges.

"Sergeant Grosvenor apologized for not performing per plan. My response—'We got the job done—end of conversation.' It was never mentioned again.

"While proceeding with the placement of the charges, I just happened to be looking eastward into the pre-sunrise sky, when an artillery round hit the sand sixty feet away. It ricocheted twenty feet into the air and its pointed nose was clearly visible against the morning sky before exploding. It split along its length and sent a two foot long 'V-shaped' chunk of steel flopping over and over toward the northeast! High explosive artillery rounds are designed to produce multiple high velocity fragments, so this was a faulty round—the result of slave labor sabotage? If so, it was much appreciated! We were under heavy small arms fire almost immediately and machine guns, mostly unseen by me, were tracking our movement. I saw three riflemen slinking to my left, in defilade behind the natural sandbank seawall above the high water line. They were heading east toward the fortified house near the mouth of les Moulins draw, but I was too busy to monitor their progress. These men may have been from our infantry covering force—the first contingent ashore from the 116th Infantry—and if so, may have been attempting to silence the enemy machine gun fire from the fortified house. We began suffering casualties soon after landing, mostly from small arms fire, but our medics were unbelievably efficient and began taking care of the casualties where they lay. Many of the less seriously wounded didn't even bother calling for help. Minden Ivey, a rugged little Texan, took a bullet through the wrist, resulting in a compound fracture; but he kept right on shooting, refusing medical aid in favor of the more seriously wounded—although he did accept some assistance in reloading his M1 rifle.

"Without warning and from ten yards out, our tank-dozer fired an HE [high explosive] round into the left jamb of the right window in the fortified house two hundred yards to our left front—and me without earplugs! That silenced the machine gunners who had been giving us so much trouble. We had been engaged, and until that blast, I was unaware that tank-dozer number 8 had finally landed—about fifteen minutes late. It was one of eight scheduled to land in the 146th ECB sector—one for each primary gap assault team, and was put ashore from LCT 2075, from which we had debarked at 03:30.

"Less than twenty minutes after landing Gap Assault Team 8 had the fifty yard section of the wooden obstacles consisting of posts and ramps, ready to blow. Sergeant Garland and I then tied forty-five second detonators to opposite ends of the ring main, tossed out the purple smoke canisters as warning signals to the infantry, and moved a short distance inland. The blast made quite a bunch of kindling and poles, but several of the obstacles were not destroyed in this initial effort. Garland and I then tied 22-second detonators to opposite the end of the remaining ring main and tried again. Two posts survived that blast, so I ran back and attached an 8-second detonator to the short fragment of ring main, pulled the igniter and splashed shoreward in water up to mid-calf. It was a successful blast—our fifty yard gap was now clear through the wooden obstacles. Only the steel hedgehogs remained to be blown! I have no way of knowing, but suspect that the primacord ring main had been cut by artillery, mortar, or small arms fire—or possibly by our tank-dozer.

"Ensign Blean then asked what his NCDU team should do. Since the NCDUs had Hagensen packs and no fifteen pound Tetrytol satchel charges destined for use on the heavy steel hedgehogs, I released him and his eleven man NCDU team to take cover behind the sand bank seawall.

"A short time later, I noticed a soldier sitting upright on the sand fifty feet to the west, facing seaward at the water's edge. Small arms fire was kicking up sand around him and I yelled for him to take cover behind one of the steel obstacles. Either he did not hear me or was disoriented and could not react; or he may have already been wounded. Soon after, he slumped over on the sand and the water sloshing around him slowly turned a delicate pink. He probably was killed and may have been from our NCDU 137, as I later learned that Wayne Carroll and Jessie Cleveland—two engineers from the NCDU—were killed that morning. Heading for the seawall, Tom Wilkins yelled for Jessie Cleveland to take cover from the heavy enemy fire. Jessie airily replied, 'I'll still be going when you're dead and gone!' Soon after, Tom was shot through the hip while attempting to rescue a wounded infantryman—for which he was awarded the Silver Star; and Jessie was decapitated by a direct hit from a mortar round. His body was picked up the next day.

"By the time Garland and I moved shoreward to the hedgehogs, our demolition team had positioned the Tetrytol satchel charges and tied them to the ring main, and we were ready to watch them disappear as if being swept away by an oversized broom! Just as Garland and I were attaching the forty-five second detonators, an infantry LCVP landed 150 yards seaward near the east border of our gap. They were probably the infantry force scheduled to arrive at 07:00. Initially I had thought them to be our late arriving 06:30 infantry cover, but probably was in error—the time was about 07:00.

"From a past experience at the ATC [Assault Training Center], I knew how deadly explosive driven steel fragments could be, and in the forty-five seconds until detonation, those men would have been nestled in and around the hedgehogs about to be blown. So even though I agonized about a delay, I could not bring myself to shred our own infantry. The steel fragments would surely have killed or wounded a number of them—so the demolition was delayed, and eventually postponed when the incoming tide inundated the hedgehogs before our infantry had cleared the area. They were destroyed by healthy members of Gap Assault Team 8 without incident when the tide receded shortly after noon.

"As the water was lapping at our feet, we began gathering our wounded and transferring them past the three foot deep runnel to an area in defilade below the natural sand seawall. As I was preparing to follow, I noticed Sergeant Roy Arn (in charge of a mine detector crew) lying on the sand a short distance to the west. He had severe wounds from an artillery round which had landed so close by that his uniform was gray from the explosive residue. A chunk of meat had been gouged from the rear of his right thigh; and another artillery fragment had torn open and broken his right shoulder and clavicle, causing a bubbling puncture wound. He was also bleeding heavily from his forehead where the edge of his helmet had been driven down by the blast. Arn's right arm and leg were useless, so he held on as we began hunching forward like wiggle-worms on the sand.

"As we neared the runnel, a machine gun burst splattered sand in our faces, so we slithered behind a nearby hedgehog—with the Tetrytol still attached. The machine gunner found other targets of opportunity and we were able to slip unnoticed into the runnel—now about four feet deep and thirty feet wide—and cross with our noses just above the water.

"Arn was carried up the bank and given further attention by our medics. Just prior to being wounded he had been shooting at the Germans in the fortified house. A bullet struck nearby kicking sand in his face, so he flattened down on the sand just as the artillery shell arrived. Had there been no small arms near miss, he likely would have been mortally wounded by the large artillery fragment that had ripped into his back. After receiving medical attention, Roy watched from about thirty feet away as one of our tanks moved over a dead soldier lying on the sand. Although dead, Roy still worried that the soldier would be squashed—but the tanker managed to straddle him…

"At midmorning Roy was carried to a collection station at les Moulins draw and then transferred to the water's edge by stretcher on his way to the LST hospital ship…

"It was now plain that my decision to delay the demolition of the hedgehogs was a mistake. Sergeant Bill Garland and I had already attached the forty-five second detonators to opposite ends of the ring main, and we should have proceeded per plan. I could have reinforced the demolition warning to the infantry by tossing out an additional canister of purple smoke and or sent a runner down to guide them further east on their way up to the seawall. Flying steel may still have killed some of these men, but this might have reduced the overall death toll by allowing a succession of landing craft to quickly disgorge their men through our blown gap. My decision at the time seemed to make sense—now it does not—I should have been better attuned to our mission…After a quick check on my men, I hurried eastward along the beach to find Lieutenant Colonel Isley for further orders. Why I went east is a mystery to me, as I was on the eastern border of the 146th ECB sector, so I may have been more than slightly excited. This was not too bright a move—out in the open with small arms, mortar, and artillery fire incoming. I had gone about seventy-five yards, and as I stopped and twisted to my right to check again on my crew, a mortar round hit the shingle eight feet to my front. Had I not stopped, the mortar crew would have dropped that round on my helmet!

"There were small fragments on my right great toe, foot, instep, calf, both knees, and a slug of fragments in my left mid-thigh. Being sideways to the blast reduced my exposure area and surely saved me from being further spiculed. Despite what I had heard, the thigh wound was quite painful—possibly because the fragments were red hot and were traveling at fairly low velocities. Conversely, I was unaware of the fragments in my feet and lower legs until that night on the hospital ship. Once an experienced mortar crew registers on a target, they normally fire several more rounds in rapid succession. Knowing that, I quickly hopped inland above the shingle, just as two more rounds dropped into the area just vacated.

"I had been scared spitless while in the LCM, but once we landed I was too busy to bother being terrified. Now finding I was not indestructible, I again became concerned about my welfare. I began digging a foxhole in the sand with my hands and then with my helmet—after slicing my hands on buried barbed wire—this gaining protection from the fierce enemy fire. Max Norris [our medic] found me sometime later and we enlarged the foxhole to a two man job. He then poured sulfanilamide powder into the thigh wound hole, bandaged it, and gave me a morphine injection…Max then brought me up to date on our casualties."[44]

Sergeant Robert H. Young was a member of the boat team and saw Ross after he was wounded by the mortar fragments. "Several attempts were made to remove him to the evacuation area, but he insisted that he stay and continue his command. The extraordinary heroism displayed by Lieutenant Ross in directing the men in the evacuation of wounded and the further clearance of the beach area despite his wounds until evacuated himself that evening, aided markedly in clearing that section of the beach."[45]

Private First Class John R. Heenan
Company B, 146th Engineer Combat Battalion, Special Engineer Task Force, Provisional Engineer Special Brigade, V Corps
Gap Support Team Number C

Private Albert J. Tucker
Company B, 146th Engineer Combat Battalion, Special Engineer Task Force, Provisional Engineer Special Brigade Group
Gap Support Team C

The four gap support teams landed about an hour late on the Easy Red sector to the east of the planned locations along the 116th Infantry's four beach sectors. Corporal Elmer C. Morrison with Company B, 146th Engineer Combat Battalion, "was a member of Boat Team C, under the command of 1st Lieutenant Donald P. Latendresse, which arrived at the beach when the obstacles which were to be removed were already awash in the rising tide. The water was then too high for any work on the obstacles. We left the boat under fire and immediately waded out of the water and ran across the beach to a place above the high water line in defilade of enemy fire. It was seen immediately that our boat team leader was missing and he was spotted trying to make his way in from the water. Private First Class Heenan and Private Tucker, without hesitancy and disregarding their own safety, ran out on to the beach and carried their wounded leader [Lieutenant Latendresse], under heavy enemy fire, to cover."[46]

Lieutenant Colonel Carl J. Isley
Headquarters, 146th Engineer Combat Battalion, Special Engineer Task Force, Provisional Engineer Special Brigade Group

Lieutenant Colonel John T. O'Neill was the commanding officer of the Special Engineer Task Force, which was responsible for obstacle clearance on Omaha Beach. "Lieutenant Colonel Isley was in command of a group of demolition teams for the removal of underwater obstacles in the initial assault of the beaches. Upon landing, Lieutenant Colonel Isley recognized the necessity of reinforcing his demolition teams. Organizing his command team and equipping it with reserve explosives and accessories, he personally employed it on the obstacles. In the face of sustained and heavy small arms and observed artillery fire, Lieutenant Colonel Isley succeeded in clearing a fifty yard gap. This display of aggressive leadership, magnificent courage and utter disregard for his own personal safety was an example to his officers and men and inspired them to complete their mission."[47]

SIMULTANEOUSLY AT H-HOUR, THE FIRST WAVES of the 16th Infantry Regiment were landing on two sectors to the east. The 741st Tank Battalion was attached to the 16th Infantry for the assault landing. The sixteen duplex drive swimming tanks of Company B, under the command of Captain James G. Thornton, Jr., were assigned to land on the Easy Red sector at H-5 minutes. Company B was attached to the 16th Infantry Regiment's 2nd Battalion landing team. Company C's sixteen DD tanks, under the command of Captain Charles R. Young, were attached to the 16th Infantry's 3rd Battalion landing team and were assigned to land at the Fox Green sector at H-5 minutes. Company A, with its sixteen wading tanks, plus eight tank-dozers would land at H-Hour astride the boundary between Easy Red and Fox Green.

At H-60 minutes the DD tanks being transported in eight LCTs were approximately six thousand yards offshore. At that time, the two tank company commanders spoke by radio to discuss launching the tanks in the extremely rough sea and agreed that the advantage to be gained by launching the tanks outweighed the risk of the rough sea. At H-50 minutes, orders were issued to launch the tanks. LCT 57, transporting four Company B tanks, incurred a damaged ramp and was unable to launch three of the tanks. All of the other twenty-nine tanks were launched. The canvas flotation skirts of the tanks were buffeted by the pounding waves and suffered catastrophic damage to the struts and incurred ripped canvas. Some tanks also experienced engine failures. Only two of the Company B tanks that were launched made it to shore. The remaining eleven Company B tanks and all sixteen of the Company C tanks sank. Most of the crews escaped from their tanks and were picked up by rescue boats. The LCT with the damaged ramp took the three tanks in and landed them on the beach. The Company A wading tanks and tank-dozers landed at H-Hour, except for two tanks and one tank-dozer which were lost when their LCT was sunk by an explosion of undetermined origin. Some of the other Company A wading tanks landed in water which was too deep and the crews were forced to abandon them.

Second Lieutenant Gaetano R. Barcellona
Company A, 741st Tank Battalion

Lieutenant Colonel Robert W. Skaggs, the commanding officer of the 741st Tank Battalion, witnessed the courageous actions of Lieutenant Gaetano R. Barcellona on June 6. "Second Lieutenant Barcellona commanded a platoon of tanks in the assault on the coast of France on 6 June 1944. He landed with the assault force. His tank sustained several hits and it became immobilized. He continued [to keep] his tank in operation and continually exposed himself to severe enemy machine gun fire in order to select enemy targets and direct the fire of his unit. When his ammunition supply was exhausted he left his tank and in spite of the intensive hostile fire, proceeded to a tractor to secure additional ammunition. He then returned to his tank and continued to carry on the fight."[48]

Lieutenant Gaetano Barcellona would later lead his platoon during the early stages of the Battle of the Bulge in destroying the armored spearhead of SS Panzer Division 2.

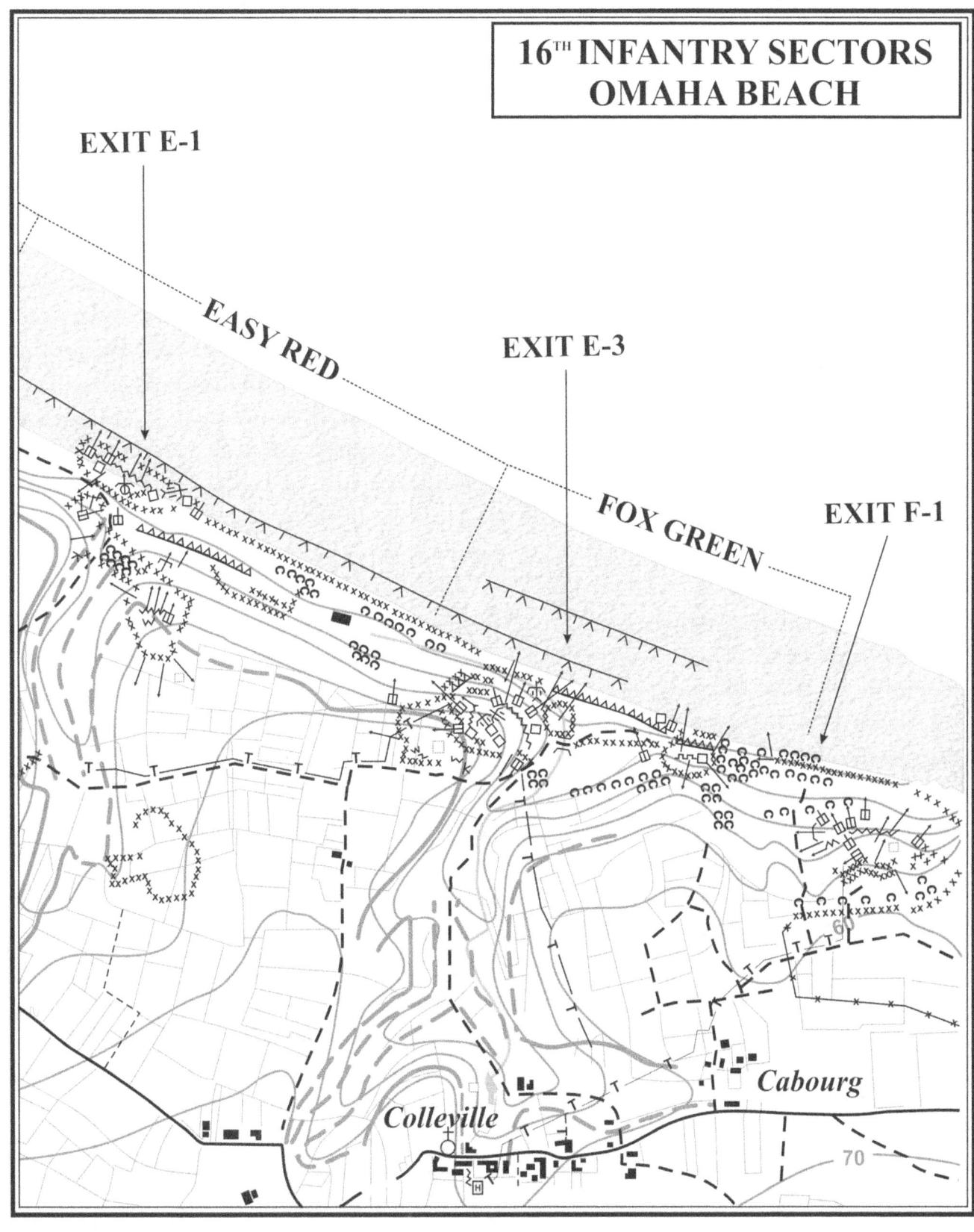

LANDING DIAGRAM 16TH RCT

FOX GREEN | EASY RED

Time	FOX GREEN	EASY RED
H-5	Co C (DD) 741 Tank Bn	Co B (DD) 741 Tank Bn
H HOUR	Co A 741 Tank Bn	Co A 741 Tank Bn
H+01	Co I 16 Inf / Co L 16 Inf	Co F 16 Inf / Co E 16 Inf
H+03	299 ECB / Demolitions Control Boat	299 ECB / 146 ECB
H+30	Co K 16 Inf / HQ 3 Bn 16 Inf / Provisional 397 AAA (AW) Bn	Provisional 397 AAA (AW) Bn / HQ 2 Bn 16 Inf / Co G 16 Inf
H+40	Co M 16 Inf	Co H 16 Inf
H+50	Co C 81 Chem Bn	HQ 116 Inf / Co C 81 Chem Bn
H+60	Bulldozers - Halftracks - Misc Units	Bulldozers - Halftracks - Misc Units
H+65	37 ECB	Det V Corps / 37 ECB
H+70		Co C 16 Inf / Co A 16 Inf

OMAHA BEACH

Time	FOX GREEN	EASY RED
H+80		[V] [V] [V] [V] [V] [V] HQ HQ Co Co A Co B 16 Inf 1 Bn 1 Bn 1 Eng Bn 16 Inf 16 Inf Co A 20 Eng Bn
H+90	[T] [T] [T] 62 FA Bn Armd	[V] [V] [V] [V] [V] HQ 1 Bn HQ and HQ Co Co D 16 Inf 37 Eng Bn Med Sec 1 Bn 16 Inf
H+95		[M] HQ and HQ Co 16 Inf
H+105	[D] [D] HQ Co 3 Bn 16 Inf	[D][D][D] [D][D][D] [D][D][D] HQ Co Btry B Btry C 1 Bn 16 2f 7 FA Bn 7 FA Bn [D][D][D] HQ Co 2 2 Bn 16 Inf
H+110		[D] [D] [D] [D] [D] [M] [V] Cannon Co 16 Inf 1 Sig Co HQ and HQ Co 1 Div 1 Sig Co
H+120	[T] [T] [T] [T] Co B 29 Btry D 197 AAA (AW) Bn Btry C 197 AAA (AW) Bn Eng Bn	[T] [T] [T] [T] [T] [T] [T] [T] HQ Btry Btry B Btry A AT Co 1 Eng Bn Co A 1 197 AAA (AW) Bn 16 Inf Med Bn
H+130		Misc Units and Vehicles
H+135	[V] [V] [V] [V] Co C 20 Eng Bn	
H+140	[R] [R] Misc Units and Vehicles	

◇ DD Tanks [T] LCT [A] LCA [V] LCVP [M] LCM [I] LCI [D] DUKW [R] Rhino Ferry

Private First Class Lawrence G. Sweeney
Company A, 741st Tank Battalion

Private First Class Lawrence G. Sweeney was the gunner of the tank commanded by Lieutenant Barcellona, who wrote the following recommendation. "Private First Class Sweeney, a cannoneer of a medium tank, landed with the initial assault wave under heavy enemy rifle, machine gun, mortar, and artillery fire. Though on landing, his tank received several hits, he continued it in operation. When his [tank's] ammunition supply became exhausted, Private First Class Sweeney, completely disregarding his own safety, boldly dismounted from his tank and moved across the fire swept beach to secure additional ammunition. After reloading his tank, he was sent on a mission to check the Easy-3 exit of the beach. On arrival, he found the exit well fortified and under terrific enemy fire which had the infantry pinned down. Fearlessly he crawled to positions which were under direct fire from the enemy in order to determine where enemy positions were located. He then proceeded under a hail of enemy fire to an abandoned tank and secured another man to load the gun while he himself engaged the enemy targets. After neutralizing several positions he reported back to his platoon leader with the information that the exit was heavily fortified with antitank guns and mines.

"He was given another mission to contact the tanks at the other end of the beach as radios had become inoperative and his platoon leader desired to rally his tanks. In route, he encountered a tank that was unable to move forward through the beach that was cluttered with wounded and dead. Unmindful of the fact that men were constantly being hit in this area, Private First Class Sweeney cleared a path [by moving the dead and wounded] and despite the devastating enemy fire, personally directed the tanks forward. He then completed his mission."[49]

Lieutenant Roger J. McDonough, another platoon leader with the 741st Tank Battalion, "observed the actions of Private First Class Lawrence Sweeney. He made his way to the beach exit Easy-3 under heavy enemy fire. On arrival at this well fortified position which had the infantry pinned down, Private First Class Sweeney crawled to positions where the infantry were engaging targets and in so doing, located several enemy emplacements. He then ran under heavy fire to an abandoned tank, climbed into the turret, called an assistant gunner and immediately proceeded to engage the targets. He repeated this action several times in order to check neutralization of targets and get additional targets."[50]

Lieutenant Frank A. Klotz was the platoon leader of the 741st Tank Battalion's tank-dozer platoon. "My tanks and several others were unable to contact any other tanks of our unit when Private First Class Lawrence Sweeney, under heavy enemy fire came running to the side of my tank. He advised me of the location of our other tanks and volunteered to lead us forward. Although men were constantly being hit in the area he proceeded to clear a path, dragging dead and wounded to the side and led my tanks forward. On arrival at the assembly area he immediately went out to complete his mission."[51]

Sergeant George A. Habib
Company A, 741st Tank Battalion

Lieutenant Colonel Robert W. Skaggs, the commanding officer of the 741st Tank Battalion, observed Sergeant George A. Habib audaciously perform a repair of his tank-dozer in the open, despite extremely heavy enemy fire. "Sergeant Habib was in command of a tank-dozer for the removal of beach obstacles in the initial assault of the beaches. Shortly after landing, both tracks of the tank-dozer were thrown. Although under heavy and sustained small arms and observed artillery fire, Sergeant Habib energetically directed the crew in repairing the thrown tracks. After successfully repairing the tank-dozer, Sergeant Habib continued removing obstacles and the unloading of vitally needed supplies and equipment with his tank-dozer. The resourcefulness, aggressive leadership, courage and extraordinary heroism displayed by Sergeant Habib were an inspiration to his crew and the officers and men in his vicinity."[52]

Technician Fourth Grade Bolick Smulik
Company A, 741st Tank Battalion

Lieutenant Colonel Skaggs also witnessed incredible heroism on the part of Technician Fourth Grade Bolick Smulik, the driver of another of the 741st Tank Battalion's tank-dozers. "Shortly after landing, his tank-dozer was disabled due to the intense German fire being placed on the beach. Though the fire on the beach was terrible he, in full view of the enemy, left his disabled tank-dozer and mounted a bulldozer. The crewmen of the bulldozer were all casualties. In this exposed position he experimented with the controls of the bulldozer until he was able to get it in operation. He then proceeded to assist in preparing a lane through the beach obstacles, which permitted the beaching of landing craft. Technician Fourth Grade Smulik's action took place under constant machine gun and artillery fire."[53]

This 88mm PAK 43/41 antitank gun, taken out of the casemate (below) at the WN 61 resistance nest, inflicted a great deal of damage to landing craft, tanks, tank-dozers, and other vehicles. *United States Coast Guard photograph, National Archives.*

This casemate, type H677, protected the 88mm antitank gun and was sited to place enfilade fire across the eastern end of Omaha Beach. Note the thick wing wall (left) that prevented observation of the gun and its muzzle blast by warships and protected the antitank gun from naval gunfire. The damage to the face of the casemate was inflicted by a tank under the command of Staff Sergeant Turner Sheppard, with Company B, 741st Tank Battalion, which reportedly knocked the gun out of action by around 7:20 a.m. *United States Army Signal Corps photograph, National Archives.*

Two duplex drive M4 Sherman tanks (right center) of Company B, 741st Tank Battalion are likely the survivors of the swim to the Easy Red sector of Omaha Beach, since their canvas floatation skirts are still partially inflated. One of the Company A, 741st Tank Battalion's wading tanks (left) designated with a "10" on the extended rear exhaust stack provides protection for a group of 16th Infantry Regiment soldiers. Other soldiers take cover behind tetrahedron obstacles while others wade through the surf to reach the shingle or shelf which provided defilade from most direct enemy fire. *Photograph by Robert Capa, Library of Congress.*

Lieutenant Colonel Robert W. Skaggs
Headquarters, 741st Tank Battalion

Much of the tank support from the 741st Tank Battalion that Colonel George A. Taylor expected for his regiment never made it to the beach. However, Colonel Taylor observed its commander courageously braving enemy fire to reorganize the battalion and bring close fire support from the battalion's surviving tanks into action. "Two companies of DD tanks and one company of assault tanks were landed with the assault echelons to support the landings. Heavy seas swamped many of the DD tanks and enemy fire held the initial landings to the beach. Lieutenant Colonel Robert W. Skaggs, 741st Tank Battalion, landed about 08:30 with the reserve echelon. Finding the assault echelon held to the fire swept beach and that only thirteen of his tanks had been able to move into a firing position and were considerably disorganized, Lieutenant Colonel Skaggs immediately initiated steps to rally his tanks and get them into action. Constantly exposing himself to fire, he moved along the beach directing the fire and moving his tanks into better firing positions. His efforts were a great inspiration to his men and assisted materially in forwarding the advance of the assault units."[54]

The plan for the 16th Infantry Regiment called for the 2nd and 3rd Battalions to land abreast, with each battalion landing two rifle companies abreast in the first infantry assault wave. Company E was assigned to land on the western half of Easy Red. Company F would land on the left of Company E on the eastern half of the Easy Red sector. Company I would land on the western half of the Fox Green sector to the left of Company F. Company L was assigned to land on the left of Company I, on the eastern half of the Fox Green sector on the extreme left flank of the Omaha Beach.

Second Lieutenant John M. Spalding
Company E, 16th Infantry Regiment, 1st Infantry Division

Staff Sergeant Curtis Colwell
Company E, 16th Infantry Regiment, 1st Infantry Division

Sergeant Clarence Colson
Company E, 16th Infantry Regiment, 1st Infantry Division

Sergeant Kenneth F. Peterson
Company E, 16th Infantry Regiment, 1st Infantry Division

Sergeant Philip Streczyk
Company E, 16th Infantry Regiment, 1st Infantry Division

Private First Class George H. Bowen
Medical Detachment, Company E, 16th Infantry Regiment, 1st Infantry Division

Private First Class Richard J. Gallagher
Company E, 16th Infantry Regiment, 1st Infantry Division

The infantry companies of the assault elements of the 1st, 29th, and 4th Infantry Divisions were organized into thirty man sections in order fit into LCVPs, which were the standard infantry landing craft. A typical section consisted of an officer section leader, an NCO assistant section leader, five riflemen, two BAR teams of two men each, two bazooka teams of two men each, a four man 60mm mortar squad, a four man wire cutting team, a two man flamethrower team, and a four man demolition team. The composition of the sections, also known as boat teams, had variants according to the needs of the units and their tasks.

Lieutenant John Spalding was a replacement platoon leader with Company E who would experience his first combat on Omaha Beach. "We loaded into LCVPs from larger ships at 03:00. The companies were divided into sections and each LCVP had thirty-two men, including a medic, plus two navy men. I was [section] leader of the First Section of Company E and we were scheduled to go in on the first wave. My assistant section leader was Technical Sergeant Philip Streczyk. The sergeant, who was wounded in the Hürtgen Forest action, was the best soldier I have ever seen. He came into the army as a selectee and worked his way up to platoon sergeant. He was in on landings at Oran and in Sicily. If we had more men like him the war would soon be over. We loaded into LCVPs in a very rough sea. It took us much longer to load than it had during the practice landings because of the rough water. After entering the LCVPs, we went an undetermined distance to a rendezvous point. Here, the navy crew took us around and around, getting us soaked to the skin. Many of the men got sick immediately and others got sick as we went in towards shore.

"About 04:00 our boats lined up in a V formation and headed towards shore. As we went towards shore we could see the outlines of other boats around us and overhead we could hear a few planes. Between 05:45 and 06:00 we saw the first flashes from the shore. We didn't know whether they were our planes bombing, as we had been told to expect, or whether the flashes were from German artillery. We caught sight of the shore about 06:15. We also saw a few of our fighter planes. About 06:30 the rocket ships began to fire, but most of their rockets hit in the water. In the meantime, the navy had been firing and the dust from debris plus the early morning mist made it difficult to see the coast. There was a very good basis for the failure of the navy crew to hit the right part of the coast.

"As we came in, there was considerable noise from the shore and the sea. En route to the shore we passed several yellow rubber boats. They had personnel in them, but we didn't know what they were. They turned out to be personnel from the DD tanks, which had foundered. About 800-1,000 yards out, we began to receive machine gun fire from the shore but it was not effective. As we neared the shore we came to the line of departure and here the odd numbered boats swung out abreast on one side, while the even numbered boats went to the other side. In this formation the boats came into shore.

"Our instructions were to land just to the right of the house at [map coordinate] (677900). This house was to be the left boundary of my position. We were to go across the antitank ditch near the E-1 entrance and scale the seawall. Once this was done, we were to send patrols into St. Laurent-sur-Mer, where we were to contact E Company of the 116th [Infantry], which was supposed to land to our right, and then to push on to the high ground behind the town. It was assumed that the air force would have destroyed the beach defenses by this time and thus we could land without any great opposition.

Troops with Company E, 16th Infantry Regiment wade ashore on Easy Red shortly after H-Hour in an iconic photo taken by Robert F. Sargent. *United States Coast Guard photograph, National Archives.*

"About 06:30 we hit the line of departure and someone gave a signal and we swung into line. When we got two hundred yards offshore, the boat halted and a member of the navy crew yelled for us to drop the ramp. Staff Sergeant Fred A. Bisco and I kicked the ramp down. Shortly before this, a navy man had mounted the machine gun on the rear of the LCVP and had started to return fire. We were now receiving not only MG [machine gun] fire, but also mortar and some artillery fire. We had come in at low tide and the obstacles were noticeable. They stuck out of the water and we could see Teller mines on many of them. No path had been cleared through them, so we followed a zigzag course in.

"Because we were carrying so much equipment and because I was afraid that we were being landed in deep water, I told the men not to jump out until after I had tested the water. I jumped out of the boat slightly to the left of the ramp into water about waist deep. It was about 06:45. Then the men began to follow me. We headed ashore and the small arms fire became noticeable. We saw other boats to our left, but nothing to our right. We were the right front of the 1st Division. We had seen some tanks coming in, but didn't know what they were. As we left the boat we spread out in a V formation about thirty yards across. There was soon a noticeable decline of sand beneath our feet and we were soon over our heads, so we tried to swim. Fortunately, when I pulled the valve of my lifebelt it inflated and saved me. I lost my carbine. We lost none of our men, but only because they helped each other or because they got rid of their equipment. There was a strong undercurrent carrying us to the left. I had had experience with the strong current of the Ohio River as a swimmer, but this was much stronger.

"Sergeant [Philip] Streczyk and the medic, Private George Bowen, were carrying an eighteen foot ladder, which was to be used for crossing the antitank ditch or for any purpose which might arise. They were struggling with it in the water just about the time that I was having my worst trouble afloat. As the ladder came by me I grabbed it. Streczyk yelled and said, 'Lieutenant, we don't need any help,' but hell I was busy trying to get help, not to give it. I told them to leave the thing [the ladder], so it was abandoned in the water. About this time we were able to put down our feet and touch bottom; the water was about up to our mouths at this time. I had swallowed about half of the ocean and felt like I was going to choke.

"As we were coming in I looked at the terrain and saw a house which looked like the one which we were supposed to hit, so I said, 'Damn, the navy has hit it right on the nose.' Later I found that we had landed near another house 1,500 yards to the east at a point about [map coordinate] (689893).

A closer view of the previous photograph showing one of the Company A, 741st Tank Battalion's wading Sherman tanks (designated with a number 9 on the rear exhaust stack) is at the center and a number of rubber rafts used by the naval combat demolition units are at the edge of the shore with prone figures lying just beyond (left center), indicating that a gap assault team had landed in this sector ahead of Company E. *United States Coast Guard photograph, National Archives.*

"Our first casualty came at the water's edge. Private William C. Roper, rifleman, was hit in the foot by small arms fire just as he hit the beach. He kept trying to get his legging off, but couldn't reach the lacing so I helped him get it off. Just after we got ashore, one of my two BAR men was hit. Private First Class Virgil Tilley was hit in the right shoulder by a shell fragment, which drove a hunk of the shoulder out towards the back, but did not come all the way through. By this time, I noticed a number of my men on the beach all standing up and moving across the sand. They were too waterlogged to run, but they went as fast as they could. It looked as if they were walking in the face of a real strong wind. Down near the water's edge we ran into wire. Staff Sergeant Curtis Colwell blew a hole in the wire with a Bangalore [torpedo]. We picked our way through; I personally didn't see the gap he had blown, but I was still in a daze. I didn't see any mines on the beach except AT [antitank] mines.

"As we went across the beach my runner, Private First Class Bruce S. Buck, came over to me. I tried to get E Company with my 536 radio. I took the 536 off my shoulder, worked the antenna out as I walked across and tried to get contact, but it didn't work. I looked down and saw that the mouthpiece was shot away. Although the radio was useless and I should have thrown it away, training habits were so strong that I carefully took the antenna down as I had always been taught to do and put the 536 back on my shoulder. Your training stays with you even when you are scared.

"We moved on across the shale to a house which was straight inland. The first place we stopped was at a demolished building [where] there was some brush around. We were halted there by a minefield at the first slope. My section was spread out. The men in accordance with orders had deployed the minute they hit the beach. They had been told to get off the beach as soon as possible. They walked on across because nobody stopped them. When we got up to the rubble by the demolished house we were built up as skirmishers and were returning what fire we could. [Sergeant] Streczyk and Private First Class Richard J. Gallagher went forward to investigate the minefield. They decided we couldn't cross it. There was pretty heavy brush around there. Streczyk and Gallagher now went to the left to a defilade (apparently a little stream had washed it out at one time) and tried to work their way through."[55]

Sergeant Streczyk cut through several aprons of barbed wire as enemy small arms and machine gun fire was concentrated on him. Streczyk then led the way as he and Private First Class Gallagher worked their way up a small path which had been created by the small streambed that led through a minefield to the top of the slope overlooking the beach. Upon reaching the top, Streczyk set off a yellow smoke grenade to signal to those below that a way up the slope had been found. Streczyk then sent Gallagher down to bring Lieutenant Spalding and the 1st Section up the path.

Down below, Sergeant Clarence Colson had watched them ascend and had been able to make out that faint path. "When I looked and saw that path…there was this pillbox way over there that wasn't manned. They didn't have anybody manning that pillbox. Enemy fire was all coming from this way. So when I saw that path and all these wires, I knew there were minefields there. I told [Private Richard] Sims. We got a BAR from a guy who was wounded. And we got a few magazines. I brought the extra magazines and we got some bandoleers of ammunition that we carried. And I said, 'I'll head for the hill.' [It was] quite a steep hill. So I went up the path. There were no wires across the path—that's what I was looking for—and running as fast as I could run. And when I got over there, I motioned him to come and Sims came up. He had some more bandoleers. So we got to the top of the hill and that's where all the trenches were.

"And here this one [German] was running back and forth in that trench. I hollered at him and he threw a potato masher, a German hand grenade. I ducked down, put my hands up, my head down. It didn't go off right quick and I kind of glanced and I see he hadn't unscrewed the back and pulled the string. So I nailed him.

"But the one that was holding the [rest of the] company up [was] the pillbox down there. I could shoot right down the back end [of it]. The pillbox had a door that goes downstairs then you have your gunner slots. So, I got the BAR. It had a bipod on it and I got it set right up and started spraying that back door. I told Sims, 'Just as soon as I kick that magazine out, put another one in.' There were twenty rounds, I think, in those magazines. So we shot about three or four of them—maybe more, maybe less. I know it was more than three. We shot quite a few rounds.

"All of sudden a white flag came out and we quit firing and they came out. I motioned for them to come on up and they came up. I don't know how many more were dead in there or anything. That's why we got all the troops up pretty soon on that part of the beach.

"[Private First Class Lewis J.] Raimundo got killed; in fact he was the first guy. They came the same way we did up the hill. He came up right after we got the prisoners.

"He said, 'I'll go back down to get the company.'

"And I said, 'Don't go down there, there are snipers and stuff around there, too. Raimundo stay here. They'll come up.'

"But he said, 'No, I'm going after them.' He went down.

"I heard one shot, I said, 'Yeah, he's had it.' A sniper got him."[56]

Meanwhile at the demolished building, Lieutenant Spalding and the rest of his boat section had been waiting for Streczyk and Gallagher to find a route through the minefield to the top of the slope. "In the meantime, we were getting heavy small arms fire. One burst from a [machine gun] left a series of dots along the wall in front of us (at some places the demolished wall was 1½-2 feet high and we were hiding behind that and the brush). [Private] Lewis J. Raimundo was killed here, the only man killed in my section on the beach D-Day. One other man was killed later on the hill. On our left we had bypassed a pillbox, from which MG [machine gun] fire was coming and mowing down F Company people a hundred yards to our left. There was nothing we could do to help them. We could still see no one to the right and there was no one up to us on the left. We didn't know what had become of the rest of E Company. Back in the water, boats were in flames. I saw a tank ashore about 07:30 to 07:45. After a couple looks back, we decided we wouldn't look back anymore.

This is the demolished building with the brush around it as described in the account by Lieutenant John M. Spalding. It was here that his Company E section was halted by a minefield beyond. Note the rocky shingle or shelf strewn with the supplies and equipment along the lower portion of the photograph. Thick rolls of barbed wire and the posts that secure them are to the right of the building. *Photograph by Lieutenant (jg) Stuart L. Brandel, United States Navy, courtesy of Tom Lane.*

This is a wider view of the same area with the demolished building at right. Sergeant Philip Streczyk and Private First Class Richard J. Gallagher cut through the wire to the left of the building and followed a dry streambed up the slope of the ridge in a slight saddle to reach the top of the bluff. *Photograph by Lieutenant (jg) Stuart L. Brandel, United States Navy, courtesy of Tom Lane.*

"About this time, Gallagher said to follow him up the defilade, which was about four hundred yards to the right of the pillbox. We were getting terrific small arms fire, but few were hit. About this time, we were nearly at the top of the hill. We returned fire, but couldn't hit them. We were also getting rifle fire. When Gallagher found the way up, I sent word back for my men to come up to the right. Sergeant Hubert W. Blades, [Staff] Sergeant Grant Phelps, Sergeant Joseph W. Slaydon, and Private First Class Raymond R. Curley went first. I went next; Sergeant [Fred] Bisco followed me and the rest of the section came along.

"I couldn't take my eye off the machine gun above us, so Sergeant Bisco kept saying, 'Lieutenant, watch out for the damn mines.' They were a little box type mine and it seemed that the place was infested with them, but I didn't see them. We lost no men coming through them, although H Company coming along the same trail a few hours later lost several men. The Lord was with us and we had an angel on each shoulder on that trip.

"Trying to get the machine gun above us, Sergeant Blades fired his bazooka and missed. He was then shot in the left arm almost immediately. Private First Class Curley, rifleman, was shot down next. Sergeant Phelps who had picked up Tilley's BAR on the beach, moved into position to fire and was shot in both legs. By this time practically all my section had moved up. We decided to rush the machine gun about fifteen yards away. You may say why hadn't we hit it? I don't know. As we rushed it, the lone German operating the gun threw up his hands and yelled, 'Kamerad.' We would have killed him, but we needed prisoners for interrogation, so I ordered the men not to shoot him.

"He was Polish. He said that there were sixteen Germans in the area; that they had been alerted that morning and were told they had to hold the beach. They had taken a vote on whether to fight and preferred not to, but the German non-coms made them. He said that there were sixteen Germans in the trench to the rear of his machine gun. He also said that he had not shot at Americans, although I had seen him hit three. I turned the PW [prisoner of war] over to Sergeant Blades, who was wounded. Blades gave his bazooka to Sergeant [Kenneth F.] Peterson and guarded the prisoner with a trench knife.

"We moved Curley, Blades, and other wounded into a defile and the medic, Private George Bowen, gave them first aid. He covered the whole beach [that our section crossed] that day; no man waited more than five minutes for first aid. His action did a lot to help morale. He got the DSC for his work.

"Coming up along the crest of the hill Sergeant Clarence Colson, who had picked up a BAR on the beach, began to give assault fire as he walked along firing the weapon from his hip. He opened up on the [enemy] machine gun to our right, firing so rapidly that his ammunition carrier had difficulty getting ammo to him fast enough. At this point Lieutenant [Kenneth] Bleau of G Company came up and contacted me. He had come up our trail. His company had landed in the second wave behind us. Just a few minutes later Captain [Joseph T.] Dawson of G Company came along. We still saw no one on the right. Captain Dawson asked if I knew where E Company was and I told him that I didn't know. He said that E Company was five hundred yards to my right, but he was thinking in terms of where they were supposed to land; they were actually 500-800 yards to our left…Dawson said that he was going into Colleville and told us to go in to the right. He had about two sections. Said he had just seen the battalion commander. This was about 08:00.

"I went over and talked to Lieutenant Bleau about the information we had gotten from the prisoner. I asked him to give us some support where the sixteen Germans were supposed to be. As we went up in this direction we hit a wooded area. We found a beautifully camouflaged trench which ran along in zigzag fashion, but we were afraid to go in. We went along the top of the trench spraying it with lead. We used bullets instead of grenades since we had very few grenades, and thought that the bullets would be more effective. We did not fix bayonets at any time during the attack.

"We turned to the right and hit a wooded area; got no fire from there, so we yelled to Lieutenant Bleau to shove off and he started for Colleville. There I stood, like a damn fool, waving him a fond farewell. We were headed for St. Laurent; G Company went on to Colleville-sur-Mer. H Company came up next under Lieutenant [John D.] Shelby.

"We were on top of the hill by 09:00. We advanced cautiously. We were the first platoon of the 16th to hit the top. I now had 21-22 men in my section. We had spent more time at the rubble than anywhere else and had taken up some time with the prisoner. As we went inland we heard rifle and machine gun fire to our right. Streczyk and Gallagher volunteered to check on the situation. Our men were spread out over an area 200-300 yards. They located a machine gunner with a rifleman on either side of him. Streczyk shot the gunner in the back and the riflemen surrendered. The two prisoners were German and refused to give us any information.

"With them in tow we continued to the west. We still saw no one [from the 116th Infantry] to the west. We were now in hedgerows and orchard country. We were watching our flanks and to the front and scouring the wooded area. We tended to send a sergeant with 3-4 men to check up on suspicious areas. We usually set up someone with an automatic weapon to cover them (we did not have any MGs at this time, however). We crossed through two minefields—one had a path through it which looked like it had been made for a long time. When we got through it we saw the 'Achtung Minen' sign. No one was lost; we still had an angel on each shoulder.

"We now found a construction shack near the strongpoint overlooking the E-1 draw. Sergeant Kenneth Peterson fired his bazooka into the tool shed, but no one came out. We were about to go on when I spied a piece of stovepipe about seventy yards away, sticking out of the ground. I formed my section into a semi-circular defensive position. We were now getting small arms fire again. Sergeant Streczyk and I went forward to investigate. We discovered an underground dugout. There was an 80mm mortar, a position for a 75[mm gun] and construction for a pillbox. All this overlooked the E-1 draw. The dugout was of cement, had radios, excellent sleeping facilities, and dogs. We started to drop a grenade in the ventilator, but Streczyk said, 'Hold on a minute,' and fired three shots down the steps into the dugout. He then yelled in Polish and German (he had interrogated the prisoners earlier) for them to come out. Four men, disarmed, came up. They brought 2-3 wounded. I yelled for Colson to bring 5-6 men. We began to get small arms fire from the right (west). I yelled for [Private First Class Edwin F.] Piasecki and [Private First Class Alexander] Sakowski to move forward to the edge of the draw. A firefight took place. The navy now began to place timed fire in the draw; this was about 10:00. Piasecki deployed 6-7 men; shot several Germans and chased a number down into the draw where they were taken care of by navy fire. (The 80mm was not manned; it had beautiful range cards and lots of ammunition.)

"When Colson came over I started down the line of communications trenches. The trenches led to the cliff over the beach. We were now behind the Germans, so we routed four out of a hole and got thirteen in the trenches. The trenches had Teller mines, hundreds of grenades, numerous machine guns. They were firing when we came up. We had a short fight with the thirteen men; they threw three grenades at us, but they didn't hit anyone. We found one dead man in the trenches, but don't know if we killed him. If we did, he was the only German we killed. We turned the prisoners over to Strecyk. Several of us went to check the trenches. I did a fool thing. After losing my carbine in the water, I had picked up a German rifle, but found I didn't know how to use it too well. When I started to check on the trenches I traded the German rifle to a soldier for a carbine and failed to check it. In a minute, I ran into a Kraut and pulled the trigger, but the safety was on. I reached for the safety catch and hit the clip release, so my clip hit the ground. I ran about fifty yards in nothing flat. Fortunately, Sergeant [Kenneth] Peterson had me covered and the German put up his hands. That business of not checking guns is certainly not habit forming.

"We next took out an AT [antitank] gun near the edge of the draw. There was little resistance. We now had the prisoners back near the dugout. We had split the section into three units. We got a little ineffective machine gun fire from the draw to the right at this time. We tried to use the [German] 80mm mortar, but no one could operate the German weapon. For the first time, I saw people across the draw to the right (west). I supposed that they were from the 116th. They seemed to be pinned down.

"About this time, two stragglers from the 116th came up. I didn't ask what company they were from, but just took them along. We went back and checked trenches since we were afraid of infiltration by the Germans. In the meantime, I sent the 17-19 German prisoners back with two men the way we had come. I told them to turn them over to anyone who would take them and to ask about our company. At this point I saw Lieutenant [Robert A.] Hutch of Company E (2nd Section, which had been directly to my left in the boats) coming up. I pointed out a minefield to him and he told me that there was a sniper near me. We had sniper fire every few feet now; we were getting pretty jittery. We set off our last yellow smoke grenade to let the navy know that we were Americans, since their timed fire was getting very close.

"About 10:45 Captain [Edward] Wozenksi of Company E came up from the left. He had come along practically the same route we had used. I was very happy to see him. We had orders to contact Major [William R.] Washington, 2nd Battalion executive officer, just outside Colleville. Our objective was changed; there were to be no patrols into Trévières that afternoon as we had been told originally. We never crossed the E-1 draw. Instead, we went along the trail towards Colleville. We were to swing into the fields to the right of Colleville.

"Lieutenant Hutch and I had about thirty men; he was in charge (I was a second lieutenant and he was a first lieutenant). Lieutenant James McGourty had also come with Captain Wozenski. We ran into Major Washington, executive officer, 2nd Battalion, near Colleville; he was in a ditch outside town. Captain Dawson had come up to Colleville, his original objective, earlier. G Company was already in and around the town. We got some small arms fire in this area, but no one was hurt.

"Lieutenant Hutch and I contacted Major Washington about 13:00. He told us we were to go to the right of Colleville and guard the right flank of the town. We went out and were surrounded in about forty minutes. Lieutenant [James A.] Krucas of G Company, with about fourteen men, came up and said he had the right flank, so we reinforced him (altogether Lieutenant Hutch, Lieutenant Krucas, and I had about forty-five men).

"In the position to the west of Colleville, we had set up our defensive position. We selected a position where no digging was necessary; used drainage ditches; we were now in orchards and hedgerows. We moved cautiously; didn't know where anybody was. About 15:00 we got German fire. [Private First Class Vincent] DiGaetano was hit in the [thigh] by shrapnel; we told him that he was too big to be missed. Sergeant [Fred] Bisco was killed; rifle fire hit him in the face and throat. Only one round of artillery came in; we thought it was from one of our ships—exploded about three hundred yards from us and had an orange and yellow flame. As we looked back towards the beach we saw several squads of Germans coming towards us. We had no contact with the battalion. Just as a G Company runner started over to us and got to the edge of our defenses they opened fire on him. After he fell they fired at least one hundred rounds of machine gun fire into him. It was terrible, but we do the same thing when we want to stop a runner from taking information.

"Of course, we didn't find out what he was coming to tell us. We fired until we were low on ammunition that afternoon. I had six rounds of carbine ammunition left. Some of the fellows were down to their last clip. We were still surrounded. We called a meeting of Lieutenants Krucas, Hutch, Technical Sergeant Ellis, Sergeant Streczyk and myself. About 17:00, we decided to fight our way back to the battalion. We sent word for the men to come to us in the ditch where we were; we were several hundred yards south and west of Colleville. At about 19:00 or 20:00, we set up automatic weapons to cover us as we crawled down the ditch back towards Colleville. Lieutenant Hutch went in front. We got back to battalion and ran into C Company of the 16th on the way to reinforce us. We didn't know where we were. We found Major Washington in a little gully at the west of town. He said we were to go back to about the same point with C Company in support.

"We took up defensive position about 500-700 yards from our original positions—this was closer to Colleville. We were still in hedgerows; we guarded roads and avenues of approach. I think that part of the company area bordered on the roads into Colleville. We now had machine guns (I believe from Company H). This was about 21:00, [and it was] nearly dark. It was quiet except for some aerial activity. We had heard American machine guns earlier in the afternoon; it is possible that they drove Germans towards us. We spent the night of the first day in the positions near Colleville."[57]

Captain Edward F. Wozenski
Company E, 16th Infantry Regiment, 1st Infantry Division

The other five sections of Company E landed to the east of Lieutenant Spalding's section, in the Fox Green sector and in front of the Colleville draw (Exit E-3), near the WN 62 resistance nest located on the west side of the draw. As his landing craft's ramp dropped, Captain Edward Wozenski had no way of knowing that the newly issued assault jackets he and his troops were wearing would contribute to the deaths of many soldiers that terrible day. "Just before the landing all of our web gear, standard web gear, issue gear, fine battle proven gear, was taken away from us because some theorist figured that it would be far easier and much more practical to wear a hunting-type jacket. So at the last minute we were issued these canvas jackets with elastic pockets all over the place and we transferred all our gear into these pockets.

"When we hit bottom, we had approximately four hundred yards to struggle through the water to the beach. There was small arms fire all around so you were up and down, ducking down, as terrified as anyone could be. Every time I got up I thought it was pure terror that was making my knees buckle until I finally hit the beach and realized I had about one hundred pounds of sand in the pockets of my jacket, sand that had accumulated on top of the fifty or sixty pound load we were all carrying in. When I finally got up to the shale I had my first sergeant with me and I asked him, 'For God's sake get a packet of cigarettes out,' and he had to dig out handfuls of sand before he could get a pack out for me…

"I was praying for smoke, any kind of smoke, so that we could get up through the wire. Heroics have nothing to do with it—their automatic weapons were trained on us and people cannot advance in daylight against automatic small arms. There were tanks burning, some landing craft had caught fire, and the general smoke and haze of a battlefield began to develop, and then through all this, off on a flank, I saw a yellow smoke flare. I knew this was one of our basic signals. All platoon leaders and platoon sergeants had yellow smoke flares and I had said the first son of a gun that gets up on top of that bluff will set off a smoke flare. I thought I would try and assemble as many people as I could and move down to the point where I thought the smoke flare went off and make a move up there because I knew I couldn't get up [the bluff] where I was.

"I remember distinctly taking my trench knife and pressing [the tip of the blade of] it into people's backs to see if they were alive. If they were alive, I would kick them or roll them over and say, 'Let's go!' I picked up half a dozen people this way, but I didn't realize that terror could be so great in a man that he would not turn around to see who was sticking a knife into him. Later on, it dawned on me that two or three of them were alive, but just wouldn't turn around because of absolute terror.

"We assembled maybe a dozen people, and about opposite the point where I saw the yellow smoke flare I started working my way up a path. Halfway up, I was climbing the bluff and I saw one of my platoon sergeants [Sergeant Philip Streczyk] coming down the other way with a big grin on his face. Right in front of my nose, as he steps down and puts his foot on a Teller mine. I said, 'My God, how stupid can you be?' and he said, 'Oh, don't let it worry you; it didn't go off when I stepped on it going up.' When we got to the top of the cliff I had a head count. I landed 180 men and eight officers. I counted thirteen men and one other officer besides myself."[58]

Upon reaching the top of the bluff, Captain Wozenski learned that Sergeant Streczyk had been the soldier who had sent up the yellow smoke. "If Sergeant Streczyk did not earn a Congressional Medal of Honor, no one ever did. Thousands of men were on the beach being killed like flies—to lift your head over the shale was to invite quick death. Yet, Sergeant Streczyk led a small group up the bluffs, cleared out enemy pillboxes, and released a flare indicating his breakthrough, which I and others followed. To the best of my knowledge the major part of the 1st Division and even the corps went up the path cleared by Streczyk."[59]

The commander of the 2nd Battalion, 16th Infantry, Lieutenant Colonel Herbert Hicks, was an eyewitness to much of the actions of Captain Wozenski and wrote the following in his recommendation for the award of the Distinguished Service Cross. "The assault craft of his company were severely battered by the intense fire and underwater mines, and terrible casualties were inflicted upon the helpless men. Despite the fact that comparative safety lay shoreward, and that his craft were the target for vicious fire, Captain Wozenski, with utter disregard for his personal safety, remained in the fire swept surf, directing and helping his heavily laden men in their struggle to reach shore. On reaching shore, Captain Wozenski found the remnants of his company scattered over a thousand yards of beach, with equipment and weapons lost or destroyed. Disdaining cover or rest, Captain Wozenski moved up and down the beach collecting serviceable weapons and reorganizing his company.

"Heedless of the fact that his movements over the beach drew constant fire, he set an inspiring example of calm courage when he worked his way on to the flat, open meadow directly under enemy guns in search of a breach through the heavy, fire covered [barbed wire] entanglements. When his depleted company was reformed, Captain Wozenski led the way through the breach in the face of extremely heavy fire concentrated on this exit. This breach, forced by Captain Wozenski was, for many hours, the only exit for the hard hit assault units on beach Easy Red.

"During the torturous slow advance up the face of the high ridge, enemy fire was poured on this serious threat. Particularly severe fire came from a well dug in, protected emplacement on the slope protecting Exit E-1. When the intense demoralizing fire from the powerful enemy installation threatened to completely stop the attack, Captain Wozenski displayed magnificent courage. Ordering his men to deploy to the flanks of the position, Captain Wozenski advanced to within one hundred yards directly in front of the embrasure and engaged the fortification with his rifle. The machine gun immediately directed its fire at him, but with complete disregard for his own safety, he held his position until his men could take advantage of his fearless diversion to destroy the enemy strongpoint, freeing the exit of a great portion of the heavy fire which swept it.

"Once more, Captain Wozenski paused only long enough to reorganize his company, adding to them the remnants of other organizations which had passed through the breach. The fanatically resisting enemy made progress inland extremely costly and slow. Constantly at the head of his forward attacking elements, Captain Wozenski led assault after assault on the enemy, until his company objective was finally seized and held."[60]

First Sergeant Lawrence J. Fitzsimmons
Company E, 16th Infantry Regiment, 1st Infantry Division

Captain Edward Wozenski was standing next to his company's first sergeant at the front of the landing craft transporting the Company E headquarters section when it touched down on Fox Green. "When his craft beached on the fire swept shore, First Sergeant Fitzsimmons exposed himself to the direct vicious artillery, mortar, and machine gun fire concentrated on the craft to forcefully pry open a defective landing ramp. He then led the men to the protection of the seven yard shale shelf. Without the slightest regard for his personal safety he repeatedly exposed himself to enemy fire in organizing his company. On three separate occasions with utter disregard for his own personal safety he dashed back into the fire swept surf to aid wounded and struggling men to reach the shore.

"First Sergeant Fitzsimmons during this period exposed himself to the vicious enemy fire to search a thousand yards of beach to locate the platoons of his company in an effort to help in their reorganization. When his organization had reached the comparative safety of the heights above the beach, First Sergeant Fitzsimmons voluntarily returned to the extremely dangerous beach, through two uncharted enemy minefields to locate those still missing from the ranks of the company. On this mission he thoroughly searched the entire beach and returned not only with several men and desperately needed radio equipment, but brought back an almost complete report of his company's dead and wounded still on the heavily shelled beach. First Sergeant Lawrence Fitzsimmons' extraordinary heroism under demoralizing fire and his calm issuance of vital orders were an inspiration to the men of E Company and were instrumental in his company's successful assault on its objectives."[61]

Technical Sergeant Calvin L. Ellis
Company E, 16th Infantry Regiment, 1st Infantry Division

Captain Wozenski was also an eyewitness to the courage of Technical Sergeant Calvin L. Ellis, one of the Company E assistant section leaders, who "was aboard a landing craft which came under intense enemy fire as it neared the shore. When the craft grounded the accurate hostile fire inflicted heavy casualties on the section, including the section leader. Technical Sergeant Ellis unhesitatingly assumed command of the unit and prepared to lead the section to land. Although a constant target for incessant enemy fire, he remained in the water, getting his section back under control and assisting the wounded through the surf. While remaining in the sea to assist members of his section to shore, Sergeant Ellis was seriously wounded in the head, but he persisted in efforts and got the entire section ashore and behind the cover of a low shale bank.

"Despite the great pain of his wounds, he refused to stop for medical aid or evacuation, and coolly maintained control and organization in his section. When he saw one of his men, wounded and weighed down with heavy equipment, still in the surf and struggling for his life, Sergeant Ellis unhesitatingly left the covered position and reentered the deadly area. Completely ignoring the hail of fire about him, he proceeded to the side of the helpless man. Picking up the wounded comrade, Sergeant

Ellis, although weakened by his own wounds, carried him back across the fire swept beach and to cover where he could be given medical aid.

"Refusing to stay in the covered position, Sergeant Ellis immediately began a hazardous reconnaissance of the area, to locate men of his section who had become separated during the landing. During a period when the slightest movement on the beach brought additional accurate fire crashing into the area, he repeatedly exposed himself to reach his men and to assemble the group. With the section again intact, Sergeant Ellis proceeded on another fearless trip up the beach to locate an exit for his men. Returning to the group, he rapidly led them across the beach and through a breach just blown in the enemy wire and across the remaining beach to join the section of his company which had effected the initial breakthrough. Enemy resistance in the area of this first breakthrough was especially fierce and determined efforts were made to prevent Sergeant Ellis' group from getting through. When direct fire from an enemy emplacement pinned his section down, he unhesitatingly advanced alone in the face of the intense fire and assaulted the position. With the enemy knocked out, he led the section on inland and up into the high ground.

"Company E, 16th Infantry was at this time almost entirely surrounded by the enemy, and fire from numerous concealed snipers and machine guns was inflicting heavy casualties on the company. The terrain, full of hedgerows and ditches, was ideally suited to the purpose of the enemy. Sergeant Ellis, after fighting through to the organization, was placed on the right flank where enemy action was fiercest. In addition to maintaining numerous concealed positions, the enemy was attempting to infiltrate into the newly won territory. A constant target for the accurate enemy fire, Sergeant Ellis moved throughout the exposed area and placed his men in positions to hold off the enemy. He then proceeded personally to find the concealed positions of snipers firing at his company. Upon ascertaining the position of one [of the snipers], he fearlessly advanced upon the dug in enemy until he could get within grenade range and knocked the position out. This heroic solitary assault into prepared positions was repeated successfully on three separate occasions and Sergeant Ellis' personal bravery and aggressive actions were largely responsible for the maintenance of the flank. With the company flank secured, Sergeant Ellis moved his section into new positions to cover not only his own company, but his entire battalion's right, and personally led repeated attacks on groups of infiltrating enemy, stopping every attempt to penetrate the line."[62]

Captain Edward Wozenski made recommendations for members of Lieutenant John Spalding's 1st Section, no doubt with Spalding's input regarding those actions. However, it is apparent that these recommendations contain some assertions which don't square with Lieutenant Spalding's account.

Staff Sergeant Curtis Colwell
Company E, 16th Infantry Regiment, 1st Infantry Division

Captain Wozenski wrote the following recommendation regarding Staff Sergeant Curtis Colwell's heroic actions. "Staff Sergeant Colwell fearlessly moved from behind the protecting shelf and while under withering machine gun and mortar fire, calmly cut a gap in the wire sufficiently large to allow his men to pass through. Advancing rapidly across the beach, he skillfully led his section over the unmarked minefield. Pressing forward under an unceasing hail of machine gun and sniper bullets, he directed his men up the side of the cliff toward a powerful and dangerous nest of machine guns. The remainder of the company followed at some distance the path which Staff Sergeant Colwell was blazing through the enemy defenses. As he and his section approached their objective the direct fire from the emplacements became unceasingly fierce. Displaying a superb courage and complete disregard for his own safety, Staff Sergeant Colwell led the advance against the enemy emplacements and successfully destroyed the machine gun positions. By eliminating this obstacle, Staff Sergeant Colwell made an exit available for his company in its advance from the beach towards their inland objectives. Staff Sergeant Colwell's action in breaching the enemy beach defenses supplied one of the first urgently needed breakthroughs for the invading forces."[63]

Sergeant Clarence Colson
Company E, 16th Infantry Regiment, 1st Infantry Division

Captain Wozenski wrote the following regarding Sergeant Clarence Colson's actions as part of the recommendation for the award of the DSC. "The LCVP carrying Sergeant Clarence Colson and the mortar unit he was leading, grounded some four hundred yards from shore. The men soon reached deeper water and were forced to swim. Sergeant Colson moved from one weakened man to another, encouraging and aiding them shoreward despite the enemy machine gun bullets which raked them. On reaching the beach Sergeant Colson discovered that his weapon had been made unfit for use by the accumulation of sand in the moving parts. Determined to continue the attack as soon as possible, Sergeant Colson secured the automatic rifle of a wounded man and moved across several hundred yards of the exposed fire swept beach, locating and reorganizing his scattered section as he went. With complete disregard for his own personal safety and ignoring cover, Sergeant Colson took up a firing position on top of the shelf in clear view of the enemy and directed his fire at the nearest enemy machine gun emplacement while one of his men cut a gap in the wire. Firing as he advanced, Sergeant Colson then led his section through the thickly strewn minefield, up the steep cliff like slope to attack the enemy machine gun emplacement firing on them. Despite enemy hand grenades thrown at him, Sergeant Colson reached the parapet of the strongpoint and leaped into it with his automatic rifle blazing. In the ensuing action against overwhelming odds, Sergeant Colson killed several of the enemy and secured seventeen prisoners."[64]

Sergeant Kenneth F. Peterson
Company E, 16th Infantry Regiment, 1st Infantry Division

Captain Wozenski wrote the following as a part of the recommendation for the Distinguished Service Cross for Sergeant Kenneth F. Peterson. "Sergeant Kenneth F. Peterson, rocketeer of the E Company first assault section, played a major part in the success of the entire operation and was directly responsible for his own company's successful completion of its mission. Armed with a bazooka, he showed utter disregard for his own personal safety by constantly exposing himself to enemy fire while leading the assaults on the concrete positions. Sergeant Peterson displayed complete determination, great personal bravery and fierce devotion to duty as he charged alone into the countless machine gun positions, troop trenches and communication tunnels across an uncharted minefield. He alone killed or captured the emplaced enemy in at least two pillboxes. He continued to lead the assault through the blanket of direct enemy fire until he reached the top of the hill where he took emplacements and held a dangerously exposed position from which he covered the troops."[65]

Sergeant Philip Streczyk
Company E, 16th Infantry Regiment, 1st Infantry Division

Captain Wozenski wrote this recommendation for the Distinguished Service Cross for Sergeant Philip Streczyk, who led the way to the top of the bluff, behind whom much of the 16th Infantry followed. "On 6 June 1944, the 16th Regimental Combat Team assaulted the coast of France north of Colleville-sur-Mer against a determined prepared enemy, who dominated the beach from concrete pillboxes and emplacements. The landings were viciously opposed and thousands of troops were pinned down on a seven yard beachhead by intense accurate artillery, machine gun, and sniper fire. There was no exit for the assault troops and the beachhead appeared to be threatened with annihilation. The only cover was afforded by the high water level and the incoming tide was driving the hard hit fire swept troops onto the enemy dominated and mine strewn flats. The situation was extremely critical and the success of the V Corps invasion efforts dangerously imperiled. Sergeant Streczyk, Company E, 16th Infantry, landed in the assault and with his company cut down by fifty percent casualties, found himself pinned down on a beach crowded with men shoulder to shoulder with no means of egress. In the face of vicious enemy fire, Sergeant Streczyk led his platoon across the beach, setting an example of extraordinary courage and heroism. He cut through the enemy wire, led his platoon through a minefield and up a steep hill overlooking the beach. This was the only beach exit available to the troops of the 1st Division and V Corps for almost forty-eight hours. It was the reason for the saving of thousands of lives, and was vital in the successful assault that followed. Although landed at the wrong part of the beach, Sergeant Streczyk then led his section to attack the key strongpoint of beach Exit E-1 and in a vicious costly fight, cleared it out, killing a score of Germans, and further insured the success of the regimental and division invasion."[66]

Private First Class George H. Bowen
Medical Detachment, Company E, 16th Infantry Regiment, 1st Infantry Division

Captain Wozenski wrote the following regarding the courageous actions of Private First Class George H. Bowen in this recommendation for the Distinguished Service Cross. "The long prepared hostile emplacements dug into the cliffs behind the beaches laid a withering fire of artillery, machine guns, and small arms over the entire beach area and the waters approaching it. These waters were strewn with heavily mined, almost impassable obstacles, and many of the landing craft were burning or sinking from direct artillery hits or contact with the mines. Severe losses of personnel and equipment were inflicted upon the regiment before the beach was gained and once on the sands the assault troops were pinned down onto a seven yard beachhead by sweeping machine gun crossfire and bursting artillery; and barbed wire and uncharted minefields prevented further advance.

Wave after wave piled onto the beach until thousands of men lay packed into the shallow strip, confused and scattered by the losses of their leaders and equipment. The only cover afforded was that of a slight shale shelf at the high water level.

"When the assault craft on which Private First Class Bowen was coming in neared the shore and began disembarking its men they were subjected to intense automatic weapons fire. As the men waded into the waist to shoulder high deep water, laden with heavy equipment, some were wounded and were in grave danger of drowning. When a seriously wounded soldier, weakened to the point where he could not progress, almost drowned, Private First Class Bowen, completely disregarding the gravest personal danger, stopped in his efforts to reach the shore and waded through the heavily mined and fire swept water to the stricken comrade's assistance. Despite the never ceasing hail of fire, he dragged the man to the shore. After treating the man and leaving him in a position of comparative safety, Private First Class Bowen proceeded to the aid of the many wounded [troops] lying about the beach. Repeatedly dashing into the fire swept areas, he administered aid to numerous casualties on the shore. Throughout the entire period of his stay on the beach, he ignored completely the constant bursting mortar shells and machine gun fire in his efforts to aid and pull into cover the wounded, [and] refusing to rest or take cover.

"As the reorganization progressed and Company E, to which he was attached, prepared to lead the assault through a breach in the wire on the positions to the rear of the beach, Private First Class Bowen stayed in the intense fire throughout the advance in order to be near the men whose medical aid he was responsible. During the attack, comrades were wounded in an assault on an enemy machine gun nest high on the slopes of the dominating cliffs. The wounded men lay helpless and exposed to the vicious fire. In order to reach these wounded comrades, Private First Class Bowen crossed an uncharted minefield. Friendly and enemy fire was striking all about him as he moved forward on his difficult mission. Displaying the highest courage, he approached to within fifteen yards of the enemy's machine gun nest and rendered first aid to the stricken men. Still completely exposed to the heavy fire, Private Fist Class Bowen returned to his unit and continued to work unceasingly. His calm and courageous attitude inspired the men to continue the costly advance."[67]

Private First Class Richard J. Gallagher
Company E, 16th Infantry Regiment, 1st Infantry Division

Captain Wozenski wrote the recommendation for the award of the Distinguished Service Cross to Private First Class Richard J. Gallagher, who along with Sergeant Streczyk, led the way to the top of the bluff, behind whom much of the 16th Infantry followed. "On 6 June 1944, Company E of the 16th Infantry assaulted the coast of France near Colleville-sur-Mer. The entire company, along with thousands of men, was pinned down on a seven yard strip of beach with a two foot shale bank affording the only protection from a concentrated hail of enemy fire. The enemy was delivering artillery and mortar fire from reinforced concrete pillboxes strategically located on the cliffs overlooking the shore and supplemented this with raking machine gun bursts and sniper fire from well dug in positions. Under this fierce barrage Private First Class Gallagher left his partially protected position and advanced across an uncharted minefield toward enemy emplacements. Undeterred by the continued withering fire, mines, and barbed wire entanglements, he continued up the slope toward a machine gun nest which had been inflicting heavy casualties on his company. Using hand grenades and his rifle Private First Class Gallagher wiped out the machine gun nest.

"Private First Class Gallagher returned to the fire swept beach. Upon reaching the beach, he worked his way over to several men in his section who were pinned down by enemy fire and led them through the minefield. When he had once more scaled the cliff under the constant sniper and machine gun fire, he proceeded along the top of the cliff to a wooded area from which a machine gun had been pouring forth a deadly stream of fire. In a short time, Private First Class Gallagher located the weapon and captured not only the German firing the machine gun, but also captured an enemy rifleman who was sniping from the cliff. All of these actions were performed by Private First Class Gallagher while the greater part of his company was still pinned down on the beach, and the enemy's firepower and defensive positions had suffered little damage."[68]

Company F, 16th Infantry was the other rifle company of the 2nd Battalion assigned to land in the first infantry wave. It was supposed to land on the eastern half of the Easy Red sector. However, only the 2nd Section landed at the planned location. The 1st, 3rd, and Company Headquarters Sections of Company F landed on the eastern edge of the Easy Red sector, just west of the Colleville draw E-3 and almost in front of the WN 62 resistance nest. The 4th and 5th Sections landed to the east directly in front of the E-3 draw on the western edge of the Fox Green sector, which was the responsibility of the 3rd Battalion, 16th Infantry Regiment.

Two sections of Company F, 16th Infantry Regiment disembark from LCVPs 18 and 19 on the eastern edge of the Easy Red sector shortly after H-Hour. *United States Coast Guard photograph, National Archives.*

Staff Sergeant David N. Radford
Company F, 16th Infantry Regiment, 1st Infantry Division

Staff Sergeant David N. Radford's extraordinary heroism was witnessed by Lieutenant Colonel Herbert C. Hicks, Jr., the commanding officer of the 2nd Battalion, 16th Infantry Regiment. "Staff Sergeant David Radford was the only member of the Company F wire team to successfully complete the long and torturous trek from the landing craft to the beach, through thickly strewn fields of floating and sunken mines and innumerable delaying obstacles of all types. Crawling up on the sandy shore, Radford saw thousands of men pinned down behind a narrow shelf of shale by streams of machine gun and small arms fire and being pounded unmercifully by well directed mortar and artillery fire. In the face of this terrific fire, minefields, and triple aprons of barbed wire, further advance was seemingly impossible. Arming himself with two Bangalore torpedoes and disregarding the great personal danger involved, Staff Sergeant Radford climbed over the shale and advanced through the thirty yards of open terrain to the aprons of barbed wire. Finding the depth of wire too great for the Bangalores he retraced his steps back to the fire swept beach where he secured another torpedo. Still ignoring his own safety and defying the murderous fire directed at him by a score of enemy weapons, Radford returned to the barbed wire, attached his three Bangalores in the most advantageous position and then set them off, blowing a huge gap in the triple apron. After creating the opening in the wire, he signaled to his section on the beach that the mission was completed and then personally led them through the wire in the face of ever increasing machine gun fire, across a strategically laid enemy minefield and hence to a position on the hill from where it was possible to direct fire upon the enemy's left flank. This position proved to be a vital factor in the success of the entire invasion operation, while the gap blasted in the wire by Radford was the main avenue through which the American troops poured to fight and pursue the enemy."[69]

Private First Class Theodore T. Wilk
Company F, 16th Infantry Regiment, 1st Infantry Division

Lieutenant Andrew D. Hanley was one of the Company F, 16th Infantry section leaders. "When the men finally struggled through the treacherous seas and reached the shore, they sought what little cover they could find, and the entire wave piled up behind a low shale shelf on the beach. With many of their leaders [becoming] casualties and much of their valuable equipment lost, the men huddled in the slight cover from flat trajectory fire while artillery and mortar fire continued to inflict casualties. The need for firepower to engage the enemy was acute; the entire 1st Division effort was threatened by the critical situation on the beach.

"Acting entirely on his own initiative, Private First Class Wilk unhesitatingly left his relatively safe position and moved forward to fire upon the embrasures of the enemy positions above and less than four hundred yards from him. During this crucial period, every motion on the beach drew additional accurate fire crashing into the area and expert snipers fired at every individual who attempted to change position. Completely ignoring the great danger, Private First Class Wilk persisted in his efforts and pushed forward over entirely exposed terrain until he could fire upon the enemy effectively. Private First Class Wilk sniped from this position, in clear view of the enemy and under constant fire, with extreme accuracy. His fire was instrumental in making the powerful emplacements reduce fire and button up. In the course of this heroic action, Private First Class Wilk was painfully wounded, but he ignored the wound, refusing to leave his post for medical aid.

"When the company was able to move, Private First Class Wilk left his extremely dangerous post and pushed inland with his comrades, taking always a leading part in the bitter hand to hand fighting for the strongpoints blocking the way. Despite the pain of his early wound, he maintained throughout the push a brilliant example of skillful and determined effort to close with and to wipe out the enemy. When the company's advance was halted by the direct fire of a well dug in machine gun, Private First Class Wilk volunteered to join a small group in the advance upon it. Again, with utter disregard for his personal safety, he moved forward through the hail of fire directed at him in his effort to get within grenade range of the enemy. When the enemy laid a mortar barrage on the group, Private First Class Wilk refused to take cover or abandon his effort. He was determinedly pushing forward when one of the exploding shells caught him, inflicting serious wounds and totally blinding him."[70]

Staff Sergeant Raymond F. Strojny
Company F, 16th Infantry Regiment, 1st Infantry Division

Staff Sergeant Raymond F. Strojny, with the 3rd Section of Company F, landed on Fox Green, slightly west of Exit E-3, the Colleville draw and in front of the WN 62 resistance nest. "I saw that our sector was too vulnerable to enemy fire, so I gave the word for all to move to the left to get behind [low sand dune] hills for protection…I was doing this because all my superiors were dead or wounded. Someone had to take over—I had lots of combat experience; all relied on me…

"I saw an enemy gun knocking three of our tanks out in a matter of minutes. That was the end of our tank support. I spotted the gun emplacement, called for a bazooka team. None were available, as they were dead or wounded. So I went searching for a bazooka on the beach, knowing that that gun had to be knocked out to make our sector a success. I found a bazooka and ammunition, came back to the original position, then figured a way as to best fire at the gun emplacement, and then crossed a minefield all alone with bazooka and ammunition. I got a good field of fire, was ready to fire, [then] discovered the bazooka was damaged, but I had to try it. Maybe it was not damaged enough. I had to take the chance. I was alone, so I loaded it and fired it alone. I fired it till I ran out of ammunition, then went back to the beach, found more ammunition, came back to the bazooka, and took up firing again. On the last round I saw the gun emplacement blow up. I believe I hit ammunition in the gun emplacement, as it was opening up to fire again. On the last round fired I was wounded. The bullet entered [my helmet] above my left eye, circled my head, and left [the helmet] above my left ear."[71]

The first wave of the 3rd Battalion consisted of Company I, which was assigned to land on the western side of the Fox Green sector and Company L, which was assigned to land on the eastern half of Fox Green at H+1 minute. However, as the LCAs carrying Company I approached the coast, Captain Kimball R. Richmond could see that they were clearly more than a mile to the east of the correct beach sector and heading for cliffs with no beach. He ordered the landing craft to take his company to the correct beach. On the way, the landing craft carrying the 4th and 5th Sections of Company I became swamped and began to sink. A control boat picked them up and took them to a troop transport ship. With Company I now thirty minutes late, Captain Richmond contacted Lieutenant Colonel Charles T. Horner, Jr., the commanding officer of the 3rd Battalion, 16th Infantry, by radio and informed him of the situation. Horner then ordered Company K to take over Company I's assignment. The four remaining LCAs transporting Company I touched down at around 8:00 a.m., well after the 3rd Battalion's other rifle companies had landed.

This 50mm PAK 38 pedestal mounted antitank gun in an open concrete lined emplacement was part of the WN 61 resistance nest which guarded the eastern side of the Colleville draw (Exit E-3). This type of gun could rapidly fire both antitank and high explosive rounds. It was sited to cover the length of the antitank ditch (in the background beyond the gun running diagonally in the photograph) which blocked the entrance to the draw and together with 50mm antitank gun at WN 62 (prior page) place in a crossfire tanks or other vehicles such as bulldozers approaching the entrance to the draw. This is possibly the gun that Staff Sergeant Raymond F. Strojny knocked out using a damaged bazooka. *Photograph by Lieutenant (jg) Stuart L. Brandel, United States Navy, courtesy of Tom Lane.*

Captain Kimball R. Richmond
Company I, 16th Infantry Regiment, 1st Infantry Division

Because of the delay, Lieutenant Colonel Horner, the battalion commander, was already ashore as the four landing craft transporting Company I approached the Fox Green sector beach. "On 6 June 1944 at about 08:30 hours, I Company, 16th Infantry was attempting to land on the beach near Colleville-sur-Mer. While still some distance from the shore, enemy batteries opened up on the boats destroying two of the [four] company assault craft. The other [two] boats continued coming in until about 250 yards from the beach, they struck mines and went up in flames. Captain Richmond jumped from his boat and swam to shore through a hail of machine gun bullets and artillery fire from reinforced concrete pillboxes in impregnable commanding positions. Upon reaching the shore, he gathered together the remainder of his company on the beach, exposing himself constantly to the vicious fire which had pinned down thousands of the assault troops on the 7½-yard beachhead.

This antitank gun positioned in an open emplacement on the west side of the Colleville draw (Exit E-3) was sited to place fire along the length of the antitank ditch which blocked the entrance to the draw and the beach to the east of the draw. This gun and the one in the previous photo were sited to place approaching tanks, bulldozers, and other armored vehicles in a crossfire. Note the netting to camouflage the gun from observation. *Photograph by Lieutenant (jg) Stuart L. Brandel, United States Navy, courtesy of Tom Lane.*

"With two officers and ten enlisted men of his company he worked his way along the fire swept crowded beach to contact remnants of K Company, where he found their commanding officer and executive officer casualties, and the company disorganized. Captain Richmond quickly organized the men for an attack against an enemy strongpoint about two hundred yards to the left flank. Displaying inspirational courage, he led his men forward through a mine strewn field in a magnificent assault on the enemy strongpoint. In the face of withering direct fire, Captain Richmond himself drove into the enemy emplacements, and smashed the fanatically resisting enemy forces. This action constituted the first large scale breakthrough and the way cleared by Captain Richmond enabled the 3rd Battalion to move forward off the fire swept deathtrap beach.

"By knocking out the enemy weapons the flanking fire which had been inflicting heavy casualties on the entire regimental combat team was removed. Without rest, Captain Richmond pushed inland against the enemy. With a magnificent display of courage, he led assault after assault against the Germans. Completely disregarding his own safety, he moved across open terrain in spite of concentrated fire to stop the advance. With a small group of men, he led in the seizure of Le Grand Hameau and held it for five hours before other units of the combat team caught up with him. In holding this town, Captain Richmond brilliantly led his men in fighting off several attacks by a full company of reinforced enemy infantry."[72]

Company L also lost an LCA when the landing craft transporting the 4th Section sunk a couple of miles offshore due to the rough sea. The men were in the water for between two and three hours before being picked up. Four of them drowned and four others were missing and presumed drowned. The other five landing craft transporting Company L approached the beach around 7:00 a.m., some thirty minutes late.

Captain John R. Armellino
Company L, 16th Infantry Regiment, 1st Infantry Division

Captain John R. Armellino was the commanding officer of Company L, 16th Infantry Regiment. "About a quarter-mile from the beach, all hell broke loose. The landing craft came under an intense attack, including mortar and artillery fire. One of my landing craft took a direct hit from enemy fire as it was unloading onto the beach. Half the men on this craft had already left the boat when it was hit. Some of these men crossed the beach. The remainder were either killed or wounded. As we landed, enemy fire peppered the ramps as they were lowered to allow my men to disembark and cross the two hundred yards of open beach. The German pillboxes and machine gun nests were laying a vicious crossfire on the beach. Many men were cut down as they left the landing craft. Small arms, mortar, and artillery fire were all concentrated on the landing area, but we suffered our greatest casualties just after touching down because of the crossfire of the German automatic weapons.

"Few of the landing craft were able to make a dry landing. Most of them grounded on sandbars fifty to one hundred yards off the beach. The water was neck deep. Some men climbed over the sides of the landing craft trying to avoid enemy fire. We lost some of these men because in the excitement they failed to open their garrison belts and the weight of their equipment took them under water. Some of these men drowned while others shed the equipment and swam to shore. The water was loaded with obstacles to which mines were attached. Those who reached shore started running across the beach through heavy machine gun crossfire, mortars, and artillery fire. We headed towards a bluff to give us cover. I lost many of those young soldiers who joined my company right before the invasion in England. They had no fear and failed to hit the ground after every few yards, running directly for cover. The more seasoned men hit the ground very often and as a result avoided being hit by enemy fire. After reaching the cover of the bluff, I began to reorganize my company. I had approximately 125 men left of the 200 I started with. I directed my lieutenants to organize their sections for the start of the attack to knock out the pillboxes and to advance to and capture our objective—Colleville-sur-Mer.

"I directed one of my officers, Lieutenant [Jimmie W.] Monteith, to move his section up a draw to take out a pillbox that was laying heavy automatic fire on the beach. The other sections were ordered to move up on his flanks towards the village of Colleville-sur-Mer. Lieutenant Monteith accomplished his mission, knocking out the pillbox, and taking several German prisoners. In the process of doing so, Lieutenant Monteith was killed by German automatic fire coming from this bunker. He had exposed himself to enemy fire time and time again while repeatedly standing up to lead his section. I recommended Lieutenant Monteith for the Congressional Medal of Honor, which he received posthumously for his brave deeds.

"As my combat sections were moving forward, I went over to one of our tanks to direct supporting fire. I had already called regimental headquarters for additional naval fire on the German positions, which was badly needed. As I was directing the tank commander where to fire, I was hit and knocked down by enemy fire. My right leg was gushing blood. A piece of shrapnel from an antitank grenade had severed the main artery. An antitank grenade is designed to pierce a tank and explode inside, killing its crew. In this case, it exploded prematurely and a piece of shrapnel hit me. A medic came to my assistance quickly. He applied a tourniquet to stop the bleeding, treated the wound with penicillin, and wrapped it with bandage. He then told me to remain on the beach and I would be evacuated after dark.

"I stayed on the beach the entire day under cover of the bluff and witnessed the successive waves of our troops cut down by the savage crossfire laid down by the Germans. By dusk, the beach was covered with dead and wounded soldiers. You could hardly walk the beach without stepping on the body of a dead or wounded soldier. While I was waiting to be evacuated, I sent some men to the low water mark to carry the wounded or dead off the beach towards the bluff, so that they would not be carried out to sea with the tide change. It was the last order I ever gave."[73]

Lieutenant Colonel Charles Horner, the 3rd Battalion commander, was an eyewitness to the extraordinary heroism of Captain Armellino that morning. "From carefully prepared positions and pillboxes, the enemy swept the entire invasion area with artillery, mortars and machine guns. Expert snipers, their rifles equipped with telescopic sights, were strategically placed on the cliff overlooking the beach. Carefully laid minefields and numerous booby traps, as well as double apron bands of barbed wire, covered the area between the waterfront and the hill, while the channel itself was strewn with floating and submerged mines and hindering obstacles of all kinds, in addition to being constantly raked by mortar, artillery, and heavy machine gun fire. Of the five craft carrying Company L, two were set afire and the other three suffered hits which killed and injured many of the troops. Upon reaching the beach, the troops were mowed down before they could leave their landing craft and the success of the entire operation in this sector was seriously threatened by the inability of the men to reach the shores in organized fighting units.

"Captain Armellino, commanding Company L, moved among his men with inspiring coolness and leadership, assembling them behind the slight cover afforded by a three foot shelf of shale. The unceasing, accurate fire from the cliffs pinned his company on the crowded narrow strip of beach. At a time when any movement drew deadly fire from snipers and machine guns, Captain Armellino traversed the exposed beach for 250 yards to a group of four tanks, which had been rendered immobile by enemy shells. Upon reaching the tanks, which were a prime objective for the enemy gunners, he stood before the tanks on the flat open ground below the enemy, coolly disregarding the hail of shells falling about him, and directed their fire on the enemy strongpoints. For forty-five minutes, Captain Armellino continued to move between his company and the tanks, coordinating their action.

Each dash across the open beach was met with fierce concentration of enemy fire by the watchful and numerous gunners on the cliff. On his last dash back to his company, Captain Armellino was hit by enemy fire and severely wounded. Despite his serious wounds, he directed his men in their assault against the enemy emplacement, which was successfully attacked and destroyed."[74]

Staff Sergeant James A. Wells
Company L, 16th Infantry Regiment, 1st Infantry Division

Captain John Armellino observed Staff Sergeant James A. Wells as he paved the way for the Company L advance. "The intensity of the enemy fire was so great that the first wave, upon reaching the sands, took cover behind a slight shale shelf, and there they were pinned down; the fire swept beach wired and mined, a seemingly impassable obstacle. Succeeding waves piled up behind the first until there were thousands of men concentrated on the strip of sheltered beach only a few yards deep and several hundred yards long. The unanswered enemy fire was causing great numbers of casualties among the men as the whole invasion effort of the 1st Division was threatened by the seemingly hopeless situation along the beach. Company L, 16th Infantry was among the units there, pinned down by the fire, and unable to advance through the wire and over the mined beach to its objective. Staff Sergeant Wells with two other men from his company volunteered to leave the relative safety afforded by the shale and proceeded to crawl through the constant fire on the beach to the wire. Completely ignoring the deadly fire falling all about him, he chopped his way through the double apron fence and out onto the beach beyond. This area was mined so heavily that it seemed impossible to pass through it safely.

"He picked his way through the field, safely reaching the ground at the base of the slope under the commanding enemy positions. He laid most accurate rifle fire on the openings of the pillboxes above and on the occupants of open emplacements. So effective was his rifle fire that the numerically superior enemy was forced to cease firing for a long enough period of time to allow ten men from Sergeant Wells' company to make their way through the wire and to follow safely through the minefield [using] the path he had shown.

"Immediately upon being joined by his comrades, Staff Sergeant Wells instructed them to take up the fire he had been delivering upon the enemy, and again proceeded to get closer to the hostile emplacements. Another minefield blocked the way, but he worked his way to the top of the hill. Alone he drove into the midst of the enemy emplacements, stopping only when he was actually behind the enemy and in the area of their communications trenches and dugouts. From this position, he again renewed his own fire, again with such great accuracy that the occupants were forced again to cease their frontal fire. Under cover of such splendid marksmanship, the ten men he had left at the bottom of the hill worked their way up to where he stood and joined in the fight. The combined firepower of the group was sufficient to stop enemy fire altogether and to allow the rest of the company, still lying on the beach behind the wire, to come forward, climb the hill, and reorganize at the top of it to continue the advance.

"Later in the same day, the enemy counterattacked in force the positions gained by L Company. Again, acting entirely on his own initiative, Sergeant Wells worked his way around the enemy to engage them from the flank. In order to reach a position from which he could fire without imperiling the lives of our men, he crossed hundreds of yards of exposed terrain before he stopped. From this position he again laid upon the enemy the deadly fire which had characterized his actions in the morning. Persistently resisting all efforts to dislodge him with fire, he remained at his post for almost five hours, sniping at every exposed enemy, until the counterattack was driven off, and he was able to rejoin his unit. Sergeant Wells' action on the beach and in supporting his comrades in their attempts to hold their objectives later in the day, were an inspiration to all."[75]

Private First Class Aaron B. Jones
Company L, 16th Infantry Regiment, 1st Infantry Division

Private First Class Aaron B. Jones was one of the two enlisted men who voluntarily accompanied Staff Sergeant Wells in crossing the beach to cut through the barbed wire and then in moving through the minefield to the base of the slope above the beach. Lieutenant Robert R. Cutler, one of the Company L section leaders, witnessed his heroic actions. "Private First Class Jones volunteered to leave the relative safety afforded by the shale and proceeded to crawl through the constant fire on the beach to the wire. Completely ignoring the deadly fire falling all about him, he chopped his way through the double apron fence and out onto the mined beach beyond. This area was mined so heavily that it seemed absolutely impossible to pass through it safely. Jumping to his feet, he picked his way through the field, safely reaching the ground at the base of the hill behind, and making a path for his comrades to follow. At the base of the hill, under the commanding enemy positions, he laid most accurate rifle fire on the openings in the pillboxes above and on the occupants of open emplacements. So effective was this rifle fire that the numerically superior enemy was forced to cease firing for a long enough period of time to allow ten men from Private First Class Jones' company to make their way through the wire and to follow safely through the minefields [on] the path he had shown. Immediately upon being joined by his comrades, Private First Class Jones instructed them to take up the fire he had been delivering upon the enemy, and again proceeded to get closer to the hostile emplacements. Another minefield blocked the way, but he worked his way to the top of the hill. Alone, he drove into the midst of the enemy and in the area of their communications trenches and dugouts. From this position he renewed his own fire and again with such great accuracy that the occupants were forced to again cease their frontal fire. Under cover of such splendid marksmanship, the ten men he had left at the bottom of the hill worked their way up to where he stood and joined in the firefight. The combined firepower of this group was sufficient to stop enemy fire altogether and to allow the rest of the company, still lying on the beach behind the wire, to come forward, climb the hill, and reorganize on top of it to continue the advance.

"Later in the same day, the enemy counterattacked in force the positions gained by L Company. Again, acting entirely on his own initiative, Private First Class Jones worked his way around the enemy to engage them from the flank. In order to reach a position from which he could fire without imperiling the lives of our men, he crossed hundreds of yards of exposed terrain before he stopped. From this position he again laid upon the enemy the deadly fire which had characterized his actions in the morning. Persistently resisting all efforts to dislodge him with fire, he remained at his post for almost five hours, sniping at every exposed enemy, until the counterattack was driven off, and he was able to rejoin his unit. Private First Class Jones' action on the beach and in supporting his comrades in their attempts to hold their objectives later in the day, were an inspiration to all."[76]

Private First Class John V. Griffin
Company L, 16th Infantry Regiment, 1st Infantry Division

Captain Armellino also witnessed the actions of the second volunteer, Private First Class John V. Griffin, who joined Staff Sergeant Wells in crossing the fire swept beach to cut through the barbed wire and advance across the minefield beyond it. "Private First Class Griffin with two other men from his company volunteered to leave the relative safety afforded by the shale and proceeded to crawl through the constant fire on the beach to the wire. Completely ignoring the deadly fire falling all about him, he chopped his way through the double apron fence and out onto the mined beach beyond. The area was mined so heavily that it seemed impossible to pass through it safely. He picked his way through the field, safely reaching the ground at the base of the hill behind, and making a path for his company to follow.

"At the base of the slope, under the commanding enemy positions, he laid most accurate rifle fire on the openings in the pillboxes above and on the occupants of open emplacements. So effective was this rifle fire that the numerically superior enemy was forced to cease firing for a long period of time to allow ten men from Private First Class Griffin's company to make their way through the wire and to follow safely through the minefield [on] the path he had shown.

"Immediately upon being joined by his comrades, Private First Class Griffin instructed them to take up the fire he had been delivering upon the enemy, and again proceeded to get closer to the hostile emplacements. Another minefield blocked the way, but he worked his way to the top of the hill. Alone, he drove into the midst of the enemy emplacements, stopping only when he was actually behind the enemy, and in the area of their communications, trenches, and dugouts. From this position, he again renewed his own fire, again with such great accuracy that the occupants were forced again to cease their frontal fire.

"Under cover of such splendid marksmanship, the ten men he had left at the bottom of the hill worked their way up to where he stood and joined in the fight. The combined firepower of the group was sufficient to stop enemy fire altogether and to allow the rest of the company still lying on the beach behind the wire to come forward, climb the hill, and reorganize at the top of it to continue the advance.

"Later in the same day, the enemy counterattacked in force the positions gained by L Company. Again acting entirely on his own initiative, Private First Class Griffin worked his way around the enemy to engage them from the flank. In order to reach a position from which he could fire without imperiling the lives of his own men, he crossed hundreds of yards of exposed fire swept terrain, before he stopped. From this position he again laid upon the enemy the deadly fire which had characterized his actions in the morning. Persistently resisting all efforts to dislodge him with fire, he remained at his post for almost five hours, sniping at every exposed enemy, until the counterattack was driven off, and he was able to rejoin his unit."[77]

Lieutenant Robert R. Cutler
Company L, 16th Infantry Regiment, 1st Infantry Division

Lieutenant Robert R. Cutler took command of Company L after Captain Armellino was wounded. Lieutenant Colonel Charles Horner, the commander of the 3rd Battalion, was an eyewitness to Cutler's courageous leadership. "Despite the fact that every leader on the entire beach was being subjected to intense and accurate sniper fire in addition to the machine gun and artillery action, Lieutenant Cutler unhesitatingly assumed command of his company. He completely ignored the vicious fire falling all about him and moved up and down the beach, collecting and consolidating the remnants of his company until he had a unified striking force. When he observed friendly tanks not firing at the enemy, Lieutenant Cutler proceeded to make his way to them across the wide area of fire swept beach. Despite the concentrated hostile machine gun and antitank gun fire the vehicles were drawing, he stayed beside them in the midst of the withering fire until such time as he was able to get their fire directed effectively upon the enemy. Throughout the entire period on the beach, both in assembling his own men and in getting the tanks into action, he acted with complete disregard for his safety in the midst of concentrated fire. Returning to his company, Lieutenant Cutler led them through the first available breach in the wire, and personally led the furious assault on the enemy emplacements in the high ground behind the beach. An uncharted minefield lay in the way, but he rapidly picked a path through it and led his entire unit across the dangerous area. Breaking through the beach defenses, he paused only long enough to reorganize the company before pushing on inland. The fanatically resisting enemy retreated slowly across the country, making a bitter stand at each of the numerous hedgerows and ditches. Lieutenant Cutler personally led the assaults on these positions despite the intense machine gun and sniper fire constantly directed at him, and continued the push inland to Le Grand Hameau and cut the main highway between Colleville-sur-Mer and Port en Bessin. Despite the most determined enemy resistance he consolidated his position and held it till other friendly units fought through [to get] on line with L Company."[78]

First Lieutenant Jimmie W. Monteith, Jr.
Company L, 16th Infantry Regiment, 1st Infantry Division

Lieutenant Colonel Charles Horner, the commanding officer of the 3rd Battalion, was a witness to much of Lieutenant Monteith's conspicuous gallantry and intrepid actions during the assault which led to the posthumous award of the Medal of Honor. "Lieutenant Jimmie Monteith disembarked from his landing craft in the initial assault under a furious barrage of enemy fire which caused heavy casualties in his craft. Calmly and efficiently he organized his men for the bitter struggle to shore and then, fully exposed to the hail of bullets and shrapnel, led his charge through the pounding surf to the beach. Here, while his surviving men gained momentary respite from the enemy fire, Lieutenant Monteith continued to ignore his own safety as he dashed up and down the beachfront, reorganizing for further assault. When all was in readiness for the attack, he again demonstrated his sterling qualities of leadership and magnificent courage by personally leading the assault over the narrow protective ledge and across the flat, exposed terrain that led to the comparative safety of a cliff.

"With complete disregard for himself, Lieutenant Monteith retraced his steps across the flat fields to the beach where two tanks had touched down and were 'buttoned up' and blind under violent enemy artillery and machine gun fire. Completely exposed to the violent fire directed at the tanks, Lieutenant Monteith led them on foot through a minefield into firing position. Coolly, he repeatedly pointed out targets on the enemy dominated cliffs. Under his direction, several of the enemy positions were destroyed and a part of the terrible crossfire laid on the crowded beach was eliminated. Lieutenant Monteith rejoined his company and led his men through heavy bands of barbed wire and through another uncharted thickly strewn minefield. Attacking against several more emplacements, Lieutenant Monteith and his men captured an advantageous position on the hill, from which point the enemy had been exacting a heavy toll from the men on the beach. Supervising the defense of this newly won position against repeated vicious counterattacks, he continued to ignore his personal safety, crossing 200-300 yards of open terrain under heavy fire repeatedly to strengthen links in his defensive chain. At one time during this activity, the enemy succeeded in completely surrounding Lieutenant Monteith and his unit and while leading the fight out of this situation, he was killed by enemy fire, only after he had destroyed three machine gun positions and successfully beaten off the enemy attack."[79]

Most of the gap assault teams in the 16th Infantry Regiment's sectors landed ahead of the assault infantry wave or the infantry was landed in the wrong locations. The DD tanks which were also supposed to land ahead of these teams to provide suppressive cover fire had mostly sunk to the bottom of the English Channel. The result was that the gap assault teams were subjected to especially intense enemy fire concentrated almost solely upon them.

Lieutenant Raymond E. Lanterman
Company C, 146th Engineer Combat Battalion, Special Engineer Task Force, Provisional Engineer Special Brigade Group
Gap Assault Team Number 9

In the predawn darkness, Lieutenant Raymond E. Lanterman and Gap Assault Team Number 9 transferred from their LST to the LCM (Landing Craft Mechanized) that would transport them to Omaha Beach. When all of the LCMs transporting the gap assault teams had assembled, the landing craft maneuvered into a wave formation and began movement toward the beach. The LCMs were close enough to one another that Lieutenant Lanterman and his men "could converse with the people in the neighboring boats; we gradually drew apart, however, spacing out to the prescribed intervals for landing. Our course took us past an enormous battleship whose big guns were blasting away in a softening up mission. Great balls of fire and clouds of black smoke belched from her guns as she fired in rapid succession, sending shells screaming over our heads to explode on the mainland of Europe. As we drew near Omaha Beach in the early morning light, we easily recognized the landmarks and features we had seen on the scale model, and were beginning to receive fire from shore. At this distance, shells from German [artillery] were plopping into the sea around us, sending up geysers of spume as they exploded in the water. Some boats, of course, were hit; one unfortunate craft blew up when a shell dropped into it and set off the explosives aboard.

"The timing of each phase of the enormously complicated Operation Overlord had been carefully worked out to the last minute: at H-Hour [+03] the first infantry units were to go ashore; at H-Hour plus five minutes we demolition engineers were to land. As thus scheduled, the infantry would have engaged the enemy, hopefully pushing him back, [and] leaving us free to proceed with our mission without the necessity of defending ourselves…It happened that we arrived first in our particular sector, at H-Hour, at lowest tide, about 6:30 a.m. The LCM went aground before we touched shore, and the coxswain told us he could go no further; he was stuck on a sand bar. He lowered the ramp and we saw that we'd have to wade a distance of perhaps fifty or seventy yards to get to the beach. I gave the order to disembark and jumped off the end of the ramp. The sand bar was under the shallow draft boat, but it wasn't in front of the ramp. Loaded down with explosives, carbines, binoculars, primacord, and what-all, we sank like stones. Fortunately, the water was only up to our necks; fortunately also, there was very little wave action, and we started to wade in. The spatter pattern of a cone of machine gun fire was hitting the water's surface off to our right and we detoured to the left in order to give it as wide a berth as possible. That cone of fire never moved closer to us, to our relief, and we all made it to the beach intact, where we immediately set to work amid the THUNK of exploding mortar shells and the whistle of small arms bullets.

"The intensive training grind we had gone through so recently tended to make robots of us. We could think of nothing but the tasks we were assigned to carry out, and working under withering fire was something we had never experienced before. It was all so very unreal. One of our men had been a goof-off and a thorn in our flesh throughout his time in the outfit; he had even tried to climb over the fence in the sealed off final briefing area to go to town. But here, when the chips were down, he was as calm as if he were in his own backyard at home, going about his assigned duties completely ignoring the danger, as if it were a commonplace thing to work under desperate conditions.

"The obstacles we demolished were wooden poles standing upright in the sand. Each pole was taller than a man, for tides are deep on that coast and many had Teller antitank mines secured to their tops which at high tide would be awash or perhaps just slightly under water. Any boats coming in at high tide would strike the mines and be disabled or destroyed. Our mission was to cut down the poles with explosives, detonating the mines as well, to create a passage through which landing barges coming in could navigate without danger. For the demolition work each of us carried a quantity of a pliable explosive substance stuffed into ordinary cotton stockings. We were to wrap these around the poles, close to the ground, then connect them all with prima cord, a kind of explosive rope. A fuse was then attached to the network of cord—fuses which had been kept waterproof by being sealed in condoms. Just when we had made ready and were about to fire the charge, an infantry detachment landed. We yelled at the colonel leading them to keep his people back, for they'd be blown to bits if they came forward through the poles just then. He and his men flattened themselves out on the sand and we pulled the fuse. We must have done something right, for we got a successful blow, the blast of the charge ringing each pole pinched it in two, and they all toppled. The first part of our mission was now completed; we had felled the posts. The tank-dozer could clear them away to create a path through the obstacles, which in addition to the posts, consisted of many X-shaped iron constructions which were about two feet high, fashioned from short lengths of railroad rails. They resembled the jacks children play with.

"The next task was to search for mines in the sand. The man who carried the mine detector had soon been killed and I picked up the instrument and began to use it. By now the tank-dozer had arrived and was beginning to clear away the fallen poles and 'jacks'. I happened to be a few yards in front of the dozer when some unfriendly soul on the Wehrmacht side got a bead on me; I dropped, hit presumably by machine gun fire.

"'That tank-dozer is going to run over me,' I thought and tried to move out of its way without much success. (Later, in the hospital in England, I saw the driver and he assured me he'd seen my fall and wasn't about to run me down.) A medic came up, a terribly young looking boy, and knelt beside me to help. He was burdened with so much gear that he apologized for not being able to reach behind himself to get out medications and bandages. I told him to turn around, tell me what to look for, and I'd fish it out of his bulging knapsack. While we were doing this he muttered, 'Lieutenant, I'm scared shitless.' I assured him he wasn't the only one. The tank-dozer was put out of commission, so there was no more worry about being run over, but lying flat on my back, I felt water at my feet and realized that the tide was coming in. Now there was a new danger: I could drown here. I tried to scootch up higher, but the tide was faster than I could move; I owe my life to a couple of the men who sized up the situation and helped me to a position above the high water line.

This iconic photograph taken by Robert Capa shows soldiers of the 16th Infantry sheltering among the beach obstacles as the tide rises. In addition to the log ramps, hedgehog obstacles constructed of three welded steel channeled rails can be seen at the center and right center of the photograph. Some of the first wave of infantry landed later than the gap assault teams and sought cover behind the obstacles because of the heavy enemy fire. This prevented some of the gap assault teams from blowing obstacles to clear gaps for later incoming waves.

"Now, it looked as if I might survive, and I wished that I had my movie camera with me, since it was impossible to get up and do anything useful. The morphine which the medic had administered made me groggy, although still quite aware. I don't know how long I was there, maybe an hour, before friendly hands put me on a stretcher and carried me to a big landing barge which had just disgorged its load and was taking wounded aboard. A missile hit its superstructure and splattered fragments around, but we backed out safely and drew alongside a destroyer far out to sea, which took us wounded on and put us in sick bay bunks. Again I could only marvel at the clockwork precision of the whole operation: if you needed something, say, a destroyer for instance, there it was, waiting for you!"[80]

Lanterman and his team had successfully cleared a fifty yard gap in the obstacles in the middle of Easy Red, which would prove critical in providing landing craft arriving in future waves a clear path to the beach.

Gap Assault Team Number 10 was the only other team in the 16th Infantry's sectors of Omaha Beach to clear a fifty yard gap in the obstacles, then later was able to blow a second gap some one hundred yards wide.

First Lieutenant Joseph J. Gregory
Company C, 146th Engineer Combat Battalion, Special Engineer Task Force, Provisional Engineer Special Brigade Group
Gap Assault Team Number 10

Private Russell E. Martin served with Company C, 146th Engineer Combat Battalion and Gap Assault Team Number 10 on June 6, 1944. "Immediately after landing on the beach, Lieutenant [Joseph J.] Gregory split our boat team into two groups, sending one to the lower band of obstacles and the other, including me, remained in the seaward band. As we finished placing the charges, the infantry were moving up into the band of obstacles for protection, so Lieutenant Gregory sent us on up above the water line while he stayed behind to try to persuade the men to follow him in so he could pull the fuse. However, he was unsuccessful and joined us shortly afterwards. Later on, he saw the men leave the obstacles and advance across the beach.

"Lieutenant Gregory then moved hastily across the beach to the outer band of obstacles, pulled the fuse and headed for the shore, pulling the fuse on the inner band of obstacles as he passed through them. The gaps were blown, but Lieutenant Gregory noticed that there were still several obstacles remaining in the gap which would prevent landing craft from entering. Since the tank-dozer was not there to push the remaining obstacles aside, Lieutenant Gregory left the shingle area with some charges that he collected from us and headed for the outer gap, refusing to let any of us go with him. Still under heavy fire for about twenty minutes, he placed the charges on the remaining obstacles, firing them individually with thirty second delay fuses. It was necessary for him to run toward the water each time in order to keep the landing troops from running into the explosives. When he completed this, he returned to our team above the high water line, and began preparing more charges. In the meantime, two tanks had moved up into our area and were drawing heavy enemy fire where a large number of wounded infantrymen were being cared for.

"Lieutenant Gregory tried to get the tanks to move from that sector of the beach, but they refused and it was at this time that an [artillery shell] landed nearby, wounding him and three more of his men. In spite of the fact that he had a bad shrapnel wound in his thigh, he helped the medical aid men administer aid to his men, refusing aid himself. After locating a gap through the minefield, above the beach, he had our staff sergeant take us through it to the protection of the hill beyond and wait for a change of tide. We tried to tell him to leave when the others were evacuated, but he told us to go ahead and he would join us as soon as he got his [wounded] men to an evacuation ship. We went up on the hill, as we were instructed. About 14:00 hours that day, the naval officer that came in on our boat came up and told us that we would find Lieutenant Gregory between the hill and the beach. Another enlisted man and I went back and found Lieutenant Gregory had been killed while trying to rejoin us."[81]

Ensign Lawrence S. Karnowski
Naval Combat Demolition Unit 45, Naval Combat Demolition Group, 6th Naval Beach Battalion, Assault Force O, Task Force 124, Eleventh Amphibious Force, 12th Fleet
Gap Assault Team Number 10

Ensign Lawrence Karnowski was the team leader of NCDU 45, which was attached to Lieutenant Gregory's Gap Assault Team Number 10 and assigned to demolish the seaward most obstacles. "Lieutenant Gregory and his men pulled off the rubber boat then headed for the dune line and their obstacles. We disembarked as two shells dropped near our LCM and we got busy tying charges to the obstacles…The first fired at 06:50, went magnificently. Machine gun fire erupted, keeping us on our bellies. Chief Conrad C. Millis couldn't resign himself to crawling and placing charges…so he took off with a roll of primacord and placed several charges, but machine gun fire cut him down, the only man I lost that day and the best one I had.[82]

"It took a lot longer to prepare and detonate the second shot because the tide was coming in fast, and infantry, ten minutes behind schedule, were filtering through us. I just had enough time, as our danger flare went up to grab a soldier from behind one of the charged pilings before our second shot went off at 07:05 hours. During this time Gunner's Mate Bob Svendsen carried wounded fellow Gunner's Mate Gale Fant all the way to the dune line with machine gun fire chasing him the whole way. Now in water up to our knees, we were almost to where Lieutenant Gregory and his men had started. They'd done a great job, clearing the entire fifty yard wide gap. Several pilings remained between our two sectors and Lieutenant Gregory insisted on getting them. A tall man, he waded and swam to each piling as we threw the charges to him. Triggering each one separately, he destroyed all three. Jerry shellfire was now really pouring in. Coming in on the almost high tide were bodies. Jeeps, tanks and small boats were piling up on the beach. Three LCIs (Landing Craft Infantry) spotted our gap and came on in. While they unloaded, we loaded out our wounded. (By this time Millis had been lost and five others from NCDU 45 wounded.) The situation became worse as we lay behind the dunes. Then one of the soldiers spotted a Jerry to our front on a footpath and took off after him. His fellow infantrymen followed. Lieutenant Gregory and I rounded up our remaining men and sent them ahead to the hillside for protection. An emergency first aid station had been set up near the path and wounded were being treated. We were nearing it when a large shell scored a direct hit. Gregory, five feet in front of me, was hit badly in the stomach and legs. I rolled him over to attend to his wounds. He kept saying he wouldn't recover. We talked about the beach job. He was happy that we had completed our assignment. Then he collapsed and died."[83]

Gap Assault Team Number 11 landed on the eastern portion of Easy Red and lost over half of its men killed or wounded, but the survivors were able to clear a partial gap.

Chief Machinist's Mate Jerry N. Markham
Naval Combat Demolition Unit 46, Naval Combat Demolition Group, 6th Naval Beach Battalion, Assault Force O,
Task Force 124, Eleventh Amphibious Force, 12th Fleet
Gap Assault Team Number 11

The LCM transporting Chief Machinist's Mate Jerry Markham and his NCDU 46 team and the rest of Gap Assault Team Number 11 touched down at the Easy Red sector at 6:33 a.m. "Now we had been briefed that the air force would carpet the beach with thousands of tons of bombs. Big naval guns would lay on a massive bombardment just prior to our landing. Rocket ships would fire off their salvos. Most of the rockets were duds or fell short. Naval gunfire had little or no effect on the convex shaped pillboxes. Most of the bombs landed too far inland to have any effect. The Germans had the beaches zeroed in and our unit ran into the strongest opposition. By the time our LCM reached the low water mark, which was dry, the machine guns opened up. The army combat engineers were the first off the ramp ashore and they were pretty badly shot up. Then it was our turn. The seamen unloaded our rubber boat with the extra explosives. Each of us carried forty pounds of Hagensen packs. I was the last one out. My job was to tie up the primacord from all the charges so that they could all be detonated simultaneously. I carried the detonators under my armpit for safety's sake. All of a sudden a mortar round hit our rubber boat, killing one of the seamen. When I turned back around I saw [Ensign] John Bussell lying face down in the water. I turned him over. He had been mortally wounded by shrapnel. The machine gun fire was really heavy now. The only cover was the mined obstacles. The tide was coming in and we kept moving forward. Two more men from my unit were killed. Four were killed in all and one of the engineers. The crosscurrent was strong, and units to the left and right were being shot up pretty badly. I was able to pull together survivors from one of them and combine them with ours. Together we salvaged enough explosives to blow a partial gap through the mined obstacles. I spent the rest of the time trying to help the wounded reach the high water mark dune line where there was a little bit of cover from the machine guns. It took three hours all told just to get there. At the dune line, I noticed four soldiers in a shallow foxhole. A mortar round had hit right behind them and shoved sand forward, practically burying them. I ran over there and helped dig them out, not realizing I had just run through all that machine gun fire."[84]

Gap Assault Team Number 12 managed to clear a thirty yard wide gap on Easy Red, but a German mortar shell detonated a line of primacord, prematurely setting off the explosive charges which were attached to a band of obstacles, killing six army combat engineers and four navy demolition men and wounding nine other members of the team.

Aviation Chief Ordnanceman Loran E. Barbour
Naval Combat Demolition Unit 22, Naval Combat Demolition Group, 6th Naval Beach Battalion, Assault Force O,
Task Force 124, Eleventh Amphibious Force, 12th Fleet
Gap Assault Team Number 12

Lieutenant Commander Joseph H. Gibbons was the commanding officer of Assault Force O's naval combat demolition units that were attached to the sixteen gap assault teams. Gibbons went ashore with the command group of the Special Engineer Task Force and was an eyewitness to the heroism of several of his sailors. "Loran Eli Barbour was placed in command of Naval Combat Demolition Unit 22. The officer originally in command of this unit was placed in command of Group II of the naval combat demolition units which comprised ten such units. Facing heavy machine gun and artillery fire, he showed exceptional leadership and initiative in directing the placing of charges and blowing a [thirty] yard gap in enemy obstacles on Easy Red Beach. Severely wounded, he calmly directed marking of the gap through which troops could be landed, continuing to direct his men after completion of their mission, to assist in aiding the wounded and evacuating casualties until exhausted, he was evacuated from the area."[85]

Gap Assault Team Number 13 was especially unlucky as an artillery shell struck a rubber boat loaded with explosives just as the team landed on Easy Red, killing or wounding all eight members of NCDU 23. The team also lost one of its army combat engineers as well. Incoming waves of infantry sought shelter behind the obstacles, preventing the team from detonating the charges it had set.

Staff Sergeant George Schneider
299th Engineer Combat Battalion, Special Engineer Task Force, Provisional Engineer Special Brigade Group
Gap Assault Team Number 13

Major Milton A. Jewett was the commanding officer of the 299th Engineer Combat Battalion. "Staff Sergeant Schneider landed during the initial assault of the beaches. As second in command of a demolition team, Staff Sergeant Schneider directed the placing of charges for the removal of underwater obstacles. He was exposed to heavy and sustained small arms and observed artillery fire while working in a heavy surf. When the demolitions endangered friendly troops, Staff Sergeant, with complete disregard to his own safety, continued the removal of obstacles by attaching a towing chain from an armored bulldozer working nearby."[86]

A German artillery shell exploded in Gap Assault Team Number 14's LCM, detonating the explosives loaded in a rubber boat, killing most of the navy team members and setting the LCM on fire. The half strength team wired some of the obstacles on the eastern edge of Easy Red, but incoming infantry landed and took refuge among them before they could detonate them. Similar fates befell the two gap assault teams assigned to the Fox Green sector. An enemy mortar round struck an explosives laden rubber boat used by Gap Assault Team Number 15, setting off a secondary explosion, killing or wounding most of the team members of NCDU 138. The LCM which landed Gap Assault Team Number 16 was blown up by a direct hit shortly after the team had exited. There were wounded infantrymen among and behind the obstacles which prevented teams from preparing and setting off charges to clear paths.

With the chaos and slaughter taking place among his combat engineers, Major Milton Jewett, aboard Command Boat II, landed to help reorganize and rally his 299th Engineer Combat Battalion engineers to finish the job of blowing gaps in the obstacle belt, despite the horrendous casualties already suffered.

Major Milton A. Jewett
Headquarters, 299th Engineer Combat Battalion, Special Engineer Task Force, Provisional Engineer Special Brigade Group

Lieutenant Colonel John T. O'Neill, the commander of the Special Engineer Task Force, observed the heroism displayed by Major Jewett in leading his combat engineers in accomplishing the mission. "The actual conditions on the beach required the highest degree of leadership and courage to gain control of and weld half drowned and badly shaken troops into command units amid the chaos and carnage of the beach. Major Jewett, upon landing immediately established contact with his units and unmindful of any personal danger, personally reconnoitered his beach area and directed the operations of his battalion. Major Jewett was apparently unmindful of self and [acted] beyond the line of duty as battalion commander. He exposed himself to withering fire, personally supervising the placing of charges, setting an example of extraordinary heroism to his officers and men, which aided materially in the accomplishment of an extremely critical and hazardous mission."[87]

Gap support teams were scheduled to land at H+8, but delays in transferring to their respective LCMs caused them to land between H+10 and H+75. Instead of landing on the western portion of the beach, the four gap support teams assigned to the 146th Engineer Combat Battalion landed on the Easy Red sector far to the east of their planned locations. The other four gap support teams, which were assigned to the 299th Engineer Combat Battalion also landed late on Easy Red instead of evenly spaced along the eastern portion of the beach. Two artillery shells struck the LCM transporting Gap Support Team F, killing fifteen men. Only four of the team members, including its commanding officer, Captain Edwin R. Perry, made it ashore.

Captain Edwin R. Perry
Company A, 299th Engineer Combat Battalion, Special Engineer Task Force, Provisional Engineer Special Brigade Group
Gap Support Team F

Major Jewett, the commander of the 299th Engineer Combat Battalion, saw the tragedy that struck Gap Support Team F as it unfolded before his eyes. "Captain Perry was in command of a demolition party for the removal of underwater obstacles in the initial assault of the beaches on 6 June 1944. The LCM on which Captain Perry and his party were loaded was hit by an artillery shell while approaching the beach. As a result of this, many pre-packed demolition charges exploded. Several men were killed and the remainder of the party thrown into the sea when the craft sank. Captain Perry swam ashore and under heavy and sustained small arms and observed artillery fire reorganized the remnants of his demolition party.

This French 75mm FK231 (f) howitzer, capable of rapid fire, was located at WN 60 on the left flank of the troops landing on the Fox Green sector. Lieutenant (jg) Stuart L. Brandel, a naval gunfire liaison officer with Naval Shore Fire Control Party 9, 294th Joint Assault Signal Company, called in rapid fire for one minute from the French cruiser F.S. *Montclair* and knocked it out of action. *Photograph by Lieutenant (jg) Stuart L. Brandel, United States Navy, courtesy of Tom Lane.*

"Unable to proceed with the demolition of obstacles because of the rise of the tide, Captain Perry directed the salvage of explosives scattered along the beach and prepared to breach the obstacles as soon as tidal conditions permitted. During all of this time Captain Perry was subjected to intense enemy fire. With utter disregard for his own personal safety, he exposed himself [to enemy fire] continuously. The magnificent courage, aggressive leadership and extraordinary heroism displayed by Captain Perry was an inspiration to the remnants of his party which enabled them to accomplish their mission."[88]

One of the vital elements of the assault landing was communication between the beach landed forces and the naval forces, especially for naval gunfire, since it would be the army's artillery support until it could land and deploy its artillery units. The naval shore fire control parties (NSFCP) were expected to play a key role in providing the communications and coordination of this powerful naval gunfire support. These NSFCPs consisted of an army forward observation team of one artillery officer, an NCO, and three radio operators; and a naval gunfire liaison observation party consisting of a naval gunfire liaison officer and three radio operators; and a section of radio operators equipped with jeeps.

This is a Panzerstellung located at WN 60 on the eastern end of Omaha Beach, which was a Tobruk open concrete position almost flush with the ground, topped with a tank turret from a French Renault tank mounting a 37mm gun. *United States Army photograph.*

Lieutenant (jg) Stuart L. Brandel
Naval Shore Fire Control Party 9, 294th Joint Assault Signal Company, Assault Force O, Task Force 124, Eleventh Amphibious Force, 12th Fleet

Lieutenant Stuart L. Brandel, a naval gunfire liaison officer, and his NSFCP were assigned to support the 3rd Battalion, 16th Infantry. "The forward elements of the party landing at H+10 minutes and the NGLO [naval gunfire liaison observation] party at a later time. The place of the landing was Omaha Beach on Fox Green. The forward party had communications by SCR 609 [radio] at H+35 minutes. The NGLO party established communications with the firing ship and forward party at H+60 minutes. The FS *Montclair* fired for us on D-Day. Both parties suffered heavy casualties; the forward party with First Lieutenant Anthony C. Lascola suffered four wounded out of five men. The two men evacuated for this party were the army officer and his sergeant. The NGLO party was also hit hard. This party of seven men had five wounded including myself.

"Four of the men had to be evacuated and I managed to carry on with the remaining two men. We salvaged essential radio equipment, including SCR 609 and SCR 284. The SCR 609 worked and we set up communications with the ship. The AM and FM communications results were very good at all times. There wasn't any need for a SCR 284 radio, at least in the initial days. We got as far as fifteen miles with the 609. It was impossible to get ashore on Fox Green Beach at H+30. Our forward party was ashore and in communication with the ship. After making several unsuccessful runs at the beach, the colonel of the 3rd Battalion of the 16th Infantry decided to lay off the beach a few hundred yards and direct the three infantry companies by radio as he was in communication with them.

"He asked us to set up and fire because we could see the enemy and gun positions at times and also the forward party was ashore and could observe our fires which would have to be close to our own troops and could give us [instructions to] cease fire if necessary. It was very rough water and nobody except my own men would cooperate, so after much trouble we finally got communication with the ship and the forward party on the beach. Our first target was up the draw to the left of Fox Green leading up to St. Honorine des Pertes. This was observed fire on enemy activity and was good effective fire. We ended this problem with rapid fire for one minute. We fired several other successful problems as requested by the colonel, who was in communication with his troops. The fire on D-Day seemed to be very valuable to the landing teams and good effect was had on the targets."[89]

Private Neville R. Wood, with the 294th Joint Assault Signal Company, was one of two men with Brandel's naval gunfire liaison party who was not wounded by enemy mortar fire after the party landed. "After landing he continued with his two remaining unwounded men, although painfully wounded himself. After going inland he directed naval fire on enemy targets and installations with such accuracy that our groups were able to advance successfully. His determination and clear thinking was an inspiration to all men about him."[90]

THE SECOND WAVE OF INFANTRY was scheduled to land at H+30 in order to give the gap assault teams the necessary time to clear paths through the obstacles. The tide was rising rapidly and the coxswains of the landing craft transporting the second wave of infantry would have to avoid the obstacles which had not been blown. Only five gaps of fifty or more yards wide had been cleared, far less than the sixteen planned gaps. The second wave of infantry of the 116th Infantry Regiment waded ashore under fire from the still intact German positions on the bluffs above, with the remnants of the regiment's initial infantry wave pinned down along the seawall, in the water behind obstacles and wrecked tanks and landing craft, or staying low in the water and coming in with the rise of the tide. The dead and badly wounded littered the beach and bodies floated and rolled back and forth with the incoming waves of water rising toward the seawall.

Company B, 116th Infantry was slated to land on Dog Green where Company A had been effectively destroyed within the last half hour. However, smoke, dust, and haze obscured the landmarks. The LCA carrying Lieutenant Leo A. Pingenot's section of Company B troops landed on the far right slightly west of the Vierville draw where some boulders gave them some protection against the enemy fire. This section miraculously lost only one killed and three wounded, and the twenty-eight remaining troops joined Captain Ralph Goranson's Company C, 2nd Ranger Battalion at the base of the cliffs just west of the Vierville draw. They climbed ropes up the steep cliffs with the Rangers and fought along side of them all day long, helping them destroy the fortified house and the Germans at WN 73, overlooking the west side of the draw. The LCA transporting Captain Ettore V. Zappacosta and his headquarters section touched down and just as the ramp was dropped, machine gun fire enveloped it. Captain Zappacosta took just a few steps off of the ramp before he was killed. Practically every other man in the craft was killed or wounded. The survivors who were able to do so stayed down in the water and took several hours to come in with the tide and took refuge behind the seawall. Soldiers in other landing craft touching down nearby met similar fates.

First Lieutenant William B. Williams
Company B, 116th Infantry Regiment, 29th Infantry Division

Second Lieutenant Walter P. Taylor, Jr.
Company B, 116th Infantry Regiment, 29th Infantry Division

With Captain Zappacosta dead, command of Company B fell to Lieutenant William B. Williams, the company executive officer, who was unaware of this as his section landed well to the left on Dog White, where the enemy fire was relatively light, except for mortar fire which bracketed their LCA as it approached the beach. Williams and his section debarked just before a mortar round exploded in the middle of the LCA. Lieutenant Williams and ten of his men made it to the seawall as their landing craft burned behind them. Williams led them across the road which ran parallel to the seawall just as mortar shells exploded around them. Williams and seven of his men made it to the base of the bluff. Lieutenant Williams then led his section to the left along the base of the bluff until he found a trail that appeared to be in defilade to enemy observation and fire. He then led them up the trail which topped the bluff west of the les Moulins draw, which was designated as Exit D-3.

Technical Sergeant William H. Pearce, the assistant section leader of Lieutenant Williams' boat section, was near the front of the column as it climbed the slope. "Approaching the top of the hill overlooking Vierville-sur-Mer beach, our section was pinned down. To our front on top of the hill was an enemy mortar emplacement intact. Through heavy fire, Lieutenant Williams worked himself close to the emplacement and single handedly fought that strongpoint. He threw grenades at the enemy and in turn they threw their grenades and wounded him. He succeeded in knocking out the emplacement. This enabled the section to move forward. I found Lieutenant Williams lying wounded on the ground on the other side of the emplacement. He told me to take over and to continue on to the objective."[91]

Technical Sergeant Pearce led the section forward to the crest of the hill, where it engaged a group of Germans behind a hedgerow, killing five of the enemy. Pearce and his men continued south to the coastal road which ran from St. Laurent to

Vierville-sur-Mer, where they followed it west to Vierville where they joined a group led by Lieutenant Walter P. Taylor, now the senior officer in Company B still in the fight. Lieutenant Taylor had lost four killed and four wounded crossing the beach, but had led twenty men from his section up the bluff and into Vierville, where they were mopping up the village when Technical Sergeant Pearce and his six man group arrived. The Company B troops led by Lieutenants Williams and Taylor were likely the first to make it to the top of the bluffs in the 116th Infantry sectors east of the Vierville exit.

Taylor decided to move south to Château de Vaumicel five hundred yards south of Vierville. The group was engaged by Germans positioned behind a hedgerow about a hundred yards from the chateau and after a close quarter firefight, Taylor's men took twenty-four prisoners. Taylor sent the prisoners back to the beach guarded by one of his men and then led his group into the chateau where he found a German doctor and a medic. Lieutenant Taylor then led them on to a crossroads beyond the chateau, making the deepest penetration in the 116th Infantry's zone of any troops on D-Day. His group was soon attacked by three truckloads of German troops, forcing Taylor and his men back to the chateau, where they held them off until just before sundown, when fifteen Rangers arrived, forcing a German withdrawal. Taylor was determined to reach his objective a half a mile west of the chateau and courageously led his small group and the Rangers west toward the company's D-Day objective. Staff Sergeant Frank M. Price had joined Taylor at Vierville and fought as part of his group for much of D-Day. "We saw no sign of fear in him. Watching him made men of us. Marching or fighting, he was leading. We followed him because there was nothing else to do."[92]

Technical Sergeant John A. Roach
Company B, 116th Infantry Regiment, 29th Infantry Division

Lieutenant Donald Caspulla, the adjutant of the 116th Infantry, observed one of the Company B platoon sergeants take charge of a leaderless group of men from his platoon. "Sergeant Roach was wounded in the forearm and [was] instructed to await evacuation with other wounded when he saw remnants of his platoon without leadership, demoralized and making no advance. Sergeant Roach seized a weapon and despite his wound and without regard for his personal safety, reorganized his platoon and rallied them to the attack. He led them forward across the beach, driving and destroying the enemy before them until the high ground beyond the beach was reached, where he again reorganized the platoon to continue the attack."[93]

Second Lieutenant Leo D. Van De Voort
Company B, 116th Infantry Regiment, 29th Infantry Division

Sergeant William Lewis and other Company B soldiers who made it in the slight defilade afforded by the shingle and the seawall waited for a leader to tell them what to do next, since the planned assault they had rehearsed so carefully had gone terribly wrong. "We were just trying to stay alive. There was nothing we could do except keep our butts down. Lieutenant Leo Van De Voort said, 'Let's go, there ain't no use staying here, we're all going to get killed!' The first thing he did was to run up to a gun emplacement and throw a grenade through the embrasure. He returned with five or six prisoners. So then we thought, 'Hell if he can do that, why can't we?' That's how we got off the beach."[94]

Lieutenant Van De Voort's single handed capture of the enemy pillbox galvanized his section, which he now led forward to attack other German positions. Lieutenant Donald Casapulla, the adjutant of the 116th Infantry, witnessed the assault. "At the time of the attack by Lieutenant Van De Voort's platoon—shortly after dawn—the beach was covered by a withering artillery, automatic weapons, and rifle fire from enemy emplacements. In the face of extraordinary hazards, Lieutenant Van De Voort was a constant inspiration to his men, exhorting them and leading them on to advance across the beach. With utter disregard for his own safety, Lieutenant Van De Voort on numerous occasions exposed himself to devastating fire in order to control his platoon."[95]

Wooden launchers for the 320mm Wurfgerät rockets (left photo) were dug in and connected by trenches to allow movement among the various launchers. These massive 320mm Wurfgerät rockets (right photo) rained down on the western portion of Omaha Beach. This battery of rockets was located near St. Laurent at WN 69 and was destroyed by naval gunfire directed by First Sergeant William M Presley, with Company B, 116th Infantry Regiment.

First Sergeant William M. Presley
Company B, 116th Infantry Regiment, 29th Infantry Division

Later that day on the bluff near WN 71, Lieutenant Van De Voort witnessed heroism by another Company B leader, First Sergeant William M. Presley. "At about H+5 hours D-Day, 6 June 1944, I saw First Sergeant William M. Presley show extreme coolness in neutralizing an emplacement protecting an artillery observation point overlooking the beach at Vierville-sur-Mer. He was leading a small party of four men who were held up by fire from other emplacements. First Sergeant Presley organized the party from the seaward edge of the cliff and without waiting for orders he returned down the cliff alone under direct short range enemy fire into a concentration of artillery fire which had forced everyone else in the area to take cover.

"With utter disregard for his personal safety, he located the [naval] shore fire [control] party, reconnoitered a covered approach up the cliff and brought the fire control party to the position occupied by his men. From this point of vantage the naval party was able to observe and bring fire to bear which not only caused a portion of the enemy to flee but made easy for the rest to take prisoners; and also neutralized another enemy position further along the cliff. The result of his action caused neutralizing of this enemy OP which was bringing fire down on the beach where men and equipment were landing."[96]

Evidently, the naval liaison officer was killed subsequently to calling in the fire on the German observation post. Sergeant Robert Slaughter, with Company D, 116th Infantry, remembered passing the dead officer. "Strapped to his back was a huge radio. He had been observing a battery of Nebelwerfers—screaming meemies—firing from a few hundred yards away. The rocket shells were playing havoc with later waves coming into the beach. Presley remembered the radio, retrieved it from the dead officer, and made contact with a destroyer out in the channel. He radioed the ship he had a target and to fire at a certain coordinate on the map. We heard the report of the 5-inch naval gun and then followed where the shell landed. Getting the pattern closer to the target, he fired for effect. We heard the salvo. 'Boom-b-b-boom-ba-ba-boom!' Soon the shells screamed overhead on the way to the target. 'Kerwhoom-kerwhoom-kerwhoom!' The ground trembled beneath us. The exploding shells saturated the area to our right front, some landing too close for comfort. But that action put the gun emplacement out of action."[97]

Major Sidney V. Bingham, Jr.
Headquarters, 2nd Battalion, 116th Infantry Regiment, 29th Infantry Division

Major Sidney V. Bingham, Jr., commanding officer of the 2nd Battalion, 116th Infantry, was scheduled to land on Dog Red at H+30. "We ground ashore and the ramp went down and we found we were on a runnel and we took about two steps and boom, we were in over our heads. Fortunately, we had life jackets on, but even so, quite a number of people were having trouble, and several of us did what we could and I think were successful in getting them started and headed towards shore where they could get their feet back on the ground.

"The naval gunfire had set the grass and weeds afire on the high ground just behind the beach. There was a strong wind coming from the west to the east, which did a great job of providing us with all kinds of concealment, very fine concealment from the smoke. This was really a godsend. Otherwise, we would have been dead ducks for sure. As soon as I got ashore and on the way in, I was most impressed by all the noise that was taking place on the beach and I thought, in my naive fashion, 'Boy, those engineer special brigade underwater obstacle people are really doing a job.' We were on an incoming tide and while I was making my way across the several hundred yards of flat sand rejoicing in the noise that I heard, thinking it was all a combination of naval gun fire and underwater demolition activity. I noticed one of the underwater obstacles was that not under water at the time (it was made out of telephone poles) sort of spitting slivers of wood. It occurred to me that this was machine gun fire that was probably aimed at me and fortunately didn't hit any of us. Anyway, this sobered me up quite a bit.

"When I got up to the shingle, which is the gravel type stuff up toward the low sea wall, there were quite a number of young men, many of whom were huddled up seeking shelter. Everyone was cold, completely soaked and still seasick, and I noticed that weapons would not fire. The water was sandy and as a consequence the carbines and rifles would not fire. So we had, believe it or not, right behind the seawall at 7:30 or 7:15 in the morning of 6 June 1944, we had weapons disassembled and had a weapons cleaning operation going on. This is sort of hard to believe, but nevertheless was pretty effective and they got to work. We had no communication. It was just total absence of any organization. Units were badly scattered. A good bit of the battalion was to the left in the 1st Division zone. We didn't get them back with us until the next day. The battalion headquarters group that was with me landed right on target at the les Moulins draw, and as I say, we were pretty much on our own and nothing in our plans and none of the things that we had rehearsed came to pass, I'm ashamed to say. The medics were outstanding. They were all over the place tending the wounded. I was most impressed by the work of a destroyer. I wish I could remember its name and number, but I thought a couple of times it must have had wheels on it and was running up and down the beach. It was so close in and those high velocity five-inch guns certainly were heartening, as far as I was concerned. Of the twelve howitzers in our direct support artillery battalion, one got ashore. We had no communications whatsoever. After a confusing day, we got off the beach in the late afternoon after having unsuccessfully tried to round up people and get some type of organization in hand.

"In the lower floor of a large concrete house, two or three stories high—it was not too badly damaged—I came upon Colonel Paul W. Thompson, commander of the 6th Engineer Special Brigade, whose mission was to clear the underwater obstacles on the beach. Colonel Thompson was very badly wounded. As I recall, he had a wound in his shoulder and another wound in his neck. One of my lieutenants was a Lieutenant Jim Bagley, whose nickname was 'Bucket Head.' He got that name because his head was so big that it was alleged that he could wear a helmet without a helmet liner. Here was Bagley looking over Colonel Thompson and Bagley took Thompson's first aid packet and applied it to the wound on his neck, where upon Thompson gesticulated to the wound on his shoulder and pointed at Bagley's first aid packet. Bagley said, 'Screw you, colonel! I might need this later today on myself.' Well, I'm happy to say that both Bagley and Colonel Thompson survived.

"I'm getting pretty much to the end of my recall, but I do want to emphasize that there were many, many acts of great heroism that took place on 6 June, 1944, most of which were unrecorded. But, you may be sure that some incredible things took place on that beach on that gloomy morning.

"One thing that I didn't mention, that I'm sure you're well aware of is the fact that the air preparation did not occur. Weather prevented the bombing that we were to expect. In fact, the beach and the 2nd Battalion, 116th Infantry were scheduled to get some three hundred tons of bombs on its small piece of beach. There weren't any. Some of my air force friends, I've mentioned this to them and they say, 'OK, that's certainly true, but how much enemy air did you see that day?' I must admit that we saw virtually none. I think one or two single German airplanes came by. They must have been on a reconnaissance flight of some kind. They didn't bother us a bit with any sort of a bombardment or strafing action. One of the things that we were concerned about before we hit the beach was getting through the bomb craters with some of our vehicles. We didn't have that problem at all. The beach was absolutely untouched. As I said earlier, the smoke that came from the burning weeds on the high ground just behind the beach was a real godsend. If it hadn't been for that accidental smoke, as I say, the smoke was occasioned by the brush and grass being set on fire by the very fine naval gun fire support, we'd have been in worse shape than we were.

"Another item was the tremendous confusion. We had these magnificently trained young men who had been through these rehearsals time and time again who, when they got on the beach were so seasick, so confused, no communication, that as many chimpanzees could have probably done as much of a job. I've often felt that if the enemy had shown any sort of enthusiasm and moved toward us that they could have run us right back into the ocean without any trouble.

"It was…chaos is not a good word for it…something perhaps even less effective than chaos. It wasn't a lot of running around and screaming and shouting and waving of arms. It was just complete lack of control and everything else, and I'm as much to blame as the next guy. In fact, I've often felt very ashamed of the fact that I was so completely inadequate as a leader on the beach on that frightful day.

"I must at the outset, with candor and honesty point out that what I, and I suspect most of all my superiors, associates, and subordinates were fighting for was not ideas. But rather an overwhelming desire to kill Germans [in order] to avoid being killed oneself and to achieve the terrain objectives we had trained so hard and so long to reach. At this late date, it would be easy for me to say that every man in the 116th infantry waded ashore with a burning desire to overcome the forces of evil and promote the principles of freedom and democracy. Unfortunately, the job at hand is considerably more down to earth and my impressions remain on that plane.

This stone building, in which German machine guns were emplaced, stood at the entrance to Exit D-3 at les Moulins, which was the objective of the 2nd Battalion, 116th Infantry Regiment, under the command of Major Sidney V. Bingham, Jr. This is the building where a badly wounded Colonel Paul W. Thompson, the commanding officer of the 6th Engineer Special Brigade, was found by Major Bingham. More German defensive positions which were a part of the WN 66 resistance nest sat on the bluffs and can be seen in the photo on the left beyond the barbed wire. This photo was taken shortly after the fighting as the body of a dead American soldier lies on the rocky shingle. *United States Army Signal Corps photograph, National Archives.*

"In this regard in late May, General Bradley visited the 29th Division and in a pep talk he made to the 116th he said, 'You men should consider yourselves lucky and are to be congratulated. You all have ringside seats at the greatest show on earth.' The men of the 116th were predominantly from rural Virginia, [and] in large measure were steeped in the traditions of the confederacy and were proud that the 116th Infantry was a direct descendant of the Stonewall Brigade of Civil War fare. They were magnificently trained, had confidence in each other, and confidence in the ability to do the job assigned to them. The variables of wind, waves, and tide landed some of our folks far removed from their assigned touch down points.

"The failure of friendly air to carpet bomb the landing beaches as planned—air strikes were diverted as you know inland, because of a low [cloud] ceiling and poor visibility. The necessity to traverse some two to three hundred yards of tidal flat after debarking from the assault craft with the well armed and determined enemy occupying the hundred foot high bluffs just behind the beach. Shooting was abandoned rapidly which neutralized much of our combat effectiveness resulting from the aforementioned training and high morale. And reduced this fine unit to a bunch of seasick, overloaded, frightened, confused, wet, and cold individuals whose only thought was to get off the beach as soon as possible and seek what little cover there might be at the base of the bluffs overlooking the beach. To make matters worse, many, when they did reach the shingle and a low sea wall, discovered their weapons had become clouded with sand and would not function. Communications were virtually non existent.

These deep narrow trenches atop the bluff overlooked the beach east of the les Moulins draw (Exit D-3) and connected fighting positions, underground shelters (left, left center, lower right), and observation posts and facilitated movement while under fire. From these positions, machine gunners and riflemen looked down the throats of the troops landing near the les Moulins draw. This type of trench system was present along the bluffs at every resistance nest overlooking the beach. *United States Army Signal Corps photograph, National Archives.*

"Unit integrity was also in short supply and if you get the idea that chaos was present, you're quite correct. An impression that overcame me at this junction was one of complete futility. Here I was, the battalion commander, unable for the most part to influence action or do what I knew had to be done. Another impression that I had, as I'm sure others did as well, was the shock of seeing dead and wounded comrades in substantial numbers and being unable to help in any way. I can't give too much credit to our company aid men and battalion medics who worked heroically against awesome odds. A few swimming tanks got ashore. They were Sherman tanks that had been modified to serve in an amphibious mode. One howitzer of the twelve in our direct support artillery battalion survived. The navy destroyer coursed up and down the beach just off shore delivering the most heartening fire from her five-inch high velocity guns and we managed to remove the sand from our clogged carbines, rifles, and machine guns. NCOs, lieutenants, and captains were able to assemble varying size groups of individuals without regard to unit assignment and make their way through minefields, up over the bluffs in some cases, and up the road through the les Moulins beach exit.

"Moving oneself on the beach was the main imperative. Many unheralded acts of initiative, improvisation, and heroism took place throughout 6 June and the total in dead and wounded was horrendous. The casualty toll would have been worse in my judgment had not the navy inadvertently come to our assistance. What occurred was this: the navy put banks of rockets on LCTs to provide covering fire for the landing craft taking us ashore. They provided the fire alright, and in so doing set fire to the tall grass and brush on the bluffs overlooking the beach. Smoke from these fires carried along by a brisk wind blowing from west to east very effectively screened us on our way to and across the beach.

"When and how did casualties occur? It is likely that landing crafts, LCVPs, were hit before touching down and that there were casualties. I can't cite any specifics on this. After touching down, there were men drowned, despite the fact that we all wore life belts. Some were hit while still in the water after debarking. The others were making their way across the beach, others on the shingle, and others after they got off the beach. Enemy artillery and automatic weapons and mines all played their part. The statistics after forty years have pretty much deserted me, but just to impart a rough idea of the attrition that took place that day: my S-3 was killed, headquarters company commander was wounded, E Company commander killed, F Company commander wounded, H Company commander killed, and in E Company, there were some fifty-five killed in action out of a total of something just over two hundred who landed."[98]

This is a pedestal mounted 50mm PAK 38 antitank gun positioned inside of an open concrete emplacement that was almost flush to the ground level. The gun shown was located east of the mouth of the les Moulins draw (Exit D-3) on the edge of the beach in order to fire at troops attempting to seek shelter along the shingle and seawall. It could also effectively engage incoming landing craft and tanks. This gun also covered the antitank ditch at Exit D-3 from the east so that any tank-dozer or bulldozer attempting to fill in the ditch in order to allow armor to cross it would be taken under enfilade fire. *Photograph by Lieutenant (jg) Stuart L. Brandel, United States Navy, courtesy of Tom Lane.*

This is one of two Panzerstellungs located on the west side of the les Moulins draw (Exit D-3) as part of WN 68. *United States Army Signal Corps photograph, National Archives.*

This is the second of the two Panzerstellungs located on the west side of the les Moulins draw (Exit D-3) as part of WN 68. *United States Army Signal Corps photograph, National Archives.*

Lieutenant Donald Casapulla, the adjutant of the 116th Infantry Regiment, was an eyewitness to at least one of the heroic actions of Major Bingham that day on Omaha Beach. "Major Sidney V. Bingham commanded the 2nd Battalion, 116th Infantry, in the assault on the French coast near Vierville-sur-Mer, 6 June 1944. The enemy was well emplaced on the cliffs behind the beach and was covering the beach with devastating artillery, automatic weapons, and small arms fire. Severe casualties were being inflicted upon our own forces who were pinned to the beach. One machine gun position whose location could not be determined from the beach was inflicting deadly fire on one of the companies of Major Bingham's battalion. With utter disregard for his own safety, Major Bingham gathered five of his men and in the face of terrific fire led his party across the beach and up the cliff. Although unable to reach the enemy machine gun position, he was nevertheless able to determine its location. He, therefore, returned to the beach and, with a part of his command, organized a flank and rear attack which succeeded in taking the enemy position and which permitted his own troops to advance. The outstanding heroism and leadership displayed by Major Bingham were an inspiration to the entire command and were largely instrumental in converting a disorganized group into a strong attacking force."[99]

First Lieutenant Robert C. Hargrove
Headquarters Company, 2nd Battalion, 116th Infantry Regiment, 29th Infantry Division

Lieutenant Robert C. Hargrove landed around H+30 along with Major Bingham. Lieutenant Donald Casapulla, the 116th Infantry's adjutant, wrote the following recommendation concerning Hargrove's actions on D-Day. "Lieutenant Hargrove was a platoon leader in the 116th Infantry. The beach [that was] assaulted was strongly defended by a determined enemy who was well emplaced in positions on the cliffs behind the beach and was covering the beach defenses and underwater obstacles with a devastating fire from artillery, automatic weapons, and rifles. The assault troops suffered heavy casualties and initially were pinned to the beach by this terrific fire. Lieutenant Hargrove, with utter disregard for his own safety and at the risk of his life, exposed himself on numerous occasions to encourage and lead his platoon across the beach."[100]

Captain John J. Cotter
Medical Detachment, 116th Infantry Regiment, 29th Infantry Division

First Lieutenant Forrest Zanlow
Medical Detachment, 116th Infantry Regiment, 29th Infantry Division

Lieutenant Donald Casapulla, the 116th Infantry Regiment's adjutant, wrote identical recommendations for two extremely courageous medical officers with the 116th Infantry Regiment who risked their lives time and again to save the wounded troops on the beach. "The 116th Infantry had severe casualties. Captain Cotter [and Lieutenant Zanlow] landed early in the assault as part of the regimental medical detachment. With a gallant and personal bravery beyond the call of duty, Captain Cotter and [Lieutenant Zanlow] attended the wounded upon the beaches, administering medical attention under heavy fire. [Their] personal bravery saved the lives of many American soldiers. [Their] heroic conduct inspired those who saw [them] to a more determined effort in meeting the enemy. Captain Cotter [and Lieutenant Zanlow were] clearly distinguished by conspicuous bravery and fearless care for the wounded in the face of enemy fire which the normal call of duty would have justified [them] avoiding."[101][102]

Lieutenant Colonel Thornton L. Mullins
Headquarters, 111th Field Artillery Battalion, 29th Infantry Division

Private Jack Manpel with Headquarters Battery, 111th Field Artillery Battalion, landed with Lieutenant Colonel Thornton Mullins and an advance team to prepare for the arrival of the battalion on Easy Green, which was scheduled for H+110. "The command party, commanded by Lieutenant Colonel Mullins, reached the beach at 07:00 hours 6 June 1944. As the ramp of our LCVP fell we were taken under heavy machine gun, mortar and [artillery] gunfire, as well as sniper fire. The infantry that had landed before had stopped on the beach and apparently were unable to move inland. Consequently, our party had to stop close to the water line and wait for the troops ahead to make room.

"Colonel Mullins went ahead to the edge of the beach where he waited for his party to catch up. When he saw that the infantry was not moving forward, he calmly stood up and walked back about 250 yards to the middle of the beach. He then waved his arm and shouted, 'Come on, let's go.' Colonel Mullins then proceeded to walk off the beach. When everyone saw that he made it without harm there was a general movement forward and the beach was cleared. Colonel Mullins then took charge of two tanks and gave them direction and range to several enemy strongpoints upon which they fired. The tanks were unable to neutralize all of the strongpoints. Fire from [artillery], machine guns and snipers was still very heavy. Colonel Mullins then made up a party of infantrymen and proceeded up the hill behind the beach in search of snipers. After about thirty minutes he returned and since small arms fire was still heavy on the beach, he organized another party and went up the hill once more. It was then that he was killed."[103]

Captain Richard F. Brush was also a member of the 111th Field Artillery Battalion command group, which landed along with Mullins. "Lieutenant Colonel Mullins landed with elements of the 2nd Battalion, 116th Infantry at H+30, 6 June 1944. Immediately upon landing he displayed tremendous aggressiveness in attempting to get our troops off the beaches. Standing exposed to enemy small arms fire and in the midst of heavy artillery barrages, he constantly urged all behind him to move forward. Because of Colonel Mullins' aggressiveness, many followed and saved themselves from being drowned or killed by enemy artillery. While accomplishing this, the colonel was wounded, but did not let this interfere with his purpose of making our troops move forward. On at least two occasions Colonel Mullins penetrated into enemy held ground in an attempt to knock out snipers in dug in positions. On one occasion he was pinned down for over an hour, his pistol shot from his hand, and was slightly wounded for the second time.

"Later, Colonel Mullins returned to the beach where he ordered a tank into firing position and in the face of enemy small arms, machine gun, and artillery fire, he directed the tank's fire at enemy strongpoints on the hill overlooking the beach. When last seen the colonel, severely wounded and refusing medical attention, was again going forward in an effort to knock out enemy resistance and accomplish his reconnaissance mission."[104]

THE SECOND WAVE OF THE 16TH INFANTRY was scheduled to land at H+30. Company G, 16th Infantry was scheduled to land on the western half of Easy Red, with one battery of the Provisional 397th Antiaircraft Artillery (Automatic Weapons) Battalion landing on the eastern half of Easy Red. One LCVP carrying Headquarters, 2nd Battalion, 16th Infantry was scheduled to land in the center of Easy Red. A second battery of the Provisional 397th Antiaircraft Artillery (Automatic Weapons) Battalion was assigned to land on the western half of Fox Green, with one LCVP of Headquarters, 3rd Battalion in the center, and Company K, 16th Infantry scheduled to land on the eastern half of Fox Green.

Lieutenant Colonel Herbert C. Hicks, Jr.
Headquarters, 2nd Battalion, 16th Infantry Regiment, 1st Infantry Division

The commander of the 2nd Battalion, 16th Infantry, Lieutenant Colonel Herbert C. Hicks, Jr., and the battalion headquarters group landed with Company G at about 7:15 a.m., some fifteen minutes late. Colonel George A. Taylor, the commanding officer of the 16th Infantry Regiment, was an eyewitness to the heroism of Hicks during the initial stages of the assault. "Finding parts of his battalion leaderless and pinned down by the intense fire, Colonel Hicks immediately made an effort to reorganize his companies. With complete disregard for his own safety, he moved up and down the fire swept beach, constantly exposing himself to the withering fire. When his hard hit organization began to take form, Colonel Hicks formed a group of leaderless soldiers and took command of them for an assault on the enemy strongholds. Displaying magnificent courage, he led his little combat group through a break in the wire over a thickly strewn uncharted minefield. In spite of the intense fire Colonel Hicks gained the cliffside directly under the enemy guns.

"Colonel Hicks assaulted and destroyed an enemy pillbox and two machine gun nests using only hand grenades and his rifle. Reaching the top of the cliff, Colonel Hicks strategically placed his men, and then retraced his dangerous route back to the beach. Again traversing the shell pounded shoreline Colonel Hicks collected the remainder of his battalion and organized them. He guided them off the beach trap to the cliff heights, and then led a superb, courageous forward advance of the remnants of his battalion in the securing of Colleville-sur-Mer."[105]

All six LCVPs transporting Company G, 16th Infantry touched down east of the assigned location and at about the same place where Lieutenant John Spalding's section of Company E had landed earlier midway between the Exit E-1 and Exit E-3 draws and between resistance nests WN 62 and WN 64. As a result of this fortunate occurrence, enemy fire was less intense than to the left or right, where the resistance nests were concentrated.

Captain Joseph T. Dawson
Company G, 16th Infantry Regiment, 1st Infantry Division

As Captain Joseph T. "Joe" Dawson waded through the surf to the shoreline he "found total chaos as men and material was literally choking the sandbar just at the water's edge. Lieutenant Colonel (and battalion commander) Hicks was already ashore and as soon as my men got off their boats I was ordered by Hicks to advance. A minefield lay in and around a path extending to my right and upward to the crest of the bluff overlooking the beach. Upon blowing a gap in the concertina wire, I led my men gingerly over the body of a soldier who had stepped on a mine in seeking to clear the path. I collected my company at the base of the bluff and proceeded ahead with my communications sergeant and another soldier. Midway toward the crest, I met Lieutenant Spalding, who was to my right and moving parallel to the crest of the bluff, with what was left of his platoon. He informed me that he had some prisoners who had surrendered to him. He had managed to clear his men from the beach to a point midway to the top of the bluff when he encountered direct fire from above. Returning the fire, nine soldiers surrendered to him. I sent one of my men to see that the prisoners were delivered to my executive officer.

"I proceeded toward the crest, asking Spalding to cover me, and at the same time sent my communications sergeant back to direct my executive officer with my men to move up to meet me as quickly as possible. Nearing the crest of the bluff, the terrain becomes almost vertical and is almost twenty feet in height. This afforded complete defilade from the entrenched enemy above. A machine gun nest was busily firing at the beach and one could hear rifle and mortar fire coming from the bluff crest. I tossed two grenades aloft into the enemy trench and upon exploding the machine gun nest became silent. I waved my men and Spalding to proceed as rapidly as possible and I then proceeded to the crest where I saw the enemy moving out toward the E-3 exit and dead Germans in the trenches. To my knowledge, no one had penetrated the enemy defenses until this moment. As soon as my men reached me, we debouched from that point, firing on the retreating enemy and moving toward a gate to the right corner at the open field. There was a roadway leading from the field through a heavily wooded area toward Colleville. Entering the wooded area we were immediately fired on by the enemy and this became a battleground extending all the way into town.

It was small units firing and falling back that constituted our opposition and was both deadly and time consuming, so we did not reach Colleville until noon. By the time we reached the outskirts of Colleville we had picked up several men from E Company, 16th Infantry and men from the 116th Infantry Regiment of the 29th Division. Company G worked its way within a kilometer of Colleville, where a very friendly French woman welcomed us with open arms and said, 'Welcome to France.'

"Major [William R.] Washington, 2nd Battalion executive officer, established a forward battalion command post at the point where we encountered the E Company and the 116th Regiment [troops], and I took charge of the men from G Company [and] proceeded into Colleville in an assault formation, giving and receiving fire as each wall and house seemed to be occupied by the enemy. The dominant building, as always in the Normandy villages, is a Norman church (built of stone). Its steeple stretches into the sky. Sure enough, in the steeple of the church there is an artillery observer. I entered the church with a sergeant and a private. Immediately, three of the enemy inside the church opened fire. Fortunately, we were not hit by this burst. But as we made our way through the church the private was killed, shot by the observer in the tower. I turned and we secured the tower by eliminating him. My sergeant shot the other two Germans and thus we eliminated the opposition at that point. As I ran out of the church, a German rifleman fired at me. I fired back with my carbine, but not before the German got off a second shot. The bullet went through my carbine and shattered the stock. Fragments went through my kneecap and leg, which caused my knee to swell and caused me to be evacuated the next day. Beyond the church, G Company ran into heavy fire from a full German company occupying the houses in Colleville. Built of stone, the positions were all but impregnable to small arms fire. By 15:00 hours, we secured Colleville and a battalion of the 18th Infantry passed through us and occupied positions east of Colleville. However, the haze of battle and the overcast sky cleared about this time and our navy proceeded to sweep the area of Colleville with deadly fire and shelling, causing a number of casualties and a most tragic loss. Their excuse upon inquiry was the orders they followed stated that they would fire on Colleville at H+60 minutes or as soon thereafter as visibility would permit. H-Hour+60 minutes was 07:30, and we fought and cleared the village some six hours later. Obviously, the navy was not informed of G Company's position, but there can be little to justify their action at such a late hour! After G Company secured Colleville for the night it took up defensive positions throughout the town."[106]

Captain Dawson had led the first company sized element to reach the top of the bluff in the 16th Infantry zone of Omaha Beach. Sergeant Philip Streczyk and Private First Class Richard J. Gallagher were the pathfinders who discovered the crack in the German defenses and made a breakthrough possible. Lieutenant Spalding and Captain Dawson led the exploitation of that small crack, with Spalding and his section widening the gap by attacking the enemy defenses all the way to the eastern side of Exit E-1 while Dawson penetrating the defense to prevent the Germans from reinforcing the defenses in that area and from making a counterattack to close the gap in their beach defenses in that area. These men led the way and were the difference makers in the Easy Red sector of Omaha beach.

Second Lieutenant Kenneth Bleau
Company G, 16th Infantry Regiment, 1st Infantry Division

Captain Dawson had plenty of help from other leaders in Company G, 16th Infantry Regiment in crossing the beach and making the breakthrough on the bluffs above Easy Red. "Lieutenant Bleau, an assault section leader of Company G, landed on Beach Easy Red at about 07:15 during the most critical period of the landing to find his company scattered and depleted by casualties. Although any movement on the beach drew fierce and terribly accurate automatic and sniper fire, desperate attempts were being made to reorganize, but these were severely impeded by the fire from the still intact enemy strongpoints on the high ridges overlooking the beach. Pausing only long enough to gather his section and place them in readiness for an advance, Lieutenant Bleau left the cover of the high water mark and completely exposed to direct intense enemy fire, moved along the heavily mined entanglements until he found a slight breach. Then with his small group following, he started across the open, uncharted minefield to attack the strongpoint. Lieutenant Bleau was at this time one of the first to pass through the beach wire. With a great portion of the initial wave still pinned down to the beach, Lieutenant Bleau, well in advance of his section reached the enemy dominated ridge.

"At approximately 11:00 hours, his unit was completely surrounded by the enemy and two strongly emplaced concealed enemy machine guns opened fire at pointblank range and threatened his small, desperately fighting section with annihilation. Displaying magnificent courage, Lieutenant Bleau continued forward alone, directly into the face of the enemy weapons. He approached to within twenty yards of one enemy nest and destroyed it with hand grenades. Without hesitation, despite the fact that vicious fire was concentrated on him, he fearlessly attacked the second enemy machine gun next and destroyed it also, allowing his own unit to withstand the enemy and enabling his company on the beach to reorganize for the attack inland. Twice during the critical period of the inland push, the enemy counterattacked with superior forces and threatened to break through the thin line of the battered company. On each occasion, Lieutenant Bleau went out to meet the enemy thrust and engaged the Germans in violent hand to hand combat in a superb demonstration of courage that was inspirational to our forces. In these savage encounters, Lieutenant Bleau killed five of the enemy and was the central figure in the repulse of the enemy thrusts."[107]

This casemate housing a 50mm PAK 38 antitank gun defended the west side of Exit E-1 as part of WN 65. *United States Army Signal Corps photograph, National Archives.*

Sergeant Arthur B. Buschlen
Headquarters Company, 2nd Battalion, 16th Infantry Regiment, 1st Infantry Division

Sergeant Arthur B. Buschlen, the 2nd Battalion message center chief, landed with the battalion command group. Lieutenant Neville A. Chandler was the battalion's S-2 (intelligence) officer. "Sergeant Arthur B. Buschlen, Headquarters and Headquarters Company, 2nd Battalion, 16th Infantry, was approaching the beach with one of the initial assault waves when his boat struck an underwater obstacle and capsized. Although thrown into deep water and subjected to fierce artillery and mortar bombardment, Sergeant Buschlen, refusing to consider personal safety, immediately swam to the aid of a wounded comrade and dragged him to shore. After securing medical attention for the casualty, Sergeant Buschlen observed another wounded man some one hundred yards from shore, struggling unsuccessfully to reach the beach with a cumbersome radio transmitter. Without hesitation and fully aware that he was inviting almost certain death, Sergeant Buschlen reentered the rough and densely mined surf and through a constant hail of machine gun and small arms fire waded to the side of the helpless man. Carrying the heavy radio and assisting the casualty, he again made his way through the curtain of fire to the shore where the transmitter was immediately pressed into service as a vital link in regimental communications. Still refusing to seek cover from the murderous concentrations of enemy fire and continuing to display courage and loyalty far beyond the normal call of duty, Sergeant Buschlen once again entered the channel to salvage additional equipment which had become entangled on barbed wire barriers and abandoned. While performing this heroic, self imposed mission, he was mortally wounded."[108]

Staff Sergeant Philip C. Clark
Headquarters Company, 2nd Battalion, 16th Infantry Regiment, 1st Infantry Division

Lieutenant Colonel Herbert Hicks, the commander of the 2nd Battalion, 16th Infantry, had landed in an LCVP along with a number of his battalion staff and headquarters company personnel. "Staff Sergeant Clark landed with a battalion section, but voluntarily joined a rifle company to aid in the assault. Leaving the slight cover of the shale shelf behind, Sergeant Clark crept to the barbed wire entanglements while under deadly raking machine gun fire and forced a breach. With mortar and artillery fire bursting about him he led his group across an uncharted minefield to the foot of the heavily defended cliffs. The intense fire from the machine gun emplacement, which was his objective, pinned down his entire platoon, but Sergeant Clark rose and ran in a frontal assault over a hundred yards of open, difficult, fire swept ground directly toward the gun position. With magnificent courage he engaged the five enemy soldiers in hand to hand combat, killing three and taking the other two prisoners."[109]

Also landing with the second wave of infantry were three man teams from the 18th Infantry Regiment to provide information to the regiment regarding the situation on the beach prior to its scheduled landing beginning at 9:30 a.m. and to coordinate its movement from the beach through the available exits.

PRIVATE CARLTON W. BARRETT
Headquarters Company, 18th Infantry Regiment, 1st Infantry Division

Lieutenant John P. Foley and two men with the Intelligence and Reconnaissance Platoon of the 18th Infantry Regiment, Privates William B. Carter and Carlton W. Barrett, landed about 7:00 a.m., in the vicinity of the St. Laurent draw, Exit E-1. Lieutenant Foley and his men were to access the situation on the beach and inform the 18th Infantry via radio before it was scheduled to land beginning at 9:30 a.m. (H+180). "As the LCM that Private Barrett was on came in to the beach, it was hit by mortar and machine gun fire from emplacements approximately two hundred yards inland from the beach. Private Barrett, [myself], and Private Carter, the other member of the set, made it to the beach in safety. As we abandoned the LCM and were coming in to the beach, Private Barrett stopped on many occasions to lift survivors to their feet when they lost their footing in the rough water. This set of the 18th Infantry had the mission of reconnoitering for an assembly area for a battalion that was to follow up the assault wave.

"As [we] made the beach [I] realized that the mission could not be accomplished until the enemy machine guns, mortars, and artillery observers were cleared from the high ground overlooking the beach. At this time, the beach was under constant machine gun, mortar, and artillery fire. It was apparent that the mission could not be accomplished for some time. Private Barrett and [I] started to work dragging soldiers from the surf who were in danger of drowning and assisting them to the meager security that the beach offered.

"Private Barrett was also dispatched with a message to contact another liaison set who were also on the beach. In full view of the enemy and under a constant barrage from enemy guns, he delivered the message. Upon his return he rendered first aid to the wounded, quieted the hysterical, and found them what little shelter was available."[110]

Lieutenant Foley was wounded while pulling survivors to the beach. "When [I] was wounded, Private Barrett skillfully bandaged [my] wounds and probably saved [my] life, as the shrapnel wounds were above the left eye, and [I] was bleeding profusely. As other men were hit by the same shell, they were pulled to shore by Private Barrett. He then went to secure aid men to administer to their needs.

"Private Barrett then waded out to contact landing boats to get litters to evacuate the casualties, then assisted in carrying the wounded to the boats. As the last of the wounded were being removed from the beach, [I] noticed our craft coming in to land. [I] called Private Barrett and sent him to contact the boats who were about to beach. He was instrumental in furnishing information in regard to the situation. He kept up this work on the beach until he became a casualty, suffering wounds in the left foot, both legs, and hips. Private Barrett is small in stature, about five feet four inches in height, and weighs 125 pounds. He truly exemplified the saying: 'No sacrifice too great. No mission too difficult. Duty first.'"[111]

On the morning of June 6, Private William B. Carter was still suffering from the effects of tonsillitis and had only been able to consume soup. "I got into the boat, crouched between some radios in the back, and put my head between my knees. I didn't see anything, but I heard the bullets bouncing off [the landing craft]. I didn't look up until I felt the boat run aground. I saw everyone was off, and I didn't want a repeat of the landing in Sicily, where I nearly drowned. I ran as hard as I could and jumped as far as I could. I came down in a few inches of water and damn near drove my knees up into my shoulders. We got up on the beach; Barrett was on one side of me and the lieutenant on the other. Mortar shells were falling all around. Shrapnel nicked Barrett on the arm and scratched the lieutenant's face. But I wasn't touched.

"We moved up the beach past a halftrack. I saw a pair of coveralls with hands coming out of the sleeves, but there was no head. Bodies were all over the place. The 16th Infantry had gotten off the beach and the lieutenant told us to stay and direct the 18th to the path that was cleared of mines. There was no hardware, tanks, or halftracks moving anywhere. Barrett and I started pulling guys out of the water, moving bodies so that boats could come in without running over them. We dragged as many as we could out of the way, while the Germans kept shelling the beach hitting first one end and then the other. We'd wait and move to the area they'd just finished pounding."[112]

Private Carlton Barrett was wounded in both legs, the buttocks, and left foot during his intrepid actions. "When I was hit I could not feel anything or I would not have run over two hundred yards up the beach and then swam out to an LCI."[113]

Private Barrett would be awarded the Medal of Honor for his conspicuous gallantry above and beyond the call of duty for saving so many lives on Omaha Beach on June 6, 1944.

First Lieutenant Howard P. MacConchie
Headquarters Company, 18th Infantry Regiment, 1st Infantry Division

Lieutenant Howard P. MacConchie was the leader of another three man team from the 18th Infantry's Intelligence and Reconnaissance Platoon, which was to provide information to the regiment prior to its landing. First Sergeant Lawrence J. Fitzsimmons, with Company E, 16th Infantry, "was an eyewitness of the actions of First Lieutenant Howard MacConchie, part of the 18th Infantry advance party which landed thirty minutes after H-Hour with the second wave of the 16th Infantry on 6 June 1944, near St. Laurent, France. Lieutenant MacConchie had been on an LCVP which was sunk about 150 yards off shore by a mortar shell. After swimming in to the beach he took immediate action on the chaotic situation there. It was crowded with bodies, many wounded and dead, the rest lying flat to escape the terrific fire being directed on them. They too, were gradually becoming casualties. Lieutenant MacConchie was waiting for a radio team, for his mission was transmitting information of the progress of the assault to his regimental commander. While waiting for his radio, he organized a firing line with the men around him, and succeeded in eliminating much of the enemy's small arms fire on the beach.

"He then went forward himself over open ground to blow out a section of barbed wire so that these men could get off the beach and press the attack on the foe's beach defenses. In accomplishing this, he survived a terrific mortar barrage. The men willingly followed him until they had reached other elements of the 16th Infantry, when he left them to find that regiment's CP. His own men having been lost, Lieutenant MacConchie attempted to contact his unit by radio at this CP, but mechanical difficulties prevented his sending his message. Then, despite being in a comparatively safe place, he decided to return to the beach to assist in anything he could until his regiment would land. The beach looked much as it had the first time he came upon the scene and Lieutenant MacConchie at once set about organizing squads of men, directing them over the safest route inland toward their respective organizations. He helped the medical men in treating and evacuating the wounded. He carried on in the same tireless manner as before, exposing himself completely to an increasingly heavy and accurate artillery barrage in order to clear the beaches for the oncoming waves of troops. He directed the organizations of his own regiment when they landed, and after contacting a representative of his CO, he joined his own battalion after six gory and toiling hours on the beach."[114]

Lieutenant Colonel Donald V. Bennett
Headquarters, 62nd Armored Field Artillery Battalion

Lieutenant Colonel Donald V. Bennett was a 1940 graduate of the United States Military Academy from Lakeside, Ohio. On the morning of June 6, he was leading an advance team of fourteen officers and men, consisting of his executive officer, reconnaissance officer, forward observers, and signals personnel ashore at H+30, ahead of his 62nd Armored Field Artillery Battalion. Bennett and his team stood at the very front of the LCVP transporting them, with infantrymen of the 3rd Battalion, 16th Infantry standing behind them as the landing craft touched down on Fox Green. "The ramp dropped. Even as it rattled down, I scrambled upward, dodging around the cable winching out and leapt, hitting the water, going under, feet hitting bottom, pushing back up, gulping for air. The memories are a kaleidoscope now, the sound of incoming bullets zipping past, the cold of the water, that horrid feeling of trying to run when one is chest deep in water, except it is not a nightmare, it is real, and someone is trying to kill you. I know I cleared the side of the ramp and scrambled through the surf to get away from that boat. I think I looked back, or maybe the memory is what someone told me later. The infantry that had been behind me in the boat had panicked under fire and piled into the back as machine gun fire tore into them, tracers flickering past, sparks flashing, rounds hitting bodies. In their last seconds no one was going forward. I think I was screaming for them to move, to go over the sides, but they didn't. In an unrelenting stream of fire those poor souls did not stand a chance. They were slaughtered to a man. Mortar rounds were dropping in the water around me. I surged forward, staggering, falling, getting up, and pushing forward and away from that doomed boat, for when the slaughter was done there, the gunners would pick off whoever was left around it.

"Years later a comrade—one of my men from the 62nd—said that he was floundering in the surf, looking for cover, and suddenly saw me standing in front of him. 'Damn it, come on,' he said I screamed at him, 'You're holding up the war!'

"I was up on the beach, out of the water and looked back again at my boat. Everyone aboard was dead, a mortar round hitting it; the boat exploding, burning, wallowing in the surf and going down. There wasn't a damn thing I could do now, and I turned away. Before me was hell on earth. The first wave had all but been annihilated. A scattering of men was visible here and there, crouched behind barriers, the dead littering the edge of the surf, which was creeping ever higher, a heroic few racing out to drag wounded comrades to higher ground…It was frightfully lonely—a few men here—others there. Up on the bluffs, three hundred yards away, I could see at least a half dozen strongpoints, tracers zipping down from them, kicking up that damn sand, which seemed to engulf and trap you so that you took four steps just to slither one step forward. It was obvious to me that any semblance of order and coordination of plan was dead at the water's edge."[115]

Despite the initial shock, Bennett's training and conditioning quickly took over. "If I thought about my personal safety, I was doomed. Any rational man at that moment would find the nearest place to hide and curl up. But war is a continuing act of irrationality, a transcending of all our instincts to preserve our own lives. Everywhere I looked, men were dead, wounded, screaming.

"My own men were loosely gathered around me, eyes fixed on me, silently asking, 'What the hell do we do now, sir?' I had to act, to do something, anything, and everything within me screamed that I had to do it quickly. I felt at that moment that we were all dead men anyhow, and the training and the pride in what I was supposed to be told me that if I was going to die, I might as well do something, anything, in those few remaining minutes that just might make a difference…

"It is a bit embarrassing to write this now, for in a way it is a violation of 'the code.' Veterans who were there know what I mean. We don't like to talk about what we did; for we survived. Far too many of our comrades who did what had to be done died doing it. In our hearts we wish not to speak of ourselves, but rather of them, if we wish to speak at all… Standing up, I started forward. It was that simple. Someone has to stand up. Once that is done, from that moment it becomes almost easy. He has crossed a line. He no longer thinks of himself or what he is doing. He no longer thinks of the possible pain, of his wife, his kids; for to do that would paralyze him. He thinks of the mission. He thinks of the men he must lead and prays that in leading them more will live than will die through his actions versus his inaction.

"I stood up. Down the beach I spotted a couple of antiaircraft guns. How they ever got on the beach was beyond me, but there they were, beautiful quad .50 caliber machine guns mounted on a light vehicle. I told my XO to head down to them and get them to start laying in suppressive fire along the top of the bluffs. I told the rest of my command to follow me up the beach. It was a long, laborious zigzag run as we moved from obstacle to obstacle. About half of my men were hit. Amazingly though, none were killed. At some point, I took a round or shell fragment through the wrist, a remarkable wound. It didn't touch a bone, a major vein, or an artery, just went clean through. I didn't even feel it at first.

"Elements of at least four companies of the 16th Infantry were scattered on the beach without any real semblance of organization. As I went up the beach, I found the captain of one company, who must, across all these years, remain nameless. He was in a blind panic frantically digging a hole, refusing to move. I left him behind. At last I found Captain [Kimball R.] Richmond of Company I, 3rd Battalion of the 16th, and a true hero…We hunkered down together, all hell roaring about us, and hurriedly worked out a plan. Several of my officers I detailed off to him as infantry commanders, slotting them in to take over whatever men they could round up…The plan Richmond and I came up with was damn simple and straightforward. We had to get those men off the beach. Once under the bluffs, we'd have some defilade, ground out of reach of their [artillery] and mortars and we could then close on the German bunkers dug in along the bluffs—easier said than done. There were still at least two hundred yards of open ground ahead. Most of the other officers with the 3rd of the 16th were dead, so I put my people in and sent them out to get the men moving…

"I started to push forward myself. A sharp clear memory is of coming across an entire squad of infantry, all but one of them dead, most likely caught by a machine gun and riddled. I went up to the one man still alive and knelt down and said something about how he'd be all right.

"'No sir,' he sighed, 'all my buddies are dead. It's okay about me. I just want to go with them.' There was nothing I could do. A few minutes later I crawled back to him and he was dead.

"The next two hours are a blur as we tried to get across that two hundred yards of open ground. Many have seen extant fragments of film of that fight, of four or five men getting up out of the surf, heavily laden, and trying to stagger forward. Within seconds two of them go down… It was like that. Four of five men getting up, dashing half a dozen yards, a man or two drops, the rest go to ground. They take a deep breath and then sprint forward again. And they are burdened with upward of a hundred pounds of equipment; they are soaking wet and cold, and trying to get up a sloping beach of wet loose sand.

"I was obsessed with getting the men to start fighting back. Most of the guns were jammed with sand and grit in spite of the plastic wrappings (and condoms) on the muzzles. If you want to do a truly maddening task, field strip a Garand under fire. You could see the Germans up there, for the trench connecting the strongpoints was only about waist deep. They'd pop up, fire, duck back down, then pop up again a few seconds later to the left or right and fire again. I started getting men to lay down suppressive fire to start throwing off the aim of the Krauts. The bluffs were so damn close and yet the final sprint to them felt like an eternity. By ones and twos, men gained the momentary protection of the base of the bluffs, a trail of casualties behind them clear back to the waterline, where the wreckage of landing boats rolled and bobbed, debris and bodies littering the high water line as the surf crept up behind us…

"Wire entanglements, mines, and deadly fields of crossfire were still ahead of us on the face of that bluff. Captain Richmond and I started to grab men to push up the bluffs, but now we got into a true short range killing zone. All the Krauts had to do was lob grenades down at us, and every approach was covered by interlocking fields of fire, barbed wire, and mines.

"I'm not sure where it came from, but out in the surf there was a beached Sherman, stalled and half submerged. The gun was still operational though, and by waving and pointing I got their attention. The guys in that tank had guts. We pointed out targets to them and they just poured it in, and they in turn became a target for every German gunner on the heights. The tank kept on firing until it was finally swamped by the rising tide.

"And then came a miracle. Even now, as I recall it, the memory brings tears to my eyes. A United States Navy destroyer came to our rescue. The men of Fox Green will forever be indebted to their comrades aboard that ship, for it was obvious that they came in not just to fight, but also to draw fire away from us, to give us a needed breather so we could get up that slope. The destroyer came slicing in out of the smoke so close that I swore it was going to beach itself not two hundred yards away [from the beach]. At that range it suddenly looked huge, like a battleship going in harm's way and every damn gun on that ship opened up, from five-inchers, to 20mm and 40mm antiaircraft, to machine guns, and I suspect more than one man had a rifle or pistol out. They just blasted that crest and the bunkers at near pointblank range. Rounds were literally shrieking in a few feet over our heads, tearing across the cliff face, rubble raining down. My God, how we cheered them. We had not been forgotten. Some sailors out there were risking their lives to give us a fighting chance. That beautiful ship came almost to a stop, the water around it foaming as the Krauts, unable to resist the target, foolishly lifted their fire from us and poured it out to sea. That was our signal to go. Richmond and I started to urge the men forward, to get the hell up that bluff while we had the chance, charging upward with the naval shells striking above us. The destroyer slowly, ever so slowly worked its way down the length of Fox Green, firing away with everything it had. It reached the edge of the front, turned sharply about, closed back in, and opened up again.

"Across forty years of service I've had a lot of rivalry with the United States Navy, but always in my heart I've felt that debt of gratitude for that ship whose name I do not know. I would not be alive now if it had not been for them. I would gladly embrace every man on that boat if I ever had the chance to meet them. They tore the crap out of that crest and under their protective fire we rushed the high ground, taking casualties, but pushing forward to the bitter close in killing range, wiping out the Kraut bunkers with nothing more than rifle fire, a few light machine guns, and grenades. And suddenly we were on the crest, the few Germans still alive up there giving back—abandoning their position, running into the fields and woods. Captain Richmond had command of the top of the bluffs."[116]

Major James W. Bowman, the executive officer of the 62nd Armored Field Artillery Battalion, spent much of the morning with Bennett. "Lieutenant Colonel Bennett landed on Omaha Fox Green and Easy Red Beach with the second wave at 07:20 hours. His party was mercilessly attacked by a tremendous volume of machine gun fire as their craft approached the beach and as they disembarked. When he and the personnel that were on his craft reached the shingle at the base of the cliff adjoining the beach, fifty percent of the personnel who had disembarked from the landing craft were casualties from machine gun fire. From his position of cover he observed that the infantry assault companies were pinned down on the beach.

"Lieutenant Colonel Bennett immediately left cover and exposed himself to extreme danger from machine gun and sniper fire to contact the company commanders. He found that two of the three company commanders were casualties and that one company had lost all of its officers. He also learned that all companies [had] lost assault equipment, except individual arms. He then rounded up all of the remaining infantry officers and directed that they be redistributed among the companies and the companies reorganized and prepare to assault the ridge.

"He continually moved along the beach gathering information and frequently exposing himself to fire. He learned that four tanks had reached a hill defiladed spot along the beach. Casualties among tank personnel were high and no officer could be found in charge. He ordered the tank personnel to fire direct fire on the pillboxes and strongpoints on the ridge during the time that the infantry was organizing. He then again exposed himself to contact an antiaircraft unit that had managed to bring six .50 caliber machine guns ashore and ordered them to place their guns in positions where they could give the infantry assault companies close heavy weapons support when they assaulted the ridge as well as protection against enemy aircraft.

"During this time, his party had made contact by radio with his battalion of artillery that was lying offshore in LCTs, and he instructed his forward observers to fire the battalion direct from the LCTs to give the infantry all support possible. At about 10:00, the infantry had organized and with the aid of the machine guns, the fire from the four tanks, and the artillery support, they successfully assaulted the cliff. Lieutenant Colonel Bennett then gave his S-3, on board one of the LCTs, orders to bring his battalion in as soon as possible on any part of the beach and he began moving down the beach to Easy Red in an effort to find a place to bring in the battalion. As he approached the beach Easy Red, he found it impossible to move along due to the low defilade and heavy machine gun and sniper fire, except by short rapid dashes of crawling. At every sign of movement the enemy would cover the area with fire and only by lying perfectly flat could one avoid being hit. In this vicinity another tank was on the beach and he ordered it to fire on some emplacements. The result of this fire silenced considerable small arms fire and one sniper in particular, that caused four casualties in less than minutes' time.

"By this time a few LCTs were coming in on the right edge of Easy Red Beach. Three LCTs had been knocked out by artillery fire, which was becoming more intense in this area causing many casualties and the destruction of many vehicles. Although shell fragments from enemy artillery fire were continuously covering the area and fragments from burning vehicles that were exploding were intense, Lieutenant Colonel Bennett continued moving down the beach trying to find a place to bring in his battalion. At 14:00 hours he was able to bring in two LCTs. One was completely unloaded and the other partially unloaded, but was driven back to sea by a tremendous concentration of enemy artillery fire.

These M7 Priests with 105mm howitzers mounted on a fully tracked armored chassis were the initial army artillery support, firing while aboard LCTs beginning at H-30. Both the 62nd Armored Field Artillery Battalion, which supported the 16th Infantry and the 58th Armored Field Artillery Battalion, which supported the 116th Infantry, both utilized M7s on D-Day. *United States Army Signal Corps photograph, National Archives.*

"He immediately formed a composite battery of four [M7 Priest 105mm self propelled] guns and went into position on the beach. Even though enemy artillery fire was constantly falling in the area, this battery was in position and able to support the infantry. Lieutenant Colonel Bennett kept moving about the beach disregarding the intense enemy fire, looking for an exit to move off the beach to a better position. By 18:00 hours, a new position was located and the composite battery had cleared the beach. Lieutenant Colonel Bennett, in disregarding his own safety under such heavy enemy fire throughout the day and his clear thinking contributed immeasurably to the success of establishing the beachhead."[117]

The Provisional 397th Antiaircraft Artillery (Automatic Weapons) Battalion was scheduled to land across all sectors of Omaha Beach at H+30 in eighteen LCVPs to deploy thirty-six .50 caliber machine guns every 150 yards spread across the entire length of the beach intended for antiaircraft defense. The battalion lost twenty-eight of its thirty-six machine guns as it disembarked. However, it did provide suppressive fire on German beach defenses with its remaining .50 caliber machine guns as the German Luftwaffe did not conduct an attack on the Omaha Beach landings.

Private First Class Henry H. Hall, Jr.
Medical Detachment, Provisional 397th Antiaircraft Artillery (Automatic Weapons) Battalion

Captain Arthur L. Meyer was temporarily assigned to the Provisional 397th Antiaircraft Artillery (Automatic Weapons) Battalion for the Normandy invasion. "Between the hours of 07:15-11:00, Private Hall, a member of the medical detachment of this organization, performed the duties of his profession under the most hazardous circumstances. Although he was faced with a staggering number of casualties lying in the safety of a twenty foot cliff which blocked the enemy's observation; casualties who would have occupied all of his time and exhausted his supplies were he to only treat them, Private Hall chose to rescue and aid those wounded and drowning in the shallows. Disregarding all personal safety and fully aware of the certain death that awaited him, he made repeated trips out into the face of direct enemy machine gun fire to aid and save many men. While on one of these trips Private Hall fell mortally wounded."[118]

Company K, 16th Infantry Regiment was scheduled to land on Fox Green at H+30 and as it did, vicious automatic weapons fire tore into it, cutting down four officers and almost fifty men while on the landing craft, in the water, and crossing the beach.

First Lieutenant James L. Robinson
Company K, 16th Infantry Regiment, 1st Infantry Division

Lieutenant Colonel Charles Horner was the commanding officer of the 3rd Battalion, 16th Infantry. "As the company's assault craft neared the beach, they became separated, and the various assault sections could not land in the planned order. The company commander and executive officer were wounded and put out of action by sniper bullets as soon as the men were off the craft. Leaderless, the scattered sections of the company waded ashore, and the remnants sought whatever cover they could find on the beach. Despite the fact that every leader in the entire area was being subjected to intense and accurate sniper fire in addition to the machine gun and artillery action, Lieutenant Robinson unhesitatingly assumed complete command of the company. He ignored the vicious fire falling all about him and moved up and down the exposed beach, collecting and consolidating the men of his unit until he again had a unified striking force of about sixty men. The particularly bitter fire on the Company K sector came mostly from a six foot thick reinforced concrete casemate on the high ground overlooking beach exit E-3. Protected by machine guns and strongly dug-in snipers, the position resisted all long range efforts to neutralize it. Displaying superb courage, Lieutenant Robinson worked his way through a slight breach in the wire and well in advance of any of his men, crawled through a minefield to the base of the hill. Intense fire was directed on him, but deigning cover or rest, he worked his way forward. Approaching to within one hundred yards of the enemy position, he engaged it with his carbine. The enemy fire concentrated on him, but with complete disregard for his own life, he continued to fire. Under this diversion, his men approached the enemy position from the flanks. Just as his men closed in on the strongpoint, Lieutenant Robinson was hit and mortally wounded. But the strongpoint was destroyed and the men on the beach, pinned down by its fire, were able to continue the attack."[119]

THE NEXT WAVE OF THE 116TH INFANTRY was scheduled to land at H+40. Company D and Headquarters Company, 1st Battalion were assigned to land on Dog Green. Combat engineers with the 121st and 149th Engineer Combat Battalions, which were assigned to open Exit D-1 to Vierville were scheduled to land on Dog White. In the Dog Red sector, Company D, 81st Chemical Battalion (Motorized) was slated to land with their 4.2 inch mortars. The 112th Engineer Combat Battalion was assigned to land on both the Dog Red and Easy Green sectors with the mission of opening up Exit D-3 at les Moulins.

Second Lieutenant Verne V. Morse
Company D, 116th Infantry Regiment, 29th Infantry Division

Lieutenant Donald Casapulla, the adjutant of the 116th Infantry, wrote the following regarding the courageous leadership of Lieutenant Verne V. Morse, as he led his troops across the fire swept beach. "Lieutenant Morse was a platoon leader in the 116th Infantry. The beach assaulted was strongly defended by a determined enemy who was well emplaced in positions on the cliffs behind the beach and was covering the beach defenses and underwater obstacles with devastating fire from artillery, automatic weapons, and rifles. The assault troops suffered heavy casualties and initially were pinned to the beach by this terrific fire. Lieutenant Morse with utter disregard for his own safety and at the risk of his life exposed himself on numerous occasions to encourage and lead his platoon across the beach."[120]

Sergeant Raymond E. Nicoli
Company D, 81st Chemical Battalion (Motorized)

Company D, 81st Chemical Battalion (Motorized) was transported to the beach in four LCVPs. The LCVP carrying the battalion's command group was heavily shelled, seriously wounding the battalion commander, Lieutenant Colonel Thomas H. James, and lost its engine and rudder and floated aimlessly before beaching in a protected spot. As a result, Captain W. R. Johnson became the acting battalion commander. "The mission of Company D in the initial operations on the beach was to deploy their 4.2 [inch] mortars in close support of the assault infantry. It was Sergeant Raymond E. Nicoli's duty as leader of a mortar squad to see that his gun, together with the ammunition, was unloaded off the landing craft, carried across the beach to a position of safety, and then moved into firing position. Although painfully wounded in the hand by shrapnel exploding on his landing craft, Sergeant Nicoli refused medical aid and with total disregard for his personal safety, remained at his post, making a number of trips across the beach under heavy machine gun and mortar fire, and successfully directed his squad in the removal of the mortars and ammunition from the landing craft safely to shore. Afterwards, Sergeant Nicoli's wound proved serious enough to require his being evacuated."[121]

Private Donald B. McLaren
Company D, 81st Chemical Battalion (Motorized)

Captain Johnson also recommended Private Donald B. McLaren for the Distinguished Service Cross for his actions on Omaha Beach. "Private Donald B. McLaren's assignment was that of ammunition handler. In addition, he was to assist in unloading guns, ammunition, and equipment from the landing craft, carrying these across the beach to a position of safety. When McLaren's boat hit the beach, it came under direct machine gun fire. Private McLaren was seriously wounded in the hips. Although at the time he refused to be evacuated it was subsequently observed that McLaren was hobbling painfully and barely able to walk. Nevertheless, Private McLaren, together with other soldiers, remained on the job, making several trips across the beach under heavy machine gun and mortar fire, helping in the removal of the mortars and ammunition from the landing craft safely to shore. When the guns were finally in position to fire, Private McLaren was evacuated. Subsequent examination showed that one of his legs was partially paralyzed. Private McLaren's outstanding bravery and self sacrifice were of great inspiration to his fellow soldiers, and his actions materially aided his company in getting their mortars in position to support the infantry."[122]

Private Benton L. Porter
Company D, 81st Chemical Battalion (Motorized)

Captain Johnson wrote a recommendation for Private Benton L. Porter, who also helped unload one of the landing crafts, despite being wounded. "Private Benton L. Porter's assignment was that of ammunition handler. In addition, he was to assist in unloading guns, ammunition, and equipment from the landing craft, carrying these across the beach to a position of safety. Shrapnel fire exploding directly on Private Porter's landing craft seriously cut his forehead, causing profuse bleeding. When the craft finally hit the beach, Private Porter refused to be evacuated. With total disregard for his personal safety, Private Porter, together with other soldiers, remained on the job, making a number of trips across the beach, under heavy machine gun and mortar fire, helping in the removal of the mortars and ammunition from the landing craft safely to shore. When the guns finally were in position to fire, Private Porter, extremely weak from loss of blood, consented to be evacuated."[123]

Technician Fifth Grade Felice J. Savino
Company D, 81st Chemical Battalion (Motorized)

Captain Johnson also witnessed the actions of Technician Fifth Grade Felice J. Savino. "Technician Fifth Grade Savino's normal assignment was that of lineman, but for this phase of the operations he was to assist in unloading guns, ammunition and equipment from the landing craft, carrying these across the beach to a position of safety and then act as an ammunition handler. Shrapnel fire exploding directly on Technician Fifth Grade Savino's landing craft seriously wounded him through the nose. When the craft finally hit the beach, Technician Fifth Grade Savino refused to be evacuated. With total disregard for his personal safety, Savino, together with other soldiers, remained on the job making a number of trips across the beach under heavy machine gun and mortar fire, helping in the removal of the mortars and ammunition from the landing craft safely to shore. When the guns finally were in position to be fired, Technician Fifth Grade Savino continued to act as an ammunition handler until he was unable to carry on. Only then, did he permit himself to be evacuated."[124]

Major William A. Richards
Headquarters, 112th Engineer Combat Battalion, 1121st Engineer Combat Group

Sergeant Major Joseph P. Medved and the rest of the 112th Engineer Combat Battalion landed at H+40 near Exit D-3, at les Moulins. "Major Richards walked over to a tank-dozer which was parked near Beach Exit D-3. He stood alongside the tank-dozer and yelled for the driver. When the driver stuck his head out, Major Richards instructed the driver to start clearing a way through the wire. Major Richards walked ahead of the tank-dozer and directed its course through the wire. All this was done under sniper fire and I heard at least five bullets ricochet from the tank-dozer."[125]

Private Arnold Roll, with Company C, 112th Engineer Combat Battalion, lost contact with his company after crossing the beach and dug in behind the seawall. "Major Richards approached a group of us, mainly 29th Division troops, and asked for two volunteers to accompany him on a reconnaissance to locate the German 88mm gun. Nobody was willing to go. Major Richards then asked me if I was from the 112th, and I answered yes.

This eighteen feet wide antitank ditch protected Exit D-3 from a direct approach up the les Moulins draw. Filling in this ditch was assigned to Lieutenant William A. Richards' 112th Engineer Combat Battalion as one of many obstacles it would have to clear to open the draw to vehicular traffic. *United States Army Signal Corps photograph, National Archives.*

"He said, 'You come with me.' I paused awhile because my rifle was filled with sand and I felt very doubtful if it would fire, but I said, 'Alright, sir.' We started down the road keeping as low as possible. About fifty yards down we then moved toward the hills off the road to take advantage of better cover. A sniper opened up on us about one hundred yards inland, firing at least three shots, the last shot just missing the major. He then ordered me to get that sniper who was about 150 yards from us. I shot him and fired another shot at him for safety. About a half a mile inland we found the 88mm on the base of the hill, well camouflaged, only the barrel showing. We then realized that the major himself was only about twenty-five yards from what seemed to be another sniper. I covered the major as he slowly moved back without the German noticing him. We arrived back at the beach and he thanked me and told me to dig in and wished me good luck. He then looked up at the cliff and was shot and wounded on the left forearm. A medical captain took him away for treatment."[126]

When Sergeant Major Medved "next saw Major Richards, he was wounded and Captain Graham, CO, Company C, 112th Engineer Combat Battalion, was giving him first aid. Right after this, Major Richards climbed over the seawall into some trenches right behind the beach. He started aggressive action against the small arms fire by personally supervising the fire of a small group of men already in the trenches."[127]

Lieutenant Colonel John T. O'Neill, the commander of the Special Engineer Task Force, received a report a short time later that Major Richards had "proceeded to the entrance of Beach Exit D-3 to organize the mine clearing and obstacle removing parties. While organizing these parties he was killed by artillery fire."[128]

The les Moulins Exit D-3 had a thick concrete wall roadblock which extended from the building (right center) and had to be demolished in order for vehicular traffic to use the exit. This was a major obstacle that the 112th Engineer Combat Battalion had to clear to open the exit. *United States Army Signal Corps photograph, courtesy of Tom Lane.*

THE 16TH INFANTRY REGIMENT units which were scheduled to land at H+40 included Company H transported in six LCVPs assigned to land on Easy Red; elements of the 2nd and 3rd Battalion Medical Detachments, advance groups from artillery, antitank units, and 5th Special Engineer Brigade, and other miscellaneous troops in two LCMs astride the Easy Red and Fox Green sectors; and Company M carried in six LCVPs on Fox Green.

First Lieutenant John D. Shelby
Company H, 16th Infantry Regiment, 1st Infantry Division

Lieutenant Colonel Herbert Hicks, commander of the 2nd Battalion, 16th Infantry, observed Lieutenant John D. Shelby take command of otherwise leaderless troops and lead them against the German defenses. "Landing on the beach amid heavy shelling, fierce flat trajectory fire, and scenes of utter confusion, Lieutenant Shelby, Company H, 16th Infantry, an assault section leader, found himself separated from his unit which was inextricably intermingled in the thousands of troops huddled behind a narrow shelf of shale—dazed, exhausted, leaderless, and suffering heavy casualties as shells burst continuously in their midst. Hesitating only long enough to gather five men into an assault team, Lieutenant Shelby in utter disregard for his safety, led his newly formed unit in a two hundred yard dash through the withering fire and across deadly exposed minefields to attack one strategically emplaced antitank gun which was delivering accurate murderous fire on incoming landing craft. Displaying superb courage, he alone assaulted the gun position and engaged the enemy crew in a vicious hand to hand battle, killing one man and taking six prisoners. Leaving the defense of the gun and position to his men, Lieutenant Shelby then took over command of a group of G Company troops who were advancing leaderless up the hill and led them in a bold attack on the nearby town of Colleville-sur-Mer. Under almost constant direct fire from the scores of snipers concealed in the town's buildings, Lieutenant Shelby never once faltered and personally accounted for seven snipers during the perilous mopping up drive, which cleared the way for the advance of our troops."[129]

Private Peter Cavaliere
Company H, 16th Infantry Regiment, 1st Infantry Division

Private Joseph P. Parke
Company H, 16th Infantry Regiment, 1st Infantry Division

Private Joseph P. Parke found another Company H soldier, Private Peter Cavaliere, "about twenty minutes after we had broken through the barbed wire defenses on the beach in the vicinity of Colleville-sur-Mer. Together, we started along the road toward the objective, the town of Colleville-sur-Mer. A short way inland we met Lieutenant Shelby and a group of other men who were with him. We continued along until we reached almost to the edge of the town. Here the advance was stopped by enemy mortar and artillery fire, plus sniper fire."[130]

Lieutenant John Shelby led a group of Company H troops who "pushed a savagely fighting enemy steadily back and into the town itself. As the company prepared to assault and drive the hostile forces out of the town, the enemy laid an intense artillery barrage in the area. Coupled with the artillery, came a fierce counterattack with approximately two hundred men and one Mark IV tank."[131]

The barrage and counterattack forced Lieutenant Shelby and the other troops in Colleville-sur-Mer to withdraw from the town. "Despite the fact that their entire unit was moving out, Private Cavaliere and Private Parke remained behind, entirely on their own initiative, to cover the movements of their company."[132]

Private Parke knew that someone had to cover the withdrawal. "When it was decided to pull back and look for a different way into town, enemy riflemen started an attack in order to break up the withdrawal. Private Cavaliere and I ran into a building on the outskirts of the town. From the second story of this building, we could deliver rifle fire on the enemy who had to pass from behind a hedgerow in order to get at our men. As they showed themselves, we shot them down. This stopped the enemy for a while and our men were able to pull back. At this point, an enemy machine gun on high ground opened up on us, but we fired at it and after a while it was silent. The main group of the enemy then started toward us in order to clear us from this building which controlled the best road into town. Their plan was to get behind a four foot stone wall about fifteen yards away from our building, which would permit them to throw hand grenades into a very large window in the wall. In order to reach this spot, they would have to show themselves across the thirty yards of open ground between the nearest hedgerow and the wall. As they came into the open we got them. Private Cavaliere and I accounted for at least twelve of the enemy in this spot. They also tried to get behind the building, but this was pretty much open ground and Private Cavaliere picked them off as they tried to move up. Then the enemy moved off, and artillery started to come in. They were using a church steeple about thirty yards from us as a sighting stake, and they leveled that off in short order, then they brought the fire onto our building.

"We couldn't lie down as the enemy was still trying to rush in and finish us with grenades, so we put on our gas masks to keep out all the dust and rubble and protect our faces and continued shooting. The shelling kept up for about four hours and our building was ruined, but we weren't hit. Just before dark, some riflemen [from our group] were able to get into town and they checked to see if we were still alive, and then took us out of town. All through this time, Private Cavaliere stayed in place firing on the enemy, and made no attempt to leave, holding a position which he knew controlled the best and maybe the only way into town. If the enemy had been able to take this position, they could have dug in and made it very hard for anyone to come in through this way."[133]

After capturing the town for the final time, Lieutenant Shelby could hardly believe the two men had survived the intense artillery barrage directed upon their building. "Over three hundred shells had exploded in the immediate vicinity of Private Cavaliere and Private Parke, but they never left their posts. Although the building in which Private Cavaliere and Private Parke were situated had been virtually destroyed, they were still firing upon the enemy whom they had forced to scatter. They had held this position for a period of almost four hours against a force that greatly outnumbered them and had vastly superior firepower. Due to the confusion caused in the enemy's ranks by this continued resistance, we were able to enter the town and quickly overcome the widespread enemy force."[134]

Private Cavaliere was subsequently promoted to corporal and awarded the Distinguished Service Cross during a ceremony conducted near Balleroy, France on July 2, 1944. However, the paperwork recommending Private First Class Parke was submitted on July 15, 1944. When the award file was submitted, it was indicated that it was a companion case to the Cavaliere award. The order awarding the DSC to Parke, who had been promoted to private first class, was published on July 31, 1944. When the citation was submitted to General Omar Bradley for signature, he signed it and then crossed it out and directed that Private Parke be recommended for the Medal of Honor. The 1st Infantry Division requested permission to resubmit Cavaliere's for the Medal of Honor as well and paperwork for both men was resubmitted in October 1944. However, the War Department did not approve the award of the Medal of Honor to either man, so Private First Class Parke was subsequently awarded the Distinguished Service Cross.

Major Charles E. Tegtmeyer
Headquarters, 1st Medical Battalion, 1st Infantry Division

Major Charles E. Tegtmeyer and an advance party of his medical battalion were transported to the beach aboard two LCM landing crafts. "As we neared the beach, machine gun bullets beat a tattoo against the plate of the LCM and whistled angrily around our heads. The men crouched toward the floor. The craft stopped suddenly on command from the colonel's LCVP which was alongside us and began to back water. A lane through the mines and beach obstacles had not been cleared. The boat turned toward the west following the beach line. The din of exploding artillery shells to our left along the shore and in the water was terrific. Suddenly, the LCM moved sharply to the left toward the beach and gathered speed. A few minutes later we grated along the sandy bottom, the ramp dropped and the men passed down into the water.

"I yelled to [First] Sergeant [Herbert] Goldberg to lead my men into the water and keep going—I would meet them on shore. The men ahead of me thinned in density, I worked my way forward and yelled to my men to hurry but to bring along the extra medical supplies. I reached the edge of the ramp, carefully descended it and found myself in icy cold rough water, which reached my lower chest. Ineffectually, I slowly worked my way shoreward, passed a Belgian gate obstacle with a large Teller mine attached to it and banged my knee against a tetrahedral of rail steel, beneath the water. Anxiously, I felt about it for a mine or a booby trap wire, while a cold clammy sweat oozed from under my helmet band. Finding neither, I climbed over it but became entangled in its five outthrust arms, slowly I extricated myself from its tentacles and touched bottom again with my feet. Using all my strength, I thrust myself forward and cursed my slow progress. The water became shallower and I pushed on, my equipment dragging me forward and downward. Abruptly, I stepped from the water to the beach shale and fell face downward. Breathing laboriously, I rested face downward for a moment, oblivious to all that was going on about me. As my oxygen debt became less, the explosion of shells and the sharp whistle of bullets forced their sound on my consciousness.

"I lifted my head and crawled up the shale bank. Just beneath its upper ledge, I rolled over and sat up. The shelf on which I rested was about ten yards in width sloping upward from the water's edge to a height of from two to ten feet at an angle of roughly thirty-five degrees. Face downward, as far as eyes could see in either direction were the huddled bodies of men; living, wounded, and dead, as tightly packed together as a layer of cigars in a box.

"Some were frantically but ineffectually attempting to dig into the shale shelf, a few were raising themselves above the parapet like edge and firing toward the concrete protected enemy and those on the cliff above, but the majority were huddled together face downward. Artillery shells exploded on the beach and in the water with sharp explosions and threw fragments in all directions. Uncomfortable close overhead machine gun and rifle bullets grazed the top of the ledge with the buzz of a million angry hornets and plunged into the water behind us with innumerable sharp hisses or whined away into the distance as they ricocheted off the stones of the beach. At the water's edge floating face downward with the arched backs were innumerable human forms eddying to and from with each incoming wave, the water about them a muddy pink in color. Floating equipment of all types, like flotsam and jetsam, rolled in the surf mingled with the bodies.

"Units of infantry and amphibious engineers were inextricably mixed together, officers without men and men without their officers lay perplexed awaiting orders. The enemy gun emplacements of reinforced concrete at the base of the cliff like slope, untouched by aerial bombing, naval and rocket shelling, continued to pour artillery and machine gun fire across the beach and into the figures struggling through the obstacles to reach it, decimating the ranks of the assaulting troops with every fusillade. Snipers were picking off every head, whether officer or enlisted man, which became lined in their sights. Everywhere, the frantic cry, 'Medics, hey medics,' could be heard above the horrible din. I called Sergeants [Herbert] Goldberg and [Edward] Bailey over to me and the three of us crept about rounding up our detachment. Within a very few minutes, all of our group excepting Captain Tierney, my dental surgeon, was accounted for. Colonel George A. Taylor, the regimental commander, had landed fifty yards to the right of us. He passed us walking erect, followed by his staff and yelled for me to bring my group along. I instructed the men to follow me up the beach and to render aid to the wounded as we passed. Crouching, running, crawling, and stumbling over the prone tightly packed bodies, we slowly worked our way up the beach, answering the cry, 'Medics' as we went.

"My men were superb as time and time again they plunged into the surf, regardless of the hail of steel fragments whistling about them, to pull wounded ashore. The wounded were hastily dressed and pulled to the shelter of the shale shelf and left with instructions to call to the landing craft for help as they grounded. I examined scores as I went, telling the men who to dress and who not to bother with. The number of dead killed by mines, shell fragments, machine guns and sniper bullets was appalling. Sergeant Herbert Goldberg, bringing up the rear, supervised the work as he came and no doctor could have done more or could have done it better.

"Every man who lifted his head above the level of the shale was asking to be shot and every man who moved along the beach had utter disregard for his own personal safety. We followed the colonel and covered a thousand yards of it, just asking for it. Father [Lawrence] Deery was having a busy day too, for many of the men had more need of him than of me.

"When we reached the extreme eastern edge of the regimental beach, the colonel called a halt. Three radios were brought up, their antennae shot into the air and the operators frantically sought contact with the battalion commanders. Staff officers and messengers were sent out to locate officers and bring them back. Slowly the reorganization of the regiment was begun. As officers were located, orders were issued and they moved out. Soon, despite the decimating enemy fire, platoons and companies were organized, small groups began blowing out the aprons of wire at the top of the ledge and columns began to crawl over it through the gaps. The attack was launched!

"Chaplain Deery and I looked at each other and in one breath exclaimed, 'And we criticized those birds at Tarawa for being green.'

"We both gave a couple of sickly laughs and Larry said, 'It's about time for Jerry to turn on his Nebelwerfer.'

"'That or a strafing plane,' I replied, 'is all that we need.' The words were no more uttered than six shells, preceded by the peculiar sound of the Nebelwerfer exploded a hundred yards away in the water.

"'Oh-oh, here it comes,' I exclaimed and ducked my head.

"A fragment whistled by grazing the sleeve of my jacket, bounced off the stone and disappeared.

"Three of the thirty-two amphibious DD tanks reached the beach a few hundred yards to our east. Lieutenant Colonel Skaggs, commanding the 741st Tank Battalion, worked his way from them to us, received instructions and departed. The tanks were doing no firing, but soon Colonel Skaggs could be seen belaboring his men with a life preserver while they ran for the tanks and scrambled into them. A few minutes later they began firing at enemy strongpoints while the enemy frantically tried to counter battery them with 88s, 75s and 47s.

"Around Colonel Taylor and his three radios the bullets began to whistle more viciously than ever. I yelled at the colonel, 'For Christ's sake colonel, get down, you're drawing fire.'

"He grinned at me, ordered the antennae pulled down and said, 'There are only two kinds of men on this beach, those who are dead and those who are about to die, let's get the hell out of here.'

"He started back along the shale to the west, the headquarters group behind him. I told Sergeant Goldberg to take the lead while I followed the rear of the crouching file. The tide had come in during this interval and the shelf had narrowed to about seven yards. We worked our way westward alternatively on the shale and knee deep in water. My men continued giving aid to the new crop of wounded that had been reaped since our trip eastward. A hundred yards from our starting point, I stumbled over an engineer, fell on my face and stayed there, too exhausted to get up.

"When I decided to move on ten minutes later, I was so tangled in my field equipment that movement was impossible. Five minutes later, I had the various straps readjusted and was able to move on. Fifty yards further on I was glad to rest again. Throughout this time the fire along the beach was as harassing as ever and the rising tide kept narrowing the beachhead. My only thought was to find the exit and get the hell off the beach. The one thing I was sure of was that I would not get back into the icy cold water to swim, no matter what happened. I'd be a guest of the Third Reich first.

"Another stop to help a wounded man and I reached the first tank, rested a few seconds and dashed across the open gap to the second, another momentary rest and a dash to the third. The vicinity of those tanks wasn't choice either. The Heinie antitank guns were still trying for them. Beyond the last tank, a wounded lieutenant stopped me. I examined the wound in his arm and told him to follow me off of the beach. Twenty yards further on, we reached the gap in the wire, hurried through it and entered the minefield.

"The building which had been visible in the aerial photographs of the place had been reduced to rubble. Engineers were using mine detectors and had cleared a single footpath through the meadow. We followed them, climbed the steep slope and came upon the regimental CP in a hollow, forty feet below the crest of the plateau. I reported to the colonel and then led my patient to my men and then dug into the steep bank twenty yards away.

"My men had all reached the aid station excepting Captain Tierney. I was greatly concerned about him, but *C'est le Guerre*. The men had salvaged two litters and some extra cases of supplies from the wreckage along the beach. Five patients had already come in, one of whom had a nasty wound of the chest."[135]

Major Tegtmeyer's improvised aid station located on the slope of the bluff near the regimental command post was safe from German artillery fire. "The enemy kept shelling the beach, even though by this time our troops had driven them back from the cliff edge and had knocked out the five strongpoints guarding the beach. Enemy fire was concentrated on the two vehicle exits and the engineers could not reach them to remove mines and blow the roadblocks. Landing craft kept bringing in personnel and vehicles even though the enemy shelling was knocking hell out of them. Crowds of leaderless men of the engineer shore brigade were still huddled along the beach and many of them were being killed by the exploding shells. Shells were just clearing the forty foot bank over our heads to hit craft, the beach and, the meadows behind us. Morale at the CP was excellent despite the reported deaths of many of the group. We were all glad to get off the beach and glad to be alive. There was no doubt in anyone's mind but that the invasion would be a success at the first try.

"Fragmentary reports, verbal and radio, kept coming in of action near Le Grande Hameau and Colleville-sur-Mer. Although the regiment had been reduced below its effective strength, with a loss of thirty percent of its officers and men, the attack was still going on. A trickling of prisoners were passing through the CP. The constant cover of our own fighter planes overhead and the constant firing of our destroyers and cruisers at inland targets were reassuring, even though the enemy artillery was raising hell with deadly accuracy along the beach behind us.

"Captain Bill Friedman, the regimental adjutant, asked me to have a look at Major Dave McGovern, our air liaison officer who had been hit on the beach. Dave had lived with us for the past months in England, had taken a terrific ride on the subject of his branch of the service and its failure to give us support in Africa and Sicily. However, with his ready wit and pleasant personality, he had been able to hold his own even on that tenderest of subject, 'Pay and a half for the air corps.'

"I scrambled up to Dave's foxhole and before I could ask him about his injury he pointed upward to the planes flying overhead and said, 'Look at them, you guys should be damn thankful they're there.' I agreed readily enough and he continued, 'You guys said this would be rough, but God I didn't think it would be this rough. You guys can have my pay and a half anytime.' I admitted it had been rough, a hell of a lot rougher than Africa and Sicily, in fact rougher than anything I ever want to go through again. I examined his wound; it was a jagged shell fragment wound just to the left of the heart and the fifth and sixth ribs were broken. Sergeant Goldberg dressed it. I asked Dave if he wanted to be evacuated and he replied, 'No.' He didn't want morphine either, but he was having a helluva time getting a decent breath.

"Captain John Finke came in with a compound fracture of the right arm and a wound of the right leg; both wounds already dressed, but he needed morphine. All through the afternoon the wounded kept coming in; my men went out to get and carry them in. Every shell that landed anywhere near the area was getting someone.

"A frantic cry came up from the mined meadow below us, 'Hey medics, hey medics.' Someone had run into the minefield and exploded a mine in an attempt to get away from a shell. Sergeant Ed Bailey and Bernie Friedenberg volunteered to go and get him, but I wouldn't let them go until I found an engineer with a mine detector to go with them. Several minutes later I watched them remove mine after mine, with crossed fingers until they reached the stricken man. They worked over him for several minutes and then carried him off in the litter. Mercifully, no shells landed in the field while they were working. Fifteen minutes later, they reported and told me that the man had two broken legs; they had left him with a naval beach unit in the ruins of the house below us. Eight mines had had to be removed before they reached the man."[136]

Colonel Taylor wrote the following in his recommendation of Major Tegtmeyer for the award of the DSC. "Immediately upon landing, Major Tegtmeyer took command of the situation and organized his medical section, although he was constantly exposed to the vicious sniper and machine gun fire. While thousands of men were pinned down behind the slight cover of a shale shelf, Major Tegtmeyer covered the length of the beach administering aid to the wounded lying all along the shore. Time and again he went into the mine strewn waters and pulled the wounded in to comparative safety behind the shale barrier. While bringing the men in from the sea, Major Tegtmeyer was surrounded by machine gun fire which churned the waters about him. For two full hours, he remained on the beach under an unceasing hail of fire. Major Tegtmeyer, heedless of the great danger all about him, treated more than eighty men under drastic conditions. As the troops advanced, Major Tegtmeyer moved forward to maintain close contact with the assault men in order to render immediate and effective treatment. Throughout all of the battles, he continued performing his duties without regard for his own safety."[137]

Some of the bravest men on Omaha Beach and indeed, of the invasion were the medics, who time and again risked their lives to aid wounded men and comfort the dying. Medics attached to the infantry regiments and medical personnel with the naval beach battalions, army combat engineer battalions, and other support units worked together under the most dangerous of circumstances to treat and evacuate the wounded while under intense enemy fire.

Captain John Settineri
Medical Detachment, 16th Infantry Regiment, 1st Infantry Division

Lieutenant Colonel Edmund F. Driscoll, the commanding officer of the 1st Battalion, 16th Infantry, witnessed Captain John Settineri's heroism and life saving actions on June 6. "Captain Settineri landed with the assault troops at about 07:15 hours, at a time when enemy fire was reaching the highest degree of intensity. The extremely rough surf hurled many of the landing craft into the mine capped obstacles and the water was filled with heavily laden wounded men struggling to reach the shore. Displaying superb courage, Captain Settineri left the cover of the beach high water level shelf and plunged into the sea. Despite the fact that he was in constant, self-imposed danger from the concussion and fragments of the exploding enemy mines, despite the terrible volume of fire directed at the incoming craft, Captain Settineri waded and swam far out into the surf to rescue the helpless wounded and carry them back through the mined and bullet-flayed water to the beach. Pausing only long enough to administer first aid and to make the soldiers as comfortable as possible, Captain Settineri went back into the water to repeat his magnificent deed. On nine separate occasions, Captain Settineri went from the beach to where the small craft, still a target for heavy artillery, were sinking or had sunk, each time carrying back to safety a wounded soldier. Throughout the day, Captain Settineri heroically continued to expose himself to the vicious enemy fire in his treatment of the wounded and dying. By his magnificent courage, his utter selflessness in the outstanding performance of his vital duties, Captain Settineri saved numerous lives."[138]

Medical personnel with the 1st Medical Battalion, including a captain (right center) treat wounded soldiers on the Fox Green sector of Omaha Beach. *United States Army Signal Corps photograph, National Archives.*

Technician Fourth Grade Stanley P. Appleby
Medical Detachment, 16th Infantry Regiment, 1st Infantry Division

Major Tegtmeyer observed the actions of Technician Fourth Grade Stanley P. Appleby during the landing of elements of the Medical Detachment, 16th Infantry. "Technician Fourth Grade Stanley Appleby disembarked from his LCM some fifty yards from the beach under a hail of artillery shells and machine gun fire. A large majority of his comrades were hit and seriously wounded while leaving the craft and, but for Appleby's prompt and courageous action, would have perished in the surf. However, with complete disregard for his own personal safety, he waded through the rain of fire to lead them ashore, while those so critically injured as to be unable to walk he literally pulled and dragged to the beach where he administered immediate first aid. Displaying extraordinary heroism, Technician Fourth Grade Appleby plunged back into the channel on at least two known occasions, swimming some fifty yards through fierce merciless fire to carry back other wounded men from the LCMs which were then being torn to shreds by well directed artillery shells. After completing these self appointed missions, Appleby continued to ignore his own safety while administering first aid to at least twenty-five other men who had been wounded on the beach. Through all of these daring exploits, Appleby knowingly and willingly placed himself under the greatest possible danger in order to save the lives of his comrades."[139]

A medic moves along the rocky shingle or shelf next to cliffs that overlook the Fox Green sector of Omaha Beach looking for wounded men to treat. The bodies of those who have been killed or drowned are in the background, along with a man sitting next to the cliffs with the hooded jacket. *United States Army Signal Corps photograph, National Archives.*

These are the dead soldiers seen in the background of the prior photograph, lying on the shingle of Fox Green. *United States Army Signal Corps photograph, National Archives.*

A medic treats a wounded man under the bluffs on the Fox Green sector of Omaha Beach. *United States Army Signal Corps photograph, National Archives.*

This antitank ditch was turned into an aid station on the afternoon of June 6, 1944. The width and depth took bulldozers to fill in these obstacles before vehicles could exit the beach. *United States Army Signal Corps photograph, National Archives.*

In this sequence of photographs, 5th Engineer Special Brigade troops rescue men from a sinking LCVP. An individual has taken a rope line out to the stricken craft. Some men from the landing craft can be seen swimming toward the shore (right). *United States Army Signal Corps photograph, National Archives.*

Combat engineers with the 5th Engineer Special Brigade pull cold water soaked soldiers from a rubber life raft. *United States Army Signal Corps photograph, National Archives.*

There were many unrecognized heroes on Omaha Beach like these troops with the 5th Engineer Special Brigade who helped these wet and cold soldiers to the shingle, where they were subsequently treated medically. The proximity of the water's edge to the shingle indicates that this action occurred at or near high tide. *United States Army Signal Corps photograph, National Archives.*

The cold wet soldiers pulled from the water have been covered with blankets in attempts to raise their body temperatures, ward off hypothermia, and prevent shock. *United States Army Signal Corps photograph, National Archives.*

First Lieutenant Carl K. Giles, Jr.
Company M, 16th Infantry Regiment, 1st Infantry Division

Lieutenant Charles Horner, the commanding officer of the 3rd Battalion, 16th Infantry, witnessed the heroic actions of Lieutenant Carl K. Giles on D-Day. "Company M, 16th Infantry, assaulted the coast of France in the vicinity of Colleville-sur-Mer on LCVPs. The long prepared enemy, who had built impregnable installations on high cliffs commanding the coast, leveled withering machine gun and artillery fire on the incoming. One of the company assault boats was badly hit and sank swiftly. The occupants of the boat, heavily laden with mortars and ammunition, were all thrown from the craft. Lieutenant Giles, section leader of this assault element, immediately went to the assistance of the panicky men, helping to land their equipment and quieting their fears. For forty-five minutes, Lieutenant Giles remained in the water, constantly under fierce machine gun and unceasing artillery fire, and where large numbers of mine capped obstacles endangered every shoreward trip. Throughout this period, he aided the men about him, never once considering his own safety. Displaying extraordinary courage and exceptional coolness, Lieutenant Giles succeeded in getting all of his men safely on the beach and in salvaging great quantities of equipment. While on the beach, Lieutenant Giles observed three severely wounded soldiers lying near the water's edge slowly being covered by the rising tide. Without a moment's hesitation, he left the protection of the shale bank and moved across the exposed beach covered by intense enemy fire and by making several highly hazardous trips, carried the stricken men to safety. At this critical point in the battle, the officers of Company K had all become casualties, and the scattered remnants of the company lay leaderless on the beach. Lieutenant Giles immediately turned over his section to another officer and assumed command. Quickly organizing the men, he led them through an uncharted minefield while under fierce enemy machine gun fire and sniper action and led the advance up the cliffside to outflank an enemy pillbox and casemate which were pouring a devastating fire on the 16th Infantry sector. Advancing in the face of the intense fire he gained his objective and personally assaulted the casemate containing a 75mm gun with hand grenades and a rifle. He and his newly organized unit completely destroyed the enemy strongpoint. Pausing only long enough to reorganize his men, Lieutenant Giles forced his way on against a savagely tenacious enemy until he reached the town of Le Grand Hameau. In this town, he joined forces with another small group of our men, and together they held the town for five hours against repeated enemy attacks by numerically superior forces until the main body of our forces made contact with them."[140]

AT H+50, THE 116TH INFANTRY was scheduled to land Company C transported in seven LCVPs along with elements of the 121st Engineer Combat Battalion carried in an LCM on Dog Green, with six LCVPs bringing in Company K on Dog White, with seven LCVPs conveying Company I to Dog Red, and Company L in seven LCVPs to touch down on Easy Green.

Second Lieutenant Leonard A. Anker
Company K, 116th Infantry Regiment, 29th Infantry Division

The landing craft transporting Company K came in together about ten minutes early on a portion of the beach where no other American troops were present. As the landing crafts dropped the ramps, Lieutenant Donald Casapulla, adjutant of the 116th Infantry Regiment, saw German machine gunners concentrate their fire on the disembarking infantrymen of Company K. "At the time of the landing of Lieutenant Anker's platoon the beach was under the withering fire from enemy artillery, automatic weapons, and small arms. After proceeding about two hundred yards, all troops in the vicinity of Lieutenant Anker were pinned down by the devastating fire. Lieutenant Anker located an enemy strongpoint that was delivering much of the direct fire. With utter disregard for his own safety Lieutenant Anker, aided by an enlisted man, whom he inspired to action by his gallant leadership, fearlessly charged and destroyed the enemy strongpoint with hand grenades, killing sixteen Germans and capturing five. The outstanding heroism displayed by Lieutenant Anker on this occasion was an inspiration to all troops in the immediate battlefront. As a result they rallied to Lieutenant Anker and drove across the beach."[141]

Technical Sergeant Carl D. Proffitt
Company K, 116th Infantry Regiment, 29th Infantry Division

Technical Sergeant Carl D. Proffitt was the assistant section leader on the LCVP transporting his section. "Anyone who had never been in combat before actually couldn't feel what was going to be happening when he hit the beach and you didn't realize until after you actually hit the beach. The shells bursting and the machine guns firing and airplanes overhead and people coming in behind you on other craft and all this type thing was so confusing. What made it so difficult, too, was that we landed at low tide and we had about three hundred yards of beach to cross. They had barbed wire entanglements and all these obstacles. That was the reason we had to go in at low tide because all of those things were mined and if we'd gone in at high tide the water would have gone over top of them and your boat would hit it and it would explode. So that's why we went in at low tide because of those obstacles on the beach. Everything was so loud. It was so loud you couldn't give a word of mouth order. You had to give hand signals or come in behind or something like that. You couldn't hear.

"Everybody was afraid. Anybody that wasn't afraid was either crazy or a damn fool one, I'll tell you. I was afraid. I didn't realize that it was actually the real thing until bullets started whizzing down, hitting in the water and hitting the side of your craft and all that type of thing, boats being blown up out there in the water, and guys going off in water over their heads.

"Some of the crafts hit sandbars and as soon as they hit a sandbar the guy who was in charge of the ramp just dropped it and off they went. They estimated that each guy was carrying somewhere about eighty pounds—ammunition, food, and equipment, and everything [else]. When they'd go off and some of the places they'd hit a sandbar and they'd drop their ramp and go off in water over their heads and how could you swim with all that weight on you? We lost a lot of guys through drowning. Well, ours ran into one of those sandbars, but the guy that was tending the ramp, he started to drop it and a coxswain yelled at him, 'Don't drop that ramp.' And he threw the LCVP in reverse and backed off of it and went around the loop there and he put us in water about ankle deep. He shot up right up on the beach at full speed. That's a lonely feeling when you saw it hit and you're moving and you turn around and look back and the boat was backing out and heading back to the mother ship out there. It was scary, pretty scary. Boats being blown up, guys dropping all over the place, and bodies being mangled all to smithereens. Rifle fire, machine gun fire and everything—it opened fire before we made our landing because we were actually supposed to have been in the second wave, but where we landed, nobody touched down.

"Everything was so confused. I guess they had fields of fire you see, and they were firing whether anybody was in that field or not. Of course they would see some people in the field and maybe sometimes it would be ten people and maybe sometimes it would be thirty people in that field, because everything was so confused. You lost your unit. We lost guys that were in our boat team. Other guys were in with another company and other boat teams would fall in together and everything jammed up against that seawall [and it] was unreal.

"Those emplacements and those pillboxes and that barbed wire held us up like you wouldn't believe. Of course we had special training in blowing up that barbed wire with those Bangalore torpedoes. Long tube, you know, and you stuck it up under it and ignited it and it would go off and blow a hole through it. In some units, they had guys that had this gear that they put on with padding under the jacket so they'd just jump up on top of the barbed wire and mash it down and guys would leapfrog right over on their back. Just step right on and go over. But they wore that particular type gear just for that purpose.

"Of course, you couldn't run all the way across the beach. You had to just go so far and then drop and breathe for a few seconds and get up and go again. Everybody was instructed to go as hard as they could go to the seawall, which we did. Fortunately, we didn't lose the first man in our boat team until we got inland about half a mile. We didn't lose anybody on the beach at all."[142]

As the LCVPs transporting Company I came to within about one hundred yards of the beach it received machine gun and small arms fire. The landing craft came in closely grouped about a thousand yards to the left of the planned area. Company G was already on the beach to their front when the Company I boats touched down.

Sergeant Douglas A. Orndorff
Company I, 116th Infantry Regiment, 29th Infantry Division

As the landing craft transporting Sergeant Douglas Orndorff, a squad leader with Company I from Winchester, Virginia, approached the beach he could feel the tension rise. "When you swallowed, it felt like your heart was up in your throat. But you had to hold yourself together."[143]

After Company I made its way to the seawall, Sergeant Orndorff led his platoon through the barbed wire entanglements, the minefield beyond, and up to the top of the bluff where he "spotted a German's head. I can see him yet. He was dug in. I saw him raise his head up."[144]

Seconds later he was hit in the face by an enemy bullet which severely wounded him, destroyed his left eye, damaged his right eye, and left him almost blind. He was given life saving first aid and carried by stretcher later that afternoon to a landing craft for evacuation.

Staff Sergeant Ozias C. Ritter
Company I, 116th Infantry Regiment, 29th Infantry Division

Lieutenant Donald Casapulla, the adjutant of the 116th Infantry, wrote the following concerning the heroic actions of Staff Sergeant Ozias Ritter, who "was a machine gun section leader in Company I, 116th Infantry. The enemy was well emplaced in fortified positions behind minefields, obstacles, and covering the approach of the 116th Infantry with a deadly small arms, machine gun, mortar and observed artillery fire. Staff Sergeant Ritter led his machine gun section with utter disregard for his own safety and with a gallantry that inspired and heartened his men, despite terrific casualties. He kept them unceasingly pressing forward by leading them and coolly placing fire on the enemy. In one instance, he purposely exposed himself to draw fire to provide his section with positive location of the enemy guns. Another time he entered a sector of observed mortar fire to carry out the wounded of his command."[145]

Technical Sergeant Louis M. Armstrong
Company L, 116th Infantry Regiment, 29th Infantry Division

When Company L landed, Lieutenant Rudolph Skrek, the section leader of the 5th Section, was killed while crossing the beach. Technical Sergeant Louis M. Armstrong immediately took command of the section. Lieutenant Casapulla wrote the following regarding Sergeant Armstrong's heroism. "When Allied forces invaded continental Europe on 6 June 1944, Sergeant Armstrong was a member of one of the rifle companies which made the invasion assault on the French coast near Vierville. At this point, the enemy was well emplaced behind mines and obstacles, and had small arms, machine gun, and observed mortar and artillery fire on all approaches to and from the beaches over which the American troops had to pass. Sergeant Armstrong was in one of the early waves of infantry that waded ashore from landing craft in the face of withering enemy fire. Despite severe casualties, he gallantly stepped to the head of his men. With a great risk of his own life and utter disregard for personal safety, set an example and shouted encouragement to others to follow in a heroic manner that clearly distinguished him as a leader in the face of the greatest of hazards. His conduct inspired all, contributed to the great success of the 116th Infantry in defeating a stubborn enemy, and was conspicuous for the great effect it had upon all who saw him in pressing forward against an enemy with superior advantages being quickly defeated."[146]

Staff Sergeant Ralph S. Coffman
Company L, 116th Infantry Regiment, 29th Infantry Division

Lieutenant Casapulla, 116th Infantry's adjutant, was a witness to the heroism of Staff Sergeant Ralph S. Coffman. "When Allied forces invaded continental Europe, 6 June 1944, Sergeant Coffman was a member of the 116th Infantry Regiment, which made the initial assault on the beaches of France near Vierville. At this place, the enemy was dug in behind minefields and skillfully emplaced obstacles, and had small arms, mortar and artillery fire on all parts of the beach and their approaches. During the early landings our infantry was pinned down in many cases by a withering machine gun and small arms fire from both front and flanks. Sergeant Coffman landed to find all troops about him thus pinned down. With an absolute disregard for his own safety, and with a great risk of life, he led a group of soldiers forward, fired on and destroyed several close range enemy machine guns which were inflicting heavy casualties on American troops. His gallant conduct inspired all about him and the success of the mission he led enabled many infantry to advance. Sergeant Coffman's heroic conduct materially contributed to the success of his regiment."[147]

ON THE EASTERN PORTION OF OMAHA BEACH, Company A, 81st Chemical Battalion (Motorized), with its 4.2 inch mortars, was transported in eight LCVPs and scheduled to land on Easy Red, while another eight LCVPs carrying Company C, 81st Chemical Battalion (Motorized) was assigned to land on Fox Green at H+50. One LCM transporting an advance command post element of the 16th Infantry, including the regimental commander, Colonel George A. Taylor was scheduled to land astride the boundary of Easy Red and Fox Green as a part of this wave.

Private Kenneth P. Kidwell
Company A, 81st Chemical Battalion (Motorized)

Captain W. R. Johnson became the acting commander after the battalion commander was seriously wounded while still aboard his landing craft. "Private Kenneth P. Kidwell, first aid man attached to one of the platoons, was wounded in the right foot as he dashed from the LCVP. Although wounded, he refused to become a casualty and would not allow himself to be evacuated until D+1. He placed his duty of rendering first aid to the wounded above all else and remained with the platoon throughout D-Day, crossing the beach numerous times administering aid to not only those men of his own unit, but to all units landing in the vicinity of his own landing. Private Kidwell's acts of heroism all through D-Day were a constant source of inspiration to the men of his unit and a source of comfort to the men whom he treated."[148]

Colonel George A. Taylor
Headquarters, 16th Infantry Regiment, 1st Infantry Division

The 16th Infantry's commanding officer, Colonel George A. Taylor, landed with the advanced command post element of his regimental headquarters at H+50 astride the boundary of Easy Red and Fox Green. Don Whitehead was a correspondent who landed with the 16th Infantry Regiment that morning. "There were many heroes on Omaha Beach that bloody day, but none of greater stature than [Brigadier General Willard] Wyman and Taylor. They formed the core of the steadying influence that slowly began to weld the 1st Division's broken spearhead into a fighting force under the muzzles of enemy guns. It's one thing to organize an attack while safely behind the lines—and quite another to do the same job under the direct fire of the enemy."[149]

Technician Fifth Grade John E. Bistrica, with Company C, 16th Infantry, was pinned down by enemy fire at the shingle when he observed Colonel Taylor "roaming up and down along the beach. He yelled, 'There are two kinds of people who are staying on this beach—those who are dead and those who are going to die! Now let's get the hell out of here!'

"I said, 'Well, somebody has finally got this thing organized. I guess we're going to move out now.'"[150]

Private First Class Victor E. Peterson
Headquarters Company, 16th Infantry Regiment, 1st Infantry Division

An LCM carrying the 16th Infantry Regiment's forward command post personnel and equipment was scheduled to land in the center of the regiment's zone. Captain George F. Wilder, with Headquarters Company, 16th Infantry, was Private First Class Victor E. Peterson's company commander. "Private First Class Peterson, Headquarters Company, 16th Infantry, had been assigned the task of bringing ashore vital equipment for the establishment of communications to assure coordination in the efforts of the attacking units. The LCT on which he was coming ashore touched down on Easy Red Beach at H+50, and immediately came under cross fire from the numerous shore emplacements. The boat was hit almost instantly, and several casualties were suffered by the men on board. Private First Class Peterson leaped off the craft, and with the assistance of a fellow soldier, began carrying the heavy equipment through the violent seas that were infested with intricate, almost impenetrable barriers of mine capped underwater obstacles and were continually being raked by fire from pillboxes, machine guns and artillery. The progress toward shore was slow, and the man assisting Private First Class Peterson was killed by the accurate enemy fire. Continuing in his assigned mission, Private First Class Peterson struggled shoreward, retaining all of the cumbersome equipment while seeking refuge from the fire behind the many obstacles. While progressing in this slow, tedious manner, he was wounded in the chest, stomach, and leg by enemy machine gun fire. With superhuman effort and outstanding determination, he dragged his burden to the beach, and then refusing medical aid, returned into the shell beaten waters, assisting his comrades ashore. Bleeding profusely, he ignored the vicious sniper fire and constant shell bursts, going time and time again into the surf to help wounded men onto the beach, where they could receive medical attention. Although implored by his comrades to submit to treatment, Private First Class Peterson disregarded his own safety and continued his fearless rescue work until he collapsed on the beach and died from loss of blood."[151]

Technician Fifth Grade John J. Pinder, Jr.
Headquarters Company, 16th Infantry Regiment, 1st Infantry Division

June 6, 1944 was Technician Fifth Grade John J. "Joe" Pinder, Jr.'s 32nd birthday. Pinder had been valedictorian of his 1931 high school class at Butler, Pennsylvania and had been a pitcher with several minor league professional baseball teams. He had completed the National Radio Institute's course in practical radio communications in 1938. His knowledge of communications resulted in Pinder being assigned to the regimental headquarters company's communications platoon. He was a veteran of the 16th Infantry Regiment's amphibious landings in North Africa and Sicily. Captain Stephen V. Ralph was the commander of Headquarters Company, 16th Infantry. "Technician Fifth Grade John J. Pinder, a member of the Radio Section of Headquarters Company, 16th Infantry, landed on Easy Red Beach one hundred yards off shore in a terrible hail of machine gun and artillery fire which caused severe casualties among his boat load. Technician Fifth Grade Pinder, carrying a SCR 284 radio, a heavy and sorely needed piece of equipment. Waist deep in water, swept off his feet by heavy currents, Technician Fifth Grade Pinder struggled toward shore. Only a few yards from his craft he was hit and seriously wounded. The left side of his face was shot completely away and suffered severe shrapnel wounds elsewhere in his body."[152]

Sergeant Robert A. Michaud, with Headquarters Company, 16th Infantry, saw Pinder get hit. "While leaving the assault boat on which he had come in, Technician Fifth Grade Pinder was struck by a shellburst. Although the side of his face was left hanging and he could see only from one eye, he held his hanging flesh with one hand and the other gripped the radio and dragged it to shore."[153]

Captain Ralph didn't think that Pinder could make it to the beach after being so severely wounded. "Technician Fifth Grade Pinder never stopped. Still carrying his radio, he made shore and delivered it to where it was needed. Then, refusing to take cover afforded or to accept medical attention for his terrible wounds, and in defiance of the murderous fire, Technician Fifth Grade Pinder went into the bullet flayed surf to salvage communications equipment floating in the water. Three times he made his self appointed missions, although terribly weakened by loss of blood and pain. He rescued many vital parts and equipment, including another workable radio. On the third trip to the water, he was again hit, suffering severe machine gun wounds in his leg. Still, he would not stop for rest or medical attention. He crawled to shore with a lost load of equipment rescued from the sea. Remaining exposed to enemy fire, growing steadily weaker, he aided in establishing vital radio communications on the beach. While so engaged, Technician Fifth Grade Pinder was hit for a third time and killed by enemy fire. Technician Fifth Grade Pinder's indomitable courage, his superhuman efforts, above and beyond the call of duty was magnificently inspirational to the men with whom he served."[154]

The Medal of Honor was awarded posthumously to Technician Fifth Grade Pinder for his conspicuous gallantry and intrepidity while refusing to stop carrying out his mission until his last breath.

Private First Class Sanford Rosen
Headquarters Company, 16th Infantry, 1st Infantry Division

During the movement from the LCM to the beach, Captain Ralph saw another member of the communications platoon bring critical equipment ashore despite being badly wounded. "Private First Class Rosen, a member of the Communications Platoon, Headquarters Company, 16th Infantry, disembarked from his landing craft amid bursts of artillery fire and, together with another man, started for the shore carrying a heavy drum of wire. Hardly had they taken their first step, when Rosen's partner was hit and instantly killed. Rosen did not hesitate. Realizing the vital necessity of getting the wire to shore, and with utter disregard for his own safety, he rescued the heavy drum of wire from the rough surf and struggled through the shoulder-deep water to the beach.

"Seconds later another burst of fire shot away his left arm at the elbow. Even this could not shake his magnificent courage nor his determination to complete his vitally important mission at any and all costs. Unable to lift the drum with his one good arm, he managed to drag it in the remaining distance, bleeding profusely, but never faltering despite the withering hail of fire directed at him by the enemy. The drum of wire so gallantly brought ashore by Rosen was one of the very few initially landed. It was quickly put to use for the establishment of regimental communication and was vitally important to the success of the entire assault operation."[155]

Staff Sergeant Leeward W. Stockwell
Headquarters Company, 16th Infantry Regiment, 1st Infantry Division

Later that day, Captain Ralph dispatched a patrol by the Intelligence and Reconnaissance Platoon to gather information about the enemy situation in front of the 16th Infantry. "A small reconnaissance patrol, led by Staff Sergeant Stockwell, penetrated deep into enemy held territory. When well within the enemy lines the patrol was suddenly brought under the fire of a deeply entrenched German mortar company. Despite the lack of cover and concealment from the intense enemy fire, Staff Sergeant Stockwell accompanied by another man, moved forward to close with the enemy. He worked his way to within twenty yards of the enemy position, at which point he threw hand grenades into the enemy dugouts causing heavy casualties. Without hesitation he and his comrade immediately charged into the enemy emplacements and fearlessly closed with the enemy forces. In this attack, several of the enemy soldiers were killed and twelve prisoners were taken."[156]

Lieutenant Colonel George W. Gibbs
Headquarters, 7th Field Artillery Battalion, 1st Infantry Division

The LCM carrying the 16th Regimental Combat Team's forward command post group included the forward command post group of the 7th Artillery Battalion, which was the artillery support for the 16th Infantry Regiment. Upon getting to the beach, Colonel George Taylor quickly realized that the situation was critical and that leadership was going to be the key to reorganizing the combat team, attacking the beach defenses, and ultimately moving off of the beach. "The entire invasion effort of the 1st Division was threatened by the seemingly hopeless situation along the beachhead. Lieutenant Colonel Gibbs, commanding officer, 7th Field Artillery Battalion, landed with the assault waves during this most critical period, long before his vitally needed artillery was scheduled to land. Displaying superb courage, Lieutenant Colonel Gibbs left his place of comparative safety, and under the intense direct fire of the still intact fortifications overlooking Exit E-1 moved down several hundred yards of exposed beach to where his unit was to land. Deigning cover in his movements—although a constant target for the deadly accurate fire of the numerous snipers—Lieutenant Colonel Gibbs was a vital factor in the reorganization of the confused, hurt men huddled on the beach, and was inspirational to them in his calm, steady assurance. Arriving at his destination, which was under particularly terrible fire, Lieutenant Colonel Gibbs, completely disregarding his own safety, made several reconnaissances under the intact guns of the enemy to find positions for his artillery as it arrived. On foot, he searched for a route through a still uncharted minefield covered by enemy fire and then organized his incoming command. He then retraced his perilous route over the fire swept beach in search of a breach in the heavy wire. Finding a small breach which led through a heavily strewn minefield, Lieutenant Colonel Gibbs and a comrade officer gathered a few men and led them across the field on a magnificent frontal assault against two enemy gun emplacements. With complete disregard for his own safety, Lieutenant Colonel Gibbs entered the maze of underground tunnels and fortifications, and led his desperately fighting group in the neutralization of the fanatically resisting enemy. Lieutenant Colonel Gibbs was among the first to reach the enemy dominated ridge line, and was highly instrumental in opening the way inland from the beach to the incoming troops."[157]

Later that morning, Lieutenant Lawrence Johnson, Jr. and three enlisted men with the 7th Field Artillery Battalion were pinned down on the shingle, unable to move forward. "To our direct front was a mass of barbed wire. Finally, some brave infantryman blew holes in this barbed wire with Bangalore torpedoes. As luck would have it, just as this hole on the wire was blown, Lieutenant Colonel George Gibbs, C.O., 7th Artillery, appeared behind us, standing as tall as if he was at West Point on parade. He asked us what we were doing lying on the beach and ordered us up the hill. Obediently, I started through the wire and marsh beyond, telling Corporal Harold Bechtel and the others to wait until I radioed them that it was safe to follow. I was no more than fifty yards on my way when I turned and saw the other three following me. 'I told you guys to wait,' I shouted. Bechtel shouted back, 'The colonel told us not to let you go alone.'"[158]

Technician Fourth Grade Lowell L. Dock
7th Field Artillery Battalion, 1st Infantry Division

Technician Fifth Grade Dennis J. Molbert was a member of the 7th Field Artillery Battalion forward command post group which landed at H+50. "We landed from our LCM on the beach at about 07:15 hours, 6 June 1944. Just as the boat crew let the ramp down, enemy machine gun and rifle crossfire started landing in and around the boat. Before we left the boat, one officer was seriously wounded. Sergeant Dock, without hesitation, and at grave personal risk, left the boat and waded to the beach under the heavy enemy fire. Sergeant Dock crawled up to and about fifty yards directly in front of the enemy pillbox and commenced firing his rifle on the pillbox, which inspired other men to do the same and Sergeant Dock's actions enabled other men to move forward against the enemy."[159]

Technician Fourth Grade William L. Kidwell also landed with the battalion's forward command post group. "After the CP had been established, Sergeant Dock volunteered to establish communications with the 16th Infantry CP and proceeded to lay the wire. The terrain over which he had to cross was being heavily shelled at the time and he had to lie flat several times to avoid flying shell fragments. About half way across, while being pinned down, Sergeant Dock saw a man lying nearby, hit in the arm by a fragment, and immediately went to his aid. After he administered first aid and secured further aid for the wounded man, Sergeant Dock continued to crawl with wire and reel about six hundred yards to the infantry CP. There he checked in, but found that the line had been cut by the enemy shelling. He then started to retrace his steps, checking the wire as he went, finding four breaks which he repaired. On the way back, the enemy was still shelling the beach and shell fragments were flying all around. Finally, he reached the CP and checked in again and the line was intact."[160]

Captain Robert W. Woodward
7th Field Artillery Battalion, 1st Infantry Division

Upon crossing the beach and reaching the shingle, Captain Robert W. Woodward, "acting at first mechanically, attempted to dig in. Then tiring, I stopped and remembered from air photo study that there was excellent cover in an abandoned trench system about fifteen feet ahead. I remember going up and down the beach organizing a firing line and kicking the bodies on the beach. Some were corpses and some were just petrified with fright."[161]

Lieutenant Colonel Gibbs and his command group of the 7th Field Artillery Battalion later made their way up the slope of the bluff. "At 13:00 hours, 6 June 1944, the command group of the 7th Field Artillery Battalion was off the beach, directly opposite of beach Exit E-1. Fire from the enemy strongpoints [to the] right of the beach exit, which had been bypassed by assault infantry, was still holding up the advance of personnel already landed.

"Captain Woodward discovered two sources of the enemy fire. One was a slot through which a machine gun was firing in bursts between which its aperture was closed; the other source was enemy infantry entrenched. Exposing himself fully to view at less than three hundred yards range, Captain Woodward jumped into one of the tanks on the beach, required it to be moved a few yards, and directed its fire on the machine gun and then the rifle slots. Captain Woodward, still amazingly unscathed, then proceeded (exposed and in the open) toward the enemy strongpoint, which was on a sharp slope surrounded by barbed wire.

"Personnel who had remained in open mouthed awe at his outstanding display of courage were inspired to follow him through the barbed wire and up the sharp slope directly towards the fortification. Captain Woodward fired his pistol into successive casemate openings and took the surrender of twenty-three enemy enlisted men. Three seriously wounded enemy soldiers were taken from their quarters in the casemates. Seven bodies were found, five of them killed by the tank's fire. One of these was an officer. In this fortification, made of reinforced concrete with built-in quarters for twenty-two persons, were three high velocity weapons which had apparently expended about 160 rounds of ammunition; innumerable machine guns, machine pistols, grenades, and small arms. Range tables for a 7.96cm gun and a map showing plotted locations of four enemy batteries on the Longueville-Formigny road were found. This action was entirely upon the initiative of Captain Woodward and displayed a zeal and disregard of self characteristic of the soldier in the finest military tradition."[162]

AT H+57, COMPANY B, 81ST CHEMICAL BATTALION (MOTORIZED) transported in four LCVPs was scheduled to land on Dog Green, while Company M, 116th Infantry and Headquarters Company, 3rd Battalion, 116th Infantry carried in nine LCVPs were scheduled to land on the Dog Red sector. At H+60, three LCTs loaded with elements of the 121st Engineer Combat Battalion aboard were slated to land on Dog Green, an LCVP with the advance command post group of the 116th Infantry Regiment on board was planned to touch down on Dog White, and five LCTs and one LCVP carrying elements of the 112th Engineer Combat Battalion were to land on the Dog Red and Easy Green sectors.

In addition, Companies A and B and elements of Headquarters Company, 2nd Ranger Battalion, part of the Provisional Ranger Group's floating reserve, were also scheduled to land on Dog Green at H+60 if the success signal was not received by H+30 from the Ranger Force A troops making the initial assault at Pointe du Hoc. This element of the 2nd Ranger Battalion would provide point and flank security for the 5th Ranger Battalion during a drive west to Pointe du Hoc, which would follow them ashore. The plan called for the combined Ranger force to move west and assault the German battery at Pointe du Hoc.

Captain Archibald A. Sproul
Headquarters, 3rd Battalion, 116th Infantry Regiment, 29th Infantry Division

Captain Archibald A. Sproul was the S-1 (personnel) staff officer of the 3rd Battalion, 116th Infantry. Lieutenant Donald Casapulla, the regimental adjutant, wrote the recommendation for the award of the DSC to Captain Sproul. "At the time of the attack the beach was covered by a withering artillery, automatic weapons, and rifle fire from enemy emplacements. Captain Sproul with utter disregard for his own safety exposed himself on numerous occasions to encourage and lead our troops across the beach. The extraordinary heroism displayed by Captain Sproul was an inspiration to the entire command and was a major contributing factor in converting a disorganized group of soldiers into a strong attacking force."[163]

Technical Sergeant John W. White
Company A, 2nd Ranger Battalion, Provisional Ranger Group

Major General Leonard T. Gerow, the commander of the V Corps, personally recommended Technical Sergeant John W. White for the award of the Distinguished Service Cross. "In the assault on the coast of France on 6 June 1944, Technical Sergeant White was initially a platoon sergeant of Company A, 2nd Ranger Battalion. Sergeant White's unit landed under a devastating fire of enemy artillery, automatic weapons, and small arms, which was being delivered from well emplaced positions. All officers of Technical Sergeant White's company became casualties and Technical Sergeant White assumed command of machine gun positions on the beach."[164]

Technical Sergeant White also assumed the responsibility of acting company commander as Rangers fell all around him. "Quite a few men got hit as soon as the ramp went down. Men died right in the water. We could not do anything until we got to the top of the hill. It didn't take long for them to realize that. We crossed about thirty yards of sand and about fifteen yards of shale. There were wrecked houses nearby, probably beach villas. We decided to get into the shelter of those houses as quickly as possible. It was all pretty confused, of course, and men were scattered in small groups. I do remember that as our group hit the second house, Germans inside opened fire on us. Those Germans did not last long, we got them."[165]

Brigadier General Norman D. Cota
Headquarters, 29th Infantry Division

The landing craft transporting Brigadier General Norman Cota, the assistant commander of the 29th Infantry Division, and Colonel Charles D. W. Canham, the commanding officer of the 116th Infantry Regiment, as well as various headquarters and liaison officers and enlisted personnel approached the beach east of the Vierville exit at about H+56 minutes. Lieutenant Jack Shea, General Cota's aide-de-camp, was one of those on board the craft, LCVP 71. "The incoming tide was about two-thirds full; having reached the band of angled timbered groins that had been erected as beach obstacles. These obstructions, which were to have been eliminated by the 146th [Engineer Combat] Battalion commanded by Lieutenant Colonel [John T.] O'Neill still stood. The engineers had been landed two thousand yards east of their appointed landing place. Approximately one-third of these obstacles had Teller mines crudely wired to the face of the timber facing seaward, fastened with bindings of bailing wire that had already been badly rusted.

"LCVP 71 was losing seaway as coxswain Feliciano cut the throttle before beaching and was swept against one of these mines by the three knot cross current, which went in an easterly direction across the face of the beach. The surf, the waves being four to six feet in height thrust the craft against the timber several times and nudged the Teller mine loose from the timbers. However, the mine failed to explode. The coxswain gunned his motor, maneuvered the boat free, and dropped the ramp. Moderate small arms fire was directed at the craft as the ramp was lowered; this consisted of rifle, and judging from the sound, machine gun fire. It continued to cover the ground as the group waded ashore. During this phase of the landing, which necessitated wading through about fifty yards of water, Major John Sours, the regimental S-4, was killed. He was hit in the chest and upper body by automatic fire and fell face down in the water. His body was recovered later as it floated in the shallows.

"The first available cover was the partial screen provided by a DD amphibious tank of C Company, 743rd Tank Battalion, which had landed at H-6. There were about eighteen tanks standing just above the water line on Dog [White] beach. They were faced towards the mainland at an interval of seventy to one hundred yards and about twenty-five yards from the seawall. They were firing at enemy positions to their immediate front.

"Two tanks near the Vierville exit were afire. One of these tanks was 'C-5'. It was a DD tank of C Company and it had been hit by several rounds from an 88mm artillery piece located in the concrete emplacement at the Vierville exit. Hit in the right side, the tank had been immobilized, but its commander, Lieutenant Williams, and his crew escaped unharmed. The tank that screened us was firing to its right front rather than engaging its previously assigned target—the enemy strongpoint at Pointe ét Raz de la Percée. This was necessary as the tank was evidently seeking to protect itself from the fire of several antitank guns which had survived the air and naval pre-landing bombardment. The antitank guns were also shooting at some other tanks, preventing them from directing their fire towards the above mentioned strongpoint and gun positions…

"Small arms fire from the flanks which wounded one of the group seeking cover behind the tank caused the group to rush forward to the cover of the low timber seawall approximately nine hundred yards east of the Vierville exit. This wooden seawall was about four or five feet high. From it at about fifty feet intervals, simple two railed timber fences were projected towards the sea to act as breakwater braces or baffles for the easterly cross current which ran across the face of the beach. These fences had been battered by the sea. They were about twenty to thirty feet long. Against the base of the seawall was heaped shingle. All of the troops that had landed up to this time, H+60 minutes, were crowded against the seawall, sprawled there, seeking protection from enemy rifle and machine gun fire that came from foxholes and fire trenches on the crest of the bluffs that rose behind the beach.

In each of the bays formed by these fences an average of eighty to one hundred troops had gathered. Members of all units were hopelessly jumbled. One could distinguish members on the beach, the 1st Battalion, 116th Regiment, the 2nd Rangers, naval beach maintenance men, naval aide group, naval shore fire control party, and members of the various landing crafts that had been destroyed by fire or had broached upon beaching. The troops were firmly pinned down."[166]

About ten minutes after landing, Lieutenant Shea witnessed LCI 91 get struck by German fire and set ablaze as it touched down. "Shortly after this occurrence, the enemy's Nebelwerfers and mortar fire thickened. Most of it landed on the sandy section of the beach and occasionally a round would land in the midst of the troops huddled together. Shell fragments of the Nebelwerfers (six-barreled mortars, nicknamed 'Screaming Meemies') resulted in unusually large chunks of shrapnel, the average size being about as large as the blade of an ordinary engineer's shovel. One of the fragments, striking a man in the small of the back, almost completely severed the upper portion of his body from his trunk. However, because of the fewer pieces of shrapnel resulting from Nebelwerfers, it did not cause as many casualties as the smaller caliber mortars. The latter named weapons had a much higher percentage of fragmentation.

"First aid men of all units were the most active of the groups that huddled against the seawall. With the limited medical facilities available to them, they did not hesitate to treat the most severe casualties. Gapping head and belly wounds were bandaged with the same rapid efficiency that was dealt to the minor wounds.

"Colonel Canham and General Cota conferred and decided that Cota would reconnoiter to the right, Canham to the left flank, to locate a suitable exit from the beach. They realized that the enemy was aware of the concentration of troops in the area of the seawall and that further high trajectory [mortar and artillery fire] could be expected. It was necessary to get the troops off the beach immediately.

"Colonel Canham was shot through the left wrist by a rifle bullet as he made his reconnaissance. He returned, refused Cota's suggestion of evacuation, and had the wrist bandaged while reporting heavy automatic fire to the left. General Cota had found a section of the seawall that had a low mound of earth some five yards beyond it. He directed the placing of a Browning Automatic Rifle there after having crawled forward to reconnoiter the firing position. This was to provide covering fire for the men who would then attempt to get off the beach. He next supervised the placing of a Bangalore torpedo in the double aproned barbed wire fence that had been erected along the inner border of the promenade, a ten foot wide tar surfaced road which paralleled the seawall along the beach. This barbed wire fence was the ordinary variety, not the heavy or squarish barbed wire, which the troops had anticipated.

"Lieutenant Colonel Max Schneider, commander, and Major [Richard P.] Sullivan, executive officer, of the 5th Ranger [Battalion] were met by General Cota at this point. He verbally directed them to blow similar gaps in the wire to the west and lead their troops against the enemy fortifications at Point et raz de Percee. Having blown a gap in the wire, Cota decided to take advantage of the partial smoke screen caused by the craft burning beneath the base of the bluff. It seemed to be hindering enemy observation and there was a chance that we could break through off the beach and reach the base of the bluff. The first soldier to go through the gap was hit by a heavy burst of machine gun fire and died in a few minutes. 'Medic,' he yelled when hit, 'Medic, I'm hit. Help me.' He moaned, cried for a few minutes, [and] finally he died, after sobbing 'Mama' several times.

"The troops had again stalled. In order to urge them on, General Cota dashed through the gap next. He and the troops that followed him crossed through the wire unharmed, dropped down from the level of the promenade to a field of marsh grass beyond. Here, a system of shallow communication trenches had been dug in the sandy soil. Using these, we advanced to the tall grass that grew near the base of the bluff. No antipersonnel mines or booby traps were discovered in these trenches. The single file of troops composed of riflemen of the 116th, 1st Battalion and headquarters; Rangers; and some members of the 81st Chemical Mortar Battalion, armed with carbines, then ascended the bluff diagonally and to the right. They reached the crest of the point about one hundred yards to the west of a small concrete foundation, evidently a summer house, which lay twenty-five yards below the crest of the bluff. A few antipersonnel mines were detonated during the ascent, but they were not great in number. Colonel Canham established his first CP at the foot of the bluff at 08:30 hours. Here, an unsuccessful attempt was made to contact the 1st Division on the left by radio channels on the SCR 300. This command post was scattered and forced to displace hurriedly when five or six rounds of extremely well placed mortar fire fell in their midst. The enemy had cross observation on this point and obviously had its two-inch mortars ranged in on it. The fragments of these mortar shells killed two enlisted men within three feet of General Cota, fiercely wounded his radio operator, Technician Fifth Grade [C. A.] Wilson, throwing him twenty or thirty feet up the bluff, and his aide also seventy-five feet below it…

"The troops ascending the bluffs stalled as its leading elements reached the crest. General Cota worked along towards the head of the column, intending to urge them on. This would be about 9:00 to 9:15. From the point just below the cliff, the attention of the troops was drawn to a single American rifleman who walked around the promenade directly below them. Before him marched five German prisoners who had been stripped of their weapons and who held their hands above their heads. In as much as they were the first Germans the men had seen they caused particular interest. As they reached a point about eight hundred yards east of the Vierville exit on the promenade, the two leading prisoners crumbled under a burst of machine gun fire that was obviously of German origin. Their captor dove towards the protecting cover of the seawall, while two of the remaining three sank to their knees. They seemed to be pleading with the operator of the machine gun situated on the bluff not to shoot them.

The next burst caught the first kneeling German in the chest and as he crumbled the remaining two took to the cover of the seawall with their American captor. Reaching the head of the column of troops, General Cota found that they had stalled in the face of enemy machine gun fire, which was sweeping a grazing fire across the flats that stretched back about three hundred to four hundred yards from the rim of the bluff. This was about 09:00. In the face of this fire, [General Cota] passed through the men and personally led them on a charge across the field, instructing them to fire at the hedgerows and houses as they advanced. Several times he had tried to move them by calling for an officer or an NCO who was in charge; but none of the leaders seemed to be in evidence. When he crossed the open field, it finally convinced them that it could be done, and they followed. The machine gun fire stopped as soon as the troops started across the open field towards them.

"Working along the margins of the field under cover of the hedgerows, General Cota reached the secondary road 150 yards west of Hamel du Pretre road junction and at about four hundred yards east of Vierville-sur-Mer. Troops of the 116th, 1st Battalion, mixed with elements of the Ranger group, B Company were strung out on both sides of this road, working westward. With little opposition, they reached Vierville, crossed the main intersection at the head of the Vierville beach exit, and continued on towards Point et raz de Percee and Grandcamp les Bains. Light enemy machine gun fire interrupted the advance of the column when they reached a point five hundred yards west of Vierville. General Cota again caught up with the head of the column and directed that a flank patrol be sent out to outflank this fire. It withdrew as our troops began to maneuver…"[167]

Major Richard P. Sullivan, the executive officer of the Provisional Ranger Group, felt that "the activities of Brigadier General Cota seemed to be stupid at the time, but it was actually nothing but sheer heroism and dedication of a professional soldier and fine officer that prompted him to walk up and down the landing beach urging the men forward. I remember his aide-de-camp being a nervous wreck trying to get the general to stop his activities."[168]

Colonel Charles D. W. Canham
Headquarters, 116th Infantry Regiment, 29th Infantry Division

Major Thomas D. Howie, the 116th Infantry Regiment's S-3 (plans and operations) officer, landed with the regimental command group. "At 07:45, Colonel Charles D. W. Canham landed with his staff on the shores of France, at Vierville-sur-Mer. Shortly after he landed, he was shot through the wrist, but after field first aid, continued on. At this time the beach was under withering artillery and machine gun fire and the initial assault waves had not yet moved off the beaches. The casualties were mounting and no relief was in sight. With apparent utter disregard for his own safety, Colonel Canham moved through the intense enemy fire across the beach, organizing groups and assigning their new objectives. The result of this forceful leadership is difficult to ascertain. The men, inspired and heartened by Colonel Canham's presence, leadership, and actions at this time in the face of this fire, broke through the heavy defenses and secured the area."[169]

Technician Fifth Grade Cecil G. Breeden, a medic with the Medical Detachment 116th Infantry, made his way to the area of the huge steel reinforced concrete casemate which had earlier inflicted heavy casualties with an 88mm PAK 43/41 antitank gun, but had now been captured. "Colonel Canham, Colonel Metcalfe, and some other officers had set up a command post. Canham was shot through the hand. I fixed it."[170]

After spending almost an hour in the water, Sergeant Bob Slaughter, a machine gun squad leader with Company D, 116th Infantry, beat the odds and made it to the shingle without being wounded. "The first thing I did was to take off my assault jacket and spread my raincoat so I could clean my rifle. It was then I saw bullet holes in my raincoat. I lit my first cigarette. I had to rest and compose myself because I became weak in the knees. Colonel Canham came by with his right arm in a sling and a .45 Colt in his left hand. He was yelling and screaming for the officers to get the men off the beach. 'Get the hell off this damn beach and go kill some Germans.' There was an officer taking refuge from an enemy mortar barrage in a pillbox. Right in front of me, Colonel Canham screamed, 'Get your ass out of there and show some leadership.' To another lieutenant he roared, 'Get these men off their dead asses and over that wall.'"[171]

AT H+60, EIGHT LCTs brought ashore bulldozers, halftracks, and combat engineers of Company C, 37th Engineer Combat Battalion at both Easy Red and Fox Green. Company B, 37th Engineer Combat Battalion aboard six DUKWs and an LCI was scheduled to land on Easy Red, Company A, 37th Engineer Combat Battalion was assigned to land on Fox Green, and a V Corps detachment transported in a DUKW was slated to land on Easy Red at H+65.

Ensign William L. Wilhoit
LCT(6) 540, Group 55, LCT Flotilla 19, Assault Force O, Task Force 124, Eleventh Amphibious Force, 12th Fleet

Ensign William L. Wilhoit was second in command of LCT(6) 540, which was carrying fourteen vehicles and fifty-seven troops of Company B, 37th Engineer Combat Battalion, 5th Engineer Special Brigade, was scheduled for landing on Easy Red at H+60. "The troops we were carrying had all participated in landing in Sicily and Italy and I remember their being particularly careful not to discuss possible German resistance in any form.

"The officer in charge of my ship, Ensign [Frederick] Nye Moses, from California, was killed during the landing. As we approached the beach after leaving the line of departure, we were both on top of the conning tower watching for activities on the beach which was still too distant to see clearly in the early morning light, when a spout of water shot up about fifty yards to port. Since neither of us had experienced enemy fire, we had a brief conversation concerning the cause of the spout, which must have seemed ridiculous to the army troops aboard, since they were well aware that the spout was caused by a shell. Our conversation was interrupted and quickly settled when a second shell whirred overhead and we both scrambled for the protection of the pilothouse."[172]

Just after they entered the pilothouse, an antitank shell struck LCT 540, killing Ensign Moses and wounding Ensign Wilhoit, who quickly realized that he had been hit by shrapnel. "The shell explosion occurred inside the pilothouse and there must have been several seconds in which we were all dazed or semiconscious. I recall scrambling to my feet and seeing the back half of the pilothouse blown out, then checking the men and realizing only one was seriously injured before someone told me my legs were bleeding. Ensign Moses had trained our crew exceptionally well prior to my being assigned to the ship and our crew performed perfectly even though the communications to the pilothouse had been knocked out. Without this perfect teamwork, our ship could not have reached the beach, much less backed off from the beach under such circumstances. After we had removed the ship from the beach a machinist's mate came up to the deck and asked if we had been hit. He was totally unaware that we had been hit a total of nine times."[173]

Despite his wounds, Wilhoit took command of the LCT as German antitank fire continued to strike it. "A stack of five gallon Jerry cans filled with gasoline was ignited by a tracer projectile and the burning gasoline spread across the deck. Everyone saw the danger, but seemed immobilized by confusion, shock or just plain fear. An army sergeant, whom I never knew by name, grabbed a fire extinguisher and with a scream ran across an exposed catwalk and began fighting the fire. This act was enough to bring the ship's fire fighting crew into action and the fire was quickly extinguished. This man, through his courage, saved the ship and cargo, possibly from serious damage and set an example of leadership that I shall always remember."[174]

This is LCT(6) 540 on Omaha Beach on June 7, 1944. Ensign William L. Wilhoit assumed command after the landing craft's officer in charge was wounded during the assault landing. *Photograph courtesy of John Kellers and http://www.navsource.org.*

Private Vinton W. Dove
Company C, 37th Engineer Combat Battalion, 5th Engineer Special Brigade, Provisional Special Engineer Brigade Group

Private William J. Shoemaker
Company C, 37th Engineer Combat Battalion, 5th Engineer Special Brigade, Provisional Special Engineer Brigade Group

Although their wave was scheduled for landing at H+60, eight LCTs carrying jeeps, halftracks, and bulldozers along with Company C, 37th Engineer Combat Battalion touched down about 8:30 a.m. Private Vinton W. Dove was one of the company's bulldozer drivers. Private William J. Shoemaker was his relief driver and mechanic. As the LCT approached the beach, Private Dove sat on his bulldozer, which was positioned behind a couple of jeeps on the landing craft. "When the front gate of the boat dropped, machine gun fire swept in and killed most of those on board. I had to push the jeeps off the boat so that we could get off, because the operators were dead. The boat couldn't get very close to shore because of the hedgehogs (obstacles) the Germans had put in the water. The water was over six feet deep, with waves over my head when we left the boat. The only thing above the waterline was the air intake, the exhaust and us, from the chest up. I knew that the bulldozer would have no trouble getting through the water to shore. Shoemaker was a top rate mechanic and could take the bulldozer apart and put it back together blindfolded. Plus, we had taken all the time we needed before we left England to waterproof it, including extending the air intake up to the level of the superstructure. We had also put as many sandbags on the sides of it as we could, and had named the bulldozer 'Hellcat' since it was made by Caterpillar. We had painted the name on the back and sides of it.

"Everyone who was alive started across the beach. My first duty was to pull the hedgehogs out of the water so that the ships could reach the shore; then rid the beach of mines and make a road to exit the beach. So Shoemaker hooked a cable from the winch on the back of the bulldozer to the hedgehogs, and I did the driving. The ships could not make it past the obstacles in the water, but the bulldozer could maneuver, so we just hooked the cable on the end of the obstacles and pulled them around until we had cleared enough room for the ships to make it to shore. The hedgehogs were long strands of steel I-beams welded together. You didn't have to pull them out of the water, just swing them around until there was an opening between them big enough for the ships to reach the shore. Then we took to the beach and began to clear it of mines.

"There were sixteen bulldozers that assaulted Omaha Beach that morning, but only three of them made it to shore. I saw one get hit immediately by an artillery shell and blown up, with both operators killed. The second was hit a few moments later and disabled. Both operators grabbed their rifles and headed for the hills with the infantry. That left us. I realized that we must be the Germans next target, and since I was driving straight down the beach, we would be easy to hit, so I turned left. A few seconds later, a shell hit right where we would have been, so I turned right. Again, right where we would have been, a shell hit. Next I backed up, and another shell hit right where we had been. At that point, the Germans stopped aiming for us. I never did figure out why. I think there must have been something bigger than us coming in from the channel. So we continued; I drove Hellcat flat on my back, sitting on the seat, leaning back almost level with the ground. I had to keep my rear end on the seat so that I could push the foot pedals. We had to keep moving at all times. The machine gun fire was incessant and kept sweeping across the bulldozer just inches above my head, and the artillery guns really cut everyone to pieces. At some point in time, I got separated from Shoemaker, so I just kept driving and clearing the beach.

"There were mines all over the beach, so I let the blade roll about two feet of sand over and over in front of Hellcat, so that the sand would set off the mines ahead of us. The blade protected us from the exploding mines and some of the enemy machine gun fire. A soldier asked me to help him knock out a machine gun nest, so I got a couple of soldiers on the supports behind the blade and drove up in front of the nest. The soldiers threw grenades over and around the blade until they killed the Germans in the nest. I left the nest intact for the Allies to use.

"My next task was to clear Exit E-3. It was a narrow road carved out of the side of a cliff, which the Germans had blocked with old cars, trucks, and even a cement mixer. I just let the blade shove the obstacles off the side of the road down. When I got up to the top, I looked back and discovered that nothing was following me—no trucks, tanks or soldiers. Looking around, I saw a German soldier come out of what appeared to be a guard shack. He looked me over and turned away. I think the sandbags acted as a disguise and made him think I was a German. As soon as he turned away, I grabbed my M1 rifle and shot him. And still there was nothing coming up the road. So I backed down the road and resumed my beach duties."[175]

Riding on the bulldozer, Private Shoemaker wondered "how I could have stayed so calm when I was going up the hill on a Caterpillar dozer. The Germans were all around, shooting to kill. I picked up my gun and prepared to fire—to my dismay it wouldn't fire. It was filled with saltwater. I jumped off the dozer, picked up a gun from one of the boys who had been killed and jumped back on the dozer and kept going."[176]

In this grainy photo, a bulldozer towing a trailer loaded with demolition materials, including high explosives to be used for obstacle clearance by combat engineers, disembarks from an LCT on Omaha Beach on June 6, 1944.

Private Dove continued to work throughout the day to clear obstacles to allow vehicular traffic off of Omaha Beach. "I had to clear a shingle and fill in a tank trap at the entrance to the exit road before I could go up the hill, pushing away the old cars, trucks and any other junk the Germans found to block the road. It was the second road off Omaha Beach (Exit E-1), and they were the only two roads exiting Omaha Beach [in the 1st Infantry Division zone]. When I got to the top of the hill there was some enemy sniper fire, and I got under the bulldozer with my rifle until the infantry took over and the Germans started running. There was lots of traffic following me, so I made a dirt road straight through the fields and hedgerows for about a mile, until I got to a paved road. At that point I backed off, out of the way, and the trucks and heavy equipment really rolled off the beach. At that point I realized that I had been shot in the hand, and had shrapnel wounds on my face and lips. That was late morning or early afternoon as near as I could figure."[177]

Brigadier General Willard G. Wyman, the assistant commander of the 1st Infantry Division, personally witnessed some of the actions of Private Dove and wrote the recommendation of the Distinguished Service Cross. "Private Dove landed with the assault troops on Omaha, the 1st Infantry Division's designated beach, and distinguished himself by his efforts to operate his bulldozer despite constant enemy artillery, mortar, machine gun, and small arms fire. In this immediate vicinity he encountered severe enemy fire and congested traffic, but he could not be deterred from his purpose. Throughout all of this enemy action on the heavily congested beach, with men falling everywhere and enemy shells dropping all around him, he furiously continued to expose himself and courted death by boldly operating his bulldozer, which was in a large measure responsible for expediting our movement on the Normandy beach. Private Dove's exemplary conduct, splendid initiative, and wholehearted devotion to duty under intense hostile fire inspired all who witnessed his deeds and represented the highest traditions of the military service."[178]

Don Whitehead, a war correspondent who landed with one of the early assault waves that morning, witnessed the heroism of Private Dove. "I remember vividly Private Vinton Dove of Washington, D.C. His name has remained with me to this day. He drove a bulldozer from a landing craft and then he began bulldozing a road from the beach as calmly as though he were grading a driveway at home. He sat there with only a sweatshirt to protect him from bullets and shell fragments."[179]

This is an aerial view of part of the antitank ditch protecting Exit E-1 (upper left). These obstacles were designed to prevent vehicles from exiting the beach and to channel armor into areas covered by antitank guns. Privates Vinton W. Dove and William J. Shoemaker filled in this antitank obstacle while under heavy enemy fire to facilitate the movement of vehicles off of the beach in this sector. *United States Air Force photograph, National Archives.*

A bulldozer of the type used on Omaha Beach by the 37th and 299th Engineer Combat Battalions. *United States Army Signal Corps photograph.*

This photograph taken on the Dog White sector on June 7, 1944 shows the obstacles cleared by the bulldozers the prior day to allow clear lanes for landing craft to reach Omaha Beach. The logs from the ramps can be seen (lower left) along with the remains of Element C or Belgian gates (center and right center). Tetrahedrons (center) are stacked in front of two beached landing craft. A bulldozer can be seen in the background (center) in the surf working to tow an obstacle to the shore. *United States Army Signal Corps photograph.*

First Lieutenant Robert P. Ross
Company C, 37th Engineer Combat Battalion, 5th Engineer Special Brigade, Provisional Engineer Special Brigade Group

Captain Johnson D. Howard, the commanding officer of Company C, 37th Engineer Combat Battalion, landed with his unit about H+120, about an hour late due primarily to the congestion caused by the lack of cleared paths through the obstacle belts. "First Lieutenant Robert P. Ross landed on Easy Red sector of Omaha Beach with thirty-two men with the mission of preparing beach Exits E-1 and E-3 for passage of vehicles from the beach. Strong enemy artillery, mortar, and small arms fire from fortified positions on the hills commanding the beach prevented him from starting upon this work. Upon observing that many infantry soldiers were held up on the beach, he took charge of one company which was without an officer, combined these troops with his own and organized fighting units with which he forced the surrender of two machine guns and killed forty of the enemy's troops. After this clearance of resistance, he proceeded to accomplish his assigned mission."[180]

FORCE C, consisting of the 5th Ranger Battalion, reinforced by two companies of the 2nd Ranger Battalion was the floating reserve of the Provisional Ranger Group and was assigned to land at Pointe du Hoc if it received a radio transmission by H+30 of a code word that indicated success from the elements of the 2nd Ranger Battalion making the initial assault. When the signal was not received, it proceeded toward Omaha Beach where it planned to land at the Dog Green sector in three waves. Companies A and B and elements of Headquarters Company, 2nd Ranger Battalion would land at H+60. Companies A, B, and E, along with Headquarters, 5th Ranger Battalion would land at H+65, followed by Companies C, D, and F, 5th Ranger Battalion and a group of Headquarters, Provisional Ranger Group at H+70. After landing, Force C would drive west to attack the German coastal artillery at Pointe du Hoc.

Lieutenant Colonel Max F. Schneider
Headquarters, 5th Ranger Battalion, Provisional Ranger Group

Technician Fourth Grade Herbert Epstein, with Headquarters Company, 5th Ranger Battalion, was the unit's intelligence sergeant and spoke German fluently. "We started in on our initial objective to support the 2nd Battalion on cliffs at Pointe du Hoc. They were then supposed to signal us by radio to follow them in to take the guns at the tops of the cliffs; that is what we had trained for. We never got the signal. So, our second objective was to land on Omaha Beach and attack Pointe du Hoc from the rear. This is something we had trained for with the commandos in Scotland many times, including live ammunition exercises. As we made our way into the beach there were a lot of obstacles in the water. We were getting a large of amount fire. Fortunately, we were also receiving a lot of naval gunfire as we were heading in from the battleship *Texas* and some of the smaller ships. They were hitting the shore pretty consistently. I didn't notice any close in air support.

"As A and B [Companies, 2nd Ranger Battalion] were preceding us into the beach, Colonel Schneider decided not to land at the Vierville draw, because the men who [had] preceded us in the 29th Division were under murderous fire on the beach and having a hard time getting out of the boats.[181] We landed at Dog White. I was in the lead boat and by Schneider's side the whole time. Schneider, by the way, was my god. Max to me was the savior of not only the 5th Ranger Battalion on D-Day, but of the entire sector of Omaha Beach. It wasn't just guts, it was combat savvy. He was the only one of the two Ranger battalions to have combat experience. We were in the front of the lead boat together and he saw what was happening on the beach when we started to go in. He ordered the flotilla commander to turn the boat to the left and go parallel to the beach to an area that looked like it wasn't so heavy. He told the flotilla commander to get us in and get us in fast. And he did! He got us in pretty good shape. He just made the decision and gave the order. Max was very direct. Max knew exactly what to do!"[182]

"After we left the boat, we had to run about one hundred yards across the beach to the seawall. When we hit the seawall, which was roughly about four feet high, we laid down prone behind the wall. We were there a very short time and General Cota, the assistant division commander of the 29th Division came over to our position. I was lying on the sand next to Colonel Schneider as Cota walked up and called for him. Schneider stood up and the two were standing there while all this firing was going on and General Cota said to him, 'Colonel, we are counting on the Rangers to lead the way.' Schneider said, 'Yes sir!' and Cota walked back east. And as Schneider dropped down to the ground near me I said to him, 'What the hell were you doing?'

"And he said to me, 'Well, he was standing and I wasn't going to be laying down here.' Anyway he got a hold of a couple of company officers and told them to get going. Using Bangalore torpedoes, they blew the holes in the wire and we pushed forward."[183]

Lieutenant Francis W. Dawson
Company D, 5th Ranger Battalion, Provisional Ranger Group

The landing craft transporting Lieutenant Francis W. Dawson and Company D, 5th Ranger Battalion, landed with the third wave of Ranger Force C on Dog White. "The LCAs formed a skirmish line parallel to the beach. I could not make out the shore of the beach due to the haze and smoke. I could see a building, but couldn't make out what type it was. As the LCA engines roared and we gathered speed, my eyes were still glued to the shoreline. Then I began to notice the obstacles ahead. Just ahead were four posts set at angle, with mines attached to the tops, and we were just about upon them, and in the boat there was no one talking at this time. Every man was quiet. I imagine each had his own thoughts of what would happen when the ramp fell. One of the posts with the mine attached loomed just ahead. The skipper made an abrupt turn to the left and a tremendous wave hit the craft and we were lifted over several obstacles. Then, the ramp dropped and I was out and running for all I was worth. Luckily, the craft had nearly beached itself, and the water as I exited the boat was probably two feet deep. I could see my immediate destination. It was a seawall about a hundred yards ahead across a flat beach. Five days on ship had taken its toll on my legs. After standing for several hours with the sea pounding, my legs just would not move fast enough. Being the first out, I was a guide for the platoon to follow, and we all ended up behind the seawall. It was crowded, the men from the 29th Division were there and you just had to push in for space. The wall was probably four feet high, made of wood. Being six foot four, I had to keep my head down.

"Our runner, Private First Class Robert Stein, who was killed on Point du Hoc June 8 by U.S. tank fire, was next to me behind the wall. And I sent him to inform Lieutenant George Miller, D Company commander, of where we were located. There was a lot of confusion—people there that I did not know; people wounded; some people in shock. Our platoon location on the beach was more of a left position than the remainder of the company. By that time, word had filtered down to me it was time to move. With that, my two Bangalore torpedo men, Elwood Dorman and Ellis (Bill) Reed, shoved the explosives over the wall and under the triple barbed wire and pulled the fuses. Even behind the wall, with the shells exploding, and a lot of machine gun fire sounding, tanks burning, ships burning, one of the Bangalore torpedo men sounded off, 'Fire in the hole!' And as in training, everyone ducked, waiting for the explosive sound."[184]

The Bangalore torpedoes exploded with a tremendous roar as Lieutenant Dawson prepared to move through the gap in the wire. "Immediately, I saw the situation and with the help of First Sergeant Herlihy, who formed his hands as a cup for me to place my boot, I was lifted over the wall. And on the double, I went through the dust and a path the explosives had torn through the wire. I could still smell that powder smell as I traveled through the trail that the explosives had made. The ground was very flat, grassy, and in full view of the enemy. Knowing I was being fired on, I twice hit the ground, rolled over, sprang up, and continued. I chose to go to my right about fifty yards and then picked a route to climb. The bluff was steep but it wasn't a cliff. I knew there were mines in the area, but I took a chance. I was alone while climbing the bluff, having outdistanced my platoon following in single file. I hadn't looked back because I was too busy looking forward, right, and left. I knew they were coming behind me; I just had that feeling.

"Beyond the top lay a battery of German rockets, which were firing. As I neared the crest, smoke started to drift towards me, but not enough to block my sight. So far, I had not seen any Germans, and I continued to climb, using my hands on the ground to help me. Suddenly I reached the top and traversed to the right, where there were trenches and German soldiers. One in particular, a huge man, came straight at me. He was my first kill. Having a Thompson sub [machine gun], I kept it hot. Several prisoners came out of a trench, and I got them spread eagled on the ground. By then, members of my platoon took over. One young German emerged with a hand blown off. We were not instructed regarding prisoners. It is rather difficult to go into an assault and use your men to guard prisoners. But we were attacking in a narrow column, so we passed the prisoners back, hoping they got to the rear. As I continued along the crest I saw below, active machine gun positions still firing on the beach. These Germans had not seen my platoon."[185]

"Just forward over the crest toward the beach, I could see a machine gun position with two men, about seventy-five yards away, firing onto the beach. They did not see me and I turned to the direction of my platoon. I wanted an automatic rifle, which had more firepower and range than my Thompson. I motioned for my BAR man to bring the automatic rifle, Private First Class Harry Bolton, came forward. In the meantime, the machine gunner had spotted us and before we could take him under fire, he turned the machine gun and killed my BAR man. I then retrieved the BAR, and opened fire on the Germans, killing them as they retreated carrying the machine gun with them through some wire they had to cross."[186]

"Others in the area were making a hasty retreat towards Vierville."[187]

"By now, my platoon was on the move. So were others of the battalion who also had followed my movement up the bluff. Everyone was following the leader, as the route did cross mined areas. And we had been trained to follow a lead man's footsteps. Thus, it slowed the platoon's advance. From the top of the bluff, I could look down on the beach and see artillery shells hitting the beach and watched as two large craft were coming in to land and discharge the troops. They were hit and burned.

"Now, the battalion was on the move. Originally my platoon of D Company was supposed to be the rear guard of the battalion if we had to move and make a beach landing and move inland. Now we were leading the battalion. Since we were up front, we continued. No enemy action was received until we received some machine gun fire as soon as we got to the Vierville road, [which was] approximately 150 yards. We failed to eliminate this gun, as it was moved back through the hedgerows as we attacked it. We withdrew and came back to the Vierville road. Our movement at this time was to outskirt the enemy around Vierville and strike out at Point du Hoc [by going] around Vierville. But as night fell, we were not too far from Vierville. We dug in and formed a perimeter for the beachhead south of Vierville, reinforced by some elements of the 116th Infantry and other scattered remnants of other units. The only action my platoon had for the night of the 6th was several stray cows, which caused some alarm."[188]

First Lieutenant Joseph R. Lacy
Headquarters Company, 5th Ranger Battalion, Provisional Ranger Group

Captain John Raaen, the commander of Headquarters Company, 5th Ranger Battalion, was on the same landing craft as the battalion's Catholic chaplain. 'This was our Ranger chaplain…old, probably in his late thirties or early forties—short, he couldn't have been over 5'6"—fat, at least thirty pounds overweight—thick glasses…He was assigned to my boat, so I checked him and his equipment out a dozen times as we went through our boat drills. The next time I saw him, I was kneeling on Omaha Beach right next to the seawall, looking back at my LCA as my men still poured out of it and began running toward me and the safety of the wall. There was Father Lacy, the last man out. He was no more than ten feet clear of the boat when a German shell hit the fantail of the LCA…I looked away and did not see Father Lacy again until much later. Others saw him and like minstrels, sang his praises. Lacy didn't cross the beach like we heroes did. He stayed down there at the water's edge pulling the wounded forward ahead of the advancing tide. He comforted the dying; calmly said prayers for the dead…Father Lacy stayed behind at the water's edge, doing the work for which God had chosen him."[189]

When Lieutenant Charles H. Parker, a platoon leader with Company A, 5th Ranger Battalion, looked back from the safety of the seawall he saw "bodies lying all over the beach. There were bodies still alive in the water, washing back and forth with the tide's waves. I could see Father Lacy trying to pull those bodies from the water onto the beach."[190]

Major Richard P. Sullivan, the executive officer of the Provisional Ranger Group, landed with the 5th Ranger Battalion and witnessed the heroism of Lieutenant Lacy in saving countless lives of the wounded troops endangered by the fast rising tide. "Chaplain Lacy, while under a constant hail of machine gun, mortar, and artillery fire, with utter disregard for his own safety, assisted every wounded man that he could find near the water's edge, to the comparative safety of the nearby seawall. Chaplain Lacy, by continually exposing himself for the benefit of others inspired a high degree of disregard for the enemy fires falling around him and was in part responsible for the rapid movement of troops from the beach to assault the enemy installations. He was a credit to the corps of chaplains, and holds the admiration and respect of all his associates."[191]

Private First Class Alexander W. Barber
Medical Detachment, 5th Ranger Battalion, Provisional Ranger Group

Lieutenant Colonel Max Schneider, the commander of the 5th Ranger Battalion, witnessed the heroic actions of one of his battalion's medics. "Private Barber's unit landed on a beach well defended by obstacles and mines, behind which was a well emplaced enemy. The beach was at the time under devastating fire from enemy artillery, automatic weapons, and rifles which had inflicted heavy casualties on the attacking troops. In spite of the hazards involved and with utter disregard for his own safety, Private First Class Barber repeatedly went along the fire swept beach giving aid to the wounded."[192]

Private First Class Barber's "first wounded case made me frightened, for I had to run to the soldier through the machine gun fire and artillery fire. When I arrived at the injured soldier's side, I felt relieved and administered medical attention and carried him to safety without being hit myself. From then on, I felt I was leading a charmed life and defied all dangers in my efforts to save lives."[193]

First Lieutenant Charles H. Parker
Company A, 5th Ranger Battalion, Provisional Ranger Group

Lieutenant Charles H. Parker was the platoon leader of the 1st Platoon, Company A, 5th Ranger Battalion. "The coxswain of our boat put us off in waist deep water. He then held his boat in and used his machine gun, trying to suppress enemy fire to give us a better opportunity for crossing the beach. I don't think it did much good, because the Germans were all shooting from massively prepared positions. Still it was an incredibly brave thing for him to do. We had to get across what seemed an endless expanse of sand and then an area of shingle—small rocks with bad footing. Behind us, boats were being blown up and burning—artillery and mortar shells were exploding, machine gun bullets ricocheting around. The water looked dimpled from the shrapnel and bullets. By the seawall, the first thing was to get the company under control. The damage reports showed I had virtually no losses. In addition to [Colonel Max F.] Schneider picking Dog White, we got another break. The grass and low bushes that grew on the flat portion of the land behind the beach and up the sides of the bluffs themselves were on fire. Smoke covered the whole area, and the Germans couldn't put much observed fire on us. The fire also revealed the mines when the grass burned off…There was concertina wire behind the seawall and we had to blow that with Bangalore torpedoes."[194]

After the wire was blown, Lieutenant Parker led his platoon up and over the steep bluff to the flat field beyond. There, he halted his platoon and conferred with a lieutenant with Company E, while Parker's runner, Technician Fourth Grade William J. Fox stood close by. Looking across the field, Parker could see some trees on the far side of it. "We didn't know it at first, but there were snipers in those trees. One of them got us in his sights and we all went down. Fox squatted while the lieutenant and I went prone. A bullet hit Fox in the shoulder, leaving a small blue hole, and then angled down. Another one struck the lieutenant [from Company E] in the right side of his head, blowing out a piece of his skull, leaving his brains partially exposed. I kept trying to wriggle out from under my pack while lying flat. It was a huge one, with enough in it for me to survive for a month. I finally got my pistol out and unbuckled the pack, although meanwhile that sniper put several bullets in it. I rolled over into a ditch and we roped the legs of the two wounded and pulled them into the ditch also. We stayed in that ditch for about three and a half hours before we could get to the rallying point, a chateau. Every man behind Fox had to crawl over him in that ditch. He waved to everyone and smiled. We gave him a canteen of water and went on our way, on our bellies. There wasn't anything we could do for them [the wounded]. Later, they picked up the lieutenant, who somehow survived, hospitalized him, and he eventually regained his ability to speak and function. We didn't know, on the other hand, that the bullet which hit Fox had ranged down and cut his spine. He died in that ditch."[195]

Lieutenant Parker and his 1st Platoon "finally reached the chateau and farmhouse, our first rendezvous point. Out of 560 men, only 23 had gotten there. But, we had more challenges ahead of us. Our long day had only just begun. No one else was at the chateau except for a couple of regular soldiers gathered in a group of trees to the side. No one had seen the rest of the Ranger battalion. Considering the amount of time we were on our bellies in that ditch, I imagined that the rest of my Ranger battalion had been there and gone on, not being able to wait for us. It also occurred to me that I had virtually no knowledge as to the well being or successes of the rest of my battalion. I knew they had gotten off the beach, but knew nothing of what had happened to them since. We had been functioning on our own now for many hours. The last time I saw my group had been at the beach. And that was literally a mess. So we took off. We figured that maybe we'd catch them, not knowing what was ahead. This time we were following a secondary road."[196]

Lieutenant Parker led the twenty-two Rangers of his platoon westward through hedgerow lined roads and fields toward Pointe du Hoc. "We would jump around and we would use farmer's trails—some of them wide enough for a wagon—some of them just wide enough to carry a bicycle. We were jumping around following a hedgerow for awhile then jumping to another one. We were using our compasses. We weren't worried about mines. They were on the coastal areas. The dirt roads appeared as tunnels located between the hedgerows. We were following a secondary road when we started running into pockets of German soldiers, a dozen here, six there. There would be a sharp firefight. We would either knock them out or pick up some prisoners. We had a considerable number of prisoners actually, twenty or so. We were making a lot of noise as we went along, having to overcome a lot of Germans. We had disarmed the prisoners as we captured them by throwing their rifles over the hedgerows. I had told my men previously that if a man is disarmed, then he is not to be shot. That would be murder. I didn't want to hear about anyone killing a prisoner who had already been disarmed. Prisoners, however, can be a hindrance. We were not equipped to handle them, at least not with the few men and limited equipment we had. Our objective as Rangers was to carry out a specific mission; it was not to take prisoners along the way. Nearing a French hamlet that the Germans had been occupying, we were running into more and more resistance from the Germans. Soon, we ran into a much larger pocket of Germans. It became apparent as we were walking along the road that we were nearly surrounded. We could hear the Germans talking on either side of the hedgerows. Realizing we were there, they started to throw their 'potato mashers' [grenades] over the hedgerows at us."[197]

Lieutenant Parker made a quick decision. "We needed to get out of there and right now. If we waited too much longer they would pinch in behind us and easily capture us. We couldn't keep going forward, however, since it was apparent that there were too many Germans ahead. We still had the prisoners with us, so we told them, 'Get out of here!' I was not going to murder them. They had no guns. We communicated the plan amongst us with very little words, mostly hand signals. Then we bugged out, quickly running one hundred yards back along the road from where we had just come. I mean we really ran. I don't know what happened to our prisoners as I never looked back to find out. We wanted to clear those Germans soldiers as fast as we could. When we estimated we had gone far enough, we climbed over the hedgerow towards the side of the sea. This direction would take us to the Pointe. We took off across country then, leaving the secondary road. In front of our group were our company's scout or point man and then his backup man. We cautiously moved forward, calculating carefully the status of the area. Time passed. It was now nine o'clock. (Two hours of daylight remained.) Up until that time I had wondered, 'Are we all that's left?' We were inland away from the channel and heard no battle sounds on Omaha.

"Suddenly an English speaking voice challenged us, its owner well hidden in the bushes. 'What's the password?'

"We had come upon the outpost line of the 2nd Rangers guarding the *pointe* on the other side of the tar road. Oh, my Lord, I've never heard such a nice sound in all my life as an American asking what the password was! So I gave it: 'Tallyho!'"[198]

Lieutenant Parker had brought in twenty-three Rangers, including himself, who were desperately needed to reinforce the hard pressed 2nd Rangers defending Pointe du Hoc. "The word was sent back to Rudder that we were there. He immediately sent a message back. 'Where are the rest of them?'

"I replied, 'I don't know. I thought they were here. They must be right behind me,' but, of course they weren't. The 5th and the rest of the 2nd Ranger Battalions were held up on the coastal road from Vierville-sur-Mer headed for Grandcamp le Bain and Cherbourg, pinned down by the Germans. They would not make it through to us until two days after D-Day."[199]

Captain George P. Whittington, Jr.
Company B, 5th Ranger Battalion, Provisional Ranger Group

Lieutenant Colonel Schneider also observed the actions of Captain George P. Whittington, commander of Company B, 2nd Ranger Battalion. "Despite devastating enemy fire, Captain Whittington personally supervised the breaching of hostile wire and obstacles by the use of Bangalores. He then led his company and the remainder of his battalion through the gap created. He led his company up the cliff and personally crawled to and destroyed a German pillbox. He then reorganized his company and continued to advance. Throughout the entire operation he displayed extraordinary heroism and aggressive leadership, thus paving the way for the success of the operation."[200]

Private First Class Carl Weast, with Company B, 5th Ranger Battalion, felt that "in our outfit, we were fortunate, we had leaders. George Whittington was one of the first ones over that seawall. The officers went first. Later on, I heard our adjutant criticizing Captain Whittington for unnecessarily exposing himself and I remember he says, 'You saw it happen back on that beach. Now when you know how the hell you lead men from behind, you tell me. It just doesn't work.'

"Believe me, on Omaha Beach there was precious little leadership anywhere. It was simple fear that stopped those guys at the seawall and they lay there and got butchered by rocket fire and by artillery fire for no damn reason other than the fact that there was nobody to lead them off that beach. We were fortunate we had some of the best officers in the army. Those guys did it, they led us."[201]

AT H+65, COMPANY B, 37TH ENGINEER COMBAT BATTALION, loaded in six amphibious DUKWs, was scheduled to land on Easy Red along with one DUKW carrying a detachment from Headquarters, V Corps, commanded by Colonel Benjamin B. Talley, which was to land and report the situation on the beach.

Colonel Benjamin B. Talley
Headquarters, V Corps

Prior to the invasion, Major General Leonard Gerow, the commanding officer of V Corps, knew that he was going to need up to the minute information about the situation on Omaha Beach. "During the planning phase of the assault on the continent of Europe, Colonel Talley volunteered to organize and command a detachment of officers and enlisted men (all volunteers) to go ashore behind the assault wave and furnish to the commanding general afloat, by radio, current information regarding the progress of the operation. All of the individuals concerned knew that the service for which they were volunteering might well be a suicide mission. This detachment was organized by Colonel Talley into two teams loaded into radio equipped DUKWs and two teams loaded in ¼ ton cars aboard an LCT. Colonel Talley commanded the detachment from one of the DUKWs."[202]

During the predawn darkness, Colonel Talley boarded the DUKW that would transport him and part of his detachment to Easy Red. "Our LST was dragging its bow anchor due to wind and sea so rough the crew dared not open the bow door. Later the heavy stern anchor was dropped, the bow anchor was lifted, and we swung about with the bow downwind where the door could be safely opened. Each passing swell brought water almost over the sill of the ramp, then lifted the end of the ramp fourteen or fifteen feet above the water only to submerge it when the ramp went down. We drove onto the ramp and were signaled to disembark. We cleared the ramp at 04:00. It was still dark. We were nearly three hours behind schedule and twelve miles from shore. Our radio operators, cooped up in a small boxlike cabin, became desperately seasick, but it affected their operations only when they had to go out to vomit into the sea.

A DUKW amphibious vehicle was a versatile craft and was used extensively in the Normandy landings. *United States Navy photograph, National Archives.*

"To facilitate secure communications, we had prepared a 'one time' code consisting of the letters of the international phonetic alphabet: 'Able, Baker, Charlie,' etc. Each letter had a special meaning. Copies were given to all headquarters concerned. Other messages would be encoded by machine. We went on the air on schedule at 06:00 and transmitted, 'Peter Item King,' meaning DUKW Number 1 afloat.

"Soon we met empty LCTs returning from the direction of the beach. By their numbers we knew they had carried DD tanks (Duplex Drive Amphibious Tanks) suspended on canvas caissons which held the tanks ten to twelve feet below the water surface. They were driven by two propellers powered by the tank engine. We were surprised that the tanks had been launched in the rough water, but reported the passage of the returning LCTs without comment. As we approached the beach, we saw small units of the 1st Division on our extreme left hugging the vertical cliff to escape grenades being dropped on them by the enemy on top the hill. I made several attempts to land, but the three long antennas extending nearly fifteen feet into the air above the DUKW drew such intense machine gun and mortar fire that I would withdraw. In any event, we could see little from the beach, whereas we had a complete panorama while at sea. The bullets hitting the sea around us reminded me of hail. I was in almost continuous radio contact with headquarters on the *Ancon* in the channel behind us.

"At 09:00, I sent the message: 'From 1,000 yards off Dog and Red (the beaches were named from letters of the phonetic alphabet), I see several companies of the 16th Infantry on Easy, Red and Fox Beaches. Enemy fire still effective. LCTs shifting to Dog. About ten LCTs standing by to land. Obstacles appear thicker than in photos. LCI 85 hit and smoking after unloading. Have seen two LCTs burn. Count ten tanks on Fox. Landing resuming on Dog.' This message is in the Situation Report of V Corps for about 09:20, 6 June, 1944.

This photo shows a DUKW on land transporting Generals George Marshall, Eisenhower, Hap Arnold, and other high ranking military officers during a tour of Omaha Beach in early July of 1944. *United States Army Signal Corps photograph, National Archives.*

"Quickly the situation changed and the landing stopped altogether. I radioed General Gerow that the landing had stopped and more than one hundred landing craft were milling around like a herd of cattle before a storm and dared not approach the beach due to heavy artillery and mortar fire. In another message, I said I believed the Germans were using a church steeple at Vierville as an observation post. This message was passed by hand from DUKW Number 2, with Lieutenant Colonel Kilburn Houston in charge, to a destroyer which immediately fired two salvos at the church steeple, cutting it off at the roof line and blowing it apart. Effective German artillery and mortar fire ceased shortly thereafter and the landing resumed. I landed shortly thereafter and within fifty feet of where I had gone ashore, met General Willard Wyman, commanding the 1st Division troops. He told me that he had no radio communications; that he had either lost his radio equipment or his operators. I sent a message for him, and as we lay on the ground, mortar shells struck nearby. Six of us were lying close, together. Of these, three were wounded and three unhurt. My driver, Private James Mildenberger, lying beside me, was hit by a shell fragment which otherwise would have hit me. I was unhurt save for some loss of hearing."[203]

Major General Gerow later wrote the following recommendation regarding the actions of Colonel Talley for the award of the Distinguished Service Cross. "The DUKWs stations were launched twelve miles offshore in darkness and successfully reached shore, under Colonel Talley's direction through rough seas wherein many DUKWs carrying lighter loads from the same ships were swamped and lost. Upon attempting to land, the two DUKWs under Colonel Talley's command came under heavy enemy artillery and machine gun fire. In as much as the DUKWs were without armor and armament except for individual weapons, and the accomplishment of the mission depended upon protecting the equipment, Colonel Talley properly decided at that time to withdraw the DUKWs and proceeded to cruise parallel to the beach three hundred to five hundred yards off shore. During this time Colonel Talley continued to furnish information by radio to me aboard the U.S.S. *Ancon*. Three further attempts to land the DUKWs were made before the fire had diminished sufficiently to permit a successful landing. Even so, after going ashore, one DUKW received a direct hit from enemy artillery which killed one enlisted man and seriously wounded two others. This DUKW burned and was a total loss. The other DUKW successfully escaped damage, although the driver was wounded by an artillery shell bursting a few yards away. The two ¼ ton stations were brought ashore in an LCT. Upon attempting to land and after the ramp was lowered this LCT received a direct hit from enemy artillery, causing several casualties among other passengers aboard. The radio equipment was drowned out in deep water going ashore, but the personnel comprising these teams continued to perform their mission of collecting information on the tactical and supply situation for transmission to me through the one station remaining in operation. The detachment operated under Colonel Talley's command and personal supervision, afloat and ashore, from H-15 minutes until approximately H+15 hours when the V Corps command post was established ashore.

"During this period Colonel Talley furnished me with reliable and current information as to the progress of the assault and for a portion of the time involved, the radio under his control was the only effective means of communication between the troops ashore and the command echelons afloat."[204]

AT H+ 70, the remainder of the 121st Engineer Combat Battalion was scheduled to touch down on Dog Green, along with an LCI transporting the bulk of Headquarters and Headquarters Company, 116th Infantry, which was scheduled to land on Dog White, another LCI carrying the rest of the 112th Engineer Combat Battalion was assigned to land on Dog Red, and an LCI transporting the 149th Beach Battalion Group, consisting of the 149th Engineer Combat Battalion and numerous other attached units was assigned to land on the Easy Green sector.

Technician Fourth Grade Elmer G. Shindle
Headquarters Company, 116th Infantry Regiment, 29th Infantry Division

Technician Fourth Grade Elmer G. Shindle, a medic attached to Headquarters Company, 116th Infantry, was aboard the LCI that was scheduled to land on Dog White. Lieutenant Donald Casapulla, the adjutant of the 116th Infantry, wrote the following recommendation for the award of the DSC based upon Shindle's heroic actions during the assault landing. "The LCI in which Technician Fourth Grade Shindle was approaching struck a mine, damaging the boat. Then it received a direct artillery hit. Men abandoned ship in water too deep to wade, sprayed with rifle and machine gun fire. Technician Fourth Grade Shindle swam ashore, aiding others to reach shore. There, under a withering enemy fire with disregard for his own safety, he rescued many wounded and near drowned soldiers from the water, took them to the most safe cover available on the beaches, aided in caring for their wounds. By his gallant and heroic efforts, he saved the lives of many comrades and inspired others to face the enemy fire both in rescue work and in carrying the fight forward."[205]

While tending the wounded on shore, Technician Fourth Grade Shindle was "caught in a crossfire of machine guns while I was dressing someone's wounds, and putting my Red Cross arm band up on one of the obstacles on the beach where I was, thinking this would stop the firing. I remember the only one who was any help to me on the beach was the medical man from the LCI we came in on. There were quite a few near me, but they were so frightened they were hugging the seawall. They were from another outfit. This man was really a hero and should have been decorated. I never did get to know his name."[206]

The medic with whom he worked on the beach wasn't the only unsung hero Shindle saw that terrible day. "I was pinned down by machine gun fire while trying to get to a wounded man, when a first sergeant came crawling up to me and found out where the firing was coming from. He went up the hill to the machine gun nest and soon there was silence. I often wondered what happened since I never saw him again."[207]

ON EASY RED, two companies of the 1st Battalion, 16th Infantry were scheduled to land at H+70. Company A, carried in six LCVPs was slated to land on the western half, while Company C, also in six LCVPs, was scheduled to land on the eastern half of the sector.

Captain James L. Pence
Company A, 16th Infantry Regiment, 1st Infantry Division

Major Edmund Driscoll, the commander of the 1st Battalion, 16th Infantry Regiment, witnessed the actions of Captain James L. Pence during the landing on D-Day. "Captain Pence was hit immediately upon debarkation from his craft, but ignoring his painful wounds, he persisted in his efforts to reach the beach. He immediately set about reorganizing his men, exposing himself repeatedly to the intense machine gun and artillery fire in his efforts to reach them. Absolutely refusing all efforts to get him under cover and to dress his severe wounds, he continued in his movements up and down the fire swept area, getting small groups together, supplying weapons for those who had lost their arms in landing, bending every effort toward getting the attack under way again. His forceful actions and splendid leadership under the most adverse and painful conditions were directly responsible for the reorganization of the units on the beach from the time he reached the sand until he collapsed from the effects of his wounds."[208]

Private First Class Leroy Herman, pinned down on the beach with most of the other soldiers on the beach, watched as "Captain Pence stood up in the beach area and yelled, 'Come on you bastards, let's go! If we're gonna die, we might as well die a little further inland!'"[209]

First Lieutenant William T. Dillon
Company A, 16th Infantry Regiment, 1st Infantry Division

Lieutenant T. Dillon and Company A, 16th Infantry landed on the right flank of the regimental sector. "Our orders were to punch a hole through; don't stop until you get to a hill one mile inland. We were to land on a high ebbing tide at 7:30 a.m. I looked over the ramp and could see the little valley which was to be our right [boundary], but I could see that the engineers hadn't been there to blow the mined ramps about six hundred yards from the beach. By now, we were getting all kinds of fire. There wasn't a footprint in the sand, nor a dead man on the beach—we were supposed to be the [support] wave! Where was the [assault] wave of troops?

"As we got to the top of the dune, there was a big concertina barbed wire entanglement. Where did the navy go? Our one Bangalore torpedo wouldn't go through. Soon, some men came up and we got two more torpedoes from them. We slid all three under the barbed wire, pulled the fuse, and jumped behind the sand dune. It went off and made a hole big enough to drive a truck through. As we went through the gap we came to bullrushes, waded through them and came to a wide canal or tank ditch. I stepped into the water and went in over my head. That's when I found out what the CO^2 tubes in my Mae West were for! I pulled both triggers and up I popped! I paddled across and started up the hill. I looked at the ground and could see both types of foot mines—one looked like a horse chestnut and would blow your leg off, the other had three prongs sticking out of the ground and would pop up face high and go off.

"Off to my right Lieutenant [Atwood M.] McElyea, Pat Ford, Sergeant [William R.] Benn, and Babcock the aid man, kept going a few steps at a time until Ford stepped on one of the horse chestnuts. It blew Ford's leg off, threw him into the air and he came down on his shoulder on another one that tore up his arm and threw him onto a third mine…Babcock gave him three morphine shots intermuscular. This is also where McElyea had some of his brains shot out. I thought he was dead…

"We couldn't go up that hill and our orders were to punch through, so we couldn't go back. We slid left and stayed close to the ground. At this point, the captain's runner came crawling up and said Captain Pence had been shot and he says you are to take over the company. I knew then why I'd been made first lieutenant in England. As I lay there, I realized that now I was responsible for 275 men, or what was left of them. I knew the Germans had to have a path up the hill that was clear of mines. I looked around. When I was younger, I'd been a good hunter and could trail a rabbit easily. I studied the ground and saw a faint path zigzagging to the left up the hill, so I walked up the path very carefully. Something blew up behind me. I looked back and a young soldier had stepped on a mine and it had blown off his foot up to his knee. I brought the others up the path. At the top we saw the first and only Russian soldiers I have ever seen."[210]

Major Edmund Driscoll, the 1st Battalion commander, was an eyewitness to the heroism of Lieutenant Dillon. "When the landing craft carrying Lieutenant William T. Dillon, Company A, 16th Infantry, and his assault section neared the shore it was the target for bitter machine gun and artillery fire. Completely disregarding the intense enemy action, he calmly gathered his section and led them through the mine strewn and bullet flayed waters to the shore. Upon reaching the relative safety of the shale shelf with his section and finding his company commander had become a casualty in the landing, Lieutenant Dillon unhesitatingly assumed responsibility for the company and took over the command. Although every movement on the beach drew additional fire and all leaders were constant targets for accurate sniper action, he proceeded to move up and down the fire swept beach, collecting the scattered assault sections and reorganizing the entire company into a fighting unit. With rapid reorganization completed, Lieutenant Dillon led a section of the company through the wire and over an uncharted minefield to a position from which they could launch an attack on a strongpoint above them. When this section too was pinned down, Lieutenant Dillon, completely disregarding the gravest personal danger, moved forward in the face of the concentrated fire to assault the commanding hostile emplacements. With hand grenades and a carbine, he assaulted the network of mutually covering emplacements, knocking out personally at least two of the weapons pinning down his men. From the very midst of the enemy, he effectively sniped at the pillbox apertures, interfering with their fire to such an extent that his men were able to resume the forward movement and join him. Minefields and wire protected the various hostile positions, but ignoring the danger, Lieutenant Dillon fearlessly found paths over which his men could safely advance through the area. He led the section in repeated frontal assaults on the still intact emplacements; personally taking the leading role in the bitter hand to hand fighting for each one. Due to his fearless personal attacks and brilliant leadership, the strongpoint was eliminated, and the men pinned down on the beach were able to begin their movement inland. His selfless determination and supreme devotion to duty during the most critical period of the invasion were instrumental in making one of the first breaks in the almost impenetrable defenses."[211]

Second Lieutenant Atwood M. McElyea
Company A, 16th Infantry Regiment, 1st Infantry Division

Lieutenant Robert F. Chambers, an officer with the 16th Infantry, witnessed the actions of Lieutenant Atwood McElyea on Easy Red. "Long prepared and determinedly held enemy positions commanded the entire beach and approach area. As soon as the landing craft came within range, they were subjected to the concentrated artillery, machine gun, and sniper fire of the still intact shore emplacements. Just above the high water mark, the beach was covered with an apron of intricate barbed wire defenses, and the area between the wire and the slope behind the sands was heavily mined and uncharted. The only semblance of cover on the entire beach was provided by a slight shelf of shale and rubble approximately seven yards from the water line. Wave after wave came ashore, only to be halted by the withering fire, until thousands of troops lay in that narrow beachhead, many of their leaders casualties. On reaching the shore Lieutenant McElyea, an assault section leader of Company A, 16th Infantry, found his section scattered over the beach and pinned down by intense crossfire of the enemy positions. Despite the fact that he was under constant observation and that movement, particularly that of an officer, drew terribly accurate fire from the numerous snipers, Lieutenant McElyea calmly moved up and down the beach to reorganize his section. Having gathered them into a position of relative safety, Lieutenant McElyea himself, displaying superb courage, searched the completely exposed line of barbed wire above the high water mark until he found a slight breach. Lieutenant McElyea was one of the first of the assault troops to go through the wire. Once in the heavily mined flat meadow beyond the beach, Lieutenant McElyea led the way across, setting an example of outstanding courage. Ignoring the hail fire directed at him, he calmly picked a path through the field, stopping only to neutralize numerous mines. A deeply booby-trapped antitank ditch lay in the way and he unhesitatingly plunged into it, clearing the way for his men through the complicated antipersonnel obstacles. Leading them out of the ditch, Lieutenant McElyea again encountered another thickly strewn, uncharted minefield covered by deadly accurate fire. Never stopping for a longer length of time than it was necessary for his men to catch up to him; he proceeded through the minefield and safely led his section to the base of the ridgeline. The persistent advance of this courageous determined leader had made him the target for the most intense sniper fire the enemy could direct upon him. Undeterred, Lieutenant McElyea started to close with the enemy. With extraordinary daring, he himself approached to within fifty yards of an enemy machine gun position and engaged until his section could get into position. During this action, Lieutenant McElyea was hit in the head and severely wounded."[212]

Technical Sergeant William R. Benn, Jr.
Company A, 16th Infantry Regiment, 1st Infantry Division

Major Edmund Driscoll, the commander of the 1st Battalion, 16th Infantry, observed Sergeant William Benn take control of his assault section after his section leader was wounded. "Completely disregarding the hail of fire about him, he exposed himself repeatedly to gather and reorganize his scattered men. Rapidly reorganizing the men under fire, he proceeded to lead them into the assault. An unmarked minefield lay in the way, but he picked a path through it and led the platoon safely across the area and to the base of the slope beyond. In the face of direct fire of the hostile emplacements above him, he led the way directly up the steep barren slope and into the midst of the enemy. The deadly fire caused heavy casualties among his section and threatened to stop the advance. Displaying superb courage and with complete disregard for his own safety, Sergeant Benn advanced alone towards the enemy positions. Armed with a rifle and some grenades, he approached through the hail of fire and from a distance of twenty-five yards threw the hand grenades with such accuracy that the positions were silenced and his comrades were enabled to advance and finish wiping out the enemy. In the course of this action, Sergeant Benn was seriously wounded, but he persisted in his efforts until the enemy was completely silenced."[213]

Staff Sergeant Paul R. Shorter
Company A, 16th Infantry Regiment, 1st Infantry Division

Sergeant Paul R. Shorter was in charge of the wire party of his Company A, 16th Infantry assault section. "I was to crawl through the minefield, clear the way for the other men. I knew it was not safe on the beach, for it was my third invasion, so the best thing a person could do was to get to land as quick as possible. I was running across the beach, men were being hit left, right, front, and rear. All I could think of was, 'I would be next.' We had no time to think of the sad part—we had a job to do. I crossed the beach, blew the barbed wire with the torpedoes."[214]

Lieutenant William Dillon, the executive officer of Company A, 16th Infantry, saw another of the company's NCOs take control of his section during the landing. "When Staff Sergeant Shorter's section reached the beach, he was the only non-com left; his section leader was often engaged elsewhere, and in his absence the entire problem of keeping the section intact and advancing fell upon Staff Sergeant Shorter. Repeatedly exposing himself to the sweeping enemy machine gun and sniper fire, he moved among his men, always at the front and leading them forward across the beach. When the order came to move out and assault the hostile strongpoints on the high ground behind the beach, he was at the head of his men and led the advance through the uncharted minefields and right into the face of the fire from the emplacements. Throughout the bitter fighting, he exposed himself repeatedly to the direct fire of the enemy, forcing them to disclose their positions, then attacking and destroying several machine gun and sniper nests. Later in that same day, as the fighting progressed inland, the fanatically defending enemy retreated slowly, making a last bitter stand at each of the many hedgerows and ditches encountered. On numerous occasions throughout the day, Staff Sergeant Shorter, acting entirely on his own initiative, organized and led patrols to wipe out nests of snipers and machine guns firing on the flanks of his unit. In each of these patrol actions he was the direct target of both machine gun and sniper activity, but completely disregarding the hail of fire about him, he personally assaulted right into the center of the emplacements, and eliminated the resistance. On at least five different occasions when organized resistance threatened to stop the advance of his organization, he moved out ahead of the unit, and despite constant enemy fire, proceeded to lead the assault on the enemy."[215]

Captain Victor H. Briggs
Company C, 16th Infantry Regiment, 1st Infantry Division

Major Driscoll, the commander of the 1st Battalion, 16th Infantry, witnessed the heroism of Captain Victor H. Briggs, the commanding officer of Company C, 16th Infantry. "During the initial assault against the beach defenses, Captain Briggs displayed superb leadership and outstanding personal bravery. With utter disregard for his own safety, he exposed himself to heavy enemy fire while leading men ashore from the landing craft and after reaching the beach, continued to ignore his own welfare while organizing an assault team from the groups of confused troops pinned down by the merciless fire. After organizing his group, Captain Briggs again braved the withering fire and personally led the advance through a dense enemy minefield and into a strategic position on the slope of the hill. Here, too, he was exposed to deadly fire from pillboxes, machine gun positions, and snipers equipped with telescopic sights. But, through his magnificent leadership and inspiring personal courage, the position was successfully defended until additional troops could be moved forward."[216]

Six LCVPs transporting Company B, 16th Infantry, were scheduled to land on the western half of Easy Red, while three LCVPs carrying members of Headquarters and Headquarters Company, 1st Battalion, 16th Infantry, was supposed to land on the eastern side of Easy Red, and three other LCVPs combat engineers with the 1st and 20th Engineer Combat Battalions were slated to land in the center of Easy Red at H+80.

Captain Thomas N. Merendino
Company B, 16th Infantry Regiment, 1st Infantry Division

Major Edmund Driscoll, the commanding officer of the 1st Battalion, 16th Infantry Regiment, along with his battalion staff and headquarters company troops landed in the same wave as Company B, 16th Infantry. "On the morning of 6 June 1944, the 16th Infantry Regiment invaded the shores of France near Colleville-sur-le-Mer, facing a firmly emplaced and fanatically determined enemy. Artillery, mortars, and machine guns swept the entire invasion area from carefully prepared positions and pillboxes. Expert snipers, their rifles equipped with telescopic sights, were strategically spotted on the ridge overlooking the beach. Carefully laid mines and countless booby traps, as well as double apron bands of barbed wire blanketed the area between the waterfront and the hill, while the channel itself was littered with floating and submerged mines and delaying obstacles of all types, in addition to being constantly raked with fire from artillery, mortars, and heavy machine guns. Troops were mowed down before they could leave their landing craft and the success of the entire landing operation in this sector was seriously threatened by the inability of the men to reach the shores in organized assault units. Only inspired leadership and superb courage prevented the whole mission from being turned into a tragic failure. Captain Merendino, commanding Company B, 16th Infantry, disembarked from his landing craft in the initial assault wave and with complete disregard for his own safety, hastily organized the confused men who were struggling in the shell chopped surf into a unit and led them through the intense fire to the shore. Upon reaching the shore, Captain Merendino refused to take cover from the enemy fire as he again organized an assault group for a further advance. Fully exposed to sweeping fire from commanding enemy pillboxes and machine gun nests, and a constant target for the snipers on the hill, he personally led the charge up the slope, guiding the men through the enemy minefield without thought to his own safety. Inspired by his great courage and devotion to duty, his unit surged forward to capture their objective."[217]

AT H+90, FIVE LCTs transporting the 58th Armored Field Artillery Battalion were scheduled to touch down on Dog White, in support of the 116th Infantry Regiment.

Captain Kenneth E. Beitler
Battery C, 58th Armored Field Artillery Battalion

Captain Paul K. Switzer, the battalion surgeon of the 58th Armored Field Artillery Battalion, was on the same LCT with Captain Beitler. "Captain Kenneth E. Beitler was in charge of an LCT carrying M7 105mm self-propelled howitzers and halftracks of this battalion in the assault landing on Omaha Beach, Normandy. About fifteen miles out from shore, the craft developed a leak in the left compartment, and was soon listing markedly. Shortly thereafter the steering gear broke, Captain Beitler moved among the men, encouraging and reassuring them, and at 09:00 an attempt was made to land on Dog White Beach. As the LCT approached the shore, it was met by a hail of machine gun fire and artillery fire. The beach was completely disorganized, and it quickly became apparent that a landing could not be made. At Captain Beitler's suggestion the craft moved back out to attempt a run in on an adjacent beach. At 10:00 the LCT approached Easy Green Beach. Going in to the beach, it struck an underwater obstacle, exploding two mines and grounding on a sandbar, separated from shore by about thirty yards of water. Artillery shells were breaking around the boat, but Captain Beitler calmed the men and directed that the ramp be lowered. Calculating the depth of the water, he ordered a halftrack off, which was barely covered [by water]. Deciding the M7s could make it, he ordered them ashore; and the two halftracks to remain [aboard the LCT]. All four of the M7's made shore successfully. Then, with enemy artillery and small arms fire still sweeping the beach, Captain Beitler directed his four guns rapidly into a firing position at 10:30 hours. Chaos and confusion still reigned on the beach, but by virtue of his courage, calmness, and leadership, Captain Beitler had his guns laid and ready to support the infantry at a time when it was critically in need of such support."[218]

COMPANY D, 16TH INFANTRY, riding in five LCVPs, along with three LCVPs carrying miscellaneous units, as well as the assistant commander of the 1st Infantry Division, Brigadier General Willard G. Wyman, were scheduled to land on Easy Red, while five LCTs transporting ing the 62nd Armored Field Artillery Battalion was assigned to land on Fox Green at H+90. The bulk of Headquarters Company, 16th Infantry, transported in one LCM and one LCVP, was scheduled to land on Easy Red at H+95.

Brigadier General Willard G. Wyman
Headquarters, 1st Infantry Division

Lieutenant Alfred Ely and a group of division headquarters personnel were in the same landing craft as General Wyman as it landed on Easy Red under intense enemy fire. "Brigadier General Willard G. Wyman landed during a heavy concentration of enemy fire during the early hours of the attack directly behind the leading waves. With total disregard for his personal safety, Brigadier General Wyman personally took charge of the situation. Due to enemy action at this time, many organizational leaders were casualties. The exits to the beaches were blocked, supporting weapons could not be landed, and the attack was halted. Brigadier General Wyman personally directed the movement of men and vehicles which had landed. Although his command post had been established during this period in a comparatively safe desolate area, not under artillery and small arms fire, General Wyman chose to remain on the beach in order to personally make instant disposition of troops as they landed on the beach and maintain control of leaderless groups. During this period, the fire delivered by enemy weapons was exceptionally intense.

General Wyman's aide and another officer with him were wounded on either side of him while in conference. Notwithstanding this loss, and with total disregard for his personal safety, General Wyman continued to direct personally the operation on the beach, and as each succeeding wave of vehicles and men would land, he would direct their disposition. During this whole time, General Wyman did not once raise his voice or shout. He quietly and calmly gave orders to the men in a casual manner. This example did much to steady the men and encourage them to greater efforts."[219]

Don Whitehead was one of several correspondents who landed that morning with the 1st Infantry Division. "'We've got to get these men off the beach,' Wyman said, 'This is murder!' Wyman studied the situation for a few minutes and then with absolute disregard for his own life and safety, he stood up to expose himself to the enemy's fire. Calmly, he began moving lost units to their proper positions, organizing leadership for leaderless troops. He began to bring order out of chaos, out of confusion, and to give direction to this vast collection of inert manpower waiting only to be told what to do, where to go…

"Up and down that bloody strip of beach he went from group to group, from soldier to soldier. Under Wyman's direction, messengers began moving between unit commanders. They stepped over dead and wounded, flung themselves flat as shells whistled in to splatter them with mud and gravel, and then jumped up to carry out their orders. And gradually the fog of battle began to lift a little."[220]

Lieutenant Robert J. Riekse, with Headquarters Company, 1st Infantry Division, had a clear memory of General Wyman "moving up and down the beach, talking, moving men, redeploying troops, urging them to use their equipment, trying to locate a radio that operated, meeting the incoming troops and always exposed."[221]

AT H+100, AN LCI carrying elements of the 6th Engineer Special Brigade, including its commanding officer, Colonel Paul W. Thompson, was scheduled to land on Dog White.

Colonel Paul W. Thompson
Headquarters, 6th Engineer Special Brigade, Provisional Engineer Special Brigade Group

Commander Lawrence C. Leever, with the United States Navy, was the commanding officer of the 7th Naval Beach Battalion. "At approximately 09:30 hours, Colonel Paul W. Thompson, commanding officer of the 6th Engineer Special Brigade, and I were together on the beach near St. Laurent, France. The assault on exit D-3 in the Omaha sector was being held up by heavy machine gun fire. Upon discovering the situation, and ascertaining that assault units were not pressing the attack, Colonel Thompson called for volunteers to assist him in wiping out the snipers. Several infantrymen volunteered. Colonel Thompson blew a gap in the wire obstacle, led his party into the exit and prepared to assault a house in which the nearest snipers were located. While approaching the house from the rear, Colonel Thompson was seriously wounded in the face and shoulder by enemy fire from another emplacement. Colonel Thompson was thus incapacitated from carrying out his mission, but the other troops, inspired by his fearless example, later stormed the exit and pushed through it."[222]

Colonel Thompson along with his headquarters group "landed a few hundred yards off from the spot where we should have landed. That was par for the course that day. We stepped out into water shoulder deep. It was midmorning, even at that early hour things weren't going well for our side. Foolishly trying to help some engineer soldiers push a Bangalore torpedo under a wire obstacle; I was hit twice by rifle fire, once through the right shoulder, and the other time through the jaw."[223]

At H+110, Cannon Company, 116th Infantry and a platoon of the Antitank Company, 116th Infantry, transported in a total of ten amphibious DUKWs, were scheduled to land at Dog Green. The other two platoons of the Antitank Company, 116th Infantry, loaded in six DUKWs, plus elements of the 29th Signal Company in another DUKW were assigned to land at Dog Red. The 111th Field Artillery Battalion carried in twelve DUKWs was assigned to land at Easy Green.

Private First Class William M. Riggs
Cannon Company, 116th Infantry Regiment, 29th Infantry Division

Lieutenant Donald Casapulla was the adjutant of the 116th Infantry Regiment. "Private First Class Riggs was coming ashore with a rough sea in a DUKW, which was struck by enemy shell fire, when it was a substantial distance offshore. The small craft was nearly capsized and appeared lost; no rescue was near. With utter disregard for his own safety, and involving a risk of life beyond the call of duty, Private First Class Riggs plunged into the turbulent sea, swam about five hundred yards further out to sea, intercepted another landing craft, and directed it to his comrades in the out of control DUKW. His gallant act of service resulted in saving the lives and equipment of his comrades. The rescue craft towed the DUKW to the beach where the occupants debarked with their equipment and took up the fight against the enemy."[224]

Second Lieutenant Forest K. Ferguson
Antitank Company, 116th Infantry Regiment, 29th Infantry Division

Lieutenant Donald Casapulla, the 116th Infantry's adjutant wrote the recommendation for Lieutenant Forest K. Ferguson, who had been an All American football player at the University of Florida and the state's collegiate boxing champion prior to America's entry into the war. "Lieutenant Ferguson was a member of the AT Company of 116th Infantry, one of the assault regiments. The enemy held coast was fortified behind minefields and extensive wire emplaced obstacles and with small arms, machine gun, mortar and observed artillery fire covering the Vierville beach sector where Lieutenant Ferguson's organization landed. He reached the shore to find the assault infantry pinned down in front of skillfully placed obstacles, receiving a withering fire, with many casualties being inflicted. With utter disregard for his personal safety, Lieutenant Ferguson, with three men he encouraged to assist him, bravely moved forward under fire with a Bangalore torpedo to the obstacles holding up large numbers of infantry. This involved a great risk of life. He exploded the torpedo with a hand grenade. It blew a gap in the obstacles. He gallantly rose from his position, shouting, 'Let's go men,' and by this heroic example inspired and heartened those about him to charge through the opening. This touched off the slowed down attack with an impetus that enabled the troops to carry the enemy held positions behind the obstacles. After reaching the enemy firing positions about one hundred yards forward, Lieutenant Ferguson received a head wound. His leadership, his courage, and his fearless and gallant conduct contributed in a great measure to the success of his regiment."[225]

Lieutenant Ferguson never recovered from his severe head wound, dying on May 15, 1954. An award is given in his name annually to the senior football player selected by the University of Florida coaching staff who displays outstanding leadership, courage, and character.

SCHEDULED TO LAND ON EASY RED AT H+110, were elements of Headquarters and Headquarters Company, 1st Infantry Division riding in two LCMs and one LCVP along with the 1st Signal Company and Cannon Company, 16th Infantry in eight DUKWs on Easy Red.

Captain Thomas F. O'Brien
Cannon Company, 16th Infantry Regiment, 1st Infantry Division

Colonel George A. Taylor, the commanding officer of the 16th Infantry Regiment, realized that the situation on Omaha Beach was still critical two hours after the initial assault waves landed. "Cannon Company, 16th Infantry, had lost nearly all of its equipment when the craft on which both personnel and equipment were loaded sunk. The men were scattered and were straggling ashore in small leaderless groups. Captain O'Brien, commanding Cannon Company, landed on the beach at 08:15 hours. At that time his unit had not begun to land, and he found himself part of the pinned down assault waves. He refused to take cover and await the landing of the remainder of his men. Absolutely disregarding the gravest personal danger, he moved up and down the beach, shouting orders and encouragement to his men, and by his brilliant example of fearless leadership restoring some semblance of order wherever he went. Several hundred yards down the beach from the position he was then in, several intact tanks were stopped a few yards from the water and buttoned up, none of them were firing. Immediately, he worked his way down the fire swept beach to them, found their crews, and led them back up the beach to a point which they could engage enemy guns firing from concrete emplacements.

"With the guns returning enemy fire for the first time, he repeatedly exposed himself to the full fury of the enemy fire by going up over the shale shelf on to a flat mine strewn field to observe and direct the fire of the hastily formed tank unit. With the tanks firing successfully at the enemy, he left them and continued his trip down the beach, ordering mortar crews to set up and begin firing, and staying with them until they became effective, then moving on to other bewildered men. Many mortar and gun crews from other organizations were halted on the beach, helpless in the loss of key personnel. Wherever he found such units, he set them into action, firing them with his own fearless determination to form again a fighting unit. Wounded men were struggling in the surf, helpless from their heavy equipment and weak from wounds and shock. Repeatedly, he dashed into the surf, dragged the men out to places of safety, and immediately rendered medical aid. On returning down the beach, he found several of the tanks had been driven back to their former useless positions by the intense enemy fire. Once more he clambered onto them, drove their crews into action and led them back to fire upon the strongpoints blocking exit E-3. Not only in observing and directing fire did Captain O'Brien deliberately leave every sign of cover, but rather he had cover only when it happened to be where he felt his leadership and control was needed.

"By this time, his own men were coming ashore, a cannon company without a single gun, thoroughly disorganized and lost amid the many other units scattered throughout the length of the beach. He collected and consolidated these small groups of men, moving up and down the beach until he had gotten all of his company together. Then, he returned to them and right on the beach and under constant fire, reorganized the company into a rifle unit. The reorganization completed, the company was attached to and fought with the 1st Battalion. When they were more urgently needed with another organization, he removed his company and attached them to the 2nd Battalion for the remainder of the fighting period. Captain O'Brien led his men in several critical actions, and by his inspiring leadership, helped turn a threatened catastrophe into a magnificent victory."[226]

Private First Class Henry Berkowitz
Cannon Company, 16th Infantry Regiment, 1st Infantry Division

One of the critical needs on Omaha Beach was radio communications. Therefore, German snipers targeted the radio operators, just as they did officers and NCOs. Captain Thomas O'Brien had one radio operator, Private First Class Henry Berkowitz, who refused to let a severe wound keep him from getting his radio into action to facilitate communications with other units. "Under the deadly artillery barrage, Private First Class Berkowitz, Cannon Company, 16th Infantry, approached the shore. The landing craft which carried him was sunk while about one hundred yards from the beach. He jumped from the sinking boat, carrying his SCR 300 radio, and began making his way ashore through the heavy surf under a constant hail of enemy fire. Just as he left his craft, Private First Class Berkowitz was severely wounded. Displaying a superb courage and singleness of purpose, he retained his hold on the vitally important radio and continued shoreward through the bullet churned sea. Upon reaching shore, he refused treatment and dragged himself and the radio along the exposed fire swept shore and over a minefield until he caught up with his forward observation party. Heedless of his painful wound and the sniper and machine gun fire all about him, he insisted upon setting up his radio set and carrying out his assignment. Private First Class Berkowitz remained at his radio throughout the period his section was on the beach and relayed vital information back to his unit. This information given in a calm concise manner by the wounded man under the most trying conditions was invaluable to the conduct of the battle."[227]

At H+120, an LCM carrying the 1st Medical Battalion landed on the Easy Red sector, which was still under tremendous enemy fire. In addition, the 1st Engineer Battalion and the Antitank Company, 16th Infantry were scheduled to land on Easy Red. In addition, the 197th Antiaircraft Artillery (Automatic Weapons) Battalion was scheduled to land on both the Easy Red and Fox Green sectors, plus an LCI(L) carrying Company B, 20th Engineer Battalion, was slated to land on the eastern end of Fox Green. LCT(5) 195, along with LCT(5) 18, LCT(5) 20, and LCT(5) 305, transporting Batteries C and D, 197th Antiaircraft Artillery (Automatic Weapons) Battalion, was scheduled to land at H+120 on Fox Green.

Captain Emerald M. Ralston
Company A, 1st Medical Battalion, 1st Infantry Division

Major Charles Tegtmeyer, the commanding officer of the 1st Medical Battalion, witnessed the arrival of an LCI carrying much of his battalion. "On 6 June 1944 at about 08:30 hours LCI 85 carrying ninety officers and enlisted men of Company A, 1st Medical Battalion neared the beach of Colleville-sur-Mer, France. Immediately on touching shore the enemy opened fire on the LCI with machine gun, 47mm, and heavy artillery from commanding, long prepared positions. Several direct hits were made on the vessel, going through the front holds, the control room and the forward deck, killing several men and wounding several more. The craft pounded with this fierce fire was forced to withdraw and seek a more suitable spot to land. While the craft maneuvered near shore still under heavy shelling, fire spread in Hold Number 2 and caused panic among the men who were trying to escape. Captain Ralston rushed into the burning hold without a moment's hesitation and with complete disregard for his own safety, organized the men in fighting the fire. His instant action not only resulted in extinguishing the fire, but by giving the men calm and rational orders, Captain Ralston wiped out all signs of panic. Although Captain Ralston was painfully burned about his face in this action, he did not take treatment, but went among the men administering aid to the wounded, personally carrying a badly wounded man to safety. The LCI once more came in for a landing and again came under intense enemy shelling, which broke the ramp off of the boat and set two holds on fire. Captain Ralston, heedless of the falling shells, ran across the deck littered with dead and wounded to rescue a critically injured patient in the officer's cabin immediately over the burning hold. Blinded by smoke and scorched by the terrific heat, he entered the cabin and displaying superb courage, carried the patient onto the deck. Captain Ralston remained on the shell swept deck to administer to the wounded. The ship put out to sea again, and transferred the wounded and dead to the U.S.S. *Chase*. Although enjoined by the naval authorities to remain on board the *Chase*, Captain Ralston reorganized and transferred the remnants of his organization to an LCM, which immediately returned to the beach. This time, in the face of vicious enemy artillery fire, which killed and wounded many of the men before they were disembarked, a landing was effected. Captain Ralston was wounded again in this landing. Refusing to take treatment or to seek cover from the withering fire sweeping the beach and mine filled water, Captain Ralston, heedless of himself, made trip after trip into heavy surf rescuing his wounded, struggling men. En route to the aid station Captain Ralston treated many of the wounded along the beach, although he was under hostile machine gun and sniper fire all the while. Captain Ralston reported to the regimental CP with twelve of his original ninety men."[228]

Lieutenant (jg) John R. Rock
LCT(5) 195, Group 53, Flotilla 18, Assault Force O, Task Force 124, Eleventh Amphibious Force, 12th Fleet

Lieutenant (jg) John R. Rock was the officer in charge of LCT(5) 195 on the morning of June 6, 1944. "Upon reaching the beach, no marked channels through the obstacles could be observed. This channel was crowded and many LCTs were milling nearby waiting for a turn to beach. The wave stood by in this area. At 09:45 LCTs 20 and 195 were able to beach. The Number 20 discharged her total load, but due to congested beach, the Number 195 was able to land only five of her ten vehicles. At 12:00 orders were received from an LCT to return to the line of departure. About 14:00 the LCT 305 tied alongside the 195. The officer in charge, Ensign John W. McClellan, had been wounded in the leg by a small caliber bullet during the morning. He was suffering from loss of blood and severe pain. The ship had hit a mine, the quarters were flooded, there were holes above and below the water line, the generator was out, the port screw had been blown off, and the engine room was filling [with seawater]. In spite of these handicaps, Ensign McClellan had attempted several beachings without success. In as much as Ensign McClellan's condition was serious, the wave leader insisted that he leave the ship to receive medical attention and he was evacuated by small boat."[229]

With no relief officer on board LCT(5) 305, Lieutenant Rock decided to board LCT 305, which was gradually sinking. Upon inspecting the damage to the craft, Rock "decided to beach her, feeling that if the load was discharged it would be possible to save the ship. At about 15:00, the 305 was beached and the load discharged. By this time the beach had been cleared, LCT 195 beached the remainder of her load (now in charge of the relief officer, Ensign [Thomas] Shand) as did LCT 18. While the 305 was retracting, she was hit by an explosive shell, which entered the quarters and caused devastating damage. The hull was broken in two by the explosion. Seven men and the wave leader were injured."[230]

Lieutenant Rock was one of those wounded by the explosion. However, despite his wounds Lieutenant Rock "went ashore in an unsuccessful attempt to get medical aid."[231] Upon his return to the badly damaged LCT 305 he found that the men aboard it had been evacuated. Lieutenant Rock then decided to abandon the stricken LCT and was taken to the U.S.S. *Capricornus* (AKA-57) for treatment.

Elements of the 5th Engineer Special Brigade, consisting of the 37th, 336th, and 348th Engineer Combat Battalions, plus other attached units to support the landings and the supply operations afterward, and transported in fourteen LCVPs and five LCAs were scheduled to land on Fox Green at H+230.

Technician Fifth Grade Edward Shaffer
Company C, 348th Engineer Combat Battalion, 5th Engineer Special Brigade, Provisional Engineer Special Brigade Group

Captain Joseph R. Kaufmann was the commanding officer of Company C, 348th Engineer Combat Battalion and was an eyewitness to the actions of one of his bulldozer operators. "Technician Fifth Grade Shaffer landed with his bulldozer on the central section of Omaha Beach at approximately 10:30 hours. He unloaded his machine in the face of extremely heavy enemy artillery, mortar, machine gun, and small arms fire, and finding that the main elements of his unit had been unable to land because of this heavy fire. He immediately volunteered his services to the flanking engineer battalion whose bulldozers and operators had suffered heavy losses from enemy fire. With complete disregard for his own personal safety, Technician Fifth Grade Shaffer, under sustained artillery, mortar, and sniper fire, operated his bulldozer continuously until he had successfully cleared the initial obstacles from the beach Exit E-1, and had cut a gap through the dune line which allowed incoming and stranded vehicles means of escape from the devastating effects of zeroed in enemy artillery and mortar fire which swept the beach. In accomplishing this voluntary mission Technician Fifth Grade Shaffer worked for approximately four hours in an absolutely exposed position in full view of enemy artillery observers and snipers on the high ground back of the beach. At any time during this period he could have taken cover with honor and without fear of censure, but with unwavering courage and determination he resolutely pursued the task at hand until the exit was opened. Then he reported to his own unit which had subsequently come ashore, and under the direction of company officers, he assisted in the opening of the second vital beach exit, an operation was again conducted in an exposed position on the beach."[232]

Major William R. Washington
Headquarters, 2nd Battalion, 16th Infantry Regiment, 1st Infantry Division

Colonel George Taylor, commander of the 16th Infantry, was already on the beach when Major William Washington arrived on Omaha Beach with badly needed infantrymen who were meant to be brought in as replacements for casualties suffered by the assault troops. Colonel Taylor needed Washington's leadership. "Major Washington landed with the regiment's over strength, which were to have come in very shortly after the initial assault. Instead, Major Washington landed to become inextricably mixed with the first waves on the bitterly contested beach line. Exposing himself fearlessly to the raking fire along the shore at a time when any movement drew the terribly accurate fire of the snipers, he swiftly reorganized his group into a compact fighting force. Then unhesitatingly he led his men through barbed wire entanglements, over an uncharted minefield, and up the heavily fortified cliffs under the direct fire of powerful machine gun emplacements and snipers. Exhibiting the greatest personal bravery, Major Washington led his men in destroying several enemy fortifications and forged his way forward to the top of the cliff through a hail of automatic fire.

"At the point where the regiment had stopped for reorganization, he turned over the replacements to their organizations. Major Washington then left the main body of troops on his own initiative and went forward to establish an observation post. He worked his way through the enemy to a vital crossroads near Colleville-sur-Mer. At this strategic point surrounded by enemy, he established an observation post and reported vital information for the advance of the regiment. Enemy snipers located his position and leveled heavy fire, but Major Washington remained at his post. Although Major Washington was badly wounded in this encounter, he still held his position for twenty-four hours, reporting invaluable observations. He fought off enemy patrols and ignored his own [friendly naval gun] fire, which struck near his isolated position. When the troops advanced, Major Washington was still in position and directed their assault along the least difficult routes."[233]

Technical Sergeant Gerald M. Henderson
Antitank Company, 18th Infantry Regiment, 1st Infantry Division

The 18th Infantry Regiment followed the 16th Infantry ashore at Omaha Beach on D-Day. Lieutenant Thomas M. Ennis witnessed the heroism of Technical Sergeant Gerald Henderson, with Antitank Company, 18th Infantry, on the afternoon of June 6. "From about 17:00 to 18:00 hours, as TQM of LCT 50, he supervised the unloading of men and vehicles off his craft upon the coast of France in the vicinity of St. Laurent, under heavy fire from enemy artillery and mortars. He remained in a most hazardous position until all trucks, tracked prime movers, and guns were on the way through deep and rough water toward shore. As Technical Sergeant Henderson was himself driving toward safety inland from the beach, he was halted by a man from Cannon Company, 18th Infantry who informed him that one of the vehicles from Cannon Company was stalled in the deep water and that several members of the crew had been wounded by artillery fire. At that very moment the enemy was lobbing mortar shells not over twenty yards from his truck, yet he turned around and placed it in position to tow out the stalled personnel carrier. He plunged into the water, dragging the winch cable behind him as he struggled against a rough sea churned not only by a stormy wind, but the constant explosion of artillery shells. When the halftrack was brought in, he immediately got the wounded men, carrying several who could not walk themselves to a place offering some shelter, and then returned to the beach. Many of the halftrack prime movers of Antitank and Cannon Companies were stalled in the deep water and for half an hour, Technical Sergeant Henderson, in order to supervise the towing of these vehicles to shore, braved the most severe pointblank shelling by [artillery] that was ever concentrated on such a limited sector. When most of the trucks, tracks, and guns of his company were safely on land, it was still impossible to move off the beach because the way forward was uncleared. Rather than go inland to a place of greater safety, Technical Sergeant Henderson chose to remain with his vehicles and guns and meanwhile, gave what aid he could to the wounded on the beach. Under the heavy enemy artillery fire that opened up on Technical Sergeant Henderson's immediate area, one of his comrades was hit and seriously wounded. Technical Sergeant Henderson went to the man while shrapnel and smoke was so thick as to black out the area, and carried him back to his own slit trench. It was after he laid the wounded man in his trench and had begun to treat him that a shell landed only a few yards away, cutting Technical Sergeant Henderson's body so badly that death from great loss of blood was only a matter of minutes."[234]

Electrician's Mate First Class Arthur V. Shields
LCI(L) 415, Group 35, Flotilla 12, Follow-up Force B, Task Force 126, Eleventh Amphibious Force, 12th Fleet

Lieutenant (jg) John F. Schereschewsky was the officer in charge of LCI(L) 415, which brought members of the 3rd Battalion, 26th Infantry Regiment to Omaha Beach on the evening of June 6. "As we neared the beach, a strong shore current made itself felt by tending to sweep our bow to the left. We touched down with about fifty yards of water between our bow and the water's edge. The ramps were lowered. Shields, Electrician's Mate First Class, went ashore with the light line and grapnel attached to the bridle. A few yards from our bow Shields began to swim. We had beached on a [sand]bar with water well over a man's head between the ship and shallow water. By swimming strongly against the current, Shields made shallow water with the grapnel. Shields signaled with his hand that the water was too deep. He appeared unconcerned by the shrapnel which splashed the water, although he had been under fire in the Pacific landings and well understood their meaning. We recalled Shields to the ship. For some two or three minutes we attempted to work over the bar without success.

"At that point, two soldiers appeared in the water to our starboard drifting parallel with the beach. Two or three others were there also, but sank (they had rushed off, I was told later before the depth had been tested). One had lost his life preserver and the other was attempting to support them both. Lieutenant Colonel [John] Corley sent one of his men with a rubber boat to help. The rubber boat putting out from our port side was swept down faster than the men, and the paddler had difficulty in getting it squared away in the right direction. By that time the man without the life preserver was definitely panicked and drowning his companion and himself. Without suggestion, Shields, still panting from his previous swim, ran down the starboard ramp and jumped in to their aid. Shields reached them in time and supported them until the rubber boat could be reached by drifting down to it. He helped heave one man into the boat and helped the other reach shallow water. Few knew until it was too late that Shields had left our ship a second time and the order had been given to retract for a further beaching at Easy Red. Shields was left on the beach.

"The ship beached fifty yards to our starboard, the [LCT] 416, had been disabled by a mine on the way to the beach. Shields went aboard her. When the order was given to abandon the 416, he stayed behind to assist two of the 416's officers and the 416's pharmacist's mate to remove a wounded crew member. It was while the party was carrying the wounded man along the beach to find another landing craft to take them off that several shells burst in succession near at hand; tore a great hole in Shields' back [killing him]."[235]

OMAHA BEACH was a bloody scene of carnage for those who landed that day. However, the exceptional courage of the average American soldier, led mostly by sergeants, lieutenants, and captains, carried the day as it always has throughout the history of the United States military. The name Omaha Beach will always rank with the greatest of American battles—the names of which will ring down through the ages—Bunker Hill, the Alamo, Gettysburg, San Juan Hill, Belleau Wood, Midway, Iwo Jima, the Chosin Reservoir, LZ X-Ray, 73 Easting, and Fallujah.

Major Sidney V. Bingham, Jr. commanded the 2nd Battalion, 116th Infantry Regiment of the 29th Infantry Division on June 6, 1944 and was himself awarded the Distinguished Service Cross for extraordinary heroism on Omaha Beach. In 1947, he wrote a letter about that terrible day on Omaha Beach. "Everything that was done was done by small groups led by the real heroes in any war. Most of them were killed, and very, very few were decorated chiefly because no one was left to tell what they did. The minefields behind the beach were strewn with these guys. They were lying around the hedgerows on top of the bluffs and of course, they were piled—literally—on the beach proper."[236]

Decades later in his autobiography, General Omar N. Bradley, the commander of the United States First Army during the invasion, reflected on the fighting at Omaha Beach and honored both the recognized and unsung heroes of that day. "Omaha Beach was a nightmare. Even now it brings pain to recall what happened there on June 6, 1944. I have returned many times to honor the valiant men who died on that beach. They should never be forgotten, nor should those who lived to carry the day by the slimmest of margins. Every man who set foot on Omaha Beach that day was a hero."[237]

When Lieutenant Colonel Donald V. Bennett was informed that he would be awarded the Distinguished Service Cross for his heroism on Omaha Beach he recalled the men who had fought alongside him that day. "The medal rests with the memory of all of those who were with me, Captain Richmond, the kid of a coxswain who died with our landing craft, the men of the 3rd of the 16th Regiment, the captain and crew of the destroyer, the sergeant who calmly made a cup of coffee, and that boy who told me not to be concerned, for all his comrades were dead and he was ready to go with them. That is where the medal rests."[238]

This is just a small part of the terrible price paid by courageous soldiers and sailors to seize Omaha Beach on June 6, 1944. The bodies of some of those killed during the assault are collected for burial. *United States Army Signal Corps photograph.*

THE EFFECT OF WHAT THE HEROES OF THAT DAY DID lives on through the free people of Europe and the American people to this day. President Bill Clinton spoke eloquently in Normandy on June 6, 1994, during a ceremony commemorating the 50th anniversary of the invasion, about the meaning to today's generations of the loss of the heroes who died that day and the days that followed to the war's end. "They were the fathers we never knew, the uncles we never met, the friends who never returned—the heroes we can never repay. They gave us our world. And those simple sounds of freedom we hear today are their voices speaking to us across the years.

Sergeant John Ellery landed on Omaha Beach with the 16th Infantry Regiment and had seen first hand the heroism and leadership that it took to win the day. "My contribution to the heroic tradition of the United States Army might have been the smallest achievement in the history of courage, but at least for a time I had walked in the company of very brave men. When you talk about combat leadership under fire on the beach at Normandy, I don't see how the credit can go to anyone other than the company grade officers and senior NCOs who led the way. It is good to be reminded that there are such men, that there always have been, and that there always will be. We sometimes forget, I think, that you can manufacture weapons and you can purchase ammunition, but you can't buy valor and you can't pull heroes off an assembly line. True courage is found in those who believe that there are things in life that are worth fighting for, and worth dying for. And there are men who are willing to do the fighting and the dying. There are those who will tell you today that patriotism is an eroded word. When I hear such talk, I think of Normandy and I know that it's not true."[239]

THE STORIES of those who were awarded the Navy Cross, Distinguished Service Cross, and Medal of Honor for their acts of extraordinary heroism, intrepidity, and conspicuous gallantry on June 6, 1944 tell only a part of the story. There were countless others who parachuted into the predawn sky, waded ashore, were a member of a tank crew, or were a crewman of a landing craft who were just as heroic. However, many of them died during those selfless acts or shortly afterward and many others who witnessed their actions were killed before they could testify to their valor. Though we do not know their names, we should always remember them. By remembering and honoring the heroes and their deeds described in this book, you are also remembering and honoring all such men and their heroism of that momentous day. The glory of their courage should live on in the hearts of future generations of Americans and the descendents of the people of France who they came to liberate. Never forget.

APPENDIX I
MEDAL OF HONOR CITATIONS

Private Carlton W. Barrett
Headquarters Company, 18th Infantry Regiment, 1st Infantry Division

Citation: Private Carlton W. Barrett, 12005025, Headquarters Company, 18th Infantry, United States Army, for gallantry and intrepidity at the risk of his life above and beyond the call of duty on 6 June 1944, in the vicinity of St. Laurent-sur-Mer, France. On the morning of D-Day, Private Barrett, landing in the face of extremely heavy enemy fire, was forced to wade ashore through neck deep water. Disregarding the personal danger, he returned to the surf again and again to assist his floundering comrades and save them from drowning. Refusing to remain pinned down by the intense barrage of small arms and mortar fire poured at the landing points, Private Barrett, working with fierce determination, saved many lives by carrying casualties to an evacuation boat lying offshore. In addition to his assigned mission as guide, he carried dispatches the length of the fire swept beach; he assisted the wounded; he calmed the shocked; he arose as a leader in the stress of the occasion. His coolness and his dauntless daring courage while constantly risking his life during a period of many hours had an inestimable effect on his comrades and is in keeping with the highest traditions of the United States Army. Entered military service from New York.

War Department, General Orders No. 78 (October 2, 1944)

Lieutenant General J. C. L. Lee (right) congratulates Corporal Carlton W. Barrett (center), from Saratoga Springs, New York, after Brigadier General R. B. Lord (left) read the citation for the award of the Medal of Honor, November 17, 1944. *United States Army Signal Corps photograph, National Archives.*

Opposite: Private Carlton Barrett served with the Intelligence and Reconnaissance Platoon of Headquarters Company, 18th Infantry and ventured from the beach into the surf numerous times to save the lives of wounded and drowning soldiers. *United States Army Signal Corps photograph, National Archives.*

First Lieutenant Jimmie W. Monteith, Jr.
Company L, 16th Infantry Regiment, 1st Infantry Division

Citation: First Lieutenant Jimmie W. Monteith, Jr., 01285793, 16th Infantry, United States Army, for conspicuous gallantry and intrepidity above and beyond the call of duty on 6 June 1944, near Colleville-sur-Mer, France. First Lieutenant Monteith landed with the initial assault waves on the coast of France under heavy enemy fire. Without regard to his own personal safety he continually moved up and down the beach reorganizing men for further assault. He then led the assault over a narrow protective ledge and across the flat, exposed terrain to the comparative safety of a cliff. Retracing his steps across the field to the beach, he moved over to where two tanks were buttoned up and blind under violent enemy artillery and machine gun fire. Completely exposed to the intense fire, First Lieutenant Monteith led the tanks on foot through a minefield and into firing positions. Under his direction several enemy positions were destroyed. He then rejoined his company and under his leadership his men captured an advantageous position on the hill. Supervising the defense of his newly won position against repeated vicious counterattacks, he continued to ignore his own personal safety, repeatedly crossing the two hundred or three hundred yards of open terrain under heavy fire to strengthen links in his defensive chain. When the enemy succeeded in completely surrounding First Lieutenant Monteith and his unit, and while leading the fight out of the situation, First Lieutenant Monteith was killed by enemy fire. The courage, gallantry, and intrepid leadership displayed by First Lieutenant Monteith is worthy of emulation.

War Department, General Orders No. 20 (March 29, 1945)

Lieutenant Jimmie W. Monteith, Jr., from Richmond, Virginia, graduated from Virginia Tech University in 1938, where he was a varsity football player. *United States Army photograph, National Archives.*

Technician Fifth Grade John J. Pinder, Jr.
Headquarters Company, 16th Infantry Regiment, 1st Infantry Division

Citation: Technician Fifth Grade John J. Pinder, Jr., HQ Company, 16th Infantry, United States Army, for conspicuous gallantry and intrepidity above and beyond the call of duty on 6 June 1944, near Colleville-sur-le-Mer, France. On D-Day, Technician Fifth Grade Pinder landed on the coast one hundred yards off shore under devastating enemy machine gun and artillery fire which caused severe casualties among the boatload. Carrying a vitally important radio, he struggled towards shore in waist deep water. Only a few yards from his craft he was hit by enemy fire and was gravely wounded. Technician Fifth Grade Pinder never stopped. He made shore and delivered the radio. Refusing to take cover afforded, or to accept medical attention for his wounds, Technician Fifth Grade Pinder, though terribly weakened by loss of blood and in fierce pain, on three occasions went into the fire swept surf to salvage communication equipment. He recovered many vital parts and equipment, including another workable radio. On the third trip he was again hit, suffering machine gun bullet wounds in the legs. Still this valiant soldier would not stop for rest or medical attention. Remaining exposed to heavy enemy fire, growing steadily weaker, he aided in establishing the vital radio communication on the beach. While so engaged, this dauntless soldier was hit for the third time and killed. The indomitable courage and personal bravery of Technician Fifth Grade Pinder was a magnificent inspiration to the men with whom he served.

War Department, General Orders No. 1 (January 4, 1945)

Major General Philip Hayes, the commander of the Third Service Command, presents the Medal of Honor, posthumously to Technician Fifth Grade John J. Pinder, Jr. at a ceremony at Baltimore, Maryland on January 27, 1945. Mr. John J. Pinder, Sr. accepts the medal on behalf of his son. *United States Army Signal Corps photograph, courtesy of the Pinder family and Emily Keating.*

Technician Fifth Grade John J. Pinder, Jr., from Butler, Pennsylvania, was the class valedictorian of his Butler High School's class of 1931 and played professional baseball prior to his military service. *Photograph, courtesy of the Pinder family and Emily Keating.*

Brigadier General Theodore Roosevelt, Jr.
Headquarters, First Army

Citation: Brigadier General Theodore Roosevelt, Jr., 0139726, United States Army, for gallantry and intrepidity at the risk of his life above and beyond the call of duty on 6 June 1944, in France. After two verbal requests to accompany the leading assault elements in the Normandy invasion had been denied, Brigadier General Roosevelt's written request for this mission was approved and he landed with the first wave of the forces assaulting the enemy held beaches. He repeatedly led groups from the beach over the seawall and established them inland. His valor, courage, and presence in the very front of the attack and his complete unconcern at being under heavy fire inspired the troops to heights of enthusiasm and self sacrifice. Although the enemy had the beach under constant direct fire, Brigadier General Roosevelt moved from one locality to another, rallying men around him, directed and personally led them against the enemy. Under his seasoned, precise, calm, and unfaltering leadership, assault troops reduced beach strong points and rapidly moved inland with minimum casualties. He thus contributed substantially to the successful establishment of the beachhead in France.

War Department, General Orders No. 77 (September 28, 1944)

This was purportedly the last photograph of Brigadier General Theodore Roosevelt, Jr. (left) taken before his death. His aide, Lieutenant Marcus Stevenson (right), is driving the jeep named "Rough Rider" for President Roosevelt's famous unit of the Spanish American War. *United States Army Signal Corps photograph courtesy of Paul Clifford.*

Next Page: Brigadier General Theodore "Teddy" Roosevelt, Jr., the son of the former president, landed with the first wave of infantry on Utah Beach. Roosevelt, a World War I veteran and former assistant commander of the 1st Infantry Division, was a supernumerary general officer assigned temporarily to the 4th Infantry Division in an unofficial capacity. The photograph was taken at Ste.-Mère-Église on July 12, 1944, just hours before his death. *United States Army photograph, National Archives.*

APPENDIX II
DISTINGUISHED SERVICE CROSS CITATIONS

First Lieutenant John L. Ahearn
Company C, 70th Tank Battalion

Citation: First Lieutenant John L. Ahearn (Army Serial No. 01011621), Cavalry, United States Army, for extraordinary heroism on 6 June 1944. First Lieutenant Ahearn fearlessly led his company to the beach, his tank being the second to land on H-Hour. Although the enemy defenses were nearly impenetrable, he continued forward through a blown gap in the seawall in pursuit of the enemy. At this point his tank struck a mine and was disabled. However, with utter disregard for his own personal safety, he dismounted under heavy enemy fire to make a foot reconnaissance to observe the enemy, who were close to his front. When so engaged, he heard the cries of distress of an infantryman, who was seriously injured by an antipersonnel mine about forty yards inside a minefield. Although he knew that this area was heavily mined and had seen an aid man wounded in attempting to reach the other man, he ran recklessly and without fear to the man's assistance and was himself seriously wounded by the explosion of a mine. Realizing the danger involved in his rescue, he ordered members of his tank crew not to venture into the field to rescue him, but to throw him a rope and pull him to safety. First Lieutenant Ahearn's actions throughout the entire operation reflect great credit upon himself, and his conduct was in accordance with the highest traditions of the armed forces of the United States. Entered military service from New York.

Headquarters, European Theater of Operations, United States Army, General Orders No. 124 (December 11, 1944)

First Lieutenant John L. Ahearn, the commanding officer of Company C, 70th Tank Battalion, was aboard in the second tank to land on Utah Beach on June 6, 1944. This photo was taken after his promotion to captain. *Photograph from www.fold3.com.*

Lieutenant John L. Ahearn (left), after being presented with the Distinguished Service Cross by Major General Raymond O. Barton (center), the commanding officer of the 4th Infantry Division, to which Ahearn's 70th Tank Battalion was attached on June 6, 1944. Lieutenant Ahearn was recuperating at Walter Reed Hospital in Washington, D.C. from his wounds, which resulted in the amputation of both of his lower legs, when the ceremony was conducted on January 26, 1945. *United States Army Signal Corps photograph, National Archives.*

Second Lieutenant Walter G. Amerman
Company B, 506th Parachute Infantry Regiment, 101st Airborne Division and 101st Provisional Pathfinder Company

Citation: Second Lieutenant Walter G. Amerman 01307632, Parachute Infantry, United States Army, for extraordinary heroism in action against the enemy on 6 June 1944, in France. Second Lieutenant Amerman with complete disregard for his own personal safety attacked an enemy machine gun nest that was firing upon a pathfinder group while they were trying to set up their equipment. After destroying the machine gun nest, Second Lieutenant Amerman organized a defensive position permitting the pathfinders to set up the equipment and guide the planes to their drop zone. The courage and personal bravery of Second Lieutenant Amerman reflects great credit on himself and is in keeping with the highest traditions of the armed forces. Entered military service from Illinois.

Headquarters, First Army, General Orders No. 31 (July 1, 1944)

General Dwight D. Eisenhower, the commander of the Allied Expeditionary Force, awards the Distinguished Service Cross to Lieutenant Walter G. Amerman, from St. Louis, Missouri, during a ceremony conducted at Hungerford Common, England on August 10, 1944. *United States Army Signal Corps photograph, courtesy of Mary K. Yoe.*

This is another view of the ceremony conducted at Hungerford Common, England on August 10, 1944, at which Lieutenant Walter G. Amerman was awarded the Distinguished Service Cross. Major Generals Maxwell Taylor (right center wearing jump boots), the commanding officer of the 101st Airborne Division and Matthew B. Ridgway (third from right wearing jump boots), the commanding general of the new formed XVIII Airborne Corps, *United States Army Signal Corps photograph, courtesy of Paul Adamic.*

Second Lieutenant William A. Anderson
Company A, 146th Engineer Combat Battalion, Special Engineer Task Force, Provisional Engineer Brigade Group, V Corps Gap Assault Team Number 2

Citation: Second Lieutenant William A. Anderson, 01110743, 146th Engineer Combat Battalion, United States Army, for extraordinary heroism in action against the enemy on 6 June 1944, in France. Second Lieutenant Anderson, commanding a demolition team, landed on the coast of France with the initial assault wave under heavy enemy rifle, machine gun, mortar, and artillery fire. Second Lieutenant Anderson promptly directed his team in the removal of obstacles. During this time he was wounded in the back. Despite this painful wound, Second Lieutenant Anderson continued to direct the removal of obstacles until he had completed his mission in this section of the beach. While leading his men to another part of the beach, Second Lieutenant Anderson was again wounded. The valor, devotion to duty, and courageous leadership displayed by Second Lieutenant Anderson reflects great credit upon himself and is in keeping with the highest traditions of the armed forces.

Headquarters, First Army, General Orders No. 37 (July 21, 1944)

Next Page: Lieutenant William A. Anderson, with Company A, 146th Engineer Combat Battalion, was born in Rockwell, Iowa and grew up in Tennessee. Anderson pursued graduate studies, performed humanitarian work with the International Organization for Migration, and worked for Bechtel Power Corporation after the war. *Photograph courtesy of Erica Beedle.*

Major General Leonard T. Gerow, the commanding officer of the V Corps, awards the Distinguished Service Cross to Lieutenant William A. Anderson, September 11, 1944. *United States Army Signal Corps photograph, courtesy of Erica Beedle.*

Second Lieutenant Leonard A. Anker
Company K, 116th Infantry Regiment, 29th Infantry Division

Citation: Second Lieutenant Leonard A. Anker, 0529110, 116th Infantry, United States Army, for extraordinary heroism in action against the enemy on 6 June 1944, in France. At the time of the landing of Second Lieutenant Anker's platoon, the beach was under withering fire from enemy artillery, automatic weapons, and small arms. After proceeding about two hundred yards, all troops in the vicinity of Second Lieutenant Anker were pinned down by the devastating fire. Second Lieutenant Anker located an enemy machine gun that was inflicting heavy casualties. With complete disregard for his own safety, Second Lieutenant Anker, aided by an enlisted man whom he inspired to action by his own gallantry, fearlessly charged and destroyed the enemy strongpoint with hand grenades, killing sixteen and capturing five of the enemy. The outstanding heroism displayed by Second Lieutenant Anker reflect great credit on himself and was in keeping with the highest traditions of the armed forces.

Headquarters, First Army, General Orders No. 29 (June 29, 1944)

Technician Fourth Grade Stanley P. Appleby
Medical Detachment, 16th Infantry Regiment, 1st Infantry Division

Citation: Technician Fourth Grade Stanley P. Appleby, 12004300, 16th Infantry, United States Army, for extraordinary heroism in action against the enemy on 6 June 1944, in France. Technician Fourth Grade Appleby disembarked from his craft some fifty yards from the beach under a hail of artillery shells and machine gun fire. A large number of casualties were sustained and, but for Technician Fourth Grade Appleby's prompt and courageous action, would have perished in the surf. With complete disregard for his own safety, he on numerous occasions waded into the surf to lead them ashore and immediately administered first aid. Despite the intense enemy fire, Technician Fourth Grade Appleby never slackened in his efforts to assist and render aid to the wounded on the beach. The courage and outstanding devotion to duty displayed by Technician Fourth Grade Appleby reflects great credit on himself and is in keeping with the highest traditions of the armed forces. Entered military service from New York.

Headquarters, First Army, General Orders No. 31 (July 1, 1944)

Captain John R. Armellino
Company L, 16th Infantry Regiment, 1st Infantry Division

Citation: Captain John R. Armellino, 0335197, 16th Infantry, United States Army, for extraordinary heroism in action against the enemy on 6 June 1944, in France. Upon landing initially on the coast of France in the face of heavy enemy rifle, machine gun and artillery fire, Captain Armellino quickly moved his men behind the slight cover afforded by a three foot shelf of shale. However, the constant and accurate fire from the cliff pinned his company down. Captain Armellino then exposed himself to this heavy enemy fire and moved up the beach to a group of four tanks which had been rendered immobile by enemy shells. Upon reaching the tanks, he placed himself before them and from this fire swept position directed their fire on the enemy strongpoints. For forty-five minutes he continued to move from his company to the tanks coordinating their action. On one of the trips back to his company, he was severely wounded by enemy fire. Despite his serious wounds he directed his men in their successful assault upon the enemy emplacement. The valor and superior leadership of Captain Armellino reflects great credit on himself and is in keeping with the highest traditions of the armed forces. Entered military service from New Jersey.

Headquarters, First Army, General Orders No. 31 (July 1, 1944)

DISTINGUISHED SERVICE CROSS CITATIONS

Technician Fourth Grade Stanley P. Appleby, from Clarksville, New York, a medic with the 16th Infantry Regiment, was one of twenty-four 1st Infantry Division soldiers awarded the Distinguished Service Cross by General Dwight D. Eisenhower during a ceremony near Balleroy, France on July 2, 1944. *United States Army Signal Corps photograph.*

Technical Sergeant Louis M. Armstrong
Company L, 116th Infantry Regiment, 29th Infantry Division

Citation: Technical Sergeant Louis M. Armstrong, 20365625, 116th Infantry, United States Army, for extraordinary heroism in action against the enemy on 6 June 1944, in France. Sergeant Armstrong came in on the initial wave of infantry that waded ashore from landing craft in the face of extremely heavy enemy fire. Despite severe casualties he fearlessly stepped to the head of his men and, with complete disregard for his own safety, set an example and shouted encouragement to the others to follow him. The gallantry and courageous leadership displayed by Sergeant Armstrong reflects great credit on himself and is in keeping with the highest traditions of the armed forces.

Headquarters, First Army, General Orders No. 29 (June 29, 1944)

Technical Sergeant Louis M. Armstrong (right center, back to camera), from Staunton, Virginia, receives the Distinguished Service Cross from Lieutenant General Omar N. Bradley, commander of the First Army, at a ceremony near Mieux, France on July 5, 1944. *United States Army Signal Corps photograph, National Archives.*

Technician Fifth Grade Billy J. Austin

149th Engineer Combat Battalion, 6th Engineer Special Brigade, Provisional Engineer Special Brigade Group, V Corps

Citation: Technician Fifth Grade Billy J. Austin (Army Serial No. 37507687), Corps of Engineers, United States Army, for extraordinary heroism in connection with military operations against an armed enemy, as a bulldozer operator, 149th Engineer Combat Battalion, during the landings on the French coast on 6 June 1944. Under heavy enemy fire, Technician Fifth Grade Austin disembarked his explosive laden bulldozer through six feet of water, rough surf, mined underwater obstacles, and wreckage. Despite concentrated artillery fire zeroed on the area and small arms fire aimed at his moving bulldozer, he grimly proceeded to the tasks of clearing the beach exit of mines, obstacles and wreckage, and of filling in a tank ditch, thereby freeing a hemmed in tank battalion. Technician Fifth Grade Austin's calm efficiency and implacable determination to complete these difficult tasks, which were of prime importance to immediate operations, reflect great credit upon himself and the armed forces of the United States. Entered military service from Missouri.

Headquarters, Communications Zone, European Theater of Operations, General Orders No. 37 (March 22, 1945)

Technician Fifth Grade Billy J. Austin (right), from Kansas City, Missouri, is awarded the Distinguished Service Cross by Major General John B. Anderson on April 9, 1945. *United States Army Signal Corps photograph, National Archives.*

Corporal James N. Barba
Company G, 502nd Parachute Infantry Regiment, 101st Airborne Division

Citation: Corporal James N. Barba, 11065409, 502nd Parachute Infantry, United States Army, for extraordinary heroism in action against the enemy on 6 June 1944, in France. Corporal Barba parachuted into France prior to dawn of D-Day and moving forward with his unit, was pinned down by a fortified roadblock, which had to be reduced in order to permit use of the road by following units. Determining that it would be necessary to attract sufficient attention from the flank in order to frontally assault the enemy, he volunteered to go into the position with hand grenades and submachine gun and to create the necessary confusion within. Completely disregarding his personal safety and displaying great fortitude, Corporal Barba crossed fifty yards of mined field and a double apron of barbed wire in the face of heavy machine gun fire to reach the inner defenses of the enemy. Rushed, as soon as he entered the first trench, he threw hand grenades and fired his gun into the enemy, killing two of them and drawing sufficient attention and fire to enable his comrades to advance and demolish the position, before he, himself, was fatally wounded. Corporal Barba's determined action, initiative, and courage constituted a demonstration of the spirit of self sacrifice and set an example in the eyes of his men long to be remembered. Entered military service from Pennsylvania.

Headquarters, First Army, General Orders No. 58 (September 15, 1944)

Corporal James Barba, with Company G, 502nd Parachute Infantry Regiment, 101st Airborne Division, was killed in action on June 6, 1944 while attacking an enemy position blocking the highway that ran from Carentan through Ste.-Mère-Église to Cherbourg, France. Barba grew up in Branford, Connecticut where he was a three sport athlete in high school. Corporal Barba's remains were repatriated after the war and buried at the St. Agnes Cemetery in his hometown. *Photograph courtesy of Patricia Nuzzo.*

Private First Class Alexander W. Barber
Medical Detachment, 5th Ranger Battalion, Provisional Ranger Group

Citation: Private First Class Alexander W. Barber, 33575048, Medical Corps, United States Army, for extraordinary heroism in action on 6 June 1944, in France. Private First Class Barber landed with his medical unit on the coast of France at a time when the beach was under heavy enemy rifle, machine gun, and artillery fire. Numerous casualties had already been inflicted by this devastating fire. In spite of this heavy fire, Private First Class Barber constantly exposed himself to the direct fire of the enemy as he went along the beach administering aid to the wounded. On one occasion he took a horse and cart into the middle of an artillery barrage to bring out three men who had been wounded. Private First Class Barber's heroic and gallant action is in keeping with the highest traditions of the service. Entered military service from Pennsylvania.

Headquarters, First Army, General Orders No. 28 (June 20, 1944)

Second Lieutenant Gaetano R. Barcellona
Company A, 741st Tank Battalion

Citation: Second Lieutenant Gaetano R. Barcellona, 01017167, 741st Tank Battalion, United States Army, for extraordinary heroism in action against the enemy on 6 June 1944, in France. Second Lieutenant Barcellona, commanding a tank platoon, landed with the assault force in the invasion upon the coast of France. Though, upon landing, his tank received several hits, he continued it in operation and fearlessly exposed himself to severe enemy rifle, machine gun and artillery fire in order to select enemy targets and direct the fire of his unit. When his ammunition supply became exhausted Second Lieutenant Barcellona, completely disregarding his own safety, dismounted from his tank and moved across the fire swept beach to secure additional ammunition. He then returned through the heavy enemy fire to his tank and continued to carry on the fight. The valor, aggressiveness, and leadership exhibited by Second Lieutenant Barcellona reflect great credit upon himself and is in keeping with the highest traditions of the armed forces.

Headquarters, First Army, General Orders No. 37 (July 21, 1944)

First Lieutenant Harold R. Beavers
Company B, 743rd Tank Battalion

Citation: First Lieutenant Harold R. Beavers, 01011362, 743rd Tank Battalion, United States Army, for extraordinary heroism in action against the enemy on 6 June 1944, in France. First Lieutenant Beavers landed on the coast of France under heavy enemy small arms, machine gun, mortar, and artillery fire with the initial assault wave. During this landing, the company commander was killed in action; First Lieutenant Beavers calmly and courageously assumed command of the disorganized company and moved forward up the beach. When another officer in the company was seriously wounded First Lieutenant Beavers, despite the intense enemy fire and without regard for his own personal safety, dismounted from his tank, placed the wounded officer onto his tank and moved the tank through an enemy minefield to a place from which the aid men could remove the wounded officer. First Lieutenant Beavers then mounted his tank and directed the company in the opening of a beach exit. The gallantry, outstanding leadership and personal bravery displayed by First Lieutenant Beavers reflects great credit upon himself and is in keeping with the highest traditions of the armed forces.

Headquarters, First Army, General Orders No. 37 (July 21, 1944)

Lieutenant Harold R. Beavers served with Company B, 743rd Tank Battalion on June 6, 1944. He was born Walter Colowski in New York City in 1918. He and his brother became orphans and were sent to Clarinda, Iowa on an orphan train in December 1922. He was adopted by the Roy Beavers family and renamed Harold R. Beavers. He grew up on a farm near New Market, Iowa. Beavers was killed in action during the Korean War in 1950 and his widow passed away during 1951, leaving two young children, Harold E. and Linda, who were subsequently raised by Roy Beavers and his wife, who were at that point in their 60s. *Photograph courtesy of Harold E. Beavers.*

Captain Kenneth E. Beitler
Battery C, 58th Armored Field Artillery Battalion

Citation: Captain Kenneth E. Beitler, 0409373, 58th Armored Field Artillery Battalion, United States Army, for extraordinary heroism in action against the enemy on 6 June 1944, in France. As Captain Beitler's landing craft approached the shore on D-Day, it was subjected to intense artillery and machine gun fire. When it became apparent that a landing could not be made, the craft was moved back from the shore at Captain Beitler's suggestion and a landing made on the next beach. Although artillery shells were landing dangerously near the craft, Captain Beitler, displaying great courage, ordered that the ramp be lowered and personally went ashore on the first artillery piece under intense and well aimed machine gun and small arms fire. Arriving on the fire swept beach, he completely disregarded the enemy's heavy shelling and braved continuous sniper fire to supervise the placement of his weapons. Throughout the entire day, Captain Beitler, the only officer remaining in his battery, heroically continued to direct exceptionally accurate artillery fire in support of the infantry. By his demonstration of outstanding leadership, personal heroism, and unflinching devotion to duty, Captain Beitler exemplified the highest traditions of the armed forces. Entered military service from Ohio.

Headquarters, First Army, General Orders No. 11 (January 18, 1945)

Captain Kenneth E. Beitler commanded Battery C, 58th Armored Field Artillery Battery on June 6, 1944. After the war he became a dentist and resided in Sycamore, Ohio. *Photograph courtesy of Dr. Claude and Marjorie Beitler.*

Sergeant Julius W. Belcher
Company C, 2nd Ranger Battalion, Provisional Ranger Group

Citation: Sergeant Julius W. Belcher, 33213927, Infantry, United States Army, for extraordinary heroism in action on 6 June 1944 at Vierville-sur-Mer, France. Upon landing with the initial assault Ranger infantry battalion on the coast of France, Sergeant Belcher immediately moved up the beach under heavy machine gun, mortar and sniper fire, and scaled a one hundred foot cliff to secure toggle ropes to barbed wire on top of the cliff. Though under constant fire on top of the cliff, he then moved into enemy positions and cleaned out six snipers. Following this he charged an enemy pillbox and mortar position and destroyed it with grenades. Sergeant Belcher's bravery and heroism are worthy of the highest tradition of the service. Entered military service from Virginia.

Headquarters, First Army, General Orders No. 28 (June 20, 1944)

Opposite: Lieutenant Colonel James Rudder, the commanding officer of the 2nd Ranger Battalion and the Provisional Ranger Group, congratulates Sergeant Julius W. Belcher, from Swords Creek, Virginia, on the award of the Distinguished Service Cross during a ceremony near Colombieres, France, June 23, 1944. *United States Army Signal Corps photograph, National Archives.*

Technical Sergeant William R. Benn, Jr.
Company A, 16th Infantry Regiment, 1st Infantry Division

Citation: Technical Sergeant William R. Benn, Jr., 12009565, 16th Infantry, United States Army, for extraordinary heroism in action against the enemy on 6 June 1944, in France. Technical Sergeant Benn landed on the coast of France with the initial assault waves under heavy enemy small arms, mortar and rocket fire. His platoon leader was seriously wounded as soon as they reached the beach, and he immediately assumed command. He led his platoon under heavy enemy fire through an uncharted minefield and up the steep slope toward enemy positions. The intense enemy fire caused severe casualties and threatened to stop the advance. Technical Sergeant Benn, completely disregarding his own safety, advanced alone towards the enemy position. He approached through the hail of fire to within twenty-five yards of the enemy guns at which point he threw hand grenades into the enemy positions, silencing their guns. Though seriously wounded in the course of this action, Technical Sergeant Benn persisted in his efforts until he had carried out his self appointed mission. The personal bravery and aggressive leadership displayed by Technical Sergeant Benn reflects credit on himself and is in keeping with the highest traditions of the armed forces. Entered military service from Pennsylvania.

Headquarters, First Army, General Orders No. 45 (August 9, 1944)

Lieutenant Colonel Donald V. Bennett
Headquarters, 62nd Armored Field Artillery Battalion

Citation: Lieutenant Colonel Donald V. Bennett, 023001, 62nd Armored Field Artillery Battalion, United States Army, for extraordinary heroism in action against the enemy on 6 June 1944, in France. When Lieutenant Colonel Bennett landed with the second wave at 07:20 on D-Day, his party was subjected to a tremendous volume of machine gun fire which inflicted fifty percent casualties before they reached the comparative safety of the shingle at the base of the cliff adjoining the beach. Observing that following units were pinned down on the beach, he immediately left his cover and moved about the beach under heavy fire in order to assemble and reorganize the infantry assault companies, four tanks, and an antiaircraft unit. By redistributing the remaining officers and equipment; by emplacing the .50 caliber machine guns of the antiaircraft unit so as to give close support to the infantry; and by radioing for tank and artillery fire support from the LCTs, he organized a sizeable force and at about 10:00 hours, successfully assaulted the ridge. He then continued moving about the beach under intense fire and succeeded in locating a protected place to bring in his battalion and move it across the beach. Lieutenant Colonel Bennett, in disregarding his own safety under such heavy enemy fire throughout the day and in his clear thinking, contributed immeasurably to the establishment of the beachhead. Entered military service from Ohio.

Headquarters, First Army, General Orders No. 45 (August 9, 1944)

Next Page: Technical Sergeant William R. Benn, Jr., from Easton, Pennsylvania, was a veteran of the 1st Infantry Division's campaigns in North Africa and Sicily. He was also a recipient of the Silver Star for single handedly capturing twenty-eight Germans and a truck during the North African campaign. Benn was killed in action on Omaha Beach on June 6, 1944 and is buried at the American Cemetery at Cambridge, England. *Photograph courtesy of Doris Bonstein and Kevin Frankenfield.*

Staff Sergeant John L. Benton
Company B, 743rd Tank Battalion

Citation: Staff Sergeant John L. Benton, 38131610, 743rd Tank Battalion, United States Army, for extraordinary heroism in action against the enemy on 6 June 1944, in France. Staff Sergeant Benton landed on the coast of France with the initial assault wave under heavy enemy rifle, machine gun, mortar, and artillery fire. When the platoon leader became a casualty, Staff Sergeant Benton immediately assumed command. In order to better direct operations and bring fire on enemy positions, Staff Sergeant Benton, completely disregarding his own safety dismounted from his tank and from this position proceeded to place fire upon the enemy positions. The courage, initiative, and leadership exhibited by Staff Sergeant Benton reflect great credit upon himself and is in keeping with the highest traditions of the armed forces.

Headquarters, First Army, General Orders No. 37 (July 21, 1944)

Private First Class Henry Berkowitz
Cannon Company, 16th Infantry Regiment, 1st Infantry Division

Citation: Private First Class Henry Berkowitz, 12006610, 16th Infantry, United States Army, for extraordinary heroism in action against the enemy on 6 June 1944, in France. When the craft upon which Private First Class Berkowitz was coming into shore was hit and sunk by enemy artillery fire, he jumped from the sinking boat with his Signal Corps radio and, under a hail of constant enemy machine gun fire, began making his way ashore through the heavy surf. Though seriously wounded as he approached the shore, Private First Class Berkowitz nevertheless retained his hold on the vitally important radio and continued ashore with it. Upon reaching the shore, he refused treatment, dragging himself and the radio along the fire-swept beach and through a minefield until he reached his forward observation party. Despite the painful wound and the intense enemy machine gun fire, Private First Class Berkowitz operated his radio throughout the period his section was on the beach. The courage and complete devotion to duty exhibited by Private First Class Berkowitz reflects great credit upon himself and is in keeping with the highest traditions of the armed forces. Entered military service from New York.

Headquarters, First Army, General Orders No. 42 (August 6, 1944)

Next Page: Major General J. Lawton Collins, the VII Corps commander, presents the Distinguished Service Cross to Private First Class Henry Berkowitz, from Brooklyn, New York, during a ceremony near Hauset, Belgium, September 27, 1944. *United States Army Signal Corps photograph, courtesy of the First Division Museum at Cantigny and the National Archives.*

Major Sidney V. Bingham, Jr.
Headquarters, 2nd Battalion, 116th Infantry Regiment, 29th Infantry Division

Citation: Major Sidney V. Bingham, Jr., 023267, 116th Infantry, United States Army, for extraordinary heroism in action against the enemy on 6 June 1944, in France. When his battalion was pinned down on the beach by the heavy and intense enemy fire, Major Bingham gathered together five of his men and personally led them across the beach and up a cliff in an attempt to seek out an enemy machine gun that had been inflicting heavy casualties on his unit. Though unable to reach the machine gun, he was, nevertheless, able to discover its location. He returned to the fire swept beach and organized a flank and rear attack which succeeded in taking the enemy position, thereby permitting his unit to advance. The heroic and superior leadership exhibited by Major Bingham reflects great credit on himself and was in keeping with the highest traditions of the armed forces.

Headquarters, First Army, General Orders No. 29 (June 29, 1944)

Sidney V. Bingham, Jr., was born at Douglas, Arizona, the son of a career army officer, and was a graduate of the United States Military Academy. Major Bingham,. *Photograph courtesy of Joseph Balkoski.*

Second Lieutenant Kenneth Bleau
Company G, 16th Infantry Regiment, 1st Infantry Division

Citation: Second Lieutenant Kenneth Bleau, 01294967, 16th Infantry, United States Army, for extraordinary heroism in action against the enemy on 6 June 1944, in France. Second Lieutenant Bleau, with complete disregard for his own safety, personally reconnoitered a path through an intricate and dense minefield under heavy artillery, mortar, and small arms fire. He then led his men through a gap to a German dominated ridge. When his unit was completely surrounded on the ridge by enemy riflemen and two hostile machine guns fired at pointblank range, threatening to annihilate his company, Second Lieutenant Bleau crawled forward to within twenty yards of one of the weapons and destroyed the gun and crew with hand grenades. He then fearlessly charged the second emplacement and knocked it out of action. Later, during two hostile counterattacks, Second Lieutenant Bleau engaged the enemy in violent hand to hand combat, personally killing five Germans and wounding many others. By his heroic achievement, exemplary bravery, and devotion to duty, Second Lieutenant Bleau acted in keeping with the highest traditions of the armed forces. Entered military service from New York.

Headquarters, First Army, General Orders No. 77 (November 9, 1944)

Sergeant Stephen Sternik (left), Sergeant Frank Baldridge (left center), and Lieutenant Kenneth Bleau from Ilion, New York (right center), all members of Company G, 16th Infantry Regiment, meet Major General Clarence Huebner, the commanding officer of the 1st Infantry Division. *Photograph courtesy of the First Division Museum at Cantigny.*

Private First Class John D. Bolderson
Company A, 505th Parachute Infantry Regiment, 82nd Airborne Division

Citation: Private First Class John D. Bolderson, 505th Parachute Infantry, United States Army, for extraordinary heroism against the enemy on 6 June 1944, in France. Private First Class Bolderson was stationed at the end of a bridge over the Merderet River as a rocketeer to repel attacks by enemy troops who controlled the other end of the bridge. This position was subject to incessant enemy rifle, machine gun, mortar, and artillery fire. After an artillery preparation, the enemy sent an assault force supported by three tanks over the bridge. Though part of the troops withdrew, Private First Class Bolderson remained at his position until the enemy tanks approached within thirty yards. In spite of the intense fire, Private First Class Bolderson rose from his position and aided by the assistant gunner, fired rockets into the three tanks. Private First Class Bolderson remained with his gun and fired it until it was pierced by enemy machine gun fire and put out of action. The courage, devotion to duty and daring displayed by Private First Class Bolderson reflects great credit on himself and is in keeping with the highest traditions of the armed forces.

Headquarters, First Army, General Orders No. 31 (July 1, 1944)

For Private First Class John D. Bolderson, from Howell County, Missouri, Normandy was his third combat jump. During the campaign, he served as a bazooka gunner with Company A, 505th Parachute Infantry Regiment, 82md Airborne Division. *Photograph courtesy of George and Diane Bolderson.*

Private First Class George H. Bowen
Medical Detachment, Company E, 16th Infantry Regiment, 1st Infantry Division

Citation: Private First Class George H. Bowen, 35643671, Medical Detachment, 16th Infantry, United States Army, for extraordinary heroism in action on 6 June 1944, in France. As the men in the initial assault upon the coast of France waded through the waist deep water, a number were wounded and were in grave danger of drowning. Private First Class Bowen, disregarding his own safety, stopped in his efforts to reach the shore, waded through the mined and fire swept water to go to a wounded man who was drowning, and dragged the man to shore. He then proceeded to the aid of the wounded men lying about the beach. He repeatedly dashed into the fire swept areas to administer to the numerous casualties. During the attack men were wounded in an assault on an enemy machine gun nest high on the slopes of a cliff. Private First Class Bowen, to reach these men, crossed an uncharted minefield and moved through vicious enemy fire to within fifteen yards of the enemy's machine gun nest to render first aid to the stricken men. The courage and fortitude displayed by Private First Class Bowen reflects credit on himself and is in keeping with the highest traditions of the armed forces. Entered military service from Kentucky.

Headquarters, First Army, General Orders No. 45 (August 9, 1944)

Private First Class George H. Bowen, from Flemingsburg, Kentucky, is awarded the Distinguished Service Cross by General J. Lawton Collins, the commanding officer of VII Corps, on September 27, 1944 during a ceremony conducted near Hauset, Belgium. *United States Signal Corps photograph, courtesy of Willa Hensley and the National Archives.*

Captain Victor H. Briggs
Company C, 16th Infantry Regiment, 1st Infantry Division

Citation: Captain Victor H. Briggs, 01286079, 16th Infantry, United States Army, for extraordinary heroism in action against the enemy on 6 June 1944 near Colleville-sur-le-Mer, France. In the initial assault against the coast of France Captain Briggs, with complete disregard for his own safety, subjected himself to heavy rifle, machine gun and artillery fire while leading his men ashore from the landing craft. He further exposed himself to this heavy fire, when, after reaching the beach, he organized an assault team from the groups of troops pinned down by the merciless fire. He then personally led this assault team through a dense enemy minefield and into a strategic position on the slope of a hill. Though attacked by superior numbers, he successfully defended this position until additional troops were moved forward. The tenacity of purpose and courage displayed by Captain Briggs reflect great credit upon himself and were in keeping with the highest traditions of the armed forces of the United States.

Headquarters, First Army, General Orders No. 31 (July 1, 1944)

Captain Victor H. Briggs, from New York City, is awarded the Distinguished Service Cross by General Dwight D. Eisenhower, during a ceremony near Balleroy, France on July 2, 1944. Another DSC recipient, Captain Thomas N. Merendino, commanding officer of Company B, 16th Infantry Regiment, is standing to Captain Briggs' left. *United States Army Signal Corps photograph, courtesy of Antion Meredith.*

This photo of Lieutenant Victor H. Briggs was taken in the United States prior to his deployment overseas with the 16th Infantry of the 1st Infantry Division. Briggs was later promoted to captain and was in command of Company C during the invasion of Normandy. Tragically, he was killed in action on November 17, 1944 during the bitter fight for the Hürtgen Forest. *Photograph courtesy of Antion Meredith.*

First Lieutenant Elton E. Brooks
Headquarters Company, 506th Parachute Infantry Regiment, 101st Airborne Division

Citation: First Lieutenant Elton E. Brooks, 01287655, 506th Parachute Infantry, United States Army, for extraordinary heroism in action against the enemy from 6 June 1944 to 8 June 1944, in France. After landing by parachute behind enemy lines, First Lieutenant Brooks gathered together one officer and fifteen men to form a patrol. For a period of sixty hours he boldly led this patrol through enemy territory which was covered by machine gun and small arms fire. Under his aggressive and valiant leadership, his unit attacked a number of hostile installations, killing thirty men and capturing twenty. On 8 June 1944, realizing the necessity of immediate medical attention for five of his men, First Lieutenant Brooks and two men courageously broke through the enemy lines and contacted friendly troops. Securing a truck, he then drove back through extremely heavy enemy machine gun and small arms fire and safely evacuated his entire group, including the wounded men and prisoners. The outstanding courage, prowess and valiant leadership displayed by First Lieutenant Brooks are in keeping with the highest traditions of the armed forces. Entered military service from Oklahoma.

Headquarters, First Army, General Orders No. 85 (November 24, 1944)

Sergeant Arthur B. Buschlen
Headquarters Company, 2nd Battalion, 16th Infantry Regiment, 1st Infantry Division

Citation: Sergeant Arthur B. Buschlen, 35011959, 16th Infantry, United States Army, for extraordinary heroism in action against the enemy on 6 June 1944, in France. Sergeant Buschlen was approaching the beach with one of the initial assault waves when his boat struck an underwater obstacle and capsized. Although thrown into deep water and subjected to fierce artillery and mortar fire, he voluntarily swam to the aid of a wounded comrade and brought him to shore. Observing another wounded man approximately one hundred yards away from shore struggling unsuccessfully to reach the beach with a cumbersome radio transmitter, Sergeant Buschlen, unhesitatingly and with complete disregard for his own safety, waded to the side of the wounded man. Although exposed to incessant machine gun and small arms fire, he carried the heavy radio and fearlessly assisted the casualty to shore. Sergeant Buschlen once again entered the channel in a vain attempt to salvage additional equipment which had become entangled on barbed wire barriers. With undiminished daring, he plunged into the water, ignoring the withering enemy fire, and struggled toward the entanglement and was mortally wounded. Sergeant Buschlen, by his display of extraordinary initiative, marked determination and great personal courage, exemplified the highest traditions of the armed forces. Entered military service from Ohio.

Headquarters, First Army, General Orders No. 94 (December 10, 1944)

Colonel Eugene M. Caffey
Headquarters, 1st Engineer Special Brigade, VII Corps

Citation: Colonel Eugene M. Caffey (Army Serial No. 09329), Corps of Engineers, United States Army, for extraordinary heroism in connection with military operations against an armed enemy on 6 June 1944, in France. Colonel Caffey landed with the first wave of the forces assaulting the enemy held beaches. Finding that the landing had been made on other than the planned beaches, he selected appropriate landing beaches, redistributed the area assigned to shore parties of the 1st Engineer Special Brigade, and set them at work to establish routes inland through the seawall and minefields to reinsure the rapid landing and passage inshore of the following waves. He frequently went on the beaches under heavy shell fire to force incoming troops to disperse and move promptly off the shore and away from the water side to places of concealment and greater safety further back. His courage and his presence in the very front of the attack, coupled with his calm disregard of hostile fire, inspired the troops to heights of enthusiasm and self sacrifice. Under his experienced and unfaltering leadership, the initial error in landing off course was promptly overcome, confusion was prevented, and the forces necessary to a victorious assault were successfully and expeditiously landed and cleared from the beaches with a minimum of casualties. He thus contributed in a marked degree to the seizing of the beachhead in France.

Headquarters, Theater Service Forces, European Theater, General Orders No. 161 (August 4, 1945)

Eugene M. Caffey, from Decatur, Georgia, was appointed as a cadet-at-large to the United States Military Academy at West Point, New York by President Woodrow Wilson, where he graduated in 1918. He commissioned as a captain in the Corps of Engineers and spent much of his early career in various assignments in Central and South America. In 1933, Caffey received a law degree from the University of Virginia and transferred to the Judge Advocate General department. At the outbreak of World War II, Caffey transferred back to the Corps of Engineers as the executive officer of the 20th Engineer Combat Regiment. He took command of the regiment shortly after America's entry into the war. He trained the regiment in the United States, and led it during the campaign in North Africa. Caffey became commander of the 1st Engineer Special Brigade in May 1943, leading it during the invasions of Sicily and Salerno, Italy. He and the brigade participated in the Utah Beach assault landing on D-Day. Colonel Caffey commanded the Utah District for five months before transferring to the Pacific Theater to take part in the invasion of Okinawa in 1945. After the war, he returned to the Judge Advocate General Corps, rising to the rank of major general and Judge Advocate General of the United States Army from 1954 until his retirement in 1956. He and his wife moved to Las Cruces, New Mexico, where he practiced law until his death in 1961. *Photograph courtesy of Mary Reistrup.*

Colonel Charles D. W. Canham
Headquarters, 116th Infantry Regiment, 29th Infantry Division

Colonel Charles D. W. Canham, 016496, 116th Infantry, United States Army, for extraordinary heroism in action against the enemy on 6 June 1944, in France. Colonel Canham landed on the beach shortly after the assault wave of troops had landed. At the time, the enemy fire was at its heaviest and had completely arrested the attack. Though wounded shortly after landing, Colonel Canham, with utter disregard for his own safety, continued to expose himself to the enemy fire in his efforts to reorganize the men. His personal bravery and determination so inspired and heartened the men that they were able to break through the enemy positions. The gallantry and outstanding leadership demonstrated by Colonel Canham reflects great credit upon himself and was in keeping with the highest traditions of the armed forces.

Headquarters, First Army, General Orders No. 29 (June 29, 1944)

Colonel Charles D. W. Canham, the commander of the 116th Infantry Regiment, was born in Kolo, Mississippi in 1901 and took competitive exams as a sergeant to attend the United States Military Academy, where he graduated in 1926. Canham retired as a major general after forty-one years of service. *United States Army photograph courtesy of Chris Profota.*

Private Peter Cavaliere
Company H, 16th Infantry Regiment, 1st Infantry Division

Citation: Private Peter (NMI) Cavaliere, 31070940, 16th Infantry, United States Army, for extraordinary heroism in action against the enemy on 6 June 1944 at Colleville-sur-le-Mer, France. As Private Cavaliere's company was about to attack the town of Colleville-sur-le-Mer the enemy laid down an intense artillery barrage and started a counterattack. This required that the attack be launched from a different sector. As his company was moving out, Private Cavaliere voluntarily remained behind to cover its movement. He took cover in a building from which he could snipe at the enemy. Though subjected in this position to heavy artillery fire, Private Cavaliere resisted every effort to dislodge him and maintained his accurate fire against the enemy and effectively hampered their attempt to cut off his company. The gallantry, tenacity of purpose and outstanding devotion to duty displayed by Private Cavaliere reflect great credit upon himself and were in keeping with the highest traditions of the armed forces of the United States.

Headquarters, First Army, General Orders No. 31 (July 1, 1944)

Private First Class John W. Ceffalo
Headquarters Company, 3rd Battalion, 505th Parachute Infantry Regiment, 82nd Airborne Division

Citation: Private First Class John W. Ceffalo, Infantry, Army of the United States, a member of Headquarters Company, 3rd Battalion, 505th Parachute Infantry Regiment, distinguished himself by extraordinary heroism in action against the enemy on 6 June 1944, near Ste.-Mère-Église, Normandy, France. Landing by parachute, he assembled, organized, and led a reinforced machine gun squad that repulsed numerous armor led hostile attacks. He personally disabled one enemy halftrack and laid a number of road mines under fire that enabled his group to drive off several armored car and infantry attacks until relieved. Private First Class Ceffalo's initiative, gallantry, and superior combat leadership made a vital contribution to the success of his unit on D-Day and reflect the highest credit on himself and the Parachute Infantry.

Department of the Army, General Orders No. 50 (July 16, 1951)

Staff Sergeant Philip C. Clark
Headquarters Company, 2nd Battalion, 16th Infantry Regiment, 1st Infantry Division

Citation: Staff Sergeant Philip C. Clark, 35011921, 16th Infantry, United States Army, for extraordinary heroism in action against the enemy on 6 June 1944 near Colleville-sur-le-Mer, France. Staff Sergeant Clark landed with the battalion headquarters but voluntarily joined a rifle company to aid in the assault. Leaving the slight cover of a shale shelf, he crept under heavy enemy machine gun fire to the barbed wire entanglements and forced a breach. He then led his group of men across a minefield to the foot of the heavily defended cliffs. Here his men were pinned down by the intense machine gun fire. Staff Sergeant Clark then charged the machine gun position killing three of the crew in hand to hand combat and taking two prisoners. The personal bravery, skill and disregard for his own safety displayed by Staff Sergeant Clark reflect great credit on himself and were in keeping with the highest traditions of the armed forces of the United States.

Headquarters, First Army, General Orders No. 31 (July 1, 1944)

Private Peter Cavaliere, with Company H, 16th Infantry, is awarded the Distinguished Service Cross during a ceremony near Balleroy, France on July 2, 1944, by General Dwight D. Eisenhower. *United States Army Signal Corps photograph, courtesy of Ronald Cavaliere.*

Technician Fifth Grade Rex D. Clark
Company E, 2nd Ranger Battalion, Provisional Ranger Group

Citation: Technician Fifth Grade Rex D. Clark, 39378566, Company E, 2d Ranger Infantry Battalion, United States Army, for extraordinary heroism in connection with military operations against an armed enemy in France. On 6 June 1944, Technician Clark was in command of an amphibious vehicle equipped with an extension ladder and mounting three machine guns which was to be used by the assault forces to scale the high cliffs near Pointe du Hoc, France. Then it was found that the vehicle could not reach the cliffs because of the rough terrain, Technician Clark gallantly ordered himself raised on the ladder, and firing his machine guns at the hostile emplacements, effectively diverted the return fire away from the assault troops. Through his intrepid actions, two enemy automatic weapons were neutralized and many of the enemy pinned down, enabling friendly forces to advance on their objective. Technician Clark's heroic actions and unselfish devotion to duty are in keeping with the highest traditions of the military service.

Headquarters, Third Army, General Orders No. 204 (August 6, 1945)

Major General E. N. Harmon, the commanding officer of the XXII Corps, awards the Distinguished Service Cross to Staff Sergeant Rex D. Clark, from Boyds, Washington, at a ceremony at Pilsen, Czechoslovakia on August 14, 1945. *United States Army Signal Corps photograph, National Archives.*

Staff Sergeant Ralph S. Coffman
Company L, 116th Infantry Regiment, 29th Infantry Division

Citation: Staff Sergeant Ralph S. Coffman, 20365662, 116th Infantry, United States Army, for extraordinary heroism in action against enemy forces on 6 June 1944, in France. Upon landing on the coast of France with the initial assault troops, Staff Sergeant Coffman observed that they were immediately pinned down by heavy enemy rifle, machine gun and artillery fire. With complete disregard for his own safety, Staff Sergeant Coffman gathered together a group of men and fearlessly led them forward to destroy several enemy machine guns which had been inflicting numerous casualties on the men pinned down on the beach. The valor, initiative and personal bravery exhibited by Staff Sergeant Coffman reflects great credit upon himself and is in keeping with the highest traditions of the armed forces.

Headquarters, First Army, General Orders No. 29 (June 29, 1944)

Sergeant Ralph S. Coffman, from Mount Sidney, Virginia, served with Company L, 116th Infantry Regiment, 29th Infantry Division. *Photograph courtesy of Donna (Coffman) Alexander.*

Sergeant Clarence Colson
Company E, 16th Infantry Regiment, 1st Infantry Division

Citation: Sergeant Clarence (NMI) Colson, 12022782, 16th Infantry, United States Army, for extraordinary heroism in action against the enemy on 6 June 1944, in France. When the landing craft carrying Sergeant Colson and his mortar squad grounded some four hundred yards offshore, the men were forced to swim to the beach under heavy enemy machine gun fire. Sergeant Colson, despite heavy enemy fire, moved from one man to another encouraging and aiding them shoreward. On reaching shore, Sergeant Colson was determined to continue the attack at once and moved across the fire swept beach, locating and organizing his scattered section. He then took up a firing position in clear view of the enemy and directed his fire at the nearest machine gun emplacement, while some of his men cut a gap in the wire. Firing as he advanced, Sergeant Colson then led his squad through an uncharted minefield to assault the enemy machine gun. Despite enemy hand grenades thrown at him, Sergeant Colson reached the parapet of the gun position and leaped into it with his rifle blazing. In the ensuing action against overwhelming odds, Sergeant Colson killed several of the enemy and forced the surrender of seventeen. The courage, initiative and leadership exhibited by Sergeant Colson reflects great credit upon himself and is in keeping with the highest traditions of the armed forces. Entered military service from New York.

Headquarters, First Army, General Orders No. 39 (July 31, 1944)

Staff Sergeant Curtis Colwell
Company E, 16th Infantry Regiment, 1st Infantry Division

Citation: Staff Sergeant Curtis (NMI) Colwell, 6662084, 16th Infantry, United States Army, for extraordinary heroism in action against the enemy on 6 June 1944, near Colleville-sur-le-Mer, France. Under the heavy rifle, machine gun, and artillery fire of the enemy, Staff Sergeant Colwell fearlessly cut a gap in the wire. He then led his section through this gap in the wire and through a minefield beyond the wire. As his section approached its objective it came under fierce enemy machine gun fire. Completely ignoring his own safety, Staff Sergeant Colwell led his section in a successful assault upon the machine gun position. The personal bravery and determined leadership exhibited by Staff Sergeant Colwell reflect great credit upon himself and were in keeping with the highest traditions of the armed forces of the United States.

Headquarters, First Army, General Orders No. 31 (July 1, 1944)

Opposite: Major General J. Lawton Collins, the commanding officer of the VII Corps, awards the Distinguished Service Cross to Staff Sergeant Clarence Colson, from Cattaraugus, New York, during a ceremony near Hauset, Belgium on September 27, 1944. After the war, Colson worked for the Cattaraugus County highway department as a heavy equipment operator and later operated a small dairy farm and was a school bus driver. *United States Army Signal Corps photograph, National Archives.*

Brigadier General Norman D. Cota
Headquarters, 29th Infantry Division

Citation: Brigadier General Norman D. Cota, 05284, 29th Infantry Division, United States Army, for extraordinary heroism in action against the enemy on 6 June 1944, in France. General Cota landed on the beach shortly after the first assault wave of troops had landed. At this time the beach was under heavy enemy rifle, machine gun, mortar, and artillery fire. Numerous casualties had been suffered, the attack was arrested and disorganization was in process. With complete disregard for his own safety, General Cota moved up and down the fire swept beach reorganizing units and coordinating their action. Under his leadership, a vigorous attack was launched that successfully overran the enemy positions and cleared the beaches. The outstanding courage and superb leadership displayed by General Cota reflects great credit on himself and were in keeping with the highest traditions of the armed forces.

Headquarters, First Army, General Orders No. 29 (June 29, 1944)

Lieutenant General Omar N. Bradley, commander of the First Army, pins the Distinguished Service Cross on Brigadier General Norman D. Cota, from Chelsea, Massachusetts and the assistant division commander of the 29th Infantry Division, during a ceremony near Mieux, France on July 5, 1944. *United States Army Signal Corps photograph, National Archives.*

Captain John J. Cotter
Medical Detachment, 116th Infantry Regiment, 29th Infantry Division

Citation: Captain John J. Cotter, 0429492, 116th Infantry, United States Army, for extraordinary heroism in action on 6 June 1944, in France. Captain Cotter landed early in the assault upon the coast of France as part of the regimental medical detachment. At this time the beach was subjected to intense enemy rifle, machine gun and artillery fire and numerous casualties had been inflicted. With complete disregard for his own safety, Captain Cotter administered medical attention to the wounded under this heavy fire. His fortitude and devotion to duty in rendering aid to the wounded under such hazardous and difficult conditions inspired those who saw him to a more determined effort in meeting the enemy. The courage and outstanding devotion to duty displayed by Captain Cotter reflects great credit upon himself and was in keeping with the highest traditions of the armed forces.

Headquarters, First Army, General Orders No. 29 (June 29, 1944)

Captain John J. Cotter, from West Wyoming, Pennsylvania, served with the Medical Detachment, 116th Infantry Regiment, 29th Infantry Division. *Photograph courtesy of Michael Cotter.*

First Lieutenant Robert R. Cutler
Company L, 16th Infantry Regiment, 1st Infantry Division

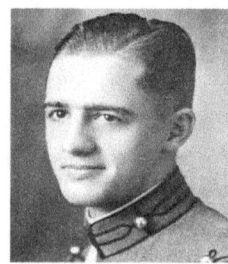

Citation: First Lieutenant Robert R. Cutler, 0384995, 16th Infantry, United States Army, for extraordinary heroism in action against the enemy on 6 June 1944, in France. Upon landing on the coast of France, First Lieutenant Cutler found that his company commander had been wounded. He immediately assumed command and reorganized the men on the fire swept beach. When he observed friendly tanks not firing at the enemy, he, completely disregarding his own safety, made his way over to them and despite the heavy enemy fire directed at the tanks, remained beside them until such time as he was able to get their fire directed effectively at the enemy. Returning to his company he led them through the first available breach in the wire to assault an enemy emplacement, and reached the high ground behind the beach. Here he reorganized his company and immediately pushed inland to his objective. Despite intense enemy fire directed at him, First Lieutenant Cutler fearlessly led the assaults on enemy strongpoints in his company's successful drive to its objective. The personal bravery and courageous leadership displayed by First Lieutenant Cutler reflects great credit on himself and is in keeping with the highest traditions of the armed forces. Entered military service from Missouri.

Headquarters, First Army, General Orders No. 48 (August 14, 1944)

Captain Robert R. Cutler, Jr., from Washington, Missouri, is awarded the Distinguished Service Cross by Major General J. Lawton Collins, commanding officer of the VII Corps, during a ceremony near Hauset, Belgium on September 27, 1944. Cutler passed away at the age of forty-one in 1958. *United States Army Signal Corps photograph, National Archives.*

Corporal Virgil E. Danforth
Company G, 501st Parachute Infantry Regiment, 101st Airborne Division

Citation: Corporal Virgil E. Danforth, 35573725, Parachute Infantry, United States Army, for extraordinary heroism in action against the enemy, in France. When two enemy machine guns opened fire on his squad, Corporal Danforth rushed forward, despite the intense enemy fire, along a hedgerow and with hand grenades inflicted severe casualties on the enemy causing them to withdraw. By this fearless action, Corporal Danforth was able to reorganize his squad and hold his assigned position. The courage, initiative and daring of Corporal Danforth reflect great credit on himself and is in keeping with the highest traditions of the armed forces.

Headquarters, First Army, General Orders No. 31 (July 1, 1944)

First Lieutenant Francis W. Dawson
Company D, 5th Ranger Battalion, Provisional Ranger Group

Citation: First Lieutenant Francis W. Dawson, 0-400036, Infantry, United States Army, for extraordinary heroism in action against enemy forces on 6 June 1944, at Vierville-sur-Mer, France. Lieutenant Dawson led his Ranger platoon ashore in the invasion of France against heavy enemy artillery, machine gun, and small arms fire. He then personally took charge of the breaching of wire entanglements. When a gap was created, he led his platoon through it and directed them in scaling a one hundred foot cliff. Upon reaching the top of the cliff, he, accompanied by one soldier, rushed forward with a submachine gun and destroyed a German pillbox, killing or capturing the enemy located therein. Lieutenant Dawson's heroic action and aggressive leadership are in keeping with the highest traditions of the service. Entered military service from South Carolina.

Headquarters, First Army, General Orders No. 28 (June 20, 1944)

Lieutenant Francis W. Dawson, from Catawba, South Carolina, was a platoon leader with Company D, 5th Ranger Battalion during the invasion of Normandy. *United States Army Signal Corps photograph, National Archives.*

Next Page: This photograph of Private Virgil E. Danforth was taken after graduation from parachute training at Fort Benning, Georgia. Danforth was from Indianapolis, Indiana. *Photograph courtesy of Michael West.*

Captain Joseph T. Dawson
Company G, 16th Infantry Regiment, 1st Infantry Division

Citation: Captain Joseph T. Dawson, 0-452348, 16th infantry, United States Army, for extraordinary heroism in action against enemy forces on 6 June 1944, in France. Captain Dawson, in the initial landing on the coast of France, disembarked under a hail of enemy machine gun and rifle fire and, with utmost calmness, proceeded to organize a large group of men who were floundering near their bullet riddled craft and led them ashore. However, upon reaching the beach, he found that his company was pinned down by direct fire from three enemy machine guns which were placed in an enemy strongpoint in a cliff immediately beyond the heavily mined sands. With absolute disregard for his own personal safety, Captain Dawson moved from his position of cover on to the minefield deliberately drawing the fire of the enemy machine guns in order that his men might be free to move. This heroic diversion succeeded and his combat group crossed the beach to move into the assault on the enemy strongpoint. During this action, Captain Dawson was wounded in the leg. In a superb display of courage in the face of heavy enemy fire, Captain Dawson although wounded, led a successful attack into the enemy stronghold. Captain Dawson's outstanding leadership and courageous actions reflect great credit upon himself and are in keeping with the highest traditions of the armed forces.

Headquarters, First Army, General Orders No. 31 (July 1, 1944)

First Lieutenant William T. Dillon
Company A, 16th Infantry Regiment, 1st Infantry Division

Citation: First Lieutenant William T. Dillon, 01301625, 16th Infantry, United States Army, for extraordinary heroism in action against the enemy on 6 June 1944, in France. Upon discovering that his company commander had been seriously wounded during the invasion on D-Day, First Lieutenant Dillon immediately assumed command of the company and proceeded up and down the fire swept beach to reorganize the scattered assault sections into a fighting unit. Under heavy enemy fire, he personally led a section through an intricate barbed wire fence and across an uncharted minefield and launched an attack on an enemy strongpoint. When his section became pinned down, First Lieutenant Dillon moved forward alone in the face of concentrated automatic weapons fire to assault the hostile emplacement. Firing his carbine and throwing hand grenades, he knocked out two machine guns, thereby permitting his men to advance. The courageous leadership and personal bravery displayed by First Lieutenant Dillon exemplifies the highest traditions of the armed forces. Entered military service from Indiana.

Headquarters, First Army, General Orders No. 77 (November 9, 1944)

Next Page: General Dwight Eisenhower pins the Distinguished Service Cross to the jacket of Captain Joseph T. Dawson, the commanding officer of Company G, 16th Infantry Regiment, 1st Infantry Division during a ceremony near Balleroy, France on July 2, 1944. Dawson was born in Temple, Texas in 1914, the son of a Baptist minister. He graduated from Baylor University in 1933 and was a geologist for two oil companies prior to enlisting in the United States Army in May of 1941. After the war, Dawson settled in Corpus Christi, Texas, where he founded Dawson Oil. He was very active in serving civic, educational, and charitable organizations. *United States Army Signal Corps photograph,, courtesy of the First Division Museum at Cantigny.*

Private First Class Dominick DiTullio
Headquarters Company, 3rd Battalion, 505th Parachute Infantry Regiment, 82nd Airborne Division

Citation: Private First Class Dominick DiTullio, 33037230, 505th Parachute Infantry, United States Army, for extraordinary heroism in action against the enemy on 6 June 1944, in France. Private First Class DiTullio, while a member of a wire section which had advanced three hundred yards beyond the front lines in attempting to establish contact with a forward unit, volunteered to lead the communications officer forward for further information and immediately set out in the lead of the party. After covering considerable territory in advance of the front line under heavy firing from friendly and enemy troops, they determined that the company they were seeking had withdrawn and, while returning, came upon two trucks loaded with Germans. Private First Class DiTullio, without a moment's hesitation, opened fire on the enemy, and forced them to take cover, thereby preventing their discovering the weakness of the party. After killing one German and forcing two to surrender, he advanced with fixed bayonet across the open road to make sure that all the enemy had withdrawn and then remained behind to cover the continued withdrawal of his own party. When the Germans drove cattle down the road in an attempt to detonate a mined roadblock, Private First Class DiTullio came out of his cover, turned the cattle back and hand grenaded the Germans behind him. He then reached the battalion aid station, which was under hostile fire so severe as to prevent aid men from securing necessary water. Without thought of his own safety, he crossed the fire-swept area to a pump and was killed in the act of pumping water for the assistance of his comrades. The high courage and absolute contempt for danger shown by Private First Class DiTullio made him an inspiring example of fortitude and heroism for his entire unit. Entered military service from Pennsylvania.

Headquarters, First Army, General Orders No. 51 (August 22, 1944)

Technician Fourth Grade Lowell L. Dock
7th Field Artillery Battalion, 1st Infantry Division

Citation: Technician Fourth Grade Lowell L. Dock, 35270134, 7th Field Artillery Battalion, United States Army, for extraordinary heroism in action against the enemy on 6 June 1944, in France. Technician Fourth Grade Dock landed on D-Day with an infantry combat team. At this time the beach was under extremely heavy enemy fire. He immediately crawled to an exposed position and commenced firing his rifle on a machine gun emplacement that was directing intense fire on the troops landing on the beach. Shortly thereafter, Technician Fourth Grade Dock rejoined his battalion command post. Although wire laying was not his duty, he voluntarily left his sheltered position and laid wire across the fire swept beach to the infantry combat team command post. While laying wire, Technician Fourth Grade Dock, despite intense enemy fire and without regard for his own safety, helped pull a wounded man off the beach to a place of safety. During the rest of the firefight, he continually crossed and recrossed the beach to repair breaks in the line. The personal bravery, aggressiveness, and initiative displayed by Technician Fourth Grade Dock reflect great credit upon himself and are in keeping with the highest traditions of the armed forces. Entered military service from Ohio.

Headquarters, First Army, General Orders No. 42 (August 6, 1944)

Next Page: General J. Lawton Collins (left foreground), the commander of the VII Corps, awards the Distinguished Service Cross to Technician Fourth Grade Lowell L. Dock, from Celina, Ohio. Dock and fifteen other 1st Infantry Division troops were awarded the DSC at a ceremony on September 27, 1944 near Hauset, Belgium. Sergeant Clarence Colson (center) stands to Dock's right. Staff Sergeant Paul R. Shorter (left center) is standing to Sergeant Colson's right. After the war, Dock returned home where he worked for the city of Celina and served his community in various civic organizations. *United States Army photograph, courtesy of the First Division Museum at Cantigny and the National Archives.*

Private Vinton W. Dove

Company C, 37th Engineer Combat Battalion, 5th Engineer Special Brigade, Provisional Engineer Special Brigade Group

Citation: Private Vinton W. Dove, 33746975, Corps of Engineers, United States Army, for extraordinary heroism in action against the enemy on 6 June 1944, in France. Private Dove landed with his bulldozer at 0830 hours, D-Day. Upon finding conditions on the beach behind schedule because of the fierce enemy opposition, he voluntarily pulled numerous drowned wheeled and track propelled vehicles out of the surf. While his bulldozer was a specific target for cannon and mortar fire, he cleared a road through the shingle at beach exits E-1 and E-3. Having completed that dangerous mission, Private Dove immediately set to the task of removing two roadblocks at exit E-1 and filling in an antitank trap at exit E-3, thereby permitting vehicles and armor to move out in support of the infantry troops. Private Dove's courage and bravery in performing his tasks under intense enemy fire reflects high credit on himself and on the Armed Forces of the United States. Entered military service from the District of Columbia.

Headquarters, First Army, General Orders No. 39 (July 31, 1944)

Private Vinton W. Dove was born in the District of Columbia in 1913. After the war, he founded and managed a concrete contracting company. This photo was taken outside of his home in Washington D.C. after the war. *Photograph courtesy of Vinton G. Dove.*

First Lieutenant Sidney W. Dunagan
50th Troop Carrier Squadron, 314th Troop Carrier Group, 52nd Troop Carrier Wing, IX Troop Carrier Command

Citation: Sidney Ward Dunagan, 0525079, First Lieutenant, Army Air Force, United States Army (Posthumous). For extraordinary heroism in action against the enemy on 6 June 1944. On this date, while leading his element in the initial invasion of France, due to cloud formations over enemy territory, Lieutenant Dunagan's airplane became separated from his entire group and was forced to continue to the drop zone as a single ship. Excellent navigation without radio aid enabled him to locate the drop zone and to drop his paratroopers in the briefed zone. Intense enemy ground fire enveloped his airplane immediately thereafter, as a result of which the ship sustained damage. Lieutenant Dunagan was notified by his crew chief that two paratroopers had failed to jump due to entangling of their chutes. Determined to complete his assigned mission, with utter disregard for his personal safety and fully cognizant of dangers to be encountered, he unhesitatingly put his ship into a three hundred sixty degree turn to the right to drop his remaining troopers. This accomplished, violent enemy ground fire was again encountered, and while engaged in evasive action and at an altitude of one hundred feet, defenseless in an unarmored plane, enemy crossfire struck and instantly killed him. The outstanding heroism displayed by Lieutenant Dunagan, his disregard for personal safety, and devotion to duty, reflect the highest credit upon himself and the armed forces of the United States.

Headquarters, United States Strategic Air Forces in Europe, General Orders No. 87 (November 2, 1944)

Lieutenants Sidney W. Dunagan (left) and Walter D. Nims (right). Dunagan, from Wilder, Idaho, was killed in action on June 6, 1944 during a troop carrier mission over the Cotentin Peninsula. He was buried at the American cemetery at Cambridge, England. *Photograph courtesy of Patrick Dunagan.*

First Lieutenant George M. Eberle
Company D, 502nd Parachute Infantry Regiment, 101st Airborne Division

Citation: First Lieutenant George M. Eberle, 025641, 502nd Parachute Infantry, United States Army, for extraordinary heroism in action against the enemy on 6 June 1944, in France. When the small force with which he was moving forward was suddenly pinned down by intense enemy machine gun fire, First Lieutenant Eberle, though seriously wounded, moved across an open road completely exposed to enemy fire in order to attack the enemy gun. Directing his fire on the enemy position, he successfully put the gun out of action. During this engagement, First Lieutenant Eberle was killed. The extraordinary heroism, aggressiveness and devotion to duty displayed by First Lieutenant Eberle reflects great credit on himself and is in keeping with the highest traditions of the armed forces. Entered United States Military Academy from New York.

Headquarters, First Army, General Orders No. 48 (August 14, 1944)

Captain Ned S. Elder
Company C, 743rd Tank Battalion

Citation: Captain Ned S. Elder, 0353313, 743rd Tank Battalion, United States Army, for extraordinary heroism in action against the enemy on 6 June 1944 in France. Captain Elder commanded a tank company which landed on the coast of France in the initial assault wave. Shortly after landing, Captain Elder was wounded. Although in great pain he refused to be evacuated and continued to command his company. The beach was covered by all types of enemy fire; machine gun, rifle, mortar, and observed artillery fire. Despite this intense enemy fire Captain Elder dismounted from his tank to select enemy targets and direct the fire of his company. Due to the effectiveness of this fire, Captain Elder was able to drive his tanks through the enemy lines and establish a vitally needed beach exit. The courage and outstanding leadership displayed by Captain Elder reflects great credit upon himself and is in keeping with the highest traditions of the armed forces.

Headquarters, First Army, General Orders No. 37 (July 21, 1944)

Captain Ned. S. Elder, from Lycoming County, Pennsylvania, was the commander of Company C, 743rd Tank Battalion, on June 6, 1944. He was killed in action on July 11, 1944 and his body was repatriated after the war and buried at the Wildwood Cemetery in South Williamsport, Pennsylvania. *Photograph courtesy of Joel Gilfert.*

Technical Sergeant Calvin L. Ellis
Company E, 16th Infantry Regiment, 1st Infantry Division

Citation: Technical Sergeant Calvin L. Ellis, 6892887, 16th Infantry, United States Army, for extraordinary heroism in action against the enemy on 6 June 1944, in France. Voluntarily assuming command after his platoon leader had been seriously wounded on D-Day, Technical Sergeant Ellis, while under heavy enemy fire, waded far out into the fire swept surf on numerous occasions to rescue wounded comrades. Although Technical Sergeant Ellis was himself severely wounded, he courageously led his men across the beach and through a barbed wire fence to join a section of his company which had made an initial breakthrough. Reaching the company's right flank, his section was pinned down by well aimed sniper fire from concealed positions. Undaunted and with indomitable fighting spirit, Technical Sergeant Ellis personally assaulted and killed three dug in Germans, and repeatedly led his section in successfully attacking groups of infiltrating enemy. By his outstanding leadership and heroic effort, Technical Sergeant Ellis acted in keeping with the highest traditions of the armed forces. Entered military service from Pennsylvania.

Headquarters, First Army, General Orders No. 81 (November 16, 1944)

Second Lieutenant Forest K. Ferguson
Antitank Company, 116th Infantry Regiment, 29th Infantry Division

Citation: Second Lieutenant Forest K. Ferguson, 01322014, 116th Infantry, United States Army, for extraordinary heroism against the enemy on 6 June 1944, in France. When Lieutenant Ferguson reached the shore he observed that the initial assault units were pinned down by the intense and heavy enemy rifle, machine gun and artillery fire, and that further advance was also blocked by an extensive barbed wire obstacle. With complete disregard for his own safety, Second Lieutenant Ferguson bravely moved forward under this heavy fire with a Bangalore torpedo with which he blew a gap in barbed wire. He then rose from his position and, while leading the troops through this gap to the enemy positions, was wounded. The personal bravery, initiative and superior leadership of Second Lieutenant Ferguson under such hazardous conditions reflects great credit on himself and was in keeping with the highest traditions of the armed forces.

Headquarters, First Army, General Orders No. 29 (June 29, 1944)

First Sergeant Lawrence J. Fitzsimmons
Company E, 16th Infantry Regiment, 1st Infantry Division

Citation: First Sergeant Lawrence J. Fitzsimmons, 6719936, 16th Infantry, United States Army, for extraordinary heroism in action against the enemy on 6 June 1944 near Colleville-sur-le-Mer, France. First Sergeant Fitzsimmons landed with the assault wave of troops. He exposed himself to the direct enemy fire when he forcefully opened a defective landing ramp. He then led his men to the protection of a small shale shelf. On at least three occasions, with complete disregard for his own safety, he dashed back into the surf to aid wounded and struggling men to reach the shore. He continually moved up and down the beach under the heavy enemy fire to locate the platoons of his company in its reorganization. The courage and leadership in battle displayed by First Sergeant Fitzsimmons reflect great credit on himself and were in keeping with the highest traditions of the armed forces of the United States.

Headquarters, First Army, General Orders No. 31 (July 1, 1944)

Captain Edward F. Wozenski (left), the commander of Company E, 16th Infantry Regiment, congratulates First Sergeant Lawrence J. Fitzsimmons (right) upon receipt of the Distinguished Service Cross. *United States Army Signal Corps photograph.*

Private First Class Richard J. Gallagher
Company E, 16th Infantry Regiment, 1st Infantry Division

Citation: Private First Class Richard J. Gallagher, 32899808, 16th Infantry, United States Army, for extraordinary heroism in action against the enemy on 6 June 1944 near Colleville-sur-le-Mer, France. While his company was still pinned down by heavy enemy fire, Private First Class Gallagher left his partially protected position and advanced across a minefield toward the enemy emplacements. Undeterred by the intense enemy fire, he continued up a slope toward a machine gun nest which had been inflicting heavy casualties on his company. Using hand grenades and his rifle, Private First Class Gallagher wiped out the machine gun emplacement. He then returned to the beach and led part of his company through the minefield. Once more, he moved up the slope of the hill to the top. Here he discovered an enemy machine gun in a wooded area. Private First Class Gallagher not only captured the man who had been firing the machine gun, but also captured an enemy rifleman who was sniping from the cliff. The tenacity of purpose, skill, and personal bravery demonstrated by Private First Class Gallagher reflect great credit on himself and were in keeping with the highest traditions of the armed forces of the United States.

Headquarters, First Army, General Orders No. 31 (July 1, 1944)

General Dwight D. Eisenhower congratulates Private First Class Richard J. Gallagher after awarding him the Distinguished Service Cross during a ceremony near Balleroy, France on July 2, 1944. Technician Fourth Grade Stanley Appleby (center), with the Medical Detachment, 16th Infantry Regiment and who has also been awarded the DSC, stands to Gallagher's right. Gallagher, from Brooklyn, New York, was killed in action on November 24, 1944 during the bitter fighting for the Hürtgen Forest. Gallagher's grave is located in the Calverton National Cemetery, Long Island, New York. *United States Army Signal Corps photograph, courtesy of the First Division Museum at Cantigny.*

Second Lieutenant Edward M. Gearing
Company A, 116th Infantry Regiment, 1st Infantry Division

Citation: First Lieutenant Edward M. Gearing, 0495585 (then Second Lieutenant), 116th Infantry, United States Army, for extraordinary heroism in action against the enemy on 6 June 1944, in France. In the initial assault upon the coast of France, First Lieutenant Gearing landed with his platoon in the face of heavy enemy rifle, machine gun and artillery fire. This intense fire pinned the men down on a narrow beachhead, inflicting numerous casualties with resultant disorganization. In the reorganization and preparation of his platoon for attack, First Lieutenant Gearing fearlessly and with complete disregard for his own safety on numerous occasions exposed himself to direct enemy fire. He then led his platoon in a successful assault upon the enemy positions. The personal bravery and superior leadership displayed by First Lieutenant Gearing reflect great credit upon himself and were in keeping with the highest traditions of the armed forces.

Headquarters, First Army, General Orders No. 29 (June 29, 1944)

Major General Charles H. Gerhardt congratulates Lieutenant Edward M. Gearing (left) after awarding him the Distinguished Service Cross during a ceremony on October 13, 1944. *United States Army Signal Corps photograph*.

Next Page: Lieutenant Edward M. Gearing was an eighteen year old officer when this photograph was taken in 1942.

Lieutenant Colonel George W. Gibbs
Headquarters, 7th Field Artillery Battalion, 1st Infantry Division

Citation: Lieutenant Colonel George W. Gibbs, 018178, 7th Field Artillery, United States Army, for extraordinary heroism against the enemy on 6 June 1944, in France. Lieutenant Colonel Gibbs landed on D-Day with the assault waves. Despite heavy enemy artillery, mortar, machine gun, and rifle fire he immediately moved several hundred yards up the beach to where his unit was to land. Locating a small breach in the heavy wire entanglements he led an officer and a small group of men through the gap and across a minefield in a frontal assault against two enemy gun emplacements. With complete disregard for his own safety, he entered the maze of underground tunnels and fortifications and led his desperately fighting group in the neutralization of the enemy. Lieutenant Colonel Gibbs was one of the first to reach the enemy dominated ridgeline and was highly instrumental in opening a way inland from the beach. The personal bravery, fearlessness, and aggressive leadership displayed by Lieutenant Colonel Gibbs reflects great credit upon himself and the military service. Entered military service from Texas.

Headquarters, First Army, General Orders No. 42 (August 6, 1944)

First Lieutenant Carl K. Giles, Jr.
Company M, 16th Infantry Regiment, 1st Infantry Division

Citation: First Lieutenant Carl K. Giles, Jr., 01286113, 16th Infantry, United States Army, for extraordinary heroism in action against the enemy on 6 June 1944 near Colleville-sur-le-Mer, France. When the landing craft containing First Lieutenant Giles and his assault section was hit by enemy fire, it quickly sank. First Lieutenant Giles remained in the water, constantly under fierce machine gun and unceasing artillery fire, until he had directed and aided his entire section through to the beach. While on the beach he observed three severely wounded soldiers lying near the water's edge slowly being covered by the rising tide. Without a moment's hesitation he left his position of cover and moved across the exposed beach and carried the stricken men to safety. When he found out that all the officers in the company had become casualties he quickly assumed command, reorganized the company and led them through a minefield under fierce enemy machine gun and sniper fire up the cliff side to outflank an enemy pillbox. He personally took part in the assault that destroyed the enemy strongpoint. The disregard for personal safety and leadership displayed by First Lieutenant Giles in battle reflect great credit upon himself and were in keeping with the highest traditions of the armed forces of the United States.

Headquarters, First Army, General Orders No. 31 (July 1, 1944)

Captain Ralph E. Goranson
Company C, 2nd Ranger Battalion, Provisional Ranger Group

Citation: Captain Ralph E. Goranson, 0-1299035, Infantry, United States Army, for extraordinary heroism in action on 6 June 1944 and 7 June 1944 at Vierville-sur-le-Mer, France. Captain Goranson landed with his Ranger Company at H-Hour on D-Day with the initial assault wave in the invasion of France in the face of heavy automatic enfilading fire from three different directions and mortar and artillery fire from cliffs overlooking the beach. In spite of extremely heavy casualties Captain Goranson calmly and courageously reorganized his company in an advance to force a junction with the main body of the assault. Though it took ten hours of the heaviest kind of fighting to reach the main body, his men, inspired by his outstanding leadership, continuously advanced until the mission was accomplished. Captain Goranson's heroic action is in keeping with the highest traditions of the service. Entered military service from Illinois.

Headquarters, First Army, General Orders No. 28 (June 20, 1944)

This photo of Captain Ralph E. Goranson, commanding officer of Company C, 2nd Ranger Battalion, was taken at Fort Dix, New Jersey in 1943. *United States Army photograph, courtesy of Lynn Towne.*

Lieutenant Colonel James E. Rudder, the commanding officer of the Provisional Ranger Group and the 2nd Ranger Battalion, congratulates Captain Ralph E. Goranson, the commanding officer of Company C, 2nd Ranger Battalion, from Chicago, Illinois, after they and other Rangers were awarded the Distinguished Service Cross during a ceremony near Colombieres, France on June 23, 1944. *United States Army Signal Corps photograph, National Archives.*

First Lieutenant Joseph J. Gregory
Company C, 146th Engineer Combat Battalion, Special Engineer Task Force, Provisional Engineer Special Brigade Group
Gap Assault Team Number 10

Citation: First Lieutenant Joseph J. Gregory, 01108697, 146th Engineer Combat Battalion, United States Army, for extraordinary heroism on 6 June 1944 in France. Lieutenant Gregory commanded a boat team which landed on the coast of France at H plus 3 minutes of D-Day. By continuously moving about the beach, placing demolition charges, and blowing gaps in the obstacles existing, he made it possible for the following waves of troops to accomplish their landing. Having completed several demolitions, Lieutenant Gregory was wounded in trying to move two tanks which were drawing considerable fire on a position where a large number of wounded men were being cared for. Despite the fragment in his thigh he continued to give instructions to his men until approximately four hours after the landing, at which time he remained behind on the beach to assist in the treatment of the wounded, refusing to be evacuated himself in order that he could continue his work. Shortly afterward, while attempting to rejoin his men, he received a second wound which proved fatal. The deed accomplished by Lieutenant Gregory, without regard for his own personal safety, was one of the deciding factors in the successful completion of the assaulting forces in his sector. The gap cut through the beach obstacles made it possible for our forces to continue to land badly needed reinforcements throughout the day regardless of the stage of the tide.

War Department, General Orders No. 87 (November 14, 1944)

Private First Class John V. Griffin
Company L, 16th Infantry Regiment, 1st Infantry Division

Citation: Private First Class John V. Griffin, 6958525, 16th Infantry, United States Army, for extraordinary heroism in action against the enemy on 6 June 1944, in France. While his company was pinned down on the beach due to the heavy enemy rifle, machine gun, and artillery fire, Private First Class Griffin with two other men volunteered to open a gap in the barbed wire. Under intense fire he cut his way through the wire and then picked his way through a minefield, marking a path for his company to follow and reached the base of a hill. From this point, he laid accurate rifle fire upon the enemy emplacements, forcing them to cease firing long enough to permit part of his company to move through the gap in the wire and the minefield and join him at the base of the hill. While this group directed frontal fire on the enemy, Private First Class Griffin moved out to the flank and from an exposed position directed his accurate fire against the enemy. Again the enemy was forced to cease firing long enough to permit the men who had been delivering the frontal fire to advance and successfully assault the enemy positions. When, later in the same day, the enemy counterattacked, Private First Class Griffin worked his way around the enemy and engaged them from the flank. Despite intense enemy fire to dislodge him, Private First Class Griffin remained at his exposed position until the enemy counterattack was beaten off. The personal bravery, initiative, and determined devotion to duty displayed by Private First Class Griffin reflects great credit on himself and is in keeping with the highest traditions of the armed forces. Entered military service from Texas.

Headquarters, First Army, General Orders No. 31 (July 1, 1944)

Sergeant George A. Habib
Company A, 741st Tank Battalion

Citation: Sergeant George A. Habib, 36230655, Infantry, United States Army, for extraordinary heroism in action against the enemy on 6 June 1944, in France. Sergeant Habib was in command of a tank dozer in the initial assault on the coast of France with the mission of removing enemy beach obstacles. Shortly after landing both tracks of the tank dozer were thrown. Although under heavy and sustained small arms and observed artillery fire, Sergeant Habib continually exposed himself in directing his crew in the repair of the thrown tracks. After successfully repairing the tank dozer, Sergeant Habib fearlessly directed the removal of obstacles. The resourcefulness, aggressive leadership and courage displayed by Sergeant Habib reflects great credit on himself and is in keeping with the highest traditions of the armed forces.

Headquarters, First Army, General Orders No. 37 (July 21, 1944)

Captain James W. Haley
Company G, 8th Infantry Regiment, 4th Infantry Division

Citation: Captain James W. Haley, 024244, 8th Infantry, United States Army, for extraordinary heroism in action against the enemy on 6 June 1944, in France. On D-Day, Captain Haley braved withering enemy artillery, machine gun, and rifle fire to reach a large group of confused and disorganized troops who congregated behind a seawall. He calmly organized them while shells were falling in the immediate area, and successfully led them across the beach. As leading elements of his own company moved forward, they encountered a minefield which caused heavy casualties. When the balance of his men froze into position and hesitated to go forward, Captain Haley, with complete disregard for his own life, courageously cleared a path and personally led his men through the obstacle. Continuing its advance, the company was pinned down by a hail of machine gun and small arms fire from a stubborn enemy group in a strongly fortified position. Displaying great personal audacity and conspicuous leadership, he once again defied intense fire and, after preparing his company for an assault, he personally led it in a vicious hand-to-hand and bayonet fight, overpowering the resistance and continuing to reach his objective. Entered military service from Louisiana.

Headquarters, First Army, General Orders No. 102 (December 28, 1944)

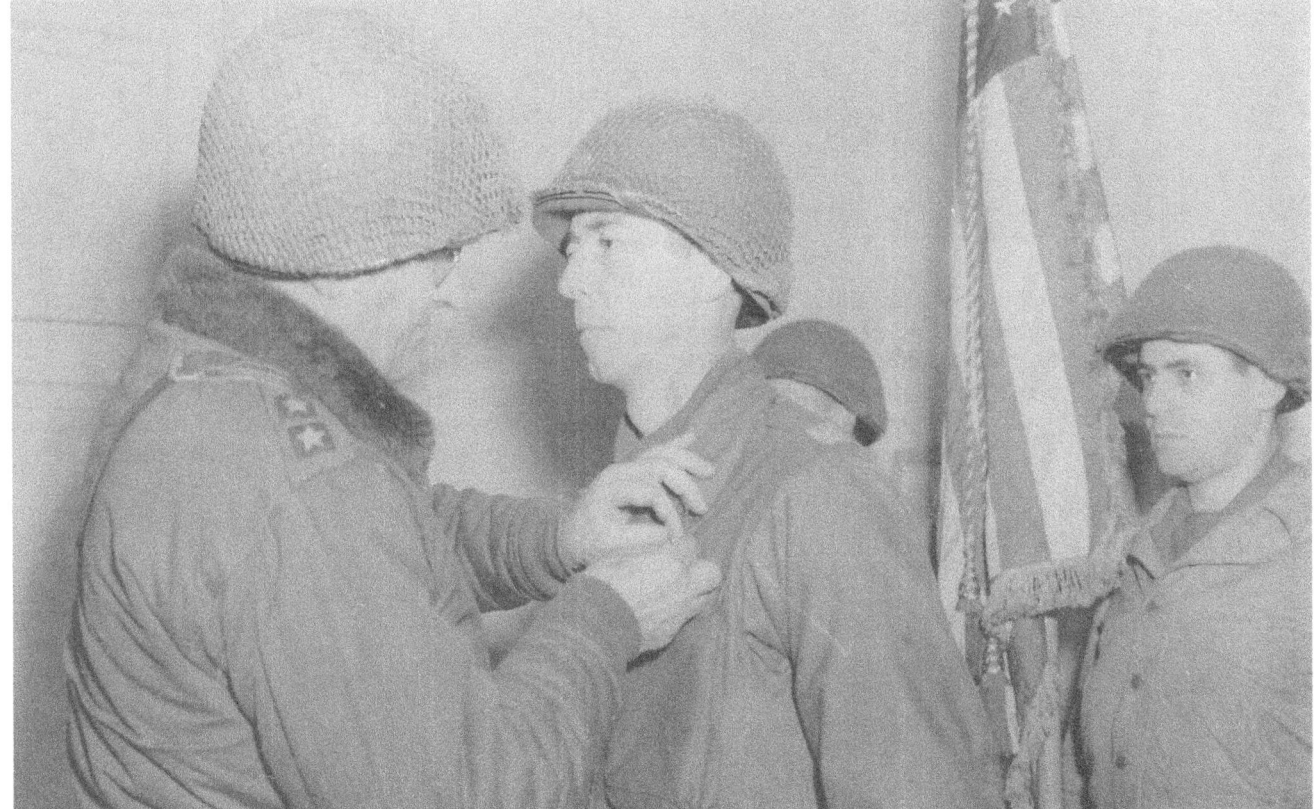

Major General Manton S. Eddy awards the Distinguished Service Cross to Major James W. Haley, from Woodruff, Indiana, on January 16, 1945. *United States Army Signal Corps photograph, National Archives.*

Private First Class Henry H. Hall, Jr.
Medical Detachment, Provisional 397th Antiaircraft Artillery (Automatic Weapons) Battalion

Citation: Private First Class Henry H. Hall, Jr., 33411015, Medical Detachment, 397th Antiaircraft Artillery (AW) Battalion, United States Army, for extraordinary heroism in action against the enemy on 6 June 1944, in France. During the early hours of the assault on the beaches of Normandy, Private First Class Hall heroically performed his duties of administering first aid to the wounded under the most hazardous circumstances. Although a number of casualties were lying in an area protected to a considerable degree from hostile fire by a twenty foot cliff—casualties which would have occupied all his time and exhausted all his supplies—Private First Class Hall chose the more dangerous duty of rescuing and aiding those wounded and drowning in the shallows. Though fully aware of the great personal danger involved, he made several trips to the water's edge and beyond, leaving the area of comparative safety in the face of direct machine gun fire, to save many lives. While thus engaged he fell mortally wounded. The extraordinary heroism of Private First Class Hall was above and beyond the call of duty and is keeping with the highest traditions of the armed forces of the United States. Entered military service from Pennsylvania.

Headquarters, First Army, General Orders No. 55 (September 3, 1944)

Private Francis L. Harbaugh
Company A, 501st Parachute Infantry Regiment, 101st Airborne Division

Citation: Private Francis L. Harbaugh, 37298441, Medical Corps, United States Army, for extraordinary heroism in action on 6 June 1944, in France. Due to heavy enemy machine gun, mortar and artillery fire, numerous casualties were suffered by the men in Private Harbaugh's company. With complete disregard for his own safety, Private Harbaugh on numerous occasions fearlessly crawled forward over open terrain to administer first aid and carry wounded personnel to safety. The outstanding courage and fortitude of Private Harbaugh reflects great credit on himself and is in keeping with the highest traditions of the armed forces.

Headquarters, First Army, General Orders No. 31 (July 1, 1944)

First Lieutenant Robert C. Hargrove
Headquarters Company, 2nd Battalion, 116th Infantry Regiment, 29th Infantry Division

Citation: First Lieutenant Robert C. Hargrove, 01296853, 116th Infantry, United States Army, for extraordinary heroism in action against the enemy on 6 June 1944, in France. In the initial assault upon the coast of France, Lieutenant Hargrove landed with his platoon in the face of heavy enemy rifle, machine gun and artillery fire. This intense fire pinned the men down on a narrow beachhead, inflicting numerous casualties with resultant disorganization. First Lieutenant Hargrove, with complete disregard for his own safety, exposed himself on numerous occasions to this direct fire in reorganizing and preparing his platoon for an attack. He then led his platoon in a successful assault upon the enemy position. The personal bravery and superior leadership exhibited by First Lieutenant Hargrove reflects great credit on himself and was in keeping with the highest traditions of the armed forces.

Headquarters, First Army, General Orders No. 29 (June 29, 1944)

First Lieutenant Ernest O. Harris
Headquarters Company, 3rd Battalion, 502nd Parachute Infantry Regiment, 101st Airborne Division

Citation: First Lieutenant Ernest O. Harris, O-463807, 502nd Parachute Infantry, United States Army, for extraordinary heroism in action against the enemy on 6 June 1944, in France. En route to the battalion assembly area after landing by parachute with a small detachment of men, First Lieutenant Harris encountered heavy machine and small arms fire from a fortified enemy garrison. Displaying superb courage and fearless leadership, he personally led an attack upon the garrison and succeeded in destroying a pillbox and several gun emplacements, killing eight men and capturing twenty-four. Still exposed to intense fire, First Lieutenant Harris, with complete disregard for his own safety, moved along the outside of the fortress and selected defensive positions for his detachment. For a period of thirty hours he skillfully directed his unit's fire upon the enemy, repelling repeated counterattacks. The personal bravery, aggressive leadership and valor displayed by First Lieutenant Harris are in keeping with the highest traditions of the armed forces. Entered military service from Missouri.

Headquarters, First Army, General Orders No. 80 (November 14, 1944)

Sergeant Bailey Harrison
Company D, 502nd Parachute Infantry Regiment, 101st Airborne Division

Citation: Sergeant Bailey Harrison, 37106743, Parachute Infantry, United States Army, for extraordinary heroism in action against the enemy on 6 June 1944, in France. While leading his squad, Sergeant Harrison was wounded. However, he refused to be evacuated and continued to lead his squad across one hundred and fifty yards of open country in the face of extremely heavy enemy fire. Despite his painful wounds, he continued to fire as he moved forward and dislodged the enemy from a prepared position, inflicting heavy casualties and successfully leading his squad to a point from which their fire forced the enemy to withdraw. The valor, courage, and aggressiveness displayed by Sergeant Harrison reflect great credit on himself and is in keeping with the highest traditions of the armed forces. Entered military service from Arkansas.

Headquarters, First Army, General Orders No. 31 (July 1, 1944)

Private First Class John R. Heenan
Company B, 146th Engineer Combat Battalion, Special Engineer Task Force, Provisional Engineer Special Brigade, V Corps Gap Support Team Number C

Citation: Private First Class John R. Heenan, 39331718, Corps of Engineers, United States Army, for extraordinary heroism in action against the enemy on 6 June 1944, in France. The demolition team, of which Private First Class Heenan was a member, landed on the coast of France under heavy enemy fire at high tide. The high tide made it impossible to work upon the obstacles. The men debarked from the landing craft and crossed the beach to a place of comparative safety to await the fall of the tide. At this time, it was noticed that the officer in charge of the demolition team was missing. He was then seen at the water's edge badly wounded attempting to make his way up the beach. Private First Class Heenan, completely disregarding his own safety, on observing the condition of his team commander, immediately left his place of cover, crossed the fire swept beach and assisted his wounded leader to safety. The gallantry, devotion to duty, and personal bravery exhibited by Private First Class Heenan reflects great credit on himself and is in keeping with the highest traditions of the Armed Forces. Entered military service from Oregon.

Headquarters, First Army, General Orders No. 37 (July 21, 1944)

Major General Leonard T. Gerow, the commanding officer of V Corps, presents the Distinguished Service Cross to Private First Class John R. Heenan, from Vernonia, Oregon, during a ceremony to award the DSC to members of the 146th Engineer Combat Battalion, conducted on September 11, 1944, in France. *United States Army Signal Corps photograph, National Archives.*

Private Marcus Heim, Jr.
Company A, 505th Parachute Infantry Regiment, 82nd Airborne Division

Citation: Private Marcus Heim, Jr., 32931497, 505th Parachute Infantry, United States Army, for extraordinary heroism in action against the enemy on 6 June 1944, in France. Private Heim, assistant gunner, was stationed at the end of a bridge over the Merderet River to repel attacks by enemy troops who controlled the other end of the bridge. This position was subject to incessant enemy rifle, machine gun, mortar, and artillery fire. After an artillery preparation, the enemy sent an assault force supported by three tanks over the bridge. Though part of the troops withdrew, Private Heim remained at his position until the enemy tanks approached within thirty yards. In spite of the intense fire, Private Heim rose from his position and with the gunner fired rockets into the three tanks. Private Heim remained with his gun and fired it until it was put out of action. The courage, devotion to duty and daring exhibited by Private Heim reflects great credit on himself and is in keeping with the highest traditions of the armed forces. Entered military service from New York.

Headquarters, First Army, General Orders No. 31 (July 1, 1944)

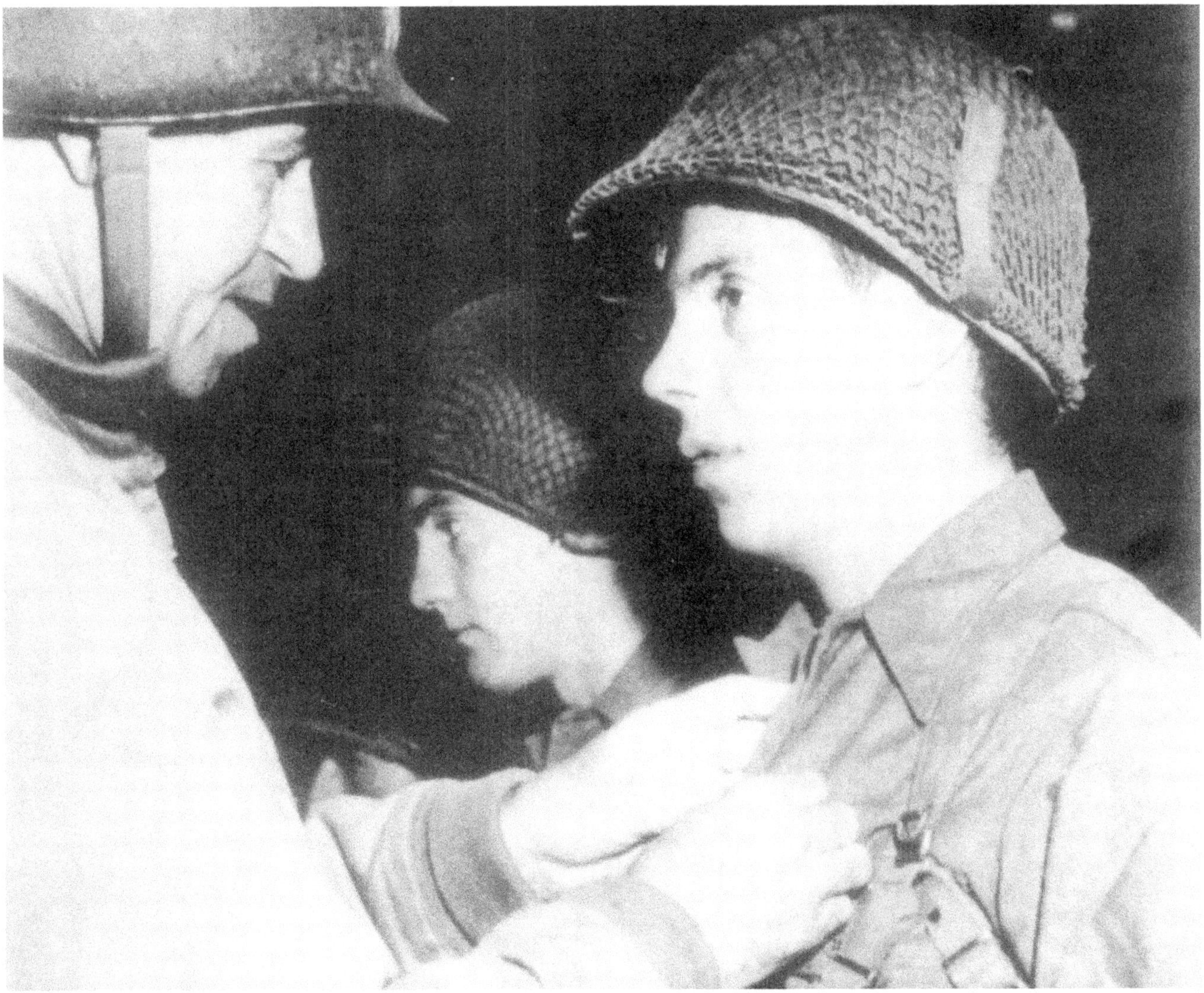

Private Marcus Heim, Jr. (right), from Buffalo, New York, receives the Distinguished Service Cross from Lieutenant General Omar Bradley during a ceremony conducted at the Chateau de Brocqueboeuf, just east of the town of La-Haye-du-Puits, France on July 10, 1944. *United States Army Signal Corps photograph.*

Technical Sergeant Gerald M. Henderson
Antitank Company, 18th Infantry Regiment, 1st Infantry Division

Citation: Technical Sergeant Gerald M. Henderson, 6292907, 18th Infantry, United States Army, for extraordinary heroism in action against the enemy on 6 June 1944, in France. On D-Day, Technical Sergeant Henderson, while exposed to intense enemy artillery, mortar, machine gun, and small arms fire, heroically supervised the unloading of men and vehicles from his landing craft. Observing that a vehicle from an adjoining craft had stalled, he voluntarily drove a truck along the fire swept beach, plunged into the water and fastened a cable to the disabled vehicle. After towing it safely to shore, he personally carried two wounded occupants to covered positions and rendered first aid. He returned to the beach and, amid bursting shells and devastating small arms fire, courageously continued his rescue work. While carrying a wounded soldier across the beach to a position of safety, a shell landed near this valiant soldier fatally wounding him. His heroic achievements during the initial landing resulted in the saving of many lives and much vital equipment. The self-sacrificing devotion to duty, personal bravery, and valorous leadership displayed by Technical Sergeant Henderson exemplified the highest traditions of the armed forces. Entered military service from Texas.

Headquarters, First Army, General Orders No. 92 (December 8, 1944)

Technical Sergeant Gerald M. Henderson, from Texarkana, Texas, was a veteran of North Africa and Sicily and had been wounded during each of those campaigns. He was mortally wounded on Omaha Beach and was later buried in the Hillcrest Cemetery in Texarkana. *Photograph courtesy of Barbara Henderson.*

Lieutenant Colonel Herbert C. Hicks, Jr.
Headquarters, 2nd Battalion, 16th Infantry Regiment, 1st Infantry Division

Citation: Lieutenant Colonel Herbert C. Hicks, 0360592, 16th Infantry, United States Army, for extraordinary heroism in action against the enemy on 6 June 1944, in France. Lieutenant Colonel Hicks, commanding one of the initial assault battalions, landed at the initial stage of the battle in the face of heavy rifle, machine gun, and artillery fire. Finding parts of the battalion leaderless and pinned down by the heavy and intense enemy fire, Lieutenant Colonel Hicks with complete disregard for his own safety moved up to the foremost elements of his unit and reorganized them for an assault on the enemy strongholds. Courageously, he led a small combat group through a breach in the wire over a thickly strewn minefield and gained the cliffsides directly under the enemy guns. Lieutenant Colonel Hicks personally assaulted and destroyed an enemy pillbox and two machine gun nests with hand grenades. Having placed the men along the cliff, Lieutenant Colonel Hicks then returned to the beach, organized the remainder of his battalion and led them off the fire swept beach to the cliff heights. From this point, he led a successful assault which gained the battalion's objective. The superior leadership and personal bravery of Lieutenant Colonel Hicks reflect great credit on himself and is in keeping with the highest traditions of the armed forces. Entered military service from South Carolina.

Headquarters, First Army, General Orders No. 31 (July 1, 1944)

The commanding officer of the 16th Infantry, Colonel George A. Taylor (left) poses with his artillery and battalion commanders; Lieutenant Colonel George W. Gibbs (second left), 7th Artillery Battalion; Lieutenant Colonel Herbert C. Hicks, Jr. (center), 2nd Battalion; Lieutenant Colonel Charles T. Horner, Jr., (second right), 3rd Battalion; and Major Edmund F. Driscoll (right), 1st Battalion. *Photograph courtesy of the First Division Museum at Cantigny.*

Major John R. Hoover
7th Reconnaissance Squadron, 8th Reconnaissance Wing, Eighth Air Force

Citation: John R. Hoover, 0732250, Major, Army Air Forces, United States Army. For extraordinary heroism in action on 6 June 1944, and from 16 June through 19 June 1944 in aerial photo reconnaissance missions over enemy held territory. On 6 June 1944, faced with low cloud formations making normal reconnaissance impossible Major Hoover elected to fly at an exceptionally low altitude in order to obtain vital photographs of enemy held territory. On 16 June 1944, he volunteered to fly the first shuttle mission to Russia, and successfully carried out his assignment in spite of hazardous weather conditions which ordinarily would have caused a pilot to return to his base. After departing from Russia, he flew to Italy and completed his flight by returning to England, bringing important photographs of installations deep in enemy territory. The courage and devotion to duty displayed by Major Hoover upon these occasions reflect highest credit upon himself and the military forces of the United States. Entered military service from Pennsylvania.

Headquarters, United States Strategic Air Forces in Europe, General Orders No. 69 (September 22, 1944)

Major John R. Hoover, from Cresson, Pennsylvania, flew aerial photo reconnaissance missions during campaigns in North Africa, Sicily, and Italy prior to the invasion of Normandy. He conducted ninety combat missions during World War II and after the war served as deputy chief of staff at the Air Force Test Center at Edwards Air Force Base, California. His awards in addition to the DSC include the Distinguished Flying Cross with one oak leaf cluster. He retired in 1969 after twenty-nine years of service. *United States Air Force photograph, www.fold3.com.*

Lieutenant Colonel Carl J. Isley
Headquarters, 146th Engineer Combat Battalion, Special Engineer Task Force, Provisional Engineer Special Brigade Group

Citation: Lieutenant Colonel Carl J. Isley, 0348085, Corps of Engineers, United States Army, for extraordinary heroism in action against the enemy on 6 June 1944, in France. Lieutenant Colonel Isley commanded a group of demolition teams for the removal of underwater obstacles. Landing with the initial assault wave, his unit was immediately met with heavy enemy rifle, machine gun, mortar, and artillery fire. Completely disregarding his own safety, Lieutenant Colonel Isley promptly reorganized his teams and though exposed to the direct enemy fire he personally supervised the placing of demolition charges on obstacles. Undaunted by the fierce enemy fire and the large number of casualties which were inflicted, Lieutenant Colonel Isley tenaciously carried on his mission of clearing a gap in the obstacles. The personal bravery, determination and aggressive leadership displayed by Lieutenant Colonel Isley reflects great credit on himself and is in keeping with the highest traditions of the armed forces. Entered military service from New York.

Headquarters, First Army, General Orders No. 37 (July 21, 1944)

Lieutenant Colonel Carl J. Isley, the commanding officer of the 146th Engineer Combat Battalion, is awarded the Distinguished Service Cross by Major General Leonard T. Gerow, commander of the V Corps. *United States Army Signal Corps photograph, National Archives.*

Major General Gerow congratulates Lieutenant Colonel Carl J. Isley, from Watkins Glen, New York, after awarding him the Distinguished Service Cross at a ceremony in France on September 11, 1944. *United States Army Signal Corps photograph, National Archives.*

Sergeant Theodore A. James
Company A, 2nd Ranger Battalion, Provisional Ranger Group

Citation: Sergeant Theodore A. James, 6938331, 2nd Ranger Infantry Battalion, United States Army, for extraordinary heroism in connection with military operations against the enemy. On 6 June 1944, during the initial landings on the beach at Vierville-sur-Mer, France, Sergeant James took command of his company when all the officers became casualties, and through his superior leadership, enabled many men to successfully cross the beach to their first objective. Here, he reorganized the company and led an assault on a heavily fortified hill to the rear of the beach. Despite being wounded severely in both hands, Sergeant James continued to direct operations and was among the first to reach the crest of the hill. Only after this objective was reached and their position secure, would Sergeant James return to the beach to receive medical treatment. His extraordinary heroism and courageous actions reflect great credit upon himself and are in keeping with the highest traditions of the military service. Entered military service from Arkansas.

Headquarters, Ninth Army, General Orders No. 27 (October 9, 1944)

Sergeant Theodore A. James (left), Private First Class Ralph Hoyt (center), and Technician Fifth Grade Richard E. Rankin (right), all veterans with Company A, 2nd Ranger Battalion, practice marksmanship with their German pistols. *Photograph courtesy of Julie Fulmer.*

Staff Sergeant Floyd M. Jenkins
Company A, 743rd Tank Battalion

Citation: Staff Sergeant Floyd M. Jenkins, 37194148, 743rd Tank Battalion, United States Army, for extraordinary heroism in action against the enemy from 6 June 1944 in France. Staff Sergeant Jenkins landed with the initial assault wave on the coast of France under intense enemy rifle, machine gun, mortar, and artillery fire. Completely disregarding his own safety he fearlessly dismounted from his tank under the heavy enemy fire and led the tanks of his platoon through the obstacles on the beach and through a minefield. When his platoon leader was killed in action Staff Sergeant Jenkins immediately assumed command and courageously led an assault against the enemy positions. In directing the fire of his tanks he completely exposed himself to the enemy fire. The personal bravery, initiative, and leadership displayed by Staff Sergeant Jenkins reflects great credit upon himself and is in keeping with the highest traditions of the armed forces.

Headquarters, First Army, General Orders No. 37 (July 21, 1944)

Next Page: Staff Sergeant Floyd M. Jenkins, Company A, 743rd Tank Battalion, shortly after being awarded the Distinguished Service Cross. *Photograph by Major Clarence Benjamin, 743rd Tank Battalion, courtesy of Joseph Keating.*

Major Milton A. Jewett

Headquarters, 299th Engineer Combat Battalion, Special Engineer Task Force, Provisional Engineer Special Brigade Group

Citation: Major Milton A. Jewett, 0-231153, 299th Engineer Combat Battalion, United States Army, for extraordinary heroism in action against the enemy on 6 June 1944, in France. Major Jewett landed with his battalion with the initial assault wave on the coast of France with the mission of clearing all of the beach obstacles. Despite intense enemy rifle, machine gun, mortar, rocket, and artillery fire, Major Jewett on landing immediately established contact with his unit and completely disregarding his own personal safety reconnoitered the beach area and directed the operations of his battalion. During this period, Major Jewett on numerous occasions exposed himself to the withering enemy fire in personally supervising the placing of charges. Under the most hazardous and difficult conditions, Major Jewett successfully organized his men in the removal and destruction of beach obstacles. By his personal bravery he set an inspiring example for his officers and men. The valor and courageous leadership displayed by Major Jewett reflect great credit on himself and is in keeping with the highest traditions of the armed forces. Entered military service from Washington.

Headquarters, First Army, General Orders No. 37 (July 21, 1944)

Major Milton A. Jewett, from Kensal, North Dakota, assumed command of the 299th Engineer Combat Battalion less than a month after its activation at Camp White, Oregon. He led it into combat on June 6, 1944 and through out the rest of the war in Europe, including a critical role in securing the first crossing of the Rhine River at Remagen. Jewett died in 1959 and is interred at Arlington National Cemetery. *Photograph courtesy of Jim Childers.*

Colonel Howard R. Johnson
Headquarters, 501st Parachute Infantry Regiment, 101st Airborne Division

Citation: Colonel Howard R. Johnson, 016673, 501st Parachute Infantry Regiment, United States Army, for extraordinary heroism in action against the enemy from 6 June 1944 to 8 June 1944, in France. Colonel Johnson was personally commanding a small group of parachute infantrymen in a bitter firefight with a large German force. Realizing that low stocks of ammunition on hand would be insufficient to engage the enemy in a prolonged battle, he made a desperate attempt to effect the surrender of the entire hostile force. Organizing a small party, he boldly led it through withering fire toward enemy lines. Moving out ahead of the party, Colonel Johnson had advanced 150 yards when the enemy fired upon him and the party, pinning them to the ground. Caught in a devastating crossfire from both friendly and enemy riflemen, he crawled back to his own lines, ceased the firing of his troops, and immediately moved toward the enemy despite continued hostile fire. Contact was effected with two German soldiers and the surrender of the entire enemy force was negotiated. As a result of his courage, perseverance, and keen strategy, approximately 350 prisoners were taken, thereby rendering an entire German infantry battalion ineffective. By his gallant leadership, bravery, and fearless devotion to duty, Colonel Johnson exemplified the highest traditions of the armed forces. Entered military service from District of Columbia.

Headquarters, First Army, General Orders No. 87 (November 27, 1944)

Colonel Howard R. Johnson, from the District of Columbia, was born in 1903. He attended the United States Naval Academy, but joined the army before graduation to become a pilot. Johnson was rejected due to poor eyesight, but remained in the army, and served in Panama, China, Fort Sill, Oklahoma and Fort Meade, Maryland. He was selected to command the newly activated 501st Parachute Infantry in November of 1942 at Camp Toccoa, Georgia. He jumped into Normandy with the 501st on June 6, 1944. The following day, Johnson and elements of the 501st destroyed Bataillon 1, Fallschirmjäger Regiment 6 near the locks at la Barquette. Johnson led his regiment in the Netherlands during Operation Market Garden, making his second combat jump. Johnson was mortally wounded by enemy shrapnel during an inspection of his regiment's positions along the Rhine River near Driel, west of Arnhem. He was buried near Nijmegen, the Netherlands, and was repatriated after the war and buried at Arlington National Cemetery. *Photograph courtesy of Michel DeTrez.*

Colonel Howard Johnson served as the commanding officer of the 501st Parachute Infantry Regiment during the invasion of Normandy. *Photograph courtesy of Michel DeTrez.*

Private First Class Aaron B. Jones
Company L, 16th Infantry Regiment, 1st Infantry Division

Citation: Private First Class Aaron B. Jones, 34357606, 16th Infantry, United States Army, for extraordinary heroism in action against the enemy on 6 June 1944, in France. On D-Day, Private First Class Jones voluntarily moved far in advance of his unit under intense enemy fire and across uncharted minefields, and placed accurate rifle fire on a hostile emplacement to cover the approach of his company. When an enemy counterattack in superior numbers threatened the unit, Private First Class Jones courageously crossed several hundred yards of open terrain alone and fired into the flanks of the hostile force. From this dangerous position, he harassed the enemy with rifle fire for a period of five hours and heroically resisted all efforts to dislodge him until the counterattack was repulsed. By his display of personal bravery and indomitable fighting spirit, Private First Class Jones acted in keeping with the highest traditions of the armed forces. Entered military service from Georgia.

Headquarters, First Army, General Orders No. 78 (November 11, 1944)

Major General J. Lawton Collins, commanding officer of the VII Corps, presents the Distinguished Service Cross to Private First Class Aaron B. Jones, from Rome, Georgia, during a ceremony on December 11, 1944, in Germany. *United States Army Signal Corps photograph, National Archives.*

First Lieutenant Henry W. Jones
Company A, 743rd Tank Battalion

Citation: First Lieutenant Henry W. Jones, 743rd Tank Battalion, United States Army, for extraordinary heroism in action against the enemy on 6 June 1944, in France. First Lieutenant Jones landed on the coast of France with the initial assault wave as a tank liaison officer with the 116th Infantry. Carrying a radio on his back, he fearlessly waded through deep water onto the beach which was being raked with enemy rifle, machine gun, mortar, and artillery fire. Rather than seek a place of cover, First Lieutenant Jones advanced in the face of this enemy fire to an exposed position from which he was able to direct the fire of the tanks. Though wounded and subjected to intense fire in his exposed position, First Lieutenant Jones, disregarding his own safety, remained at his post. His accurate direction of the tank fire reduced enemy gun positions and made possible the advance of the infantry. The valor, determination, and courage displayed by First Lieutenant Jones reflects great credit on himself and is in keeping with the highest traditions of the armed forces. Entered military service from Utah.

Headquarters, First Army, General Orders No. 37 (July 21, 1944)

First Lieutenant William J. Kehaly
Company A, 146th Engineer Combat Battalion, Special Engineer Task Force, Provisional Engineer Special Brigade Group
Gap Assault Team Number 1

Citation: First Lieutenant William J. Kehaly, 01113292, 146th Engineer Combat Battalion, United States Army, for extraordinary heroism in action against the enemy on 6 June 1944, in France. First Lieutenant Kehaly in command of a demolition team landed on the coast of France with the initial assault wave. As his boat beached it was subjected to extremely heavy enemy small arms and artillery fire. Severe casualties were inflicted on First Lieutenant Kehaly's team. Despite the intense enemy fire, First Lieutenant Kehaly, completely disregarding his own safety, promptly reorganized the remnants of his demolition team and personally led his team in the successful accomplishment of its mission of breaching a gap through the beach obstacles. Though exposed to the direct enemy fire, First Lieutenant Kehaly refused to be deterred from the completion of his mission. The valor, disregard for his own safety and determined leadership exhibited by First Lieutenant Kehaly reflects great credit upon himself and is in keeping with the highest traditions of the armed forces.

Headquarters, First Army, General Orders No. 37 (July 21, 1944)

Sergeant John J. Kelly
459th Antiaircraft Artillery (Automatic Weapons) Battalion
and the Provisional 397th Antiaircraft Artillery (Automatic Weapons) Battalion

Citation: Sergeant John J. Kelly, 6947062, Coast Artillery Corps, 459th AAA AW Battalion, United States Army, for extraordinary heroism in connection with military operations against the enemy. On 6 June 1944, upon landing at Omaha Beach, France, Sergeant Kelly saw an enemy machine gun firing into troops that were trying to get ashore. Heedless of intervening minefields, he quickly organized a party to lead against the enemy emplacement. Despite a serious hand wound he had received and with complete disregard for his own personal safety, he advanced ahead of the attacking party and hurled a hand grenade into the enemy nest, killing the entire crew. When enemy snipers directed fire against engineers who were clearing the minefields, Sergeant Kelly voluntarily and courageously led an assault which cleared the snipers from the sector. Through his inspiring example and at the risk of his own safety, he played a large part in establishing the beachhead. The extraordinary heroism and courageous actions of Sergeant Kelly reflect great credit upon himself and are in keeping with the highest traditions of the military service. Entered military service from Pennsylvania.

Headquarters, Ninth Army, General Orders No. 5 (January 6, 1945)

Major General Raymond S. McLain awards the Distinguished Service Cross to Sergeant John J. Kelly, from Philadelphia, Pennsylvania, on January 16, 1944. *United States Army Signal Corps photograph, National Archives.*

Second Lieutenant George F. Kerchner
Company D, 2nd Ranger Battalion, Provisional Ranger Group

Citation: Second Lieutenant George F. Kerchner, 0-13099569, Infantry, United States Army, for extraordinary heroism in action on 6 June 1944 at Pointe du Hoc, France. When the company commander and other company officers became casualties from the heavy enemy rifle, machine gun, and artillery fire upon landing on the coast of France, Lieutenant Kerchner assumed command of the company. By his determined leadership and outstanding heroism he led the company in the successful assault upon and captured the 155mm gun positions. While engaged in this operation, Lieutenant Kerchner and fifteen members of his organization were surrounded and cut off from the main body for two and a half days. He tenaciously and courageously held his position until relieved and was a constant inspiration and source of encouragement to his troops. The outstanding heroism displayed by Lieutenant Kerchner during the initial assault and subsequent operations are worthy of the highest traditions of the military service. Entered military service from Maryland.

Headquarters, First Army, General Orders No. 28 (June 20, 1944)

Lieutenant Colonel James E. Rudder (left), the commander of the Provisional Ranger Group and the 2nd Ranger Battalion, congratulates Lieutenant George F. Kerchner (right), Company D, 2nd Ranger Battalion, from Baltimore, Maryland, on the award of the Distinguished Service Cross at a ceremony near Colombieres, France on June 23, 1944. *United States Army Signal Corps photograph, National Archives.*

Private Kenneth P. Kidwell
Company A, 81st Chemical Battalion (Motorized)

Citation: Private Kenneth P. Kidwell, 35457322, Chemical Warfare Service, United States Army, for extraordinary heroism in action against the enemy on 6 June 1944, in France. Immediately upon leaving his landing craft, Private Kidwell was wounded in the right foot. However, he refused to become a casualty and would not allow himself to be evacuated. Despite the intense and accurate enemy fire, Private Kidwell placed his duty of rendering first aid to the wounded above all else and made numerous trips across the fire swept beach to administer aid, not only to those men of his own unit, but to all men who were in the immediate vicinity. The outstanding heroism and complete devotion to duty displayed by Private Kidwell reflects great credit on himself and is in keeping with the highest traditions of the Armed Forces. Entered military service from Ohio.

Headquarters, First Army, General Orders No. 37 (July 21, 1944)

Second Lieutenant Gustav D. Kjosness
572nd Bombardment Squadron, 391st Bombardment Group, 99th Bombardment Wing, Ninth Air Force

Citation: Gustav D. Kjosness, 0-6713272, Second Lieutenant, Army Air Forces, United States Army. For extraordinary heroism in action against the enemy, 6 June and 8 June 1944. On 6 June 1944 Lieutenant Kjosness was bombardier on a B-26 airplane on a mission over the Cherbourg Peninsula. Shortly after crossing the enemy coast Lieutenant Kjosness was hit and rendered unconscious by a shell fragment. Regaining consciousness just before reaching the target, he assumed his post and dropped the bomb load with devastating effect. Although he had not fully recovered from this wound, Lieutenant Kjosness on 8 June asked to fly as bombardier on another extremely hazardous mission. At the moment the bombs were released on the target he was hit and mortally wounded by a large shell fragment. Upon hearing the command to close the bomb bay doors, knowing that unless the doors were closed the airplane would probably fall out of formation and be a target for enemy fighters, he used the last of his fast ebbing strength to obey the pilot's orders, and died with his mangled left hand still clutching the bomb bay lever. The heroism and devotion to duty displayed by Lieutenant Kjosness was inspiring to his fellow fliers, reflecting the highest traditions of the armed forces of the United States.

Headquarters, United States Strategic Air Forces in Europe, General Orders No. 43 (July 13, 1944)

Lieutenant Gustav D. "Don" Kjosness, served with the 572nd Bombardment Squadron of the 391st Bombardment Group, 99th Bombardment Wing, Ninth Air Force and was wounded during recovered from his wound, requested to fly a mission on June 8, and was killed by flak. *Photograph courtesy of Jim Roberts.*

Lieutenant Colonel Edward C. Krause
Headquarters, 3rd Battalion, 505th Parachute Infantry Regiment, 82nd Airborne Division

Citation: Lieutenant Colonel Edward C. Krause, 0-375296, 505th Parachute Infantry, United States Army, for extraordinary heroism in action against the enemy on 6 and 7 June 1944, in France. Lieutenant Colonel Krause shortly after landing on D-Day assembled a composite group of parachutists and led a night assault on the town of Ste.-Mère-Église and successfully destroyed the immediate enemy resistance. However, the enemy immediately counterattacked with numerically superior numbers supported by tanks and artillery. In these early counterattacks, Lieutenant Colonel Krause, continually disregarding his own safety, moved from point to point directing the defense. He later received a severe wound in the leg, but again insisted on remaining with his troops and continued to direct the defense through his subordinate officers. The inspiring courage, dauntlessness, and outstanding leadership displayed by Lieutenant Colonel Krause reflects great credit on himself and is in keeping with the highest traditions of the armed forces. Entered military service from Wisconsin.

Headquarters, First Army, General Orders No. 31 (July 1, 1944)

Lieutenant General Omar Bradley (right), awards the Distinguished Service Cross to Lieutenant Colonel Edward C. Krause (second from left) at a ceremony at the Chateau de Brocqueboeuf, just east of the town of La-Haye-du-Puits, France on July 10, 1944. Lieutenant Colonel Benjamin H. Vandervoort (center), also a recipient of the DSC for heroism on June 6, is at Krause's left. *United States Army Signal Corps photograph.*

Next Page: Lieutenant Colonel Edward C. "Cannonball" Krause, from Neenah, Wisconsin, was the commanding officer of the 3rd Battalion, 505th Parachute Infantry Regiment on D-Day. Krause and his veteran paratroopers liberated Ste.-Mère-Église, the first town in France, during the predawn hours of June 6, 1944. The town lay astride the main avenues of attack from the north and west for German forces counterattacking the Utah Beach landings. The 505th repulsed attacks of two regimental sized kampfgruppen of Luftlande Division 91 and held the town until the 4th Infantry Division linked up with it on the afternoon of June 7, 1944. This photograph was taken during the defense of Ste.-Mère-Église. *Photograph courtesy of Michel DeTrez.*

First Lieutenant Joseph R. Lacy
Headquarters Company, 5th Ranger Battalion, Provisional Ranger Group

Citation: First Lieutenant Joseph R. Lacy, 0525094, Chaplain Corps, United States Army, for extraordinary heroism in action on 6 June 1944 at Vierville-sur-Mer, France. In the invasion of France, Chaplain Lacy landed on the beach with one of the leading assault units. Numerous casualties had been inflicted by the heavy rifle, mortar, artillery, and rocket fire of the enemy. With complete disregard for his own safety, he moved about the beach, continually exposed to enemy fire, and assisted wounded men from the water's edge to the comparative safety of a nearby seawall, and at the same time inspired the men to a similar disregard for the enemy fire. Chaplain Lacy's heroic and dauntless action is in keeping with the highest traditions of the service. Entered military service from Connecticut.

Headquarters, First Army, General Orders No. 28 (June 20, 1944)

Lieutenant Colonel James E. Rudder (left), commanding officer of the Provisional Ranger Group, congratulates Lieutenant Joseph R. Lacy (right), chaplain of the 5th Ranger Battalion, on the award of the Distinguished Service Cross at a ceremony near Colombieres, France on June 23, 1944. Lacy was from Boston, Massachusetts. *United States Army Signal Corps photograph, National Archives.*

First Lieutenant Raymond E. Lanterman
Company C, 146th Engineer Combat Battalion, Special Engineer Task Force, Provisional Engineer Special Brigade Group
Gap Assault Team Number 9

Citation: First Lieutenant Raymond E. Lanterman, 01110604, Corps of Engineers, United States Army, for extraordinary heroism in action against the enemy on 6 June 1944, in France. First Lieutenant Lanterman, commanding a demolition team, landed on the coast of France with the initial assault troops under heavy enemy rifle, machine gun and artillery fire. He directed the members of his team in the clearing of the gap through mined obstacles. Though First Lieutenant Lanterman was twice wounded, he refused to be evacuated and continued to direct the activities of his team until the initial task was completed. The gallantry, devotion to duty, and courageous leadership displayed by First Lieutenant Lanterman reflect great credit on himself and is in keeping with the highest traditions of the armed forces. Entered military service from Indiana.

Headquarters, First Army, General Orders No. 37 (July 21, 1944)

Raymond E. Lanterman was from Kokomo, Indiana and was a graduate of the Chicago Academy of Fine Arts prior to his enlistment in the army in 1940. He was at the Schofield Barracks in Oahu, Hawaii during the attack on Pearl Harbor. Lanterman was wounded on Omaha Beach. After recovering, he was medically discharged and returned to Hawaii where he worked as a commercial artist and illustrator and lived the remainder of his life. *Photograph courtesy of Colonel Melvin L. Turner (USAF retired) and the Lanterman family.*

Captain Frank L. Lillyman

Company I, 502nd Parachute Infantry Regiment, 101st Airborne Division and 101st Provisional Pathfinder Company

Citation: Captain Frank L. Lillyman, 0368010, Parachute Infantry, United States Army, for extraordinary heroism in action against the enemy on 6 June 1944, in France. Riding in the leading plane of the pathfinder element, Captain Lillyman was one of the first Allied soldiers to make a parachute jump in the airborne assault on the Cotentin peninsula. Although under incessant enemy fire from the time he landed, Captain Lillyman assembled his pathfinder group, located the drop zones and directed the setting up and operation of homing devices for the guiding of the following waves of parachute troop planes to the correct drop zones. When attacked by the enemy forces Captain Lillyman led his men in the successful defense of this vital area and provided cover for the landing of the follow up wave of parachute troops. The courageous leadership displayed by Captain Lillyman reflects great credit on himself and is in keeping with the highest traditions of the armed forces. Entered military service from New York.

Headquarters, First Army, General Orders No. 31 (July 1, 1944)

Private John A. Lockwood

Company D, 508th Parachute Infantry Regiment, 82nd Airborne Division

Citation: Private John A. Lockwood, 32864423, 508th Parachute Infantry, United States Army, for extraordinary heroism in action against the enemy on 6 June 1944, in France. After landing by parachute before dawn on D-Day and joining a composite group which proceeded to carry out a battalion mission, Private Lockwood and two comrades served as an outpost in a building on the edge of Gueutteville. When a battalion of German infantry, reinforced by tanks, approached from the west and placed machine guns and mortars in position, those three valiant men immediately opened fire on the enemy. Ordered to leave the post, they determined to hold out until the thirty men in the town had withdrawn. Private Lockwood assisted in holding the hostile force at bay for two hours, killing fifteen Germans and wounding many others. His voluntary and courageous action delayed the enemy sufficiently to permit the main body of parachute troops to establish defensive positions to the east from which they were able to deny overwhelming German forces the opportunity of crossing the Merderet River. Private Lockwood is missing as a result of this action. His superb heroism and unselfish devotion to duty exemplifies the highest traditions of the United States Army. Entered service from New York.

Headquarters, First Army, General Orders No. 61 (September 25, 1944)

Next Page: Captain Frank L. Lillyman, from Binghamton, New York, commanded the 101st Airborne Provisional Pathfinder Company on D-Day and was one of the first soldiers to land in Normandy. Prior to America's entry into the war, Lillyman had been an enlisted man, rising to the rank of first sergeant before attending officer candidate school in 1941. He volunteered for the airborne in 1942 and continued his military career after the war, rising to the rank of lieutenant colonel.

First Sergeant Leonard G. Lomell
Company D, 2nd Ranger Battalion, Provisional Ranger Group

Citation: First Sergeant Leonard G. Lomell, 32269677, Infantry, United States Army, for extraordinary heroism in action on 6 June 1944 at Pointe du Hoc, France. First Sergeant Lomell led a patrol of men through the heaviest kind of automatic weapons fire to destroy an enemy machine gun nest. Later on the same day while leading another patrol, he penetrated through the enemy lines to the rear and discovered five enemy 155mm guns which were shelling the beachhead. Though these guns were well guarded, nevertheless he gallantly led his patrol against the enemy and successfully destroyed the guns as well as the ammunition supply. First Sergeant Lomell's bold and outstanding leadership in the face of superior numbers is in keeping with the highest traditions of the service. Entered military service from New Jersey.

Headquarters, First Army, General Orders No. 28 (June 20, 1944)

First Sergeant Leonard G. Lomell, from Point Pleasant, New Jersey, served with Company D, 2nd Ranger Battalion on June 6, 1944. Lomell later received a battlefield commission and promotion to the rank of lieutenant. After the war, he became an attorney, founding a law firm. He also worked as a vice president and bank director and served in civic, social, and educational organizations.

First Sergeant Herman J. Lorenz
459th Antiaircraft Artillery (Automatic Weapons) Battalion
and the Provisional 397th Antiaircraft Artillery (Automatic Weapons) Battalion

Citation: First Sergeant Herman J. Lorenz (Army Serial No. 6860794), Coast Artillery Corps, United States Army, for extraordinary heroism in connection with military operations against an armed enemy on 6 June 1944. Upon landing on Omaha Beach, on the French coast, First Sergeant Lorenz noticed many men of his battery in danger of enemy fire as they huddled behind disabled tanks near the water's edge. When they failed to obey his instructions to charge forward to the beach, he left cover, returned to the wrecked vehicles, and by his superb leadership, succeeded in getting most of the men to safety. Ignoring his serious wounds, he proved such a magnificent example to his men in assuming the responsibilities of his battery commander, who had been killed, that in a short time the battery was in position. Entered service from North Dakota.

Headquarters, Communications Zone, European Theater of Operations, General Orders No. 39 (March 25, 1945)

Brigadier General E. F. Koenig, the commander of the Normandy Base Section, presents the Distinguished Service Cross to Lieutenant Herman J. Lorenz, from Cockrane, Wisconsin, on June 19, 1945 at a ceremony conducted at the Normandy Base Section in France. *United States Army Signal photograph, National Archives.*

Sergeant Worden F. Lovell
165th Signal Photographic Company

Citation: Sergeant Worden F. Lovell, 11050584, 165th Signal Photographic Company, United States Army, for extraordinary heroism in action against the enemy on 6 June 1944, in France. Sergeant Lovell, in an attempt to obtain photographs of an attack, courageously moved forward with an assault group. During an enemy artillery concentration, his camera was knocked from his hands and damaged. Moving forward, the squad encountered intense hostile machine gun fire. Sergeant Lovell secured the rifle and hand grenades of a casualty and, with complete disregard for his own safety, voluntarily charged the enemy emplacement. Upon reaching the position, he threw several of the grenades and successfully silenced the weapon. By his courage, personal bravery and devotion to duty, Sergeant exemplified the highest traditions of the armed forces. Entered military service from Massachusetts.

Headquarters, First Army, General Orders No. 92 (December 8, 1944)

Major General J. Lawton Collins (left), the commanding officer of VII Corps, talks with Sergeant Worden F. Lovell (right), from Boston, Massachusetts, after he awarded him the Distinguished Service Cross on December 17, 1944 at Kornelimünster, Germany. *United States Army Signal Corps photograph, National Archives.*

Captain George L. Mabry, Jr.
Headquarters, 2nd Battalion, 8th Infantry Regiment, 4th Infantry Division

Citation: Captain George L. Mabry, Jr., 0390036, 8th Infantry, United States Army, for extraordinary heroism in action against the enemy on 6 June 1944, in France. When Captain Mabry, the battalion S-3, observed that heavy enemy fire from the right flank had pinned down his battalion, he moved to the forward elements. There he organized a group of men and personally led them in a successful assault upon the enemy position. Despite the intense enemy fire and without regard to his own safety he at all times was in the forefront of the firefight, personally killing two of the enemy in hand to hand combat and capturing eighteen of the enemy. The personal bravery, initiative, and courageous leadership displayed by Captain Mabry reflects great credit on himself and was in keeping with the highest traditions of the armed forces.

Headquarters, First Army, General Orders No. 32 (July 12, 1944)

Captain George L. Mabry, Jr., from Sumter, South Carolina, graduated from Presbyterian College in Clinton, South Carolina in 1940. He was the S-3 (plans and operations) officer of the 2nd Battalion, 8th Infantry Regiment, 4th Infantry Division on June 6, 1944. He later commanded the 2nd Battalion and was awarded the Medal of Honor for heroism during the fighting in the Hürtgen Forest. Mabry rose to the rank of major general after the war. *United States Army photograph.*

First Lieutenant Howard P. MacConchie
Headquarters Company, 18th Infantry Regiment, 1st Infantry Division

Citation: First Lieutenant Howard P. MacConchie, 0885722, 18th Infantry, United States Army, for extraordinary heroism in action against the enemy on 6 June 1944, in France. Voluntarily assuming command on D-Day of a leaderless and completely disorganized group of men, First Lieutenant MacConchie immediately established a firing line of company strength in a desperate attempt to neutralize the enemy's devastating small arms and machine gun fire and to minimize casualties. Despite heavy artillery and mortar concentrations, he courageously moved up and down the beach directing the fire and encouraging the men. With great courage, he crawled alone along the beach gathering discarded explosives, blew a gap in a wire entanglement and heroically led the men forward to regain contact with other assaulting elements. Returning to the fire swept beach, he awaited the arrival of his own unit and directed elements to areas subjected to light resistance. By his extraordinary heroism, superb leadership and unflinching devotion to duty, First Lieutenant MacConchie exemplified the highest traditions of the armed forces. Entered military service from New Jersey.

Headquarters, First Army, General Orders No. 99 (December 17, 1944)

Major General Clarence R. Huebner, the commanding officer of the V Corps, awards the Distinguished Service Cross to Lieutenant Howard P. MacConchie, from Newark, New Jersey, at First Army headquarters at Sourbrodt, Belgium on January 23, 1945. MacConchie was the platoon leader of the 18th Infantry Regiment's Intelligence and Reconnaissance Platoon on D-Day. *United States Army Signal Corps photograph, National Archives.*

Lieutenant Colonel Carlton O. MacNeely
Headquarters, 2nd Battalion, 8th Infantry Regiment, 4th Infantry Division

Citation: Lieutenant Colonel Carlton O. MacNeely, 0262343, Infantry, United States Army, for extraordinary heroism in action against the enemy on 6 June 1944, in France. Lieutenant Colonel MacNeely landed on the beach in the invasion of the coast of France with the first elements of his battalion. Immediately upon reaching the beach the battalion was met by heavy enemy automatic weapons and artillery fire from fixed emplacements in the sand dunes and along the seawall. With complete disregard for his own safety, Lieutenant Colonel MacNeely reconnoitered the beach and ascertained his position. Coordinating the fire of all arms he personally led his battalion through the intense enemy fire and through the minefields. He exposed himself on numerous occasions in directing the successful assault on the enemy beach positions. With unceasing energy he then fearlessly led his men through the inundated area under enemy small arms and artillery fire and quickly secured the commanding terrain, thereby contributing materially to the security of the beachhead. The courage and outstanding leadership displayed by Lieutenant Colonel MacNeely reflects great credit on himself and was in keeping with the highest traditions of the armed forces.

Headquarters, First Army, General Orders No. 32 (July 12, 1944)

The commanding officer and staff of the 8th Infantry Regiment, 4th Infantry Division, three of whom were awarded the Distinguished Service Cross for heroism on June 6, 1944. Those recipients are Colonel James A. Van Fleet (sitting second from left), commanding officer of the regiment; Lieutenant Colonel Fred A. Steiner (sitting third from left), regimental executive officer; and Lieutenant Colonel Carlton O. MacNeely (standing middle), commanding officer of the 2nd Battalion. *United States Army photograph.*

Captain John S. Maloney
Service Company, 506th Parachute Infantry Regiment, 101st Airborne Division

Citation: Captain John S. Maloney, 0428979, Chaplain Corps, United States Army, for extraordinary heroism in action in France. Captain Maloney, completely disregarding his own personal safety, he assisted medical aid men in administering first aid to the wounded in intense enemy machine gun fire. He further assisted in their evacuation under continuous mortar fire. Captain Maloney's fortitude, initiative, and courage reflect great credit to himself and is in keeping with the highest traditions of the armed forces. Entered military service from New York.

Headquarters, First Army, General Orders No. 31 (July 1, 1944)

Captain John S. Maloney, from Elmira, New York, was the 506th Parachute Infantry Regiment's Catholic chaplain. Maloney graduated from St. Bernard's Seminary and was ordained June 6, 1936. He was commissioned in the army on December 23, 1941 and after attending the Chaplain's School at Fort Benjamin Harrison, Indiana, was assigned to the 506th Parachute Infantry at Camp Toccoa, Georgia in September 1942. Maloney continued to serve in the ministry after the war, living in Ithaca, New York.

Captain Otto Masny
Company F, 2nd Ranger Battalion, Provisional Ranger Group

Citation: Captain Otto (NMI) Masny, 01283639, Infantry, United States Army, for extraordinary heroism in action on 6 June 1944 at Pointe du Hoc, France. Captain Masny led his company in the face of heavy enemy fire on to the beach at H-Hour on D-Day. Although wounded in this initial landing, he refused to be evacuated and remained with his company on the narrow and insecure beachhead. Captain Masny's action was an example to his men and inspired them to put down three enemy counterattacks. A few days later, still refusing to be evacuated, he voluntarily, despite continuous enemy machine gun fire, led a patrol which destroyed an enemy ammunition dump. Captain Masny's courage and outstanding devotion to duty are in keeping with the highest traditions of the service. Entered military service from Illinois.

Headquarters, First Army, General Orders No. 28 (June 20, 1944)

This photo of Captain Otto Masny, the commanding officer of Company F, 2nd Ranger Battalion, was taken at Fort Dix, New Jersey in 1943. Captain Masny was from Arlington Heights, Illinois. *United States Army photograph, courtesy of Lynn Towne.*

Lieutenant Colonel James E. Rudder (left), commander of the Provisional Ranger Group, congratulates Captain Otto Masny (right), the commanding officer of Company F, 2nd Ranger Battalion, on the award of the Distinguished Service Cross at a ceremony near Colombieres, France on June 23, 1944. *United States Army Signal Corps photograph, National Archives.*

Second Lieutenant Atwood M. McElyea
Company A, 16th Infantry Regiment, 1st Infantry Division

Citation: Second Lieutenant Atwood M. McElyea, 02046692, 16th Infantry, United States Army, for extraordinary heroism in action against the enemy on 6 June 1944, in France. On D-Day, Second Lieutenant McElyea courageously moved across the fire swept invasion beach, located a breach in a barbed wire fence and personally led his troops through the gap. Upon reaching a deep, booby-trapped antitank ditch, he plunged into it unhesitatingly and cleared it of antipersonnel obstacles before leading his men across. When his company was pinned down a short time later by a heavy artillery concentration and intense machine gun fire from a well emplaced machine gun, Second Lieutenant McElyea, undaunted and with great personal valor, crept several hundred yards toward the weapon. Fearlessly, he engaged it singlehandedly to divert its fire, thus permitting his men to advance safely into position on the enemy's flank. When he attempted to rejoin his men to lead an assault on the position, he was severely injured by a burst of machine gun fire. By his fearless leadership, heroic achievement and unflinching devotion to duty, Second Lieutenant McElyea acted in keeping with the highest traditions of the armed forces. Entered military service from Connecticut.

Headquarters, First Army, General Orders No. 82 (November 19, 1944)

Lieutenant Atwood M. McElyea, from Knoxville, Tennessee, was wounded during combat in Tunisia, Sicily, and on Omaha Beach. In addition to the DSC, his awards included the Silver Star with an oak leaf cluster for heroism in Tunisia and Sicily and the Purple Heart medal with three oak leaf clusters. *Photograph courtesy of Barbara L. Scholar.*

Captain Tildon S. McGee
Service Company, 506th Parachute Infantry Regiment, 101st Airborne Division

Citation: Chaplain (Captain) Tildon S. McGee (Army Serial No. 0163836) United States Army, for extraordinary heroism in action during the period 6 June to 10 June 1944, near Brévands, France. Chaplain McGee, landing by parachute, made his way under heavy enemy fire to the initial objective of his unit. There he found a very small force being subjected to heavy mortar and machine gun fire, without benefit of medical aid. Chaplain McGee, with complete disregard for his own safety, evacuated approximately forty wounded men to an improvised aid station. While under direct enemy artillery fire, he rendered first aid, fed, and ministered to the needs of the wounded in his care until relieved four days later. Later, while Chaplain McGee was evacuating a wounded soldier, his unit was erroneously subjected to a bombing and strafing attack by friendly aircraft. During the actual air attack, Chaplain McGee, with complete disregard for his own safety, jumped on a high wall in the face of heavy small arms and aircraft fire, and waved a recognition flag to identify his troops to the attacking aircraft. His actions were above and beyond the normal call of duty and the outstanding courage displayed by Chaplain McGee reflects great credit upon himself, and were in keeping with the highest traditions of the armed forces. Entered military service from Mississippi.

Headquarters, European Theater of Operations, United States Army, General Orders No. 108 (October 28, 1944)

Captain Tildon S. McGee was the Protestant chaplain of the 506th Parachute Infantry Regiment. When the United States entered World War II, McGee waived ministerial exemption from the draft and enlisted as a private at Camp Shelby, Mississippi. He was eventually convinced to accept a commission and after volunteering for parachute training was assigned to the 506th Parachute Infantry Regiment, which was then undergoing training at Camp Toccoa, Georgia in September of 1942. *Photograph courtesy of Stuart Tribble.*

Private Donald B. McLaren
Company D, 81st Chemical Battalion (Motorized)

Citation: Private Donald B. McLaren, 34403080, 81st Chemical Battalion, United States Army, for extraordinary heroism in action against the enemy on 6 June 1944, in France. As Private McLaren's craft hit the beach it came under the direct machine gun fire of the enemy. Private McLaren, though seriously wounded in the hips at the time, refused to be evacuated. Though painfully wounded, he nevertheless made several trips across the beach under intense enemy machine gun and mortar fire aiding in the removal of the mortars and ammunition from the landing craft to the shore. Only when the guns were finally in position to fire did Private McLaren permit himself to be evacuated. Private McLaren's outstanding bravery, self sacrifice, and devotion to duty reflect great credit upon himself and is in keeping with the highest traditions of the armed forces.

Headquarters, First Army, General Orders No. 37 (July 21, 1944)

Brigadier General Fenton S. Jacobs, commander of the Channel Base Section, awards the Distinguished Service Cross to Private First Class Donald B. McLaren, from Miami, Florida, during a formal ceremony on February 21, 1945, at Lille, France. *United States Army Signal Corps photograph, National Archives.*

Lieutenant Colonel Louis G. Mendez, Jr.
Headquarters, 3rd Battalion, 508th Parachute Infantry Regiment, 82nd Airborne Division

Citation: Lieutenant Colonel Louis G. Mendez, Jr., (Army Serial Number O23262), Infantry, United States Army, for extraordinary heroism in combat during the period 6 June 1944 to 7 July 1944, while commanding a battalion of a parachute infantry regiment. One instance of particular note was on 20 June 1944, near Prétot, France, when Lieutenant Colonel Mendez personally led an assault on the town of Prétot through a withering concentration of observed mortar, timed artillery and machine gun crossfire. In their first attempt to win their objective, the two assault companies were pinned to the ground by a devastating artillery barrage and suffered heavy casualties. Appreciating the danger of delay, Lieutenant Colonel Mendez crawled to a position in front of his men, leaped to his feet and led the charge which drove the enemy out of the town. By his calm disregard for personal danger and his ability to act quickly and aggressively under fire, he turned imminent catastrophe into a victory. Lieutenant Colonel Mendez's courage, calmness, judgment and devotion to duty were directly responsible for the achievement of his battalion's objective and were in keeping with the highest traditions of our armed forces. Entered military service from Colorado.

Headquarters, European Theater of Operations, United States Army, General Orders No. 79 (August 8, 1944)

Lieutenant Colonel Louis G. Mendez, Jr., from Trinidad, Colorado, graduated from the United States Military Academy in 1940. He was the commanding officer of the 3rd Battalion, 508th Parachute Infantry Regiment throughout combat in Europe. Mendez continued his military career after the war, which included serving as military attaché to Spain and later with the War Histories Division of the army General Staff. *United States Army photograph.*

Captain Thomas N. Merendino
Company B, 16th Infantry Regiment, 1st Infantry Division

Citation: Captain Thomas N. Merendino, 0412675, 16th Infantry, United States Army, for extraordinary heroism in action against the enemy on 6 June 1944, in France. Captain Merendino disembarked from the landing craft in the initial assault wave and with complete disregard for his own safety, hastily organized the men who were struggling in the water and led them through the intense enemy fire to the shore. Upon reaching the shore, he refused to take cover and again organized an assault group for further advance. Fully exposed to the sweeping fire from enemy pillboxes and machine gun nests and a constant target for snipers on the hill, he personally led the charge up the slope. The personal bravery and the inspired leadership exhibited by Captain Merendino reflects great credit on himself and is in keeping with the highest traditions of the armed forces. Entered military service from New Jersey.

Headquarters, First Army, General Orders No. 31 (July 1, 1944)

Captain Thomas N. Merendino, from Atlantic City, New Jersey, was a graduate of the Pennsylvania Military College. He was awarded a Silver Star for heroism during the North African campaign and commanded Company B, 16th Infantry on June 6, 1944. *Photograph courtesy of the First Division Museum at Cantigny.*

Lieutenant Colonel Raymond D. Millener
Headquarters, 101st Airborne Division

Citation: Lieutenant Colonel Raymond D. Millener, 018140, General Staff Corps, United States Army, for extraordinary heroism in action against the enemy on 6 June 1944, in France. Lieutenant Colonel Millener and his men were dropped fifteen miles from the appointed drop zone. He assembled all the forces in the immediate vicinity and started toward the designated assembly area to join the main force. En route, the party encountered heavy enemy resistance. Despite the intense enemy fire, Lieutenant Colonel Millener repeatedly exposed himself in leading his men. Inspired by Lieutenant Colonel Millener's personal bravery and leadership, his small force successfully assaulted two machine gun positions and destroyed two enemy tanks and two enemy halftrack vehicles. The gallantry and superior leadership displayed by Lieutenant Colonel Millener reflects great credit on himself and is in keeping with the highest traditions of the armed forces. Entered military service from Pennsylvania.

Headquarters, First Army, General Orders No. 31 (July 1, 1944)

General Dwight D. Eisenhower awards the Distinguished Service Cross to Colonel Raymond D. Millener, from Williamsport, Pennsylvania, during a ceremony at Hungerford Common, England on August 10, 1944. Millener graduated from the United States Military Academy in 1930 and served as the G-3 (plans and operations) officer for the 101st Airborne Division during the Normandy invasion. He was later promoted to colonel and served as the division's chief of staff. He tragically took his life on December 7, 1944, while the division was at Camp Mourmelon, France after the Holland campaign. *United States Army Signal Corps photograph, National Archives.*

Private First Class George Montilio
Company H, 506th Parachute Infantry Regiment, 101st Airborne Division

Citation: Corporal George Montilio, 11089193 (then Private First Class), Parachute Infantry, United States Army, for extraordinary heroism in action against the enemy on 6 June 1944, in France. As a volunteer scout, Corporal Montilio carried out an assault on a footbridge under intense machine gun and small arms fire. Though the bridge was held by a superior number of the enemy, his daring and aggressiveness forced them to withdraw and thereby permitted his unit to organize and hold their objective. The personal bravery and initiative displayed by Corporal Montilio reflects great credit on himself and is in keeping with the armed forces. Entered military service from Massachusetts.

Headquarters, First Army, General Orders No. 31 (July 1, 1944)

Private First Class George Montilio was from Quincy, Massachusetts and worked at the Fore River Shipyard prior to America's entry into the war. He was promoted to the rank of corporal and then sergeant subsequent to the award of the DSC. Montilio continued to serve with Company H, 506th Parachute Infantry until his death from an accidental shooting by another trooper on April 17, 1945. *Photograph courtesy of Joseph Montilio.*

First Lieutenant William D. Moody
Company C, 2nd Ranger Battalion, Provisional Ranger Group

Citation: First Lieutenant William D. Moody, 01300357, 2nd Ranger Infantry Battalion, United States Army, for extraordinary heroism in action against the enemy on 6 June 1944, in France. On D-Day, First Lieutenant Moody led his platoon in the face of heavy and intense enemy fire across the beach to the comparative safety of the cliffs overlooking the beach. He then climbed the cliffs and secured ropes to the top for the ascent of the remainder of his platoon. Without waiting for his men to reach the top, First Lieutenant Moody valiantly moved to attack and clear the enemy out of his trenches in this vicinity. He was advancing upon an enemy position when he was killed by a sniper. The extraordinary heroism and courageous leadership displayed by First Lieutenant Moody were an inspiration to the men of his platoon and are in keeping with the highest traditions of the armed forces. Entered military service from Tennessee.

Headquarters, First Army, General Orders No. 70 (October 17, 1944)

Lieutenant William D. Moody, from Sullivan County, Tennessee, served with Company C, 2nd Ranger Battalion. This photograph was taken at Fort Dix, New Jersey in 1943. Moody was killed in action on June 6, 1944 and was buried at the National Cemetery at Knoxville, Tennessee. *United States Army photograph, courtesy of Lynn Towne.*

Second Lieutenant Verne V. Morse
Company D, 116th Infantry Regiment, 29th Infantry Division

Citation: First Lieutenant Verne V. Morse, 01292044 (then Second Lieutenant), 116th Infantry, United States Army, for extraordinary heroism in action against the enemy on 6 June 1944, in France. In the initial assault upon the coast of France, First Lieutenant Morse landed with his platoon in the face of heavy enemy rifle, machine gun and artillery fire. This intense fire pinned the men down on a narrow beachhead, inflicting numerous casualties with resultant disorganization. In the reorganization and preparation of his platoon for attack, First Lieutenant Morse fearlessly and with complete disregard for his own safety, on numerous occasions exposed himself to the direct enemy fire. He then led his platoon in a successful assault upon the enemy positions. The personal bravery and superior leadership demonstrated by First Lieutenant Morse reflects great credit on himself and were in keeping with the highest traditions of the armed forces.

Headquarters, First Army, General Orders No. 29 (June 29, 1944)

Lieutenant Verne V. Morse, from Jefferson County, Pennsylvania, served with Company D of the 116th Infantry Regiment. He was wounded near the war's end and died on June 5, 1945. Lieutenant Morse is buried at the United States military cemetery near Margraten in the Netherlands. *Photograph courtesy of Joseph Balkoski.*

Second Lieutenant Marvin F. Muir
93rd Troop Carrier Squadron, 439th Troop Carrier Group, 50th Troop Carrier Wing, Ninth Air Force

Citation: Marvin F. Muir, 0-541641, Second Lieutenant, Army Air Forces, United States Army. (Missing in action). For extraordinary heroism in action while serving as lead pilot in a wing element of C-47 type aircraft, participating in a paradrop mission behind enemy lines, immediately prior to the land invasion of the continent of Europe, 6 June 1944. After his ship was mortally hit by enemy ground fire it burst into flames while at an altitude of only 750 feet and 2½ minutes from the drop zone. Although forced to leave formation, he courageously stuck to his post and battled the controls in order that he might effectively accomplish his mission and properly accomplish the evacuation of his paratroopers in the assigned dropping zone. After evacuation of the paratroopers, he continued in an attempt to crash land the flaming aircraft in order by chance to save his crew members trapped inside. The devotion to duty, heroism, and service above self displayed by Lieutenant Muir on this occasion reflect great credit upon himself and the armed forces of the United States. Entered military service from Indiana.

Headquarters, United States Strategic Air Forces in Europe, General Orders No. 58 (August 30, 1944)

Lieutenant Colonel Thornton L. Mullins
Headquarters, 111th Field Artillery Battalion, 29th Infantry Division

Citation: Lieutenant Colonel Thornton L. Mullins, 0299488, 111th Field Artillery Battalion, United States Army, for extraordinary heroism in action against the enemy on 6 June 1944, in France. Lieutenant Colonel Mullins landed on the coast of France with the initial assault wave under intense enemy small arms, machine gun, mortar, and 88mm fire. The infantry was pinned to the beach and was apparently unable to move forward. Advancing to the end of the beach, Lieutenant Colonel Mullins then turned and though exposed to the enemy fire, walked back to the water line, urging troops to move forward and off the beach. While accomplishing this, Lieutenant Colonel Mullins was wounded but continued in his efforts until finally the assault wave of the infantry moved forward. He then took command of two tanks and directed their fire on enemy strongpoints overlooking the beach. Observing that the tanks were unable to neutralize all the strongpoints, he organized a party of infantrymen and led them in the face of intense enemy fire up a hill to assault the strongpoints. Though again wounded and forced to withdraw, he refused to be deterred. Undaunted, he organized another party, and while leading this group in an assault, Lieutenant Colonel Mullins was killed by enemy fire. The extraordinary heroism, initiative, and personal bravery displayed by Lieutenant Colonel Mullins reflects great credit upon himself and is keeping with the highest traditions of the armed forces. Entered military service from Virginia.

Headquarters, First Army, General Orders No. 42 (August 6, 1944)

Staff Sergeant Richard C. Murrin
Company B, 70th Tank Battalion

Citation: Staff Sergeant Richard C. Murrin, 33036042, 70th Tank Battalion, United States Army, for extraordinary heroism in action against the enemy on 6 June 1944 on the Cotentin Peninsula, France. In the assault on the heavily fortified beach on the Cotentin Peninsula Sergeant Murrin's tank was one of the first to land. In the face of concentrated enemy fire which consisted of flanking coastal guns, mortars, and automatic weapons, Sergeant Murrin proceeded on his own initiative across a heavily mined beach and neutralized enemy gun emplacements, thereby facilitating the advance of friendly infantry. At this early time the route of advance had not been reconnoitered. Since visibility was poor from within a tank, Sergeant Murrin fearlessly dismounted from his tank under the heavy enemy fire and reconnoitered the terrain to better direct the forward advance of his tank. The personal bravery, initiative, and leadership displayed by Sergeant Murrin reflect great credit upon himself and upon the armed forces.

Headquarters, First Army, General Orders No. 35 (July 19, 1944)

Staff Sergeant Richard C. Murrin, from Butler, Pennsylvania, was in command of a Company B, 70th Tank Battalion tank on D-Day. Butler is also the hometown of Technician Fifth Grade John J. Pinder, Jr., who was posthumously awarded the Medal of Honor for his actions on June 6, 1944. *Photograph courtesy of Kathryn L. Blum.*

Sergeant Raymond E. Nicoli
Company D, 81st Chemical Battalion (Motorized)

Citation: Sergeant Raymond E. Nicoli, 37203447, 81st Chemical Battalion, United States Army, for extraordinary heroism in action against the enemy on 6 June 1944, in France. Although painfully wounded in the hand as his landing craft was approaching the beach Sergeant Nicoli refused first aid and remained with his squad. On reaching the beach he directed his squad in the removal of the mortars and ammunition from the landing craft to the shore. With complete disregard for his own safety he made numerous trips across the beach under the intense enemy fire before he completed his mission. Although anxious to remain with his men, his wound proved serious enough to require his being evacuated. The valor, determination, and devotion to duty displayed by Sergeant Nicoli reflect great credit upon himself and is in keeping with the highest traditions of the armed forces.

Headquarters, First Army, General Orders No. 37 (July 21, 1944)

Sergeant Henry V. Nothel
Company A, 70th Tank Battalion

Citation: Sergeant Henry V. Nothel, 32120996, 70th Tank Battalion, United States Army, for extraordinary heroism in action against the enemy on 6 June 1944 on the Cotentin Peninsula, France. In the assault on the heavily fortified beaches on the Cotentin Peninsula Sergeant Nothel's tank was one of the first to land. Under extremely heavy automatic weapon, mortar, and artillery fire, Sergeant Nothel directed his tank across a mined beach and was the first to breach the enemy seawall, neutralized two enemy mortars, thereby facilitating the advance of friendly infantry. At this early time the route of advance had not been reconnoitered. Since visibility was poor from within a tank, Sergeant Nothel fearlessly dismounted from his tank under the heavy enemy fire and reconnoitered the terrain to better direct the forward advance of his tank. The personal bravery, initiative, and leadership displayed by Sergeant Nothel reflect great credit upon himself and upon the armed forces.

Headquarters, First Army, General Orders No. 35 (July 19, 1944)

Captain Thomas F. O'Brien
Cannon Company, 16th Infantry Regiment, 1st Infantry Division

Citation: Captain Thomas F. O'Brien, 0357647, 16th Infantry, United States Army, for extraordinary heroism in action against enemy forces on 6 June 1944, in France. Captain O'Brien landed on the coast of France with the initial assault wave. Severe casualties were inflicted on his company when the craft on which they were coming ashore was hit and sunk. Upon reaching the shore, he found that his men were scattered and disorganized. Despite the fact that most of the men were pinned down by extremely heavy enemy fire, Captain O'Brien, disregarding his own personal safety, moved up and down the fire swept beach shouting orders and giving encouragement to the men. By his valiant leadership, he successfully reorganized his company. When he observed that several tanks were buttoned up and not firing, he immediately worked his way through the heavy enemy fire to them, found their crews and led them up the beach to a point from which they could engage the enemy guns. The personal bravery, aggressiveness and leadership displayed by Captain O'Brien reflects great credit upon himself and are in keeping with the highest traditions of the Armed Forces. Entered military service from New Hampshire.

Headquarters, First Army, General Orders No. 42 (August 6, 1944)

Major General J. Lawton Collins, the commanding officer of VII Corps, awards the Distinguished Service Cross to Captain Thomas F. O'Brien, with Cannon Company, 16th Infantry, during a ceremony near Hauset, Belgium on September 27, 1944. Captain O'Brien had previously been awarded the DSC for heroism during the amphibious assault landing at Gela, Sicily. He was killed in action on November 16, 1944, in the Hürtgen Forest, just one day past his 34th birthday. Captain O'Brien is buried at the Riverside Cemetery in Lincoln, New Hampshire. *United States Army Signal Corps photograph, courtesy of the First Division Museum at Cantigny.*

Lieutenant Colonel John T. O'Neill
Headquarters, Special Engineer Task Force, Provisional Engineer Special Brigade Group, V Corps

Citation: Lieutenant Colonel John T. O'Neill, 0269006, Corps of Engineers, United States Army, for extraordinary heroism in action against the enemy on 6 June 1944, in France. Lieutenant Colonel O'Neill arrived on the coast of France in a small craft which was under heavy and continuous enemy small arms and artillery fire immediately after the initial assault wave. Despite the intense enemy fire, he moved close in shore and ran his craft parallel to the beach to direct the operations of the demolition battalions under his command. With complete disregard for his own personal safety, he coolly appraised the situation along the entire length of the beach and then went ashore. From an exposed position on the beach, he issued orders amending the original plan in order to provide for more expeditious removal of obstacles most dangerous to the landing craft. He then proceeded, under a hail of enemy fire, to inspect the progress of the work and to encourage the demolition teams to greater effort. During the entire day, Lieutenant Colonel O'Neill, despite extremely dangerous and hazardous conditions, moved back and forth across the beach to further the completion of the mission assigned to his battalions. The personal bravery, determination and courageous leadership displayed by Lieutenant Colonel O'Neill reflects great credit on himself and is in keeping with the highest traditions of the armed forces. Entered military service from Maryland.

Headquarters, First Army, General Orders No. 37 (July 21, 1944)

Sergeant Douglas A. Orndorff
Company I, 116th Infantry Regiment, 29th Infantry Division

Citation: Sergeant Douglas A. Orndorff, 20365289, 116th Infantry, United States Army, for extraordinary heroism in action against the enemy on 6 June 1944, in France. When Sergeant Orndorff landed with his platoon on the coast of France, he found that the heavy enemy rifle, machine gun and artillery fire had pinned down two battalions. He rallied his platoon to attack and, despite the intense enemy fire, fearlessly led them forward in an assault on the enemy positions. This action so inspired the other troops that they joined in the assault and helped carry the positions. The courage, initiative and determined leadership displayed by Sergeant Orndorf reflects great credit on himself and was in keeping with the highest traditions of the armed forces.

Headquarters, First Army, General Orders No. 29 (June 29, 1944)

Lieutenant Colonel Edwin J. Ostberg
Headquarters, 1st Battalion, 507th Parachute Infantry Regiment, 82nd Airborne Division

Citation: Lieutenant Colonel Edwin J. Ostberg, 022043, 507th Parachute Infantry, United States Army, for extraordinary heroism in action against the enemy on 6 June 1944, in France. During an assault upon a vital bridge, Lieutenant Colonel Ostberg's battalion was pinned down by heavy enemy fire. Lieutenant Colonel Ostberg, completely disregarding his own safety, placed himself at the head of a reorganized assault group and led them through the intense enemy fire. This action so inspired his men that they smashed through the enemy defenses and seized one end of the bridge. From a position lacking protection from the artillery fire falling all around him, he maintained fire against the enemy on the other side of the bridge and directed the annihilation of their forces. While directing the operation from his exposed position, Lieutenant Colonel Ostberg was seriously wounded. The personal bravery and courageous leadership displayed by Lieutenant Colonel Ostberg reflects great credit on himself and is in keeping with the highest traditions of the armed forces.

Headquarters, First Army, General Orders No. 42 (August 6, 1944)

Sergeant Douglas A. Orndorff, from Winchester, Virginia, was a squad leader with Company I, 116th Infantry who led his platoon up the bluffs above Omaha Beach and was subsequently wounded by a sniper, losing his left eye and partially blinded in his right eye. *Photograph courtesy of Robert Orndorff and Kathy Manual.*

First Lieutenant James P. Panas
Company A, 81st Chemical Battalion (Motorized)

Citation: First Lieutenant James P. Panas, 0454558, Chemical Warfare Service, United States Army, for extraordinary heroism in action against the enemy on 6 June 1944, in France. First Lieutenant Panas came ashore immediately after the assault wave for the purpose of establishing a forward observation point for his platoon. Landing under extremely heavy fire, he paused in his dash for cover to assist a wounded soldier in reaching the beach. Upon learning that his company commander was wounded and was helpless in the water, he fearlessly returned to the beach and braving the intense enemy fire, carried the wounded officer ashore. After assuming command of the company, he led them across the fire swept beach and through the minefield to a position where the mortars could be set up and fired. The gallantry, determination and leadership exhibited by First Lieutenant Panas reflect great credit on himself and is in keeping with the highest traditions of the armed forces. Entered military service from Arizona.

Headquarters, First Army, General Orders No. 37 (July 21, 1944)

Private First Class Camillus J. Paolini
Company L, 18th Infantry Regiment, 1st Infantry Division

Citation: Private First Class Camillus J. Paolini, 33313568, 18th Infantry, United States Army, for extraordinary heroism in action against enemy forces on 6 June 1944, in France. When his company commander was seriously injured by an exploding mine, Private First Class Paolini, observing that there were no medical personnel in the vicinity, entered the minefield and went to the officer's assistance. Despite increasing enemy small arms fire, he continued to administer aid. At this time, a heavy enemy artillery barrage began to descend in the immediate area setting off mines all around Private First Class Paolini. As he was preparing to return to his company, a large piece of shrapnel from an artillery shell which landed nearby, hit the company commander. Undaunted by this occurrence which nearly took his own life, Private First Class Paolini ministered to this new wound. The gallantry and heroic determination of Private First Class Paolini in administering aid under such hazardous conditions reflects great credit upon himself and is in keeping with the highest traditions of the armed forces. Entered military service from Pennsylvania.

Headquarters, First Army, General Orders No. 42 (August 6, 1944)

Private Joseph P. Parke
Company H, 16th Infantry Regiment, 1st Infantry Division

Citation: Private Joseph P. Parke, 12022214, 16th Infantry, United States Army, for extraordinary heroism in action against the enemy on 6 June 1944, in France. As Company H, 16th Infantry, was about to attack a small town, the enemy laid down an extremely heavy artillery barrage and launched an attack. This forced Company H to move back and start their attack in another direction. Despite the fact that his entire unit was moving out, Private Parke voluntarily remained behind. From a position of cover in a building he poured an extremely accurate hail of fire on the hostile force. For over four hours he engaged the enemy forces and disorganized their attack by his effective fire. During this time, over three hundred artillery shells exploded in the vicinity of the building in which Private Parke was situated. Despite this fact, he resisted every effort to dislodge him and was still in his position when Company H finally took the town. The personal bravery, determination, and devotion to duty of Private Parke reflects great credit on himself and on the armed forces. Entered military service from New York.

Headquarters, First Army, General Orders No. 39 (July 31, 1944)

First Lieutenant Charles H. Parker
Company A, 5th Ranger Battalion, Provisional Ranger Group

Citation: First Lieutenant Charles H. Parker, 012902298, Infantry, United States Army, for extraordinary heroism in action on 6, 7, and 8 June 1944 from Vierville-sur-le-Mer to Pointe du Hoc, France. In the invasion of France, Lieutenant Parker led his company up the beach against heavy enemy rifle, machine gun, and artillery fire. Once past the beach he reorganized and continued inland. During this advance numerous groups of enemy resistance were encountered. Through his personal bravery and sound leadership this resistance was overcome, and his company succeeded in capturing Pointe du Hoc, the battalion objective. The following morning Lieutenant Parker led a patrol through enemy held territory in an effort to establish contact with the balance of the battalion. Lieutenant Parker's valor and superior leadership are in keeping with the highest traditions of the service. Entered military service from South Dakota.

Headquarters, First Army, General Orders No. 28 (June 20, 1944)

Captain Lloyd E. Patch
Headquarters Company, 1st Battalion, 506th Parachute Infantry Regiment, 101st Airborne Division

Citation: Captain Lloyd E. Patch, 0364576, Parachute Infantry, United States Army, for extraordinary heroism in action against the enemy on 6 June 1944, in France. Captain Patch assembled a group of sixty parachutists from a number of different regiments into an organized fighting unit and led them in an attack against Ste.-Marie-du-Mont. Encountering heavy enemy resistance in the form of a battery of 105mm guns, he led successful assaults against these gun positions. As he moved closer to Ste.-Marie-du-Mont extremely intense enemy automatic weapons fire halted the advance. Captain Patch then directed his men back to the captured enemy gun positions, reversed the guns and placed short range direct artillery fire on the enemy positions in the town. This fire was so effective that it completely disorganized the enemy and made possible the capture of the town. The courage and outstanding leadership displayed by Captain Patch reflect great credit on himself and is in keeping with the highest traditions of the armed forces. Entered military service from Massachusetts.

Headquarters, First Army, General Orders No. 31 (July 1, 1944)

Captain Lloyd E. Patch, from Brockton, Massachusetts, was the commanding officer of Headquarters Company, 1st Battalion, 506th Parachute Infantry Regiment on June 6, 1944. He was subsequently promoted to the rank of major and commanded the 2nd Battalion, 506th Parachute Infantry during the latter days of fighting around Bastogne during the Ardennes campaign. He continued his military career after the war, serving during the Korean War with the 2nd Infantry Division. He retired from the United States Army at the rank of colonel. *United States Navy photograph, National Archives.*

The commanding officer of the 5th Ranger Battalion, Lieutenant Colonel Max F. Schneider, congratulates Captain Charles H. Parker, the commanding officer of Company A, 5th Ranger Battalion, from Hecla, South Dakota, after both were awarded the Distinguished Service Cross, near Colombieres, France on June 23, 1944. After the war, Parker returned to civilian life with a career in pharmaceutical sales. *United States Army Signal Corps photograph courtesy of Victoria Parker-Christensen.*

Sergeant Lyman K. Patterson, Jr.
Company E, 116th Infantry Regiment, 29th Infantry Division

Citation: Staff Sergeant Lyman K. Patterson, Jr., 33042869 (then Sergeant), 116th Infantry, United States Army, for extraordinary heroism in action against the enemy on 6 June 1944, in France. At the place where Staff Sergeant Patterson's squad landed on the beach, the enemy was well protected by minefields and barbed wire. Heavy enemy rifle, machine gun and artillery fire was placed on the beach, and had pinned down the invading force. With complete disregard for his own safety and, in spite of the numerous casualties that this intense enemy fire was inflicting, Staff Sergeant Patterson exposed himself to it in order to encourage and personally lead his men in the attack. This fearlessness of Staff Sergeant Patterson so inspired the troops about him, that they vigorously assaulted and overran the enemy positions. The outstanding courage and personal bravery displayed by Staff Sergeant Patterson reflects great credit on himself and was in keeping with the highest traditions of the armed forces.

Headquarters, First Army, General Orders No. 29 (June 29, 1944)

Captain James L. Pence
Company A, 16th Infantry Regiment, 1st Infantry Division

Citation: Captain James L. Pence, 01286176, 16th Infantry, United States Army, for extraordinary heroism in action against the enemy on 6 June 1944, in France. Captain Pence, although severely wounded upon debarking from his craft in the invasion, ignored his painful wounds and immediately set about in reorganizing his men. In this effort, he constantly exposed himself to intense machine gun and artillery fire. Refusing all efforts to get him under cover and dress his wounds, he continued in his movements up and down the fire swept beach spending every effort toward getting the attack under way again until he collapsed from the effects of his wounds. The courage and outstanding devotion to duty displayed by Captain Pence reflects great credit on himself and is in keeping with the highest traditions of the armed forces. Entered military service from Kansas.

Headquarters, First Army, General Orders No. 31 (July 1, 1944)

Captain Edwin R. Perry
Company A, 299th Engineer Combat Battalion, Special Engineer Task Force, Provisional Engineer Special Brigade Group
Gap Support Team F

Citation: Captain Edwin R. Perry, 0-1107033, 299th Engineer Combat Battalion, United States Army, for extraordinary heroism in action against the enemy on 6 June 1944, in France. Captain Perry, commanding a demolition party for the removal of underwater obstacles, came in with the initial assault wave in the invasion of the coast of France. The craft on which Captain Perry's party was coming ashore was hit by an artillery shell. Numerous casualties were inflicted and the remainder of the party was thrown into the sea when the craft sank. Captain Perry swam ashore and under heavy and sustained enemy small arms and artillery fire reorganized the remnants of his demolition party. With complete disregard for his own safety, Captain Perry continuously exposed himself to the intense enemy fire in directing the salvage of explosives along the beach, preparatory to breaching the obstacles as soon as tidal conditions permitted. When tidal conditions permitted, Captain Perry, though the beach was still under heavy enemy fire, fearlessly directed his men in demolishing the beach obstacles. The personal bravery, determination, and leadership displayed by Captain Perry reflect great credit on himself and is in keeping with the highest traditions of the armed forces. Entered military service from New Jersey.

Headquarters, First Army, General Orders No. 37 (July 21, 1944)

Staff Sergeant Gerard B. Peterson
Company C, 743rd Tank Battalion

Citation: Staff Sergeant Gerard B. Peterson, 37272176, 743rd Tank Battalion, United States Army, for extraordinary heroism in action against the enemy on 6 June 1944 in France. Staff Sergeant Peterson landed with his tank unit on the coast of France with the initial assault wave. He successfully directed the landing of his section under heavy enemy small arms and artillery fire. Despite the devastating enemy fire he promptly directed the fire of his section against enemy installations which were delaying the advance of the infantry. When the forward advance of his section was stopped by an antitank ditch he, without regard to personal safety, dismounted from his tank and personally directed a crossing of the obstacle. The courage, aggressiveness, and leadership demonstrated by Staff Sergeant Peterson reflect great credit upon himself and is keeping with the highest traditions of the armed forces.

Headquarters, First Army, General Orders No. 37 (July 21, 1944)

Staff Sergeant Gerard B. Peterson, from Perley, Minnesota, was fatally wounded on August 8, 1944, when his tank was mistakenly attacked by friendly aircraft. *Photograph courtesy of Jill Johnson.*

Sergeant Kenneth F. Peterson
Company E, 16th Infantry Regiment, 1st Infantry Division

Citation: Sergeant Kenneth F. Peterson, 32569088, 16th Infantry, United States Army, for extraordinary heroism in action against the enemy on 6 June 1944, in France. Sergeant Peterson, armed with a bazooka, exhibited utter disregard for his own safety by constantly exposing himself to enemy fire while leading assaults on enemy emplacements. He, alone, charged and destroyed the emplaced enemy in at least two pillboxes. He continued in the advance of the assault in the face of intense enemy fire until he reached the top of a hill. From his exposed position on the hill he covered the advance of his company. The determination, personal bravery, and devotion to duty displayed by Sergeant Peterson reflects great credit on himself and is in keeping with the highest traditions of the armed forces. Entered military service from New Jersey.

Headquarters, First Army, General Orders No. 31 (July 1, 1944)

Private First Class Lenold C. Peterson
Company A, 505th Parachute Infantry Regiment, 82nd Airborne Division

Citation: Private First Class Lenold C. Peterson, 37092874, 505th Parachute Infantry, United States Army, for extraordinary heroism against the enemy on 6 June 1944, in France. Private First Class Peterson was stationed at the end of a bridge over the Merderet River as a rocketeer to repel attacks by enemy troops who controlled the other end of the bridge. This position was subject to incessant enemy rifle, machine gun, mortar, and artillery fire. After an artillery preparation, the enemy sent an assault force supported by three tanks over the bridge. Though part of the troops withdrew, Private First Class Peterson remained at his position until the enemy tanks approached within thirty yards. In spite of the intense fire, Private First Class Peterson rose from his position and fired rockets into the three tanks. The courage, devotion to duty and daring displayed by Private First Class Peterson reflects great credit on himself and is in keeping with the highest traditions of the armed forces. Entered military service from Minnesota.

Headquarters, First Army, General Orders No. 31 (July 1, 1944)

Private First Class Victor E. Peterson
Headquarters Company, 16th Infantry Regiment, 1st Infantry Division

Citation: Private First Class Victor E. Peterson, 33117025, 16th Infantry, United States Army, for extraordinary heroism in action against the enemy on 6 June 1944, in France. As Private First Class Peterson's landing craft touched shore on D-Day it was subjected to devastating fire from heavy shore emplacements causing numerous casualties to men on board. Voluntarily and with complete disregard for his own personal safety, Private First Class Peterson plunged into the fire swept water and, assisted by a comrade, carried a heavy piece of vital communications equipment toward shore. When his companion was instantly killed by machine gun fire, Private First Class Peterson courageously and single handedly dragged the heavy equipment through the mine infested water. Midway to the beach, he was mortally wounded. With great determination, he continued forward and safely delivered the equipment upon the beach. Refusing medical attention, he made frequent trips into the water, through heavy artillery, mortar, and small arms fire, and rescued wounded comrades until he collapsed upon the beach. The self-sacrificing devotion to duty, personal bravery, and fortitude displayed by Private First Class Peterson exemplify the highest traditions of the armed forces. Entered military service from Pennsylvania.

Headquarters, First Army, General Orders No. 94 (December 10, 1944)

Captain Vodra C. Philips
Company A, 743rd Tank Battalion

Citation: Captain Vodra C. Philips, 0364786, Infantry, United States Army, for extraordinary heroism in action against the enemy on 6 June 1944, in France. Captain Philips commanded a tank company which landed on the coast of France with the initial assault wave. Although the entire beach was covered by enemy rifle and machine gun fire, Captain Philips, completely disregarding his own safety, dismounted from his tank and led the tanks from his landing craft through the beach obstacles so that they could move on above the high water mark. He, despite this enemy fire, then proceeded to mark the routes and led the remaining tanks coming from other landing craft up through the obstacles. When the battalion commander became a casualty, Captain Philips immediately assumed command of the battalion, organized a firefight on the beach and directed the movement of the battalion inland. The personal bravery, initiative and courageous leadership displayed by Captain Philips reflects great credit on himself and is in keeping with the highest traditions of the armed forces. Entered military service from Missouri.

Headquarters, First Army, General Orders No. 37 (July 21, 1944)

Captain Vodra C. Philips, from Fayette, Missouri, was the commanding officer of Company A, 743rd Tank Battalion on June 6, 1944. *Photograph by Major Clarence Benjamin, 743rd Tank Battalion, courtesy of Joseph Keating.*

Private Benton L. Porter
Company D, 81st Chemical Battalion (Motorized)

Citation: Private Benton L. Porter, 34427549, 81st Chemical Battalion, United States Army, for extraordinary heroism in action against the enemy on 6 June 1944 in France. As Private Porter's landing craft was approaching the beach exploding shrapnel fire seriously cut his forehead, causing profuse bleeding. When the craft finally hit the beach, he refused to be evacuated. With total disregard for his own personal safety and in spite of his painful wound, Private Porter made a number of trips across the beach under heavy machine gun and mortar fire aiding in the removal of the mortars and ammunition from the landing craft safely to shore. When the guns were in position to fire Private Porter, extremely weak for loss of blood, consented to be evacuated. The personal courage, self-sacrifice, and devotion to duty displayed by Private Porter reflects great credit upon himself and is in keeping with the highest traditions of the armed forces.

Headquarters, First Army, General Orders No. 37 (July 21, 1944)

First Sergeant William M. Presley
Company B, 116th Infantry Regiment, 29th Infantry Division

Citation: First Sergeant William M. Presley, 33147994, 116th Infantry, United States Army, for extraordinary heroism in action against the enemy on 6 June 1944, in France. As Sergeant Presley, whose small unit had been cut off by the heavy enemy fire, was attempting to make contact with the main body he encountered an enemy strongpoint and artillery observation post on the top of a cliff. Placing his men where they could bring fire on the enemy, Sergeant Presley set out for the beach to contact a naval shore fire control party. Completely disregarding his own safety, he moved through the intense enemy fire and successfully reached a naval shore fire control party and led the party to a position from which they could direct their fire. Sergeant Presley remained in an exposed position to cover the party while they were directing their fire. The gallantry, initiative and leadership exhibited by Sergeant Presley reflects great credit on himself and was in keeping with the highest traditions of the armed forces.

Headquarters, First Army, General Orders No. 29 (June 29, 1944)

Technical Sergeant Carl D. Proffitt
Company K, 116th Infantry Regiment, 29th Infantry Division

Citation: Technical Sergeant Carl D. Proffitt, 20365448, 116th Infantry, United States Army, for extraordinary heroism in action against the enemy on 6 June 1944, in France. When Sergeant Proffitt's company landed on the coast of France, the beach was covered by the withering enemy rifle, machine gun and artillery fire. In spite of the great number of casualties that were being inflicted on his company, Sergeant Proffitt on a number of occasions fearlessly exposed himself to this intense fire in order to encourage and lead his troops across the beach. The gallantry and disregard for his own safety displayed by Sergeant Proffitt reflects great credit on himself and were in keeping with the highest traditions of the armed forces.

Headquarters, First Army, General Orders No. 29 (June 29, 1944)

Opposite: Photograph of Lieutenant Carl D. Proffitt, from Charlottesville, Virginia, after receiving a battlefield commission and promotion subsequent to the invasion of Normandy. *Photograph courtesy of Sterling Proffitt.*

Private First Class Gordon C. Pryne
Company A, 505th Parachute Infantry Regiment, 82nd Airborne Division

Citation: Private First Class Gordon [C.] Pryne, 39291525, 505th Parachute Infantry, United States Army, for extraordinary heroism against the enemy on 6 June 1944, in France. Private First Class Pryne was stationed at the end of a bridge over the Merderet River as a rocketeer to repel attacks by enemy troops who controlled the other end of the bridge. This position was subject to incessant enemy rifle, machine gun, mortar, and artillery fire. After an artillery preparation, the enemy sent an assault force supported by three tanks over the bridge. Though part of the troops withdrew, Private First Class Pryne remained at his position until the enemy tanks approached within thirty yards. In spite of the intense fire, Private First Class Pryne rose from his position and fired rockets into the three tanks. The courage, devotion to duty and daring displayed by Private First Class Pryne reflects great credit on himself and is in keeping with the highest traditions of the armed forces. Entered military service from California.

Headquarters, First Army, General Orders No. 31 (July 1, 1944)

Staff Sergeant Darvin D. Purvis
Company A, 70th Tank Battalion

Citation: Staff Sergeant Darvin D. Purvis, 6890765, 70th Tank Battalion, United States Army, for extraordinary heroism in action against the enemy on 6 June 1944 on the Cotentin Peninsula, France. In the assault on the heavily fortified beaches of the Cotentin Peninsula, Sergeant Purvis' platoon leader was seriously wounded. Sergeant Purvis on his own initiative assumed command of the platoon and proceeded to lead his tank platoon down a mine strewn road. Since at this time the route of advance was unreconnoitered and since visibility was poor from within his tank, Sergeant Purvis despite intense enemy small arms, machine gun, and artillery fire dismounted from his tank to reconnoiter and led his unit through enemy strongpoints. At other times he advanced across heavily fortified terrain bristling with pillboxes, minefields, and tank traps. The personal bravery, initiative, and leadership demonstrated by Sergeant Purvis reflect great credit upon himself and upon the armed forces.

Headquarters, First Army, General Orders No. 35 (July 19, 1944)

Staff Sergeant David N. Radford
Company F, 16th Infantry Regiment, 1st Infantry Division

Citation: Staff Sergeant David N. Radford, 13015814, 16th Infantry, United States Army, for extraordinary heroism in action against the enemy on 6 June 1944, near Colleville-sur-le-Mer, France. When Staff Sergeant Radford observed the great number of men that were pinned down by the heavy enemy fire on the beach, he armed himself with two Bangalore torpedoes and advanced through thirty yards of open terrain to the aprons of barbed wire. Finding the depth of the wire too great for two Bangalores he returned to the beach, secured another, and returned to the barbed wire. He attached the three Bangalores in the most advantageous position and blew a huge gap in the wire. He then led his section through this gap in the wire and across an enemy minefield to the top of a hill from which position flanking fire was directed on the enemy position. The valor and unselfish devotion to duty demonstrated by Staff Sergeant Radford reflect great credit upon himself and were in keeping with the highest traditions of the armed forces of the United States.

Headquarters, First Army, General Orders No. 31 (July 1, 1944)

Captain Emerald M. Ralston
Company A, 1st Medical Battalion, 1st Infantry Division

Citation: Captain Emerald M. Ralston, 0468276, 1st Medical Battalion, United States Army, for extraordinary heroism in action against the enemy on 6 June 1944, in France. The landing craft, upon which Captain Ralston's medical company was coming ashore, was hit twice by enemy shells setting two of the holds on fire. Captain Ralston immediately rushed into one of the burning holds, calmed the men and organized them to fight the fire. Although painfully burned about the face he continued to render aid to the wounded. Despite smoke and terrific heat, Captain Ralston fearlessly entered the officers' cabin over a burning hold to rescue a critically injured man. He then returned to the shell swept deck to administer to the wounded. When a naval craft came along side to the rescue, Captain Ralston although strongly enjoined to remain with the rescue craft, refused and transferred the remnants of his company to an LCM and directed it to the beach. In the face of vicious enemy artillery fire which killed and wounded many of the men, a landing was effected. Although wounded in this landing, Captain Ralston, refusing to take treatment or seek cover from the devastating enemy fire, made trip after trip into the heavy surf to rescue his wounded and struggling men. En route to the aid station he treated many of the wounded on the beach under hostile enemy machine gun and sniper fire. The personal bravery, superb courage and outstanding leadership displayed by Captain Ralston reflect great credit on himself and is in keeping with the highest traditions of the military service. Entered military service from Nebraska.

Headquarters, First Army, General Orders No. 42 (August 6, 1944)

Major General J. Lawton Collins awards the Distinguished Service Cross to Captain Emerald M. Ralston M.D., from Stanton, Nebraska, during a ceremony conducted on October 7, 1944. *United States Army Signal Corps photograph, courtesy of the First Division Museum at Cantigny.*

Captain Knut H. Raudstein
Company C, 506th Parachute Infantry Regiment, 101st Airborne Division

Citation: Captain Knut H. Raudstein, 0428613, Infantry, United States Army, for extraordinary heroism on 6 June 1944 near Holdy, France. Captain Raudstein formed a small group of approximately twenty-five men and led them in an attack on a well camouflaged and heavily defended enemy 105mm howitzer battery. Approaching within thirty yards of the enemy position he controlled the fire of his group upon the trench system surrounding the battery. He then directed the final assault on the battery, capturing valuable enemy weapons and killing or capturing the battery personnel. Later, near St. Come-du-Mont, France, to assist one of his platoons which had been surrounded by a superior enemy force, Captain Raudstein led a small force approximately two hundred yards along a hedgerow covered by an enemy machine gun from a parallel hedgerow 150 yards away. This platoon had suffered heavy losses in men and equipment and was without automatic weapons. Captain Raudstein issued an order to hold, and while his entire platoon was under heavy enemy machine gun and mortar fire, he left cover and with a 60mm mortar fired twenty rounds in the direction of an enemy flanking attack causing the enemy to retreat. Although painfully wounded by rifle fire in this action, he refused evacuation and continued to lead his company until seriously wounded while leading his troops in a later attack. The outstanding courage and leadership displayed by Captain Raudstein reflect great credit upon himself and were in keeping with the highest traditions of the armed forces. Entered military service from Oregon.

Headquarters, European Theater of Operations, United States Army, General Orders No. 108 (October 28, 1944)

Major General Maxwell D. Taylor, the commander of the 101st Airborne Division, awards the Distinguished Service Cross to Captain Knut H. Raudstein, from Portland, Oregon, during a ceremony at Berchtesgaden, Germany on May 17, 1945. *United States Army Signal Corps photograph, National Archives.*

Major William A. Richards
Headquarters, 112th Engineer Combat Battalion, 1121st Engineer Combat Group

Citation: Major William A. Richards, 0393258, 112th Engineer Combat Battalion, United States Army, for extraordinary heroism in action against the enemy on 6 June 1944, in France. Major Richards landed on the coast of France with the initial assault waves under heavy enemy artillery, machine gun, and rifle fire. He immediately effected the removal of barbed wire by directing the operations of a tank dozer, preceding it on foot under heavy small arms fire. After removing this obstacle he personally reconnoitered inland to find the exact position of an enemy gun which was harassing troops and equipment at the entrance of one of the beach exits. After locating this gun he made his way back to the beach and reported its location. He then proceeded to organize the units of his battalion to aggressive action against the enemy on the cliffs. Though wounded, Major Richards again proceeded to a beach exit to direct the efforts of the mine clearing and obstacle removing parties. While organizing these parties he was killed by enemy fire. The courage and devotion to duty exhibited by Major Richards reflects great credit on himself and is in keeping with the highest traditions of the armed forces. Entered military service from Michigan.

Headquarters, First Army, General Orders No. 39 (July 31, 1944)

Major William A. Richards, executive officer of the 112th Engineer Combat Battalion, assumed command of the battalion prior to the invasion when the battalion commander, Lieutenant Colonel John T. O'Neill, was selected as commander of the Special Engineer Task Force. Richards, from Marquette County, Michigan, was killed during the assault landing on Omaha Beach while leading his unit. *United States Army photograph, courtesy of Amy Wooldridge.*

Captain Kimball R. Richmond
Company I, 16th Infantry Regiment, 1st Infantry Division

Citation: Captain Kimball R. Richmond, 01286184, 16th Infantry, United States Army, for extraordinary heroism in action against the enemy on 6 June 1944 near Colleville-sur-le-Mer, France. When the crafts on which his company was moving in on the initial assault upon the coast of France, were sunk by enemy fire and mines, Captain Richmond swam ashore through a hail of machine gun bullets and artillery fire. Upon reaching the shore he gathered together the remainder of his company and moved down the beach. Here he established contact with a group of men whose officers had become casualties. He quickly organized the men for an attack against an enemy strongpoint on the left flank. In the face of heavy direct enemy fire he gallantly led his men in a successful assault upon this enemy emplacement, thereby removing an enemy installation that had been inflicting heavy casualties on this part of the beach. Without hesitation, Captain Richmond then pushed inland against the enemy. Completely disregarding his own safety he led his men across open terrain and captured Le Grand Homeau and successfully defended it against superior forces until relieved. The personal bravery and determined leadership of Captain Richmond reflect great credit upon himself and were in keeping with the highest traditions of the armed forces of the United States.

Headquarters, First Army, General Orders No. 31 (July 1, 1944)

Captain Kimball R. Richmond, the commanding officer of Company I, 16th Infantry Regiment, is awarded the Distinguished Service Cross by General Dwight D. Eisenhower during a ceremony near Balleroy, France on July 2, 1944. Richmond was from Windsor, Vermont. *United States Army Signal Corps film still, courtesy of www.combatreels.com.*

Major General Matthew B. Ridgway
Headquarters, 82nd Airborne Division

Citation: Major General Matthew B. Ridgway, 05264, 82nd Airborne Division, United States Army, for extraordinary heroism in action against the enemy from 6 June 1944 to 9 June 1944, in France. Major General Ridgway jumped by parachute at approximately 02:00 prior to the dawn of D-Day and landed about 3/4 mile northeast of Ste.-Mère-Église, France, to spearhead the parachute landing assault of his Airborne Division on the Cotentin Peninsula. Throughout D-Day, he visited every point in the then surrounded area in order to evaluate the opposition and to encourage his men. He penetrated to the front of every active sector without thought of the personal danger involved. He exposed himself continuously to small arms, mortar and artillery fire; as, by his presence and through words of encouragement, he greatly assisted and personally directed the operations of one of his battalions in the important task of securing the bridgehead across the Merderet River, which required a frontal assault against strongly entrenched enemy positions. His personal bravery and his heroism were deciding factors in the success of his unit in France.

Headquarters, First Army, General Orders No. 35 (July 19, 1944)

Major General Matthew B. Ridgway commanded the 82nd Airborne Division during the Normandy campaign and was promoted in August 1944 to command the newly formed XVIII Airborne Corps, which consisted of the 82nd, 101st, and the 17th Airborne Division. Ridgway was born at Fort Monroe, Virginia on March 3, 1895, the son of a career army officer. He graduated from the United States Military Academy in 1917. After World War II, Ridgway commanded United Nations forces during the Korean War, where he turned the tide of the war. He later was Chief of Staff, United States Army. *United States Army photograph.*

Private First Class William M. Riggs
Cannon Company, 116th Infantry Regiment, 29th Infantry Division

Citation: Private First Class William M. Riggs, 34499006, 116th Infantry, United States Army, for extraordinary heroism in action against the enemy on 6 June 1944, in France. When the landing craft on which Private First Class Riggs was coming ashore was struck by enemy shell fire, it began to sink in the rough sea. With complete disregard for his own safety and despite the intense enemy small arms and artillery fire, Private First Class Riggs plunged into the turbulent sea and swam about five hundred yards to another landing craft and directed it to the sinking craft. This act permitted the men to reach the beach and engage in the firefight against the enemy. The courage, initiative and heroism displayed by Private First Class Riggs reflects great credit on himself and was in keeping with the highest traditions of the armed forces.

Headquarters, First Army, General Orders No. 29 (June 29, 1944)

Staff Sergeant Ozias D. Ritter
Company I, 116th Infantry Regiment, 29th Infantry Division

Citation: Technical Sergeant Ozias D. Ritter, 20365297 (then Staff Sergeant), 116th Infantry, United States Army, for extraordinary heroism in action against the enemy on 6 June 1944, in France. Technical Sergeant Ritter led his machine gun section ashore in the first wave of troops to attack the coast of France. With complete disregard for his own safety, he fearlessly, despite the devastating enemy fire which was inflicting heavy casualties, led his men into position and coolly placed fire on the enemy positions. In one instance, he purposely exposed himself to draw enemy fire to provide his section with positive location of the enemy guns. Another time, he entered a sector of observed enemy mortar fire to carry out the wounded. The gallantry, leadership and outstanding courage of Technical Sergeant Ritter reflects great credit on himself and was in keeping with the highest traditions of the armed forces.

Headquarters, First Army, General Orders No. 29 (June 29, 1944)

Technical Sergeant John A. Roach
Company B, 116th Infantry Regiment, 29th Infantry Division

Citation: Technical Sergeant John A. Roach, 20363889, 116th Infantry, United States Army, for extraordinary heroism in action against the enemy on 6 June 1944, in France. Sergeant Roach, who was wounded as he came in on the initial assault and was awaiting evacuation, observed that his platoon leader had become a casualty and that the leaderless platoon was fast becoming disorganized under the heavy and intense enemy fire. Sergeant Roach, despite his painful wound, seized a rifle, moved over to his platoon and reorganized it. He then rallied the men and personally led them forward in the face of the devastating fire and successfully overran the enemy positions. The outstanding courage, initiative and leadership displayed by Sergeant Roach reflects great credit on himself and was in keeping with the highest traditions of the armed forces.

Headquarters, First Army, General Orders No. 29 (June 29, 1944)

Opposite: Technical Sergeant Ozias D. Ritter, from Winchester, Virginia, served with the Virginia National Guard before the war. He was one of the stalwart NCOs with the 116th Infantry who rallied the young soldiers of the regiment to assault the bluffs. *Photograph courtesy of Isabelle Ritter Kastak, Walter Ritter, and David Ritter.*

Corporal Ernest T. Roberts
Company D, 508th Parachute Infantry Regiment, 82nd Airborne Division

Citation: Corporal Ernest T. Roberts, 18199335, 508th Parachute Infantry, United States Army, for extraordinary heroism in action against the enemy on 6 June 1944, in France. After landing by parachute before dawn on D-Day, and joining a composite group which proceeded to carry out a battalion mission, Corporal Roberts and two comrades served as an outpost in a building on the edge of Gueutteville. When a battalion of German infantry, reinforced with tanks, approached from the west and placed machine guns and mortars in position, these three valiant men immediately opened fire on the enemy. Ordered to leave the post, they determined to hold out until the thirty men in the town had withdrawn. Corporal Roberts assisted in holding the hostile force at bay for two hours, killing fifteen Germans and wounding many others. His voluntary and courageous action delayed the enemy sufficiently to permit the main body of parachute troops to establish defensive positions to the east from which they were able to deny overwhelming German forces the opportunity of crossing the Merderet River. Corporal Roberts' superb heroism and unselfish devotion to duty exemplifies the highest traditions of the United States Army. Entered military service from Texas.

Headquarters, First Army, General Orders No. 61 (September 25, 1944)

Second Lieutenant Eskell F. Roberts
Company B, 146th Engineer Combat Battalion, Special Engineer Task Force, Provisional Engineer Special Brigade Group
Gap Assault Team Number 6

Citation: Second Lieutenant Eskell F. Roberts, 01108273, 146th Engineer Combat Battalion, United States Army, for extraordinary heroism in action against the enemy on 6 June 1944 in France. Second Lieutenant Roberts, commanding a demolition team, landed on the coast of France with the initial assault wave. As he was leading his team from the boat across the beach he was wounded in the legs by enemy mortar fire. Unmindful of his painful wounds Second Lieutenant Roberts, completely disregarding his own safety, refused to be evacuated and personally directed his team in clearing a gap through the obstacles. It was only when the rising tide prevented further work on the obstacles that he allowed first aid to be administered. As the tide receded he fearlessly led his team back onto the beach under heavy enemy fire and directed their efforts until he was wounded a second time. The gallantry, devotion to duty, and courageous leadership displayed by Second Lieutenant Roberts reflects great credit upon himself and is in keeping with the highest traditions of the armed forces. Entered military service from Oklahoma.

Headquarters, First Army, General Orders No. 37 (July 21, 1944)

First Lieutenant James L. Robinson
Company K, 16th Infantry Regiment, 1st Infantry Division

Citation: First Lieutenant James L. Robinson, 01296583, 16th Infantry, United States Army, for extraordinary heroism in action against the enemy on 6 June 1944, in France. On D-Day, First Lieutenant Robinson assumed immediate control of his company after his commanding officer was wounded, and moved up and down the fire swept beach to reorganize the unit for an attack. Advancing forward, the company was pinned down by heavy machine gun and rifle fire from a concrete pillbox. First Lieutenant Robinson, displaying superb courage, crawled through a dense minefield to a point one hundred yards from the emplacement and engaged it single handedly with his rifle. Under this diversion, his men approached the hostile position from the flanks. While personally leading his company in an assault upon the pillbox, First Lieutenant Robinson was mortally wounded by sniper fire. The personal bravery, tenacity of purpose, and inspiring leadership displayed by First Lieutenant Robinson is in keeping with the highest traditions of the armed forces. Entered military service from Mississippi.

Headquarters, First Army, General Orders No. 78 (November 11, 1944)

Private First Class Thomas L. Rodgers
Company C, 504th Parachute Infantry Regiment, 82nd Airborne Division and 82nd Provisional Pathfinder Company

Citation: Private First Class Thomas L. Rodgers, 20421704, Infantry, United States Army, for extraordinary heroism in connection with military operations against an enemy of the United States. Having jumped into Normandy in the vicinity of Amfreville, France on 6 June 1944, Private First Class Rodgers, observing many of his comrades pinned down by enemy machine gun and small arms fire, moved without hesitation to destroy the enemy. Mounting a stone wall, in full view of the enemy, he neutralized the machine gun position and proceeded forward, driving back the enemy with effective fire from his Browning Automatic Rifle. During this action Private First Class Rodgers killed or wounded twenty-five of the enemy and made possible the organization and advance of our troops in the area. His personal courage, aggressive leadership and courageous inspiration contributed materially to the success of his comrades and typified the highest traditions of the service. Private First Class Rodgers was later killed in action against the enemy. Entered military service from Alabama.

Headquarters, XVIII Airborne Corps, General Orders No. 45 (June 18, 1945)

Private First Class Thomas L. Rodgers served with Company C, 504th Parachute Infantry Regiment, 82nd Airborne Division and was one of twenty-six combat experienced paratroopers of the 504th who jumped in Normandy with the 507th and 508th Parachute Infantry pathfinder teams to provide security for those teams. He was subsequently killed in action on June 15, 1944 and was buried at Andalusia, Alabama. *Photograph courtesy of Bill Rodgers.*

Sergeant Howard W. Rogers
Company F, 116th Infantry Regiment, 29th Infantry Division

Citation: Technical Sergeant Howard W. Rogers, 33047696, then Sergeant, 116th Infantry, United States Army, for extraordinary heroism in action against the enemy on 6 June 1944, in France. Soon after landing on the coast of France with the initial assault wave of troops, Technical Sergeant Rogers became separated from his unit and found himself in a group of other soldiers who were also separated from their organizations. Upon discovering an enemy pillbox from which devastating machine gun fire was being directed, he quickly organized this group of soldiers into a raiding party. With complete disregard for his own safety, he fearlessly, despite intense enemy fire, led the raiding party in an assault upon the pillbox and destroyed this enemy gun position. The courage and initiative exhibited by Technical Sergeant Rogers reflects great credit on himself and was in keeping with the highest traditions of the armed forces.

Headquarters, First Army, General Orders No. 29 (June 29, 1944)

Private First Class Sanford Rosen
Headquarters Company, 16th Infantry Regiment, 1st Infantry Division

Citation: Private First Class Sanford Rosen, 12021989, 16th Infantry, United States Army, for extraordinary heroism in action against the enemy on 6 June 1944, in France. Private First Class Rosen disembarked from his landing craft amidst bursts of artillery fire and, with another man, started for the shore carrying a heavy drum of wire. At the first move his comrade was hit and instantly killed. With complete disregard for his own safety he rescued the heavy drum of wire from the surf and struggled with it under heavy enemy fire through the shoulder deep water to the beach. Seconds later another burst of artillery fire shot away his left arm at the elbow. Unable to lift the drum with his one good arm he valiantly dragged it the remaining distance, bleeding profusely, but never hesitating despite his terrible wound and the intense enemy fire. This drum of wire so gallantly brought ashore was one of the very first initially landed and was urgently needed. In so distinguishing himself through his display of personal courage, dauntlessness, and devotion to duty, Private First Class Rosen reflects great credit on himself and on the armed forces. Entered military service from New York.

Headquarters, First Army, General Orders No. 39 (July 31, 1944)

First Lieutenant Robert P. Ross
Company C, 37th Engineer Combat Battalion, 5th Engineer Special Brigade, Provisional Engineer Special Brigade Group

Citation: First Lieutenant Robert P. Ross, 01100746, 37th Engineer Combat Battalion, United States Army, for extraordinary heroism in action against the enemy on 6 June 1944, in France. First Lieutenant Ross landed on the coast of France with the initial assault wave with the mission of preparing beach exits for passage of vehicles from the beach. Extremely heavy enemy artillery, mortar, and small arms fire from positions on the hills commanding the beach prevented him from starting on this work. Upon observing that many infantry soldiers were pinned down on the beach he assumed command of a company, which was without an officer, reorganized these troops with his own and engaged the enemy. With these troops he forced the surrender of two machine guns and killed forty of the enemy. He then proceeded to accomplish his assigned mission. The courage, initiative, and leadership displayed by First Lieutenant Ross reflects great credit on himself and is in keeping with the highest traditions of the armed forces. Entered military service from Wisconsin.

Headquarters, First Army, General Orders No. 39 (July 31, 1944)

Second Lieutenant Wesley R. Ross
Company B, 146th Engineer Combat Battalion, Special Engineer Task Force, Provisional Engineer Special Brigade Group
Gap Assault Team Number 8

Citation: Second Lieutenant Wesley R. Ross, 0472141, 146th Engineer Combat Battalion, United States Army, for extraordinary heroism in action against the enemy on 6 June 1944 in France. Second Lieutenant Ross, commanding a demolition team, landed on the coast of France with the initial assault wave. Though subjected to heavy enemy small arms, mortar, and artillery fire, Second Lieutenant Ross, completely disregarding his own safety, personally led his team in breaching the beach obstacles. While engaged in this mission Second Lieutenant Ross was wounded in the legs by enemy mortar fire. Though repeated efforts were made to evacuate him, Second Lieutenant Ross insisted upon remaining with his unit until a gap was cleared through the obstacles. The valor, devotion to duty, and determined leadership displayed by Second Lieutenant Ross reflect great credit upon himself and is in keeping with the highest traditions of the armed forces.

Headquarters, First Army, General Orders No. 37 (July 21, 1944)

Major General Leonard T. Gerow, commanding officer of the V Corps, awards the Distinguished Service Cross to Lieutenant Wesley R. Ross, from Wamic, Oregon, during a ceremony to award DSC medals to members of the 146th Engineer Combat Battalion, conducted on September 11, 1944, in France. *United States Army Signal Corps photograph, National Archives.*

Lieutenant Colonel James E. Rudder
Headquarters, 2nd Ranger Battalion, Provisional Ranger Group

Citation: Lieutenant Colonel James E. Rudder, 0294916, Infantry, United States Army, for extraordinary heroism in action on 6 June 1944 at Pointe du Hoc, France. Lieutenant Colonel Rudder, commanding Force "A" of the Rangers, landed on the beach with his unit which was immediately subjected to heavy rifle, machine gun, mortar, and artillery fire. Devastating fire was also directed from the cliffs overlooking the beach. Completely disregarding his own safety he repeatedly exposed himself in directing the reorganization of his unit to assault the cliffs. As soon as the first elements had scaled the cliffs, Lieutenant Colonel Rudder immediately scaled the cliffs in order to better direct the attack. Though wounded he refused to be evacuated and continued to direct the attack. By his determined leadership and dauntlessness he inspired his men so that they successfully withstood three enemy counterattacks. Though wounded again he still refused to be evacuated. Lieutenant Colonel Rudder's heroic leadership, courage, and complete devotion to duty are in keeping with the highest traditions of the service. Entered military service from Texas.

Headquarters, First Army, General Orders No. 28 (June 20, 1944)

Captain Francis L. Sampson
Service Company, 501st Parachute Infantry Regiment, 101st Airborne Division

Citation: Chaplain (Captain) Francis L. Sampson, 0-471891, 501st Parachute Infantry, United States Army, for extraordinary heroism on 6 and 7 June 1944 at Basse Addeville, France. On the afternoon of D-Day a small force of parachute infantry were forced to evacuate their positions to the enemy's advance. Chaplain Sampson, though strongly urged otherwise, elected to remain behind with fourteen seriously wounded men. When the enemy seized the position Chaplain Sampson immediately made his presence known so that no attack would be made on the wounded men. Granted permission to remain with the wounded, he valiantly struggled in the face of the most hazardous and difficult conditions to keep the men alive. On the second night, during an artillery barrage which lasted four hours and virtually demolished the house, he administered blood plasma and aid to the wounded. As three shells hit the building he threw his bed across the wounded to protect them. He made numerous trips across a shell swept courtyard to ascertain the conditions of the most seriously wounded men. When a shell destroyed the adjacent room, fatally injuring the two men therein, he immediately went to their assistance and attempted to dig them out from the debris. He suffered a second degree burn from a tracer bullet but continued to care for the wounded. In the morning, after the Germans left the vicinity, an evacuation party arrived. Assured that the living wounded were evacuated to the division hospital, Chaplain Sampson proceeded to the same hospital where he gave a seriously wounded man a liter of blood and spent the remainder of the day and night rendering spiritual and physical aid to the wounded. The courage, fortitude, and heroism displayed by Chaplain Sampson is worthy of emulation.

War Department, General Orders No. 91 (December 19, 1944)

Captain Francis L. Sampson, from Cherokee, Iowa, was the Catholic chaplain of the 501st Parachute Infantry Regiment. In this photo he is giving last rites to dead paratroopers wrapped in parachute canopies at the temporary American cemetery at Blosville, France. *United States Army Signal Corps photograph.*

Technician Fifth Grade Felice J. Savino
Company D, 81st Chemical Battalion (Motorized)

Citation: Technician Fifth Grade Felice J. Savino, 32796601, 81st Chemical Battalion, United States Army, for extraordinary heroism in action against the enemy on 6 June 1944 in France. Sharpnel fire exploded directly on Technician Fifth Grade Savino's landing craft and seriously wounded him through the nose. When the craft landed on the beach he refused to be evacuated. With total disregard for his own safety he made numerous trips across the fire swept beach, aiding in the removal of the mortars and ammunition from the landing craft to the shore. When the guns finally were in position to be fired, Technician Fifth Grade Savino continued to act as an ammunition handler until he was unable to carry on. Only then did he permit himself to be evacuated. The great courage and devotion to duty exhibited by Technician Fifth Grade Savino reflects great credit upon himself and is in keeping with the highest traditions of the armed forces.

Headquarters, First Army, General Orders No. 37 (July 21, 1944)

Second Lieutenant George E. Schmidt
Company E, 501st Parachute Infantry Regiment, 101st Airborne Division

Citation: Second Lieutenant George E. Schmidt, 01303955, Infantry, United States Army, for extraordinary heroism on 6 June 1944. Second Lieutenant Schmidt landed by parachute with his battalion in the vicinity of St. Come-du-Mont, France. Due to a heavy concentration of machine gun and mortar fire from nearby enemy positions, the battalion had much difficulty in assembling, but Second Lieutenant Schmidt, the first officer from his company to reach assembly area, immediately assumed command and made repeated trips to the drop zone to bring back men and equipment. By his courageous and diligent efforts, he was successful in assembling an effective fighting force. Second Lieutenant Schmidt then skillfully deployed his men along the route of advance. Extremely heavy enemy fire suddenly pinned down the entire battalion. Second Lieutenant Schmidt, displaying outstanding leadership, placed his men in advantageous positions and ordered them to maintain a fast rate of fire in order to deceive the enemy as to the strength of his force. In an attempt to locate enemy snipers who were firing on his men, he exposed himself to enemy fire. Although he received a head wound, he continued to search until he had spotted the snipers. While directing fire of his submachine gun upon those snipers, he was fatally wounded. During the entire action, he displayed outstanding courage, devotion to duty, and complete disregard for his personal safety. His conduct was in accordance with the highest standards of the military service. Entered military service from Ohio.

Headquarters, European Theater of Operations, United States Army, General Orders No. 108 (October 28, 1944)

Staff Sergeant George Schneider
299th Engineer Combat Battalion, Special Engineer Task Force, Provisional Engineer Special Brigade Group, V Corps

Citation: Staff Sergeant George Schneider, 32846999, 299th Engineer Combat Battalion, United States Army, for extraordinary heroism in action against the enemy on 6 June 1944 in France. Staff Sergeant Schneider landed in the initial assault wave in the invasion of the coast of France. The second in command of a demolition team, Staff Sergeant Schneider was continually exposed to heavy and sustained small arms and observed artillery fire as he directed the placing of charges for the removal of underwater obstacles. Despite the devastating enemy fire, Staff Sergeant Schneider personally continued to direct his detachment in the removal of underwater obstacles until his mission was accomplished. The personal bravery, determination, and courage exhibited by Staff Sergeant Schneider reflects great credit upon himself and is in keeping with the highest traditions of the armed forces.

Headquarters, First Army, General Orders No. 37 (July 21, 1944)

Colonel Ernest A. Kindervater, the commander of the Fort Hayes army base near Columbus, Ohio, awards the Distinguished Service Cross posthumously to Lieutenant George E. Schmidt. His mother (right) accepted the medal during a ceremony held on May 23, 1945. *United States Army Signal Corps photograph, National Archives.*

Lieutenant Colonel Max F. Schneider
Headquarters, 5th Ranger Battalion, Provisional Ranger Group

Citation: Lieutenant Colonel Max F. Schneider, 0384849, Infantry, United States Army, for extraordinary heroism in action on 6 June 1944 at Vierville-sur-le-Mer, France. In the initial landings in the invasion of France, Lieutenant Colonel Schneider led the 5th Ranger Infantry Battalion ashore at H-Hour on D-Day in the face of extremely heavy enemy rifle, machine gun, mortar, artillery, and rocket fire. Upon reaching the beach, Lieutenant Colonel Schneider reorganized his unit. During this reorganization he repeatedly exposed himself to enemy fire. He then led his battalion in the assault on the enemy beach positions, and having accomplished this mission led them up a steep incline to assault the enemy gun emplacements on the top of the hill. The destruction of these enemy positions opened one of the vital beach exits, thereby permitting the troops and equipment which had been pinned down to move inland from the beach, with the result that reinforcements could be landed from the sea. By his heroic leadership and personal courage Lieutenant Colonel Schneider set an inspiring example to his command, reflecting the highest traditions of the armed forces. Entered military service from Iowa.

Headquarters, First Army, General Orders No. 28 (June 20, 1944)

A group photograph of 5th Ranger Battalion recipients of the Distinguished Service Cross (left to right) Lieutenant Colonel Max F. Schneider; Captain George P. Whittington, Jr.; Captain Charles H. Parker, Lieutenant Francis W. Dawson, Sergeant Willie W. Moody, Technician Fifth Grade Howard D. McKissick, Denzil O. Johnson, and Private First Class Alexander W. Barber, June 23, 1944. All but Moody, McKissick, and Johnson were awarded for actions on June 6, 1944. Lieutenant Joseph R. Lacy, the battalion's chaplain and DSC recipient for his heroism on June 6, 1944 does not appear in this photograph. *United States Army Signal Corps photograph, National Archive*s.

Private First Class Curtis N. Schur
149th Engineer Combat Battalion, 6th Engineer Special Brigade, Provisional Engineer Special Brigade Group, V Corps

Citation: Private First Class Curtis N. Schur (Army Serial No. 37507811), Corps of Engineers, United States Army, for extraordinary heroism in connection with military operations against an armed enemy, as a bulldozer operator, 149th Engineer Combat Battalion, during the landings on the French coast on 6 June 1944. Under heavy enemy fire, Private First Class Schur disembarked his explosive laden bulldozer through six feet of water, rough surf, mined underwater obstacles and wreckage. Despite concentrated artillery fire zeroed on the area and small arms fire aimed at his moving bulldozer, he grimly proceeded to the tasks of clearing the beach exit of mines, obstacles and wreckage, and of filling in a tank ditch, thereby freeing a hemmed in tank battalion. Private First Class Schur's calm efficiency and implacable determination to complete these difficult tasks, which were of prime importance to immediate operations, reflect great credit upon himself and the armed forces of the United States. Entered military service from Kansas.

Headquarters, Communications Zone, European Theater of Operations, General Orders No. 37 (March 22, 1945)

Captain John Settineri
Medical Detachment, 16th Infantry Regiment, 1st Infantry Division

Citation: Captain John Settineri, 0490121, 16th Infantry, United States Army, for extraordinary heroism in action against the enemy on 6 June 1944, in France. On D-Day, Captain Settineri voluntarily and with inspiring valor waded and swam into the bullet-flayed and mined waters of the landing beach on nine separate occasions to rescue wounded and drowning comrades.

Disregarding completely his own personal safety, he carried the injured men through intense artillery, mortar, and machine gun fire to a place of safety and rendered medical treatment. By his unselfish devotion to duty and fearless courage, Captain Settineri saved many lives and acted in keeping with the highest traditions of the armed forces. Entered military service from New York.

Headquarters, First Army, General Orders No. 81 (November 16, 1944)

Captain John Settineri, from Syracuse, New York, served as a surgeon with the Medical Detachment, 16th Infantry Regiment of the 1st Infantry Division. *Photograph courtesy of Mary S. Gregory.*

Technician Fifth Grade Edward Shaffer
Company C, 348th Engineer Combat Battalion, 5th Engineer Special Brigade, Provisional Engineer Special Brigade Group

Citation: Technician Fifth Grade Edward Shaffer, 17088074, 348th Engineer Combat Battalion, United States Army, for extraordinary heroism in action against the enemy on 6 and 7 June 1944, in France. Technician Fifth Grade Shaffer arrived on the invasion beach on D-Day and, upon learning that his battalion had not yet landed, volunteered his services to an adjacent unit. For a four hour period he operated his bulldozer through continuous and devastating artillery, mortar, machine gun and small arms fire to clear obstacles and construct exits from the fire swept beach. On the following morning, he moved with the assaulting infantry under fierce fire and again operated a bulldozer with complete indifference to shells landing dangerously near him, widening roads and preparing transit areas which facilitated the movement inland of vital combat equipment. Entered military service from Colorado.

Headquarters, First Army, General Orders No. 32 (July 12, 1944)

First Lieutenant John D. Shelby
Company H, 16th Infantry Regiment, 1st Infantry Division

Citation: First Lieutenant John D. Shelby, 0885777, 16th Infantry, United States Army, for extraordinary heroism in action against the enemy on 6 June 1944, in France. First Lieutenant Shelby landed with the initial assault wave on the coast of France. He immediately organized five men into an assault team and, completely disregarding his own safety, led them in a two hundred yard dash through devastating enemy fire and across a minefield to attack an antitank gun. He alone assaulted the gun position and engaged the enemy crew in a hand-to-hand battle, killing one man and taking six prisoners. Leaving the defense of the gun and position to his men, he then took command of a group of troops who were advancing leaderless up the hill and personally led them, despite heavy sniper fire, in an attack upon a nearby town. The personal bravery, initiative, and courageous leadership displayed by First Lieutenant Shelby reflects credit on himself and is in keeping with the highest traditions of the armed forces. Entered military service from Texas.

Headquarters, First Army, General Orders No. 45 (August 9, 1944)

Technician Fourth Grade Elmer G. Shindle
Headquarters Company, 116th Infantry Regiment, 29th Infantry Division

Citation: Technician Fourth Grade Elmer G. Shindle, 33494073, 116th Infantry, United States Army, for extraordinary heroism in action against the enemy on 6 June 1944, in France. When the craft in which Technician Fourth Grade Shindle was coming ashore in the initial assault on the coast of France received a direct hit from an enemy shell, it quickly sank. Men were forced to abandon ship under heavy enemy rifle, machine gun and artillery fire in water too deep to wade. Technician Fourth Grade Shindle, as he swam ashore, aided others to reach the beach. Without regard for his own safety and despite the intense enemy fire, Technician Fourth Grade Shindle made numerous trips across the beach to the water to rescue many wounded and drowning soldiers and took them to the most available cover on the beach where he treated their wounds. The gallantry and personal bravery displayed by Technician Fourth Grade Shindle reflects great credit on himself and was in keeping with the highest traditions of the armed forces.

Headquarters, First Army, General Orders No. 29 (June 29, 1944)

Private William J. Shoemaker
Company C, 37th Engineer Combat Battalion, 5th Engineer Special Brigade, Provisional Engineer Special Brigade Group

Citation: Private William J. Shoemaker, 33762655, 37th Engineer Combat Battalion, United States Army, for extraordinary heroism in action against the enemy on 6 June 1944, in France. Private Shoemaker landed with his bulldozer at 0830 hours, D-Day. Upon finding conditions on the beach behind schedule because of the fierce enemy opposition, he voluntarily pulled numerous drowned wheeled and track-propelled vehicles out of the surf. While his bulldozer was a specific target for cannon and mortar fire, he cleared a road through the shingle on beach exits E-1 and E-3. Having completed that dangerous mission, Private Shoemaker immediately set to the task of removing two roadblocks at exit E-1 and filling in an antitank trap at exit E-3, thereby permitting vehicles and armor to move out in support of the infantry troops. Private Shoemaker's courage and bravery in performing his tasks under intense enemy fire reflects high credit upon himself and upon the armed forces of the United States. Entered military service from Pennsylvania.

Headquarters, First Army, General Orders No. 39 (July 31, 1944)

Next Page: Technician Fourth Grade Elmer G. Shindle, a medic with the 116th Infantry Regiment from Lancaster, Pennsylvania, is awarded the Distinguished Service Cross by Lieutenant General Omar N. Bradley, commander of the First Army, during a ceremony near Mieux, France, July 5, 1944. *United States Army Signal Corps photograph, National Archives.*

Staff Sergeant Paul R. Shorter
Company A, 16th Infantry Regiment, 1st Infantry Division

Citation: Staff Sergeant Paul R. Shorter, 33092154, 16th Infantry, United States Army, for extraordinary heroism in action against the enemy on 6 June 1944, in France. When his section reached the beach with the initial assault wave in the attack upon the European continent, Staff Sergeant Shorter was the only non-commissioned officer left. He immediately, with complete disregard for his own safety exposed himself to the sweeping enemy machine gun and sniper fire in moving about and reorganizing his men. He then led his section through minefields and into the face of the enemy fire to assault and destroy several machine gun and sniper nests. As the fighting progressed inland Staff Sergeant Shorter, on his own initiative, organized and led patrols to wipe out nests of snipers and machine guns firing on the flank of his unit. On at least five different occasions when organized resistance threatened to stop the advance of his organization he moved out ahead of his unit and despite constant enemy fire proceeded to lead the assault on the enemy. Staff Sergeant Shorter's personal bravery and repeated aggressiveness in engaging superior enemy forces without the slightest regard for his personal safety reflects the highest credit on himself and on the armed forces. Entered military service from Virginia.

Headquarters, First Army, General Orders No. 39 (July 31, 1944)

Opposite: Major General J. Lawton Collins, the commanding officer of the VII Corps, awards the Distinguished Service Cross to Staff Sergeant Paul R. Shorter, from Martinsville, Georgia, during a ceremony near Hauset, Belgium on September 27, 1944. *United States Army Signal Corps photograph, National Archives.*

Lieutenant Colonel Robert N. Skaggs
Headquarters, 741st Tank Battalion

Citation: Lieutenant Colonel Robert N. Skaggs, 0260683, 741st Tank Battalion, United States Army, for extraordinary heroism in action against the enemy on 6 June 1944 in France. Three companies of Lieutenant Colonel Skaggs' tank battalion were landed with the assault echelon in the invasion upon the coast of France. Lieutenant Colonel Skaggs landed shortly thereafter, finding the assault echelon held to the fire swept beach and considerably disorganized. Lieutenant Colonel Skaggs immediately initiated steps to rally his tanks and get them into action. Constantly exposing himself to intense enemy small arms, machine gun, and artillery fire, he moved along the beach organizing and directing the fire of his tanks. Notwithstanding the difficulties encountered and the constant enemy fire, he continued his efforts throughout the entire day of the assault. The personal bravery and outstanding leadership displayed by Lieutenant Colonel Skaggs reflect great credit upon himself and is in keeping with the highest traditions of the armed forces.

Headquarters, First Army, General Orders No. 37 (July 21, 1944)

Major General Leonard T. Gerow (center), the commanding officer of the V Corps, converses with the commanding officer of the 741st Tank Battalion, Lieutenant Colonel Robert N. Skaggs (left), from Los Angeles, California, and a member of Company A of that battalion, Staff Sergeant George A. Habib (right), from Fond Du Lac, Wisconsin, after awarding them the Distinguished Service Cross on September 12, 1944. *United States Army Signal Corps photograph, National Archives.*

Technician Fourth Grade Bolick Smulik
Company A, 741st Tank Battalion

Citation: Technician Fourth Grade Bolick Smulik, 6890110, 741st Tank Battalion, United States Army, for extraordinary heroism in action against the enemy on 6 June 1944 in France. Technician Fourth Grade Smulick landed with the assault force in the invasion upon the coast of France. Shortly after landing, the tank dozer which he was operating was destroyed by enemy fire. Completely disregarding his own safety, Technician Fourth Grade Smulik left his destroyed tank dozer, crossed the fire swept beach, and mounted an abandoned bulldozer. Though completely exposed to the heavy enemy fire, he placed the bulldozer in operation, and proceeded to assist in preparing a lane through the beach obstacles which permitted the beaching of landing craft. The outstanding courage, determination, and initiative of Technician Fourth Grade Smulik reflect great credit upon himself and is in keeping with the highest traditions of the armed forces.

Headquarters, First Army, General Orders No. 37 (July 21, 1944)

First Lieutenant Francis E. Songer
Company B, 70th Tank Battalion

Citation: First Lieutenant Francis E. Songer, 01011806, 70th Tank Battalion, United States Army, for extraordinary heroism in action against the enemy on 6 and 9 June 1944, in France. Landing with his tank company on D-Day at H-Hour ahead of friendly infantry, First Lieutenant Songer, despite heavy enemy fire, proceeded through a gap in the seawall and led his company down a mine strewn road. Dismounting from his tank, First Lieutenant Songer exposed himself to intense enemy fire as he reconnoitered the route. While advancing along a causeway, his tank was disabled by an enemy mine and struck by three enemy shells which wounded several of the crew. After rendering first aid, he commandeered the next tank and proceeded to capture his objective. When at a later date, five of his tanks became mired in a marsh and antitank ditch, First Lieutenant Songer dismounted under enemy artillery, mortar and small arms fire to supervise freeing the tanks. Though wounded in this engagement, he refused to be evacuated and continued to lead his company in a successful attack. The courageous leadership and personal bravery displayed by First Lieutenant Songer reflects great credit on himself and is in keeping with the highest traditions of the armed forces. Entered military service from California.

Headquarters, First Army, General Orders No. 60 (September 20, 1944)

Private Andrew Sosnack
Medical Detachment, 506th Parachute Infantry Regiment, 101st Airborne Division

Citation: Private Andrew Sosnack, 33501650, Medical Corps, United States Army, for extraordinary heroism in action during the period 6 June 1944 to 10 June 1944, in France. During this period, Private Sosnack made numerous trips over ground covered by intense enemy machine gun and artillery fire to administer first aid and to carry food and water to two parachutists who were severely injured in landing. Due to his ceaseless and fearless efforts, the two men were eventually evacuated on the third day. The courage, fortitude and complete devotion to duty displayed by Private Sosnack reflects great credit on himself and is in keeping with the highest traditions of the armed forces. Entered military service from Pennsylvania.

Headquarters, First Army, General Orders No. 31 (July 1, 1944)

Lieutenant Francis E. Songer, from Santa Barbara, California, was the commanding officer of Company B, 70th Tank Battalion and its sixteen duplex drive tanks which landed on Utah Beach on June 6. *Photograph courtesy of Laura Kruss.*

Second Lieutenant John M. Spalding
Company E, 16th Infantry Regiment, 1st Infantry Regiment, 1st Infantry Division

Citation: Second Lieutenant John M. Spalding, 01317433, 16th Infantry, United States Army, for extraordinary heroism in action against the enemy on 6 June 1944, in France. Upon reaching the beach in the initial landing on the coast of France, Second Lieutenant Spalding, completely disregarding his own personal safety, led his men up the beach to the slight cover of a shale shelf. Having suffered numerous casualties, he hesitated only long enough to reorganize his unit. He then led his men over the embankment, through barbed wire and across a thickly sewn minefield. Second Lieutenant Spalding led his men in the attack on a series of enemy strongpoints and successfully destroyed them. Constantly ignoring heavy enemy fire, he at all times continued in the advance and personally destroyed an antitank gun which had been firing on beach targets with deadly effect. The personal bravery and superior leadership demonstrated by Second Lieutenant Spalding reflects great credit on himself and is in keeping with the highest traditions of the armed forces. Entered military service from Kentucky.

Headquarters, First Army, General Orders No. 31 (July 1, 1944)

General Dwight D. Eisenhower awards the Distinguished Service Cross to Lieutenant John M. Spalding, from Owensboro, Kentucky, during a ceremony near Balleroy, France, July 2, 1944. Lieutenant Spalding led the Company E section that made the initial breakthrough to reach the top of the bluff in the 16th Infantry's sector of Omaha Beach. Spalding was born in 1918 in Evansville, Indiana and moved to Owensboro, Kentucky as a young child. He was a sportswriter prior to the war and received a commission as a second lieutenant at Fort Benning, Georgia in April of 1943. After the war, he served two terms in the Kentucky General Assembly's House of Representatives. Spalding tragically died in 1959 at the age of forty-four years old. *United States Army Signal Corps photograph, courtesy of Tina Gerteisen.*

Captain Archibald A. Sproul
Headquarters, 3rd Battalion, 116th Infantry Regiment, 29th Infantry Division

Citation: Captain Archibald A. Sproul, 0406823, 116th Infantry, United States Army, for extraordinary heroism in action against the enemy on 6 June 1944, in France. At a time when his battalion was pinned down on the beach due to the heavy enemy rifle, machine gun and artillery fire, Captain Sproul, with complete disregard for his own safety, exposed himself on numerous occasions in encouraging and organizing the hard pressed troops. His fearlessness in leading the men across the fire swept beach materially contributed in converting the disorganized troops into a strong attacking force. The courage and valor of Captain Sproul reflects great credit on himself and was in keeping with the highest traditions of the armed forces.

Headquarters, First Army, General Orders No. 29 (June 29, 1944)

Major Paul J. Stach
455th Bombardment Squadron, 323rd Bombardment Group, 98th Bombardment Wing, Ninth Air Force

Citation: Major Paul J. Stach (Army Serial No. 0409795), Air Corps, United States Army, for extraordinary heroism in connection with military operations against an armed enemy, as Operations Officer of the 455th Bombardment Squadron (M), on 6 June 1944. Major Stach participated in an aerial attack upon a special military target at Caen, France, which was heavily defended. Although flak bursts had knocked out his left engine and started a fire in the bomb bays, he maintained his aircraft in position until the bombs were successfully dropped on the target. He continued to maintain the craft in level flight allowing his crew to bail out before he attempted to leave the plane himself. The indomitable courage of Major Stach permitted the successful bombardment of a vital target and probably resulted in saving the lives of his entire crew. Entered military service from Texas.

Headquarters, European Theater of Operations, United States Army, General Orders No. 38 (March 17, 1945)

Lieutenant Colonel Fred A. Steiner
Headquarters, 8th Infantry Regiment, 4th Infantry Division

Citation: Lieutenant Colonel Fred A. Steiner, 0119758, 8th Infantry, United States Army, for extraordinary heroism in action against the enemy on 6 June 1944, near Germain, France. As his regiment was moving forward Lieutenant Colonel Steiner discovered a strongly fortified position near a regimental CP that had not been fully reduced and which was threatening to hold up the advance of the rear elements. Realizing the seriousness of the situation, Lieutenant Colonel Steiner immediately organized a force of the available personnel in the immediate vicinity. Despite intense enemy fire, Lieutenant Colonel Steiner exposed himself on numerous occasions in leading and directing the attack upon the strongpoint. After a severe firefight, in which Lieutenant Colonel Steiner personally took part, the strongpoint was reduced. In this attack four enemy field pieces, which were capable of effective use against the beachhead, were destroyed and numerous prisoners were taken. The courageous and superior leadership exhibited by Lieutenant Colonel Steiner reflect great credit upon himself and were in keeping with the highest traditions of the armed forces.

Headquarters, First Army, General Orders No. 32 (July 12, 1944)

Opposite: Captain Archibald A. Sproul, from Staunton, Virginia, was the S-1 (personnel) staff officer of the 3rd Battalion, 116th Infantry Regiment, 29th Infantry Division. He remained with the Virginia National Guard after the war, where he became the commanding officer of the 116th Infantry Regiment and later the commander of the 29th Infantry Division. *Photograph courtesy of Archibald A. Sproul, Jr.*

Private First Class Otto K. Stephens
Company C, 2nd Ranger Battalion, Provisional Ranger Group

Citation: Private First Class Otto K. Stephens, 20533605, 2nd Ranger Infantry Battalion, United States Army, for extraordinary heroism in action against the enemy on 6 and 7 June 1944, in France. Private First Class Stephens landed with the initial assault wave on the coast of France on D-Day under heavy enemy artillery, machine gun, mortar and rocket fire. Proceeding across the fire swept beach, he scaled a 100 foot cliff and secured ropes to the top for other men to use in ascending. Without waiting for his comrades to reach the top, Private First Class Stephens proceeded to attack the enemy positions located there. Although wounded by sniper fire, he disdained medical attention, killed the sniper who shot him, and continued on until the following day when he was evacuated for his injuries. The personal bravery and courage displayed by Private First Class Stephens reflect credit on himself and is in keeping with the highest traditions of the armed forces. Entered military service from Indiana.

Headquarters, First Army, General Orders No. 69 (October 16, 1944)

This photograph of Sergeant Otto K. Stephens was taken in 1940. He was from Henry County, Indiana and was killed in action on December 6, 1944 at Germeter, Germany. Stephens was buried at the cemetery near New Castle, Indiana. *Photograph courtesy of Mrs. Faith Groce, Mark Stephens, and James Stephens.*

Staff Sergeant Leeward W. Stockwell
Headquarters Company, 16th Infantry Regiment, 1st Infantry Division

Citation: Staff Sergeant Leeward W. Stockwell, 12005027, 16th Infantry, United States Army, for extraordinary heroism in action against the enemy on 6 June 1944, in France. A small reconnaissance patrol, led by Staff Sergeant Stockwell, penetrated deep into enemy held territory. When well within the enemy lines the patrol was suddenly brought under the fire of a deeply entrenched German mortar company. Despite the lack of cover and concealment from the intense enemy fire, Staff Sergeant Stockwell, accompanied by another man, moved forward to close with the enemy. He worked his way to within twenty yards of the enemy position, at which point he threw hand grenades into the enemy dugouts causing heavy casualties. Without hesitation he and his comrade immediately charged into the enemy emplacements and fearlessly closed with the enemy forces. In this attack several of the enemy were killed and twelve prisoners were taken. The personal bravery, aggressiveness and courage displayed by Staff Sergeant Stockwell in the face of superior enemy forces reflects great credit on himself and is in keeping with the highest traditions of the armed forces. Entered military service from New York.

Headquarters, First Army, General Orders No. 42 (August 6, 1944)

This photograph of Lieutenant Leeward W. Stockwell, of Warrensburg, New York, was taken after he had received a battlefield commission and promotion. *Photograph courtesy of Reneé Stockwell.*

Sergeant Philip Streczyk
Company E, 16th Infantry Regiment, 1st Infantry Division

Citation: Sergeant Philip (NMI) Streczyk, 32182713, 16th Infantry, United States Army, for extraordinary heroism in action against the enemy on 6 June 1944, in France. In the face of vicious enemy fire, Sergeant Streczyk led his section across the beach. He cut through the enemy wire, led his platoon through a minefield and up a steep hill overlooking the beach and by this action opened a beach exit. He then led his section in an attack on an enemy emplacement, the fire from which had prevented the establishment of a vitally needed beachhead in that sector. In a vicious fight, Sergeant Streczyk set the example for his men in leading the attack. The destruction of this enemy strongpoint contributed materially to the success of the invasion effort. The valor, initiative, and disregard for his own safety exhibited by Sergeant Streczyk reflects great credit on himself and is in keeping with the highest traditions of the armed forces. Entered military service from Massachusetts.

Headquarters, First Army, General Orders No. 31 (July 1, 1944)

Sergeant Philip Streczyk was from East Brunswick, New Jersey and a veteran of the North Africa and Sicily campaigns. In addition to the Distinguished Service Cross, he was the recipient of the Silver Star medal with two oak leaf clusters. He was promoted to the rank of technical sergeant shortly after the general orders were issued awarding him the DSC. After the war, Streczyk worked as a brick and stone mason in Florida. Sadly, he passed away on June 25, 1958, five months to the day before his 40th birthday. He is buried at the Polish Old Catholic Cemetery in his hometown. *Photograph courtesy of Stanley Streczyk.*

DISTINGUISHED SERVICE CROSS CITATIONS 375

Captain Edward F. Wozenski, the commanding officer of Company E, 16th Infantry, congratulates Sergeant Philip Streczyk, after a ceremony at which General Dwight D. Eisenhower awarded the Distinguished Service Cross to Streczyk and twenty-one other officers and men of the 1st Infantry Division near Balleroy, France on July 2, 1944. *United States Army Signal Corps photograph, courtesy of Stanley Streczyk.*

Staff Sergeant Raymond F. Strojny
Company F, 16th Infantry Regiment, 1st Infantry Division

Citation: Staff Sergeant Raymond F. Strojny, 31069497, 16th Infantry, United States Army, for extraordinary heroism in action against the enemy on 6 June 1944, in France. When his company was pinned down by the heavy and intense enemy fire, Staff Sergeant Strojny, with complete disregard for his own safety, picked up a bazooka from a wounded soldier who had been pierced by shrapnel. He then crossed the fire swept beach and took up a position in a minefield within 250 yards of an enemy machine gun pillbox. He put the pillbox under his fire until his ammunition was exhausted. Braving the small arms fire that was being directed at him, he moved back across the beach to find more ammunition. Securing the ammunition, he again took up the same position and fired until he knocked out the pillbox. The personal bravery and determined devotion to duty of Staff Sergeant Strojny reflects great credit on himself and is in keeping with the highest traditions of the armed forces. Entered military service from New Jersey.

Headquarters, First Army, General Orders No. 31 (July 1, 1944)

General Dwight D. Eisenhower awards the Distinguished Service Cross to Staff Sergeant Raymond F. Strojny, from Taunton, Massachusetts, at a ceremony near Balleroy, France, July 2, 1944. Staff Sergeant Raymond F. Strojny with Company F, 16th Infantry Regiment, served thirty-two months overseas and never missed a day of combat during seven campaigns. He was the recipient of the Distinguished Service Cross, the Silver Star, and the Bronze Star for heroism. Strojny stayed in the army after the war and retired to Lynwood, Washington in 1964. He bequeathed his entire estate to charity upon his death in 2008. *United States Army Signal Corps photograph.*

Major Richard P. Sullivan
Headquarters, 5th Ranger Battalion, Provisional Ranger Group

Citation: Major Richard P. Sullivan, 0399856, Infantry, United States Army, for extraordinary heroism in action from 6 June 1944 to 10 June 1944 near Vierville-sur-le-Mer, in France. Completely disregarding his own safety, he personally directed a successful landing operation and led his men across the beach covered with machine gun, artillery, and rocket fire. After reorganizing his men he immediately resumed his duties as battalion executive officer and was placed in command of two Ranger companies which fought their way inland against fierce opposition to join and relieve the Ranger detachment on Pointe du Hoc. After laying communications through the enemy lines under cover of darkness, Major Sullivan directed the Rangers' progress across country to Pointe du Hoc and Grandcamp. In cooperation with United States infantry an attack was begun on the Grandcamp battery. When certain elements were temporarily halted by artillery fire, Major Sullivan, who had been wounded at Pointe du Hoc, calmly and courageously rallied his officers and men, ordered a renewal of the attack, and instead of bypassing the resistance, advanced over heavily mined terrain to capture the Grandcamp battery with a loss of only fifteen men. Eighty-six prisoners and several large caliber artillery pieces in concrete bunkers were taken. Attacks by Major Sullivan's command contributed greatly to the success of the entire corps' operations. By his intrepid direction, heroic leadership, and superior professional ability, Major Sullivan set an inspiring example of his command reflecting the highest traditions of the armed forces. Entered military service from Massachusetts.

Headquarters, First Army, General Orders No. 28 (June 20, 1944)

Major Richard P. Sullivan, the executive officer of the 5th Ranger Battalion, served as the executive officer of the Provisional Ranger Group. Sullivan was promoted to the rank of lieutenant colonel and led the 5th Ranger Battalion during the fighting in the Hürtgen Forest and the Battle of the Bulge.

Staff Sergeant Harrison C. Summers
Company B, 502nd Parachute Infantry Regiment, 101st Airborne Division

Citation: Staff Sergeant Harrison C. Summers, 35275212, Parachute Infantry, United States Army, for extraordinary heroism in action against the enemy on 6 June 1944, in France. While leading a patrol, Staff Sergeant Summers was wounded. However, though wounded, he continued the fight and accounted for nine of the enemy. Later, on 11 June 1944, when his platoon leader became a casualty, Staff Sergeant Summers assumed command of the platoon. When their ammunition became exhausted he, despite intense enemy fire, made repeated trips across an open field. This replenishment of the ammunition enabled his platoon to continue in the advance. The daring, leadership and complete disregard for his own safety displayed by Staff Sergeant Summers reflects great credit on himself and is in keeping with the highest traditions of the armed forces. Entered military service from Virginia.

Headquarters, First Army, General Orders No. 31 (July 1, 1944)

Private First Class Lawrence G. Sweeney
Company A, 741st Tank Battalion

Citation: Private First Class Lawrence G. Sweeney, 33266510, 741st Tank Battalion, United States Army, for extraordinary heroism in action against the enemy on 6 June 1944, in France. Upon landing with the initial assault wave in the invasion of France, Private First Class Sweeney's tank received several direct hits. Courageously, he remained within the tank and fired at the enemy until his ammunition supply was exhausted. Dismounting, he fearlessly ran across the fire swept beach, secured additional ammunition and returned to continue his devastating fire. A short while later he was assigned the hazardous mission of reconnoitering an exit from the beach. Crawling through intense artillery, mortar, and small arms fire, he reached his objective and observed that heavy fire from the area had pinned the assaulting infantrymen to the ground. With great valor, he voluntarily mounted an abandoned tank, fired at hostile strongpoints, and neutralized several gun emplacements. On another dangerous assignment, Private First Class Sweeney, with complete disregard for his own safety, preceded several tanks in an assault and, as heavy caliber shells fell dangerously near him, coolly and calmly removed wounded men from the path of the tanks. By his great courage, selfless devotion to duty, and marked valor, Private First Class Sweeney exemplified the highest traditions of the armed forces. Entered military service from Pennsylvania.

Headquarters, First Army, General Orders No. 19 (January 31, 1945)

Colonel Benjamin B. Talley
Headquarters, V Corps

Citation: Colonel Benjamin B. Talley, 016668, V Corps, United States Army, for extraordinary heroism in action against the enemy on 6 June 1944, in France. Colonel Talley commanded a detachment that closely followed the initial assault wave in the invasion on the coast of France. The mission of his detachment was to furnish the corps commander reports as to the progress of the operation. Upon attempts to land, the two DUKWs under Colonel Talley's command came under heavy enemy artillery and machine gun fire. As the accomplishment of the mission depended upon protecting the equipment, Colonel Talley properly decided at that time to withdraw the DUKWs and proceeded to cruise parallel to the beach three hundred to five hundred yards off shore. Colonel Talley made three further attempts to land but was driven off by the heavy enemy fire. Undaunted, Colonel Talley made a further attempt into the face of the enemy fire and managed to reach the beach. Once on shore, Colonel Talley personally led his detachment into the heaviest part of the fighting so that he might transmit first hand information to his corps commander. Though exposed to enemy fire and forced to operate under extremely difficult and hazardous conditions, Colonel Talley continued to carry on his mission until the corps headquarters came ashore. The personal bravery, tenacity of purpose and determined leadership of Colonel Talley reflects great credit on himself and is in keeping with the highest traditions of the armed forces. Entered military service from Pennsylvania.

Headquarters, First Army, General Orders No. 37 (July 21, 1944)

Benjamin B. Talley was born in Oklahoma and was an engineering graduate of from Georgia Tech and then received a master's degree from the Westinghouse Graduate Engineering School. He received a regular army commission in the Corps of Engineers in 1926. On June 6, 1944, he commanded a detachment of V Corps troops with the mission of providing situation reports from Omaha Beach during the assault. He later commanded the 1st Engineer Special Brigade during the invasion of Okinawa. Talley retired at the rank of brigadier general in 1956. As a civil engineer, Talley managed reconstruction of Anchorage, Alaska after the massive 1964 earthquake. He oversaw heavy construction for the navy in South Vietnam. Talley died in 1998 and is buried at Arlington National Cemetery. *United States Army Signal Corps photograph.*

Colonel George A. Taylor
Headquarters, 16th Infantry Regiment, 1st Infantry Division

Citation: Colonel George A. Taylor, 16th Infantry, United States Army, for extraordinary heroism in action against the enemy on 6 June 1944, in France. Colonel Taylor landed during the most crucial and threatening period of the invasion operation. Thousands of men lay huddled on a narrow beachhead, their organization and leaders cut down by the disastrous enemy fire. Without hesitation, unmindful of the sniper and machine gun fire which was sweeping the beach, Colonel Taylor began to reorganize the units. While continuously exposed to this murderous fire, Colonel Taylor never slackened in his efforts in directing and coordinating the attack. By his initiative and leadership, he was able to clear an exit from the beach and begin moving groups of men from the crowded beachhead. This was the only exit opened in the early part of the assault and subsequent events proved it to be one of the most vital points contributing to the success of this operation. The high professional skill and outstanding courage exhibited by Colonel Taylor reflects great credit on himself and is in keeping with the highest traditions of the armed forces. Entered United States Military Academy from Oklahoma.

Headquarters, First Army, General Orders No. 31 (July 1, 1944)

Next Page: Colonel George A. Taylor, from Flat Rock, Illinois, was a graduate of the United States Military Academy's class of 1922. He commanded the 16th Infantry Regiment during the invasions of Sicily and Normandy and was promoted to the rank of brigadier general on August 1, 1944 and was the assistant division commander of the 1st Infantry Division from October of 1944 through July 1945. He retired from the military in 1946 due to health reasons and passed away at Palo Alto, California in 1969. *Photograph courtesy of the First Division Museum at Cantigny.*

Major General Maxwell D. Taylor
Headquarters, 101st Airborne Division

Citation: Major General Maxwell D. Taylor, 014898, (then Brigadier General), 101st Airborne Division, for extraordinary heroism in action against the enemy on 6 June 1944, in France. Landing with his parachute unit in enemy territory and in the face of intense enemy fire, Major General (then Brigadier General) Taylor quickly organized the control elements of the Division Headquarters. Perceiving that the important causeway at Pouppeville could not be taken by the unit assigned that mission, General Taylor personally led elements of the Division Headquarters and other special troops in an attack on the causeway. General Taylor led the successful assault and seized the causeway thereby clearing the way for the advance of the seaborne units. The courage and outstanding leadership displayed by General Taylor reflects great credit on himself and is in keeping with the highest traditions of the armed forces. Entered military service from Missouri.

Headquarters, First Army, General Orders No. 31 (July 1, 1944)

Major General Maxwell D. Taylor was born on August 26, 1901 in Keytesville, Missouri and graduated from the United States Military Academy in 1922. He served as the assistant commander of the 82nd Airborne Division during the invasion of Sicily. Taylor was the commander of the 101st Airborne Division on June 6, 1944 and continued as its commanding officer through the end of the war. After the war, Taylor succeeded Matthew B. Ridgway as the Chief of Staff, United States Army from 1955–1959, when he retired from the military in protest of President Eisenhower's defense policy. Taylor felt it neglected the country's conventional forces in favor of a reliance on nuclear weapons as deterrence to communist aggression. President Kennedy recalled Taylor to duty in 1961 to serve as his military advisor and then as the Chairman, Joint Chiefs of Staff from 1962–1964. He retired again in 1964 and then served as ambassador to Vietnam from 1964 until 1965, during the early stages of the American involvement in the conflict. *United States Army photograph.*

Lieutenant General Omar N. Bradley awards the Distinguished Service Cross to Major General Maxwell D. Taylor during a ceremony on July 2, 1944. *United States Army Signal Corps photograph.*

Twenty-five members of the 101st Airborne Division were awarded the Distinguished Service Cross on July 2, 1944. In this photo are three recipients for actions on June 6: Major General Maxwell D. Taylor (front left), Captain Frank L. Lillyman (front second from right), and Chaplain John S. Maloney (front right). *United States Army Signal Corps photograph.*

Second Lieutenant Walter P. Taylor, Jr.
Company B, 116th Infantry Regiment, 29th Infantry Division

Citation: First Lieutenant Walter P. Taylor, Jr., 01312356 (then Second Lieutenant), Infantry, 116th Infantry Regiment, 29th Infantry Division, United States Army, for extraordinary heroism in connection with military operations against the enemy. On 6 June 1944, Lieutenant Taylor landed with his boat section near Vierville-sur-Mer, France and led his men on to their initial objective through enemy machine gun, artillery and mortar fire. After being joined by another section, Lieutenant Taylor and his group headed for the predetermined battalion rendezvous area. In this move one of his men was wounded. Disregarding his own personal safety and in the face of enemy fire, Lieutenant Taylor moved to aid the wounded man. In so doing his weapon was shot from his hand, but he courageously proceeded with his task and evacuated the wounded man to safety. During the following days, Lieutenant Taylor displayed inspiring leadership and outstanding courage as he skillfully led his men in numerous advances on enemy positions. At one time he led the spearhead of a battalion attack across a river and up a heavily fortified enemy held hill. On 13 June 1944, Lieutenant Taylor was wounded, but his display of skillful, courageous leadership contributed immeasurably to the success of his unit and was a source of inspiration to his men. The extraordinary heroism and courageous actions of Lieutenant Taylor reflect great credit upon himself and are in keeping with the highest traditions of the military service. Entered military service from Massachusetts.

Headquarters, Ninth Army, General Orders No. 75 (December 20, 1944)

Lieutenant Walter P. Taylor, Jr., leading his Company B, 116th Infantry boat section, was likely the first man to reach the top of the bluff in the 116th Infantry's zone and made the deepest penetration of any unit of the 29th Infantry Division. Taylor had been an exchange student in Germany in 1936 and was fluent in the German language. He met and married a Red Cross nurse in France during the war. *Photograph courtesy of Geoff Taylor.*

Major Charles E. Tegtmeyer
Headquarters, 1st Medical Battalion, 1st Infantry Division

Citation: Major Charles E. Tegtmeyer, 0335197, 16th Infantry, United States Army, for extraordinary heroism in action against the enemy on 6 June 1944, in France. When Major Tegtmeyer landed with his medical section, the assaulting troops were still pinned down on a narrow beachhead. Due to the devastating fire of the enemy, numerous casualties had been sustained. With complete disregard for his own safety Major Tegtmeyer covered the length of the beach, administering aid to the wounded lying all along the shore. Time and again, he went into mine strewn waters and pulled the wounded in to comparative safety behind a shale barrier. Major Tegtmeyer, heedless of the heavy fire, worked unceasingly in rendering aid to the wounded under the most hazardous conditions. The fortitude and unhesitating devotion to duty of Major Tegtmeyer reflects great credit on himself and is in keeping with the highest traditions of the armed forces. Entered military service from New York.

Headquarters, First Army, General Orders No. 31 (July 1, 1944)

General Dwight D. Eisenhower awards the Distinguished Service Cross to Major Charles E. Tegtmeyer, from the Bronx, New York, during a ceremony near Balleroy, France on July 2, 1944. Other DSC recipients in this photograph are Lieutenant Colonel Herbert C. Hicks, Jr. (center), Captain Joseph T. Dawson (second from right), and Captain Kimball R. Richmond (right). *United States Army Signal Corps photograph, courtesy of the First Division Museum at Cantigny.*

Colonel Paul W. Thompson
Headquarters, 6th Special Engineer Brigade, Provisional Engineer Special Brigade Group, V Corps

Citation: Colonel Paul W. Thompson, 017506, Corps of Engineers, United States Army, for extraordinary heroism in action against the enemy on 6 June 1944, in France. The attack on a vital beach exit was being held up by heavy enemy machine gun fire. Upon discovering the situation and ascertaining that the assault units were pinned to the beach and were not pressing the attack, Colonel Thompson called for volunteers to assist in wiping out the machine guns. Several infantrymen volunteered. With complete disregard for his own safety, Colonel Thompson, while under heavy enemy fire, blew a gap in the wire entanglements. He then fearlessly led his party through the gap and was rushing to assault the enemy machine guns when he was seriously wounded by enemy fire from another emplacement. The inspiring leadership and personal bravery displayed by Colonel Thompson reflects great credit on himself and is in keeping with the highest traditions of the Armed Forces. Entered United States Military Academy from Nebraska.

Headquarters, First Army, General Orders No. 39 (July 31, 1944)

Colonel Paul W. Thompson commanded the 6th Special Engineer Brigade on June 6, 1944. This photo of Thompson was taken after his promotion to brigadier general. Thompson, from Alliance, Nebraska, was a 1929 graduate of the United States Military Academy. *Photograph courtesy of Jonathan Gawne.*

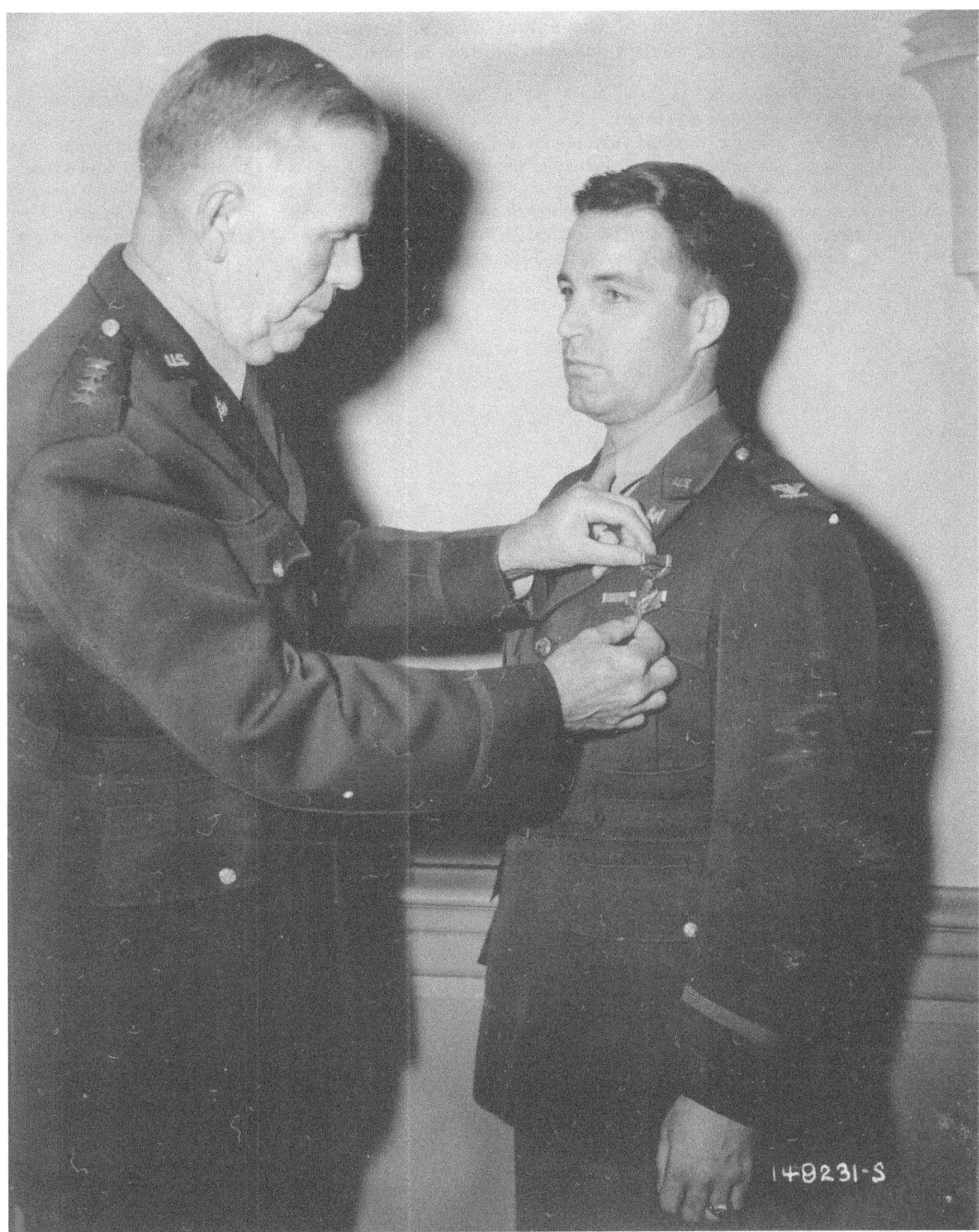

General George C. Marshall, the Chief of Staff of the United States Army, awards the Distinguished Service Cross to Colonel Paul W. Thompson in the general's office at the Pentagon, October 3, 1944. *United States Army Signal Corps photograph, National Archives.*

Second Lieutenant John N. Townsend
Company B, 70th Tank Battalion

Citation: Second Lieutenant John N. Townsend, 01015121, 70th Tank Battalion, United States Army, for extraordinary heroism in action against the enemy on 6 June 1944 on the Cotentin Peninsula, France. In the assault on the heavily fortified beaches of the Cotentin Peninsula Lieutenant Townsend's tank platoon reached that part of the beach ahead of friendly infantry. Extremely heavy enemy automatic weapons, artillery, and mortar fire was directed from the right flank on to his platoon. He immediately organized his platoon and advanced into this heavy enemy fire. Lieutenant Townsend, when he found that his advance was impeded by extremely poor visibility, with complete disregard for his own safety dismounted from his tank while under heavy enemy fire and personally directed the attack of his tank platoon from this exposed position. The courage and leadership exhibited by Lieutenant Townsend reflect great credit upon himself and upon the armed forces.

Headquarters, First Army, General Orders No. 35 (July 19, 1944)

John N. Townsend, from Mena, Arkansas, served with the Arkansas National Guard before attending officer candidate school. After graduating in January 1943, he was assigned to the 70th Tank Battalion and served with it during the campaigns in North Africa, Sicily, and Normandy. Lieutenant Townsend was awarded the Silver Star for heroism in Sicily and an oak leaf cluster to the Silver Star for his heroism in Normandy on June 23, 1944, in which he was wounded. He was discharged in December of 1945 and returned home to continue his education. Townsend tragically died in a car wreck on June 16, 1946.

First Sergeant Herbert A. Tubbs
Company I, 501st Parachute Infantry Regiment, 101st Airborne Division

Citation: First Sergeant Herbert A. Tubbs, 39195705, 501st Parachute Infantry, United States Army, for extraordinary heroism in action against the enemy from 6 June 1944 to 14 June 1944, in France. First Sergeant Tubbs and four other men landed by parachute and became separated from their group deep in hostile territory. He contacted French patriots while on a patrol and received information concerning location of enemy forces in the area. During the week-long period which followed, he personally led many day and night reconnaissance patrols and succeeded in retrieving equipment bundles containing radios, guns and ammunition. On one occasion while questioning civilians, he observed several enemy soldiers advancing toward his position. Unhesitatingly, and ignoring their fire, he rushed toward them firing his submachine gun, forcing them to flee. Later, he single handedly routed another enemy patrol near his area. After repeated attempts, First Sergeant Tubbs was successful in breaking through enemy lines and contacting friendly forces. Returning with a truck, he again passed through enemy lines and evacuated the remainder of his group, together with the accumulated equipment. First Sergeant Tubbs' courageous leadership, personal valor and unswerving devotion to duty exemplified the highest traditions of the armed forces. Entered military service from Washington.

Headquarters, First Army, General Orders No. 86 (November 25, 1944)

First Sergeant Herbert A. Tubbs was from Bellingham, Washington and served with Company I of the 501st Parachute Infantry Regiment, 101st Airborne Division during World War II. *Photograph courtesy of Loren Tubbs.*

Private Albert J. Tucker
Company B, 146th Engineer Combat Battalion, Special Engineer Task Force, Provisional Engineer Special Brigade Group
Gap Support Team Number C

Citation: Private Albert J. Tucker, 38463788, 146th Engineer Combat Battalion, United States Army, for extraordinary heroism in action against the enemy on 6 June 1944 in France. The demolition team in which Private Tucker was a member landed on the coast of France under heavy enemy fire at high tide. The high tide made it impossible to work upon the obstacles. The men debarked from the landing craft and crossed the beach to a place of comparative safety to await the fall of the tide. At this time it was noticed that the officer in charge of the demolition team was missing. He was then seen badly wounded at the water's edge attempting to make his way up the beach. Private Tucker, completely disregarding his own safety, upon observing the condition of his team commander, immediately left his place of cover, crossed the fire swept beach and assisted his wounded leader to safety. The gallantry, devotion to duty, and personal bravery exhibited by Private Tucker reflect great credit upon himself and is in keeping with the highest traditions of the armed forces.

Headquarters, First Army, General Orders No. 37 (July 21, 1944)

Private Albert J. Tucker, from Ramona, Oklahoma, receives the Distinguished Service Cross from Major General Leonard T. Gerow, the commanding officer of V Corps, during a ceremony to award the DSC to members of the 146th Engineer Combat Battalion, conducted on September 11, 1944 in France. *United States Army Signal Corps photograph, National Archives.*

Lieutenant Colonel John S. Upham, Jr.
Headquarters, 743rd Tank Battalion

Citation: Lieutenant Colonel John S. Upham, Jr., 017178, 743rd Tank Battalion, United States Army, for extraordinary heroism in action against the enemy on 6 June 1944, in France. Early on D-Day, when his tank battalion was landing in the assault, Lieutenant Colonel Upham was directing operations by radio from a craft several hundred yards offshore. The unloading of tanks and men became increasingly difficult, as under the devastating enemy fire, tanks were knocked out and the wreckage impeded movement across the beach. Realizing the gravity of the situation, he went over the side of his landing craft and waded ashore in the face of the enemy fire. He proceeded to the tanks, personally guided them across the fire swept beach, and directed their fight to open the beach exit. Though seriously wounded twice, he disdained to seek medical attention but continuously remained exposed to the enemy fire and coordinated the fire and movement of his tanks. It was only after his battalion had seized its objective that he was evacuated for his wounds. The extraordinary heroism, the personal bravery, and the determined leadership displayed by Lieutenant Colonel Upham reflects great credit upon himself and is in keeping with the highest traditions of the armed forces. Entered the United States Military Academy from the United States at large.

Headquarters, First Army, General Orders No. 68 (October 14, 1944)

This photograph of Lieutenant Colonel John S. Upham, Jr., the commanding officer of the 743rd Tank Battalion, shows him in the commander's hatch of his Sherman tank during training in the United States prior to the battalion moving overseas. Upham was a 1928 graduate of the United States Military Academy and retired from the United States Army at the rank of lieutenant general. *Photograph courtesy of Anne Upham Brown.*

Second Lieutenant Leo D. Van De Voort
Company B, 116th Infantry Regiment, 29th Infantry Division

Citation: First Lieutenant Leo D. Van De Voort, 0885530 (then Second Lieutenant), 116th Infantry, United States Army, for extraordinary heroism in action against the enemy on 6 June 1944, in France. In the initial assault upon the coast of France, First Lieutenant Van De Voort landed with his platoon in the face of heavy enemy rifle, machine gun and artillery fire. This intense fire pinned the men down on a narrow beachhead, inflicting numerous casualties with resultant disorganization. With complete disregard for his own safety, First Lieutenant Van De Voort, on numerous occasions, exposed himself to this direct fire in reorganizing and preparing his platoon for an attack. He then led his platoon in a successful assault upon the enemy positions. The personal bravery and superior leadership displayed by First Lieutenant Van De Voort reflect great credit on himself and was in keeping with the highest traditions of the armed forces.

Headquarters, First Army, General Orders No. 29 (June 29, 1944)

Colonel James A. Van Fleet
Headquarters, 8th Infantry Regiment, 4th Infantry Division

Citation: Colonel James A. Van Fleet, 03847, 8th Infantry, United States Army, for extraordinary heroism in action against the enemy on 6–8 June 1944, in France. In the initial landing and assault upon the European continent, Colonel Van Fleet quickly organized his troops and pushed them rapidly across the beach in an orderly and determined manner, brushing aside resistance and thereby greatly expediting the early establishment of the division beachhead. Colonel Van Fleet was always well forward and on numerous occasions personally went up to check his battalions. His superior leadership and personal example of courage aided in clearing the beach with a minimum of casualties and substantially contributed to the rapid advance of the division to its D-Day objectives. On 7 June 1944, while the enemy was using observed fire to vigorously shell the highways and avenues of approach in the vicinity of his unit, he displayed cool leadership and skill in maintaining order under severely trying conditions, and did so encourage and inspire confidence in all members of the combat team that they followed his example and advanced with no hesitation, and minimum losses of both men and equipment. This was at a critical time when a failure to procure advanced positions would have endangered the success of the operation. On the morning of 8 June 1944, while visiting his front line battalions, with disregard for his personal safety, he captured an enemy guard and procured important information from him which aided the regiment in successfully advancing against the enemy's strongly entrenched successive positions. The cool fearlessness, personal bravery, and leadership displayed by Colonel Van Fleet were an inspiration to his men and a great force in their battle success. Entered military service from Florida.

Headquarters, First Army, General Orders No. 20 (June 20, 1944)

Private John J. Van Valkenburg
Company I, 507th Parachute Infantry Regiment, 82nd Airborne Division

Citation: Private John J. Van Valkenburg, 32743116, 507th Parachute Infantry, United States Army, for extraordinary heroism in action against the enemy during the period 6 June 1944 through 5 July 1944, in France. On D-Day Private Van Valkenburg on three separate and distinct occasions crossed open fields swept by enemy fire to administer aid to and evacuate wounded men. On 14 June 1944, he moved out one hundred yards in front of the lines under heavy enemy mortar and machine gun fire to render aid to a wounded man and to bring him back to the safety of his own lines. On 15 June 1944, while accompanying a patrol, he left his place of cover and administered first aid in the midst of mortar and small arms fire to a wounded man. Though wounded by mortar fire, he refused to be evacuated. On 5 July 1944, he twice moved across open fields swept by machine gun fire to administer aid to wounded men. On this latter occasion Private Van Valkenburg was again wounded. The gallantry and unselfish devotion to duty without regard for his own personal safety displayed by Private Van Valkenburg reflects great credit on himself and is in keeping with the highest traditions of the armed forces.

Headquarters, First Army, General Orders No. 45 (August 9, 1944)

Lieutenant Colonel Benjamin H. Vandervoort
Headquarters, 2nd Battalion, 505th Parachute Infantry Regiment, 82nd Airborne Division

Citation: Lieutenant Colonel Benjamin H. Vandervoort, 0-22715, 505th Parachute Infantry, United States Army, for extraordinary heroism in action against the enemy on 6 June 1944, in France. Though he sustained a broken foot in his jump, Lieutenant Colonel Vandervoort refused to be evacuated. He immediately, despite his painful injury, assembled and organized all the available troops from his battalion and personally led it through enemy held territory to the initial objective. With only first aid treatment for his broken foot, he remained with his unit and directed the defense of its newly won position against a vastly superior enemy. With complete disregard for his own safety, he continually moved about the foremost elements, subjecting himself to intense enemy rifle, machine gun, and artillery fire. Inspired by his presence, his men successfully withstood repeated enemy counterattacks. The personal bravery, devotion to duty, and outstanding leadership displayed by Lieutenant Colonel Vandervoort reflects great credit on himself and is in keeping with the highest traditions of the armed forces. Entered military service from Ohio.

Headquarters, First Army, General Orders No. 31 (July 1, 1944)

Lieutenant General Omar Bradley, commander of the First Army, awards the Distinguished Service Cross to Lieutenant Colonel Benjamin H. Vandervoort, from Columbus, Ohio, in the courtyard of the Chateau de Brocqueboeuf, east of La-Haye-du-Puits, France on July 10, 1944. Three other 82nd Airborne Division paratroopers are also being awarded the DSC for their heroism on June 6, 1944. They are Lieutenant Colonel Edward C. Krause (left), Private First Class Gordon C. Pryne (second from right), and Private Marcus Heim, Jr. (partially shown at right). *United States Army Signal Corps photograph, courtesy of the 82nd Airborne Division War Memorial Museum.*

Lieutenant Colonel Benjamin H. Vandervoort, commanding officer of the 2nd Battalion, 505th Parachute Infantry Regiment, is congratulated by Lieutenant General Omar Bradley upon being awarded the Distinguished Service Cross for his heroism on June 6, 1944. *United States Army Signal Corps photograph.*

Major William R. Washington
Headquarters, 2nd Battalion, 16th Infantry Regiment, 1st Infantry Division

Citation: Major William R. Washington, 16th Infantry, United States Army, for extraordinary heroism in action against the enemy on 6 June 1944 in France. Major Washington landed with the regiment's over-strength which was to follow the initial assault. When intense enemy fire pinned down the leading waves and his troops became part of this halted group, he exposed himself fearlessly to the raking fire along the shore and unhesitatingly led his men through barbed wire entanglements, over an uncharted minefield and up the heavily fortified cliffs, destroying several enemy fortifications while forging his way forward to the top. Then, after turning the replacements over to their organizations, he left the main body of troops and, to his own initiative, went forward through the enemy line to a vital crossroad near Colleville-sur-le-Mer and established an observation post. Although badly wounded by enemy sniper fire, he held his position for twenty-four hours and his observations and directions were invaluable to the advancing troops. Major Washington's incomparable fighting spirit and magnificent valor, his extraordinary heroism and professional skill were important and decisive factors in the initial assault. Entered military service from Virginia.

Headquarters, First Army, General Orders No. 45 (August 9, 1944)

The VII Corps commander, Major General J. Lawton Collins, awards the Distinguished Service Cross to Major William R. Washington, the executive officer of the 2nd Battalion, 16th Infantry Regiment, from Croset, Virginia, during a ceremony held near Hauset, Belgium on September 27, 1944. *United States Army Signal Corps photograph, courtesy of the First Division Museum at Cantigny,*

Sergeant William W. Weir
Company G, 501st Parachute Infantry Regiment, 101st Airborne Division

Citation: William W. Weir, 16151362, Sergeant, 501st Parachute Infantry, United States Army, for extraordinary heroism in connection with military operations against an armed enemy of the United States. On 6 June 1944, he landed with a small group in the vicinity of Boutteville, France. The group was under continuous fire from the enemy, which surrounded them as soon as they had landed. Sergeant Weir, noticing the heaviest fire coming from a nearby house, attacked the house alone and captured three of the enemy. On the following day, in the vicinity of Hiesville, France, Sergeant Weir and four men volunteered to take out enemy weapons which were firing on some gliders which contained vitally needed supplies. Sergeant Weir and his four were pinned down about fifty yards from an enemy machine gun emplacement. After he expended his M1 ammunition, Sergeant Weir charged across the open field, and with hand grenades, wiped out the machine gun nest, causing the remainder of the enemy to withdraw. His actions were in accordance with the highest standards of the military service. Entered military service from Michigan.

Headquarters, XVIII Airborne Corps, General Orders No. 16 (December 18, 1944)

Sergeant William W. Weir, from Owosso, Michigan, served with Company G, 501st Parachute Infantry Regiment of the 101st Airborne Division. The photograph is of Weir as a private first class shortly after graduation from the Parachute School at Fort Benning, Georgia. Weir was killed in action during the fighting around Bastogne in the Ardennes campaign. He is buried at Oak Hill Cemetery in Owosso. *Photograph courtesy of Pierre Godeau.*

Lieutenant Colonel John C. Welborn
Headquarters, 70th Tank Battalion

Citation: Lieutenant Colonel John C. Welborn, 018863, 70th Tank Battalion, United States Army, for extraordinary heroism in action against the enemy on 6 and 7 June 1944 in France. During the initial assault on the heavily fortified coast of Normandy, Lieutenant Colonel Welborn, in order to get his assault companies on the beach at the earliest possible moment, voluntarily landed on foot. Despite the heavy enemy fire, he immediately proceeded inland. When he contacted his tank companies, he organized them for attacks against enemy pillboxes and strongpoints. When a tank of his battalion was disabled by a mine and struck three times by antitank shells that killed the driver and wounded other soldiers, Lieutenant Colonel Welborn, with complete disregard for his own safety, aided in evacuating the wounded from his damaged tank. On the 7th of June when a heavy enemy counterattack threatened vital positions Lieutenant Colonel Welborn rallied his battalion and fearlessly led a company of tanks through heavy enemy fire while mounted in a ¼-ton truck. The personal bravery and fearless leadership displayed by Lieutenant Colonel Welborn reflects great credit on himself and on the armed forces. Entered military service from Washington.

Headquarters, First Army, General Orders No. 35 (July 19, 1944)

Lieutenant General Courtney Hodges awards the Distinguished Service Cross to Lieutenant Colonel John C. Welborn, the commanding officer of the 70th Tank Battalion, at a ceremony at the 4th Infantry Division headquarters on August 16, 1944. *United States Army Signal Corps photograph, National Archives.*

John C. Welborn was born at Fort Sam Houston, Texas, the son of a West Point officer. He was a 1932 graduate of the United States Military Academy at West Point, New York. Welborn retired at the rank of colonel at the end of his postwar career in the army. *Photograph courtesy of Carl Welborn.*

Staff Sergeant James A. Wells
Company L, 16th Infantry Regiment, 1st Infantry Division

Citation: Staff Sergeant James A. Wells, 35215424, 16th Infantry, United States Army, for extraordinary heroism in action against the enemy on 6 June 1944 near Colleville-sur-le-Mer, France. While his company was pinned down on the beach due to the intense enemy rifle, machine gun, and artillery fire, Staff Sergeant Wells with two other men volunteered to cut an opening in the barbed wire. In the face of the heavy enemy fire he opened a gap in the wire, and then picked his way through a minefield to the base of a hill and proceeded to lay effective rifle fire on the enemy positions. He caused the enemy to cease firing long enough to allow his company to move through the gap in the wire and join him beyond the minefield. Then while the men who had joined him laid frontal fire on the enemy position, he, though continually exposed, moved to the flank and rear of the enemy and subjected them to his extremely accurate rifle fire. While he engaged the enemy, the company again moved forward and successfully assaulted the enemy positions. When the enemy counterattacked Staff Sergeant Wells again worked his way to the flank and from his exposed position laid effective fire upon the enemy, and remained at his post despite the heavy fire that was placed upon him until the counterattack was beaten off. The courage, initiative, and skill demonstrated by Staff Sergeant Wells reflect great credit on himself and were in keeping with the highest traditions of the armed forces of the United States.

Headquarters, First Army, General Orders No. 31 (July 1, 1944)

Technical Sergeant John W. White
Company A, 2nd Ranger Battalion, Provisional Ranger Group

Citation: Technical Sergeant John W. White, 31135430, Infantry, United States Army, for extraordinary heroism in action against the enemy from 6 to 8 June 1944 at Vierville-sur-le-Mer and Pointe du Hoc, France. When all the officers of his company became casualties in the initial landing on the coast of France from the devastating enemy fire he assumed command of machine gun positions and directed their fire on the enemy positions. Later he personally acted as the point of the column which advanced from the beach to Pointe du Hoc. On this advance Sergeant White exposed himself to the direct rifle and machine gun fire of the enemy as well as sniper fire. Technical Sergeant White's excellent leadership and gallantry under such difficult and hazardous circumstances is in keeping with the highest traditions of the service. Entered military service from Massachusetts.

Headquarters, First Army, General Orders No. 28 (June 20, 1944)

Technical Sergeant John W. White (left) and Technician Fifth Grade Richard E. Rankin (right), both members of Company A, 2nd Ranger Battalion, posed for this photograph at Arlon, Belgium during October 1944. White was from Jamaica Plains, Massachusetts. *Photograph courtesy of Julie Fulmer.*

Lieutenant Colonel James E. Rudder (left), commanding officer of the Provisional Ranger Group and the 2nd Ranger Battalion, congratulates Technical Sergeant John W. White (right) on the award of the Distinguished Service Cross at a ceremony near Colombieres, France on June 23, 1944. *United States Army Signal Corps photograph, National Archives.*

Captain George P. Whittington, Jr.
Company B, 5th Ranger Battalion, Provisional Ranger Group

Citation: Captain George P. Whittington, Jr., 0403921, Cavalry, United States Army, for extraordinary heroism in action on 6 June 1944 at Vierville-sur-Mer, France. Captain Whittington commanded a Ranger company which landed on the coast of France at H-Hour. The landing was made on the beach against heavy rifle, machine gun, mortar, artillery and rocket fire of the enemy. Despite this fire, he personally supervised the breaching of hostile barbed wire and obstacles by the use of Bangalores. He then led his company and the remainder of his battalion through the gap created. He then directed the scaling of a one hundred foot cliff by his company. When he reached the top of the cliff he crawled under enemy machine gun fire and destroyed the enemy position. Captain Whittington's bravery, aggressiveness and inspired leadership are in keeping with the highest traditions of the service. Entered military service from Arkansas.

Headquarters, First Army, General Orders No. 28 (June 20, 1944)

Captain George P. Whittington, Jr., from Hot Springs, Arkansas, commanded Company B, 5th Ranger Battalion during the invasion of Normandy. He earned a bachelor's degree in journalism after the war, settling in Henderson, Kentucky in 1947. Whittington returned to active duty during the Korean War, where he served as a battalion commander at the rank of major. He later became a farmer and also owned a cattle ranch in Costa Rica. *United States Army Signal Corps photograph, National Archives.*

Private First Class Theodore T. Wilk
Company F, 16th Infantry Regiment, 1st Infantry Division

Citation: Private First Class Theodore T. Wilk, 31272097, 16th Infantry, United States Army, for extraordinary heroism in action against the enemy on 6 June 1944, in France. On D-Day, Private First Class Wilk voluntarily left his position of safety and advanced boldly to a position from which he placed well-aimed fire upon an enemy pillbox. With utter disregard for his safety, he crawled closer through intense automatic weapons and small arms fire, and while delivering accurate fire which silenced the enemy, he was seriously wounded by sniper fire. Despite his wounds, he refused medical aid and pushed inland with his comrades. When his unit was halted by the direct fire of a well dug-in machine gun, Private First Class Wilk courageously moved through a hail of fire to get within hand grenade range of the weapon. En route to the gun position, he was caught in a heavy artillery barrage which blinded him and inflicted additional wounds. By his unflinching devotion to duty, his Spartan effort, and his personal bravery, Private First Class Wilk exemplified the highest traditions of the armed forces. Entered military service from Connecticut.

Headquarters, First Army, General Orders No. 81 (November 16, 1944)

First Lieutenant Alfred H. Williams, Jr.
Company C, 743rd Tank Battalion

Citation: First Lieutenant Alfred H. Williams, Jr., 01016166, 743rd Tank Battalion, United States Army, for extraordinary heroism in action against the enemy on 6 June 1944 in France. First Lieutenant Williams commanded a tank company, landing on the coast of France under heavy enemy small arms, machine gun, and observed artillery fire. Due to the devastating enemy fire heavy casualties were sustained and his unit became partially immobilized. First Lieutenant Williams promptly reorganized and directed his company to the opening of a beach exit. With complete disregard for his own safety he constantly exposed himself to the intense enemy fire and directed his unit in the accomplishment of its mission. First Lieutenant Williams' personal bravery and superior leadership reflects great credit upon himself and is in keeping with the highest traditions of the armed forces.

Headquarters, First Army, General Orders No. 37 (July 21, 1944)

First Lieutenant William B. Williams
Company B, 116th Infantry Regiment, 29th Infantry Division

Citation: Captain William B. Williams, 0379493 (then First Lieutenant), Infantry, 116th Infantry Regiment, 29th Infantry Division, United States Army, for extraordinary heroism in connection with military operations against the enemy on 6 June 1944. In the initial assault upon the coast of France, Captain Williams skillfully led his boat team through a hail of small arms, mortar and artillery fire to the high ground off the beach. At this point the party encountered a mortar emplacement which had to be either destroyed or neutralized before their advance could continue. Captain Williams alone charged the position but was thrown back by enemy grenades. With stubborn determination and without regard for his own personal safety, Captain Williams made four more attempts to knock out the enemy position; each time he was forced to fall back. Although wounded in his previous attempts but undaunted, Captain Williams courageously made another bold attempt; this time his grenades found their mark and the enemy position was destroyed. The extraordinary heroism and courageous actions of Captain Williams reflect great credit upon himself and are in keeping with the highest traditions of the military service. Entered military service from Pennsylvania.

Headquarters, Ninth Army, General Orders No. 75 (December 20, 1944)

First Lieutenant Richard D. Winters
Company E, 506th Parachute Infantry Regiment, 101st Airborne Division

Citation: First Lieutenant Richard D. Winters, 01286582, Parachute Infantry, United States Army, for extraordinary heroism in action against the enemy on 6 June 1944, in France. First Lieutenant Winters, with seven enlisted men, advanced through intense enemy automatic weapons fire, putting out of action two guns of the battery of four [105]mm that were shelling the beachhead. Unswerved in his determination to complete his self-appointed and extremely hazardous task, First Lieutenant Winters and his group withdrew for reinforcements. He returned with tank support and the remaining two guns were put out of action, resulting in decreased opposition to our forces landing on the beachhead. First Lieutenant Winters' heroic and determined leadership reflects great credit on himself and is in keeping with the highest traditions of the armed forces. Entered military service from Pennsylvania.

Headquarters, First Army, General Orders No. 31 (July 1, 1944)

Lieutenant Richard D. Winters, from Lancaster, Pennsylvania, was the executive officer of Company E of the 506th Parachute Infantry Regiment, 101st Airborne Division on June 6, 1944. He rose to the rank of major by the end of the war. After the war, he gained international fame when Stephen Ambrose wrote a best selling a book about Company E, 506th Parachute Infantry, entitled *Band of Brothers*, which relied heavily on his war time diary and personal interviews.

An award ceremony was held on July 2, 1944 to award the Distinguished Service Cross to members of the 101st Airborne Division. Lieutenant Richard D. Winters is seventh from the left of the recipients standing below the elevated stage. *United States Army Signal Corps photograph.*

Captain Robert W. Woodward
7th Field Artillery Battalion, 1st Infantry Division

Citation: Captain Robert W. Woodward, 0389219, Field Artillery, United States Army, for extraordinary heroism in action against the enemy on 6 June 1944, in France. Captain Woodward, while on the beach on D-Day, discovered an enemy casemate from which heavy fire was being delivered on the troops moving across the beach. Exposing himself fully to the view of the enemy at less than three hundred yards range, Captain Woodward jumped into a tank, required it to move forward and then directed its fire on this emplacement. He then left the tank and, though completely lacking cover from the intense enemy fire, proceeded through the barbed wire and up a sharp slope directly towards the fortification. Captain Woodward fired his pistol into successive casemate openings and forced the surrender of twenty-three of the enemy. Captain Woodward's initiative, personal bravery and daring set an inspiring example to his men and is in keeping with the highest traditions of the Armed Forces. Entered military service from Massachusetts.

Headquarters, First Army, General Orders No. 39 (July 31, 1944)

Captain Robert W. Woodward, from Rockland, Massachusetts, is awarded the Distinguished Service Cross by Major General J. Lawton Collins, VII Corps commander, during a ceremony near Hauset, Belgium on September 27, 1944. *United States Army Signal Corps photograph, National Archives.*

Captain Edward F. Wozenski
Company E, 16th Infantry Regiment, 1st Infantry Division

Citation: Captain Edward F. Wozenski, 0351415, 16th Infantry, United States Army, for extraordinary heroism in action against the enemy on 6 June 1944, in France. On D-Day, Captain Wozenski's company suffered numerous casualties in reaching the fire swept invasion beach. Boldly, he moved along the beach, at the risk of his life, to reorganize his battered troops. The reorganization completed, he courageously led his men through heavy machine gun and small arms fire across the beach and toward an enemy dominated ridge. Demoralizing fire from a powerful enemy installation on the ridge threatened to stop the attack. Ordering his men to deploy to the flanks of the enemy position, Captain Wozenski, with great valor, advanced alone to within one hundred yards of the emplacement. With cool and calm efficiency, he engaged the fortification single handedly with rifle fire to divert attention of the enemy from the flanking movement. Upon observing this valiant soldier, the enemy directed the fire of a number of its machine guns on him but Captain Wozenski, with complete disregard for his own safety, continued his harassing fire until his men reached their positions safely. His inspired troops charged the strongpoint vigorously and completely destroyed it, inflicting numerous casualties upon the enemy. By his superb leadership and fearless courage, Captain Wozenski exemplified the highest traditions of the armed forces. Entered military service from Connecticut.

Headquarters, First Army, General Orders No. 82 (November 19, 1944)

Brigadier General Willard G. Wyman
Headquarters, 1st Infantry Division

Citation: Brigadier General Willard G. Wyman, 012356, 1st Infantry Division, United States Army, for extraordinary heroism in action against the enemy on 6 June 1944, near Colleville-sur-le-Mer, France. At a time when the heavy rifle, machine gun, artillery, and rocket fire of the enemy seriously threatened the invasion effort on this part of the beach, Brigadier General Wyman came ashore directly behind the leading wave of troops. Due to enemy action, many organizational leaders became casualties. With disregard to his own personal safety Brigadier General Wyman moved up and down the fire-swept beach personally directing the movement of the men and the vehicles which had landed. Under his direction the men were reorganized and successfully assaulted the enemy positions. The gallantry and outstanding leadership displayed by Brigadier General Wyman reflect great credit upon himself and were in keeping with the highest traditions of the armed forces.

Headquarters, First Army, General Orders No. 31 (July 1, 1944)

Private First Class Donald E. Zahn
Company H, 506th Parachute Infantry Regiment, 101st Airborne Division

Citation: Sergeant Donald E. Zahn, 17109148, 506th Parachute Infantry, United States Army, for extraordinary heroism in action against the enemy on 6 June 1944, in France. Sergeant Zahn volunteered as a scout to make the initial crossing of a vital bridge in the face of heavy enemy machine gun and small arms fire. He advanced daringly across the bridge defended by a large force of German soldiers and poured incessant fire into their positions, forcing them to withdraw. By his courageous action, Sergeant Zahn enabled his unit to organize, establish an effective bridgehead and hold its objective. Sergeant Zahn's display of personal valor and heroic achievement are in keeping with the highest traditions of the armed forces. Entered military service from Minnesota.

Headquarters, First Army, General Orders No. 81 (November 16, 1944)

Brigadier General Willard G. Wyman, from Augusta, Maine, graduated from the United States Military Academy in 1919. He was the assistant commander of the 1st Infantry Division during the invasion of Normandy and subsequently commanded the 71st Infantry Division through the end of the war in Europe. Wyman commanded the IX Corps during the Korean War and served as Commander In Chief, NATO Land Forces South-East Europe. He retired from the army in 1958 as a four star general. He died in 1969 and is buried at Arlington National Cemetery. *Photograph, courtesy of the First Division Museum at Cantigny.*

First Lieutenant Forrest Zanlow
Medical Detachment, 116th Infantry Regiment, 29th Infantry Division

Citation: Captain Forrest (NMI) Zanlow, 0474270 (then First Lieutenant), 116th Infantry, United States Army, for extraordinary heroism in action against the enemy on 6 June 1944, in France. In the initial landings on the coast of France, Captain Zanlow landed early in the assault as part of the regimental medical detachment. Undaunted by the heavy and intense enemy fire, Captain Zanlow attended the wounded on the beach. With complete disregard for his own safety, he moved about the beach rendering aid to the numerous casualties caused by enemy fire. By his personal bravery under such hazardous conditions, he was instrumental in the saving of many lives. The courage and high devotion to duty displayed by Captain Zanlow reflects great credit on himself and was in keeping with the highest traditions of the armed forces.

Headquarters, First Army, General Orders No. 29 (June 29, 1944)

First Lieutenant Harvey J. Zeigler
Company H, 505th Parachute Infantry Regiment, 82nd Airborne Division

Citation: Harvey J. Zeigler (0-1286224), First Lieutenant (Infantry), United States Army, for extraordinary heroism in action against the enemy on 6 June 1944, near Ste.-Mère-Église, France. An American truck loaded with ammunition accidentally hit an American roadblock and minefield. The accident dislocated the minefield and damaged the roadblock. The enemy was maintaining rifle and artillery fire on the truck, which caught fire. With complete disregard for his own safety, First Lieutenant Zeigler left his position of cover and personally re-laid the minefield and reconstructed the roadblock under intense enemy fire. A short while after this action the ammunition truck exploded. The personal bravery and valor exhibited by First Lieutenant Zeigler reflect great credit on himself and were in keeping with the highest traditions of the armed forces.

Headquarters, First Army, General Orders No. 31 (July 1, 1944)

Private Otto K. Zwingman
Company D, 508th Parachute Infantry Regiment, 82nd Airborne Division

Citation: Private Otto K. Zwingman, 32815665, 508th Parachute Infantry, United States Army, for extraordinary heroism in action against the enemy on 6 June 1944, in France. After landing by parachute before dawn on D-Day, and joining a composite group which proceeded to carry out a battalion mission, Private Zwingman and two comrades served as an outpost in a building on the edge of Gueutteville. When a battalion of German infantry, reinforced with tanks, approached from the west and placed machine guns and mortars in position, these three valiant men immediately opened fire on the enemy. Ordered to leave the post, they determined to hold out until the thirty men in the town had withdrawn. Private Zwingman assisted in holding the hostile force at bay for two hours, killing fifteen Germans and wounding many others. His voluntary and courageous action delayed the enemy sufficiently to permit the main body of parachute troops to establish defensive positions to the east from which they were able to deny overwhelming German forces the opportunity of crossing the Merderet River. Private Zwingman's superb heroism and unselfish devotion to duty exemplifies the highest traditions of the United States Army. Entered service from New York.

Headquarters, First Army, General Orders No. 61 (September 25, 1944)

APPENDIX III
NAVY CROSS CITATIONS

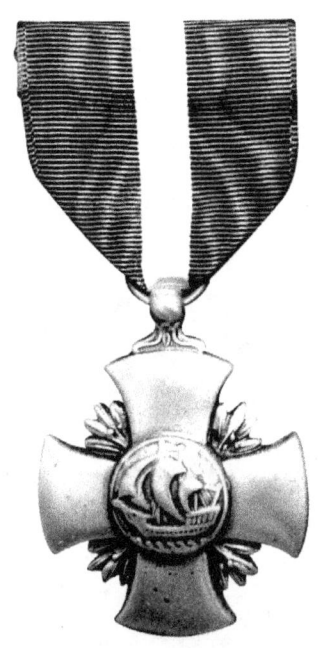

Lieutenant (jg) Grant G. Andreasen
Naval Scouts, Assault Force O, Task Force 124, Eleventh Amphibious Force, 12th Fleet

Citation: Lieutenant (jg) Grant G. Andreasen, 0-231795, United States Naval Reserve. For conspicuous bravery in the performance of outstanding services as Scout Boat officer during the amphibious assault on the coast of France, June 6, 1944. Lieutenant (jg) Andreasen embarked in one of the first craft to approach the strongly defended Normandy coast and succeeded in the highly important mission of locating the beaches to be assaulted. Despite heavy surf and harassing enemy fire, he went in close to the beach to act as a guide for the approaching wave of DD tanks. While he was in this advanced position he fired the rockets from his craft at target objectives, moved in closer to the beach, and rendered close fire support for the infantry assault waves. In addition to his assigned duties, without regard for his own personal safety and under heavy enemy fire he rescued wounded personnel from burning landing craft and carried them to safety. The outstanding devotion to duty and courage under fire displayed by Lieutenant (jg) Andreasen were in keeping with the highest traditions of the naval service.

Bureau of Naval Personnel Information Bulletin No. 334 (January 1945)

Under Secretary of the Navy, Ralph A. Bard, congratulates Lieutenant (jg) Grant G. Andreasen, from Homer, Idaho, upon the award of the Navy Cross at a ceremony at the Navy Department in Washington D.C. on January 12, 1945. *United States Navy photograph, National Archives.*

Aviation Chief Ordnanceman Loran E. Barbour
Naval Combat Demolition Unit 22, Naval Combat Demolition Group, 6th Naval Beach Battalion, Assault Force O,
Task Force 124, Eleventh Amphibious Force, 12th Fleet
Gap Assault Team Number 12

Citation: Aviation Chief Ordnanceman Loran Eli Barbour, United States Naval Reserve, for extraordinary heroism and devotion to duty in action against the enemy while serving as acting commanding officer of Naval Combat Demolition Unit Twenty-two (NCDU-22) during the amphibious assault on the Normandy coast of France on 6 June 1944. Aviation Chief Ordnanceman Barbour, facing heavy machine gun and artillery fire, showed exceptional bravery, leadership and initiative in the placing of charges and the blowing of a fifty yard gap in enemy beach obstacles. Although severely wounded, he calmly directed marking of the gap through which troops could be landed, and directed his men after completion of their mission to assist in aiding the wounded and evacuating the casualties. The conduct of Aviation Chief Ordnanceman Barbour throughout this action reflects great credit upon himself and was in keeping with the highest traditions of the United States naval service.

Bureau of Naval Personnel Information Bulletin No. 334 (January 1945)

Gunner's Mate Second Class Robert W. Bass
Naval Combat Demolition Unit 11, Naval Combat Demolition Group, 7th Naval Beach Battalion, Assault Force O,
Task Force 124, Eleventh Amphibious Force, 12th Fleet
Gap Assault Team Number 1

Citation: Gunner's Mate Second Class Robert W. Bass, 0-8298294, United States Naval Reserve, for extraordinary heroism in combat while serving as a member of a naval combat demolition unit participating in the assault on France on 6 June 1944. Bass and his crew, although subjected to heavy artillery, machine gun and rifle fire, succeeded in blowing a fifty yard gap through the beach obstacles. As a result of enemy fire seven of the twelve man crew were killed or wounded and a large share of the extra work fell on Bass who performed the duties coolly and capably without regard to personal safety. Upon completion of the mission Bass further exposed himself to enemy fire and was wounded himself while carrying injured crew mates to safety. His display of courage and devotion to duty on this occasion reflects the highest traditions of the United States naval service.

Commander Naval Forces, Europe: Serial 7562 (September 7, 1944)

Lieutenant Clarence H. Black
2nd Beach Battalion, Assault Force U, Task Force 125, Eleventh Amphibious Force, 12th Fleet

Citation: Lieutenant Clarence H. Black, 0-128964, United States Naval Reserve, for distinguishing himself by extraordinary heroism while attached to Assault Force "U" engaged in the assault upon the coast of France, 6 June 1944. Although his beach was under incessant enemy artillery fire, his executive officer killed and all personnel ordered to take cover, Lieutenant Black fearlessly exposed himself in order to direct the incoming assault waves to successful landings. By his courageous actions he made possible the beaching of twenty-seven waves of assault craft. The bravery and outstanding devotion to duty displayed by Lieutenant Black on this occasion were in keeping with the highest traditions of the United States naval service.

Commander Naval Forces, Europe: Serial 7929 (September 13, 1944)

Gunner's Mate Second Class Robert W. Bass, from Durham, North Carolina, served with the elite Combat Naval Demolition Unit 11. *Photograph courtesy of Robert W. Bass, Jr.*

Lieutenant (jg) Stuart L. Brandel
Naval Shore Fire Control Party 9, 294th Joint Assault Signal Company, Assault Force O, Task Force 124, Eleventh Amphibious Force, 12th Fleet

Citation: Lieutenant Stuart L. Brandel, 0-174133, United States Naval Reserve, for extraordinary heroism as Naval Gunfire Liaison Officer attached to the Sixteenth Regimental Combat Team during the assault on the coast of Normandy, France, on June 6, 1944. With his assault boat twice driven off by the enemy while attempting to land with the second wave and half his gallant party killed or wounded, Lieutenant (then Lieutenant, junior grade) Brandel quickly grasped the situation and setting up his radio in the boat and establishing communications with a supporting cruiser, skillfully fired several highly effective missions at this critical juncture. Finding his forward observer seriously wounded immediately after gaining the shore, he coolly took over that duty in addition to his own and rapidly reorganized his unit. Although under intense enemy gunfire, he valiantly continued to call for and adjust his devastating supporting fire against hostile positions. His superb performance of duty and inspiring leadership aided materially in the advance of our forces in this vital area and reflected the highest credit upon Lieutenant Brandel and the United States naval service.

Commander Naval Forces Europe File P15-9: Serial 7511 (September 6, 1944)

Boatswain's Mate First Class Robert A. Bridges
LCT(5) 25, Group 53, Flotilla 18, Assault Force O, Task Force 124, Eleventh Amphibious Force, 12th Fleet

Citation: Boatswain's Mate First Class Robert A. Bridges, 4124263, United States Naval Reserve, for extraordinary heroism and outstanding devotion to duty in action against the enemy during the assault phase of the invasion of France on June 6, 1944. Bridges, with disregard for his own safety, worked tirelessly in an effort to unload vehicles and personnel from a United States Landing Craft Tank, exposing himself in so doing to heavy machine gun and artillery fire. He further displayed heroism when, after assisting in the evacuation of the wounded from his own ship, he boarded another Landing Craft Tank and manned a twenty-millimeter gun to engage an enemy machine gun nest, enabling soldiers to move forward on the beach without opposition from this emplacement. The outstanding courage and initiative displayed by Bridges on this occasion were in keeping with the highest traditions of the United States naval service.

Commander Naval Forces, Europe: Serial 7517 (September 6, 1944)

Lieutenant (jg) Stuart L. Brandel, wearing the Navy Cross for his extraordinary heroism during June 6, 1944 as a member of a Naval Fire Control Shore Party. *Photograph courtesy of Tom Lane.*

Lieutenant (jg) Phil H. Bucklew
Naval Scouts, Assault Force O, Task Force 124, Eleventh Amphibious Force, 12th Fleet

Citation: Lieutenant (junior grade) Phil H. Bucklew, United States Naval (Reserve), for conspicuous bravery in the performance of outstanding services as Scout Boat Officer during the amphibious assault on the coast of France, June 6, 1944. Lieutenant (junior grade) Bucklew embarked in one of the first craft to approach the strongly defended Normandy coast and succeeded in the highly important mission of locating the beaches to be assaulted. Despite heavy surf and harassing enemy fire, he skillfully led the first wave of DD tanks to the beach and there took up his station near the beach to act as a guide. While the tanks were landing, he fired rockets over them at target objectives on the beach. After all rockets were expended he moved in closer to the beach and fired his fifty caliber machine guns at suspected machine gun nests in houses along the beach. In addition to his assigned duties, without regard for his own personal safety and under heavy enemy fire he rescued wounded personnel from the water near their burning landing craft and carried them to safety. He continued throughout the morning and afternoon of D-Day working near the beach, regulating the flow of traffic and rescuing wounded personnel. The outstanding devotion to duty displayed by Lieutenant (junior grade) Bucklew were in keeping with the highest traditions of the United States naval service.

Bureau of Naval Personnel Information Bulletin No. 333 (December 1944)

Ralph A. Bard, Under Secretary of the Navy, reads the citation for a gold star in lieu of a second Navy Cross to be presented to Lieutenant (jg) Phil H. Bucklew, at a ceremony at the Navy Department in Washington D.C. on January 12, 1945. *United States Navy photograph, National Archives.*

Chief Gunner's Mate William R. Freeman
Naval Combat Demolition Unit 11, Naval Combat Demolition Group, 7th Naval Beach Battalion, Assault Force O,
Task Force 124, Eleventh Amphibious Force, 12th Fleet
Gap Assault Team Number 1

Citation: Chief Gunner's Mate William R. Freeman, 4111797, United States Navy, for extraordinary heroism in combat under intense enemy gunfire while leading Naval Combat Demolition Unit 11 which participated in the assault on the coast of France, 6 June 1944. Freeman was placed in charge of Naval Combat Demolition Unit 11 when the original officer in charge was transferred to another group. He and his crew were charged with the task of landing on the beach at H-Hour plus three minutes and blowing a fifty yard gap in the enemy placed obstacles on the beach. This mission was accomplished in the face of heavy enemy artillery and small arms fire. In the execution of their mission four men were killed and three wounded out of a total crew of twelve. On numerous occasions Freeman exposed himself to enemy fire while removing wounded personnel to places of safety. His conduct under fire was a constant inspiration to the men in his charge. The exceptional courage and outstanding devotion to duty displayed by Freeman were in keeping with the highest traditions of the United States naval service.

Commander Naval Forces Europe: Serial 7562 (September 7, 1944)

Lieutenant (jg) Robert B. Gilfert
LCT(6) 590, Group 35, LCT Flotilla 12, Assault Force O, Task Force 124, Eleventh Amphibious Force, 12th Fleet

Citation: Lieutenant (junior grade) Robert B. Gilfert, United States Naval Reserve, for extraordinary heroism and distinguished service in the line of his profession as commanding officer of LCT Five Hundred Ninety (LCT 590), in action against enemy forces during the invasion of Normandy, France, on 6 June 1944. Braving intense hostile gunfire which holed his ship severely, rendered his unloading equipment inoperative and caused several casualties to his small crew, Lieutenant (junior grade) Gilfert succeeded in landing his craft to discharge DD tanks. Undaunted by these almost insurmountable obstacles, he retracted from the beach, effected a difficult mooring alongside an APA despite extremely rough seas and, aware of the danger of his waterlogged vessel capsizing under the weight of another cargo, unselfishly offered the services of his gallant craft to deliver additional cargo to our hard pressed forces on the beach. His outstanding courage and outstanding devotion to duty reflect great credit upon himself and are in keeping with the highest traditions of the United States naval service.

Board of Awards: Serial 1713 (July 3, 1946)

Lieutenant (jg) Frank M. Hall
Company B, 7th Naval Beach Battalion, Assault Force O, Task Force 124, Eleventh Amphibious Force, 12th Fleet

Citation: Lieutenant Frank M. Hall, 0-110137, United States Naval Reserve, for extraordinary heroism and distinguished service in the line of his profession as Medical Officer in charge of the 7th Beach Battalion, Naval Beach Party Medical Team, during the invasion of the coast of France, on 6 June 1944. Forced to swim three miles to shore when his own landing craft was sunk during the initial assault, Lieutenant Hall gallantly carried on his mission with such meager supplies as he was able to salvage from the dead and wounded. Completely unmindful of his own danger, he labored with untiring zeal under the terrific fire of the enemy, resolutely assuming command of all medical work on an additional beach when it was determined that the officer in charge was missing in action and, despite the extreme hazards and the grueling strain, skillfully covered two beaches without relief until the afternoon of D+2 day. His splendid example of leadership and courage and his valiant devotion to the fulfillment of a vital and perilous mission reflect the greatest credit upon Lieutenant Hall, his high professional integrity, and the United States naval service.

12th Fleet: Serial 10552 (October 30, 1944)

Lieutenant Robert B. Gilfert served with LCT(6) 590 during the Normandy landings on June 6, 1944. *Photograph courtesy of Joel Gilfert.*

Lieutenant William M. Jenkins
Naval Combat Demolition Unit 43, Naval Combat Demolition Group, 7th Naval Beach Battalion, Assault Force O, Task Force 124, Eleventh Amphibious Force, 12th Fleet
Gap Assault Team Number 6

Citation: Lieutenant (jg) William M. Jenkins, 140710, United States Naval Reserve, for extraordinary heroism and distinguished service in the line of his profession as officer in charge of Naval Combat Demolition Unit Forty-Three (NCDU-43), during the amphibious assault on the Normandy coast of France on 6 June 1944. Although the LCT to which he was attached sank prior to H-Hour, Lieutenant, Junior Grade, Jenkins salvaged his vital equipment and, directing his crew skillfully and with aggressive determination despite hostile gunfire, successfully accomplished the extremely difficult mission of blowing a fifty yard gap through the enemy seaward band of beach obstacles. When one of his men was killed while preparing a demolition charge, he unhesitatingly completed the task himself and personally placed a number of charges, subsequently supervising his crew in helping other groups to clear the inward band of obstacles. The conduct of Lieutenant, Junior Grade, Jenkins throughout this action reflects great credit upon himself and was in keeping with the highest traditions of the United States naval service.

Bureau of Naval Personnel Information Bulletin No. 334 (January 1945)

Artemus L. Gates, Assistant Secretary of the Navy for Air, reads the citation for the Navy Cross to be presented to Lieutenant (jg) William M. Jenkins, from Everett, Washington, during a ceremony conducted at the Navy Department in Washington D.C. on December 29, 1944. Jenkins had received an MBA from Harvard University in 1943 and after returning from the war, had a long career in the banking business. *United States Navy photograph, National Archives.*

Ensign Lawrence S. Karnowski
Naval Combat Demolition Unit 45, Naval Combat Demolition Group, 6th Naval Beach Battalion, Assault Force O,
Task Force 124, Eleventh Amphibious Force, 12th Fleet
Gap Assault Team Number 10

Citation: Ensign Lawrence S. Karnowski, United States Naval Reserve, for extraordinary heroism in operations against the enemy as officer in charge of a naval combat demolition unit participating in the invasion of France on 6 June 1944. Ensign Karnowski, although under heavy artillery and rifle fire succeeded in clearing a fifty yard gap through the enemy beach obstacles. He exposed himself to enemy fire to rescue a wounded member of his crew in danger of drowning in the rising tide and time after time returned alone to place charges to widen the gap when the rest of his crew had been killed or wounded. When tidal conditions made further demolition impossible, he tended wounded along the beach and assisted in the evacuation of casualties in the absence of sufficient medical personnel. The exceptional cool courage, leadership, and complete disregard for personal safety displayed by Ensign Karnowski were in keeping with the highest traditions of the United States naval service.

Bureau of Naval Personnel Information Bulletin No. 334 (January 1945)

Gunner's Mate Second Class John H. Line
Naval Combat Demolition Unit 22, Naval Combat Demolition Group, 6th Naval Beach Battalion, Assault Force O,
Task Force 124, Eleventh Amphibious Force, 12th Fleet
Gap Assault Team Number 12

Citation: Gunner's Mate Second Class John H. Line, United States Naval Reserve, for extraordinary heroism under fire as a member of Naval Combat Demolition Unit Twenty-Two (NCDU-22), which participated in the assault on the coast of France on 6 June 1944. Line was a member of Naval Combat Demolition Unit 22 whose mission was to land on the beach at H-hour-plus-3-minutes and blow a fifty yard gap in the enemy placed obstacles on the beach. Although half of the crew were killed before their mission was completed, Gunner's Mate Second Class Line with surviving members carried on and successfully completed their mission in the face of heavy enemy gunfire. After successfully completing this mission, Gunner's Mate Second Class Line directed incoming craft through the gap which had been blown. He exposed himself on numerous occasions while administering to and removing wounded personnel to places of safety. The exceptional courage and outstanding devotion to duty displayed by John H. Line, Gunner's Mate Second Class, were in keeping with the highest traditions of the naval service.

Bureau of Naval Personnel Information Bulletin No. 334 (January 1945)

Next Page: Lieutenant (jg) Lawrence S. Karnowski is awarded the Navy Cross for his heroism on June 6, 1944. *United States Navy photograph.*

Chief Machinist's Mate Jerry N. Markham
Naval Combat Demolition Unit 46, Naval Combat Demolition Group, 6th Naval Beach Battalion, Assault Force O,
Task Force 124, Eleventh Amphibious Force, 12th Fleet
Gap Assault Team Number 11

Citation: Chief Machinist's Mate Jerry Neal Markham, United States Naval Reserve, for extraordinary heroism and devotion to duty in action against the enemy while serving as a member of a naval combat demolition unit, during the amphibious assault on the Normandy Coast of France on 6 June 1944. When the Officer in Charge of his unit was killed on landing, Chief Machinist's Mate Markham assumed command of the remainder of his unit and blew a partial gap in the enemy beach obstacles. After leading injured members of his crew to safety, he assisted other units in demolitions, succeeded in saving three men buried as a result of a cave-in caused by a shell explosion, and for forty-eight hours directed his men in the clearance of beach obstacles with commandeered equipment after explosives for that purpose had been expended. His display of courage and devotion to duty on this occasion reflects the highest traditions of the United States naval service.

Hospital Apprentice Augustus B. McKee, Jr.
Company B, 7th Naval Beach Battalion, Assault Force O, Task Force 124, Eleventh Amphibious Force, 12th Fleet

Citation: Augustus Bernard McKee, Jr., Hospital Apprentice First Class, United States Naval Reserve, for extraordinary heroism and courageous devotion to duty while serving as a member of a naval beach party medical team landing with assault forces on the Omaha area of the Normandy coast of France, on 6 June 1944. Hospital Apprentice First Class McKee, cut off from the remainder of his unit and working under intense enemy fire with utter disregard for his own safety, attended the wounded with such skill and devotion to duty as unquestionably to have resulted in the saving of many lives. His own landing craft having been sunk at sea, he had lost all of his medical supplies before reaching the beach. Working with such meager supplies as he was able to salvage from the dead and wounded, and all the while working under intense machine gun and sniper fire, Hospital Apprentice First Class McKee attended the wounded and comforted the dying with utter disregard for his own safety until help reached him several hours later. His gallantry and outstanding devotion to duty were in accord with the highest traditions of the United States naval service.

A ceremony is conducted to award Hospital Apprentice First Class Augustus B. McKee, Jr. the Navy Cross for extraordinary heroism. *Photographs courtesy of Augustus B. McKee, III.*

Lieutenant Robert A. Morris
LCT(A) Group, Assault Force O, Task Force 124, Eleventh Amphibious Force, 12th Fleet

Citation: Lieutenant Robert A. Morris, United States Naval Reserve, for extraordinary heroism and distinguished service in the line of his profession as commander of a landing craft flotilla which spearheaded the assault on the beaches of Normandy, France on 6 June 1944. Lieutenant Morris fearlessly led his wave into the beach under intense fire from enemy guns of all calibers through un-cleared obstacles. Although the craft in which he was stationed was hit repeatedly by 88mm shells and machine gun fire and several of the personnel on board were killed, he pressed his attack relentlessly. The conduct of Lieutenant Morris throughout this action reflects great credit upon himself and was in keeping with the highest traditions of the United States naval service.

Bureau of Naval Personnel Information Bulletin No. 333 (December 1944)

Lieutenant (jg) Kenneth S. Norton
Naval Shore Fire Control Party 1, 293rd Joint Assault Signal Company, Assault Force O, Task Force 124, Eleventh Amphibious Force, 12th Fleet

Citation: Lieutenant (junior grade) Kenneth S. Norton, United States Naval Reserve, for extraordinary heroism and distinguished service in the line of his profession as Naval Gunfire Liaison Officer to the Second Ranger Battalion, during the assault on Normandy, France, on 6 and 7 June 1944. Lieutenant Norton landed with the first wave of Rangers at the base of Pointe du Hoc. He was one of the first up the cliff. When the Second Ranger Battalion was surrounded by enemy troops in superior numbers, Lieutenant Norton called for and adjusted fire in great volume and with marked accuracy and effect throughout the day. Without this accurate fire it is probable that the Rangers could not have survived. On the evening of D-Day, Lieutenant Norton's forward observer was killed and Lieutenant Norton was wounded. He nevertheless continued his efforts, organized an emergency shore fire control net and successfully directed several additional fire-support missions. After being evacuated and treated on the U.S.S. *Texas* he returned to the battlefield to take up his regular duties. The conduct of Lieutenant Norton throughout this action reflects great credit upon himself and was in keeping with the highest traditions of the United States naval service.

Bureau of Naval Personnel Information Bulletin No. 334 (January 1945)

Lieutenant (jg) John O. Parrott
U.S.S. *Corry* (DD-463), Bombardment Group, Assault Force U, Task Force 125.8, Eleventh Amphibious Force, 12th Fleet

Citation: Lieutenant (jg) John Oliver Parrott, United States Naval Reserve, for extraordinary heroism in combat against the enemy while serving as First Lieutenant in the U.S.S. *Corry* near St. Vaast, coast of France on June 6, 1944. After the word had been given to abandon ship, and while the ship was sinking under the gunfire of shore batteries, Lieutenant (junior grade) Parrott went down into the forward fire room of the ship to rescue a water tender third class trapped under the grating of the upper level who was swimming in fuel oil and water. The atmosphere of the fire room was filled with live steam. At extreme risk to his own life, Lieutenant (junior grade) Parrott went under the grating and pulled the enlisted man to safety. The courageous and prompt action displayed on this occasion reflects great credit on the United States naval service.

Bureau of Naval Personnel Information Bulletin No. 332 (November 1944)

Lieutenant Commander Herbert A. Peterson
Naval Combat Demolition Group, 2nd Naval Beach Battalion, Combined Task Group 125.2.3, Assault Force U, Task Force 125, Eleventh Amphibious Force, 12th Fleet

Citation: Lieutenant Commander Herbert A. Peterson, United States Naval Reserve, for extraordinary heroism in action against the enemy on June 6, 1944, during the initial assault on the coast of France. Lieutenant Commander Peterson was in command of eleven United States Navy Combat Demolitions Units, which landed on the beaches at 06:30 hours, four hundred yards in the rear of the initial assault wave of infantry. His command was charged with the mission of clearing the underwater mines and obstacles from the beach assigned, which was two thousand yards long and four hundred yards wide at low tide, backed by a twelve foot concrete wall surmounted by fifteen to twenty-five foot sand dunes. The beach was littered with steel, concrete, barbed wire and wooden obstacles interspersed with mines. Lieutenant Commander Peterson landed with the units and personally directed their work. Not only did the units perform their work rapidly and efficiently under his example and leadership, but the mission was accomplished with a minimum of casualties to themselves and to other personnel nearby. The personal example, high courage, and effective leadership of Lieutenant Commander Peterson on this occasion were a most material contribution to the success of the operation and reflect great credit upon the United States naval service.

Commander, 12th Fleet: Serial 2858 (March 8, 1945)

Lieutenant Charles S. Potter
2nd Beach Battalion, Assault Force U, Task Force 125, Eleventh Amphibious Force, 12th Fleet

Citation: Lieutenant Charles S. Potter, United States Naval Reserve, for extraordinary heroism against the enemy while coordinating beach activities under intense enemy shellfire during the assault of France on June 6, 1944. Lieutenant Potter, wounded by enemy shellfire, refused to be hospitalized and when all personnel had been ordered to take cover, he fearlessly exposed himself in order to direct incoming assault waves to successful landings. Lieutenant Potter's actions were conspicuous amongst his comrades and an inspiration to his men. By his courage, aggressive leadership, and unwavering devotion to duty, Lieutenant Potter reflected great credit upon himself and upheld the highest traditions of the United States naval service.

Bureau of Naval Personnel Information Bulletin No. 334 (January 1945)

Rear Admiral R. W. Christie, the commandant of the Puget Sound Navy Yard in Bremerton, Washington awards the Navy Cross to Lieutenant Charles S. Potter. *United States Navy photograph courtesy of Barbara and Trevor Potter.*

Lieutenant Charles S. Potter is wearing the French Croix de Guerre in this photo. In addition to the Navy Cross for extraordinary heroism on Utah Beach where he was a beach master and was wounded on D-Day, Lieutenant Potter was a recipient of the Silver Star for heroism during the invasion of Sicily. He grew up in New York City and graduated from the Groton School in 1932. Prior to the war, he worked for John D. Rockefeller, Jr. and restored colonial Williamsburg, Virginia. After the war, Potter worked in advertising in Detroit before becoming president of the Union Stock Yards and Transit Company in Chicago, when it was the world's largest cattle market. He was involved in a number of charitable and community service organizations. *Photograph courtesy of Barbara and Trevor Potter.*

Lieutenant (jg) John R. Rock
LCT(5) 195, Group 53, Flotilla 18, Assault Force O, Task Force 124, Eleventh Amphibious Force, 12th Fleet

Citation: Lieutenant (junior grade) John R. Rock, D-V(S), United States Naval Reserve, for extraordinary heroism and outstanding devotion to duty while engaged in action against the enemy during the initial landings on the coast of France, June 6, 1944. Lieutenant (junior grade) Rock, observing that the LCT(5) was in sinking condition, with the officer in charge severely wounded, directed the evacuation of the stricken officer and leaving his own ship in command of his assistant, boarded the sinking craft to successfully beach it, and discharge its load. He further displayed courage and heroism when after the craft was hit and completely disabled by enemy shells, swam ashore for medical assistance, despite the handicap of a broken arm sustained as a result of the concussion from enemy fire. His remarkable display of disregard for his own safety in devotion to duty is in keeping with the highest traditions of the United States naval service.

Bureau of Naval Personnel Information Bulletin No. 334 (January 1945)

Lieutenant (jg) Dean L. Rockwell
Group 35, LCT Flotilla 12, Assault Force O, Task Force 124, Eleventh Amphibious Force, 12th Fleet

Citation: Lieutenant (junior grade) Dean L. Rockwell, D-V(G), United States Naval Reserve, for extraordinary skill and courageous devotion to duty as Group Commander of LCTs carrying DD tanks to spearhead the assault on the beaches on June 6, 1944. Lieutenant (junior grade) Rockwell personally commanded a group of LCTs which were to launch DD tanks prior to H-Hour. As the sea was too rough for these tanks to keep from foundering, he quickly estimated the situation and, in the face of very heavy enemy fire, conducted the LCTs to the beach and discharged the tanks on the ground. By quick and sound decision he was able to land all these tanks at the correct spot prior to H-Hour and, by skillful handling, received only a minimum of damage to his ships. The courage and decisive action displayed by Lieutenant (junior grade) Rockwell on this occasion were in keeping with the highest traditions of the United States naval service.

Electrician's Mate First Class Arthur V. Shields
LCI(L) 415, Group 35, Flotilla 12, Follow-up Force B, Task Force 126, Eleventh Amphibious Force, 12th Fleet

Citation: Electrician's Mate First Class Arthur V. Shields, United States Naval Reserve, for extraordinary heroism and devotion to duty in action against the enemy while serving aboard Infantry Landing Craft Four Hundred Fifteen (LCL(L) 415), during the amphibious assault on the Normandy coast of France on 6 June 1944. Electrician's Mate First Class Shields unhesitatingly plunged to the aid of two drowning soldiers in water under enemy shellfire on the Omaha Beach Although tired from swimming ashore with grapnel and line to test the depth of the water before disembarking troops, and although he had voluntarily made the trip once through shrapnel splashed water, Electrician's Mate First Class Shields did not hesitate to jump in once more when he saw the two soldiers in dire need of aid. Through his efforts, the lives of these men were saved and they were carried through the deep water to the shore. Later, he went aboard LCI(L)-416, disabled on the beach because of mines and shellfire. In helping to carry a wounded member of the crew of that ship along the beach, Electrician's Mate First Class Shields was killed by shrapnel. His exceptional courage and valiant devotion to duty in the face of grave danger were in keeping with the highest traditions of the United States Naval Service. He gallantly gave his life for his country.

Bureau of Naval Personnel Information Bulletin No. 337 (April 1945)

Seaman First Class Herman J. Teeter
LCF 31, LCF Group, Assault Force U, Task Force 125, Eleventh Amphibious Force, 12th Fleet

Citation: Herman Joseph Teeter, Seaman First Class, United States Navy (Reserve), for extraordinary heroism and devotion to duty in action against the enemy while serving aboard a landing craft which struck a mine and subsequently sank during the amphibious assault on the Normandy coast of France on 6 June 1944. As a result of the explosion, Seaman First Class Teeter was thrown clear of the ship. After landing in the water he swam back to the ship, climbed aboard, cut off the float nets, and directed the abandonment of the craft, all of the officers aboard having been thrown clear or being so sorely wounded as to be incapable of commanding the crew. Under his supervision, members of the crew took off various shipmates who had been wounded and aided the wounded men in the water clinging to the nets and rafts until help arrived. The conduct of Seaman First Class Teeter throughout this action reflects great credit upon himself and was in keeping with the highest traditions of the United States naval service.

Ensign William L. Wilhoit
LCT(6) 540, Group 55, LCT Flotilla 19, Assault Force O, Task Force 124, Eleventh Amphibious Force, 12th Fleet

Citation: Ensign William L. Wilhoit, United States Naval Reserve, for extraordinary heroism as Relief Officer on board LCT 540 during landing and support operations on the Normandy coast of France beginning 6 June 1944. Severely wounded during the first moments of the assault when nine shattering blasts from German 88mm cannon crippled his ship, killed his officer in charge, killed or wounded six Army personnel and injured seven crewmen, Ensign Wilhoit unhesitatingly assumed command and despite his extreme youth and lack of combat experience, maneuvered the now unwieldy craft toward the beach through German emplaced obstacles and mines. Intrepid in the face of continued punishing gunfire and unwavering under the grueling day and night duty of the ensuing four days, Ensign Wilhoit faithfully carried on his mission and, by his own great valor, inspired his loyal crew to supreme effort in the repeated landing of equipment, supplies and troops vital to assault operations. By his dauntless leadership, resolute fighting spirit, and conspicuous gallantry in the fulfillment of an unfamiliar and perilous task, Ensign Wilhoit upheld and enhanced the finest traditions of the United States naval service.

Bureau of Naval Personnel Information Bulletin No. 334 (January 1945)

Next Page: Ensign William L. Wilhoit was a senior mechanical engineering student and a member of the Naval Reserve Officer Training Corps at Georgia Tech when that unit was activated and he was called to active duty. After the war, he finished his study at Georgia Tech, earning a degree in mechanical engineering. He spent much of his post war career as an executive with a major health insurance company. *Photograph courtesy of William L. Wilhoit.*

NOTES

101ST AIRBORNE DIVISION

1. Captain Frank L. Lillyman, "The Organization and Initial Commitment of the 101st Airborne Division Pathfinders during the Period of December 1943 to the Normandy Invasion on 6 June 1944," Officers Associate Advanced Course, Class Number 4, The Military Police School, pp. 25–27.
2. Frank L. Lillyman as quoted in George Koskimaki, *D-Day With The Screaming Eagles*, Casemate, 2002, pp. 28–29.
3. Captain Frank L. Lillyman, 101st Airborne Pathfinder Group, APO 472, "Report of D-Day Pathfinder Activities," July 1, 1944.
4. Ibid.
5. Ibid.
6. Walter G. Amerman, as quoted in "The Longest Day Was Almost Eternity" *St. Louis Post Dispatch*, November 4, 1962, p. 3H.
7. Ibid.
8. Walter G. Amerman, as quoted in "Wife Hears Paratroop Husband Tell of D Day Over KXOK" *St. Louis Star Times*, 1944.
9. Amerman, as quoted in "The Longest Day."
10. Amerman, as quoted in "Wife Hears Paratroop Husband."
11. Amerman, as quoted in "The Longest Day."
12. Ibid.
13. Ibid.
14. Ibid.
15. Lieutenant Edward Beauregard, statement, Charles H. Young, *Into The Valley, The Untold Story of USAAF Troop Carrier in World War II, From North Africa Through Europe,* PrintComm, Inc. 1995, p. 146.
16. Major John Stopka, "Certificate," August 11, 1944, award file, Lieutenant Ernest O. Harris, National Archives, Record Group 338, Stack 290, Box 13, First Army Awards, Harris DSC file.
17. Lieutenant George H. Craft, "Certificate," June 16, 1944, award file, Corporal James N. Barba, National Archives, Record Group 338, Stack 290, Box 2, First Army Awards, Barba DSC file.
18. General Maxwell Taylor as quoted in Gerald Astor, *The Greatest War*, Presidio Press 1999, p. 487.
19. Major General Maxwell D. Taylor, "Talk by Major General M. D. Taylor to First Class 12 December 1945," pp. 12–13.
20. Virgil Danforth as quoted in George Koskimaki, *D-Day With The Screaming Eagles*, Casemate 2002, p. 135.
21. Ibid, p. 138.
22. Lieutenant Carlton P. Chandler, "Statement," July 10, 1944, award file, Lieutenant George M. Eberle, National Archives, Record Group 338, Stack 290, Box 8, First Army Awards, Eberle DSC file.
23. Lemuel L. Nicholas as quoted in Koskimaki, *D-Day With The Screaming Eagles*, pp. 184–185.
24. Sergeant Eli Cole, "Statement," June 15, 1944, award file, Lieutenant George M. Eberle, National Archives, Record Group 338, Stack 290, Box 8, First Army Awards, Eberle DSC file.
25. John F. Camien, Jr., letter to Captain Hugh Roberts, November 14, 1945, courtesy of Mark Bando.
26. Donald E. Zahn, interview with author.
27. Major Knut H. Raudstein, "The Operation of the 1st Battalion, 506th Parachute Infantry (101st Airborne Division) in the Vicinity of Carentan) 6–8 June 1944 (Normandy Campaign) (Personal Experience of a Company Commander)," 1948–1949 Advanced Infantry Officers Course, courtesy of the Donovan Research Library, Fort Benning, Georgia, pp. 19–23.
28. Richard D. Winters, "Normandy / D-Day / 1944, Brécourt," Richard D. Winters Collection, Box Number 1, Folder 3, United States Army Heritage and Education Center, Carlisle, Pennsylvania.

82ND AIRBORNE DIVISION

1. Thomas J. McCarthy, as quoted in *In Their Own Words, WWII: Europe*, audio book, Topics Entertainment, Cassette 1, Side A.

2. Lieutenant Louis A. Hauptfleisch, "Recommendation for Award of Distinguished Service Cross (Posthumous)," October 25, 1944, award file, Private First Class Thomas L. Rodgers, National Archives, Record Group 338, Stack 290, Box 27, First Army Awards, Rodgers DSC file.
3. Lieutenant Norman MacVicar, "Recommendation for Award," July 3, 1944, award files, Private John A. Lockwood, Corporal Ernest T. Roberts, and Private Otto K. Zwingman, National Archives, Record Group 338, Stack 290, Boxes 18, 27, and 38, First Army Awards, Lockwood, Roberts, and Zwingman DSC files.
4. John J. Dolan, letter to James M. Gavin, March 23, 1959, courtesy of the 82nd Airborne Division War Memorial Museum.
5. Gordon C. Pryne, interview with author.
6. Marcus Heim, Jr., "D-Day, June 6, 1944," courtesy of Mrs. Marcus Heim, p. 1.
7. Dolan letter.
8. Ibid.
9. Ibid.
10. Ibid.
11. Heim, "D-Day, June 6, 1944," p. 1.
12. Ibid.
13. Dolan letter.
14. Heim, "D-Day, June 6, 1944," p. 1.
15. Dolan letter.
16. Lieutenant Colonel Edward C. Krause, "Recommendation for Award," June 29, 1944, award file, Private First Class Dominick DiTullio, National Archives, Record Group 338, Stack 290, Box 8, First Army Awards, DiTullio DSC file.
17. Benjamin H. Vandervoort, written account, courtesy of the Cornelius Ryan Collection, Alden Library, Ohio University, p. 1.
18. James J. Coyle, as quoted in *Echoes of the Warriors*, compiled and edited by George Jacobus, n. p., 1992, p. 261.
19. Dr. Lyle B. Putnam, response to questionnaire, courtesy of the Cornelius Ryan Collection, Alden Library, Ohio University, p. 2.
20. Lieutenant Colonel Benjamin H. Vandervoort, as quoted in "Debriefing Conference – Operation Neptune," courtesy of the 82nd Airborne Division War Memorial Museum, p. 2.
21. Dr. Lyle B. Putnam, as quoted in Michel DeTrez, *The Way We Were: Colonel Ben Vandervoort*, D-Day Publishing, 2004, p. 40.
22. Vandervoort, written account, p. 1.
23. Vandervoort, as quoted in *The Way We Were*, p. 36.
24. Benjamin H. Vandervoort, as quoted in Deryk Wills, *Put On Your Boots and Parachutes!*, 1992, p. 74.
25. Otis L. Sampson, unpublished manuscript, "Time Out For Combat," p. 193.
26. Vandervoort, written account, p. 1.
27. Ibid, pp. 1–2.
28. Lieutenant Colonel William E. Ekman, "Recommendation for Award," June 17, 1944, award file, Lieutenant Colonel Benjamin H. Vandervoort, National Archives, Record Group 338, Stack 290, Box 34, First Army Awards, Vandervoort DSC file.
29. Leslie P. Cruise, written account, courtesy of Leslie P. Cruise.
30. Captain Walter C. DeLong, "Recommendation for Award," June 18, 1944, award file, Lieutenant Harvey J. Zeigler, National Archives, Record Group 338, Stack 290, Box 38, First Army Awards, Zeigler DSC file.
31. Lieutenant Robert J. Wilson, "Recommendation for Award," July 9. 1944, award file, Private John J. Van Valkenburg, National Archives, Record Group 338, Stack 290, Box 34, First Army Awards, Van Valkenburg DSC file.

UTAH BEACH

1. Theodore Roosevelt, Jr., letter to wife, June 11, 1944.
2. Lieutenant Colonel Carlton O. MacNeely, "Statement," June 27, 1944, award file, Brigadier General Theodore Roosevelt, Jr., National Archives, Record Group 338, Stack 290, Box 27, First Army Awards, Roosevelt MOH file.
3. Colonel James A. Van Fleet, "Recommendation for Award," June 17, 1944, award file, Lieutenant Colonel Carlton O. MacNeely, National Archives, Record Group 338, Stack 290, Box 18, First Army Awards, MacNeely DSC file.
4. Major George L. Mabry, Jr., "Recommendation for Award," October 24, 1944, award file, Captain James W. Haley, National Archives, Record Group 338, Stack 290, Box 12, First Army Awards, Haley DSC file.

5. John L. Ahearn, oral history transcript, courtesy of the Eisenhower Center.
6. Technician Fourth Grade Anthony Zampiello, "Statement," June 25, 1944, award file, Lieutenant John L. Ahearn, National Archives, Record Group 338, Stack 290, Box 1, First Army Awards, Ahearn DSC file.
7. Ahearn, transcript.
8. Zampiello, statement.
9. Ahearn, transcript.
10. Zampiello, statement.
11. Ahearn, transcript.
12. Captain J. Stewart Williams, "Recommendation for Award," June 17, 1944, award file, Sergeant Henry V. Nothel, National Archives, Record Group 338, Stack 290, Box 22, First Army Awards, Nothel DSC file.
13. Captain J. Stewart Williams, "Recommendation for Award," June 17, 1944, award file, Staff Sergeant Darvin D. Purvis, National Archives, Record Group 338, Stack 290, Box 25, First Army Awards, Purvis DSC file.
14. Lieutenant Colonel John C. Welborn, "Recommendation for Award," June 19, 1944, award file, Lieutenant Francis E. Songer, National Archives, Record Group 338, Stack 290, Box 31, First Army Awards, Songer DSC file.
15. Lieutenant John N. Townsend, "Recommendation for Award," June 17, 1944, award file, Staff Sergeant Richard C. Murrin, National Archives, Record Group 338, Stack 290, Box 22, First Army Awards, Murrin DSC file.
16. Lieutenant Johnnie L. Casteel, "Recommendation for Award," award file, Lieutenant John N. Townsend, National Archives, Record Group 338, Stack 290, Box 34, First Army Awards, Townsend DSC file.
17. Corporal James H. Burke, "Statement," October 12, 1944, award file, Lieutenant Commander Herbert A. Peterson, National Archives, Record Group 313, Stack 370, Box 32, Peterson NC file.
18. Sergeant Paul Feheley, "Statement," October 12, 1944, award file, Lieutenant Commander Herbert A. Peterson, National Archives, Record Group 313, Stack 370, Box 32, Peterson NC file.
19. Sergeant Guido Troiano, "Statement," October 12, 1944, award file, Lieutenant Commander Herbert A. Peterson, National Archives, Record Group 313, Stack 370, Box 32, Peterson NC file.
20. Lieutenant Colonel George L. Mabry, Jr., "Operations of the 2nd Battalion, 8th Infantry (4th Infantry Division) in the landing at Utah Beach, 5-7 June 1944. (Normandy Campaign) (Personal Experience of a Battalion S-3)," courtesy of the Donovan Research Library, Fort Benning, Georgia, pp. 21–24.
21. Major General Raymond O. Barton, "Recommendation for Award," June 14, 1944, award file, Colonel James A. Van Fleet, National Archives, Record Group 338, Stack 290, Box 34, First Army Awards, Van Fleet DSC file.
22. Colonel James A. Van Fleet, "Recommendation for Award," June 17, 1944, award file, Lieutenant Colonel Fred A. Steiner, National Archives, Record Group 338, Stack 290, Box 32, First Army Awards, Steiner DSC file.
23. Van Fleet, Steiner award file.

POINTE DU HOC

1. Sidney Saloman, as quoted in Marcia Moen and Margo Heinen, *The Fool Lieutenant, A Personal Account of D-Day and World War II*, Meadowlark Publishing, 2000, pp. 64–65.
2. James E. Rudder, as quoted in W. C. Heinz, "I Took My Son to Omaha Beach," Collier's Magazine, June 11, 1954, p. 24.
3. Ibid.
4. George F. Kerchner, "Memoirs," courtesy of the Eisenhower Center.
5. Ibid.
6. Ibid.
7. Ibid.
8. Lieutenant Fred W. Trenkle, "Recommendation for Award," June 22, 1945, award file, Technician Fifth Grade Rex D. Clark, National Archives, Record Group 338, Stack 290, Box 6, First Army Awards, Clark DSC file.
9. Leonard G. Lomell, written account, courtesy of http://www.americandday.org.
10. Ibid.
11. Leonard G. Lomell, speech transcript, Brookdale Community College, New Jersey, http://www.brookdalecc.edu.
12. Leonard G. Lomell, oral history transcript, courtesy of the Eisenhower Center.
13. Leonard G. Lomell, speech transcript.
14. Leonard G. Lomell, oral history transcript.
15. Leonard G. Lomell, speech transcript.
16. Ibid.

17. Elmer H. Vemeer, oral history transcript, courtesy of the Eisenhower Center.
18. Lieutenant Colonel James E. Rudder, "Recommendation for Award," June 17, 1944, award file, Captain Otto Masny, National Archives, Record Group 338, Stack 290, Box 19, First Army Awards, Masny DSC file.
19. Lieutenant Colonel James E. Rudder, "Recommendation for Award," June 17, 1944, award file, Lieutenant (jg) Kenneth S. Norton, National Archives, Record Group 338, Stack 290, Box 22, First Army Awards, Norton DSC file. Norton was awarded the Navy Cross.
20. Lieutenant Colonel James E. Rudder, "Recommendation for Award," June 17, 1944, award file, Sergeant Worden F. Lovell, National Archives, Record Group 338, Stack 290, Box 18, First Army Awards, Lovell DSC file.

AIR POWER OVER NORMANDY

1. Staff Sergeant George W. Fobes, Casualty Questionnaire, nd, and statement, September 20, 1945, Missing Air Crew Report 5527, www.fold3.com.
2. Staff Sergeant Otis O'Neal, statement, June 7, 1944, Missing Air Crew Report 5527, www.fold3.com.
3. Fobes, statement.

OMAHA BEACH

1. Ray B. Bristol, as quoted in Chet Cunningham, *The Frogmen of World War II: An Oral History*, Pocket Books, 2005, pp. 185–186.
2. Captain Phil H. Bucklew, interview transcript, Special Collections and Archives Department, Nimitz Library, United States Naval Academy, courtesy of Coleman Strickland, pp. 114–115.
3. Ibid, pp. 115–116.
4. Bristol, *The Frogmen of World War II*, p. 186.
5. Ibid.
6. Phil H. Bucklew, as quoted in John B. Dwyer, *Scouts and Raiders*, Praeger, 1993, p. 73.
7. Bristol, as quoted in *The Frogmen of World War II*, p. 186.
8. Bucklew, interview, p. 116 and p. 112.
9. Bucklew, as quoted in *Scouts and Raiders*, p. 73.
10. Bucklew, interview, pp. 116–117.
11. Lieutenant (jg) Dean L Rockwell, "Launching "DD" Tanks on D-Day," July 14, 1944, courtesy of http://ww2lct.org, pp.1–2.
12. Dean L Rockwell, oral history transcript, courtesy of the Eisenhower Center.
13. Major William D. Duncan, "Recommendation for Award," June 17, 1944, award file, Lieutenant Harold R. Beavers, National Archives, Record Group 338, Stack 290, Box 2, First Army Awards, Beavers DSC file.
14. Major William D. Duncan, "Recommendation for Award," June 17, 1944, award file, Staff Sergeant John L. Benton, National Archives, Record Group 338, Stack 290, Box 2, First Army Awards, Benton DSC file.
15. Major William D. Duncan, "Recommendation for Award," June 17, 1944, award file, Captain Ned S. Elder, National Archives, Record Group 338, Stack 290, Box 8, First Army Awards, Elder DSC file.
16. Captain Ned S. Elder, "Recommendation for Award," June 17, 1944, award file, Staff Sergeant Gerard B. Petersen, National Archives, Record Group 338, Stack 290, Box 24, First Army Awards, Peterson DSC file.
17. Major William D. Duncan, "Recommendation for Award," June 17, 1944, award file, Captain Vodra C. Philips, National Archives, Record Group 338, Stack 290, Box 24, First Army Awards, Philips DSC file.
18. Major William D. Duncan, "Recommendation for Award," June 17, 1944, award file, Staff Sergeant Floyd M. Jenkins, National Archives, Record Group 338, Stack 290, Box 16, First Army Awards, Jenkins DSC file.
19. Major William D. Duncan, "Recommendation for Award," June 17, 1944, award file, Lieutenant Henry W. Jones, National Archives, Record Group 338, Stack 290, Box 16, First Army Awards, Jones DSC file.
20. Captain Vodra C. Philips, "Certificate," August 31, 1944, award file, Lieutenant Colonel John S. Upham, Jr., National Archives, Record Group 338, Stack 290, Box 34, First Army Awards, Upham DSC file.
21. John Barnes, oral history transcript, courtesy of the Eisenhower Center.
22. Elisha R. Nance, as quoted in Alex Kershaw, *The Bedford Boys*, Da Capo Press, 2003, p. 161.

23. Major General Leonard T. Gerow, "Recommendation for Award," June 17, 1944, award file, Sergeant Howard W. Rogers, National Archives, Record Group 338, Stack 290, Box 27, First Army Awards, Rogers DSC file.
24. Lieutenant Donald P. Casapulla, "Recommendation for Award," June 17, 1944, award file, Sergeant Lyman K. Patterson, National Archives, Record Group 338, Stack 290, Box 23, First Army Awards, Patterson DSC file.
25. Ralph E. Goranson, oral history transcript, courtesy of the Eisenhower Center.
26. Ibid.
27. Ibid.
28. Captain Ralph E. Goranson, "Recommendation for Award," June 14, 1944, award file, Lieutenant William D. Moody, National Archives, Record Group 338, Stack 290, Box 21, First Army Awards, Moody DSC file.
29. Captain Ralph E. Goranson, "Recommendation for Award," June 14, 1944, award file, Private First Class Otto K. Stephens, National Archives, Record Group 338, Stack 290, Box 32, First Army Awards, Stephens DSC file award file.
30. Captain Ralph E. Goranson, "Recommendation for Award," June 14, 1944, award file, Sergeant Julius W. Belcher, National Archives, Record Group 338, Stack 290, Box 2, First Army Awards, Belcher DSC file.
31. Ralph Goranson, transcript.
32. Sidney Salomon, as quoted in, Gerald Astor, *June 6, 1944*, St. Martin's Press, 1994, p. 183.
33. Goranson, transcript.
34. Ibid.
35. Lieutenant (jg) Frank M. Hall, "Recommendation for Award of Navy Cross," July 17, 1944, award file, Hospital Apprentice Augustus B. McKee, Jr., National Archives, Record Group 313, Stack 370, Box 30, McKee NC file.
36. Lieutenant (jg) James G. Reid, "Recommendation for Award of Navy Cross," July 17, 1944, award file, Lieutenant (jg) Frank M. Hall, National Archives Record Group 313, Stack 370, Box 30, Hall NC file.
37. William J. Kehaly, unpublished manuscript, courtesy of http://www.146thecbwwii.org.
38. Ibid.
39. Lieutenant Colonel Carl J. Isley, "Recommendation for Award," June 17, 1944, award file, Lieutenant William J. Kehaly, National Archives, Record Group 338, Stack 290, Box 17, First Army Awards, Kehaly DSC file.
40. Lieutenant Commander Joseph H. Gibbons, "Recommendation for Award of Silver Star Medal," June 24, 1944, award file, Gunner's Mate Second Class Robert W. Bass, National Archives, Record Group 313, Stack 370, Box 30, Bass NC file.
41. Sergeant James E. Lemonds, "Affidavit," June 11, 1944, award file, Lieutenant William A. Anderson, National Archives, Record Group 338, Stack 290, Box 1, First Army Awards, Anderson DSC file.
42. Lieutenant Colonel Carl J. Isley, "Recommendation for Award," June 17, 1944, award file, Lieutenant William A. Anderson, National Archives, Record Group 338, Stack 290, Box 1, First Army Awards, Anderson DSC file.
43. Lieutenant Ben G. Bartholomew, "Recommendation for Award," June 11, 1944, award file, Lieutenant Eskell F. Roberts, National Archives, Record Group 338, Stack 290, Box 27, First Army Awards, Roberts DSC file.
44. Wesley R. Ross, "146th Engineer Combat Battalion: A Journey," courtesy of http://www.6juin1944.com.
45. Sergeant Robert H. Young, "Affidavit," June 11, 1944, award file, Lieutenant Wesley R. Ross, National Archives, Record Group 338, Stack 290, Box 28, First Army Awards, Ross DSC file.
46. Corporal Elmer C. Morrison, "Affidavit," June 11, 1944, award file, Private First Class Albert J. Tucker, National Archives, Record Group 338, Stack 290, Box 34, First Army Awards, Tucker DSC file.
47. Lieutenant Colonel John T. O'Neill, "Recommendation for Award," June 17, 1944, award file, Lieutenant Colonel Carl J. Isley, National Archives, Record Group 338, Stack 290, Box 15, First Army Awards, Isley DSC file.
48. Lieutenant Colonel Robert W. Skaggs, "Recommendation for Award," June 17, 1944, award file, Lieutenant Gaetano R. Barcellona, National Archives, Record Group 338, Stack 290, Box 2, First Army Awards, Barcellona DSC file.
49. Lieutenant Gaetano R. Barcellona, "Certificate," November 20, 1944, award file, Private First Class Lawrence G. Sweeney, National Archives, Record Group 338, Stack 290, Box 33, First Army Awards, Sweeney DSC file.
50. Lieutenant Roger J. McDonough, "Certificate," November 20, 1944, award file, Private First Class Lawrence G. Sweeney, National Archives, Record Group 338, Stack 290, Box 33, First Army Awards, Sweeney DSC file.
51. Lieutenant Frank A. Klotz, "Certificate," November 20, 1944, award file, Private First Class Lawrence G. Sweeney, National Archives, Record Group 338, Stack 290, Box 33, First Army Awards, Sweeney DSC file.
52. Lieutenant Colonel Robert W. Skaggs, "Recommendation for Award," June 17, 1944, award file, Sergeant George A. Habib, National Archives, Record Group 338, Stack 290, Box 12, First Army Awards, Habib DSC file.
53. Lieutenant Colonel Robert W. Skaggs, "Recommendation for Award," June 17, 1944, award file, Technician Fourth Grade Bolick Smulik, National Archives, Record Group 338, Stack 290, Box 31, First Army Awards, Smulik DSC file.
54. Colonel George A. Taylor, "Recommendation for Award," June 17, 1944, award file, Lieutenant Colonel Robert W. Skaggs, National Archives, Record Group 338, Stack 290, Box 30, First Army Awards, Skaggs DSC file.

55. John M. Spalding, interview with Master Sergeant Forest C. Pogue, February 9, 1945, http://www.warchronicle.com.
56. Clarence Colson, interview, courtesy of http://www.warchronicle.com.
57. John Spalding, interview.
58. Edward F. Wozenski, as quoted in, Russell Miller, *Nothing Less Than Victory*, Quill, 1998, pp. 333–335.
59. Edward F. Wozenski, response to questionnaire, courtesy of the Cornelius Ryan Collection, Alden Library, Ohio University.
60. Lieutenant Colonel Herbert C. Hicks, Jr., "Recommendation for Award," July 13, 1944, award file, Captain Edward F. Wozenski, National Archives, Record Group 338, Stack 290, Box 37, First Army Awards, Wozenski DSC file.
61. Captain Edward F. Wozenski, "Recommendation for Award," June 17, 1944, award file, First Sergeant Lawrence J. Fitzsimmons, National Archives, Record Group 338, Stack 290, Box 9, First Army Awards, Fitzsimmons DSC file.
62. Captain Edward F. Wozenski, "Recommendation for Award," July 17, 1944, award file, Technical Sergeant Calvin L. Ellis, National Archives, Record Group 338, Stack 290, Box 8, First Army Awards, Ellis DSC file.
63. Captain Edward F. Wozenski, "Recommendation for Award," June 17, 1944, award file, Staff Sergeant Curtis Colwell, National Archives, Record Group 338, Stack 290, Box 6, First Army Awards, Colwell DSC file.
64. Captain Edward F. Wozenski, "Recommendation for Award," June 24, 1944, award file, Sergeant Clarence Colson, National Archives, Record Group 338, Stack 290, Box 6, First Army Awards, Colson DSC file.
65. Captain Edward F. Wozenski, "Recommendation for Award," June 17, 1944, award file, Sergeant Kenneth F. Peterson, National Archives, Record Group 338, Stack 290, Box 24, First Army Awards, Peterson DSC file.
66. Captain Edward F. Wozenski, "Recommendation for Award," June 10, 1944, award file, Sergeant Philip Streczyk, National Archives, Record Group 338, Stack 290, Box 32, First Army Awards, Streczyk DSC file.
67. Captain Edward F. Wozenski, "Recommendation for Award," June 23, 1944, award file, Private First Class George H. Bowen, National Archives, Record Group 338, Stack 290, Box 4, First Army Awards, Bowen DSC file.
68. Captain Edward F. Wozenski, "Recommendation for Award," June 17, 1944, award file, Private First Class Richard J. Gallagher, National Archives, Record Group 338, Stack 290, Box 10, First Army Awards, Gallagher DSC file.
69. Lieutenant Colonel Herbert C. Hicks, Jr., "Recommendation for Award," June 17, 1944, award file, Staff Sergeant David N. Radford, National Archives, Record Group 338, Stack 290, Box 25, First Army Awards, Radford DSC file.
70. Lieutenant Andrew D. Hanley, "Recommendation for Award," July 20, 1944, award file, Private First Class Theodore T. Wilk, National Archives, Record Group 338, Stack 290, Box 37, First Army Awards, Wilk DSC file.
71. Raymond F. Strojny, response to questionnaire, courtesy of the Cornelius Ryan Collection, Alden Library, Ohio University.
72. Lieutenant Colonel Charles T. Horner, Jr., "Recommendation for Award," June 17, 1944, award file, Captain Kimball R. Richmond, National Archives, Record Group 338, Stack 290, Box 27, First Army Awards, Richmond DSC file.
73. John R. Armellino account, courtesy of http://www.americandday.org.
74. Lieutenant Colonel Charles T. Horner, Jr., "Recommendation for Award," June 17, 1944, award file, Captain John R. Armellino, National Archives, Record Group 338, Stack 290, Box 1, First Army Awards, Armellino DSC file.
75. Captain John R. Armellino, "Recommendation for Award," June 17, 1944, award file, Staff Sergeant James A. Wells, National Archives, Record Group 338, Stack 290, Box 36, First Army Awards, Wells DSC file.
76. Lieutenant Robert R. Cutler, "Recommendation for Award," July 20, 1944, award file, Private First Class Aaron B. Jones, National Archives, Record Group 338, Stack 290, Box 16, First Army Awards, Jones DSC file.
77. Captain John R. Armellino, "Recommendation for Award," June 17, 1944, award file, Private First Class John V. Griffin, National Archives, Record Group 338, Stack 290, Box 12, First Army Awards, Griffin DSC file.
78. Lieutenant Colonel Charles T. Horner, Jr., "Recommendation for Award," June 22, 1944, award file, Lieutenant Robert R. Cutler, National Archives, Record Group 338, Stack 290, Box 8, First Army Awards, Cutler DSC file.
79. Lieutenant Colonel Charles T. Horner, Jr., "Recommendation for Award," June 22, 1944, award file, Lieutenant Jimmie W. Monteith, Jr., National Archives, Record Group 338, Stack 290, Box 21, First Army Awards, Monteith MOH file.
80. Raymond E. Lanterman, "D-Day: Personal Memories of Raymond E. Lanterman," May 20, 1984, courtesy of the Lanterman family.
81. Private Russell E. Martin, "Affidavit," July 13, 1944, award file, Lieutenant Joseph J. Gregory, National Archives, Record Group 338, Stack 290, Box 12, First Army Awards, Gregory DSC file.
82. Lawrence S. Karnowski, as quoted in Joseph Balkoski, *Omaha Beach*, Stackpole Books, 2004, p. 151.
83. Lawrence S. Karnowski, as quoted in John B. Dwyer, "On Bloody Omaha," http://www.americanthinker.com.
84. Jerry Markham, as quoted in John B. Dwyer, "The Dauntless Demolitioneers," http://www.navyfrogmen.com.
85. Lieutenant Commander Joseph H. Gibbons, "Recommendation for Award of Silver Star Medal," June 24, 1944, award file, Aviation Chief Ordnanceman Loran E. Barbour, National Archives, Record Group 313, Stack 370, Box 30, Barbour NC file.

86. Major Milton A. Jewett, "Recommendation for Award," June 17, 1944, award file, Staff Sergeant George Schneider, National Archives, Record Group 338, Stack 290, Box 29, First Army Awards, Schneider DSC file.
87. Lieutenant Colonel John T. O'Neill, "Recommendation for Award," June 17, 1944, award file, Major Milton A. Jewett, National Archives, Record Group 338, Stack 290, Box 16, First Army Awards, Jewett DSC file.
88. Major Milton A. Jewett, "Recommendation for Award," June 17, 1944, award file, Captain Edwin R. Perry, National Archives, Record Group 338, Stack 290, Box 24, First Army Awards, Perry DSC file.
89. Lieutenant (jg.) Stuart L. Brandel, "Report on Operation Neptune," July 13, 1944, http://www.purplehearts.net.
90. Private Neville R. Wood, "Affidavit," June 22, 1944, award file, Lieutenant (jg.) Stuart L. Brandel, National Archives, Record Group 313, Stack 370, Box 17, Brandel NC file.
91. Technical Sergeant William H. Pearce, "Statement," June 24, 1944, award file, Lieutenant William B. Williams, National Archives, Record Group 338, Stack 290, Box 37, First Army Awards, Williams DSC file.
92. Staff Sergeant Frank M. Price, as quoted in S. L. A. Marshall, "First Wave at Omaha Beach," The Atlantic Monthly, November 1960.
93. Lieutenant Donald P. Casapulla, "Recommendation for Award," June 17, 1944, award file, Technical Sergeant John A. Roach, National Archives, Record Group 338, Stack 290, Box 27, First Army Awards, Roach DSC file.
94. William Lewis, as quoted in, Stephen Ambrose, *D-Day*, Simon and Schuster, 1994, pp. 344–345.
95. Lieutenant Donald P. Casapulla, "Recommendation for Award," June 17, 1944, award file, Lieutenant Leo D. Van De Voort, National Archives, Record Group 338, Stack 290, Box 34, First Army Awards, Van De Voort DSC file.
96. Lieutenant Leo D. Van De Voort, "Affidavit," June 15, 1944, award file, First Sergeant William M. Presley, National Archives, Record Group 338, Stack 290, Box 25, First Army Awards, Presley DSC file.
97. John Robert Slaughter, as quoted in, Gerald Astor, *June 6, 1944*, St. Martin's Press, 1994, pp. 278–279.
98. Sidney V. Bingham, Jr., oral history transcript, courtesy of the Eisenhower Center.
99. Lieutenant Donald P. Casapulla, "Recommendation for Award," June 17, 1944, award file, Major Sidney V. Bingham, Jr., National Archives, Record Group 338, Stack 290, Box 2, First Army Awards, Bingham DSC file.
100. Lieutenant Donald P. Casapulla, "Recommendation for Award," June 17, 1944, award file, Lieutenant Robert C. Hargrove, National Archives, Record Group 338, Stack 290, Box 13, First Army Awards, Hargrove DSC file.
101. Lieutenant Donald P. Casapulla, "Recommendation for Award," June 17, 1944, award file, Captain John J. Cotter, National Archives, Record Group 338, Stack 290, Box 7, First Army Awards, Cotter DSC file.
102. Lieutenant Donald P. Casapulla, "Recommendation for Award," June 17, 1944, award file, Lieutenant Forrest Zanlow, National Archives, Record Group 338, Stack 290, Box 38, First Army Awards, Zanlow DSC file.
103. Private Jack Manpel, "Certificate," June 24, 1944, award file, Lieutenant Colonel Thornton L. Mullins award file, National Archives, Record Group 338, Stack 290, Box 21, First Army Awards, Mullins DSC file.
104. Captain Richard F. Brush, "Certificate," June 25, 1944, award file, Lieutenant Thornton L. Mullins award file, National Archives, Record Group 338, Stack 290, Box 21, First Army Awards, Mullins DSC file.
105. Colonel George A. Taylor, "Recommendation for Award," June 17, 1944, award file, Lieutenant Colonel Herbert C. Hicks, Jr., National Archives, Record Group 338, Stack 290, Box 14, First Army Awards, Hicks DSC file.
106. Joseph T. Dawson, oral history transcript, courtesy of the Eisenhower Center.
107. Captain Joseph T. Dawson, "Recommendation for Award," July 13, 1944, award file, Lieutenant Kenneth Bleau, National Archives, Record Group 338, Stack 290, Box 3, First Army Awards, Bleau DSC file.
108. Lieutenant Neville A. Chandler, "Recommendation for Award," October 11, 1944, award file, Sergeant Arthur B. Buschlen, National Archives, Record Group 338, Stack 290, Box 5, First Army Awards, Buschlen DSC file.
109. Lieutenant Colonel Herbert C. Hicks, Jr., "Recommendation for Award," June 17, 1944, award file, Staff Sergeant Philip C. Clark, National Archives, Record Group 338, Stack 290, Box 6, First Army Awards, Clark DSC file.
110. Lieutenant John P. Foley, "Recommendation for Award," June 15, 1944, award file, Private Carlton W. Barrett, National Archives, Record Group 338, Stack 290, Box 2, First Army Awards, Barrett MOH file.
111. Ibid.
112. William B. Carter, as quoted in, Gerald Astor, *June 6, 1944*, 1994, St. Martin's Press, pp. 198–199.
113. Carlton W. Barrett, response to questionnaire, courtesy of the Cornelius Ryan Collection, Alden Library, Ohio University.
114. First Sergeant Lawrence J. Fitzsimmons, "Affidavit," July 26, 1944, award file, Lieutenant Howard P. MacConchie, National Archives, Record Group 338, Stack 290, Box 18, First Army Awards, MacConchie DSC file.
115. General Donald V. Bennett (Retired) with William R. Forstchen, Ph. D., *Honor Untarnished*, Forge, 2003, pp. 202–203.
116. Ibid, pp. 203–209.
117. Major James W. Bowman, "Recommendation for Award," n.d., award file, Lieutenant Colonel Donald V. Bennett, National Archives, Record Group 338, Stack 290, Box 2, First Army Awards, Bennett DSC file.

118. Captain Arthur L. Meyer, "Recommendation for Award," n.d., award file, Private First Class Henry H. Hall, National Archives, Record Group 338, Stack 290, Box 12, First Army Awards, Hall DSC file.
119. Lieutenant Colonel Charles T. Horner, Jr., "Detailed Description," June 23, 1944, award file, Lieutenant James L. Robinson, National Archives, Record Group 338, Stack 290, Box 27, First Army Awards, Robinson DSC file.
120. Lieutenant Donald P. Casapulla, "Recommendation for Award," June 17, 1944, award file, Lieutenant Verne V. Morse, National Archives, Record Group 338, Stack 290, Box 21, First Army Awards, Morse DSC file.
121. Captain W. R. Johnson, "Recommendation for Award," June 17, 1944, award file, Sergeant Raymond E. Nicoli, National Archives, Record Group 338, Stack 290, Box 22, First Army Awards, Nicoli DSC file.
122. Captain W. R. Johnson, "Recommendation for Award," June 17, 1944, award file, Private Donald B. McLaren, National Archives, Record Group 338, Stack 290, Box 19, First Army Awards, McLaren DSC file.
123. Captain W. R. Johnson, "Recommendation for Award," June 17, 1944, award file, Private Benton L. Porter, National Archives, Record Group 338, Stack 290, Box 25, First Army Awards, Porter DSC file.
124. Captain W. R. Johnson, "Recommendation for Award," June 17, 1944, award file, Technician Fifth Grade Felice J. Savino, National Archives, Record Group 338, Stack 290, Box 28, First Army Awards, Savino DSC file.
125. Sergeant Major Joseph P. Medved, "Affidavit," June 17, 1944, award file, Major William A. Richards, National Archives, Record Group 338, Stack 290, Box 27, First Army Awards, Richards DSC file.
126. Private Arnold Roll, "Affidavit," June 17, 1944, award file, Major William A. Richards, National Archives, Record Group 338, Stack 290, Box 27, First Army Awards, Richards DSC file.
127. Medved, "Affidavit."
128. Lieutenant Colonel John T. O'Neill, "Recommendation for Award," June 19, 1944, award file, Major William A. Richards, National Archives, Record Group 338, Stack 290, Box 27, First Army Awards, Richards DSC file.
129. Lieutenant Colonel Herbert C. Hicks, Jr., "Recommendation for Award," June 25, 1944, award file, Lieutenant John D. Shelby, National Archives, Record Group 338, Stack 290, Box 30, First Army Awards, Shelby DSC file.
130. Private First Class Joseph P. Parke, "Affidavit," February 6, 1945, award file, Corporal Peter Cavaliere, National Archives, Record Group 338, Stack 290, Box 6, First Army Awards, Cavaliere DSC file.
131. Lieutenant John D. Shelby, "Detailed Description," June 17, 1944, award files, Corporal Peter Cavaliere and Private Joseph P. Parke, National Archives, Record Group 338, Stack 290, Boxes 6 and 23, First Army Awards, Cavaliere and Parke DSC files.
132. Ibid.
133. Parke, "Affidavit."
134. Shelby, "Detailed Description."
135. Major Charles E. Tegtmeyer, "Personal War Time Memoir of Major Charles E. Tegtmeyer, Medical Corps, Regimental Surgeon, 16th Infantry Regiment, 1st Infantry Division," http://history.amedd.army.mil.
136. Ibid.
137. Colonel George A. Taylor, "Recommendation for Award," June 17, 1944, award file, Major Charles E. Tegtmeyer, National Archives, Record Group 338, Stack 290, Box 33, First Army Awards, Tegtmeyer DSC file.
138. Lieutenant Colonel Edmund F. Driscoll, "Recommendation for Award," July 13, 1944, award file, Captain John Settineri, National Archives, Record Group 338, Stack 290, Box 29, First Army Awards, Settineri DSC file.
139. Major Charles E. Tegtmeyer, "Recommendation for Award," June 17, 1944, award file, Technician Fourth Grade Stanley P. Appleby, National Archives, Record Group 338, Stack 290, Box 1, First Army Awards, Appleby DSC file.
140. Lieutenant Colonel Charles T. Horner, Jr., "Recommendation for Award," June 17, 1944, award file, Lieutenant Carl K. Giles, Jr., National Archives, Record Group 338, Stack 290, Box 11, First Army Awards, Giles DSC file.
141. Lieutenant Donald P. Casapulla, "Recommendation for Award," June 17, 1944, award file, Lieutenant Leonard A. Anker, National Archives, Record Group 338, Stack 290, Box 1, First Army Awards, Anker DSC file.
142. Carl D. Proffitt, interview transcript, Cadet Ryan Koniak, February 17, 2005, courtesy of John A. Adams Center for Military History and Strategic Analysis, Virginia Military Institute.
143. Douglas A. Orndorff, as quoted in Doug O'Connell, "D-Day June 6, 1944," Winchester Star, June 2, 1984, page 9.
144. Ibid, p. 10.
145. Lieutenant Donald P. Casapulla, "Recommendation for Award," June 17, 1944, award file, Staff Sergeant Ozias C. Ritter, National Archives, Record Group 338, Stack 290, Box 27, First Army Awards, Ritter DSC file.
146. Lieutenant Donald P. Casapulla, "Recommendation for Award," June 17, 1944, award file, Technical Sergeant Louis M. Armstrong, National Archives, Record Group 338, Stack 290, Box 1, First Army Awards, Armstrong DSC file.
147. Lieutenant Donald P. Casapulla, "Recommendation for Award," June 17, 1944, award file, Staff Sergeant Ralph S. Coffman, National Archives, Record Group 338, Stack 290, Box 6, First Army Awards, Coffman DSC file.

148. Captain W. R. Johnson, "Recommendation for Award," June 17, 1944, award file, Private Kenneth P. Kidwell, National Archives, Record Group 338, Stack 290, Box 18, First Army Awards, Kidwell DSC file.
149. Don Whitehead, as quoted in Flint Whitlock, *The Fighting First*, Westview Press, 2005, p. 178.
150. John E. Bistrica, as quoted in Flint Whitlock, *The Fighting First*, Westview Press, 2005, p. 178.
151. Captain George F. Wilder, "Recommendation for Award," October 19, 1944, award file, Private First Class Victor E. Peterson, National Archives, Record Group 338, Stack 290, Box 24, First Army Awards, Peterson DSC file.
152. Stephen V. Ralph, "Recommendation for Award," June 22, 1944, award file, Technician Fifth Grade John J. Pinder, Jr., National Archives, Record Group 338, Stack 290, Box 24, First Army Awards, Pinder MOH file.
153. Sergeant Robert A. Michaud, "Affidavit," November 4, 1944, award file, Technician Fifth Grade John J. Pinder, Jr., National Archives, Record Group 338, Stack 290, Box 24, First Army Awards, Pinder MOH file.
154. Ralph, "Recommendation for Award."
155. Stephen V. Ralph, "Recommendation for Award," June 23, 1944, award file, Private First Class Sanford Rosen, National Archives, Record Group 338, Stack 290, Box 28, First Army Awards, Rosen DSC file.
156. Stephen V. Ralph, "Recommendation for Award," June 23, 1944, award file, Staff Sergeant Leeward W. Stockwell, National Archives, Record Group 338, Stack 290, Box 32, First Army Awards, Stockwell DSC file.
157. Colonel George A. Taylor, "Recommendation for Award," June 24, 1944, award file, Lieutenant Colonel George W. Gibbs, National Archives, Record Group 338, Stack 290, Box 11, First Army Awards, Gibbs DSC file.
158. Lieutenant Lawrence Johnson, Jr., as quoted in Flint Whitlock, *The Fighting First*, Westview Press, 2005, p. 211.
159. Technician Fifth Grade Dennis J. Molbert, "Eyewitness Statement," June 23, 1944, Technician Fourth Grade Lowell L. Dock, National Archives, Record Group 338, Stack 290, Box 8, First Army Awards, Dock DSC file.
160. Technician Fourth Grade William L. Kidwell, "Eyewitness Statement," June 23, 1944, Technician Fourth Grade Lowell L. Dock, National Archives, Record Group 338, Stack 290, Box 8, First Army Awards, Dock DSC file.
161. Robert W. Woodward, response to questionnaire, courtesy of the Cornelius Ryan Archive, Alden Library, Ohio University.
162. Lieutenant Colonel George W. Gibbs, "Recommendation for Award," June 21, 1944, Captain Robert W. Woodward, National Archives, Record Group 338, Stack 290, Box 38, First Army Awards, Woodward DSC file.
163. Lieutenant Donald P. Casapulla, "Recommendation for Award," June 17, 1944, award file, Captain Archibald A. Sproul, National Archives, Record Group 338, Stack 290, Box 31, First Army Awards, Sproul DSC file.
164. Major General Leonard T. Gerow, "Recommendation for Award," June 17, 1944, award file, Technical Sergeant John W. White, National Archives, Record Group 338, Stack 290, Box 36, First Army Awards, White DSC file.
165. John W. White, as quoted in, http://www.wwiirangers.com/Photo%20Galleries/Rgr%20Spotlight/WhiteJohn.htm.
166. Lieutenant Jack Shea, D-Day Narrative, courtesy of the Cornelius Ryan Collection, Alden Library, Ohio University, pp. 3–6.
167. Lieutenant Jack Shea, D-Day Narrative, courtesy of the Cornelius Ryan Collection, Alden Library, Ohio University, pp. 7–11.
168. Richard P. Sullivan, response to questionnaire, courtesy of the Cornelius Ryan Collection, Alden Library, Ohio University.
169. Major Thomas D. Howie, "Affidavit," June 15, 1944, award file, Colonel Charles D. W. Canham, National Archives, Record Group 338, Stack 290, Box 5, First Army Awards, Canham DSC file.
170. Cecil G. Breeden, as quoted in Stephen Ambrose, *D-Day*, Simon and Schuster, 1994, p. 421.
171. John Robert Slaughter, as quoted in Stephen Ambrose, *D-Day*, Simon and Schuster, 1994, p. 344.
172. William L. Wilhoit, response to questionnaire, courtesy of the Cornelius Ryan Collection, Alden Library, Ohio University.
173. Ibid.
174. Ibid.
175. Vinton W. Dove, written account, courtesy of Vinton W. Dove, Jr.
176. William J. Shoemaker, response to questionnaire, courtesy of the Cornelius Ryan Collection, Alden Library, Ohio University.
177. Vinton W. Dove, written account, courtesy of Vinton W. Dove, Jr.
178. Brigadier General Willard G. Wyman, "Recommendation for Award," June 19, 1944, award file, Private Vinton W. Dove, National Archives, Record Group 338, Stack 290, Box 8, First Army Awards, Dove DSC file.
179. Don Whitehead, "A Correspondent's View of D-Day, 1971," http://www.ww2talk.com.
180. Captain Johnson D. Howard, "Recommendation for Award," June 16, 1944, award file, Lieutenant Robert P. Ross, National Archives, Record Group 338, Stack 290, Box 28, First Army Awards, Ross DSC file.
181. Herbert Epstein, as quoted in "The Landing," courtesy of www.dropzone.org.

182. Herb Epstein, as quoted in Charles H. Parker, *Reflections of Courage on D-Day and the Days that Followed*, DeForest Press, 1999, p. 90.
183. Epstein, as quoted in "The Landing."
184. Francis W. Dawson, "Good Hunting, Rangers," courtesy of the Eisenhower Center.
185. Francis W. Dawson, as quoted in Gerald Astor, *June 6, 1944*, St. Martin's Press, 1994, pp. 208–209.
186. Dawson, "Good Hunting, Rangers."
187. Francis W. Dawson, as quoted in *June 6, 1944*, p. 209.
188. Dawson, "Good Hunting, Rangers."
189. John Raaen, as quoted in Joseph Balkoski, *Omaha Beach*, Stackpole Books, 2004, p. 176.
190. Charles H. Parker, *Reflections of Courage on D-Day and the Days that Followed*, DeForest Press, 1999, p. 25.
191. Major Richard P. Sullivan, "Recommendation for Award," June 17, 1944, award file, Lieutenant Joseph R. Lacy, National Archives, Record Group 338, Stack 290, Box 18, First Army Awards, Lacy DSC file.
192. Lieutenant Colonel Max F. Schneider, "Recommendation for Award," June 17, 1944, award file, Private First Class Alexander W. Barber, National Archives, Record Group 338, Stack 290, Box 2, First Army Awards, Barber DSC file.
193. Dr. Alexander W. Barber, response to questionnaire, courtesy of the Cornelius Ryan Collection, Alden Library, Ohio University.
194. Charles H. Parker, as quoted in Gerald Astor, *June 6, 1944*, St. Martin's Press, 1994, pp. 206–207.
195. Ibid, p. 209.
196. Parker, *Reflections of Courage on D-Day*, pp. 93–95.
197. Ibid, p. 97.
198. Ibid, p. 98–99.
199. Ibid, p. 101.
200. Lieutenant Colonel Max F. Schneider, "Recommendation for Award," June 16, 1944, award file, Captain George P. Whittington, Jr., National Archives, Record Group 338, Stack 290, Box 36, First Army Awards, Whittington DSC file.
201. Carl Weast, as quoted in, Russell Miller, *Nothing Less Than Victory*, Quill, 1993, pp. 483–484.
202. Major General Leonard T. Gerow, "Recommendation for Award," June 13, 1944, award file Colonel Benjamin B. Talley, National Archives, Record Group 338, Stack 290, Box 33, First Army Awards, Talley DSC file.
203. Colonel Benjamin B. Talley, account, courtesy of http://www.military.com.
204. Gerow, "Recommendation for Award."
205. Lieutenant Donald P. Casapulla, "Recommendation for Award," June 17, 1944, award file, Technician Fourth Grade Elmer G. Shindle, National Archives, Record Group 338, Stack 290, Box 30, First Army Awards, Shindle DSC file.
206. Elmer G. Shindle, response to questionnaire, courtesy of the Cornelius Ryan Collection, Alden Library, Ohio University.
207. Ibid.
208. Lieutenant Colonel Edmund F. Driscoll, "Recommendation for Award," June 17, 1944, award file, Captain James L. Pence, National Archives, Record Group 338, Stack 290, Box 24, First Army Awards, Pence DSC file.
209. Leroy Herman, response to questionnaire, courtesy of the Cornelius Ryan Collection, Alden Library, Ohio University.
210. William T. Dillon, "Pearl Harbor to Normandy and Beyond," United States Army Military History Institute.
211. Major Edmund F. Driscoll, "Recommendation for Award," July 12, 1944, award file, Lieutenant William T. Dillon, National Archives, Record Group 338, Stack 290, Box 8, First Army Awards, Dillon DSC file.
212. Lieutenant Robert F. Chambers, "Recommendation for Award," June 23, 1944, award file, Lieutenant Atwood M. McElyea, National Archives, Record Group 338, Stack 290, Box 19, First Army Awards, McElyea DSC file.
213. Major Edmund F. Driscoll, "Recommendation for Award," June 26, 1944, award file, Technical Sergeant William R. Benn, Jr., National Archives, Record Group 338, Stack 290, Box 2, First Army Awards, Benn DSC file.
214. Paul R. Shorter, response to questionnaire, courtesy of the Cornelius Ryan Collection, Alden Library, Ohio University.
215. Lieutenant William T. Dillon, "Recommendation for Award," June 23, 1944, award file, Staff Sergeant Paul R. Shorter, National Archives, Record Group 338, Stack 290, Box 30, First Army Awards, Shorter DSC file.
216. Lieutenant Colonel Edmund F. Driscoll, "Recommendation for Award," June 17, 1944, award file, Captain Victor H. Briggs, National Archives, Record Group 338, Stack 290, Box 4, First Army Awards, Briggs DSC file.
217. Major Edmund F. Driscoll, "Recommendation for Award," June 17, 1944, award file, Captain Thomas N. Merendino, National Archives, Record Group 338, Stack 290, Box 19, First Army Awards, Merendino DSC file.
218. Captain Paul K. Switzer, "Recommendation for Award," December 7, 1944, award file, Captain Kenneth E. Beitler, National Archives, Record Group 338, Stack 290, Box 2, First Army Awards, Beitler DSC file.

219. Lieutenant Alfred Ely, "Affidavit," June 15, 1944, award file, Brigadier General Willard G. Wyman, National Archives, Record Group 338, Stack 290, Box 38, First Army Awards, Wyman DSC file.
220. Don Whitehead, as quoted in *The Fighting First*, pp. 177–178.
221. Robert J. Riekse, response to questionnaire, courtesy of the Cornelius Ryan Collection, Alden Library, Ohio University.
222. Commander Lawrence C. Leever, "Sworn Statement," June 19, 1944, award file, Colonel Paul W. Thompson, National Archives, Record Group 338, Stack 290, Box 33, First Army Awards, Thompson DSC file.
223. Brigadier General Paul W. Thompson, address to The Society of Military Engineers, May 18, 1988, courtesy of the Eisenhower Center.
224. Lieutenant Donald P. Casapulla, "Recommendation for Award," June 17, 1944, award file, Private First Class William M. Riggs, National Archives, Record Group 338, Stack 290, Box 27, First Army Awards, Riggs DSC file.
225. Lieutenant Donald P. Casapulla, "Recommendation for Award," June 17, 1944, award file, Lieutenant Forest K. Ferguson, National Archives, Record Group 338, Stack 290, Box 8, First Army Awards, Ferguson DSC file.
226. Colonel George A. Taylor, "Recommendation for Award," June 22, 1944, award file, Captain Thomas F. O'Brien, National Archives, Record Group 338, Stack 290, Box 23, First Army Awards, O'Brien DSC file.
227. Captain Thomas F. O'Brien, "Recommendation for Award," June 24, 1944, award file, Private First Class Henry Berkowitz, National Archives, Record Group 338, Stack 290, Box 3, First Army Awards, Berkowitz DSC file.
228. Major Charles E. Tegtmeyer, "Recommendation for Award," June 24, 1944, award file, Captain Emerald M. Ralston, National Archives, Record Group 338, Stack 290, Box 26, First Army Awards, Ralston DSC file.
229. Lieutenant (jg) John R. Rock, "Action Report Wave Number 12, Green Beach," June 14, 1944, www.fold3.com.
230. Ibid.
231. Ibid.
232. Captain Joseph R. Kaufmann, "Recommendation for Award," January 18, 1945, award file, Technician Fifth Grade Edward Shaffer, National Archives, Record Group 338, Stack 290, Box 29, First Army Awards, Shaffer DSC file.
233. Colonel George A. Taylor, "Recommendation for Award," June 22, 1944, award file, Major William R. Washington, National Archives, Record Group 338, Stack 290, Box 35, First Army Awards, Washington DSC file.
234. Lieutenant Thomas M. Ennis, "Recommendation for Award," August 23, 1944, award file, Technical Sergeant Gerald M. Henderson, National Archives, Record Group 338, Stack 290, Box 13, First Army Awards, Henderson DSC file.
235. Lieutenant (jg) John F. Schereschewsky to Commander, U.S. Naval Forces in Europe, "Recommendation for Appropriate Award," August 15, 1944, award file, Electrician's Mate First Class Arthur V. Shields, National Archives, Record Group 313, Stack 370, Box 15, Shields NC file.
236. Major Sidney V. Bingham, Jr., as quoted in Joseph Balkoski, *Omaha Beach*, Stackpole Books, 2004, p. 347.
237. Omar N. Bradley, as quoted in Omar N. Bradley and Clay Blair, *A General's Life*, Simon and Schuster, 1983, p. 249.
238. Bennett and Forstchen, *Honor Untarnished*, p. 216.
239. John Ellery, oral history transcript, courtesy of the Eisenhower Center.

BIBLIOGRAPHY

PUBLISHED SOURCES

Ambrose, Stephen, *D-Day*, New York: Simon and Schuster, 1994.

Astor, Gerald, *June 6, 1944*, New York: St. Martin's Press, 1994.

Astor, Gerald, *The Greatest War*, Novato, California: Presidio Press 1999.

Balkoski, Joseph, *Omaha Beach*, Mechanicsburg, Pennsylvania: Stackpole Books, 2004.

Balkoski, Joseph, *Utah Beach*, Mechanicsburg, Pennsylvania: Stackpole Books, 2005.

Bennett, General Donald V. (Retired), with Forstchen, Ph. D., William R., *Honor Untarnished*, New York: Forge, 2003

Black, Colonel Robert W., *The Battalion*, Mechanicsburg, Pennsylvania: Stackpole Books, 2006.

Bradley, Omar N. and Blair, Clay, *A General's Life*, New York: Simon and Schuster, 1983.

Cunningham, Chet, *The Frogmen of World War II: An Oral History*, New York: Pocket Books, 2005.

Department of the Army Historical Division, *Utah Beach to Cherbourg*, Washington D.C.: Center of Military History, United States Army, 1994.

DeTrez, Michel, *The Way We Were: Colonel Ben Vandervoort*, Wezembeek-Oppem, Belgium: D-Day Publishing, 2004.

Dunford, Sue Ann and O'Dell, James Douglas, *More Than Scuttlebutt*, s.p., 2009.

Dwyer, John B., *Scouts and Raiders*, West Port, Connecticut: Praeger, 1993.

Ford, Ken and Zaloga, Steven J., *Overlord: The D-Day Landings*, Oxford, England: Osprey Publishing Limited, 2009.

Gawne, Jonathan, *Spearheading D-Day*, Paris, France: Histoire and Collections, 1998.

Hatfield, Thomas M., *Rudder: From Leader to Legend*, College Station, Texas: Texas A&M University Press, 2011.

Jensen, Marvin, *Strike Swiftly*, Novato, California: Presidio Press, 1997.

Kershaw, Alex, *The Bedford Boys*, New York: Da Capo Press, 2003.

Koskimaki, George, *D-Day With The Screaming Eagles*, Havertown, Pennsylvania: Casemate, 2002.

Lane, Ronald L., Rudder's Rangers, Altamonte Springs, Florida: Ranger Associates, Inc., 1994.

Miller, Russell, *Nothing Less Than Victory*, New York: Quill, 1998.

Parker, Charles H., *Reflections of Courage on D-Day and the Days that Followed*, Elk River, Minnesota: DeForest Press, 1999.

Whitlock, Flint, The Fighting First, Cambridge, Massachusetts: Westview Press, 2004.

Wills, Deryk, *Put On Your Boots and Parachutes!*, Deryk Wills, 1992.

Young, Charles H., Into The Valley, The Untold Story of USAAF Troop Carrier in World War II, From North Africa Through Europe, Dallas: PrintComm, Inc. 1995.

Zaloga, Steven J., *D-Day Fortifications in Normandy*, Oxford, England: Osprey Publishing Limited, 2005.

Zetterling, Niklas, Normandy 1944, Wiinipeg, Canada: J.J. Fedorowicz Publishing, Inc., 2000.

ARTICLES

Amerman, Walter G., in "The Longest Day Was Almost Eternity" *St. Louis Post Dispatch*, St. Louis, Missouri, November 4, 1962, p. 3H.

Amerman, Walter G., in "Wife Hears Paratroop Husband Tell of D Day Over KXOK" *St. Louis Star Times*, St. Louis, Missouri, n.d. 1944.

Orndorff, Douglas A., in Doug O'Connell, "D-Day June 6, 1944," *Winchester Star*, Winchester, Virginia, June 2, 1984, page 9.

Price, Staff Sergeant Frank M., in S. L. A. Marshall, "First Wave at Omaha Beach," The Atlantic Monthly, November 1960.

James E. Rudder, in W. C. Heinz, "I Took My Son to Omaha Beach," Collier's Magazine, June 11, 1954.

UNPUBLISHED DIARIES, SWORN STATEMENTS, LETTERS, EMAILS, WRITTEN ACCOUNTS, MEMOIRS, AND MANUSCRIPTS

Camien, John F. Jr., letter to Captain Hugh Roberts, November 14, 1945, Mark Bando.

Cruise, Leslie P., written account, Leslie P. Cruise.

Dawson, Francis W., "Good Hunting, Rangers," Eisenhower Center, New Orleans, Louisiana.

Dillon, William T., "Pearl Harbor to Normandy and Beyond," United States Army Military History Institute, Carlisle, Pennsylvania.

Dolan, John J., letter to James M. Gavin, March 23, 1959, 82nd Airborne Division War Memorial Museum, Fort Bragg, North Carolina.

Dove, Vinton W., written account, Vinton W. Dove, Jr.

Heim, Marcus Jr., "D-Day, June 6, 1944," Mrs. Marcus Heim.

Jacobus, George, *Echoes of the Warriors*, compiled and edited by George Jacobus, n. p., 1992

Kerchner, George F., "Memoirs," Eisenhower Center, New Orleans, Louisiana.

Lanterman, Raymond E., "D-Day: Personal Memories of Raymond E. Lanterman," May 20, 1984, Lanterman family.

Sampson, Otis L., unpublished manuscript, "Time Out For Combat."

Vandervoort, Benjamin H., written account, Cornelius Ryan Collection, Alden Library, Ohio University, Athens, Ohio.

Winters, Richard D., "Normandy / D-Day / 1944, Brécourt," Richard D. Winters Collection, Box Number 1, Folder 3, United States Army Heritage and Education Center, Carlisle, Pennsylvania.

RESPONSES TO QUESTIONNAIRES

Cornelius Ryan Collection, Alden Library, Ohio University, Athens, Ohio, questionnaires with the following veterans:

Barrett, Carlton W.
Barber, Dr. Alexander W.
Herman, Leroy
Putnam, Dr. Lyle B.
Riekse, Robert J.
Shindle, Elmer G.
Shoemaker, William J.
Shorter, Paul R.
Strojny, Raymond F.
Sullivan, Richard P.
Wilhoit, William L.
Woodward, Robert W.
Wozenski, Edward F.

UNITED STATES MILITARY DOCUMENTS, AFTER-ACTION REPORTS, STUDIES, MONOGRAPHS, STATEMENTS, AWARD FILES, AND COMBAT INTERVIEWS

Award files at the National Archives, College Park, Maryland, First Army Awards, Record Group 338, Stack 290:

Ahearn, Lieutenant John L., Box 1, Ahearn DSC file.
Anderson, Lieutenant William A., Box 1, Anderson DSC file.
Anker, Lieutenant Leonard A., Box 1, Anker DSC file.
Appleby, Technician Fourth Grade Stanley P., Box 1, Appleby DSC file.
Armellino, Captain John R., National Archives, Box 1, Armellino DSC file.
Armstrong, Technical Sergeant Louis M., Box 1, Armstrong DSC file.
Barba, Corporal James N., Box 2, Barba DSC file.
Barber, Private First Class Alexander W., Box 2, Barber DSC file.
Barcellona, Lieutenant Gaetano R., Box 2, Barcellona DSC file.
Barrett, Private Carlton W., Box 2, Barrett MOH file.
Beavers, Lieutenant Harold R., Box 2, Beavers DSC file.
Beitler, Captain Kenneth E., Box 2, Beitler DSC file.
Belcher, Sergeant Julius W., Box 2, Belcher DSC file.
Benn, Technical Sergeant William R. Jr., Box 2, Benn DSC file.
Bennett, Lieutenant Colonel Donald V., Box 2, Bennett DSC file.
Benton, Staff Sergeant John L., Box 2, Benton DSC file.
Berkowitz, Private First Class Henry, Box 3, Berkowitz DSC file.
Bingham, Major Sidney V. Jr., Box 2, Bingham DSC file.
Bleau, Lieutenant Kenneth, Box 3, Bleau DSC file.
Bowen, Private First Class George H., Box 4, Bowen DSC file.
Briggs, Captain Victor H., Box 4, Briggs DSC file.
Buschlen, Sergeant Arthur B., Box 5, Buschlen DSC file.
Canham, Colonel Charles D. W., Box 5, Canham DSC file.
Cavaliere, Corporal Peter, Box 6, Cavaliere DSC file.
Clark, Staff Sergeant Philip C., Box 6, Clark DSC file.

Clark, Technician Fifth Grade Rex D., Box 6, Clark DSC file.
Coffman, Staff Sergeant Ralph S., Box 6, Coffman DSC file.
Colson, Sergeant Clarence, Box 6, Colson DSC file.
Colwell, Staff Sergeant Curtis, Box 6, Colwell DSC file.
Cotter, Captain John J., Box 7, Cotter DSC file.
Cutler, Lieutenant Robert R., Box 8, Cutler DSC file.
Dillon, Lieutenant William T., Box 8, Dillon DSC file.
DiTullio, Private First Class Dominick, Box 8, DiTullio DSC file.
Dock, Technician Fourth Grade Lowell L., Box 8, Dock DSC file.
Dove, Private Vinton W., Box 8, Dove DSC file.
Eberle, Lieutenant George M., Box 8, Eberle DSC file.
Elder, Captain Ned S., Box 8, Elder DSC file.
Ellis, Technical Sergeant Calvin L., Box 8, Ellis DSC file.
Ferguson, Lieutenant Forest K., Box 8, Ferguson DSC file.
Fitzsimmons, First Sergeant Lawrence J., Box 9, Fitzsimmons DSC file.
Gallagher, Private First Class Richard J., Box 10, Gallagher DSC file.
Gibbs, Lieutenant Colonel George W., Box 11, Gibbs DSC file.
Giles, Lieutenant Carl K. Jr., Box 11, Giles DSC file.
Gregory, Lieutenant Joseph J., Box 12, Gregory DSC file.
Griffin, Private First Class John V., Box 12, Griffin DSC file.
Habib, Sergeant George A., Box 12, Habib DSC file.
Haley, Captain James W., Box 12, Haley DSC file.
Hall, Private First Class Henry H., Box 12, Hall DSC file.
Hargrove, Lieutenant Robert C., Box 13, Hargrove DSC file.
Harris, Lieutenant Ernest O., Box 13, Harris DSC file.
Henderson, Technical Sergeant Gerald M., Box 13, Henderson DSC file.
Hicks, Lieutenant Colonel Herbert C. Jr., Box 14, Hicks DSC file.
Isley, Lieutenant Colonel Carl J., Box 15, Isley DSC file.
Jenkins, Staff Sergeant Floyd M., Box 16, Jenkins DSC file.
Jewett, Major Milton A., Box 16, Jewett DSC file.
Jones, Private First Class Aaron B., Box 16, Jones DSC file.
Jones, Lieutenant Henry W., Box 16, Jones DSC file.
Kehaly, Lieutenant William J., Box 17, Kehaly DSC file.
Kidwell, Private Kenneth P., Box 18, Kidwell DSC file.
Lacy, Lieutenant Joseph R., Box 18, Lacy DSC file.
Lockwood, Private John A., Box 18, Lockwood DSC file.
Lovell, Sergeant Worden F., Box 18, Lovell DSC file.
MacConchie, Lieutenant Howard P., Box 18, MacConchie DSC file.
MacNeely, Lieutenant Colonel Carlton O., Box 18, MacNeely DSC file.
Masny, Captain Otto, Box 19, Masny DSC file.
McElyea, Lieutenant Atwood M., Box 19, McElyea DSC file.
McLaren, Private Donald B., Box 19, McLaren DSC file.
Merendino, Captain Thomas N., Box 19, Merendino DSC file.
Monteith, Lieutenant Jimmie W. Jr., Box 21, Monteith MOH file.
Moody, Lieutenant William D., Box 21, Moody DSC file.
Morse, Lieutenant Verne V., Box 21, Morse DSC file.
Mullins, Lieutenant Colonel Thornton L., Box 21, Mullins DSC file.
Murrin, Staff Sergeant Richard C., Box 22, Murrin DSC file.
Nicoli, Sergeant Raymond E., Box 22, Nicoli DSC file.
Norton, Lieutenant (jg) Kenneth S., Box 22, Norton DSC file.
Nothel, Sergeant Henry V., Box 22, Nothel DSC file.
O'Brien, Captain Thomas F., Box 23, O'Brien DSC file.
Parke, Private Joseph P., Box 23, Parke DSC file.
Patterson, Sergeant Lyman K., Box 23, Patterson DSC file.
Pence, Captain James L., Box 24, Pence DSC file.
Perry, Captain Edwin R., Box 24, Perry DSC file.

Petersen, Staff Sergeant Gerard B., Box 24, Peterson DSC file.
Peterson, Sergeant Kenneth F., Box 24, Peterson DSC file.
Peterson, Private First Class Victor E., Box 24, Peterson DSC file.
Philips, Captain Vodra C., Box 24, Philips DSC file.
Pinder, Technician Fifth Grade John J. Jr., Box 24, Pinder MOH file.
Porter, Private Benton L., Box 25, Porter DSC file.
Presley, First Sergeant William M., Box 25, Presley DSC file.
Purvis, Staff Sergeant Darvin D., Box 25, Purvis DSC file.
Radford, Staff Sergeant David N., Box 25, Radford DSC file.
Ralston, Captain Emerald M., Box 26, Ralston DSC file.
Richards, Major William A., Box 27, Richards DSC file.
Richmond, Captain Kimball R., Box 27, Richmond DSC file.
Riggs, Private First Class William M., Box 27, Riggs DSC file.
Ritter, Staff Sergeant Ozias C., Box 27, Ritter DSC file.
Roach, Technical Sergeant John A., Box 27, Roach DSC file.
Roberts, Corporal Ernest T., Box 27, Roberts DSC file.
Roberts, Lieutenant Eskell F., Box 27, Roberts DSC file.
Robinson, Lieutenant James L., Box 27, Robinson DSC file.
Rodgers, Private First Class Thomas L., Box 27, Rodgers DSC file.
Rogers, Sergeant Howard W., Box 27, Rogers DSC file.
Roosevelt, Brigadier General Theodore Jr., Box 27, Roosevelt MOH file.
Rosen, Private First Class Sanford, Box 28, Rosen DSC file.
Ross, Lieutenant Robert P., Box 28, Ross DSC file.
Ross, Lieutenant Wesley R., Box 28, Ross DSC file.
Savino, Technician Fifth Grade Felice J., Box 28, Savino DSC file.
Schneider, Staff Sergeant George, Box 29, Schneider DSC file.
Settineri, Captain John, Box 29, Settineri DSC file.
Shaffer, Technician Fifth Grade Edward, Box 29, Shaffer DSC file.
Shelby, Lieutenant John D., Box 30, Shelby DSC file.
Shindle, Technician Fourth Grade Elmer G., Box 30, Shindle DSC file.
Shorter, Staff Sergeant Paul R., Box 30, Shorter DSC file.
Skaggs, Lieutenant Colonel Robert W., Box 30, Skaggs DSC file.
Smulik, Technician Fourth Grade Bolick, Box 31, Smulik DSC file.
Songer, Lieutenant Francis E., Box 31, Songer DSC file.
Sproul, Captain Archibald A., Box 31, Sproul DSC file.
Steiner, Lieutenant Colonel Fred A., Box 32, Steiner DSC file.
Stephens, Private First Class Otto K., Box 32, Stephens DSC file award file.
Stockwell, Staff Sergeant Leeward W., Box 32, Stockwell DSC file.
Streczyk, Sergeant Philip, Box 32, Streczyk DSC file.
Sweeney, Private First Class Lawrence G., Box 33, Sweeney DSC file.
Talley, Colonel Benjamin B., Box 33, Talley DSC file.
Tegtmeyer, Major Charles E., Box 33, Tegtmeyer DSC file.
Thompson, Colonel Paul W., Box 33, Thompson DSC file.
Townsend, Lieutenant John N., Box 34, Townsend DSC file.
Tucker, Private First Class Albert J., Box 34, Tucker DSC file.
Upham, Lieutenant Colonel John S. Jr., Box 34, Upham DSC file.
Van De Voort, Lieutenant Leo D., Box 34, Van De Voort DSC file.
Van Fleet, Colonel James A., Box 34, Van Fleet DSC file.
Van Valkenburg, Private John J., Box 34, Van Valkenburg DSC file.
Vandervoort, Lieutenant Colonel Benjamin H., Box 34, Vandervoort DSC file.
Washington, Major William R., Box 35, Washington DSC file.
Wells, Staff Sergeant James A., Box 36, Wells DSC file.
White, Technical Sergeant John W., Box 36, White DSC file.
Whittington, Captain George P. Jr., Box 36, Whittington DSC file.
Wilk, Private First Class Theodore T., Box 37, Wilk DSC file.
Williams, Lieutenant William B., Box 37, Williams DSC file.

Woodward, Captain Robert W., Box 38, Woodward DSC file.
Wozenski, Captain Edward F., Box 37, Wozenski DSC file.
Wyman, Brigadier General Willard G., Box 38, Wyman DSC file.
Zanlow, Lieutenant Forrest, Box 38, Zanlow DSC file.
Zeigler, Lieutenant Harvey J., Box 38, Zeigler DSC file.
Zwingman, Private Otto K., Box 38, Zwingman DSC file.

Award files at the National Archives, College Park, Maryland, U.S. Naval Forces, Eastern Atlantic and Mediterranean, Record Group 313, Stack 370:

Barbour, Aviation Chief Ordnanceman Loran E., Box 30, Barbour NC file.
Bass, Gunner's Mate Second Class Robert W., Box 30, Bass NC file.
Brandel, Lieutenant (jg.) Stuart L., Box 17, Brandel NC file.
Hall, Lieutenant (jg) Frank M., Box 30, Hall NC file.
McKee, Hospital Apprentice Augustus B. Jr., Box 30, McKee NC file.
Peterson, Lieutenant Commander Herbert A., Box 32, Peterson NC file.
Shields, Electrician's Mate First Class Arthur V., Box 15, Shields NC file.

Lillyman, Captain Frank L., 101st Airborne Pathfinder Group, APO 472, "Report of D-Day Pathfinder Activities," July 1, 1944, National Archives, College Park, Maryland.

Lillyman, Captain Frank L., "The Organization and Initial Commitment of the 101st Airborne Division Pathfinders during the Period of December 1943 to the Normandy Invasion on 6 June 1944," Officers Associate Advanced Course, Class Number 4, The Military Police School, Fort Leonard Wood, Missouri.

Mabry, Lieutenant Colonel George L. Jr., "Operations of the 2nd Battalion, 8th Infantry (4th Infantry Division) in the landing at Utah Beach, 5-7 June 1944. (Normandy Campaign) (Personal Experience of a Battalion S-3)," Donovan Research Library, Fort Benning, Georgia.

Raudstein, Major Knut H., "The Operation of the 1st Battalion, 506th Parachute Infantry (101st Airborne Division) in the Vicinity of Carentan) 6–8 June 1944 (Normandy Campaign) (Personal Experience of a Company Commander)," 1948–1949 Advanced Infantry Officers Course, Donovan Research Library, Fort Benning, Georgia.

Roosevelt, Theodore Jr., letter to wife, June 11, 1944.

Shea, Lieutenant Jack, D-Day Narrative, Cornelius Ryan Collection, Alden Library, Ohio University, Athens, Ohio.

Vandervoort, Lieutenant Colonel Benjamin H., as quoted in "Debriefing Conference – Operation Neptune," 82nd Airborne Division War Memorial Museum, Fort Bragg, North Carolina.

TAPED INTERVIEWS AND ORAL HISTORIES, INTERVIEW AND ORAL HISTORY TRANSCRIPTS, AND SPEECHES

Ahearn, John L., oral history transcript, Eisenhower Center, New Orleans, Louisiana.

Barnes, John, oral history transcript, Eisenhower Center, New Orleans, Louisiana.

Bingham, Sidney V. Jr., oral history transcript, Eisenhower Center, New Orleans, Louisiana.

Bucklew, Captain Phil H., interview transcript, Special Collections and Archives Department, Nimitz Library, United States Naval Academy, Annapolis, Maryland.

Dawson, Joseph T., oral history transcript, Eisenhower Center, New Orleans, Louisiana.

Ellery, John, oral history transcript, Eisenhower Center, New Orleans, Louisiana.

Goranson, Ralph E., oral history transcript, Eisenhower Center, New Orleans, Louisiana.

Lomell, Leonard G., oral history transcript, Eisenhower Center, New Orleans, Louisiana.

McCarthy, Thomas J., in *In Their Own Words, WWII: Europe*, audio book, Topics Entertainment, Cassette 1, Side A.

Proffitt, Carl D., interview transcript, Cadet Ryan Koniak, February 17, 2005, John A. Adams Center for Military History and Strategic Analysis, Virginia Military Institute, Lexington, Virginia.

Pryne, Gordon C., interview with author.

Rockwell, Dean L, oral history transcript, Eisenhower Center, New Orleans, Louisiana.

Taylor, Major General Maxwell D. "Talk by Major General M. D. Taylor to First Class 12 December 1945," United States Army Heritage and Education Center, Carlisle, Pennsylvania.

Thompson, Brigadier General Paul W., Address to The Society of Military Engineers, May 18, 1988, Eisenhower Center, New Orleans, Louisiana.

Vemeer, Elmer H., oral history transcript, Eisenhower Center, New Orleans, Louisiana.

Zahn, Donald E., interview with author.

INTERNET WEB PAGES

Armellino, John R., account, courtesy of http://www.americandday.org.

Brandel, Lieutenant (jg.) Stuart L., "Report on Operation Neptune," July 13, 1944, http://www.purplehearts.net.

Colson, Clarence, interview, http://www.warchronicle.com.

CTF 122 Report of Naval Combat Demolition Units at Normandy, http://www.history.navy.mil.

Epstein, Herbert, in "The Landing," www.dropzone.org.

German Defenses at Omaha Beach, http://www.feldgrau.net

German Defenses at Omaha Beach, http://forum.axishistory.com.

German Defenses at Omaha Beach, http://www.omaha-beach.org.

German Defenses at Omaha Beach, http://omahabeach.vierville.free.fr.

Karnowski, Lawrence S., in John B. Dwyer, "On Bloody Omaha," http://www.americanthinker.com.

Kehaly, William J., unpublished manuscript, http://www.146thecbwwiiI.org.

Lomell, Leonard G., written account, courtesy of http://www.americandday.org.

Lomell, Leonard G., speech transcript, Brookdale Community College, New Jersey, http://www.brookdalecc.edu.

Markham, Jerry, in John B. Dwyer, "The Dauntless Demolitioneers," http://www.navyfrogmen.com.

Photographs, http://www.flickr.com/photos/photosnormandie.

Recipient Research, www.ancestry.com.

Research of 16th Infantry Recipients, http://www.warchronicle.com.

Research of 29th Infantry Division Recipients, http://www.29infantrydivision.org.

Research of 29th Infantry Division Recipients, http://www.marylandmilitaryhistory.org.

Research of 101st Airborne Division Recipients, http://triggertimeforum.yuku.com.

Rock, Lieutenant (jg) John R., "Action Report Wave Number 12, Green Beach," June 14, 1944, www.fold3.com.

Rockwell, Lieutenant (jg) Dean L, "Launching "DD" Tanks on D-Day," July 14, 1944, courtesy of http://ww2lct.org

Ross, Wesley R., "146th Engineer Combat Battalion: A Journey," http://www.6juin1944.com.

Spalding, John M., interview with Master Sergeant Forest C. Pogue, February 9, 1945, http://www.warchronicle.com.

Talley, Colonel Benjamin B., account, http://www.military.com.

Tegtmeyer, Major Charles E., "Personal War Time Memoir of Major Charles E. Tegtmeyer, Medical Corps, Regimental Surgeon, 16th Infantry Regiment, 1st Infantry Division," http://history.amedd.army.mil.

White, John W., in, http://www.wwiirangers.com.

Whitehead, Don, "A Correspondent's View of D-Day, 1971," http://www.ww2talk.com.

Various United States military orders, after-action reports, missing air crew reports, and photographs, www.fold3.com.

MAP AND CHART INDEX

NORMANDY INVASION ASSAULT PLAN 13

AIRBORNE PLAN 14

101st AIRBORNE DIVISION SECTOR 17

MARMION FARM 22

OBJECTIVE WXYZ 28

BRÉCOURT MANOIR 30

82nd AIRBORNE DIVISION SECTOR 35

UTAH BEACH SECTORS AND GERMAN DEFENSES 44

GERMAN BATTERIES AND FIRST ARMY TARGET NUMBERS 62

LAYOUT OF TYPICAL BATTERY – POINTE DU HOC 65

OMAHA BEACH SECTORS AND GERMAN DEFENSES 90

116th INFANTRY SECTORS OMAHA BEACH 103

LANDING DIAGRAM 116th RCT 104

16th INFANTRY SECTORS OMAHA BEACH 127

LANDING DIAGRAM 16th RCT 128

INDEX OF HEROES

Ahearn, Lieutenant John L., 49-51, 234–235
Amerman, Lieutenant Walter G., 19–20, 235–237
Anderson, Lieutenant William A., 122, 237–239
Andreasen, Lieutenant (jg) Grant G., 410
Anker, Lieutenant Leonard A., 190, 240
Appleby, Technician Fourth Grade Stanley P., 185, 240–241
Armellino, Captain John R., 149–150, 240
Armstrong, Technical Sergeant Louis M., 192, 242
Austin, Technician Fifth Grade Billy J., 243
Barba, Corporal James N., 23–24, 244
Barber, Private First Class Alexander W., 207, 245, 361
Barbour, Aviation Chief Ordnanceman Loran E., 156, 411
Barcellona, Lieutenant Gaetano R., 126, 245
Barrett, Private Carlton W., 172, 226–227
Bass, Gunner's Mate Second Class Robert W., 122, 411–412
Beavers, Lieutenant Harold R., 98, 245–246
Beitler, Captain Kenneth E., 216, 246–247
Belcher, Sergeant Julius W., 110-114, 247–248
Benn, Technical Sergeant William R. Jr., 214, 249–250
Bennett, Lieutenant Colonel Donald V., 173–176, 249
Benton, Staff Sergeant John L., 98, 251
Berkowitz, Private First Class Henry, 219, 251–252
Bingham, Major Sidney V. Jr., 162–167, 253
Black, Lieutenant Clarence H., 411
Bleau, Lieutenant Kenneth, 170, 253–254
Bolderson, Private First Class John D., 36–38, 255
Bowen, Private First Class George H., 133–140, 143–144, 255–256
Brandel, Lieutenant (jg.) Stuart L., 159–160, 413–414
Bridges, Boatswain's Mate First Class Robert A., 413
Briggs, Captain Victor H., 215, 257–258
Brooks, Lieutenant Elton E., 259
Bucklew, Lieutenant (jg) Phil H., 93–95, 415
Buschlen, Sergeant Arthur B., 171, 259
Caffey, Colonel Eugene M., 259–260
Canham, Colonel Charles D. W., 199, 260–261
Cavaliere, Corporal Peter, 181, 262–263
Ceffalo, Private First Class John W., 262
Clark, Staff Sergeant Philip C., 171–172, 262
Clark, Technician Fifth Grade Rex D., 74–75, 264
Coffman, Staff Sergeant Ralph S., 192, 265
Colson, Sergeant Clarence, 133–140, 142–143, 266–267
Colwell, Staff Sergeant Curtis, 133–140, 142, 266
Cota, Brigadier General Norman D., 197–199, 268
Cotter, Captain John J., 168, 269

Cutler, Lieutenant Robert R., 151–152, 270
Danforth, Corporal Virgil E., 26, 271–272
Dawson, Lieutenant Francis W., 206–207, 271, 361
Dawson, Captain Joseph T., 169–170, 273–274
Dillon, Lieutenant William T., 213–214, 273
DiTullio, Private First Class Dominick, 39, 275
Dock, Technician Fourth Grade Lowell L., 195, 275–276
Dove, Private Vinton W., 201–202, 277
Dunagan, Lieutenant Sidney W., 278
Eberle, Lieutenant George M., 26–27, 279
Elder, Captain Ned S., 98, 279
Ellis, Technical Sergeant Calvin L., 141–142, 280
Ferguson, Lieutenant Forest K., 218, 280
Fitzsimmons, First Sergeant Lawrence J., 141, 280–281
Freeman, Chief Gunner's Mate William R., 416
Gallagher, Private First Class Richard J., 133–140, 144, 281–282
Gearing, Lieutenant Edward M., 107, 283–284
Gibbs, Lieutenant Colonel George W., 195, 285, 298
Giles, Lieutenant Carl K. Jr., 190, 285
Gilfert, Lieutenant (jg) Robert B., 416–417
Goranson, Captain Ralph E., 110–114, 285–287
Gregory, Lieutenant Joseph J., 154–155, 288
Griffin, Private First Class John V., 151, 288
Habib, Sergeant George A., 130, 288–289, 382
Haley, Captain James W., 49, 289
Hall, Lieutenant (jg) Frank M., 117–118, 416
Hall, Private First Class Henry H., 176, 290
Harbaugh, Private Francis L., 290
Hargrove, Lieutenant Robert C., 167–168, 290
Harris, Lieutenant Ernest O., 21–22, 291
Harrison, Sergeant Bailey, 291
Heenan, Private First Class John R., 125, 291–292
Heim, Private Marcus Jr., 36–38, 293, 413
Henderson, Technical Sergeant Gerald M., 221, 294
Hicks, Lieutenant Colonel Herbert C. Jr., 169, 295
Hoover, Major John R., 299
Isley, Lieutenant Colonel Carl J., 126, 297–298
James, Sergeant Theodore A., 299
Jenkins, Staff Sergeant Floyd M., 106, 299–300
Jenkins, Lieutenant (jg) William M., 418
Jewett, Major Milton A., 157, 301
Johnson, Colonel Howard R., 302–303
Jones, Private First Class Aaron B., 150–151, 304
Jones, Lieutenant Henry W., 106, 305
Karnwoski, Ensign Lawrence S., 155, 419–420
Kehaly, Lieutenant William J., 119–122, 305
Kelly, Sergeant John J., 305–306
Kerchner, Lieutenant George F., 72–74, 306–307

Kidwell, Private Kenneth P., 193, 308
Kjosness, Lieutenant Gustav D., 308
Krause, Lieutenant Colonel Edward C., 309–310, 413, 414
Lacy, Lieutenant Joseph R., 207, 311
Lanterman, Lieutenant Raymond E., 152–154, 312
Lillyman, Captain Frank L., 17–19, 313–314, 401
Line, Gunner's Mate Second Class John H., 419
Lockwood, Private John A., 36, 313
Lomell, First Sergeant Leonard G., 75–78, 315
Lorenz, First Sergeant Herman J., 316
Lovell, Sergeant Worden F., 83, 317
Mabry, Captain George L. Jr., 58–59, 318
MacConchie, Lieutenant Howard P., 173, 319
MacNeely, Lieutenant Colonel Carlton O., 48, 320
Maloney, Captain John S., 321, 401
Markham, Chief Machinist's Mate Jerry N., 156, 421
Masny, Captain Otto, 83, 321–322
McElyea, Lieutenant Atwood M., 214, 323
McGee, Captain Tildon S., 323–324
McKee, Hospital Apprentice Augustus B. Jr., 117–118, 422
McLaren, Private Donald B., 178, 325
Mendez, Lieutenant Colonel Louis G. Jr., 326
Merendino, Captain Thomas N., 215–216, 257, 327
Millener, Lieutenant Colonel Raymond D., 328
Monteith, Lieutenant Jimmie W. Jr., 152, 228
Montilio, Private First Class George, 28–29, 329
Moody, Lieutenant William D., 110–114, 330
Morris, Lieutenant Robert A., 423
Morse, Lieutenant Verne V., 177, 330–331
Muir, Lieutenant Marvin F., 21, 331
Mullins, Lieutenant Colonel Thornton L., 168, 332
Murrin, Staff Sergeant Richard C., 56, 332
Nicoli, Sergeant Raymond E., 177, 333
Norton, Lieutenant (jg) Kenneth S., 83, 423
Nothel, Sergeant Henry V., 52, 333
O'Brien, Captain Thomas F., 218–219, 333–334
O'Neill, Lieutenant Colonel John T., 335
Orndorff, Sergeant Douglas A., 191, 335–336
Ostberg, Lieutenant Colonel Edwin J., 335
Panas, Lieutenant James P., 337
Paolini, Private First Class Camillus J., 337
Parke, Private Joseph P., 181, 337
Parker, Lieutenant Charles H., 207-209, 338–339, 361
Parrott, Lieutenant (jg) John O., 423
Patch, Captain Lloyd E., 29–30, 338
Patterson, Sergeant Lyman K., 108, 340
Pence, Captain James L., 213, 340
Perry, Captain Edwin R., 157–158, 340
Petersen, Staff Sergeant Gerard B., 100, 340–341
Peterson, Lieutenant Commander Herbert A., 58, 424
Peterson, Sergeant Kenneth F., 133–140, 143, 341
Peterson, Private First Class Lenold C., 36–38, 342
Peterson, Private First Class Victor E., 193, 342
Philips, Captain Vodra C., 102, 342–343

Pinder, Technician Fifth Grade John J. Jr., 193–194, 229–230
Porter, Private Benton L., 178, 344
Potter, Lieutenant Charles S., 424–425
Presley, First Sergeant William M., 162, 344
Proffitt, Technical Sergeant Carl D., 190–191, 344–345
Pryne, Private First Class Gordon C., 36–38, 346, 413
Purvis, Staff Sergeant Darvin D., 54, 346
Radford, Staff Sergeant David N., 145, 346
Ralston, Captain Emerald M., 219–220, 347
Raudstein, Captain Knut H., 29-30, 348
Richards, Major William A., 178–179, 349
Richmond, Captain Kimball R., 147–148, 350
Ridgway, Major General Matthew B., 350–351
Riggs, Private First Class William M., 217–218, 352
Ritter, Staff Sergeant Ozias C., 192, 352–353
Roach, Technical Sergeant John A., 161, 352
Roberts, Corporal Ernest T., 36, 354
Roberts, Lieutenant Eskell F., 123, 354
Robinson, Lieutenant James L., 177, 354
Rock, Lieutenant (jg) John R., 220, 426
Rockwell, Lieutenant (jg) Dean L., 96–97, 426
Rodgers, Private First Class Thomas L., 33-34, 355
Rogers, Sergeant Howard W., 108, 355
Roosevelt, Brigadier General Theodore Jr., 48, 231–232
Rosen, Private First Class Sanford, 194, 356
Ross, Lieutenant Robert P., 205, 356
Ross, Lieutenant Wesley R., 123–125, 356–357
Rudder, Lieutenant Colonel James E., 81–83, 248, 287, 307, 311, 322, 357, 400
Sampson, Captain Francis L., 358
Savino, Technician Fifth Grade Felice J., 178, 359
Schmidt, Lieutenant George E., 359–360
Schneider, Staff Sergeant George, 157, 359
Schneider, Lieutenant Colonel Max F., 205, 339, 360–361
Schur, Private First Class Curtis N., 361
Settineri, Captain John, 184, 361–362
Shaffer, Technician Fifth Grade Edward, 220–221, 362
Shelby, Lieutenant John D., 180, 363
Shields, Electrician's Mate First Class Arthur V., 222, 426
Shindle, Technician Fourth Grade Elmer G., 212, 363–364
Shoemaker, Private William J., 201–202, 363
Shorter, Staff Sergeant Paul R., 215, 365
Skaggs, Lieutenant Colonel Robert W., 132, 366
Smulik, Technician Fourth Grade Bolick, 130, 367
Songer, Lieutenant Francis E., 54, 367–368
Sosnack, Private Andrew, 367
Spalding, Lieutenant John M., 133–140, 368–369
Sproul, Captain Archibald A., 196, 370–371
Stach, Major Paul J., 87, 370
Steiner, Lieutenant Colonel Fred A., 60, 326, 370
Stephens, Private First Class Otto K., 110–114, 372
Stockwell, Staff Sergeant Leeward W., 194, 372–373
Streczyk, Sergeant Philip, 133-140, 143, 374–375
Strojny, Staff Sergeant Raymond F., 146, 376
Sullivan, Major Richard P., 377

Summers, Staff Sergeant Harrison C., 27–28, 378
Sweeney, Private First Class Lawrence G., 130, 378
Talley, Colonel Benjamin B., 209–212, 378–379
Taylor, Colonel George A., 193, 298, 379–380
Taylor, Major General Maxwell D., 25, 381–383
Taylor, Lieutenant Walter P., 160–161, 383–384
Teeter, Seaman First Class Herman J., 427
Tegtmeyer, Major Charles E., 182–184, 385
Thompson, Colonel Paul W., 217, 386–387
Townsend, Lieutenant John N., 57, 388
Tubbs, First Sergeant Herbert A., 389
Tucker, Private First Class Albert J., 125, 390
Upham, Lieutenant Colonel John S. Jr., 106, 391
Van De Voort, Lieutenant Leo D., 161, 392
Van Fleet, Colonel James A., 59, 326, 392
Van Valkenburg, Private John J., 42, 392
Vandervoort, Lieutenant Colonel Benjamin H., 39–41, 393–394

Washington, Major William R., 221, 395
Weir, Sergeant William W., 396
Welborn, Lieutenant Colonel John C., 397–398
Wells, Staff Sergeant James A., 150, 399
White, Technical Sergeant John W., 197, 399–400
Whittington, Captain George P. Jr., 209, 361, 401
Wilhoit, Ensign William L., 200, 427–428
Wilk, Private First Class Theodore T., 146, 401
Williams, Lieutenant Alfred H. Jr., 402
Williams, Lieutenant William B., 160–161, 402
Winters, Lieutenant Richard D., 30–32, 402–403
Woodward, Captain Robert W., 196, 404
Wozenski, Captain Edward F., 140–141, 282, 392, 405
Wyman, Brigadier General Willard G., 216–217, 405–406
Zahn, Private First Class Donald E., 28–29, 405
Zanlow, Lieutenant Forrest, 168, 407
Zeigler, Lieutenant Harvey J., 42, 407
Zwingman, Private Otto K., 36, 407